Handbook of Hospitality
Marketing Management

Handbook of Hospitality Marketing Management

Editor:

Haemoon Oh

Editor in Chief:

Abraham Pizam

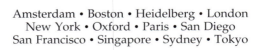

Amsterdam • Boston • Heidelberg • London
New York • Oxford • Paris • San Diego
San Francisco • Singapore • Sydney • Tokyo

ELSEVIER

Butterworth-Heinemann is an imprint of Elsevier

Butterworth-Heinemann is an imprint of Elsevier
Linacre House, Jordan Hill, Oxford OX2 8DP, UK
30 Corporate Drive, Suite 400, Burlington, MA 01803, USA

First edition 2008

Notice
No responsibility is assumed by the publisher for any injury and/or damage to persons
or property as a matter of products liability, negligence or otherwise, or from any use
or operation of any methods, products, instructions or ideas contained in the material
herein. Because of rapid advances in the medical sciences, in particular, independent
verification of diagnoses and drug dosages should be made

British Library Cataloguing in Publication Data
A catalogue record for this book is available from the British Library

Library of Congress Cataloging-in-Publication Data
A catalog record for this book is available from the Library of Congress

ISBN: 978-0-0804-5080-3

For information on all Butterworth-Heinemann publications
visit our web site at books.elsevier.com

Printed and bound in Great Britain
08 09 10   10 9 8 7 6 5 4 3 2 1

Contents

Preface

You are opening a book that hosts a collection of critical research topics in hospitality marketing. More than 20 prominent researchers and authors have worked diligently for the past 15 months or so to bring this much needed volume to life. Included in this volume are the topics that should appeal not only to hospitality researchers and students but also to sophisticated industry practitioners and managers. These topics are quintessential to understanding the mainstream issues that have been driving a broad agenda of hospitality marketing research. A collection of topics like this is an unprecedented scholarly endeavor in that it covers a number of topics not regularly found in standard marketing texts, each topic is treated in depth in both knowledge and pedagogical history, and each chapter can serve as a reservoir of essential knowledge and references on the respective topic for researchers and practitioners.

This handbook was initiated to fill the void that we had few compilations of hospitality marketing research topics to serve as a forum for advanced discussions and applications. Higher education in hospitality, especially marketing, is gradually facing a maturity stage, in quantity, of its developmental progress. Along with the increasing number of graduate programs and students worldwide, we have also witnessed an escalating importance of bricks-and-mortar as well as innovative tools to support and raise the quality of our advanced education in hospitality marketing. Industry too is demanding hospitality graduates with a unique and stronger set of marketing skills to engineer the next round of growth and managerial evolution. This handbook has taken a small initial stride to address such academic and industrial needs, though it is hoped to seed much more refined efforts in the future.

A variety of readers will find this handbook useful. First, each chapter of the handbook will provide graduate and advanced undergraduate students with either a good starting point for or a synopsis of reading on the specific hospitality marketing topic, as it covers key issues of and references on the topic. Thus, the handbook may serve as an excellent basic reading packet introducing new graduate and advanced undergraduate students to a number of important topics in hospitality marketing research. It is also intended as a solid provision of knowledge summarizing countless investigations into mainstream hospitality marketing issues and practices and, hence, may well serve the interests of advanced graduate students too as easy research notes. Second, hospitality marketing researchers and instructors will find this handbook useful in that it provides a viable collection of reading materials bound in a single volume. Researchers may obtain a quick review of critical issues for each topical area and build their reading list based on the references provided in each chapter of the handbook. Instructors of graduate hospitality marketing courses may adopt this handbook as a basic text for topical readings and discussions in their courses, and may develop and assign additional readings for each chapter's topic. Finally, the handbook will appeal to many sophisticated practitioners and managers, because it will provide them with necessary conceptual background and practical guidelines for applying topical research results to industry's daily operations. To this end, each chapter contains either a separate section or part of discussions pointing to ways to apply the ideas presented in the chapter to hospitality operations.

The handbook consists of nineteen chapters that are grouped into five sectional parts based on the chapter's discussion focus. It should be noted, though, that such a grouping of the chapters does not carry substantive scientific meanings because it was done rather for the convenience of structuring the handbook as originally conceived. In the first part, three chapters examine fundamental issues of hospitality marketing such as the philosophical and historical meanings of the concept *hospitality*, social responsibilities of hospitality marketing, and basic hospitality marketing principles. The second part features five chapters on essentials of the hospitality marketing mix including branding and brand equity, relationship/loyalty marketing, advertising and public relations, distribution channels and e-commerce, and service quality and business performance. The five chapters of the next part focus on selected hospitality consumer behavior topics pertaining to attitudes and motivations in travel decisions, the traveler's information search behavior, customer satisfaction and service recovery, hedonic and experiential consumption behaviors, and psychological and behavioral pricing. Three chapters of destination marketing issues appear in the fourth part and they discuss roles of destination marketing organizations, push and pull dynamics in travel decisions, and group decision-making in travel. In the fifth and final part, the handbook includes three chapters on special topics addressing internal marketing, strategic alliances, and casino marketing research.

Another feature of this handbook is that in general each chapter is framed to cover the contents in a similar manner so that readers can obtain a balanced set of reviews and discussions on the topics, across all chapters. All contributing authors were urged to include at least three aspects in their chapter, and the editorial review process attempted to assure each chapter's inclusion of such suggested contents. As a result, first, each chapter includes both conceptual and methodological reviews of the chapter topic, chronologically where applicable, thereby providing readers with necessary background information. These critical reviews often resulted in summarizing the mainstream research foci and presenting more widely adopted conceptual models. Second, the authors illustrate how the key concepts and theories could be applied to hospitality operations, with appropriate case examples wherever available. Such illustrations are intended mainly for industry and practitioners, and have often led the authors to pinpointing potential problems and to evoking precautions for future applications. Toward the end of each chapter, readers will also find directions for future research on the topic. In this section, the authors have typically attempted to prioritize pending research issues on the topic in order to help readers understand what should be done in the future. Consequently, this review-application-future frame of information is expected to serve the varying interests of readers.

This handbook could see the light, thanks to the inspiration and passion of many colleagues. First of all, I am grateful to Dr. Abraham Pizam at University of Central Florida for his initiation of this handbook series and for his willingness to entrust me with this particular volume. As the master editor, he has envisioned the potential contribution of this handbook to our discipline, and he did not, of course, need to convince me hard about that. He provided critical check points throughout the handbook editing and, without his guidance and presence whenever I needed, I could hardly think of moving forward. On behalf of all readers of this handbook, I also cannot thank enough the chapter authors for their scholarly contribution to the birth of this handbook. Through their inspiring chapters, they share their knowledge, experience, vision, and passion for what we were doing and what we could do together for our discipline through this volume. They were patient with my often critical, excessive editorial demands, and it was an honor for me to work with them who truly cared about how we could do things better. My special thanks go to the former graduate students of my hospitality marketing seminar course at Iowa State University who provided me with numerous valuable inputs for the design of the course whose basic format enthused me to frame this handbook. One of my graduate assistants, Seung Lee, helped me check for details in the chapter manuscripts; I thank her. I thank Elsevier and its staff involved in this project and Iowa State University for their direct and indirect support for my engagement in this handbook. Finally, thank you reader, for your interest in hospitality marketing research and this handbook.

I hope readers will find this handbook useful and consider it a ground-breaking effort that bears many more refined volumes in years to come. This handbook is far from perfect and calls for invigorated attempts to move hospitality marketing research forward. It will do its small due contribution if it sparks more debates among the readers on related issues. It will also do its small due contribution if it causes the readers to come forward with better ideas. But, for now, I proudly present this volume to all readers on behalf of the chapter authors. Enjoy the reading and let me hear from you.

July 22, 2007
Haemoon Oh

List of Contributors

David C. Bojanic is the Anheuser–Busch Professor of Tourism in the Department of Marketing at the University of Texas at San Antonio. He is the co-author of two books in hospitality and tourism marketing: *Hospitality Marketing Management* and *Hospitality Sales: Selling Smarter*. In addition, he has published many articles in hospitality and tourism journals such as the *International Journal of Hospitality Management, Journal of Hospitality and Tourism Research, Cornell Hotel and Restaurant Administration Quarterly, Journal of Travel Research*, and *Annals of Tourism Research*. He serves on the editorial review board for four hospitality and tourism academic journals, and he has served as a consultant and member of the board of directors for hospitality, tourism, and non-profit organizations.
Department of Marketing
College of Business
University of Texas at San Antonio
One UTSA Circle
San Antonio, TX 78249-0631
210-458-3113
Email: David.Bojanic@UTSA.edu

Kathryn A. Braun-LaTour is an Assistant Professor of hospitality marketing at the William F. Harrah College of Hotel Administration at the University of Nevada, Las Vegas. Kathryn received her Ph.D. in Marketing from the University of Iowa in 1997. From 1998 to 2001, she served as a visiting scholar in the Mind of the Market Lab at the Harvard Business School where she worked on applications of cognitive neurosciences to marketing. Her research focus has been on the complexity of human memory, and she is especially known for her research on the reconstructive nature of recall which has been published in the prestigious *Journal of Consumer Research*. Braun-LaTour

has also worked on and developed research methods that 'dig deeper' into the customer psyche.
Email: Kathryn.LaTour@unlv.edu.

Alan Bright is an Associate Professor in the Department of Human Dimensions of Natural Resources at Colorado State University in Fort Collins, Colorado. He earned an MBA from the University of Illinois in 1988 and Ph.D. in Recreation Resource Management from Colorado State University in 1993. He teaches in the Natural Resources Tourism Concentration and his research interests focus on social psychological aspects of attitudes and behavior related to tourism, outdoor recreation, and natural resource management.
235 Forestry Building
Department of Human Dimensions of Natural Resources
Colorado State University
Fort Collins, CO 80523-1480
Tel: 970-491-5487
Fax: 970-491-2255
Email: abright@warnercnr.colostate.edu.

Prakash Chathoth is an Assistant Professor in the School of Hotel and Tourism Management at the Hong Kong Polytechnic University. He started his career as a Management Trainee and has over 16 years of combined academic and industry experience. He worked in various management positions for luxury hotels before pursuing an academic career. Prior to moving to Hong Kong, he served as an Assistant Professor in the Department of Hospitality Management in the College of Business at San Francisco State University. Prakash has published papers in top-tiered hospitality journals and has made presentations at both global business and hospitality conferences. Prakash received his Ph.D. in 2002 from Virginia Tech, Virginia, USA, specializing in Strategic Management and Corporate Finance Applied to the Hospitality Industry. His Master's degree is from Institute de Management Hotelier International (IMHI), France.
Hung Hom, Kowloon
Hong Kong, SAR, China
Tel: (852) 2766 4613
Fax: (852) 2362 9362
Email: hmkc@polyu.edu.hk.

Christina Geng-qing Chi is an Assistant Professor at the School of Hospitality Business Management at the Washington State University, Pullman, Washington. She received her M.S. and Ph.D. degrees from the School of Hotel and Restaurant Administration at the Oklahoma State University, Stillwater, Oklahoma, and her B.A. degree from the Guang-dong University of Foreign Studies, Guangzhou, China. She teaches courses related to lodging operations, hospitality accounting, and human resources management. Her areas of research encompass hospitality and tourism marketing, tourist behavior, destination image, service quality management, and human resources management. Her research has been published in refereed journals such as *Tourism Management, International Journal of Hospitality and Tourism Administration,* and *Journal of Human Resources in Hospitality and Tourism.* Her research has also been presented at numerous international hospitality and tourism conferences.

Washington State University
College of Business
School of Hospitality Business Management
481 Todd Hall
PO Box 644742
Pullman, WA 99164-4742
Phone: (509) 335-7661
Fax: (509) 335-3857
Email: cgengqi@wsu.edu

Michael Davidson is currently a Professor and Head of Griffith University's Department of Tourism, Leisure, Hotel and Sport Management in Australia and was previously Director of the Kabacoff School of Hotel, Restaurant, and Tourism Administration, University of New Orleans. He was also the Foundation Head of Griffith's School of Tourism and Hotel Management. His research interests relate to the impact of organizational culture and climate on service quality, operational and marketing performance, employee motivation and turnover in the hospitality industry. He started his career in hotels and became a general manager of a five star hotel in the Southern England. He has undertaken many research and consultancy projects, published widely, and serves on journal editorial boards and is a reviewer for a number of journals.

Head of Department
Griffith Business School
Griffith University
Austrailia
Email: m.davidson@griffith.edu.au.

Alain Decrop is Head of the Department of Business Administration at the University of Namur, a visiting professor at the Catholic University of Louvain, Belgium, and a member of CeRCLe (Center for Research on Consumption and Leisure). He holds Master's degrees in history and economics and a Ph.D. in Business Administration. His major research interests include consumer decision-making and behavior, qualitative interpretive methods, and tourism marketing. His works have been published in journals such as *Annals of Tourism Research,*

Tourism Management, the *Journal of Travel and Tourism Marketing* and *Tourism Analysis*, as well as in many books.

Rempart de la Vierge, 8, B-5000, Namur, Belgium
Email: alain.decrop@fundp.ac.be.

Yuksel Ekinci is a Senior Lecturer in Hospitality Management at the University of Surrey. His research interests include service quality, customer satisfaction and services branding. He has published articles in the *European Journal of Marketing, Journal of Business Research, Journal of Travel Research, International Journal of Hospitality Management,* and many other hospitality journals. Yuksel is an active researcher and editorial board member of *Surrey Quarterly, Journal of Travel Research, Journal of Retailing and Consumer Services,* and *Tourism Analysis.*

Reader in Marketing
Oxford Brookes University
Wheatley, OX33 1HX,
United Kingdom
Phone: 44(0) 1865 485858
Email: yukselekinci@hotmail.com

Huimin Gu is Deputy Dean of the School of Tourism Management and Vice President of the Beijing Hospitality Institute, Beijing International Studies University. She has published in several leading Chinese and English language journals and acted in an advisory capacity for the China Tourist Hotel Association, the China National Tourism Administration, and various provincial government administrations in China and the Education Ministry. She has held a visiting position at the Conrad Hilton College, University of Houston, Texas.

No. 1 Dingfuzhuang Nanli
Chaoyang District
Beijing 100024
China
Email: bjguhuimin@sina.com.

Dogan Gursoy is an Associate Professor at Washington State University in the School of Hospitality Business Management. He teaches courses related to hospitality and tourism marketing and management. His area of research includes tourist behavior, travelers' information search behavior, community attitudes toward tourism development, mega events, cross-cultural studies, and consumer behavior and involvement. His research has been published broadly in refereed journals such as *Annals of Tourism Research, International Journal of Hospitality Management,* and *Journal of Hospitality and Tourism Research, etc.* His research has been presented at numerous international conferences and has received several best-paper awards. He serves as the editor of *Journal of Hospitality Marketing and Management* and serves on the editorial board of several journals including *Annals of Tourism Research, Journal of Travel Research*, and *Journal of Travel & Tourism Marketing*.

Washington State University
College of Business
School of Hospitality Business Management
479 Todd Hall
PO Box 644742
Pullman, WA 99164-4742
Phone: (509) 335-7945
Fax: (509) 335-3857
Email: dgursoy@wsu.edu.

Kathryn Hashimoto spent over 10 years in resort management before moving to university teaching in marketing and hospitality. During this time, Kathryn has published 3 books, written over 25 articles, and presented numerous times on casino management. Kathryn testified before the Public Gaming Sector Commission and the Rhode Island Finance Committee on the impact of casinos and was a column writer for *Casino Enterprise Management*. One of her proudest achievements was to work with the only aboriginal university in the world, First Nations University of Canada, to create their first program in hospitality and gaming. Currently, Kathryn has a new casino management textbook out and is working on a Casino Certificate series of five books, which is expected to be available by the end of 2008.

East Carolina University
Department of Hospitality Management
RW-308 Rivers Building
Greenville, NC 27858 USA
Email: hashimotok@ecu.edu.

Azilah Kasim is an Associate Professor of tourism at the Universiti Utara Malaysia, Malaysia. She is Deputy Dean of Research and Postgraduate Studies on the Faculty of Tourism and Hospitality Management. She has been on the editorial board of the *Malaysian Management Journal* since 2004 and is an active reviewer of manuscripts for a number of international journals including *Annals of Tourism Research*, *ASEAN Tourism Journal*, and *Anatolia: An International Journal of Tourism and Hospitality Research*. Azilah has researched and published a number of journal articles in the area of business social responsibility and tourism marketing. She has also written a number of books on recreation management. Besides research and writing, she also participates actively in training and consultation projects.

Associate Professor,
Faculty of Tourism, Hospitality and Environment Universiti Utara Malaysia 06010 Sintok Kedah Darulaman MALAYSIA.
Tel: 604 928 5984

Fax: 604 928 5975
Email: azilah@webmail.uum.edu.my.

Camille Kapoor completed her Master of Science degree in Hospitality Management in the Conrad N. Hilton College of Hotel & Restaurant Management at the University of Houston in May 2006. Her academic focus was on marketing, particularly in the areas of consumer behavior, loyalty, and restaurants. Her thesis, *Understanding the Antecedents and Consequences of Customer Loyalty in Restaurants*, examined the key drivers behind customer loyalty in restaurants. She currently works as a Consultant for PKF Consulting, engaging in Financial and Market Studies and Valuations involving hotels and other hospitality products.
1010 Lamar, Suite 400
Houston, Texas 77002
Email: Camille.Kapoor@pkfc.com.

Woody G. Kim is an Associate Professor and Director of International Center for Hospitality Research & Development in the Dedman School of Hospitality at Florida State University. He holds a PhD from Purdue University, an MBA from University of Houston, and a MS from University of Massachusetts. His research and teaching interests include revenue management, pricing, brand management, customer relationship marketing, hotel feasibility study, and hospitality financial management. He has published more than 50 peer-reviewed articles in the following journals: *International Journal of Hospitality Management, Journal of Hospitality and Tourism Research, Cornell Hotel and Restaurant Administration Quarterly, Tourism Management, Journal of Consumer Marketing, Journal of Travel & Tourism Marketing,* and *Tourism Economics.* He has also presented papers in more than 60 national and international conferences. He is a recipient of the 2004 *Journal of Hospitality & Tourism Research* Best Article of the Year award from Sage Publication and the best paper award at the 2004 Hospitality Information Technology Association (HITA) Conference. He serves on journal editorial boards and is a reviewer for a number of journals.
288 Champions Way, UCB 4116
P.O. Box 3062541
Tallahassee, FL 32306
Tel: (850) 644-8242
Fax: (850) 644-5565
E-mail: wkim@cob.fsu.edu.

Conrad Lashley is Professor and Director of the Centre for Leisure Retailing at Nottingham Trent University. He has researched and written extensively about hospitality studies informed by an array of social science perspectives. His work claims that traditional understanding of hospitality can better inform management practice in contemporary commercial bars, cafés, hotels, and restaurants. He is co-editor of *In Search of Hospitality: Theoretical Perspectives and Debates*, and *Hospitality: A Social Lens*. He is editor of the Butterworth-Heinemann's *Hospitality, Leisure and Tourism* series of texts as well as co-editor of the *Events Management* series. He has personally authored a number of books on hospitality and services management including *Empowerment: HR Strategies for Service Excellence*; *Hospitality Retail Management: A Unit Mangers Guide*; *Business Development for Licensed Retailing*; and *Organisation Behaviour for Service Sector Organisations*.

Centre for Leisure Retailing
Nottingham Trent University
Burton Street
Nottingham
NG1 4BU
United Kingdom
0044 115 9233855
E-mail: conradlashley@aol.com

Xiangping Li is a Ph.D. candidate in the Department of Hospitality and Tourism Management at Virginia Polytechnic Institute & State University. Her specialization is in the area of tourism development and marketing.
Blacksburg, VA 24061 USA
Phone: (540) 257 3357
Email: lxpwj@vt.edu

Andrew Lockwood is the Forte Professor of hospitality management, Associate Dean of Learning and Teaching for the Faculty of Management and Law, and Head of the Division of Hospitality and Tourism Management at the University of Surrey, where he teaches undergraduate and postgraduate courses in international hospitality management, operations management, and operations analysis. He has developed and taught short courses for the hospitality industry in the United Kingdom, Bali, Bulgaria, Crete, Cyprus, Ireland, and Mauritius. He has written or edited ten books and well over 100 articles, chapters, and conference papers on the management of hospitality operations. His longstanding research interests lie in the fields of service quality management, hospitality education, and managerial activity in the hospitality industry.
Guildford, GU2 7XH
Email: a.lockwood@surrey.ac.uk

Anna S. Mattila is an Associate Professor at Pennsylvania State University. She holds a Ph.D. from Cornell University, an MBA from University of Hartford, and a B.S. from Cornell University. Her research interests focus on consumer responses to service encounters and cross-cultural issues in services marketing. Her work has appeared in the *Journal of the Academy of Marketing Science, Journal of Retailing, Journal of Service Research, Journal of Consumer Psychology, Psychology & Marketing, Journal of Services Marketing, International Journal of Service Industry Management, Cornell Hotel & Restaurant Administration Quarterly, Journal of Travel Research, International Journal of Hospitality Management,* and in *Journal of Hospitality & Tourism Research.* She is a recipient of John Wiley & Sons Lifetime Research Award and The University of Delaware Michael D. Olsen Research Achievement Award. Web-link: www.personal.psu.edu/faculty/a/s/asm6

201 Mateer Building
University Park, PA 16802-1307
Tel: (814) 863-5757
Fax: (814) 863-4257
Email: asm6@psu.edu.

David Njite is an Assistant Professor in the School of Hotel and Restaurant Administration, Oklahoma State University. He is a graduate of The University of Strathclyde, UK and The Ohio State University. He has published articles applying consumer psychology to diverse areas of hospitality management including pricing, restaurant operations, and consumer behaviour on the Internet. His work has appeared in the *Journal of Hospitality & Tourism Research, Cornell Hotel and Restaurant Administration Quarterly,* and *Journal of Services Research.* He is a twice recipient of the best-paper awards at the I-CHRIE conferences, a finalist for the Cornell HRA Quarterly Article-of-the-Year award, and a recipient of the Bradford Wiley Best Research Paper Award (2006). His research interests include pricing in hospitality, branding and brand management, and consumer behavior.

Oklahoma State University
School of Hotel and Restaurant Administration 201C HESW Stillwater, OK USA 74078
Ph: 405-744-7675
Fax: 405-744-6299
Email: david.njite@okstate.edu

Peter O'Connor is Professor of information systems at Essec Business School France, where he also serves as Academic Director of Institute de Management Hotelier International (IMHI), Europe's leading MBA program in international hospitality management. His research, teaching, and consulting interests focus on distribution, e-commerce, and electronic marketing in hospitality and tourism. He has authored two leading textbooks – *Using Computers in Hospitality* (Cassell, UK – now in its third edition) and *Electronic Information Distribution in Hospitality and Tourism Industries* (CABI, UK) as well as countless articles in both the academic and trade press. He is widely sought after to conduct seminars on technology management, distribution, and electronic marketing by both international hospitality companies and industry associations.

E-mail: Oconnor@essec.fr

H.G. Parsa is an Associate Professor in hospitality management at the Ohio State University. He is the Honorable Editor-in-Chief of *Journal of Foodservice Business Research* and recipient of a Fulbright Visiting Scholar Fellowship. He has published and presented over 100 research papers in business and hospitality journals. He serves on the editorial boards of seven academic journals. His research has appeared in journals such as the *Cornell Hotel and Restaurant Administration Quarterly, Journal of Business Research, Journal of Hospitality & Tourism Research, Journal of Hospitality and Tourism Education, Journal of Restaurant & Foodservice Marketing, Journal of Quality Assurance in Hospitality and Tourism,* and *Journal of College and University Foodservice*. His research interests include pricing strategies in foodservice, analysis of the factors that contribute to small-business failure and success, and restaurant chain management. His research has been quoted in popular press including *Business Week, Fortune, Wall Street Journal, NPR, Chicago Tribune, USA Today,* and over 50 regional newspapers.

9907 Universal Blvd
Orlando, FL 32819
Office: (407) 903-8048
Fax: (407) 903-8105
Email: hparsa@mail.ucf.edu

Heejung Ro is an Assistant professor in the Rosen College of Hospitality Management at the University of Central Florida. Her research interests focus on consumer dissatisfaction responses with a special emphasis on negative emotions. Her current research work involves understanding the nature and structure of consumer dissatisfaction responses and linking consumption emotions to behavioral and non-behavioral consumer responses.

9907 Universal Boulevard, Orlando FL 32819
Tel: 407-903-8075
Fax: 407-903-8105
Email: hro@mail.ucf.edu

Chris Ryan is a Professor of tourism at the University of Waikato, Hamilton, New Zealand. He is an elected Fellow of the International Academy for the Study of Tourism, editor of the journal *Tourism Management*, and Honorary Professor of the University of Wales. His past publications number over 200, including over 100 publications in academic journals, 11 books, and several contributions to edited books. He also acts in a consultancy and advisory role for government, industry, and universities.

Private Bag 3105
Gate 7, Hillcrest Road
Hamilton 3240
New Zealand
Email: caryan@waikato.ac.nz.

Stowe Shoemaker is Donald Hubbs Distinguished Professor in the University of Houston's Conrad Hilton College of Hotel and Restaurant Management. He holds a Ph.D. from Cornell University in the School of Hotel Administration, an MS from the University of Massachusetts, and BS from the University of Vermont. Stowe is also a member of the Executive Education faculty at the Cornell University School of Hotel Administration. Stowe teaches strategic pricing for hotels and revenue enhancement through pricing, customer relationship and frequency management, strategic marketing, and strategic hospitality management. His research interests include the antecedents and consequences of consumer loyalty, loyalty programs, and strategic pricing and revenue management. Stowe's research has appeared in many hospitality journals and he has written two books on hospitality marketing, both published by Prentice Hall.

Room: N235-e
University of Houston
229 C.N. Hilton Hotel & College
Houston, TX 77204-3028
Tel: 713-743-7371
Fax: 713-743-2482
E-mail: sshoemaker@uh.edu

Ercan Sirakaya-Turk is a Sloan Research Professor of tourism in the School of Hotel, Restaurant, and Tourism Management at the University of South Carolina. He is the 2006–2007 recipient of US State Department's prestigious Fulbright scholarship to teach tourism and conduct destination development and branding studies for the Russian Federation in St. Petersburg. Before joining USC, Ercan was a faculty member at Texas A&M University for 8 years and at Penn State for 3 years. Ercan has published a significant number of articles in prestigious tourism journals such as the *Annals of Tourism Research*, *Journal of Travel Research, Tourism Management*, and *Tourism Analysis*.

Ercan is the founding and current Editor-in-Chief for an online tourism research bulletin, *e-Review of Tourism Research*.
Columbia, SC 29208
Phone: (803) 777-3327
Fax: (803) 777-1224
Email: Ercan@sc.edu

Karl Titz is an Associate Professor at the University of Houston Conrad N. Hilton College. He teaches services management and restaurant management. His research stream includes studies of experiential motivators in gambling and restaurant settings. Currently, he is working on service scale development for RV parks.
Email: jgnoth@business.otago.ac.nz
Karl Titz, Ph.D.
Associate Professor
229 CN Hilton College
University of Houston
Houston, TX 77204-3028
Phone: 713-743-2412
Fax: 713-743-2575
Email: ktitz@uh.edu

Muzzo (Muzaffer) Uysal is a Professor and Associate Dean for Graduate Programs and Research in the College of Hospitality, Retail, & Sport Management at the University of South Carolina. Before joining USC, Muzzo was a faculty member at Virginia Polytechnic Institute & State University for 15 years. Muzzo is a member of the International Academy for the Study of Tourism and the Academy of Leisure Sciences, and serves as Co-editor of *Tourism Analysis*, an interdisciplinary journal. In addition, he sits on the editorial boards of eight journals, including the *Journal of Travel Research* and *Annals of Tourism Research* as resource editor. His current research interests center on tourism demand–supply interaction, tourism development and marketing, and international tourism.
Columbia, SC 29208
Phone: (803) 777-7624
Fax: (803) 777-6427
E-mail: Muzzo@sc.edu

Karin Weber is an Assistant Professor in the School of Hotel & Tourism Management at the Hong Kong Polytechnic University. Karin has published on a wide range of subjects in leading international tourism and hospitality journals, with a particular focus on services marketing and convention tourism. She is lead editor and chapter author of a book on convention tourism, and serves on the editorial board of four international tourism and hospitality journals. Karin is

listed in Who's Who in the World and Who's Who in Asia. A native of Germany, Karin received her Ph.D. in services marketing from Griffith University, Australia, M.Sc. in Hotel Administration from the University of Nevada, Las Vegas, and Bachelor of Business (Hons) degree from Monash University.
Hung Hom, Kowloon
Hong Kong, SAR, China
Tel: + (852) 2766 4031
Fax: + (852) 2362 9362
Email: hmkweber@polyu.edu.hk

Dia Zeglat is a postgraduate student in the University of Surrey's School of Management, UK. Dia is conducting a research project on the relationship between service quality and profitability in the budget hotel industry. Dia worked in the Ministry of Administrative Development (MOAD) in Jordan as a researcher for 2 years. Dia was involved in a national project for improving the public sector and participated in some research projects covering issues such as service delivery improvement, procedural simplification, and customer satisfaction.
Guildford, GU2 7XH
Email: d.zeglat@surrey.ac.uk

Part One

Hospitality Marketing Concepts

Marketing hospitality and tourism experiences

Conrad Lashley

Introduction

Much of the hospitality and tourism marketing literature implies that the sector represents one more facet of the service industry. Indeed principles adapted from manufacturing and product marketing are applied to redefine marketing issues through the prism of product, place, price and promotion, by adding people, processes and place in service contexts (Parasuraman et al., 1991; Palmer, 2001). In this framework, marketing strategies and tactics in hospitality and tourism are principally concerned with adjusting each of these elements to provide a competitive offer to customers (Kotler, 2003). The same concepts apply, therefore, to marketing to hotel and restaurant customers, as those apply to marketing to laundry or financial service customers (Lovelock, 1999).

This chapter argues that these techniques fail to recognize the potentially unique relationship between guests and hosts. That is not to say that the more conventional and rational approaches do not have a place, but there is a need to recognize that hospitality and tourism experiences have important emotional dimensions that traditional marketing approaches tend to underplay. By understanding the hospitality-based transaction between guests and hosts, marketeers and commercial operators can deliver customers experiences through which to build customer loyalty and a robust business better able to withstand competitor pressure. The guest and host relationship has a long tradition, pre-dating modern hospitality and tourism businesses by thousands of years and universally evident across all societies. The study of this relationship and the mutual obligations imposed on both guests and hosts, together with the study of hospitableness, suggests that commercial practice has much to gain from traditional understanding of hospitality. The chapter briefly outlines some of the issues related to hospitality and hospitableness and discusses the implications for commercial practice. For the purposes of this discussion, I use the term hospitality to refer to transaction between host and guest, together with cultural and religious obligations associated with the two roles. Hospitableness, on the other hand, is exclusively concerned with host behavior and the personal qualities used to ensure the well-being and comfort of guests.

More than a service encounter?

The emergence of the word 'hospitality' to describe hotel and catering activities in English-speaking countries is worthy of research in its own right, but beyond the scope of this chapter. The implied intention was to present in a more favorable light, the commercial bar, hotel, and restaurant businesses through reference back to traditions, both cultural and domestic, of host's concern for the well-being of guests. Hospitality creates an impression of hosting and hospitableness, which prioritizes guest experiences. Hospitality also suggests a commitment to meeting guests' needs as the key focus in these essentially commercial operations and a nobility of purpose beyond the more venal commercial relationship implied in the hotel, the bar, or the restaurant. Hospitality implies a selfless commitment to the meeting of the emotional needs of guests whereas bars, hotels and restaurants imply commercial relationships where service comes at a price, and only if profitable (in principle).

The re-branding of bars, hotels and restaurants, and other catering activities as hospitality may not have been a totally cynical step and one that just 'sounded right'. Reference to the implied meaning does open up some interesting avenues of enquiry that may ultimately refocus commercial activities. Certainly recent academic developments, stimulated initially by *In Search of Hospitality: theoretical perspectives and debates* (Lashley and Morrison, 2000), have taken up some of the issues that the word hospitality implies, as a way of better informing the study of hospitality for those destined to manage hospitality business operations. Some commentators suggest that two alternative schools of thought have emerged (Litteljohn, 1990; Jones, 2004; Lashley, 2004). '*Hospitality studies*' refers to the study of hospitality as a social phenomenon with traditions stretching across cultures and historical time periods. An array of social scientists provides insights into the study of hospitality. The following are some examples of authors who have written about hospitality from specific social science perspectives: anthropology (Andrews, 2000; Selwyn, 2000; Cole, 2006), social history (Walton, 2000; Lomine, 2005), philosophy (Derrida, 2002; Telfer, 1996, 2000), social geography (Bell, 2006; Wharton, 2006), and sociology (Ritzer, 1993, 2006; Warde and Martens, 2001). Each helps to establish a broader understanding of hospitality as a human activity with long and widespread antecedents. In fact, Derrida says, 'Not only is there a culture of hospitality, but there is no culture that is not also a culture of hospitality. All cultures compete in this regard and present themselves as more hospitable than the others. Hospitality – this is culture itself' (2002:361).

The second school of thought can be said to be concerned with *hospitality management* and the management of hospitality business operations. This is the traditional perspective to be found across the international hospitality industry and in the educational provision for careers as managers in the sector. Here the concerns are primarily with an array of applied business management disciplines in accounting, marketing, human resources management, operations management, legal principles, etc. That said, the traditional study of hospitality management practice might involve social science inputs through disciplines in economics, psychology, and organizational behavior, for example.

In fact, the supposed dichotomy between the '*studies*' and '*management*' schools is a false one (Jones, 2004; Lashley, 2004). Sound management education and practice needs to be based on a firm grounding of critical and analytical insights from the social sciences. Hence study *of* hospitality is key to studies *for* hospitality management (Lashley, 2004; Lashley et al., 2006a; Lashley et al., 2006b). In this context, an understanding of hospitality as a human relationship involving people in host and guest roles is essential to better inform the marketing of hospitality and tourism operations. Through a better understanding of the provision of hospitality and acts of hospitableness, commercial organizations are better able to recognize the emotional experiences involved and ensure that management practice focuses on their production.

Lashley (2000) initially proposed that a three-domain model helped to set the context of hospitality using an admittedly crude Venn diagram, not only to distinguish between cultural/social, private/domestic, and commercial domains but also to show how they potentially overlap and influence each other. This is reproduced as Figure 1.1.

Whilst it was recognized that the Venn diagram was unsophisticated, it did allow a discussion of the three domains to take place, and the following paragraphs will highlight some of the emerging issues that have implications for the marketing of hospitality and tourism. Figure 1.2, which will be introduced later, suggests a model for the organization of business activities founded on the primacy of host and guest transactions as a means of building guest loyalty.

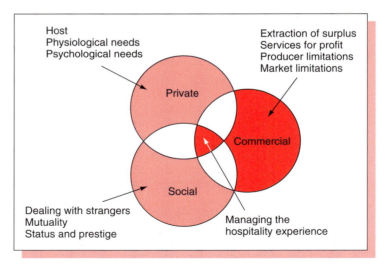

Figure 1.1
The three domains of hospitality (*Source:* Lashley (2000)).

The social/cultural domain

Destination marketing often makes reference explicitly and implicitly to the hospitality and welcome given to visitors. Failte Ireland's (2005) tourism marketing research shows that nine out of every ten overseas visitors to Ireland claim Irish friendliness and hospitality as the primary reasons for visiting the country. The Jamaican smile and welcome, and the world-famous 'Southern hospitality' in the USA are also examples of the claims about the welcome strangers will receive in different cultures, which are employed in the marketing of particular destinations. The quotation from Derrida given above suggests that these are claims made by all cultures and are indications of the human decency with which a society seeks to define itself. The problem is that both Derrida and tourism marketeers tend to downplay the extent to which these obligations to be hospitable vary between cultures, and over time.

Selwyn (2000) reminds us that a dominant culture-related definition of hospitality across societies is that it involves 'converting strangers into friends' (p. 19) and provides examples spanning continents, religions, and cultures. In Western settings, O'Gorman (2006) refers to an array of both Greco–Roman and Judeo–Christian texts extolling the religious obligations on both hosts and guests. O'Gorman says (p. 23)

Hospitality includes food, drink and accommodation and also is concerned with the approach to be adopted e.g. welcoming, respectful and genuine. Hospitality is offered and the extent or limitation of it is based on the needs and the purpose of the guests/strangers. Alliances are initially developed through hospitality between friends, households and states, and are strengthened through continuing mutual hospitality. Hospitality once granted between individuals, households and states is also granted to descendants and through extended friendships.

Apart from the general obligation to offer succor and support to travelers, strangers, and the poor, reciprocity is also an important consideration of the hospitality relationship; in other words, the host may one day be the guest. Reciprocity was an important feature of tourism in Augustinian Rome (Lomine, 2005). Families built up networks of mutual relationships through offering and receiving hospitality, and toured between the various network members.

Heal's (1990) work on hospitality in the early modern England suggests that there were strong cultural obligations to offer hospitality to strangers, travelers, and the homeless. In particular, the host was required, as a moral and sacred obligation, to offer protection and safety to the guest, as well as shelter and nourishment. Heal argues that

7

five underlying principles have governed English hospitality during the period. These are:

1. the relationship between host and guest is a 'natural' one (i.e., it is grounded in the nature of social life);
2. an intrinsic part of being a host is having regard for the 'sacred nature' of the guest (which refers, broadly, to the honor and status which a guest may bring to the host);
3. hospitality is noble;
4. 'altruistic giving' is an established and expected part of English social life; and
5. the social relationships and exchanges that hospitality engenders are at least as important as those formed in the market place (p. 22).

The obligations clearly extend back through human history and, until recently, in 'modern societies' carried strong moral sanctions for those who failed either to offer hospitality as a host or to behave appropriately as a guest. In the latter case, guests overstaying their welcome was a significant concern. Sherringham and Daruwalla (2006) remind us of an old Italian saying, which roughly translates as, 'Guests are like fish, after three days they stink'. Selwyn's account of the three varieties of coffee offered free to travelers to the city of Sarajevo showed a deteriorating quality of coffee being offered, depending on the length of the visitor's stay. 'If he has still not departed for the town having taken some cups of this second variety, the guest is served a third type which is known as *sikterusa*, which means "fuck off coffee"' (Selwyn, 2000, p. 33).

As further confirmation of these strong obligations in recent history, it is interesting to note that Shakespeare makes references to hospitality and inappropriate host and guest behaviors many times in his plays. Typically, he uses transgression of the laws of hospitality as a way on increasing the villainy of the character and action. Whilst twenty-first century audiences may well need to have the significance explained to them, it is likely that contemporary Jacobean audiences well understood that the murder of Duncan whilst he was a guest in Macbeth's house further intensified the outrage of the crime. Just in case, however, Shakespeare has Lady Macbeth feign horror on the discovery of the murder by saying, 'What in our house?' In other words, reminding the audience that the King has been murdered whilst the Macbeths should have been protecting him. In King Lear, when Buckingham is about to have his eyes removed by Lear's sons-in-law whilst he is entertaining them in his home, he says, 'But you are my guests'. In both cases, Shakespeare uses the contemporary audience's understanding of the obligations of hospitality for dramatic effect, to distance the perpetrators from normal, moral, and decent society. Clearly, current cultural and religious pronouncements rarely consider these obligations to offer protection and hospitality to guests, though Selwyn (2000) traces sermons by religious leaders stretching into the nineteenth century where the virtues of extending hospitality are extolled. Even in the 1930s, in the United States, the Catholic Workers' movement advocated re-engaging with medieval ideas of hospitality as a way of providing support for unemployed and poverty-stricken people (Selwyn, 2000). The key point here is that the obligations to be hospitable to strangers and to the poor has changed in industrial societies, though there is no reason why they cannot be a source of inspiration to hospitality and tourism marketeers, and cannot be re-introduced as models for current practice.

Similarly, it is important to remember that some contemporary cultures still place a high value on the obligations of hospitality. At the time of writing, the Iraqi individual, who betrayed Sadam Hussein's sons to the US forces for the large reward is himself a fugitive. The elders of his tribe say that he shamed the tribe by betraying the hospitality obligation to protect the Husseins whilst they were guests in his house. As a result, he is said to have dishonored the tribe. Cole's (2006) work with the Ngadha tribe in Indonesia provides some fascinating insights into contemporary hospitality and tourism in a remote community. Tribe members practice hospitality through mutual hosting of pig roast celebrations. Guests will at some time be hosts and vice versa. When small groups of tourists visit the tribe, they are welcomed and invited to join the celebration as guests, even though they themselves are not able to offer reciprocal hospitality by hosting a pig-roasting. Cole's conversations with tribe-member hosts suggest that they feel honored by the tourists' presence, and tourists bring news from the outside world. The local community does not feel that there is a lack of reciprocity.

Finally, the obligations to be hospitable to strangers may change over time, particularly as a society feels under threat, as contact with strangers increases, or as the benefits and costs of tourism are borne unevenly through a community or society. Molz (2005) and Crang (2005) have used concepts of hospitality to explore the varying responses of host communities to asylum-seekers and migrants. Supposedly hospitable communities may well refuse hospitality to certain groups that are deemed to be undeserving and unworthy. Contact with strangers can result in a abatement in the obligation to be hospitable, when guests behave in a way that fails to treat the host with respect, or when guests do not meet their obligations. It could be that the commercial relationship implicit in mass tourism and hospitality sector activities reduces the obligations on both hosts and guests. Whether 'commercial hospitality' can be 'hospitable' is a question that will be discussed further, later in the chapter. Finally, the impact of tourism on communities is not evenly spread. For some sections of a community, hospitality and tourism activities represent employment and business opportunities, but for other residents they represent noise-disturbance and a threat to their environment (Walton, 1998, 2000, 2005).

The study of hospitality in this social and cultural domain does enable both destination and individual business marketeers to develop a better understanding of the needs of visitors as guests. It also enables an understanding that the cultural obligations to be hospitable do vary over time. Those with frontline contact with guests need to be motivated and trained to deliver the guest experiences that create memorable moments which result in repeat visits and from which to build customer loyalty. Host communities need to be considered as part of the development of the hospitality experience. Feelings of exclusion or threat amongst those with no immediate perceived benefit from guest visits may well cause resentment, or even conflict, which runs counter to the message of welcome and friendly hospitality. Ultimately, it is possible to conceive hospitality and tourism operations as primarily focused on converting strangers (customers) into friends. This will be discussed more fully, later in the chapter.

The domestic/private domain of hospitality

Whilst the social/cultural domain of hospitality provides a set of broadly shared social norms and expectations about hospitality and the obligations of hosts and guests, the private/domestic domain is the key arena for learning the behaviors of being a host and being a guest. Typically most households will both entertain non-household members as guests, and be invited to be guests in other households. The expectations on acceptable behavior will be broadly shared through social/cultural norms. Most dinner party guests, for example, would feel that the obligations of hospitality had been broken by a host who expected them to pay for each glass of wine, yet in many cultures it would be expected that they bring with them wine or food as contribution to occasion. Within this broad setting, hosts have a degree of control over how they shape guest experiences and commercial hospitality operations can learn from and employ the experiences of hospitality in the private/domestic domain.

Telfer's (2000) differentiation between hospitality and hospitableness provides an important insight for marketeers because it gives an insight into being a good host, which extends beyond culturally shared obligations of hospitality. Being a good host has clear relevance to commercial contexts. Telfer says (p. 40), 'If entertaining guests is making yourself responsible for their happiness so long as they are beneath your roof, a good host is one who does make his guests happy – or as happy as a host's efforts and ministrations can make them – while they are in his care.' Telfer suggests that truly hospitable behavior is motivated by genuine needs to please and care for others. She says these include the following:

- the desire to please others, stemming from general friendliness and benevolence or from affection for particular people, concern, or compassion;
- the desire to meet another's need;
- the desire to entertain one's friends or to help those in trouble; and
- the desire to have company or to make friends, and the desire for the pleasures of entertaining – what we may call the wish to entertain as a pastime.

The key concern for hospitality and tourism marketing is the extent that these motives and desires can be captured, promoted, and delivered in a commercial context. In principle, Telfer suggests that where hosts are offering hospitality for personal gain, or for vanity or solely out of a sense of duty, the actions are not genuinely hospitable. From a twentieth-century Christian perspective, Nouwen (1975) argues that hospitality should consist of the following facets:

- Free and friendly space – creates physical, emotional, and spiritual space for the stranger.
- Stranger becomes a guest – treats a stranger as a guest and potential 'friend.'
- Guest protected – offers sanctuary to the guest.
- Host gives gifts – the host welcomes the guest by providing the best gifts possible.
- Guest gives gifts – the guest reciprocates and gives gifts to host.
- All guests are important and gifted – the host values the guest and gains value from them.
- Acceptance, not hostility – especially the kinds of subtle hostility, which makes fun of strangers or puts them into embarrassing situations.
- Compassion – hospitality is basically a sense of compassion.

It is possible to argue that hospitality offered at a price can never be genuine hospitality because it is not motivated by these desires. Genuine hospitality can only be experienced in the private/domestic domain. This is an argument supported by the work of Warde and Martens (2001), which suggested that diners regarded hospitality offered in the home to be authentic whist the hospitality offered in commercial restaurants was less than authentic. Certainly, the domestic/private domain of hospitality is important for hospitality and tourism marketeers because this domain is perceived as being authentic and more genuinely driven by altruist motives, and is a source of learning about host and guest relations, which can be used during communications with guests and with staff. For example, one UK based restaurant group required service workers to 'treat customers as though they are guests in your own home' (Lashley, 2001, p. 70).

Apart from providing a context in which individuals learn host and guest behavior, the domestic/private domain also provides some of the specific skills associated with cooking, serving drinks, and providing accommodation. O'Mahony's (2003) profile of five award-winning Australian restaurateurs revealed that a common theme was that all learnt to cook food in the domestic/private domain. Typically, they learnt to love food and to cook through the influence of a female family member. In other cases, the enjoyment of food and drink and entertaining was developed in the home. This author's (Lashley, 1985) research into leading hotel and restaurant chef profiles also revealed that they typically developed an enjoyment of food and cooking in the home with a mother, grandmother or other significant female family member.

On another level, many hospitality businesses are 'commercial' homes (Lynch and MacWhannell, 2000). Commercial homes (Lynch, 2005), particularly in the accommodation sector, including small hotels, bed and breakfast establishments, farm-stay properties, and guest houses frequently involve both the owners and guests living on the same premises. Several authors (Lynch and MacWhannell, 2000; Lynch, 2005; Sweeney and Lynch, 2006) have undertaken research on the nature of the relationship between hosts and 'paying guests' in these contexts, exploring the extent to which they share common space. At one extreme, the paying guest would have similar access to private/domestic space as would a personal guest. In other situations, private space is clearly delineated from the public space available to guests. Lynch (2005) points to some important tensions that should be of interest to marketeers. Visitors to these properties are frequently making a purchase decision based on the perceived authenticity of the hospitality experience by 'staying with a real family', whilst the operators in some establishments keep them at arm's length by keeping them away from private areas. Tourism advisors sometimes further compound this tension by advising operators to 'professionalize' the service by providing guest dining rooms, printed menus, and operating standards informed by larger hotel operations. Tourism marketeers need to understand these drives for authenticity and the implications of the domestic/private domain in shaping these purchase decisions. Although the interface between resident guest and host is at its sharpest in the accommodation sector, pubs, inns and bars, as well as some restaurant and café businesses represent close links between the home and the commercial activity.

In fact, the micro-business characteristic of the provision in hospitality and tourism industry also raises some issues for destination marketing and consistency of service quality for visitors. Internationally, hotels, restaurants, pubs, bars, and café operations are run by micro firms employing 10 or fewer persons. Typically 70 per cent or more of the businesses in these sectors are micro businesses, and a significant number employ no permanent staff other than immediate family and friends, and can be described as 'family businesses' (Getz et al., 2004). The key issue is that many of these smaller firms are more motivated by 'lifestyle' rather than classical entrepreneurial motives. In a survey of 1396 small hospitality and tourism micro businesses, Thomas et al. (2000) found that just one in eight firms recorded 'to make a lot of money' as one of their motives for being in business. Most were aiming for some personal lifestyle improvements, typically to have 'more control', or because they 'liked the life' or had life-long ambitions to run a pub, hotel, restaurant or other business in the sector. Often the domestic setting is seen as 'not having to work' or presents a business opportunity where their life skills learnt in the home provide them with an opportunity to 'work at home' (Lashley and Rowson, 2005). In their recent exploration of 17 couples buying small hotels in the British seaside resort, Blackpool, Lashley and Rowson (2005) found that 16 had sold a domestic property, typically a three- or four-bedroom house, to buy the Blackpool hotel.- For many, owning a seaside hotel had been a life-long dream. Being paid to provide hospitality with their own home is at the heart of these dreams, and many do not equate work in the commercial home with 'real work'. Lashley's and Rowson's (2002) earlier studies on those taking on a British pub franchise also confirm similar business motives and suggest that the low priority given to business growth and profit maximization was something of a limit on the ability of the franchisor pub company to expand its business.

The overlap between domestic/private and commercial domains has important implications for destination marketeers attempting to promote the quality of hospitality and service standards at a destination. Where business motives are chiefly personal, marketing and other management skills may not be developed or recognized as being important. Frequently, it is difficult to support these micro business owners because they do not recognize their own skill deficiencies and the need for formal management practice because their business agendas are primarily personal (Lashley and Rowson, 2002, 2003, 2005). In many cases, high levels of business failure and churn in ownership have a negative effect on overall business development for the tourism profile of the destination. For example, estimates of the change in ownership of Blackpool was conservatively estimated at 20 per cent per year, though some professionals suggested it could be as high as 50 percent (Lashley and Rowson, 2005), whilst estimates of change in pub tenancies in the UK were thought to be in the region of 30 per cent per year (Lashley and Rowson, 2001).

The domestic/private domain of hospitality provides valuable insights for those interested in marketing commercial hospitality experiences. It establishes a context in which individuals perform acts of hospitality and display their qualities of hospitableness. The domain also establishes the sense of authenticity of the hospitality experience. The assumption is that those who invite guests to stay or dine in their home are motivated by the desire to entertain. Telfer (2000) shows that these motives may not always be genuine. Individuals may be offering hospitality out of a sense of vanity, for ulterior motives, or because they feel an obligation to do so. Certainly, the domestic/private domain is an important setting for learning both the obligations to be a good host and guest, and the specific skills needed to run accommodation, bar, and restaurant operations. Indeed the link between cooking, serving food and drink, and providing accommodation in the home and in commercial operations in micro businesses is an important factor in persuading so many individuals that they have the skill sets to successfully run a hotel, restaurant, or bar venture. Destination marketeers have some important issues to confront because customers often perceive these independent micro businesses as offering a more authentic experience, where the skill sets of the actual business operators may, or may not, be capable of delivering the quality experience they expect.

The commercial domain

The nature of the relationship between those offering hospitality experiences in bars, hotels, and restaurant sites and the recipients of those experiences is of key importance to an analytical understanding of the commercial domain of hospitality. For some (Slattery, 2002), these are economic relationships. Customers are not guests in the sense outlined earlier in this chapter; they are customers entering into a contractual economic relationship. Customers receive a bundle of products and services, and for this they pay money in exchange. This type of thinking implies a substantially rational relationship and one in which emotional needs of the service encounter are recognized but given a subordinate role in the economic transaction. Service deliverers are required to provide emotional labor (Hochschild, 1983) through an appropriate emotional performance, but this is only one element of the service delivery.

This chapter argues that sustained customer relationships can be developed if the host and guest relationship is informed by these more traditional definitions of hospitality, concerned with delivering hospitality through the genuine hospitableness of hosts. By providing hospitality experiences that are delivered by individuals who are welcoming and hosting guests in a way that converts 'strangers into friends,' it is possible to develop a loyal base of 'customers who are friends'.

One of the key debates that has emerged over the commercial domain of hospitality is the extent to which it is possible to engage these traditional relationships in what is essentially an economic transaction. As we have seen earlier in the chapter, Telfer's comments on the motives of hospitableness suggest that commercial hospitality providers have ulterior motives. They deliver hospitality goods and services for profit; the level and extent of the service provided will always be dependent on their ability to turn in a profit. Frontline staff providing the service are doing so as employees, and customers are not their guests. Hochschild's (1983) work on emotional labor suggests that service staff are often required by their employers to provide an emotional performance they frequently do not feel and, hence, they have to engage in working at the emotions required for their job. Warde's and Martens's (2001) findings from 1000 respondents suggested that when asked about their dining-out experiences, a majority considered that dining in domestic/private venues involved genuine hospitality, whereas dining in commercial settings did not. Ritzer, through his work on 'MacDonaldization,' (1993, 2004) suggests that hospitality services are subject, like all services, to corporate pressures to increase control, calculability, predictability, and efficiency that lead ultimately to 'inhospitable hospitality' (Ritzer, 2006). These systems, informed by Taylorism (Taylor, 1947) developed in manufacturing, ultimately minimize human discretion and personal initiative, resulting in standardized and scripted service interactions, which are inconsistent with genuine hospitality and acts of hospitableness.

Although Telfer's (2000) exploration of the philosophy of hospitableness suggests that the ulterior motives associated with commercial hospitality might reduce the genuine quality of hospitableness, she hints that it might be more complex than it initially appears. When discussing commercial hospitality, Telfer suggests that it is not inevitable that commercial hospitality is inhospitable. It is possible that individuals who are naturally hospitable are attracted to work in the sector and provide hospitable behavior, even as employees of essentially 'inhospitable' firms. She also points out that many small firms may be operated for other than commercial reasons, and these may offer genuinely hospitable experiences. Lashley et al. (2005) found that interviewees were able to recognize hospitality experiences as being genuine in both commercial and domestic settings. When asked to recount their most memorable meal experiences, about half the occasions they recounted were in domestic settings, whilst the other half were in commercial settings. Interestingly, both appeared to be recognized as having authenticity, though the language of domestic hospitality was used to evaluate experiences in commercial settings. Emotional requirements to feel safe and secure, welcome, and genuinely valued dominate the assessment of authenticity in both settings.

Bell (2006) suggests that hospitality venues in the form of bars and cafes, and restaurants play an important role in providing the setting for new forms of urban cultural life. In many ways they perform as the community meeting point which, Adelmann et al. (1994) suggest, will become an increasing feature of service in cities where many people have an individualized existence. Bars, cafes and restaurants provide a service that 'creates a sense of social connection to others' (p. 140). In other words, they play a key role in providing social networking, which develops an authenticity in its own right.

The delivery of hospitality and tourism experiences can be better informed by recognizing the fundamental role that guest and host relations play in contemporary social life. This chapter argues that guest and host relations are at the heart of all hospitality transactions, irrespective of their immediate setting – the domestic/private or the commercial, or in the way destination residents interact with tourists. This chapter also argues that those wishing to market particular destinations – nation, region, or city – need to set the host–guest transaction at the centre of their marketing and service delivery strategies and manage the service in a way that pays attention to the emotional dimensions of the guest experience. In particular, the guest needs to feel like a guest in a domestic/private setting. They need to feel wanted and respected as individuals; they need to feel important and that their needs will be both recognized and met. Guests need to feel that they will be safe and secure, and comfortable. Hosts, therefore, need to be motivated by the desire to be hospitable and to ensure the happiness and wellbeing of the guest. Most importantly, commercial hospitality experiences must extend beyond formulaic standardized transactions wherein both customers and the staff hosting them are ultimately unimportant as individuals because the processes are essentially dehumanizing.

The emotions of hospitality

The emotional dimensions of the service encounter have been well understood for decades and have been incorporated into evaluations of satisfactory job performance. Typically, frontline staff in hospitality and tourism operations are required to present a 'nice day' (Mann, 1999) persona to customers irrespective of their personal feelings or moods. They should not show negative or aggressive emotions to customers, even awkward ones! Nor should they display other emotions inconsistent with the defined service standard. Many of the service quality models such as SEVQUAL incorporate 'empathy' as one of the dimensions via which to evaluate service quality and customer perceptions of the quality of service encounters (Parasuraman et al., 1991). Bitner et al.'s (1990) classic contribution prioritizes staff performance during critical incidents, such as when customers complain, or make unusual requests, or just in the manner of their interaction with customer. Performance in these situations can produce either customer satisfaction or dissatisfaction. Whilst all these concepts are helpful, they fail to recognize the key importance and uniqueness of the host–guest transaction. The nature and quality of the host–guest transaction are given high priority by the guests, though many hospitality and tourism operators tend to undervalue their importance.

Accounts of 'memorable meal occasions' (Lashley et al., 2005) suggest that the emotional dimensions of the meal were much more significant than the quality of the food. The research asked 63 first-year students to provide a written account of their most memorable meal. The texts were subjected to semiotic analysis and a multi-dimensional image of the meal emerged – nature of the occasion of the meal; fellow diners who made up the company with whom they dined; characteristics that contributed to the atmosphere; food eaten; overall setting; and the service provided. The occasion was typically some significant event in which the social dynamics of the meal reinforced the emotional significance of the event. Here the event is made more significant by the hospitality setting. The occasion of the meal or holiday is often a celebration of bonding and togetherness with family and friends. The company of others comes across strongly in these accounts, and although one account involved the company of just one other person, most involved groups of people, and none involved individual diners on their own. The atmosphere created by the setting, other people, and their treatment by the hosts provide emotional dimensions to the meal occasions that are vital to creating memorable occasions. Interestingly, few of the respondents mentioned the food consumed or quality of dishes as part of their descriptions. The dominant impression is that these emotional dimensions of hospitality are what make these meal occasions special, and it will be these emotional dimensions of their visit that make up memorable hospitality and tourism events.

Respondents in this research used language that links their experiences back to domestic/private hospitality. The need to feel welcome and friendliness from hosts,being secure in a non-threatening environment, feeling comfort and warmth, being an accepted and a valued member of the social group were all words used to describe guest's emotions. Commercial settings are not always a lesser form of hospitality; they engage guests with some different emotions, but there are some important overlaps. Fundamentally, guests evaluate hospitality experiences primarily in emotional terms, and providers of hospitality experiences in hospitality venues and resorts need to be aware of these emotional dimensions of the customer experiences and how to meet these emotional needs.

The problem is that many hospitality and tourism operators give priority to tangible aspect of what the customer is offered – the quality of the food, facilities and comforts in the room, the range and quality of the drinks on offer, etc. – but fail to see that it is the quality of the guest's emotional experience that really creates long-term customer satisfaction and loyalty. Herzberg's (1966) concept of motivation theory provides a useful metaphor; the physical aspects of the resort, the décor of the accommodation, physical facilities, the meal, and drink are potential 'dissatisfiers.' If standards do not meet expectations, customers will be dissatisfied, but exceeding their expectations in these aspects will not produce satisfaction (Balmer and Baum, 1993). Customer satisfaction will be generated by the quality of the emotions generated from their experiences with staff performance, the qualities of hospitableness, and fellow diners, and the performance of line management is the key to generating customer satisfaction through their emotional experiences as guests. Long-term customer-loyalty and repeat custom to the venue and resort are dependent on the emotions generated by these elements. Highly satisfied hospitality and tourism visitors are more likely to return or to recommend the establishment to family and friends.

Hochschild's (1983) seminal work suggests that service workers suffer job stress which results in 'burn-out,' and staff retention problems emerge because of the requirement to supply emotional labor. From a service perspective, 'emotional harmony' – where the individual genuinely feels that the emotion they are expected to display is the desired state – requires less emotional labor; it causes less stress and is more acceptable to customers, because the emotions expressed are those genuinely felt and required of the jobholder. Langhorn's (2004) study of emotional performance and emotional intelligence in a popular UK restaurant chain is interesting. Emotional Intelligence is the ability of individuals to recognize both their own emotions and those of others in their interactions with other people. Langhorn's study found that staff who were able to display 'service emotions' which they genuinely felt were perceived by customers as giving better service and better value. Customers also stated such staff increased their desire to return to the restaurant. Langhorn's study suggests that customers are less impressed with staff performance where the person appears to be acting and trying to hide emotions felt as in the case of 'surface acting'. Hospitality and tourism operators need to consider these dimensions of the service interaction and how to support their emotional laborers, because they are key to offering good hosting experiences that will engender positive emotional responses in guests. They are crucial to converting customers into friends.

The work on emotional labor has stimulated interest in the emotional dimensions of organizational life (Fineman, 1993, 2000). The impact of emotional intelligence has been seen as a key influence on business success in commercial organizations, with particular relevance for services. *Emotional Intelligence* has been described as key to organizational success as well, again with particular relevance in organizations like hospitality and tourism services where employee (internal customer) relations impact so directly on external customer experiences. Goleman (1998) puts emotional intelligence at the leading edge of business success. 'The business case is compelling: companies that leverage this advantage [emotional intelligence] add measurably to their bottom line' (p. 13).

The notion of an Emotional Intelligence Quotient is being widely promoted by many consultants and is said to underpin the most effective business performance and successful lives (Cooper and Sawaf, 1997). Those who are emotionally intelligent are said to have abilities in five domains. They

1. recognize their own emotions and express them to others;
2. recognize and understand the emotions of others;
3. use emotions with reason and emotional information in thought;
4. regulate and manage their own and the emotions of others; and
5. control strong emotional states – anger, frustration, excitement, anxiety, etc.

Hospitality and tourism operators are able to improve business performance and customer satisfaction with management practices rooted in emotional intelligence practices. Langhorn's (2004) study also explored the impact of emotional intelligence scores of managers in the same restaurant group. He found that mangers with higher emotional intelligence scores were positively related to improved profit performance, customer satisfaction, employee satisfaction, and team performance. Improvements can be made in operational performance through recruitment and training practices, as well as performance and service quality monitoring that use emotional intelligence as a key business concern.

The emotional dimensions of hospitality and tourism make the relationship between host and guest more than an ordinary service encounter. Guests are likely to evaluate the totality of their experiences on the basis of the feelings generated in their various encounters with immediate resort frontline staff and managers as well as the personnel from other organizations involved in the complete visit experience. An awareness of these emotional dimensions leads on to a concern for the emotional labor undertaken by frontline employees and the conditions needed both to remove negative impacts and generate emotions that are genuinely hospitable. Recent interest in assessing, recruiting, and developing the emotional intelligence of service workers offers one interesting avenue for improvement of service encounters. Frontline staff and immediate unit management are the crucial elements of marketing hospitality and tourism experiences to guests. They deliver the host contact that can develop positive guest emotions and experiences from which customers become loyal because they have an emotional attachment to the establishment or destination.

Making customers into friends

Acceptance of the central importance of the guest experience has some major implications for the management of hospitality and tourism service providers. Policies that train, support, and empower frontline staff become essential and have to be seen as core to the management task. Training frontline staff in how to build friendly relations with a stranger/guest is not just a nice idea, or an expensive luxury to be jettisoned when times get tough. Similarly, the management of staff retention is core to being able to build the relationship. It is impossible to train frontline staff appropriately if there is a constant churn of new employees through the organization. The returning guest will not feel like a friend if there is no continuity amongst the people who meet, greet, and serve them. There is now a well-proven link between employment practices, employee satisfaction, and customer satisfaction. Acceptance of the emotional importance and the need to establish friendly relations with guests intensify the needs for stable employment relationships and recognition of the asset value of service personnel.

Figure 1.2 suggests a model for the management of commercial hospitality assuming the primacy of the guest experience. The performance

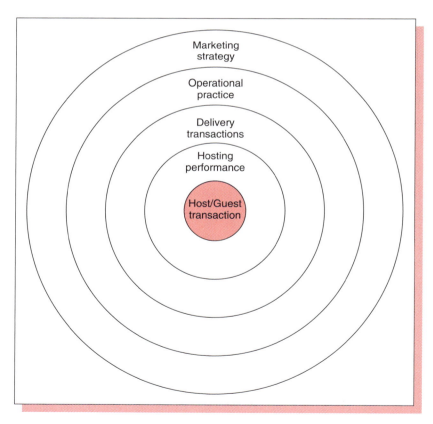

Figure 1.2
Modeling the management of commercial hospitality

of the immediate frontline team, including unit management, or all potential destination contacts in a tourism setting is key to success. Traditional ways of managing these operations have tended in the past to be priorities of a cost minimization strategy and labor has been a key area for cost minimization (Lashley et al., 2002; Lashley and Rowson, 2003, 2005).

Similarly, marketing strategy has tended to be given a higher budget and priority than the quality of the customer experience or the skills needed to deliver those experiences. In some cases, marketing activities deliver increased customer footfall, but also create more dissatisfied customers, because appropriate service quality standards and employee performance have not been established first. The approach being advocated in this chapter suggests that this must be reversed. As Figure 1.2 shows, the quality of the guest experience must be at the core of commercial strategy, and hosting skills are crucial elements of delivery of those experiences. Marketeers have to be concerned with these people management and operational issues as dimensions of the marketing mix. There is a need for a more multi-disciplinary approach to the role of the marketeer than is found in more traditional functionally specialized organizations.

The guest–host transaction

If the guest experience is to be such as to create memorable experiences and ultimately enable the guest to feel a bond of friendship, hosting behavior needs to reflect the traditions of hospitality and hospitableness. In addition, hosts need to have high levels of emotional intelligence and ability to predict and connect with guests' emotional needs. Table 1.1 lists some of key qualities required of hosts.

A culture of hospitality within commercial hospitality and tourism organizations would reflect traditional hospitality values and obligations. Accepting all visitors as guests irrespective of their likelihood of becoming regular visitors is at the heart of this approach. All strangers and guests are treated as potential friends. They are included into the host's setting and accepted as a right without fear. There is no hostility or threat to the guest, and developing a sense of security and safety is a priority. The hosting community is keen to ensure that all strangers are made to feel comfortable and personally welcome. A culture of welcome by gifting to the visitor involves unexpected and spontaneous gifting beyond formulaic 'give-aways' and 'promotional offers,' which have an ulterior motive and are given out to guests on an impersonal basis. A culture of hospitality would reject uneven and unfair treatments of individuals on the basis of gender, ethnicity, sexual orientation, or any other prejudgment. Ethical business policies promote and support all individuals.

Table 1.1 Key hosting qualities

A culture of hospitality

- The stranger is treated as a guest and potential 'friend'
- Guest included into the social context without limits
- Acceptance of all guests as equally valued individuals irrespective of guest characteristics
- No evidence of hostility to guests
- Guest protected and provided with a safe and secure environment
- Host gives gifts – the host welcomes the guest by providing the best gifts possible
- Host expresses compassion for the needs of others

Qualities of hospitableness

- The desire to please others
- General friendliness and benevolence
- Affection for people; concern for others and compassion
- The desire to meet another's need
- A desire to entertain
- A desire to help those in trouble
- A desire to have company or to make friends
- A desire for the pleasures of entertaining

Displaying emotional intelligence (Cooper and Sawaf, 1997)

- Hosts recognize their own emotions and are able to express them to others
- Hosts recognize and understand the emotions of guests
- Hosts use emotions with reason and emotional information in thought
- Hosts regulate and manage their own and the emotions of others
- Hosts control strong emotional states – anger, frustration, excitement, anxiety, etc.

Individuals practice hospitableness. They are selected, recruited, trained, appraised, and rewarded based on the display of qualities such as the desire to please others and being open, friendly, and benevolent, as well as compassionate and concerned about others with a desire to help. They must be keen to entertain others and willing to accept responsibility for the comfort and wellbeing of guests. They must be open and friendly, willing to make friends irrespective of the characteristics of the guest. They must enjoy entertaining and take pleasure in the happiness of others, without ulterior or egocentric motives. The organization must give high priority to the emotional dimensions of service and value emotional intelligence amongst frontline staff and managers. Emotionally intelligent frontline staff will better understand and manage their own emotions and will be supported by emotionally intelligent managers, who will manage in a way that supports staff in dealing with potential emotional disharmony and encourages them to be sensitive to the emotional needs of guests.

Hosts will understand the emotional needs of guests. These include the need to feel welcome as an individual, together with the need to feel respected and valued and the need to feel that the welcome and service by the host(s) are genuine and heartfelt. Guests also need to feel that hosts are sympathetic to the occasion of the visit and that hosts understand their different needs on different occasions, sometimes to be left alone and at other times to be embraced into the community. The establishment and tangible elements of the offer to guests must be at least in line with guest expectations, and, if faults do occur, these must be dealt with quickly. Guest must feel, therefore, that their wellbeing and comfort are of paramount concern driven by a genuine desire to entertain and provide hospitality. Guests need to feel that hosts know what they want before they themselves do. Most importantly, guests must feel comfortable and at-home. They must have a shared understanding of the context and the setting, as well as the hidden rules and expectations of them as guests and what they might reasonably understand from hosts and other guests. They must feel more than customers of the commercial setting; they must feel like friends.

Delivering host–guest transactions

Given the crucial importance of host performance in the delivery of guest experiences that will develop friendly relations with guests and ultimately loyal customers, the management of frontline personnel is of paramount importance. Recruiting staff that have a positive profile as hosts, with clear qualities of hospitableness and with a good level of emotional intelligence, will enable a commercial hospitality or tourism organization to build a workforce committed to deliver remarkable guest experiences. A planned program of training, role modeling, and best practice sharing will reinforce and further develop the culture of hospitality and commitment to guest experiences. Similarly, prioritizing staff retention is crucial because guests will not feel welcome and important if they never see the same person twice. Ensuring that staff are recruited, trained, supported, and retained is not just a nice idea, somehow 'other worldly' in a 'tough commercial environment;' it is an essential element of the business strategy on which to base competitive advantage and long-term profitability. Loyal customers are more profit yielding and lost customers are costly to replace. Staff retention builds up the store of human capital to the firm, and lost employees are expensive to replace. Recent figures by the UK-based Chartered Institute of Personnel and Development suggest that it costs £1000 (approximately US$2000) to replace each 'routine unskilled employee' (2005). Appraisal and reward systems must encourage and support hosting and the qualities of hospitableness.

Frontline staff need to be empowered. The form of the empowerment may vary between empowerment through participation, through involvement, or through commitment (Lashley, 2001), but in all circumstances staff must feel empowered. That is, they need to feel they have opportunities to do whatever is necessary to ensure guest experiences exceed expectations. They need to feel they have the skills needed to do whatever it takes and they are trusted by supervisors and managers. Effective empowerment involves feeling empowered. It is likely that the form of empowerment will be consistent with the type of service offer being made to guests. In other words, the extent to which employees are instructed, consulted, or democratically involved in making decisions will depend on the amount of discretion they need to meet guests' needs (Lashley, 2001). That said, the general principles of hospitality and hospitableness can be applied in any context, even in MacDonald's, Pizza Hut, and Kentucky Fried Chicken.

Operational practice

Fundamentally, the approach demands a concern for emotional intelligence amongst management. Emotional intelligence amongst managers assists them to have empathy with the workforce and with customers. Langhorn's (2004) work with a British restaurant chain indicated that managers who registered higher scores on the Emotional Intelligence Quotient had better employee retention, improved employee satisfaction score, and more satisfied customers and registered better profitability than managers with lower scores.

Emotional leadership actively engages the emotions of the followers (Mann, 1999). It recognizes the importance and inevitability of emotional dimensions of working life. Mann draws on interview responses from people at work: 'A good leader should be fair and treat people well'; 'They should be approachable, not distant. You should be able to discuss anything with a good leader'; 'They should nurture their staff not hold them back'; 'A truly great leader is one who demands the best but who rewards you fairly'; 'Leaders communicate their vision to those around them in ways that emotionally enroll others'; 'Leadership is about emotion' (p. 13).

Emotional leadership recognizes and supports staff engaged in emotional labor. The leader is in a crucial position to limit emotional dissonance that is at the heart of emotional labor. That is, they are in a position to create conditions whereby emotions that are expressed to the guest are the same as those being felt. If frontline personnel are to provide the emotional context in which customers feel secure, welcomed, and valued as friends, emotional leadership should provide employment experiences that make employees feel happy. Empowerment and participative forms of management have the potential to create the 'happy workers who will create happy customers,' summed up in Marriott's famous phrase (Lashley, 2001).

The operational context needs also to be sensitive to the emotions of the guest who is to become a friend. Information technology, already available but frequently not used by frontline staff, is essential in building the profile of the stranger as friend. In particular, subsequent visits provide opportunities to communicate the importance of the guest as an individual. Too few hotels use the information about the guest that they have already gathered; preferred newspaper, room type, and dining requirements, for example, are rarely referred to when a guest registers at the hotel for second and subsequent visits. The technology available is not appropriately used by staff because they do not recognize the importance of, nor are accountable for, developing a relationship with customers that recognizes them as individuals.

Often the rational commercial models of business control are not consistent with the mutual respect and trust required of friends. The overly secure mini-bar, for example, may well please the accountant concerned with cost minimization and increasing shareholder value, but does communicate a lack of trust of guests. There needs to be a complete audit of procedures so as to ensure that all processes involving guests communicate a trust and a relationship that is consistent with friends.

This way of thinking about the guest relationship needs to drive the whole management agenda, and it requires a fundamental shift in management thinking and priorities. Many hospitality organizations tend to prioritize shareholder concerns when making operational decisions (Lashley et al., 2002). Decisions to limit number of staff on duty, or to pay minimum wage rates, ultimately put both physical and emotional pressure on employees and limit their ability to develop appropriate relationships with customers. Reduced service to customers is unlikely to lead to the guest feeling important and like a friend. Hospitality service providers need to shift priorities so that guests' emotions are paramount. Guests are important as individuals, and they must be welcomed and made to feel at home. Lashley et al. (2005) suggests that these emotions are important in all settings, and the most successful hospitality experiences for guests are those in which emotions expressed by staff appear to be genuinely felt toward customers.

Operational management practices need to be informed by and fit with the model of service offer being made to guests. Based on work by Lashley and Taylor (1998), which established four service types, Lashley (2000) identified three service types that are being offered in hospitality and tourism contexts. In each case, the marketing offer to customers, staff performance, and the operating system need to be consistent with the reasons why customers visit the particular venue or destination. In addition to these variations in the nature of the offer to hospitality and tourism guests, the concept of 'occasionality'

(Lashley, 2000) suggests that the same customers may visit the same establishment with different needs on different occasions. These result in different 'critical success factors' which determine the perception of a successful or unsuccessful visit. Operations management needs to understand these occasionalities and ensure that service standards and service performance are flexible and capable of meeting these different sets of expectations.

Marketing strategy

Making traditional hospitality and the emotional dimensions of guest experiences at the heart of commercial hospitality and tourism marketing is, in principal, advocating a business strategy which aims to gain competitive advantage through the uniqueness of the service quality. Conventional services (Kotler, 2003) marketing literature suggests that a strategy that aims to compete via quality is less easily replicated than a strategy that aims to compete on low prices. A quality strategy is likely to develop more loyal customers and will be less susceptible to competitor pressures. The approach advocated here adds a further dimension to this because traditional hospitality suggests that good hosting leads to strangers becoming friends. In commercial context the approach suggests that making customers into friends intensifies the levels of loyalty because of the emotional attachment of the relationship.

Communications with customer/friend needs to be consistent with friendship. In other words it has to be sensitive to the needs of each individual customer, their likes and dislikes, preferences and needs. Sending out birthday, wedding anniversary, and Christmas cards is consistent with how friends operate, but these need to avoid overly formulaic and corporate outputs that often lack the personal touch. Invites to special events and being given special access to corporate events as honored friends are all examples of building ongoing contacts and communications that help to establish the special relationship. The British pub company JD Wetherspoon has an incentive scheme for bar staff who get to know the personal details of one hundred of their regular customers. A hotel known to the author provides regular guests with a complimentary favored drink in their room after they have dined in the hotel's dining room. The key point is that communications at corporate, unit, and individual level are consistent with 'guests as friends' rather than as customers.

Public relations outputs, advertising messages, and the brand image must link to values and obligations of traditional hospitality. This practice can be illustrated in the following quote from the brochure of Le Petit Hotel, St. Martin: 'Enjoy the spirit of our intimate island home, where you arrive a stranger and leave as our cherished friend'. In some cases, the hotel name is used to underscore the potential relationship. The names of some present day accommodation providers such as the *Welcome Stranger Motel* in Bendigo, Australia and the *Hotel Huincahue* (translates as Stranger's Place) in Pucon, Chile reflect these traditional concepts of hospitality and duties of hosts.

Frontline staff and management are the crucial marketing interface with guests. Under this approach, staff are more than service deliverers, they are the hosts who provide guest with experiences. It is vital, therefore, that staff are recognized as performing this marketing role, not just up-selling and complaint handling, but delivering the core brand values to guests. They are also the means of responding to each customer's needs and the variations amongst service types (Lashley, 2001) and of recognizing the potential service needs of the same guests when they arrive with different service needs in mind. They must recognize and respond to the critical success factors relevant to that customer's visit.

Conclusion

Traditional notions of hospitality can inform hospitality and tourism marketing strategies in commercial organizations and the business' relationship with customers. By recognizing the core importance of the host–guest transaction and the emotional dimensions of the guest's experiences, it is possible to build a loyal customer base of individuals who have a friendly or friend like relationship with the brand. These traditional concepts of hospitality are universal and are defining features of a society and its culture. That said, an investigation of the obligation to offer hospitality does show variation between societies and in the same society in different time periods. Many industrialized societies no longer have strong cultural, religious, and moral obligations to offer hospitality to strangers, and in some cases there are examples of communities who are positively hostile to tourists, migrants, and asylum seekers.

Whilst recognizing this cultural context of hospitality in many of the cultures that are both major tourism exporters and importers, these traditional concepts of hospitality can be employed to redefine the way commercial organizations device their marketing strategies. This chapter has advocated an approach which develops competitive advantage through the quality of the guest experience and by developing emotional bonds with guests that will convert strangers into friends in the manner of traditional hospitality.

Setting the host–guest transactions at the core of commercial hospitality and tourism organizations requires some fundamental changes in the way many commercial organizations operate. In many cases, and despite the rhetoric of stakeholder interests and balanced score cards, shareholder interests are paramount and dominate short-term financial targets. The model suggested here requires customers to be seen as the key stakeholders, with staff as a key resource through which to deliver the experiences necessary to convert guests into loyal friends. To succeed, organizations will need to be much more prepared to use an array of different techniques to evaluate business value. Retained customers and staff have a genuine value to the business organization and this needs to be recognized in spirit, and in management priorities, if not in tangible financial terms.

References

Adelmann, M.B., Ahavia, A., and Goodwwin, C. (1994) 'Beyond Smiling: social support and service quality', in Rust, R.T. and Oliver, R.L., eds, *Service Quality: new directions in theory and practice*, London: Sage.

Andrews, H. (2000) 'Consuming Hospitality on Holiday', in Lashley, C. and Morrison, A., eds, *In Search of Hospitality: theoretical perspectives and debates*, Oxford: Butterworth-Heinemann.

Balmer, S. and Baum, T. (1993) 'Applying Herzberg's Hygiene Factors to the Changing Accommodation Environment', *International Journal of Contemporary Hospitality Management*, Vol. 5 No. 2, pp. 34–45.

Bell, D. (2006) 'Hospitality and Urban Regeneration', in Lashley, C., Lynch, P., and Morrison, A. eds, *Hospitality: a social lens*, Oxford: Elsevier.

Bitner, J., Booms, B.H., and Tetreault, M.S. (1990) 'The Service Encounter: Diagnosing Favorable and Unfavorable Incidents', *Journal of Marketing*, Vol. 54, January, pp. 71–84.

Chartered Institute of Personnel and Development (2005) *CIPD Labor Turnover 2005 Survey Results*, London: CIPD.

Cole, S. (2006) 'Hospitality and Tourism in Ngadha: an ethnographic Exploration', in Lashley, C., Lynch, P., and Morrison, A., eds, *Hospitality: a social lens*, Oxford: Elsevier.

Cooper, R. and Sawaf, A. (1997) *Executive EQ*, London: Orion Business.

Crang, P. (2005) 'Hospitality, the City, and Café Culture: cosmopolitanism, conviviality and contemplation in Chueca, Madrid', Conference Abstracts, *Mobilizing Hospitality: the ethics of social relations in a mobile world*, Lancaster University.

Derrida, J. (2002) *Acts of Religion*, New York: Routledge.

Fineman, S., ed. (1993) *Emotion in Organizations*, London: Sage.

Fineman, S., ed. (2000) *Emotion in Organizations*, London: Sage.

Getz, D., Carlsen, J., and Morrison, A. (2004) *The Family Business in Tourism and Hospitality*, Wallingford: CABI Publishing.

Goleman, D. (1998) *Working with Emotional Intelligence*, London: Bloomsbury.

Heal, F. (1990) *Hospitality in Early Modern England*, Oxford: Oxford University Press.

Herzberg, F. (1966) *Work and the Nature of Man*, New York: Staple Press.

Hochschild, A.R. (1983) *The Managed Heart: commercialization of human feeling*, Berkley: University of California Press.

Ireland, F. (2005) *Strategy Statement 2005–2007*, Dunlin: Failte.

Jones, P. (2004) 'Finding the Hospitality Industry? Or Finding Hospitality Schools of Thought?', *Journal of Hospitality, Leisure, Sport and Tourism Education*, Vol. 3, No. 1, pp. 33–45.

Kotler, P. (2003). *A Framework for Marketing Management*, Oxford: Prentice Hall.

Langhorn, S. (2004) *The Role of Emotion in Service Encounters*, DBA Thesis, Luton: University of Luton.

Lashley, C. (1985) *Why Women Don't Become Chefs*, unpublished MA Thesis, Warwick: University of Warwick.

Lashley, C. (2000) *Hospitality Retail Management: a unit manager's guide*, Oxford: Butterworth Heinemann.

Lashley, C. (2001) *Empowerment: HR strategies for service excellence*, Oxford: Butterworth-Heinemann.

Lashley, C. (2004) *Escaping the Tyranny of Relevance: some reflections on hospitality management education*, paper presented at CAUTHE 2004, Alice Springs.

Lashley, C. and Morrison, A., eds (2000) *In Search of Hospitality: theoretical perspectives and debates*, Oxford: Butterworth-Heinemann.

Lashley, C. and Rowson, B. (2001) 'When is a Franchise not a Franchise? When it's a Pub!', *Strategic Change*, Vol. 11, No. 3, pp. 411–425.

Lashley, C. and Rowson, B. (2002) 'A Franchise by any Other Names? Tenancy Arrangements in the Pub Sector', *International Journal of Hospitality Management*, Vol. 21, No. 4, pp. 353–369.

Lashley, C. and Rowson, B. (2003) *The Benefits of Pub Retailer Training: a report for the Punch Pub Company*, Nottingham: Nottingham Trent University.

Lashley, C. and Rowson, B. (2005) *Developing Management Skills In Blackpool's Small Hotel Sector: a research report for England's North West Tourism Skills Network*, Nottingham: Nottingham Trent University.

Lashley, C. and Taylor, S. (1998) 'Hospitality Retail Operations Types and Styles in the Management of Human Resources' in *Journal of Retailing and Consumer Services*, Vol. 5, No. 3, pp. 59–84.

Lashley, C., Lynch, P., and Morrison A. (2006a) 'Hospitality: an introduction', in Lashley, C., Lynch, P., and Morrison, A., eds, *Hospitality: a social lens*, Oxford: Elsevier.

Lashley, C., Lynch, P., and Morrison, A. (2006b) 'Ways of Knowing Hospitality', in Lashley, C., Lynch, P., and Morrison, A., eds, *Hospitality: a social lens*, Oxford: Elsevier.

Lashley, C., Morrison, A., and Randall, S. (2005) 'More Than a Service Encounter? Insights into the Emotions of Hospitality Through Special Meal Occasions', *Journal of Hospitality and Tourism Management*, Vol. 12, No.1, pp. 80–92.

Lashley, C., Thomas, R., and Rowson, B. (2002) *Employment Practices and Skill Shortages in Greater Manchester's Tourism Sector*, Leeds: Leeds Metropolitan University.

Litteljohn, D. (1990) 'Hospitality Research: philosophies and progress', in Teare, R., Moutinho, L., and Morgan, N., eds, *Managing and Marketing Services in the 1990s*, London: Cassell, pp. 209–232.

Lomine, A. (2005) 'Tourism in Augustinian Society (44BC–AD69)' in Walton, ed., *Histories of Tourism*, Clevedon: Channel View Publications.

Lovelock, C. (1999). *Principles of Service Marketing and Management*, London: Prentice Hall.

Lynch, P.A. (2005) 'Reflections on the Home Setting in Hospitality', *Journal of Hospitality and Tourism Management*, Vol. 12, No. 1, pp. 37–49.

Lynch, P. and MacWhannell, D. (2000) 'Home and commercialized hospitality', in Lashley, C. and Morrison, A., eds, *In Search of Hospitality: theoretical perspectives and debates*, Oxford: Butterworth-Heinemann.

Mann, S. (1999) *Hiding What We Feel, Faking What We Don't: understanding the role of emotions at work*, Shaftesbury: Element.

Molz, J.G. (2005) 'Cosmopolitans on the Couch: mobilizing hospitality and the internet', Conference Abstracts, *Mobilizing Hospitality: the ethics of social relations in a mobile world*, Lancaster University.

Nouwen, H. (1975) *Reaching Out: the three movements of the spiritual life*, New York: Doubleday & Co.

O'Gorman, K.D. (2006) 'Dimensions of Hospitality: exploring ancient and classical origins', in Lashley, C., Lynch, P., and Morrison, A., eds, *Hospitality: a social lens*, Oxford: Elsevier.

O'Mahony, B. (2003) 'Social and Domestic Forces in Commercial Hospitality Provision: A View from Australia', *Hospitality Review*, Vol. 5, No. 4, pp. 37–41.

Palmer, A. (2001) *Principles of Services Marketing*, McGraw Hill: London.

Parasuraman, A., Berry, L.L., and Zeithaml, V.A. (1991) 'Understanding Customer Expectations of Service', *Sloan Management Review*, Vol. 32, No. 3, pp. 39–48.

Ritzer, G. (1993) *The MacDonaldization of Society*, Thousand Oaks, CA: Pine Forge.

Ritzer, G. (2004) *The Mcdonaldization of Society Revised New Century Edition*, Thousand Oaks: Pine Forge Press.

Ritzer, G. (2006) 'Inhospitable hospitality?' in Lashley, C., Lynch, P., and Morrison, A., eds, *Hospitality: a social lens*, Oxford: Elsevier.

Selwyn, T. (2000) An Anthropology of Hospitality, in Lashley, C. and Morrison, A., eds, *In Search of Hospitality: theoretical perspectives and debates*, Oxford: Butterworth-Heinemann.

Sherringham, C. and Daruwalla, P. (2006) 'Transgressing Hospitality: Polarities and Disordered Relationships', in Lashley, C., Lynch, P., and Morrison, A., eds, *Hospitality: a social lens*, Oxford: Elsevier.

Slattery, P. (2002) 'Finding the Hospitality Industry', *Journal of Hospitality, Leisure Sport and Tourism*, Vol., 1, No. 1, pp. 19–28.

Sweeney, M. and Lynch, P. (2006) 'Explorations of the Host's Relationship with the Commercial Home' 15th *CHME research Conference Proceedings*, Nottingham: Nottingham Trent University.

Taylor, F.W. (1947) *Scientific Management*, New York: Harper & Row.

Telfer, E. (1996) *Food for Thought, Philosophy of Food,* London: Routledge.

Telfer, E. (2000) The Philosophy of Hospitableness, in Lashley, C. and Morrison, A., eds, *In Search of Hospitality: theoretical perspectives and debates,* Oxford: Butterworth-Heinemann.

Thomas, R., Lashley, C., Rowson, B., Guozhong, X., Jameson, S., Eaglen, A., Lincoln, G., and Parsons, D. (2000) *The National Survey of Small Tourism and Hospitality Firms: 2000 – Skills Demand and Training Practices,* Leeds: Leeds Metropolitan University.

Walton, J.K. (1998) *Blackpool,* Edinburgh: Keele and Edinburgh University Press.

Walton, J.K. (2000) *The British Seaside: holidays and resorts in the twentieth century,* Manchester: Manchester University Press.

Walton, J.K. (2005) *Histories of Tourism*, Clevedon: Channel View Publications.

Warde, A. and Martens, L. (2001) *Dining Out*, London: Sage.

Wharton, A. (2006) 'Commodifying Space: hotels and pork bellies' in Lashley, C., Lynch, P., and Morrison, A., eds, *Hospitality: a social lens*, Oxford: Elsevier.

CHAPTER 2

Socially responsible hospitality and tourism marketing

Azilah Kasim

Introduction

As one of the fastest growing sectors of the global economy, the extent and scope of hospitality and tourism (H&T) growth raise issues on its negative environmental and social impacts. This chapter aims to highlight these impacts, with a special reference to the hotel sector. The relevance and importance of addressing social responsibility and ethical issues in the H&T context are emphasized. In addition, ways to engage in the management and marketing of a socially responsible and ethical image will also be suggested to enhance awareness among readers on the issue.

By nature, H&T offerings depend greatly on environmental and cultural resources, as the industry involves activities that are constantly interactive with the natural systems. For example, tourists' desire for a secluded and scenic accommodation may result in increased clearance of natural areas for the purpose of development of resorts and hotels (Wahab and Pigram, 1997). In addition, the transportation of tourists from one destination to another requires the use of some form of transport and, hence, the use of fossil fuel, which releases significant amounts of greenhouse gases and other air pollutants (Holden, 2000). Solid and organic wastes produced by food and beverage operators could also contribute to environmental problems at particular destinations.

H&T has the capacity to initiate significant changes in the physical environment (Wahab and Pigram, 1997; Hassan, 2000). This is particularly true for the hotel sector whose impacts have clearly been identified (see International Hotel Environmental Initiative's [IHEI] *Environmental Action Pack for Hotels*, 1995; Kirk, 1995; Green Hotelier, 1999; Green Globe 21 Asia Pacific, 2000; World Travel and Tourism Council [WTTC], 2002; Kasim, 2005) as involving: (1) energy consumption; (2) water consumption; (3) waste production; (4) wastewater management; (5) chemical use and atmospheric contamination; (6) purchasing/procurement; and (7) local community initiatives. A broader outlook on other negative impacts of the industry is available in the United Nations Environment Programme (UNEP) report (2002).

Besides interactions with the natural systems, H&T activities also involve direct or indirect contacts between tourists and the local people. Homestay tourism, agro-tourism, and eco-tourism, for example, generally involve direct interactions between the visitors and the locals (villagers, farmers, local guides, etc.). In contrast, conventional mass tourism requires less involvement of the local people, thereby minimizing direct interactions. In both cases, however, contacts between tourists and the local people could lead to problems such as conflict of values, over-commercialization of arts and crafts at the expense of authenticity, and importation of new lifestyle and culture, with possible negative consequences to local values, particularly among the youth

(Hong, 1985; Wahab and Pigram, 1997; In Malaysia, for example, the first strains of the 'drug culture' were found among the hippie tourists who came in big groups to Penang. The tourists were also observed to impose their culture and way of life on places they visited, through activities such as swimming nude and having marijuana parties, which are against the local beliefs and values (Hong, 1985).

The negative social impacts of H&T may begin even before tourists arrive at a destination. Rapid and often poorly planned developments of H&T in developing countries catalyze rapid transitions of lifestyles from traditional to western-style modernization. This implies a rapid loss of cultural identity and degradation of traditional values. It could lead to far-reaching negative impacts such as the disruption of family and social cohesion (e.g., people work harder to improve social status, thereby spending less time with families), the abandonment of traditional economies (e.g., activities such as farming and fishing are replaced by H&T-related activities), substance abuse, prostitution, and more (Hong, 1985; Mathieson and Wall, 1992; German NGO Forum on Environment and Development, 1998).

The inevitable link between H&T and the physical and social environments implies that H&T's survival depends critically on its ability to not only maximize its benefits but also minimize its negative impacts on environments and societies. In other words, the quality of tourists' interaction with locals and environments will diminish considerably, if the natural setting of H&T activities is polluted, degraded, or lost in its aesthetic qualities as a result of a poorly planned H&T development. Similarly, a destination may lose its tourist appeal if there are social problems such as increased crimes (from drugs/alcohol abuse and prostitution) and societal antagonism. Therefore, the mitigation of these possible negative impacts is essential in order to sustain the quality of H&T services.

Indeed, it would be impossible to solve all the environmental and social impacts already mentioned, in absolute terms. However, key players in H&T can choose to pursue growth in a way that allows them the flexibility to respond positively to the changing global environment and societal structure, while being responsive to the principles and practices of sustainable development. In other words, H&T needs a new direction that involves all the key players in order to address the flaws of its conventional (mass) form. Goeldner and Ritchie (2006: 470) state that:

From the standpoint of the tourism sector, the reality is that all questions related to nature and extent of tourism development must be supported by the community at large. This means that whatever direction tourism development takes in a community, region, or country, it must have the support of citizens who are affected by it.

As one of the 'citizens' affected by tourism development, the H&T business needs to contribute to sustainable development. Sustainable efforts from the industry and all its segments – hospitality, travel agency, air transport, tour operators, and others – are key to ensuring that the industry is sustainable. With support for sustainable development in mind, the H&T business must therefore be managed and marketed in a more responsible manner. Under the concept of business social responsibility (BSR), key trading partners of the industry including the H&T business are asked to show more accountability or social responsibility in their management. Consequently, they can engage in social or relationship marketing with the aim of benefiting the target audience or the wider public.

Social responsibility and ethical issues in H&T

Having established the relevance of ethical issues related to the social responsibility of H&T, it is also crucial to further understand what social responsibility entails, how it fits into the H&T context, how to engage in it, and how to portray a socially responsible image through marketing. The following subsections will deal with each of these, in further detail.

Social responsibility (SR) and examples

SR is an increasingly important concept in the business world today. It expands business priority beyond something simply financial, to consider a range of stakeholders in business planning and operations (including marketing activities), with the goal of forming an alliance beneficial to both the business and its relevant stakeholders. A key aspect of SR is to work with the local community/destination, to develop practices suitable to the local context, contribute to the local economy, and benefit the local people in some ways.

In developed countries, the concept was first explored via the 'eco-efficiency' approach, which, according to DeSimone and Popoff (1997), was a business concept that emphasized: (1) value creation for consumers, society, and business itself; (2) reduction of externalities (e.g., waste generation, pollution, and over-consumption of non-renewable resources); (3) addressing the requirements of all key stakeholders; and (4) pollution control beyond on-site measures.

In the 1990s, the concept of 'voluntary initiatives' was promoted to encourage self-regulated activities that pre-empt governmental regulations. It provides an avenue for businesses to negotiate and develop mutually agreeable ethical standards with the government and Non-Government Organizations (NGOs). In approaching the new millennium, big businesses started to account for social factors such as consumer demands, NGO pressures, political pressures, and media reports in their decision-making (Welford, 1994).

Finally, following the Johannesburg Summit in 2002, business's definition of sustainable development firmly included elements such as the economy, environment, and society. Economically, sustainable development is linked to profitability, wages and benefits, labor productivity, job creation, expenditures on outsourcing, and human capital. Environmentally, sustainable development concerns the impacts of processes, products, and services on air, water, and land, biodiversity, and human health. Socially, sustainable development relates to workplace health and safety, community relations, employee retention, labor practices, business ethics, human rights, and working conditions (World Business Council on Sustainable Development [WBCSD], 2003). These definitions show that businesses are required to pay greater attention to the social dimension of their responsibility.

This raises the question of what exactly is meant by the term 'social responsibility.' Earlier expectation of SR of tourism business, according to the Green Globe 21 standard, was confined to environment-related social issues such as 'environmental awareness of staff, customers and communities' and 'partnership for sustainable development' (see World Travel and Tourism Council, World Tourism Organization and Earth Council, 1995). Similarly, in the Manila Declaration on the Social Impact of Tourism (1997) made by governmental and private representatives from 77 countries and territories, the following declaration is the only statement spelling out clearly the role of business:

[To] cooperate with and encourage the business community engaged in tourism and travel trade to create the right image and develop appropriate marketing tools for the destination countries, and to undertake education, information and communication services to sensitise visitors to the culture and behavioural expectations of host communities.

(Manila Declaration on Social Impact of Tourism, 1997: 2)

However, the more recent definitions of SR of business are broader in nature. According to the Organization for Economic Cooperation and Development (OECD), SR of business is the actions to nurture and enhance their relationships with the societies in which they operate (Gordon, 2002). Similarly, the BSR emphasizes that SR for business denotes doing business without dishonoring ethical values and respect for people, communities, and the natural environment. This means addressing the legal, ethical, commercial, and other expectations society has of business and fairly treating all key stakeholders (BSR, 2003). Similarly, the American Society for Quality defines SR as people and organizations behaving and conducting business ethically and with sensitivity toward social, cultural, economic, and environmental issues. Striving for SR helps individuals, organizations and governments to have a positive impact on development, business, and society (American Society for Quality, 2004). In sum, SR is no longer limited to environmental aspects, but extends further to include social, cultural, and economic aspects as well.

For tourism in general, and the H&T business in particular, a framework for 'Ten Top Priority Areas for the Tourism Business' has been proposed by World Tourism Organization (WTO), WTTC, and Earth Council (EC) for businesses to become more responsible for:

1. waste minimization, reuse, and recycling;
2. energy efficiency, conservation, and management;
3. management of freshwater resources;
4. wastewater management;
5. hazardous substances control;
6. transport;
7. land-use planning and management;
8. involvement of staff, tourists, and communities in environmental issues;
9. design for sustainability that makes or uses less polluting, highly efficient, socially and culturally appropriate, and readily accessible new products; and
10. partnership for sustainable development between the government and civil organizations (WTTC/WTO/EC, 1995).

Green Globe 21 (GG21), a global standard for tourism businesses, was set up in 1994 to 'enable tourism firms to seek advice on environmental matters from experts who also understood the travel trade' (Forsyth, 1996: 6). GG21 standard tackles global environmental issues in travel and tourism through consultation with key stakeholders such as employees, tourists, communities, and suppliers of the tourism industry. For H&T, a more specific framework for engaging in SR is also available (see Exhibit 2.1). One such framework is IHEI's *Environmental Action Pack for Hotels, 1995*, which allows hotels to compare their environmental performance with that of hotels with similar facilities, in three major climate zones.

IH&RA *Environmental Good Practice in Hotels*, 1996, is another publication that provides a persuasive confirmation on the feasibility of utilizing and managing change in an effort to achieve environmental excellence. Some of the basic 'responsible activities' being proposed for the hotel sector include use of recyclable office paper supplies, use of cleaning solution products that are biodegradable and environmentally sensitive, implementation of some form of energy saving programs, and implementation of active recycling programs. Websites such as www.greenhotels.org and www.ceres.org, and www.iblf.org

---

Exhibit 2.1 Best practice guides and case studies available for engaging on SR

Document type	Examples
Websites	• Green Hotels Association (www.greenhotels.com) • Coalition for Environmentally Responsible Economies (CERES) Corporate Outreach Committee (2000) – Best Practice Survey for Institutional purchasers (www.ceres.org) • Coalition for Environmentally Responsible Economies (2006). Investor and environmentalist for sustainable prosperity (www.ceres.org) • Green Hotels Association (2006). Green Hotels (www.greenhotels.com) • Green Globe 21, Green Globe Manual 1994 (www.wttc.org/Publications.htm) • International Hotels and Restaurant Association (IH&RA) (2005) (http://www.ih-ra.org/awards/2005/index.php)
Corporate reports	• Inter-Continental Hotels and Resorts with Grecotel • Canadian Pacific Hotels and Resorts' Green Partnership Guide • Scandic Hotels' 'Resource Hunt'—a 3-year program to address resource efficiency
Institutional publications	• IH&RA and UNEP: *Environmentally Good Practices in Hotels* (1996) – case studies • Tour Operators Initiative for Sustainable Tourism Development: *A Practical Guide to Good Practice—Managing Environmental and Social Issues in the Accommodations Sector* (2003)
Other publications	• Kirk, 1995 • Meade and Monaco, 1999

Adapted from: Kasim (2005)

---

also provide specific guidelines on environment-friendly measures suitable for hotel operations. Nonetheless, it must be noted that such information is often accessible only through membership.

The case study in Exhibit 2.2 provides a comprehensive example of how the framework can be adopted by hotels. More examples can also be accessed through various UNEP joint publications on the matter (see http://www.uneptie.org/pc/tourism/library/training-hotel.htm).

Exhibit 2.2   Case Study on Hotel Nikko, Hong Kong

About Hotel Nikko Hongkong

Hotel Nikko Hongkong is situated on the waterfront of the Victoria Harbor next to the famous Kownloon shopping district. It has a total of 462 rooms of which 19 are suites in its 17 floor building. The ballroom, with four additional function rooms, can accommodate up to 460 people. Each of the room has a seating capacity from 55 to 230 people. The hotel has four restaurants and two bars, a business center, a swimming pool, a health club, and a shopping arcade.

Water

Reducing water consumption
To reduce water consumption, the hotel has been using, since 1995, a calibrated water control system, called the 'Platypus System.' The core element of this system is a compact valve that is inserted into the hydraulic system of each tap or shower to control the flow and temperature balance. The correct type and size of valve is chosen for each tap or shower, depending on factors such as required water temperature, pressure and flow rate. The advantages of this system are:

- Water flow is constant; flow fluctuations from each tap or shower are eliminated
- Changes in water temperature are eliminated
- Water hammer, velocity noise, and splashing are substantially reduced when taps are turned on.
- Filters improve the quality of the water delivered to guests.

Economic and environmental benefits
The reduced water consumption has brought both economic and environmental benefits to Hotel Nikko even in the first year the system was installed. For example, between July 1995 and June 1996, despite an average occupancy increase of 4% over the previous year, water consumption per guest decreased by an average of 13%, equating to saving of HK$13 000 (US$1688) per month. (Note: This figure could be as high as 30% as it does not include water consumption for laundry)

Hot water consumption fell correspondingly and the use of fuel for the hot water boilers decreased by an average of 4% or 2000 liters per month in that year. This led to savings of approximately HK$5600 (US$724) in fuel costs. Taking into account the energy saved, the investment return period is estimated to be about 30 months. However, if the savings on the Trade Effluent Discharge which the hotel had imposed in April 1995 and the Sewerage Discharge fees are included, the payback period could have been considerably shorter.

Reducing the use of fresh water
By using seawater in the chiller plant and placing towel re-use tent cards in all guest-bathrooms, the hotel managed to limit the use of scarce fresh water resources.

Energy

Key-card master switch
Estimating that approximately a third of its guests forget to turn off the master switch controlling electrical units when leaving the room, the hotel installed a key-card-controlled master switch to replace the button previously used. This automatically turns off all electrical units when rooms are vacant.

Economic and environmental benefits
The key-card system brings an average saving of HK$2.36 (US$0.30) per day per room. Switches cost HK$165 (US$21) per units to install and the payback period for this investment is estimated to be about 70 days.

Maintaining indoor temperatures
Indoor temperatures are maintained by daily thermometer readings (20° Celsius in summer and at 21–22° Celsius in winter).

Reducing boiler operating hours and water temperatures
To reduce boiler operating hours, the hot-water boilers are switched off between 0100 and 05.00 a.m. Water temperature is reduced from 60 to 55°C, i.e. an ideal temperature for personal use and to prevent legionella growth.

Economic and environmental benefits
By reducing the boiler operating hours and water temperatures, gas consumption of the hotel is reduced by 11% and associated costs are reduced by 6% each year.

Wider benefits and networking

Collaboration with the Hong Kong Polytechnic University
The hotel collaborates closely with the Hong Kong Polytechnic University by allowing it to be used as a practical study program for students in their final year of the Department of Building Services at the university. This partnership began in 1992 when the students performed an audit on Hotel Nikko Hongkong's water and energy consumption efficiency and on indoor air quality. It has since

produced a number of environment-related student research applicable to the hotel industry.

A 'Guide to energy and water conservation in hotels'

With the help of the Hong Kong Polytechnic University, the hotel published *A Guide to Energy and Water Conservation in Hotels*, to provide managers and engineering staff a practical guide based on the experience gained from auditing hotels in Hong Kong.

Networking and sponsorship

To garner support from the public and potential partners, the hotel's general manager often makes presentations on environmental management in hotels at national and international workshops and conferences. In addition, the hotel sponsors the Hong Kong Annual Business and Industry Environment Conference and participates in tree-planting efforts and fund-raising activities for environmental charities.

Support measures

Visitor communication

Visitors can clearly see the environmental awards won by Hotel Nikko Hongkong, which are displayed in the reception area. The awards are also listed on hotel stationery, brochures, and other promotional materials.

Staff

Environmentally sound housekeeping measures are enforced among staff, in their daily tasks: turning off equipment when not in use, closing curtains in unoccupied bedrooms to reduce heat transfer, using equipment (especially washing machines) according to manufacturers' specifications, and reporting leaks and other defects.

Engineering and maintenance staff who are actively involved in improving the operating efficiency of all equipment are given special treatment.

Staff are kept informed through the distribution of *Guidelines for Energy Efficiency Advisory Committee of the Government of Hong Kong*.

Adapted from: UNEP/IH&RA publication 'Environmental Good Practice in Hotels: Case Studies from the IHRA Environmental Award.' Retrieved on August 4, 2006 from http://www.eco-pages.org/frame_main/Champions_05/Hotel_ Nikko_eng.htm

Other success stories can be seen through award schemes such as the IH&RA Environmental Award conducted in association with the UNEP. In 2005, The Meliá Jardim Europa in São Paulo, Brazil was chosen as the winner in the chain category notably for its innovative 'Green Floor Project,' which re-creates the tropical Brazilian forest inside the hotel. The Green Floor Symbol is displayed throughout the property and is comprised of three green leaves symbolizing the three Rs – reduce, reuse, and recycle. Guests are encouraged to contribute to the World Wildlife Fund and the hotel would then match each donation. This makes the project a holistic approach to sustainability where all the actions adopted by the management are clearly visible to the guests and are fortified by their contribution.

The same award recognized The Monterey Inn Resort and Conference Center in Ontario, Canada for its 'Carbon Neutral program' that inculcates consumer awareness through encouraging them to calculate the carbon dioxide (CO_2) emission produced during their own travel and offers ways to offset the CO_2 emissions by taking part in the Tree Canada Foundation's carbon credit program. The hotel collects the cost of planting trees from the customer and facilitates the planting of trees with the Tree Canada Foundation. Consequently, hundreds of trees are being planted on behalf of guests. Spice Village in Kerala, India was awarded for using customer feedback to improve the hotel's environmentally best practice initiatives. The guests are encouraged to pen down their valuable suggestions on environmental issues, which make their stay an engaging experience. The 3 Rivers Eco Lodge & Sustainable Living Centre in Dominica, West Indies was recognized for integrating communication 'as a structural part of its offer by setting up a "sustainable living centre" that also extends the discussion beyond the "travel" experience to the guests' every-day lives.' The work of Fairmont Hotels & Resorts in designing a comprehensive corporate environmental policy, to be implemented at the property level, is also commended by the judges (more details are available at http://www.ih-ra. org/awards/2005/index.php).

The above examples are admittedly focusing on the environmental management of H&T businesses. Examples of social management, though not as abundant, are also available. One such example can be seen through Six Continental Hotel's guideline on community development initiatives (see Exhibit 2.3).

Exhibit 2.3   An example of award-winning best practices in community development initiatives

Six continental hotels

Philanthropic initiatives system
1. Identify areas of focus – the hotel chain focuses on five areas of concern 1. children; 2. diversity; 3. education; 4. environment; and 5. well-being

2. Develop a 'giving criteria' – the Six Continental's giving criteria include that:
   a. the receiving non-profit organization be serving and providing health and human services, education, arts and culture, or community development initiatives;
   b. the focus of donations and sponsorships be on communities where the hotel chain is operating;
   c. the charity organizations be legal; and
   d. the donation be used solely by the receiving organization and solely for the purpose the donation was being made.
3. Develop a 'restriction criteria' – for the hotel chain, restriction criteria include:
   a. non-profit organizations that constitute a conflict of interest for the chain or any of its brand;
   b. political or politically affiliated organizations;
   c. individuals seeking personal sponsorships;
   d. governmental organizations; and
   e. religious organizations, except when the activity being sponsored is sectarian, such as shelter.

Employee friendly system

1. establish the firm's core value in relation to employee development
2. establish the firm's policy on the qualities that different people bring to their jobs
3. establish the firm's policy on interests and demands of employees outside work
4. decide the firm's policy on increasing understanding and motivation of employees
5. develop appropriate strategies based on the firm's priorities regarding (1)–(4).

Adapted from: Six Continents Environmental and Social Report (2002)

The above example demonstrates the possibility of integrating social responsibility into the management of an organization. In fact, through awards and recognition schemes such as the IH&RA award, business can gain extra miles on being recognized for doing so. This is, of course, very good for a business's image and reputation.

The marketing sense of being a socially responsible business

From the discussions above, it seems that there are many examples to help guide the H&T business through social responsibility engagements. Ideally, all business organizations should be 'jumping into the bandwagon'. But the reality is that business responsiveness often relates to anticipations about future changes as a result of changing government policies or market demands. In other words, business would only change if it makes business sense to do so. From a marketing point of view, a greater market share and an improved overall image to stakeholders are what the H&T business is most concerned about. Greenhotels, for example, proposed that the growing niche of discerning and environmentally conscious business travelers in the United States was the major reason why more hotels should offer environment-friendly attributes. Another example is Coalition for Environmentally Responsible Economies' (CERES) Green Hotel Initiative that aims at raising the industry's awareness about meeting planners' and travel buyers' environmental concerns and encouraging hotels to take advantage of these growing markets (CERES, 2000). At an intra-regional level, the Green Leaf program, which was developed by the Pacific Asia Travel Association (PATA) and later integrated into the Green Globe program in March 2000, was another example of an initiative to capture the new market (Cheney and Barnett, 2001). These and many more positive reactions, particularly by big chain hotels worldwide, relate to increasing reports of 'green demand' and 'green consumerism' as explained below.

Green consumerism

Green consumerism is a major driver for business to be green. As stressed by Lave and Matthews (1996), without the existence of market niches for green products and services and green demand from the customer, even a well intentioned business would be reluctant to raise its production or operation costs for the good of the environment. In the United Kingdom, green consumerism has increased significantly in recent years. This is seen in the rise of 'green' product supply ranging from ethical finance to fair trades of coffee, tea, and chocolates. According to 'The Green and Ethical Consumer' market research reports published in 2000 and 2002, green and ethical consumer markets in the United Kingdom were found to be rising due to the increasing importance of green and ethical criteria in purchasing patterns. However, price was still an overriding factor particularly in purchasing non-food goods and financial services.

Several studies on consumerism have proven that there is a growing demand for products and services that are offered by environment-friendly and socially responsible firms. According to European, North American and Oceanic research, care for the environment and sub-themes like social responsibility have become an increasingly significant consumer value (Conner, 2000; Faulk, 2000). Marketing experts have discovered that consumers are willing to act on their environmental values (Post and Altma, 1994) and are willing to pay increased tariffs for goods and services that provide assurances of environmental responsibility (Creyer and Ross, 1997; Wolfe and Shanklin, 2001; Wearing et al., 2002). According to one survey, as many as eight out of ten American consumers claimed that they were environmentalists (Grove et al., 1996). Another more recent survey cites that 70% of consumers occasionally consider environmental issues when purchasing products or services (Wearing et al., 2002; Miller, 2003).

The Hong Kong Trade Development Council (2004) has reported that the proportion of green consumers who actively seek out and buy green products are on the rise, accounting for more than 20% of the population in the United States and the United Kingdom and around 50%, in west Germany. The study also revealed that green consumers usually have higher incomes and are better educated, with the younger generation being relatively more concerned about environmental protection. Supporting the findings of Wolfe and Shanklin (2001), Wearing et al. (2002), and Creyer and Ross (1997), the Council reported that an increasing number of consumers were willing to pay more for products with green attributes and that the price premium enjoyed by green businesses could be as much as 20% in the US market. Realizing this increasing trend in green consumerism, Hong Kong firms have been advised to tap the green market in a more effective way.

In a detailed analysis of factors influencing the consumer's purchasing decision, carried out by Creyer and Ross (1997), the findings have pointed out that consumers are concerned about corporate ethics and believe that they will take actions to promote it. Consumers also would reward ethical corporate behaviors with their willingness to pay higher prices for that firm's product. They may also buy from an unethical firm, but would do so at lower price which, in effect, punishes unethical business conducts by firms. These findings can strongly pressure firms to act more responsibly.

In contrast to the findings related to the willingness of consumers to pay higher premiums for green goods and services, the latest Green and Consumer Market Assessment, carried out in 2005, noted that consumers are actually unwilling to purchase excessively for greener alternatives (Key Note Publications, 2005). The consumer research conducted for this report demonstrates that the demand for ethical business conducts and greater corporate responsibility is being channeled more effectively through consumer boycotts and more sophisticated campaigning by protest groups.

Tourism also has its share of ethical consumerism, with firms such as German-based Touristik Union International (TUI), First Choice, and British Airways Holidays adopting sustainable developments in their corporate policy. Several studies have tried to prove the existence of green tourists and understand their behavior. Environmental issues that concern the green tourist include wildlife, transport, conservation, use of natural resources, pollution, construction and planning, sports activities, and practices of tourism firms themselves (Faulk, 2000). The argument of whether or not pressure from tourists, especially green tourists, can change tourism industry practices to be more eco-friendly has been put forward by Forsyth (1996), Wearing et al. (2002), Hjalager (1999), Diamantis (1998) and Miller (2003). Some of their findings support the view that tourist demands are important drivers of sustainable tourism, whereas others have concluded that only a small number of tourists want holidays that are 'green'.

In the United States, evidence of tourist demand for environment-friendly hotels is quite significant. According to a report by Guadalupe-Fajardo (2002), a survey by Small Luxury Hotels of the World has found that 80% of American travelers place importance on hotels preserving and protecting the environment. The survey also found that 55% of American tourists are more likely to book a hotel that establishes itself as an environment-friendly hotel, while 70% of them are willing to pay more to stay in a hotel with a responsible environmental attitude. The survey also looked at the attitude of tourists toward other social issues and found that Americans place importance on hiring hotel employees to help communities and on sharing of resources between hotels and local communities. The report also mentioned about initiatives by both the Caribbean Hotel Association and the Puerto Rico Hotel and Tourism Association to honor hoteliers for their environmental efforts.

The Green and Ethical Consumer Market Assessment 2000 has provided a more detailed account of the demographic factors influencing consumer behavior (Key Note Publication, 2000). The survey carried out during this assessment showed that older respondents (35 or older) attached greater priority to ethical issues than their younger counterparts. Those aged between 45 and 54 were most likely to have refused to purchase an item of clothing on ethical grounds. The results of the survey also showed that women consistently demonstrated a more positive attitude toward green and ethical issues than men. This market assessment also identified, to the contrary, that low priority was attached to the environment-friendly aspects of holidays in that only less than a third of the respondents would choose a holiday that was advertised with environment-friendly features (Key Note Publications, 2000).

In a survey of UK consumers conducted by Miller (2003), consumers were already making decisions based on environmental, social, and economical qualities for the purchase of day-to-day products and were keen to transfer these habits to the purchase of tourism products. The survey results also showed that 78% of the respondents either 'always' or 'sometimes' look for environment-friendliness of their intended destination, thus providing evidence that consumers were seeking out green product information and using it to make decisions about their destinations. The research highlighted the need for the tourism industry to capitalize on the demand for a wider range of product information, including environmental information, and promote moves toward greater levels of tourism sustainability.

Wearing et al. (2002) studied Australia's backpacker market to explore the tourists' environmental concerns and behaviors and suggested that although environmental concerns existed among the backpackers interviewed, this did not always translate into environmentally and socially responsible behaviors. Inconsistencies between environmental concerns and actual behaviors were due to three major factors: lack of education and awareness about eco-friendly tourism products and accreditation programs, the need to internalize locus of control in terms of environmental responsibility, and apparent abandonment of environmental responsibility by tourists while on holiday. To increase the conversion of environmental concerns into responsible purchases, it was recommended that the promotion of 'green' tourism products and accreditation programs should be undertaken through national tourism organizations during the pre-departure stage of a holiday taking.

In terms of factors influencing the consumer's choices of holiday destinations, Hjalager (1999) reported that the response was highly correlated with four basic factors – mode of accommodation preferred, nationality, gender and age. Vacationers with a high interest in environmental issues were more open to accept less sophisticated accommodation in coastal or rural areas whereas vacationers with less interest on the environment tended to prefer hotel or youth hostel instead. Relating to nationality, the Germans assigned significantly greater importance to environmental issues than any other nationalities. Gender wise, both men and women were equally sensible to environmental matters, while tourists aged between 25 and 46 attached more importance to the environment than tourists outside that age category. It is certain that environment plays an important role in tourists' destination selection and, accordingly, action will have to be taken to meet this new demand (Hjalager, 1999).

However, the majority of tour operators did not believe that consumer demand had changed (Weeden, 2002) and were very critical of the survey's finding that consumers were willing to pay more for ethical tourism products. Weeden (2002) suggests that although tourists may be willing to pay more, these altruistic ideas about ethical issues may not necessarily transform into actions when making buying decisions. Her findings suggest that price-based competitive strategies remain important even for specialist holiday markets.

According to Mintel (2005) – an international research company – the majority of the 2008 holidaymakers surveyed were apathetic toward ethical issues. In fact, they were more concerned with standards of accommodation and weather, wanting to relax during a holiday and not be bothered with ethical issues (40%). For these holidaymakers, the main priorities were self-indulging concerns such as high standards of accommodation (64%), nice weather (60%), convenient transport (35%), uncrowded beaches (34%), reasonably priced drinks (30%), and good tour representatives/guides (29%).

In short, even if research has shown high levels of consumer awareness, there is no sure evidence that the awareness will turn into actions through selective purchasing based on responsible criteria. In practice, too, there is no evidence that the awareness led to actual purchase behaviors. As explained by Dodds and Joppe (2005), there is an obvious contradiction between intention and behavior because the consumer's decisions are often dominated by other factors, mostly by price.

With the anecdotal and contrasting findings on green consumerism as described above, perhaps the suggestion by Dodds and Joppe (2005) has merit in that a socially responsible image should be projected in marketing to other businesses rather than to individual consumers. According to these authors, owing to low consumer awareness about environmental issues, it is more sensible to focus an organization's resources on marketing such an image to the business market rather than the consumer market. This is because the growing importance of 'corporate governance' in business cause buyers to increasingly seek out the suppliers who have strong sustainability credentials and evidence of social responsibility. A conference organizer, for example, is more likely to choose its conference venue (hotel) based on selected responsible criteria (such as use of recyclable paper and energy-friendly setting).

Engaging in socially responsible behavior

Although evidence of green consumerism remains sketchy and anecdotal, engaging in socially responsible behavior remains important for business-to-business marketing and for the improvement of overall image to stakeholders. IHEI, for example, maintains the need to incorporate environmental principles and standards or policies in the management, service delivery, and marketing of hotel companies, as there are clear savings to be made by using resources more efficiently by reducing waste and cutting costs.

Before an organization's socially responsible image can be marketed successfully, it must first be embedded into daily practices. A key aspect of ethical practices is to work with the local stakeholders to develop practices suitable to the local context, contribute to the local economy, and benefit the local people in multiple ways. Ethical practices must also include minimizing damage and any other form of possible negative impacts resulting from tourism activities. Thus, social responsibility may begin by minimizing environmental damage from a business's operations. A hotel, for example, needs to have a specifically designed environmental policy that is not viewed merely as an additional measure to the corporate strategy (Brown, 1994), but rather as an integral policy that commands constant evaluations to ensure effectiveness. The adoption of an environmental policy, Brown (1994) stresses, would help ensure that any necessary changes to implement the policy are embedded in the existing structure of the organization.

The adoption of an environmental management system (EMS) that extends throughout the business organization and between the business and its clients, to local community, and even to its suppliers is an important mechanism of becoming a responsible business. Welford and Young (2000) propose that a successful and well-communicated EMS can enhance a business's image in the marketplace. For tourism businesses such as hotels, this could translate into the ability to reach the growing, environmentally sensitive tourist market (see Cater, 1993; Wahab and Pigram, 1997) whose members may be interested to stay at properties with environmental policies and programs. A well-placed EMS, compliant with such standards as International Standardization Organization (ISO) and GG21, can also lead to improving efficiency and reducing operating costs (Meade and del Monaco, 1999). Savings will demonstrate the financial benefits of the systematic application of environment-friendly practices. Hotels, just like any other businesses, could certainly benefit from such savings and improved operational efficiency.

To ensure a successful environmental efficiency initiative, BSR (2001) suggests the following six steps to be taken as a continuous and cyclical process for best results:

a. Create an energy policy/mission statement which will act as a foundation for programs and initiatives;
b. Audit the performance of all facilities, industrial processes, and equipment to determine current energy consumption and future savings and to provide information for firms in setting their priorities;
c. Start with basic improvements such as basic equipment tune-ups, building insulation, and installation of timing devices for lighting and HVAC systems;
d. Educate employees and create cross-functional efficiency teams – employees most often have the best ideas for energy efficiency improvements, and this will also provide room for employee participation in the organization's efficiency efforts;
e. Seek outside expertise and opinions – private consulting firms are useful to perform audits and suggest more efficient energy processes, and non-governmental organizations could help firms understand environmental issues; and
f. Evaluate performance – proper monitoring will ensure that energy saving efforts are not wasted. It will also enable the identification of opportunities for further savings or refinement of the existing measures (BSR, 2001).

In addressing ethical practices related to community development, the H&T business can address labor issues raised by the United Nations', which include low wages, insecurity of work (according to seasonality), and irregular working hours. Specific to the hotel sector in Pacific Asia, domination of the expatriate staff in key managerial and professional positions at the expense of potential domestic talents is an important issue (WTTC, 1994). Organic waste management and green procurement are two ethical issues that affect the restaurant business. The former requires creative ways of disposing waste without harming the environment; two possible practices are to donate the waste to pig farmers (Kasim, 2005) or turn the waste into compost. Green procurement is more complicated as it requires the availability of cheap and widely distributed organic produce for restaurant needs. In many countries including the United Kingdom, there are few organic farms available (Revell and Blackburn, 2004). The availability of higher quality, lower price non-organic produce also makes green procurement less feasible.

Indeed, identifying relevant issues that can be effectively addressed is not easy; it depends on the priorities and financial capability of each business. Yet, it is crucial prior to any attempt to market a responsible image. Only after relevant issues have been identified and addressed can a business go to the next step, i.e., marketing a responsible image to a target audience(s). Choosing a right target audience(s) depends on the objectives of the H&T business. Nonetheless, the responsible image must be marketed both internally and externally as discussed below.

Letting people know – Marketing SR internally

Once a business decides to engage in a socially responsible behavior, it needs to, first and foremost, ensure that all levels of the organization embrace the idea and support it. This begins with a strong portrayal of the socially responsible image by the top management. In other words, organization leaders have to lead by example, particularly, when it comes to any attempt to make socially responsible practices an organizational culture. In a panel discussion on corporate ethics in the restaurant industry, at the Multi-Unit Foodservice Operators conference in Atlanta (*Nations Restaurant News*, 2003), Margaret Waldrep, Chief Administrative Officer of Madison, a Georgia-based Avado Brands Inc., has implied that any attempt to show social responsibility must start at the top, and the challenge is to model the behavior for the workers to follow. Phillip Hickey Jr, Chairman and Executive of Atlanta-based Rare Hospitality International, supported this by saying that the extent to which a socially responsible culture could successfully permeate an organization is usually set by the behavior of the top management. According to Stevens and Brownell (2000), acting ethically by top managers is the primary approach to communicating standards and influencing people's behavior.

Once management has set the tone through leadership, the idea of being socially responsible then needs to be marketed to the middle management and the workers. This is probably the most challenging because not only do the top management have to specify what constitutes social responsibility, but it also has to clearly communicate and market this idea to the workers. The more clearly and more explicitly the idea is marketed, the more likely a shared culture will develop (Singhapakedi et. al., 1996).

Marketing the idea of being a socially responsible organization requires clear, consistent, frequent, and effective communications with the workers. For this reason, Stevens and Brownell (2000) provide four methods that may be adapted:

a. Create social responsibility codes and publish these through the organization's Standard Operating Procedures, employee manuals, and other documents. Many hospitality companies have developed such codes (see IHEI, 1996).
b. Conduct training on social responsibility. This can be embedded in the new staff orientation program and other formal trainings as those programs are major channels for communicating managerial expectations. The programs also deliver managerial messages in a systematic and consistent manner.
c. Coach employees and ask them to coach people under their care. This is a way of reinforcing managerial messages. It is also a way to assess employee performance and provide a constructive feedback in an effort to clarify performance standards and motivate employees to improve job performance. Coaching is less formal and could encourage workers to take responsibility for their action and understand how each of them fits into the organizational framework.
d. Model desired behavior. This goes back to the idea of leading by example, where top and middle managers have to consistently display socially responsible behaviors to earn respect and continuously teach workers about social responsibility.

As the H&T business is primarily service-oriented, workers constitute the most important asset. Therefore, marketing SR internally through the means described above is one of the best investments that an organization can make in order to further develop this asset. The service providers – hotel frontliners, restaurant waiters, tourist guides – need to understand what it means to be socially responsible and accept this as part of their duties. This is an important precedent to establishing a business organization with a strong responsible image.

Letting people know – Projecting a responsible image to the market

A company with a strong BSR image would be able to differentiate itself and its products from its competitors and their products, to the market and investors alike. A strong BSR image may be established through publicizing the company's socially responsible actions. Small operators in the Association of Independent Tour Operators in the United Kingdom, for example, implement an SR practice of paying a high proportion of profits to charity, offering more training to local operations, and increasingly developing partnerships with the local community. The association has now developed an SR policy that may be used to determine membership in the future (www.aito.co.uk). The UNEP developed a Tour Operator's Initiative for Sustainable Development to assist international tour operators in adopting and projecting a more responsible image. A guideline has been developed to measure and report responsible practices among members. This allows a more systematic reporting among participating tour operators, such as Thomson Holidays. Thomson Holidays has a Sustainable Tourism Manager to manage the ethical aspects of its operations. Its ethical initiatives include working with destinations to develop and provide a sustainable quality holiday. A more innovative approach has been adopted by Responsibletravel that provides the market with access to tour operators that successfully produce a code of practice and meet the minimum standards. It gives the market a peace of mind in choosing their holidays and allows them to comment on a company's responsible practices (Tearfund, 2002).

In the hotel business, a number of other large hotel corporations, such as Canadian Pacific, InterContinental, and Ramada, have implemented a range of effective environmental measures (Checkley, 1992; Hawkes and Williams, 1993; IHEI, 1996) in their effort to project a responsible image. The Canadian Pacific Hotels and Resorts' 12-steps program in its *Green Partnership Guide* is a good example of an independently developed initiative. The environmental programme has set the target for a reduced landfill waste by 50% and reduced paper use by 20% in 2 years. It saves energy by retrofitting light bulbs, showerheads, and taps with 'Environmental Choice' equipment and by purchasing environment-friendly products for cleaning and running the hotels (Theobald, 1998). The Inter-Continental has received awards for its attempts to make its properties 'green' by reducing plastic throw-aways and waste, while the Scandic hotels, a Scandinavian hotel chain, has opened two eco-hotels in Oslo that saves energy and therefore energy cost (BSR, 2001). All these initiatives must however, be effectively communicated to all stakeholders and the market. Without effective communication, it would be difficult for a hotel to project its responsible image.

There are several possible marketing channels for a firm to promote and communicate its responsible behaviours (a detailed account of these is available in the UNEP report published in 2005). Some tourist boards such as those in Scotland and Costa Rica have been known to give added promotions for the tourism firms that achieve and maintain certain sustainability standards. Businesses certified as sustainable by the boards will be endorsed with an additional logo in their promotional materials or special brochures for sustainable products. Some tour operators in Germany, Italy, and Holland also provide similar promotional advantages for responsible businesses as tourists do demand information on sustainable products. However, this channel is quite restricted as tour operators will not want to promote a responsible tourism firm until a significant proportion of its products have met the necessary standards set by tour operators. Compared to the broad standards of the tourist boards, the standards set by tour operators are more specific and comprehensive. For example, the Dutch Tour Operator Association requires members to develop and implement a responsible tourism policy, appoint and train a responsible tourism coordinator, and report annually to the association at least one sustainable measure in accommodation, transport, recreation/excursions, consumer information, and internal sustainability.

Guidebooks may also be a possible channel for marketing a responsible tourism firm. They identify and evaluate tourism products objectively for the benefit of both conventional tourists and business travelers. They emphasize the products that align with the principle of sustainability and emphasize more the uniqueness of the products and excitement that the products would bring. Lonely Planet's Shoestring Guides and the *Good Alternative Travel Guide* by Tourism Concern are examples of such guidebooks.

Media such as newspapers and travel magazines are also possible marketing channels for responsible businesses. However, media tend to emphasize excitement and uniqueness of products rather than sustainability standards of the products *per se*. For example, tourism firms need to design their message by first emphasizing why it is exciting. This has to be done from the tourist's point of view (fun, adventurous, interesting, and unique) rather than from a more mundane fact such as conservation.

Conclusion

Social responsibility is fast becoming an important business agenda in H&T, coupled with increasing evidence of consumer demands for it. The interactions between H&T and the environments imply the need to minimize negative impacts of H&T's developments and operations to ensure tourism's long-term survival. Otherwise, the quality of tourists' experience will diminish considerably over time. Therefore, mitigation of negative impacts is essential to sustain the quality of tourism services. BSR is an important management concept that could help the H&T business address those impacts. It expands business priority from simply financial to socially responsible by considering a range of stake-holders in business planning and operations with a goal of forming an alliance beneficial to both the business and the stakeholders.

Once social responsibility is integrated into a business's manage-ment, it needs to be marketed both internally and externally. Internal marketing requires top management to 'lead by example' if social responsibility is to be an organization culture. It also entails communi-cating the idea clearly and consistently to the workers through train-ing and education. Workers have to 'buy' the idea that being socially responsible is good for business and that they play important roles in helping the organization realize the objectives.

From the external marketing point of view, a greater market share and an improved overall image to stakeholders are what tourism busi-nesses are concerned about. Although evidence on 'green demand' and 'green consumerism' is inadequate and current consumer awareness of BSR is relatively low, business-to-business marketing based on BSR still holds a promising future. There are several possible marketing channels for a firm to promote its responsible behaviours to its target market. Tourist boards, guidebooks, and the media such as newspa-pers and travel magazines are possible marketing channels to publicize the firm's responsible business.

In sum, SR and ethics are relevant and important issues to be addressed by the fast growing H&T business. What is probably lacking is a driver for the H&T business to begin addressing at least some of its SR and ethical issues. The driver could be in the form of govern-ment incentives and/or regulations, the details of which are beyond the scope of this chapter. Nevertheless, addressing social responsibility and ethical issues is important for the H&T business's own sustainability.

References

American Society for Quality (2004). Social responsibility: Doing the right thing. Retrieved on October 12, 2006, from http://www.asq.org/social-responsibility/

Brown, M. (1994). Environmental auditing and the hotel industry: An accountant's perspective. In Seadon, A. V. (ed.), *Tourism: The state of the art*, Chichester: John Wiley and Sons, pp. 675–681.

Business Social Responsibility (2003). Overview of corporate social responsibility. Retrieved on October 11, 2006, from http://www.bsr.org/CSRResources/IssueBriefDetail.cfm?DocumentID=48809

Cater, E. (1993). Sustainable tourism in the third world: Problem for sustainable tourism development. *Tourism Management*, 14(2), 83–93.

Checkley, A. (1992). Accommodating the environment: The greening of Canada's largest hotel company. Proceedings of ISEP Conference on *Strategies for reducing the environmental impact of tourism*, Vienna: International Society for Environmental Protection, pp. 178–189.

Cheney, J., & Barnett, S. (2001). The greening of accommodation: Stakeholders perspectives of environmental programs in New Zealand hotels and luxury lodges. *The Journal of Corporate Citizenship*, 1, 115–126.

Coalition for Environmentally Responsible Economies (CERES) Corporate Outreach Committee (2000). *Green hotel initiative: Overview*. Retrieved on April 25, 2001 from http://www.ceres.org

Conner, F. L. (2000). Hoteliers and corporate travel buyers to promote 'green' hotels together. *Cornell Hotel and Restaurant Administration Quarterly*, 41(5), 16.

Creyer, E. H., and Ross, W. T. (1997). The influence of firm behavior on purchase intention: Do customers really care about business ethics? *Journal of Consumer Marketing*, 14(6), 421–433.

DeSimone, L., and Popoff, F. (1997). *Eco-efficiency: The business link to sustainable development*, Cambridge Massachusetts: The World Business for Sustainable Development (WBCSD), and MIT Press.

Diamantis, D. (1998). Consumer behavior and ecotourism products. *Annals of Tourism Research*, 25(2), 515–528.

Dodds, R., and Joppe, M. (2005). *CSR in the tourism industry? The status of and potential for certification, codes of conduct and guidelines*. Research Paper. Foreign Investment Advisory Service, Investment Climate Department.

Faulk, E. S. (2000). *A survey of environmental management by hotels and related tourism businesses*. Research Paper. Switzerland: University of St Gallen.

Forsyth, T. (1996). *Sustainable tourism: Moving from theory to practice*, London: Tourism Concern.

German NGO Forum on Environment and Development (1998). *Tourism and sustainable Development: Report to the 7th Meeting of the Commissions on Sustainable Development (CSD)*. November.

Goeldner, C. R., and Ritchie, J. R. (2006). *Tourism: Principles, practices, philosophies*. New Jersey: John Wiley & Sons, Inc.

Gordon (2002). The OECD guidelines for multinational enterprises. Contribution to the *International Conference, Governance and Sustainability – New challenges for the state, business and civil society*, organized by the Institute for Ecological Economy Research, Berlin, Friedrich-Ebert-Stiftry (FES) Berlin on 30th September and 1st October, 2002.

Green Hotelier *Magazine of International Hotels Environment Initiative* (1999), Issue No. 16.

Grove, S. J., Fisk, R. P., Picket, G. M., and Kangun, N. (1996). Going green in the service sector: Social responsibility issues, implications and implementation. *European Journal of Marketing* MCB University Press, 30(5), 56–66.

Guadalupe-Fajardo, E. (2002). American tourists prefer green hotels and are willing to pay more to stay in them. *Caribbean Business*, 19, 13.

Hassan, S.S. (2000). Determinants of market competitiveness in an environmentally sustainable tourism industry. *Journal of Travel Research*, 38(3), 239–246.

Hawkes, S., and Williams, P. (1993). *The greening of tourism from principles to practice: A casebook for environmental practice in tourism*, Burnaby BC: Simon Fraser University, Center for Tourism and Policy Research.

Hjalager, A. (1999). Consumerism and sustainable tourism. *Journal of Travel and Tourism Marketing*, 8(3), 1–20.

Holden, A. (2000). *Tourism and Environment*, London: Routledge. Green Globe 21 Asia Pacific (2000) Introduction to Green Globe Standard, retrieved 02/03/01 from www.ggasiapacific.com.au

Hong, E. (1985). *See the Third World while it lasts: The social and environmental impact of tourism with special reference to Malaysia*, Penang: Market Association of Penang.

International Hotels Environmental Initiatives (1995). Environmental Management for Hotels: The industry guide to best practice. Oxford: Butterworth-Heinemann *Business Social Responsibility (BSR) official website*, retrieved in 2001 from www.bsr.org

International Hotels Environmental Initiatives (1996). *Environmental Management for Hotels*, Oxford: Butterworth-Heinemann.

International Hotels and Restaurant Association (IH&RA) and United Nations Environment Project (UNEP) (1996). *Environmental good practice in hotels: Case studies*, Paris: UNEP.

International Hotel & Restaurant Association's Environmental Good Practice in Hotels: Case Studies from the IH&RA Environmental Award (2005) IH&RA and United Nations Environment Programme (UNEP).

Kasim, A. (2005). *Business environmental and social responsibility: Factors influencing the hotel sector in Penang, Malaysia*, Sintok: Monograph University Utara Malaysia Press.

Key Note Publications (2000). *Green and ethical consumer market assessment 2000*. Available online at www.researchandmarkets.com.

Key Note Publications (2005). *Green and ethical consumer market assessment 2005*. Available online at www.researchandmarkets.com.

Kirk, D. (1995). Environmental management in hotels. *International Journal of Contemporary Hospitality Management*, 7(6), 3–8.

Lave, L. B., and Matthews, H. S. (1996). It's easier to say green than be green. *Technology Review*, 99(8), 68–69.

Mathieson, A., and Wall, G. (1992). *Tourism: Economic, physical and social impacts*, Harlow: Longman.

Meade, B., and Del Monaco, A. (1999, May). *Environmental Management: The Key to Successful Operation*, Pan American Proceedings.

Miller, G. A. (2003). Consumerism in sustainable tourism: A survey of UK consumers. *Journal of Sustainable Tourism*, 11(1), 17–39.

Mintel (2005). *Ethical Holidays-UK*. Mintel International Group Limited, UK: London.

Nations Restaurant News (2003). Corporate ethics: Best behavior should start at the top. Retrieved on July 14, 2006 from http://www.hm.com.

Post, J. E., and Altma, B. W. (1994). Managing the environmental change process: Barriers and opportunities. *Journal of Organizational Change Management*, 7(4), 64–81.

Revell, A., and Blackburn, B. (2004). The environmental practices of restaurants in the UK. Small Business Research Centre, Kingston University. Retrieved on July 3, 2006 from http://business.kingston.ac.uk/research/sbrc/respapersrestex.pdf.

Singhapakedi, A., Roa, C., and Vitell, S. (1996). Ethical decision-making: An investigation of services-marketing processions. *Journal of Business Ethic*, 15, 635–644.

Six Continents Environmental and Social Report (2002). Guidelines. Retrieved on April 4, 2003 from http://www.sixcontinents.com/environment/2 . . . /employee_policies.html and www. sixcontinentshotels.com/h/d/6c/c/2/dec/6c/1/en/sr.html.

Stevens, B., and Brownell, J. (2000). Ethics: Communicating standards and influencing behaviors. *Cornell Hotel and Restaurant Administration Quarterly*, 41(2), 39–43.

Tearfund (2002). World's apart: A call to responsible global tourism. Retrieved on March 22, 2006 from http://www.tearfund.org/webdocs/Website/Campaigning/Policy%20and%20research/Worlds%20Apart%20tourism%20report.pdf.

Theobald, W. F. (1998). *Global tourism in next decade*. Oxford: Butterworth-Heinemann.

The Manila Declaration on social impact of tourism (1997). Retrieved on June 23, 2003 from http://www.eco-tour.org/info/w_10196_de.html.

United Nations Economic and Social Council (1999, 15 January). Tourism and Sustainable Development: Report of the Secretary-General, retrieved on 24/6/03 from ods-dds-ny.un.org/doc/UNDOC/GEN/N99/010/96/PDF/N9901096.pdf? OpenElement

United Nations Environment Programme (UNEP) report (2002). *Sustainable tourism*. Retrieved on July 12, 2006 from http://www.uneptie.org/pc/tourism/sust-tourism/env-3main.htm.

United Nations Environment Programme (UNEP) (2005). *Marketing sustainable tourism products*. Nairobi: UNEP.

Wahab, S., and Pigram, J. J. (1997). *Tourism, development and growth: The challenge for sustainability*. London: Routledge.

Wearing, S., Cynn, S., Ponting, J., and McDonald, M. (2002). Converting environmental concern into ecotourism purchases: A qualitative evaluation of international backpackers in Australia. *Journal of Ecotourism*, 1(2/3), 133–148.

Weeden, C. (2002). Ethical tourism: An opportunity for competitive advantage? UK *Journal of Vacation Marketing*, 8(2), 141–153.

Welford, R. (1994). *Environmental strategy and sustainable development: The corporate challenge for the 21st Century*, London: Routledge.

Welford, R., and Young, C. W. (2000). Towards sustainable production and consumption: from products to services. In Welford, R (ed.) *Corporate environmental management: Towards sustainable development.* London: Earthscan Publications Ltd.

Wolfe, K. L., and Shanklin, C. W. (2001). Environmental practices and management concerns of conference center administrators. *Journal of Hospitality and Tourism Research*, 25(2), 209–216.

World Business Council on Sustainable Development (2003). *Sustainable development reporting: Striking the balance*, retrieved on May 1, 2003 from http://www.wbcsd.ch.

World Travel and Tourism Council (1994). *Gearing up for growth. A study of education and training for careers in Asia Pacific travel and tourism*, London: WTTC.

World Travel and Tourism Council (2002). *Agenda 21 for the Travel & Tourism Industry: Towards environmentally sustainable development*, retrieved on February 12, 2002 from http://www.wttc.org/promote/agenda21.htm.

World Travel and Tourism Council, World Tourism Organization and Earth Council (1995). *Agenda 21 for the Travel and Tourism Industry: Towards Environmentally Sustainable Development*, London: WTTC.

Websites

Coalition for Environmentally Responsible Economies (2006). Investor and environmentalist for sustainable prosperity. Website address: http://www.ceres.org

Green Hotels Association (2006). 'Green' hotels association. Website address: www.greenhotels.com

International Business Leaders Forum (2006). IBLF is at the heart of sustainable business. Website address: http://www.iblf.org

Hospitality marketing mix and service marketing principles

David Bojanic

Introduction

The concept of marketing is based on the premise that firms should determine consumer wants and needs before designing products and services. This consumer-orientation results in greater demand for a firm's products and services and higher levels of customer satisfaction after the purchase. Marriott International followed this approach in developing their Courtyard and Residence Inns hotels. For example, the Courtyard concept is supposed to attract business travelers and transient customers who do not really like staying at hotels (Wind et al, 1992; Hart, 1986). The researchers recruited individuals for focus groups representing these two market segments to determine the hotel attributes that were most important to them. Next, a tradeoff analysis was performed on a larger sample of people from the target groups to determine the utility, or value, placed on each of the attributes and its possible level. The final result of this study was the concept of a hotel that would have a high level of appeal to the target markets, created using consumer inputs.. The hotel possessed all of the attributes that were important to the target market in adequate levels, at a price they were willing to pay.

This chapter focuses on the marketing mix and its use in contemporary marketing. The traditional marketing mix, also referred to as the four Ps of marketing or the marketing program, consists of: price, product, place, and promotion. These four components of the marketing mix represent the decision-making variables that are available to marketing managers. In other words, decisions concerning the marketing mix are controlled by the firm that is marketing the product or service in question. However, all firms operate within an external environment that is dynamic and cannot be controlled by the firm or its employees. The external environment can be divided into five areas: economic, social, technological, political and legal, and competitive.

There have been alternatives to the traditional marketing mix offered in the marketing literature in response to differences that exist between tangible products (i.e., goods) and services. Services have four major characteristics that affect the design of marketing programs: intangibility, inseparability, perishability, and variability. These characteristics led to the creation of an expanded marketing mix for all services with 7 Ps (the original 4 plus physical evidence, participants/people, and process) and a hospitality marketing mix that is thought to be more relevant for hospitality services firms, tourism organizations, and other travel-related firms. The three components of the hospitality marketing mix are the product–service mix, the presentation mix, and the communication mix. The similarities and differences between the traditional marketing mix and the hospitality marketing mix are discussed later in this chapter. In addition, the criteria used by consumers to evaluate services are introduced and explained in detail using real world examples.

Marketing mix

Traditional marketing mix

The concept of a marketing mix originated in the 1950s and was first published in the marketing literature in the 1960s (Borden, 1964). However, the most common form of the marketing mix (i.e., four Ps) used in most textbooks was developed by McCarthy in the 1970s (McCarthy, 1975). McCarthy's four Ps consisted of price, product, place, and promotion. The overall marketing process involves the use of the four decision-making variables within the context of the firm's macro-environment, while focusing on the target market(s). The marketing mix is controlled by the firm, while the macro-environment cannot be directly controlled. The main objective for the firm is to determine a 'mix,' for each product, that satisfies consumer wants and needs and affords the firm a unique position in the marketplace. Firms try to develop marketing strategies utilizing the marketing mix that will establish sustainable competitive advantages leading to long-term growth and profitability. Figure 3.1 is a diagram, used by Reid and Bojanic (2006) in their textbook, that provides a visual presentation of the marketing process.

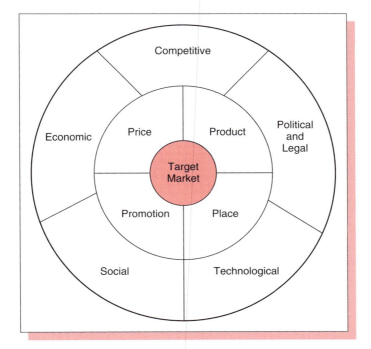

Figure 3.1
The marketing mix and external environments

Price. Price is the value placed on a product or service. Other terms that can be used to refer to the price component of the marketing mix are: fee, rate, tuition, premium, and toll. There are non-monetary elements to price as well as the more obvious monetary elements. Some examples of non-monetary price are the time it takes to search and evaluate alternative products or services and the convenience of location. If a consumer drives to several locations to shop for a product or service, then there are costs associated with time, gas, and depreciation on the car. Also, there could be tolls for highways, bridges, or subways. In the end, it is the perceived price or the perceived value the consumer associates with a product or service that influences the purchase and the level of customer's satisfaction. Value is the tradeoff between price and quality – the benefits the consumer receives for the price paid.

Some of the other variables, in addition to the list-price, that are considered are discounts, allowances, and payment options. Some of the possible reasons for price segmentation and offering discounts include purchase quantity (i.e., volume), time of purchase (e.g., early-bird specials), buyer identification (e.g., AARP, AAA, etc.), purchase location, and bundling (e.g., vacation packages) (Nagle and Holden, 2002). Allowances are most prevalent in the business-to-business part of the channel of distribution and are common in the travel sector between hospitality suppliers (e.g., hotels) and tour operators or travel agencies. Finally, the most popular payment options for large ticket purchases are credit cards and/or the ability to pay over time. For example, it is often necessary to book a cruise several months before the scheduled departure date, requiring the consumer to purchase the service well in advance of its consumption. In response, cruise lines allow passengers to make a small deposit in lieu of paying the entire amount. The remainder of the cost is due on the date of departure.

Product. The product element of the marketing mix includes the tangible good and all of the services that accompany that good to produce the final product. A product is a package, or bundle, of goods and services that comprise the total offering. For example, the purchase of a hotel room includes the guest room, fitness center, pool, restaurants, valet service, concierge, housekeeping service, etc. A restaurant meal consists of the actual food, host/hostess, and waiters, etc. Finally, a travel experience consists of a chain of products and services starting at the time of purchase and ending upon returning from the trip. Everything in between, such as hotel service, restaurants, and transportation (including taxis and buses), affect the overall experience.

Some of the variables that are part of the 'product' decision include variety, quality, design, features/amenities, brand name, packaging, supporting services, and warranties. As stated earlier, the decision regarding the proper mix of goods and services is based on the wants and needs of consumers (the concept of marketing). A tradeoff must be determined that provides the most utility for consumers at a price that is profitable for the firm offering the product. Hotels are segmented, by the level of amenities and services offered, into full service and limited service. Limited service hotels lack services such as restaurants, valet parking, and concierge. There is also a designation that separates hotels, motels, and inns based on the size of the property and the available amenities. Similarly, restaurants are segmented into quick-service, casual, and fine-dining based on the atmosphere and the level of service. Quick-service restaurants do not have waiters, and customers are often required to perform some of the service (e.g., get their own drinks). Finally, travel agents and tour operators create 'bundles' or 'packages' by combining the services of different vendors into products with various levels of quality.

Place. The place element of the marketing mix includes the distribution and logistics of producing a product or service and making it available to the final consumer. The location of a manufacturing or wholesaling facility is determined by considering the costs of resources such as labor, raw materials, and real estate. In addition, it is necessary to have access to the preferred mode(s) of transportation for delivering the products to wholesalers and retailers. The location of a retail establishment is based mainly on accessibility to the final consumers. Services have relatively short channels of distribution and focus most of their efforts on finding retail locations that are convenient for consumers. For example, restaurants tend to choose high traffic areas close to shopping and other attractions. Similarly, hotels locate their facilities in areas such as airports, urban centers, industrial centers, and tourist attractions that are accessible to their respective target markets.

Some of the variables that are part of the 'place' decision include the type of channel, location, assortments, coverage area, inventory, and transportation. Many service providers overlook the importance of this variable in the strategic planning process. The channel of distribution tends to be shorter for the marketing of services than that for goods, and most service providers act as manufacturer and retailer. Many managers in service firms assume that once the initial location is determined this variable diminishes in importance. However, hotels and restaurants do switch their operations to a more favorable location on occasion. This is a major decision involving company time and resources, but it can result in long-term growth and increased profit if handled properly. Another good example of a 'place' decision for a hotel is the Harborside Hyatt in Boston, Massachusetts. The hotel is located near the airport and the normal route to the downtown area that serves as a tourist attraction, government center, and financial district is to fight airport traffic. The hotel decided to offer a boat shuttle to take guests to the downtown area in an attempt to 'improve' the guests' perceptions of the hotel's location. Finally, Internet travel agents like Expedia and Travelocity have provided hotels and restaurants, especially independent operators, with an alternative channel for delivering their services.

Promotion. The promotion element of the marketing mix includes all of the communications associated with marketing a product or service. The promotion mix consists of four elements: advertising, personal selling, publicity, and sales promotion. Advertising and publicity are forms of mass communication using a variety of mediums such as television, radio, newspaper, magazines, direct mail, and the Internet. Advertising is a paid form of mass communication with an identified sponsor, while publicity is a non-paid form of mass communication without a sponsor (i.e., it is free and objective). Personal selling is a form of interpersonal communication sponsored by the firm. Sales promotion is a short-term inducement to purchase a product or service. Some examples of sales promotions are contests, sweepstakes, premiums, and product bundles.

Hospitality firms determine their promotion mixes based on their clientele and trading areas. Restaurants tend to draw customers from the local, or regional, population and benefit from using local media such as newspapers and radio stations. Only large chain restaurants, owing to their wide geographic coverage, can benefit from national advertising in magazines and on television. Conversely, hotels tend to draw customers more from regional, national, and international markets. Therefore, most hotels advertise in national media such as magazines and television, unless they are marketing their restaurants on weekend packages. However, the advent of the Internet has provided the smaller, independent hotels and restaurants with a cost-effective medium to reach international audiences. There are also differences based on the market the hotel is targeting. For example, larger hotels market their meeting and banquet facilities to meeting planners using sales people, direct mail, the Internet, trade shows, and trade magazines. In contrast, it is not cost-effective to use some of these same means for transient customers (e.g., personal selling), and the promotion mix is focused mainly on advertising and some sales promotions.

Marketing environment

Environmental scanning is an important element of any firm's strategic planning. The components of the marketing mix (i.e., the four Ps or marketing program) are controlled by the managers within the firm. However, the external environment cannot be controlled by the firm, and changes in the environment result in both opportunities and threats. Savvy firms are able to take advantage of the opportunities and minimize the threats. The external environment consists of five basic areas: economic, social, technological, political and legal, and competitive.

Economic Environment. The economic environment consists of factors that affect consumer's purchasing power and spending patterns. Purchasing Power Parity (PPP) is a measure used to compare incomes across countries by examining the prices for a group of standard products using the exchange rate with the US dollar. Most service firms, especially hospitality and travel, rely heavily on consumers' disposable and discretionary incomes. Disposable income represents the amount of income left after the consumer pays his taxes and other required deductions. Discretionary income represents the amount of disposable income left after the consumer pays for other necessities such as housing, food, and clothing. Consumers in developed countries have higher standards of living and more discretionary income than those in developing or under-developed countries.

Spending patterns are also important and they differ by country and/or culture. For example, people in the United States save much less of their income than people in Asian countries like Japan or South Korea. In addition, US consumers tend to have high debt-to-income ratios resulting from expenditures on housing and transportation (i.e., automobiles). This willingness on the part of US consumers to spend their discretionary income and incur debt identifies them as good prospects for hospitality and travel services. However, these consumers are also susceptible to changes in the economy leading to inflation or a recession. For example, recent increases in gasoline prices have led to reduction in discretionary income and the ability to purchase travel services. In some cases, it results in decreasing the level of quality and taking cheaper vacations, while in other cases the result is eliminating travel altogether.

Social Environment. The social environment consists of the changing trends in the population in terms of demographics and cultural norms. According to the US Census Bureau, the world population is currently estimated at approximately 6.5 billion in 2006, and it is expected to increase to approximately 7.9 billion by 2025, with the current annual growth rate being 1.14%. Most of the increase is expected in developing or under-developed countries in Asia, Africa, and Latin America. Many companies from the United States, Japan, Korea, and Western Europe are targeting high-growth countries like China and India. The average age of the population is also expected to increase, and there is an anticipated shift from rural to urban areas. It is important for firms to determine how these changes in demographics and living conditions are going to affect their businesses. For example, hospitality and travel firms can focus resources on marketing to the aging population.

This social environment is probably the least dynamic of the external environments. In other words, most of the changes take place over a long time period and do not require immediate attention. The values and norms of cultures and subcultures have been developed over hundreds, or thousands, of years and are not likely to change drastically over short time periods. However, some of the recent trends that affect the hospitality and travel industry include healthier diets, women's roles in society, physical fitness (especially for seniors), and concern for the environment. This has led to restaurant menu changes and alliances (e.g., Weight Watchers and Applebee's), 24-hour room service, an increase in motor-coach tours, and eco-tourism.

Technological Environment. The technological environment consists of factors that change the way consumers live and the production and delivery of products and services. The changes in the technological environment over the last 50 years have been remarkable, and the rate of technological change has been increasing. These changes have resulted in more product variety and convenience for consumers. The areas with some of the most technological advances include electronics and telecommunications. For example, hotels, restaurants, airlines, and rental car agencies have all seen improvements in reservation management and point-of-sale systems in the form of computer software programs that streamline the process and provide information for revenue management.

In particular, the advent of the Internet has had a profound effect on hospitality and travel firms. As mentioned earlier, the Internet offers hospitality and travel firms a way to reach new target markets (e.g., price-sensitive consumers). In addition, firms can create databases and e-mail lists in an effort to increase consumer loyalty. Finally, the new technology as allowed firms to relinquish some of the service responsibilities to consumers, while at the same time giving them a sense of control. For example, once an airline ticket is purchased, consumers can choose their seats and print boarding passes through Internet web sites. Consumers also benefit from the convenience of using the Internet for information search, comparing alternative products, and making hospitality and travel purchases.

Political and Legal Environment. The political and legal environment consists of the government, lobbyists, and other individuals and groups involved in the creation and implementation of laws and regulations. Government legislators create laws and regulations to avoid unfair competition among firms, to protect consumers from unfair business practices, and to make sure products and services are safe. However, many critics feel that too much government regulation can lead to an unnecessary financial burden on firms, barriers to entry for competition, and/or a lack of choice for consumers, resulting in higher prices. In addition to regulating industries, the governments have had to deregulate some industries in the past. For example, in the United States the airline industry was deregulated in the late 1970s in an attempt to increase competition, lower prices, and increase overall volume.

Government regulations affect many industries by setting tariffs and quotas for imports and exports and by regulating taxes. Hotels in the

United States face taxes from the state and local governments that can range from single-digit percentages to the high teens when combined. In particular, this affects a city's ability to attract large meetings and conventions. The restaurant industry in the United States has been affected by changes in tax credits for business meals and non-smoking regulations. Obviously, these industries cannot control the government's decisions in these areas, but they are able to influence these decisions through lobbying. Most industries have trade associations like the American Hotel and Motel Association (AHMA) and the National Restaurant Association (NRA) that employ paid lobbyists, whose sole mission is to maintain a favorable operating environment for their members.

Competitive Environment. The competitive environment consists of all individuals and organizations that are marketing similar, or substitute, products and services to the same target markets. These firms compete for resources such as labor and supplies, as well as for sales volume and revenue. There are basically four possible competitive structures:

- Pure monopoly – one seller and many buyers
- Oligopoly – a few sellers and many buyers
- Monopolistic competition – many sellers with differentiated products and many buyers
- Pure competition – many sellers with similar products and many buyers

The most common competitive structure in developed countries with a capitalist economy is monopolistic competition. Pure monopolies and oligopolies normally require favorable government regulations (or lack of regulations), in order to exist. Pure competition is more prevalent during the maturity stage of the product life cycle when industry sales has stagnated and weaker competitors are forced into decline.

Firms must be able to identify indirect, or 'latent' competitors, as well as their direct competitors. There are threats from potential new entrants and substitute products that should not be overlooked. For example, restaurants face competition from other restaurants, but there is also competition from convenience stores and supermarkets that offer sandwiches and prepared meals. Similarly, hotels might analyze their competition from other hotels, but they might underestimate the potential threat from motels, inns, bed and breakfasts, and time-shares. Finally, major airlines must monitor the activities of budget and regional airlines, trains, buses, and rental car agencies as well as of other major airlines. The Internet has leveled the playing field for smaller, independent operations, and this form of electronic commerce has also made it easy for firms and consumers to compare the alternatives.

Applying the marketing-mix concept

It is necessary with any concept or theory that purports to be an abstraction of reality that it demonstrates an ability to be applied in practice. Shapiro (2001) suggests that the marketing-mix concept must be used to answer the following questions:

- Are the marketing-mix elements consistent with one another?
- In addition to being consistent, do the elements add up to a harmonious, integrated whole?
- Is each element being given its best leverage?
- Are the target market segments precisely and explicitly defined?
- Does the total program meet the needs of the target market segment?
- Does the marketing mix build on the organization's strengths and compensate for its weaknesses?
- Does the marketing mix create a distinctive competitive advantage?

These questions are based on Shapiro's discussion of the interaction within the marketing mix. Specifically, there are three degrees of interaction: consistency, integration, and leverage. Consistency refers to the logical and useful fit between two or more of the marketing-mix elements. Integration refers to an active, harmonious interaction among the elements (in addition to the coherent fit implied by consistency). Leverage is the use of each element to the best advantage of the overall marketing mix. Finally, in addition to the relationships between the elements within the marketing mix, it is important to evaluate the relationship of the marketing program with the market, the company, and the competition.

Marketing-mix customization

The paradigm shift from transaction marketing to relationship marketing has led many firms, especially service firms, to involve their customers in the product development process. The advances in technology (i.e., computers and telecommunications) have enabled firms to create databases that are used to contact consumers via the Internet, telephone, or direct mail. This personal information and access to consumers allow firms to customize their marketing programs. Table 3.1 is a framework for marketing-mix customization adapted from an article by Logman (1997).

The first column in Table 3.1 lists the four elements of the marketing mix. The second column identifies whether the customization is handled by the company, or left to the consumer. The third column lists the possible types of customization for each of the marketing-mix elements. The fourth column includes hospitality examples of the types of customization. These are just a partial list of customization options and

Table 3.1 Marketing-mix customization and customizability options

Marketing-mix elements	Focus	Type of customiza-tion/customizability	Hospitality examples
Product	By Company	• Offering enhanced and/or bundled products	• Buffets, vacation packages
	By Customer	• Offering products with different options • Offering a menu of product components	• Rental car agencies • Online travel agencies
Price	By Company	• Offering segmented price discounts • Offering a customized product	• Group business, seniors • Fast food 'value' meals
	By Customer	• Offering a customizable product • As a result of bargaining power	• Banquet/catering menus • Meeting planners
Promotion	By Company	• Use one-to-one communication tools	• Frequent flyer programs
	By Customer	• Offering an interactive information network	• Hotel web sites
Place	By Company	• Offering multiple channels and locations	• Online hotel reservations
	By Customer	• Offering an interactive distribution network	• Online airline check-in

examples used as an introduction. There is more detailed information on the customization process in the original article (Logman, 1997), and there are more examples pertaining mostly to tangible products, or goods.

Managing the marketing mix over the product life cycle

The dynamic nature of the marketplace for products requires firms to continually monitor the environment and adapt the marketing mix to take advantages of opportunities and minimize the impact of threats. In addition, products move through a 'life cycle' that takes them through four stages: introduction, growth, maturity, and decline (see Figure 3.2). The elements of the marketing mix are adjusted

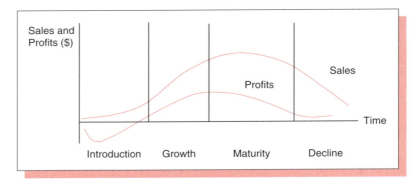

Figure 3.2
The product life cycle

throughout the product's life cycle, based on changes in the market-place (Bass, 1969).

Introduction. New products enter the market with low sales volume and accumulated costs in the form of research and development, capital costs for buildings and supplies, production, etc. This leads to negative profits, and firms often use a 'price skimming' strategy that results in larger profit margins because of the higher price. The higher price is justified if the product is unique and/or the level of quality is high. At this point, there are few, if any, substitutes or competitors. There are typically a small number of distribution outlets (i.e., selective) and the main objective of the promotion mix is to create awareness and trial.

Growth. The next stage occurs once the level of awareness and trial has increased and the sales volume begins to grow. The accumulated sales volume and the high profit margins result in positive profits. However, this profit potential attracts more competitors and prices start to decline (as do costs per unit). The firm increases the number of distribution outlets, including direct mail and Internet web sites, and enhances the product by offering more features and options. The focus of the promotion mix is on continuing to educate consumers about the benefits of the product and starting to differentiate it from the competitors' offerings.

Maturity. Most products are in the maturity stage of the product life cycle (PLC), evidenced by a large number of sellers with relatively similar products. At this stage, the number of distribution outlets is at its peak (i.e., intensive) and the heavy competition keeps prices low. The overall sales for the product category becomes 'stagnant' and the growth rate levels off. Competitors with weaker positions begin to leave the marketplace, and the product and promotion strategies focus on differentiating the firm's product from those of its competitors.

Decline. The final stage of the PLC is the decline stage. The market growth rate for the product category is negative, improvements in technology are limited, and the profit margins are low. Only the strongest competitors remain, and the prices continue to decline. The number of distribution outlets decreases as less profitable operations are shut down or sold off. The amount spent on promotion is decreased in an attempt to maintain decent profit margins, and the focus is on simply reminding consumers the product is still available. Finally, only the most successful versions of the product are maintained, and standardization is used to decrease production costs.

Table 3.2 summarizes the marketing-mix strategies for each of the stages in the PLC. The PLC has been criticized for being a self-fulfilling prophecy – firms might make decisions based on a belief that the product is moving through the life cycle, and these decisions might actually become the catalyst for the movement from stage to stage. In reality, there is no set length of time that a product spends in each stage. For example, many products are in the maturity stage of the PLC, and they have been in the stage for decades. The industry sales for fast food hamburger restaurants stagnated years ago, but McDonald's continues to reinvent itself by adding new services such as breakfast and healthier foods.

One of the other problems associated with the PLC is that it tends to emphasize new product development, often to the detriment of existing products. Resources are shifted from the existing products, or strategic business units, into the research and development for new products. However, it is also possible to extend the PLC for existing products by

Table 3.2 Marketing-mix strategies over the product life cycle

Marketing-mix element	Introduction	Growth	Maturity	Decline
Product	Offer unique, high quality	Improve quality	Add features	Use profitable design
Price	Charge high skimming price	Reduce	Discount	Reduce
Promotion	Focus on raising awareness and trial	Stress benefits	Differentiate	Remind
Place	Selective	Intensive	Intensive	Selective

increasing sales to current customers, increasing the number of users, and/or finding new uses for the product.

Criticisms of the marketing-mix concept

The critics of the marketing mix point out its inability to fulfill the requirements of the marketing concept. This is particularly true in the case of services. The debate will continue over the applicability of the marketing-mix concept and its treatment of the interactions between elements and market-orientation. However, it still appears in textbooks as a cornerstone of marketing theory.

Lack of proper identification

The properties or characteristics that are the basis for classification have not been identified (Van Waterschoot and Van den Bulte, 1992). Early coverage of the marketing mix views the elements of the marketing mix as processes or activities (Borden, 1964), while the more recent view in textbooks is that they are objects or tools that are used by marketing managers in developing marketing programs to target specific markets with a product or brand. The proposed solution is to devise a clear definition of the dimensions used to classify the activities and objects into the four marketing-mix elements.

Overlap between marketing-mix elements

There has also been some question regarding the lack of characteristics used to classify the marketing-mix elements and the fact that the elements are not mutually exclusive (Van Waterschoot and Van den Bulte, 1992). McCarthy's four Ps were chosen to simplify Borden's original list of 12 elements, but there was no attempt made to identify a basis on which to extract the four elements. For example, sales promotion is a subcategory under the promotion element, but there are areas where sales promotion overlaps with product, pricing, and distribution strategies. One could also question whether the four 'P' categories are collectively exhaustive. That is, can every component of the marketing program fit into one of the four elements? Once again, sales promotion is an example of a category that includes all of the items that don't fit nicely into one of the other categories in the promotion mix, or the marketing mix. In other words, McCarthy recognized the interactive nature of the elements in the marketing mix, but did not explicitly state the interrelationships among the elements.

Production-oriented approach

The marketing-mix concept is based on a production-oriented definition of marketing rather than a market-oriented approach (Gronroos, 1989). That is, the traditional marketing mix views customers as an entity *to* which something is done, rather than an entity *for* which something is done. Also, the marketing-mix paradigm supports the notion of a separate marketing department within a firm, leading to the marketing function being isolated from other activities of the firm. The proposed solution is to initiate a paradigm shift toward relationship marketing, which recognizes the importance of integrating the activities of the firm and incorporating services marketing principles in an attempt to achieve a true market-orientation (Gronroos, 1997).

Service marketing principles

There does not seem to be one agreed-upon definition of services in the marketing literature. In fact, most authors skip directly to discussing the nature and classification of services and avoid the issue altogether. One of the few authors who offered a relatively straightforward definition is Berry (1980), who defined a service as a deed, act, or performance. The academic field first addressed services marketing in the 1950s and 1960s, but most of the advances started in the 1970s (Brown et al., 1994). The early studies in services marketing tended to focus on the unique service features, or characteristics that separate services from goods or tangible products. The fact that services are 'intangible' leads to most of the issues surrounding the debate regarding the differences between marketing services and 'typical' products (Shostack, 1977). The names or descriptions of the unique service features vary slightly, but most authors agree on the following four characteristics of services.

Characteristics of services

Intangibility. Services are intangible and cannot be evaluated before they are purchased. The consumer cannot see, taste, hear, or feel the service before it is purchased. Therefore, service firms often try to 'tangibilize' the service, or offer some evidence of the service. One of the best examples of a service industry that provides tangible evidence for a service that is intangible is the insurance industry. Customers are 'in good hands,' 'get a piece of the rock,' or the 'protection of a cavalry' when they purchase insurance. Similarly, restaurants place colorful pictures of the appetizers, entrees, and desserts on their menus, and/or provide descriptions of the menu item so customers can attempt to evaluate the service before it is consumed. Japanese restaurants go a step further and place replicas of their meals in the window of the restaurant to entice consumers to enter and try the food. Hotel services contain more attributes and cannot be as easily displayed. The strategy followed by most hotels is to maintain an appealing external appearance and lobby – the first things a consumer sees upon approaching, and entering, the hotel. It is difficult for hotels to give every prospective guest a tour of the property, but they do provide site inspections for meeting planners who book volume business. In Europe, hotels have 'runners' at the train stations who offer to take travelers to the property so that the travelers can actually see the hotel before making a decision. If the traveler is not pleased with the hotel, the 'runner' will return him to the train station, free of charge. Finally, the Internet has become a useful supplement to other promotional materials in 'tangibilizing' hospitality services. For instance, hotels and tourism destinations are able to provide detailed information, high quality pictures, and visual tours on their web sites.

Inseparability. Another difference between tangible products and services is that services are typically produced and consumed simultaneously. In other words, services do not go through the traditional channel of distribution that involves a manufacturer, a wholesaler, and a retailer. Service firms are normally retailers that produce the service and deliver it to the consumer while it is being produced. In fact, the consumer is often part of the production process. For example, the consumer must be present for a service such as an airline flight or cruise to take place. The consumer is checked in, he boards the mode of transportation, and the service is completed. Similarly, food service firms normally prepare meals as customers order them, unless they are involved in 'grab-and-go' like in some convenience stores and supermarkets.

Perishability. The fact that services are intangible means that they cannot be stored, or placed in inventory. A good, or tangible product, can be stored in a warehouse and then shipped to the retailer where it can continue to be stored for some time period. Some supermarket products such as produce and meat have a limited shelf-life and are considered quickly perishable as well. However, other goods such as automobiles and computers can be stored almost indefinitely. Hospitality and travel services cannot be inventoried at all, similar to haircuts and doctors appointments. Seats on an airplane, hotel rooms, and rental cars perish the moment an airplane takes off, when the day ends and the hotel room is unsold, or if the automobile is still on the lot. All these represent lost sales that can never be recouped because each of these services has a finite capacity that cannot be exceeded. This particular characteristic of services has led to the development of yield-management and revenue-management models. Hospitality firms alter their prices in reaction to fluctuating demand in an attempt to maximize potential revenue, or 'yield.' It is also important for hospitality and travel firms to manage supply under these conditions by planning their facilities (i.e., capacity) and scheduling labor, to meet demand.

Variability. The characteristic of services to be discussed last is the variability in the delivery of services. The marketing of both goods and services is situational. That is, the consumer decision-making process is influenced by many factors such as the reason for the purchase, how much time is available, and the consumer's involvement with the product or service category. The fact that services are intangible and consumers are part of the production process makes it difficult to be consistent in the delivery of a service. Many quick-service restaurants have mechanized the preparation of their menu items in an attempt to provide a consistent service, but they cannot fully control the atmosphere in the restaurant at the time of delivery. For example, you could have a bus load of children who fill the tables and slow the queue, a fight could break out between two patrons, or the restaurant could be almost empty. All these represent different situations that would affect the production and consumption of a 'fast food' purchase. Similarly, hotels could have varying occupancies, different types of groups could be staying at the hotel, or there could be a major event in the city or town. Once again, all these would affect the delivery and quality of the service. In summary, a consumer could dine at the same restaurant on the same night every week and have a different experience on every occasion. The same holds true for staying at a particular hotel on every business trip. Hospitality firms 'blueprint' their services, mechanize certain components of the service, and train employees to deliver the service in a consistent manner in hopes of reducing the variability.

These four unique service features, or characteristics, are the reason why most critics believe services and goods are different, and that 'typical' product marketing techniques do not work well for services. Table 3.3 is adapted from an article by Zeithaml et al. (1985) discussing the specific problems and strategies associated with services marketing.

The validity and usefulness of this paradigm based on the four unique service features has been questioned by Lovelock and Gummesson (2004), who offer three options for moving forward: (1) declare victory and abandon the notion of a separate field, (2) focus on specific service subfields, and (3) search for a new, unifying paradigm. The first option accepts the fact that many manufacturing firms include an array of services as part of their offerings and suggests that the discussion of services should be integrated throughout textbooks rather than confined to one chapter. The second option maintains status quo in terms of having services marketing as a separate discipline and suggests the creation of meaningful subfields under the services marketing umbrella. The third option is to search for a new paradigm, or reconstruct the current foundation of the discipline. To this end, Lovelock and Gummesson (2004) present the idea of having a new paradigm based on the fact that some marketing transactions (i.e., services) do not involve a transfer of ownership. Ironically, this was the focus of discussions in the early stages of services marketing.

Table 3.3 Problems and strategies related to unique service features

Unique service features	Resulting marketing problems	Marketing strategies to solve problems	Hospitality strategy examples
Intangibility	• cannot protect services through patents • cannot display services • prices are difficult to set	• stress tangible cues • stimulate word-of-mouth • create strong image • use cost accounting to help set prices • engage in post-purchase communications	• Motel 6 – 'We'll keep a light on for you' • restaurant critics/publicity • Hertz Rental Car Agency • menu engineering • frequent-flyer programs
Inseparability	• consumer involved in production • other consumers present during production • difficult to mass produce	• good selection and training of contact personnel • manage consumers • use multiple locations	• Marriott's continuous training program • airline practices • franchising and chain operations
Perishability	• services cannot be stored	• use strategies to cope with fluctuating demand • manage demand and supply	• yield management • early-bird specials
Variability	• standardization and quality control are difficult	• industrialize service • customize service	• pre-packaged vacations • fast-food preparation

Service evaluation

Most of the relationships between variables in the field of marketing are situational and change continually. For example, there are different influences on the choice of a restaurant if it is for a special occasion (e.g., first date, anniversary, birthday, etc.) versus a normal family dinner. Similarly, the choice of hotels depends on whether it is a business trip or a family vacation. In addition, the intangible nature of services that relates to perishability and variability makes it difficult to evaluate the final product. The following discussion focuses on the various attributes used in evaluating products (both goods and services).

Search Attributes. These represent the characteristics of a product that the consumer can evaluate prior to purchase. It is possible to find restaurant or hotel locations, menus, and the amenities offered through telephone books or Internet web sites. One can also find information on airline routes, type of plane, seating charts, on-time percentage, and baggage handling policies. Tourism destinations use brochures and web sites to provide information on tourist attractions, restaurants, and lodging.

Experience Attributes. These represent the characteristics of a product that the consumer can only evaluate after purchase. For example, the actual quality of a meal or hotel as a meeting venue cannot be determined from search attributes. The consumer can form expectations, but it is only after the purchase and consumption of the service that the consumer forms a perception of the final service. A visit to a tourism destination depends on the weather, transportation, lodging, restaurants, etc. and can be very different from the consumer's original expectations.

Credence Attributes. These represent the characteristics of a product that are difficult to evaluate even after purchase. It is possible to evaluate most hospitality and tourism services after consumption because they are heavy in experience attributes. However, the 'pure' intangible services like health care, lawyers, and accountants are difficult to evaluate even after consuming the service. For example, you assume your accountant did a good job on your taxes, but you never really know without an audit or a review by a second accountant. Similarly, patients might need a second opinion (or more) to evaluate a doctor's performance.

In general, the demand is more elastic for services that have a 'tangible' component with more search attributes. These tangibility-based services are easier to evaluate and compare among competitors. The demand for services becomes more inelastic as they exhibit more experience, and then credence, attributes. One of the subsequent chapters in this text covers the service evaluation process in more detail, including service quality and customer satisfaction. The remainder of this chapter focuses on frameworks for classifying services based on various characteristics such as the degree of intangibility.

Classifying services

There are many classification schemes in the services-marketing literature based on the level of ownership (e.g., rented vs. owned), the mix of tangible goods and intangible services, whether the service is equipment-based or people-based, and the extent of customer contact

(Judd, 1964; Hill, 1977; Shostack, 1977; Chase, 1978; Thomas, 1978). Lovelock (1983) presented five classification schemes based on a review of previous literature and posited the following questions:

1. What is the nature of the service act?
2. What type of relationship does the service organization have with its customers?
3. How much room is there for customization and judgment on the part of the service provider?
4. What is the nature of demand and supply for the service?
5. How is the service delivered?

The topic of discussion in this chapter is hospitality and tourism services. Therefore, the rest of this section focuses on the application of the above classification schemes to these services.

Nature of the Service Act. The issues involved in this classification scheme are at whom (or what) is the act directed, and is the act tangible or intangible in nature? Hospitality and tourism services are designated as tangible actions directed at people who need to be physically present throughout most of the service delivery process. This differs from services like accounting and insurance that do not require the consumer's physical presence during service delivery. This high-contact system for hospitality services requires providers to locate near the consumer, manage the atmosphere or environment, schedule around consumers' preferences, hire and train employees with good interpersonal communication skills, and maintain quality control (Chase, 1978). It is interesting to note that hospitality services are often 'mixed,' in terms of contact. For example, airlines are high-contact regarding check-in and boarding, but low-contact for baggage handling and services that are available via the Internet such as ticketing and choosing seats. Similarly, restaurants are high-contact for dine-in consumers, but low-contact for take-out and delivery services.

Relationship with Customers. This classification scheme is based on the nature of service delivery (i.e., discrete or continuous) and the type of relationship between the service organization and its customers (i.e., membership or no formal relationship). Some service firms, such as banking and telephone services, have formal relationships, or memberships, with customers. Other service firms have a continuous delivery of service like insurance companies and police departments. Hospitality and tourism firms tend to focus on discrete transactions without formal relationships, or memberships. For example, consumers use rental car services, eat at restaurants, or stay at hotels only on a need basis (i.e., discrete transactions). Also, consumers are able to purchase these services without having a formal relationship with the firm. However, many hospitality firms offer frequent user programs in an attempt to create formal relationships with consumers and build brand loyalty.

Degree of Customization. This classification scheme is based on the extent to which the characteristics of services are customized and the extent to which contact personnel exercise judgment in meeting individual customer needs. Hospitality and tourism employees do not have as much latitude to exercise judgment in delivering services as employees in health care or education (i.e., low discretionary ability). Instead, hospitality firms focus on customizing the tangible elements of the service, while limiting the variability in service delivery. For example, luxury hotels and fine dining restaurants offer their customers a myriad amenities and options (i.e., high customization). In contrast, limited service hotels and quick-service restaurants are more standardized and do not offer as many options (i.e., low customization). Similarly, travel agents offer various types and levels of vacation packages, but they do not have much flexibility in pricing or adding value through special services.

Nature of Demand and Supply. This classification scheme is based on the extent of demand fluctuations and the extent to which supply is constrained. Professional services such as insurance and banking have consistent demand over time and usually have the capacity to meet the demand. Utility companies like telephone and electricity do experience fluctuations in demand, but they are normally able to meet demand. However, hospitality and travel firms like airlines, rental car agencies, lodging facilities, and restaurants have fluctuations in demand, but cannot always meet the demand during peak periods. For example, there are seasonal peak periods in demand for many tourism destinations based on weather (e.g., beach areas), during which lodging facilities and restaurants operate at capacity and turn consumers away. Similarly, airlines and rental car agencies in these areas are affected by the demand among tourists, but they have also short-term fluctuations based on day of the week and time of the day. Yield management models are used to manage this relationship between demand and supply (i.e., limited capacity) in order to maximize potential revenue. Remember, services are perishable and cannot be stored.

How the Service is Delivered. This classification scheme is based on the number or availability of service outlets and the nature of the interaction (i.e., does the consumer have to be physically present?). As stated in the first classification scheme, consumers of hospitality and tourism services need to be physically present for at least part of the delivery process. In most cases, the consumer goes to the service organization (e.g., hotel or restaurant), and there are usually multiple sites available given the number of franchises and chains. Independent lodging facilities and restaurants do not necessarily offer multiple sites, and tourist attractions are normally single entities within a given destination, but they still require the physical presence of consumers. By exception, travel agents, meeting planners, and tour operators are able to provide services without the physical presence of the consumer.

This is due to the fact that they operate as intermediaries rather than as retailers that deliver the final products to the consumers.

Alternatives to the traditional marketing mix

Expanded marketing mix

An expanded marketing mix was developed as a result of the debate over the differences between product (i.e., goods) and services marketing (Booms and Bitner, 1982; Magrath, 1986; Collier, 1991). The expanded marketing mix consists of seven Ps, including the traditional four Ps, aimed at solving the deficiency associated with the categories in the traditional marketing mix, of not being collectively exhaustive. Finally, the concept includes more discussion of the characteristics used to identify the proper category for the activities and objects being assigned. The additional three elements of the expanded marketing mix are: physical evidence, participants/people, and process.

Physical Evidence. This element includes the atmosphere of the service operation and any tangible evidence used to market the product. For example, restaurants decorate their dining rooms in an attempt to promote a 'theme' and they use this theme in their marketing materials. Applebee's promotes its chain as a neighborhood restaurant, and Subway promotes itself as providing fresh food that is healthy. The casinos in Las Vegas are especially adept at 'tangibilizing' their services and creating themes based on the physical surroundings (e.g., Treasure Island, Excalibur, and the Venetian).

Participants/People. This element recognizes that people are part of the service production and delivery process. The employees and the consumers must both be present for the service encounter to take place. Service firms must train their employees, educate consumers, and manage consumer expectations. Service firms can add 'value' to the product through their employees, who are part of the service experience. Also, consumers are more likely to be satisfied if they have reasonable expectations (i.e., if the firm can meet, or exceed, their expectations). Ritz-Carlton is known for its total quality management program and is a former winner of the Malcolm Baldridge Award for quality. The hotel chain gives every employee a credo with over 20 items that give guidance as to how customers should be treated. Employees 'own' problems until they are resolved and are empowered to be able to solve normal issues.

Process. This element deals with the delivery of the services to consumers and includes process design elements such as supply cycles, franchising policies, payment policies, and employee training procedures. Hospitality firms like McDonald's and Marriott try to standardize their service delivery processes in an attempt to provide consistent service throughout their operations. Airlines and rental car agencies have also standardized their operations through computer reservation systems and inventory control systems.

Hospitality marketing mix

The inherent differences between goods and services led to the development of an alternative marketing mix for the hospitality industry. Renaghan (1981) felt that the traditional marketing mix had little utility for the service industries (i.e., hospitality) and presented an alternative marketing mix with the following three components:

Product–service Mix. The product–service mix refers to the combination of products and services, whether free or for sale, aimed at satisfying the needs of the target market. The term 'product–service mix' is supposed to capture the fact that hospitality firms offer a blend of products and services. Renaghan (1981) alludes to the intangible nature of services and suggests that consumers are more likely to measure services by performance rather than possession. The inclusion of 'service' in the category title supports the notion that the marketing mix needs to include services marketing principles and take a market-oriented approach. The marketing function in service firms is not limited to the marketing department as in most manufacturing firms. It is important for all employees to focus on customers and form long-term relationships. For example, hospitality and travel firms attempt to accomplish this through the use of programs aimed at frequent flyers/guests/diners. This element also allows for the fact that employees and customers are actually part of the service offering because the production and consumption is simultaneous.

Presentation Mix. The presentation mix refers to all of the elements used by the firm to increase the tangibility of the product–service mix in the perception of the target market, at the right place and time. The presentation mix is used to differentiate a firm's offering from other products in the market. Some of the major elements of the presentation mix are the physical plant, location, atmospherics, price, and employees. It should be noted that the price and place components from the traditional marketing mix are included in this hospitality marketing-mix component. The place element in this context refers more to the service delivery process rather than the normal distribution process associated with product (i.e., goods) marketing that focuses on logistics and supply chain management. This element provides a category for many activities and objects that are specific to services (especially hospitality services) and that could not be easily assigned to one of the categories of the traditional marketing mix.

Communication Mix. The communication mix is very similar to the promotion component of the traditional marketing mix. The communication mix refers to all communications between the firm and the target market that increase the tangibility of the product–service mix, that establish or monitor consumer expectations, or that persuade consumers to purchase. This is accomplished by 'tangibilizing' the service using visual media to simulate the service experience. This approach addresses the criticisms dealing with the handling of sales promotion as a subcategory of the promotion element and provides a more encompassing element, focused on promotion and communication, than the traditional marketing mix. One of the service quality gaps involves the lack of communication with consumers concerning the nature of the service and what to expect. Managing consumer expectations is a critical activity in the marketing programs for services that is not explicitly identified in the traditional marketing mix. Service employees are also responsible for communicating with consumers in their boundary spanning capacities. For example, reservation agents at hotels and waiters at restaurants are frontline employees who are relied on to describe (i.e., tangibilizing) the firm's services.

Chapter summary

It seems as though the marketing-mix concept has been around forever. The concept started in the 1950s as a list of ingredients used to make marketing decisions and evolved into the four controllable elements that comprise the marketing program that is used to formulate marketing strategies for each of the firm's target markets. In addition to managing the marketing mix, firms must also engage in environmental scanning. This chapter discusses the five external environments (social, economic, technological, political and legal, and competitive) and their influence on the firms' marketing strategies. Managers cannot control the environment the way they control the marketing mix, but they need to monitor the environment for opportunities and threats, and then react appropriately. The chapter also examines the application of the marketing mix through customization and managing over the product life cycle. There are examples provided and baseline recommendations given for general situations in hospitality and tourism. It is the responsibility of each firm to determine the best way to customize its product–service mix and establish a unique position in the market with sustainable competitive advantages.

The unique nature of services, relative to other products (i.e., goods), is addressed. Services are intangible (they cannot be held), which leads to the other characteristics. Services are produced and consumed simultaneously (inseparability), they are difficult to standardize (variability), and they cannot be inventoried (perishability). These unique service features also make it difficult to evaluate services. Search, experience, and credence attributes are used to evaluate products, but services rely heavily on experience and credence attributes. In other words, most services are difficult to evaluate until after consumption, and even then it might be difficult to evaluate them. Several schemes exist for classifying services and each has its merits. The chapter covered five possible classification schemes and their relevance to the hospitality and tourism industry.

There have been critics of the marketing-mix concept and some alternative models presented in an attempt to incorporate the special nature of services. In fact, there was even an attempt to establish a unique marketing mix for the hospitality industry, and a suggested paradigm shift from the marketing mix to relationship marketing. The expanded marketing mix and the hospitality marketing mix addressed the criticisms associated with the traditional marketing mix and provided services marketers with tools for making marketing decisions that are market-oriented. The hospitality marketing mix consists of three elements: product–service mix, presentation mix, and communication mix. These elements are more flexible for making hospitality marketing decision, but while being collectively exhaustive, they are not mutually exclusive. Also, more emphasis should be placed on identifying the characteristics and properties that serve as the basis for classification of activities and objects into marketing-mix elements.

References

Bass, F. M. (1969). A new product growth model for consumer durables. *Management Science*, 15(5), 215–227.

Berry, L. L. (1980 May–June). Services marketing is different. *Business Week*, 24–29.

Booms, B. H. and Bitner, M. J. (1982). Marketing strategies and organizational structures for service firms. In J. H. Donelly and W. R. George (Eds). Marketing of Services (pp. 47–51). Chicago, IL: American Marketing Association.

Borden, N. H. (1964). The concept of the marketing mix. *Journal of Advertising Research*, 4, 2–7.

Brown, S. W., Fisk, R. P., and Bitner, M. J. (1994). The development and emergence of services marketing thought. *International Journal of Service Industry Management*, 5(1), 21–48.

Chase, R. B. (1978 November–December). Where does the customer fit in service operation? *Harvard Business Review*, 56, 137–142.

Collier, D. A. (1991). New marketing mix stresses service. *Journal of Business Strategy*, 12(2), 42–45.

Gronroos, C. (1989). Defining marketing: A market-oriented approach. *European Journal of Marketing*, 23(1), 52–60.

Gronroos, C. (1997). From marketing mix to relationship marketing – Towards a paradigm shift in marketing. *Management Decision*, 35(3/4), 322–340.

Hart, C. W. L. (1986). Product development: How Marriott created Courtyard. *The Cornell Hotel and Restaurant Administration Quarterly*, 27(3), 68–69.

Hill, T. P. (1977 December). On goods and services. *Review of Income and Wealth*, 23, 315–338.

Judd, R. C. (1964 January). The case for redefining services. *Journal of Marketing*, 28, 59.

Logman, M. (1997 November–December). Marketing mix customization and customizability. *Business Horizons*, 39–44.

Lovelock, C. H. (1983 Summer). Classifying services to gain strategic marketing insights. *Journal of Marketing*, 47, 9–20.

Lovelock, C. and Gummesson, E. (2004). Whither services marketing? In search of a new paradigm and fresh perspectives. *Journal of Service Research*, 7(1), 20–41.

Magrath, A. J. (1986 May–June). When marketing services, 4 Ps are not enough. *Business Horizons*, 29, 44–50.

McCarthy, J. (1975). *Basic marketing: A managerial approach*. Homewood, IL: Richard D. Irwin.

Nagle, T. T. and Holden, R. K. (2002). *The strategy and tactics of pricing: A guide to profitable decision making* (3rd ed., pp. 227–252). Upper Saddle, NJ: Prentice-Hall.

Reid, R. D. and Bojanic, D. C. (2006). *Hospitality marketing management* (4th ed.). Hoboken, NJ: John Wiley & Sons, Inc.

Renaghan, L. M. (1981). A new marketing mix for the hospitality industry. *The Cornell Hotel and Restaurant Administration Quarterly*, 22(2), 30–35.

Shapiro, B. P. (2001). Getting things done: Rejuvenating the marketing mix. *Harvard Business Review*, 63(5), 28–34.

Shostack, G. L. (1977 April). Breaking free from product marketing. *Journal of Marketing*, 41, 73–80.

Thomas, D. R. (1978 July–August). Strategy is different in service Businesses. *Harvard Business Review*, 56, 158–165.

Van Waterschoot, W. and Van den Bulte, C. (1992 October). The 4P classification of the marketing mix revisited. *Journal of Marketing*, 56, 83–93.

Wind, J., Green, P. E., Shifflet, D., and Scarbrough, M. (1992). Courtyard by Marriott: Designing a hotel facility with consumer-based marketing models. In C. H. Lovelock (Ed.). Managing services: Marketing, operations, and human resources (2nd ed., pp. 118–137). Englewood Cliffs, NJ: Prentice Hall.

Zeithaml, Valerie, A. Parasuraman, Leonard L. Berry (1985). "Problems and Strategies in Services Marketing," *Journal of Marketing*. Vol. 49 (Spring), pp. 33–46.

Part Two

Hospitality Marketing Functions and Strategies

CHAPTER 4

Branding, brand equity, and brand extensions

Woody G. Kim

Introduction

Brand management is a topic of considerable interest for both academia and industry. Building and managing strong brands is considered to be one of the crucial tasks of brand managers for the success of any hospitality and tourism organization. Strong brands provide a series of benefits to service firms, such as greater customer loyalty and higher resiliency to endure crisis situations, higher profit margins, higher market value (O'Neil and Xiao, 2006), more favorable customer response to price change, and licensing and brand extension opportunities (Keller, 2001). Ries and Ries (1998, p. 2) argue that branding has possibly been one of the most critical marketing strategies that serve as 'the glue that embraces the wide range of marketing functions collectively.'

In the past 20 years, the hotel industry has observed the proliferation of new brands. The rapid growth in hotel branding, totaling approximately 285 brands around the world in 2006, poses some problems to customers. Many hotel guests are confused with an explosion in the number of brands, and they may not be able to distinguish many similar brands offered by different hotel companies, in the same price range. According to *Hotel & Motel Management magazine* (2004), the total number of lodging brands in the extended-stay segment alone was over 25. For example, Residence Inn by Marriott was the front-runner in this segment, closely followed by Homewood Suites by Hilton, Extended StayAmerica, and Candlewood Suites by InterContinental.

There are plenty of newly launched hotel brands such as Starwood's 'XYZ', Choice Hotel's chicCabmira Suites and InterContinetal's Indigo (Weinstein, 2005). Starwood typically focuses on operating luxury brands, namely, St. Regis, the Luxury Collection, 'W' and upper upscale segments such as Sheraton and Westin. It developed Four-Point brand categorized as a midscale hotel with food and beverage (F&B) in 1995, and the brand was successful with a rapid expansion in positioning in the mid-priced market. Starwood recently introduced a new brand, Aloft, in a select-service hotel segment developed by W Hotel's development team. Shortly after launching 'Aloft,' Starwood introduced another upscale extended-stay brand, Element. It intends to be positioned closely to an upper upscale brand, Westin. Nylo is another newly launched hotel brand in a boutique hotel concept. Nylo hotels' primary market segments are business travelers and weekend leisure guests in their early 20s to mid 50s (Nylohotels, 2007). Nylo hotels feature 24-hour restaurants, bars, libraries, business centers, and game rooms.

Evidence suggests that independent hotels have lost ground in market share to branded hotels. A study by Forgacs (2003) showed that branded hotels in the United States accounted for more than 70% of the total room supply in 2000, as compared to approximately 61% in 1990. Forgacs (2003) also revealed that branded hotels in the United States led by American hotel chains has spread to all over the world and dominate the total room supply; more than 70% of the hotels in the United States have a brand name relative to 40% in Canada, 25% in Europe, and approximately 10% in the rest of the world. The significant increase is attributed to the benefits associated with branding. Previous research disclosed that a majority of business and leisure travelers preferred to stay at branded hotels rather than at 'unflagged' operations (Yesawich, 1996). Hotel guests perceive relatively lower risk when they choose an internationally well-recognized brand than when choosing an independent hotel. Compared to independent operations, branded hotels have competitive advantages in trusted brand names, sophisticated revenue management system, and frequent guest programs. In addition, obtaining financing for a branded hotel is much easier than for an independent hotel (O'Neil and Xiao, 2006). Lending institutions are generous in financing a hotel project affiliated with an internationally recognized brand. Keeling (2001), as reported in O'Neil and Xiao (2006), stated that obtaining financing for an unflagged hotel, however, is a challenge owing to more strict underwriting criteria and higher interest rates.

As in the lodging industry, building and managing brands has become a main focus of restaurant brand managers and marketers. Many restaurants are restructuring their corporate missions to reflect branding orientation rather than product orientation (Muller, 1998). Siguaw et al. (1999) argued that developing a clearly defined brand personality for quick-service and casual dining restaurants is an overriding goal of restaurant brand managers. They maintain that unique brand personality can serve as an effective vehicle by which to distinguish one restaurant brand from another. Njite et al. (in press) studied how consumers perceive restaurant brands and explored to identify brand dimensions specifically attributed to fine dining restaurants. They also investigated the extent to which these restaurant brand associations are prioritized in preference among fine dining restaurants.

Branding has recently started to be considered one of the top issues and challenges facing the tourism industry. It was not until 1990s that branding as a concept in tourism destination marketing started drawing attention from tourism practitioners (e.g., top mangers of destination management organizations) and academics (Blain et al., 2005). Ritchie and Ritchie (1998) define destination brand as: 'a name, symbol, logo, word, mark or other graphic that both identifies and differentiates the destination; furthermore, it conveys the promise of memorable travel experience that is uniquely associated with the destination; it also serves to consolidate and reinforce the recollection of pleasurable memories of the destination experience' (Goeldner et al., 2000, p. 653). Despite significant works about branding as a concept in tourism destination marketing, research on destination branding is relatively new and more is needed to further implement the concept.

The rest of this chapter is structured as follows. Section 2, background, starts with basic definitions of popular terms in the brand literature: branding, brand equity, brand extension, and co-branding. The benefits and pitfalls of using brand extensions and co-branding strategies in the hotel and restaurant industry are described. Three different approaches to brand equity measurement and review of previous hospitality and tourism studies follow. Section 3, application, presents hospitality firms ranked among the top 100 global brands. It illustrates the case of hotel and restaurant companies that have successfully adopted brand management strategies. Section 4 describes suggested directions for future research, followed by a concluding section.

Definitions

Branding

Farquhar (1989, p. 24) defines brand as 'a name, symbol, logo, or mark that enhances the value of a product beyond its functional value.' Kotler et al. (2005, p. 315) refers to a brand as 'a name, term, sign, symbol, design, or a combination of these elements that is intended to identify the goods or services of the seller and differentiate them from competitors.' Kotler et al. (2005, p. 315) define brand mark as 'the elements of the brand that cannot be articulated (e.g., a symbol, design, or unique color or lettering).' MSH Marketing Group (2006) defines branding as a marketing function that identifies products and their source and differentiates them from all other products. Jaffe Associates (2006) state that branding is important for consumer decision-making, as it provides a road map to identifying professional services with high value. The more differentiated the brand, the less likely the customer will switch to a substitute.

Examples of brand are Marriott, Burger King, TGI Friday's, KFC, and Wendy's. Some examples of brand mark are Marriott's M, Burger King's English king, TGI Friday's red-and-white stripes, KFC's Colonel Sanders, and Wendy's country girl (a daughter of the founder). A trademark is a legal designation to which the owner has exclusive rights for the brand or part of the brand.

Kotler et al. (2005) describe five desirable characteristics of a brand name:

1. brand name should deliver the qualities and benefits of the product or service;
2. it must be easy to recognize, recall, and articulate;
3. it should be unique;
4. in order to be a global brand, brand name should be easily and positively interpreted into foreign languages;
5. brand name may be legally protected under the trademark, patent, and/or copyright laws.

Brand equity

Key definitions of brand equity are summarized below. Aaker (1991, p. 15) stated that brand equity is 'A set of brand assets and liabilities linked to a brand, its name and symbol, that adds to or subtract from the value provided by a product or service to a firm and/or to the firm's customers.' Blackston (1995) defined brand equity as brand value and brand meaning, where brand meaning implies brand saliency, brand associations, and brand personality and brand value is the outcome of managing the brand meaning. Keller (1993, p. 2) defined brand equity as 'the differential effect of brand knowledge on consumer response to the marketing of the brand.' Brand knowledge consists of brand nodes in memory to which a variety of associations are linked. The core components of brand knowledge are brand awareness, brand favorability, and strengths and uniqueness of the brand associations in the consumer's memory.

An initial step to building a company's brand equity is to ensure that the consumer is well aware of the brand and holds some favorable, strong, and unique brand image in memory (Keller, 1993). Based on Keller's (1993) definition of customer-based brand equity, Lassar et al. (1995) describe five important characteristics in defining brand equity.

First, brand equity refers to consumer perceptions rather than objective indicators. Second, brand equity refers to a global value associated with a brand. Third, the global value associated with the brand stems from the brand name and physical aspects of the brand. Fourth, brand equity is not absolute but relative to competition. Finally, brand equity positively influences financial performance.

(pp. 12–13)

According to Aaker (1991), brand equity provides value to customers by enhancing their interpretation and processing of information, increasing confidence in the purchase decision, and raising the level of satisfaction. Brand equity also provides value to the firm by enhancing efficiency and effectiveness of marketing programs, prices and profits, brand extensions, trade leverage, and competitive advantage.

Brand extension

Brand extension refers to 'the use of well-recognized brand names to enter new product categories or classes' (Keller and Aaker, 1992, p. 35). VentureRepublic (2006), a leading branding strategy firm, defines brand extension as the application of a brand beyond its initial range of products, or outside of its category. This becomes possible when the brand image and attributes have contributed to a perception with the consumer/user, where the brand and not the product is the decision driver. A brand extension strategy can be used when a firm leverages a well-known brand name to introduce a new product or service. A new brand created from an existing brand through such a brand extension is a sub-brand or baby brand. The parent brand is an existing brand that gives birth to a new brand extension (Lee and Widdows, 2007).

Co-branding

Brand equity can be leveraged via co-branding and brand alliance (Kotler et al., 2005). Although co-branding has existed for many years, the concept has not been widely accepted as a popular strategy for service marketing until the 1990s (Khan, 1999). Boone (1997, p. 34) defines co-branding as 'the pairing of two or more recognized brands within one space.' The benefit of co-branding is 'that several different brands can command more power through customer awareness and traffic than can a single brand-name operation (e.g., a restaurant or hotel by itself) or an independent, "no name" operation.' (Boone, 1997, p. 34). Stewart (1995) defines co-branding as multiple business partners collaborating in promotion, technology development, and production, while maintaining their independence as a separate brand.

Benefits and pitfalls of branding, brand extension, and co-branding strategies

Dorsey (1994), as reported in Morrison (1996, p. 262) summarizes the benefits of branding for both customers and companies (i.e., service providers). The benefits to customers are:

1. it helps customers assess quality of products or service, particularly, if customers are not able to judge them;
2. it aids in reducing customers' perceived risk of purchase;
3. customers are willing to try the branded concept due to their higher acceptance for the established product or service; and
4. it helps reduce the search time and cost needed for purchase.

The benefits of branding to the service provider are that it:

1. facilitates market segmentation by creating tailored images;
2. facilitates promotional efforts;
3. gives the company the potential to attract customers who are willing to pay a premium for the brand;
4. enhances the firm's image, if their brands are successful;
5. assists in cultivating brand loyalty and stabilizing market share; and
6. reduces launching costs of a new product or service.

Kotler et al. (2005) mentioned that economy of scale is an important condition for building a strong brand. The examples of cost savings that branded hospitality operations could accomplish from the economies of scale include reduced promotional costs, lower central reservation system costs, purchasing economies, and oftentimes advantageous financing packages.

Benefits of a brand extension are also summarized here. First, when executed successfully, time and promotional costs of a newly launched concept (i.e., an extended brand or concept) are significantly reduced. Second, the newly extended brand will draw quicker customer awareness and willingness to adopt the product than an unfamiliar brand. Third, consumers perceive lower risks with a new concept if it carries a familiar brand name. Fourth, customers associate the quality of the well-known parent brand with the newly launched brand and are more likely to trust the new concept. Thus, brand extension allows higher success rates when launching a new concept.

Brand managers should understand that brand is one of the most valuable assets and it needs to be managed with great caution if they choose to extend the brand. Brand managers should ensure that brand extension is based on consumer needs rather than brand developers' perspective. Attracting new users to the brand is one of the advantages of brand extension but brand developers should be cautious enough to retain existing customers as well. Keller and Sood (2003, p. 12) caution that 'brand extension could be a double-edged sword.' A well-managed brand not only increases profit, but also strengthens brand meaning and brand equity. However, poorly-executed brand extensions will be a risky venture cannibalizing the sales of the parent brand and causing a considerable risk of brand equity dilution. If the extended brands do not fit with the original personality of the parent brand, the focal point of the parent brand's personality might get distorted in the minds of the consumers. Aaker (1990, pp. 50–52) delineates the pitfalls of brand extensions:

When a brand name is extended just to offer recognition, credibility, and a quality association, there is oftentimes a significant risk that, even though initially successful, a brand extension may be susceptible to competition. Extensions should improve the core brand, but there is a risk that an extension could arouse negative attribute association. The extension must fit the brand; a meaningful association that is common to the brand and the extension can provide the basis of fit. An extension usually will create new brand associations, some of which can hurt the brand. The brand association created by the extension can also blur a sharp image. Possibly, the worst potential outcome of a brand extension is a foregone opportunity to create new brand equity.

Yip (2005) also mentioned the challenges of adopting a co-branding strategy:

Adopting a co-branding strategy in the hospitality industry is not easy and [it is] complex. One of the primary weaknesses of implementing a co-branding strategy is potential introduction of new variables that can complicate daily operations. Hotel management teams have to ensure that partnering with a branded food and beverage, for example, will not result in direct competition with the hotel's existing in-house food and beverage services; rather, the coalition should complement the hotel's established amenities. Other challenges include, but are not limited to: negotiating monetary commitment and upfront investment between the two parties; the fear of damaging brand reputation or of experiencing a decrease in quality levels during the term of the alliance; and the concern of collaborating with the wrong brand. Many examples of failed alliances have been the result of miscommunication between the partners.

Dimensions of brand equity

Within marketing research, operationalization of customer-based brand equity is generally categorized into two types (Cobb-Walgren et al., 1995; Yoo and Donthu, 2001): consumer perception (brand awareness, brand associations, perceived quality) and consumer behavior (brand loyalty, willingness to pay a high price). Brand equity is operationalized by Lassar et al. (1995, p. 13) as 'the enhancement in the perceived utility and desirability a brand name confers on a product.' According to them, customer-based brand equity indicates only perceptual dimensions, excluding behavioral or attitudinal dimension such as loyalty or usage intention. Lassar et al. (1995) also developed a scale to measure customer-based brand equity. This scale consists of the five underlying dimensions of brand equity: performance, social image, value, trustworthiness, and attachment.

Aaker (1991, 1996b) proposed four components of brand equity – perceived quality, brand awareness, brand image (association), and brand loyalty – and his conceptualization has been widely accepted and employed by many scholars (Keller, 1993; Motameni and Shahrokhi, 1998; Low and Lamb, 2000; Prasad and Dev, 2000; Yoo and Donthu, 2001). Each component is discussed briefly below.

Perceived quality

Perceived quality is 'the customer's judgment about a product or service's overall excellence or superiority' (Zeithaml 1988, p. 3). It is based on the consumer's subjective evaluation of a product or service quality.

Product's or service's perceived quality is frequently used as a strategic instrument by a firm. Yoo et al. (2000) stated:

High perceived quality means that, through the long-term experience related to the brand, consumers recognize the differentiation and superiority of the brand. Zeithaml [1988] identifies perceived quality as a component of brand value; therefore, high perceived quality would drive a consumer to choose the brand rather than other competing brands. Therefore, to the degree that brand quality is perceived by consumers, the enhancement level brand equity value will be decided.

(p. 197)

Brand awareness

Brand awareness is 'the ability for a customer to recognize or recall that a brand is a member of a certain product category' (Aaker 1991, p. 91). Even if consumers are fully aware of a specific brand, it does not necessarily mean they prefer the brand, attach a high value to it, or associate any superior attributes to the brand; it just refers to recognizing the brand and identifying it under different conditions. Awareness can affect perceptions and attitudes, and it may drive brand choice and loyalty. Awareness has several levels such as unawareness of the brand, brand recognition, brand recall, and the top-of-mind brand. Brand recognition relates to the consumer's ability to confirm prior exposure to the brand as a cue (e.g., Have you heard about Club Med?). Brand recall relates to the consumer's ability to retrieve the brand when given a product category as a cue (e.g., What brands of pizza restaurants can you recall?). Brand recall reflects more correctly a brand's position in the market because it requires that consumers generate the brand from memory. The top-of-the mind brand is the first named brand in a recall test. There is no doubt that greater awareness of the brand is the major element driving brand equity.

Brand associations or brand image

Aaker (1991, p. 147) defines brand associations as 'anything that is linked in memory to a brand.' Brand associations imply not only the impression of individual brand but also the image of the company that offers the product or service. It also contains the concept of value that customers may confer a brand and brand personality as well. Therefore, it is possible to create brand associations, although the customer does not have direct experience with the product or service. A link to a brand will be stronger when it is based on frequent experiences or exposures. When one association is easily linked to additional associations, the former gets stronger. For example, McDonald's is strongly linked to various images – the yellow arch of character 'M', Ronald McDonald of Disney World, children, fun, Big Mac, and so on. Keller (1998) defines brand associations as informational nodes connected to the brand node in memory that holds the meaning of the brand for consumers. These associations contain perceptions of brand quality and attitudes toward the brand. Brand associations are useful to marketers. Marketers use brand associations to differentiate, position, and extend brands, as well as to create positive attitudes and feelings toward a brand and to suggest attributes or benefits of purchasing or using a specific brand (Aaker, 1991).

Brand image is a set of brand associations held in consumer memory. Keller (1993, p. 3) defined brand image as 'perceptions about a brand as reflected by the brand associations held in consumer memory.' Keller (1998) and Aaker (1991) postulate that consumer perception of a brand is a multi-dimensional concept. Different types of brand associations making up brand image include product-related or non-product-related attributes, functional, experiential, or symbolic benefits, and overall brand attitudes. Some research has concentrated on product attributes or benefits. Aaker and Stayman (1990) investigated whether two different beer brands had invoked different associations to consumers. The findings indicated that one brand was strongly associated with 'warm' and 'friendly' dimensions, while the other was evaluated higher as being 'healthy' and 'wholesome'.

These associations can vary according to their favorability, strength, and uniqueness. High levels of brand awareness and a positive (favorable, strong, and unique brand associations) brand image should increase the probability of brand choice, as well as enhance consumer loyalty and reduce vulnerability to competitors' promotional activities. A positive brand image also has specific implication for the pricing, distribution, and promotion activities related to branding (Keller, 1993).

Brand loyalty

Brand loyalty is defined as 'the attachment that a customer has to a brand' (Aaker, 1991, p. 65). Aaker (1991) suggests that brand equity relies on the number of people who patronize the brand. Zeithaml and Bitner (2002, p. 49) describe factors affecting brand loyalty: 'the degree to which consumers are committed to particular brands of goods or services relies upon the four factors – switching cost, the availability of substitute, the perceived risk associated with the purchase, and the previous satisfaction level.'

Odin et al. (2001) propose the level of sensitivity to differentiate loyalty from inertia. In other terms, a repeat purchasing behavior under conditions of strong sensitivity will be considered as brand loyalty; a consumer who tends to repurchase the same brand and who attaches great importance to brands of his choice is said to be brand loyal. By contrast, a repeat purchasing behavior under conditions of weak brand sensitivity is considered as purchase inertia. In this case, the consumer does not attach any importance to the brand of the purchased product or service. The consumer is not able to distinguish the brand from other alternative brands.

Approaches to measuring brand equity

Understanding how to measure brand equity is an important issue facing hospitality brand managers. The brand equity has primarily focused on exploring customer-based brand equity. This chapter extends the focus to include two additional perspectives: financial and comprehensive.

Customer-based aspect

According to Aaker (1991), brand equity is a complex concept comprised of brand loyalty, brand awareness, perceived quality, brand associations, and other proprietary assets. Yoo and Donthu (2001) developed a multi-dimensional consumer-based brand equity scale (MBE) drawn from Aaker's (1991) and Keller's (1993) conceptualizations. They postulate that brand equity can be measured by four dimensions: brand loyalty, brand awareness, perceived quality, and brand associations. However, their findings suggest that consumer-based brand equity scale must be measured with three dimensions: brand loyalty, perceived quality, and brand awareness/associations.

Total Research (1998), acquired by HI Europe in 2002, developed EquiTrend, a measure based on a small set of simple, yet powerful, questions. The EquiTrend measure is based on three dimensions of brand equity. The first is salience, the percentage of respondents who have an opinion about the brand. The second, perceived quality, is at the heart of EquiTrend. Quality is measured on an 11-point scale that ranges from 'outstanding' to 'unacceptable.' The third, user satisfaction, is the average quality rating a brand receives among consumers who use the brand most often. Analysis of the EquiTrend data has shown that perceived quality is associated with premium price and usage rate. When a perceived quality rating goes down, so does the usage.

Young and Rubicam (Y&R), a major global advertising agency, measured brand equity of 450 global brands and more than 8,000 local brands in 24 countries. The measure is named as the Brand Asset Valuator. Each brand was estimated through a questionnaire made up of 32 items, which included four sets of measures. Y&R postulates that brands are built sequentially along the four dimensions – differentiation, relevance, esteem, and knowledge.

Financial aspect

The financial viewpoint aims to determine a brand's valuation for purposes of licensing agreements or acquisition decisions. It is based on the incremental discounted future cash flows that would result from a branded product's revenue over the revenue from an unbranded product (Simon and Sullivan, 1993). The asset representing the brand is recorded in the company's balance sheet. The financially-fair market value of a company is based on its tangible and intangible assets' ability to generate cash flow (Simon and Sullivan, 1993). The tangible assets consist of (1) property, plant, and equipment, (2) current assets – cash equivalent, inventories, and marketable securities, and (3) investments and stocks and long-term bonds. Intangible assets include patents, trademarks, franchises, R&D, good will, and brand equity (Simon and Sullivan, 1993). The estimation method extracts the value of brand equity from the value of the firm's intangible assets by first breaking down the value of a firm's total financial market value into tangible and intangible assets and then carving brand equity out from the intangible assets. In other words, the value of intangible assets can be calculated by subtracting the value of its tangible assets from the market value of a company (Simon and Sullivan, 1993). Thus, brand value of a company can be derived as the market value (stock price × number of shares) minus its tangible and the remaining intangible assets.

Let us try to estimate the brand value of Marriott International as of December 2005. The total market value (capitalization) was approximately $18.5 billion; tangible assets were estimated to be about $15.5 billion and the remaining intangible assets were worth $1.4 billion. The brand value of Marriott can be calculated from market value ($18.5 billion) minus tangible ($15.5 billion) and its remaining intangible assets ($1.4 billion). Its brand value, thus, was approximately $1.6 billion. Brand value of $1.6 billion can also be derived by simply subtracting its remaining intangible assets of $1.4 billion (e.g., goodwill, franchises) from its total intangible assets of $3.0 billion.

Comprehensive aspect

Lastly, the comprehensive aspect of measuring brand equity incorporates both customer-based brand equity and financial brand equity. This method has appeared to make up for the insufficiencies that may exist when only one of the two techniques is emphasized. Dyson et al. (1996), for instance, adopted a survey approach designed to place a finance-related value on the consumer-based equity of brand images and associations. Motameni and Shahrokhi (1998) suggested global brand equity (GBE) valuations, which combine brand equity from a marketing viewpoint and brand equity from a financial aspect. GBE can be computed by simply multiplying the brand's net earnings by the

brand's multiple. The brand's net earnings, which are based on a financial approach, are the incremental profit of a branded product over an
unbranded product. In contrast, the brand multiple is derived from
brand strength, which will be determined based on a multiple-step
process using an in-depth-assessment consumer survey and utilizing
a combination of techniques to measure brand equity (Motameni and
Shahrokhi, 1998). A more detailed explanation as to how to measure
brand equity in marketing practices will be provided in the next section.

Financial World uses one of the most publicized financial methods
in its annual listing of worldwide brand valuation (Ourusoff, 1993).
Financial World's formula computes net brand-related earnings and
assigns a multiple based on brand strength. Obviously, the stronger
the brand, the higher the multiple applied to profits. Brand strength
refers to a combination of leadership, stability, trading environment,
internationality, ongoing direction, communication support, and legal
protection. The fact that the full value of brand-owning companies was
neither explicitly shown in the accounts nor always reflected in the
stock market value led to a reappraisal of the importance of intangible
assets in general, and brands in particular. The estimation technique
is based on a discounted cash flow (DCF) analysis of forecasted incremental cash flows earned as a result of owning a brand – the brand's
contribution to the business. DCF analysis is a valuation method used
to estimate the brand value of any company. DCF analysis uses future
free cash flow projections and discounts them to arrive at a present
value, which is used as a proxy for brand value.

For example, let us attempt to estimate the brand value of Marriott by
using DCF analysis. First of all, future cash flow generated from owning
multiple brands should be estimated. We need to project the future
15–20 year cash flow streams and discount them to come up with a sum
of the present value of each future cash flow stream, which is equivalent
to brand value. The projection period depends on the longevity of the
brand. Suppose the brand manager of Courtyard by Marriott predicts
that future cash flow expected from owning the well-established hotel
brand will be as given below – a mixed stream of cash flows for
15 years. Also suppose that the discount rate (weighted average cost of
capital) is 7%. The brand value today of Courtyard by Marriott should
equal the sum of present value of all future cash flow received from
owning the brand. Table 4.1 illustrates how the total brand value of
$308 million is derived with the given 15 year future cash flow streams.

Depending on the stakeholders, a different method may be adopted
to measure brand equity. For example, financial institutions, bankers,
and merger and acquisition specialists are more likely to see the equity
value from a financial perspective. However, hospitality marketers,
brand management team, and managers are more likely to find that
a consumer-based approach is more useful for their decision-making,
than the financial approach.

Table 4.1 Discount cash flow analysis

Year	Cash flow (in millions)	Discount factor (7%)	Present value (PV)
1	25.0	0.935	23.36
2	26.3	0.873	22.93
3	27.6	0.816	22.50
4	28.9	0.763	22.08
5	30.4	0.713	21.67
6	31.9	0.666	21.26
7	33.5	0.623	20.86
8	35.2	0.582	20.47
9	36.9	0.544	20.09
10	38.8	0.508	19.72
11	40.7	0.475	19.35
12	42.8	0.444	18.99
13	44.9	0.415	18.63
14	47.1	0.388	18.28
15	49.5	0.362	17.94
		Sum of PV	308.13

Table 4.2 summarizes previous research on brand equity from customer-based, financial, comprehensive, and consulting companies' institutional research.

Table 4.2 Summary of past research on brand equity

Researchers	Concept	Measurement
Customer-based aspect		
Aaker (1991, 1996b)	Brand awareness Brand loyalty Perceived quality Brand associations	Perceptual and behavioral Conceptualization
Srivastava and Shocker (1991)	Brand strength	Brand strength (customers' perception and behavior) + Fit = Brand value (financial outcome)

Table 4.2   (Continued)

Researchers	Concept	Measurement
Keller (1993, 2001)	Brand knowledge	Brand knowledge = Brand awareness + Brand image
Blackston (1995)	Brand meaning	Brand relationships model: Objective Brand (personality characteristics, brand image) + Subjective Brand (brand attitude)
Kamakura and Russell (1993)	Brand value	Brand Value = Tangible Value + Intangible Value Segmentwise logit model on single-source scanner panel data
Swait et al. (1993)	Total utility	Equalization Price measuring
Park and Srinivasan (1994)	Difference between overall preference and preference on the basis of objectively measured attribute levels	Brand Equity = Attribute based + Non-attribute based
Francois and Maclachlan (1995)	Brand strength	Intrinsic brand strength Extrinsic brand strength
Lassar et al. (1995)	Performance Social image Commitment Value Trustworthiness	Evaluated only perceptual dimensions Discovered a halo effect across dimensions of brand equity
Agarwal and Rao (1996)	Overall quality Choice intention	Brand perception/brand preference/brand choice paradigm
Yoo & Donthu (2001)	Brand loyalty Brand awareness/associations	Validating Aaker's conceptualization
Cobb-Walgren et al. (1995)	Brand awareness Perceived quality Brand associations	Relationship with brand preference and usage intentions
Prasad and Dev (2000)	Brand performance Brand awareness	Hotel brand equity index = Satisfaction + Return intent + Value perception + Brand preference + Brand awareness

(Continued)

Table 4.2 (Continued)

Researchers	Concept	Measurement
Kim and Kim (2004)	Brand loyalty Perceived quality Brand awareness Brand image	Relationship between four components of brand equity and restaurant firms' performance
Atilgan et al. (2005)	Brand loyalty Perceived quality Brand awareness Brand association	Four determinants of overall brand equity in the beverage industry
Kim and Kim (2005)	Brand loyalty Perceived quality Brand awareness Brand image	Relationship between brand equity and firms' financial performance in luxury hotels and chain restaurants.
Financial aspect		
Simon and Sullivan (1993)	Incremental cash flows which accrue to branded products	Brand equity = Intangible assets − (Nonbrand factors + Anticompetitive industry structure)
Comprehensive aspect		
Farquhar (1989)	Added value with which a given brand endows a product	Respective evaluation on firm's, trade's, and consumer's perspective
Dyson et al. (1996)	Brand loyalty Brand attitude	Consumer Value model: Proportion of expenditure × Weight of consumption
Motameni and Shahrokhi (1998)	Global Brand Equity (GBE)	Brand strength (customer, competitive, global potency) × Brand net earnings
Institutional Research		
AGB Taylor Nelson	Consumers' association with a particular faith (Brand Vision)	
Total Research		Brand salience, perceived quality and user satisfaction (EquiTrend)
Millward Brown		Brand loyalty (BranDynamic)
Young & Lubicom		Brand stature and brand strength (Brand Asset Valuator)

Source: Reprinted from Tourism Management, 26, Kim, H and Kim, W. G. (2004). The relationship between brand equity and firms' performance in luxury hotels and chain restaurants, p. 553, Adapted by permission with Elsevier.

Brand equity research in the hospitality industry

There is relatively little research focused on the consumer-based equity of service brands (Smith, 1991). Muller and Woods (1994) emphasized brand management rather than product management in the restaurant industry. Muller (1998) recommended three major issues that a service brand should concentrate on in order to build equity and acceptance in the marketplace: high quality products and services, execution of service delivery, and a symbolic and evocative image. He insisted that through the combination of these three fundamentals in restaurant-brand development, the opportunity would come for charging a price premium and enhancing customer loyalty.

Davis (1995) showed an excellent example of a hospitality company that charges price premiums. He reported that Starbucks was successful in providing quality, consistency, and the image of authenticity to their customers. It permitted Starbucks to price an average middle-size coffee at approximately $1.60, which is at least 60 cents more than a similar size coffee available at other stores (Leiser, 2003).

Another study by Cobb-Walgren et al. (1995) focused on a consumer-based, perceptual measure of brand equity. The study employed the perceptual components of Aaker's (1991) definition of brand equity: brand awareness, brand associations, and perceived quality. Holiday Inn and Howard Johnson were studied to examine the impact of brand equity on consumer preferences and purchase intentions. They found that, of the five features examined, brand name was ranked fourth following price, bed size, and availability of pool. Brand equity (i.e., preference) of Holiday Inn was found to be approximately 10 times greater than that of Howard Johnson. After comparing Holiday Inn and Howard Johnson, they discovered that the higher the promo-tion budget, the higher the value of brand equity. In addition, the higher the brand equity, the higher the preference and purchase intentions.

Considering customers as source of all cash flow and resulting prof-its, Prasad and Dev (2000) developed a customer-centric index of hotel brand equity. This customer-centric brand equity index is a measure for converting customers' awareness of a brand and their view of the brand's performance into a numerical index. This is based on actual customer satisfaction data, intent to return, perception of the price–value relationship, brand preference, and top-of-mind awareness of the brand.

Kim and Kim (2004) examined the four underlying components of brand equity: brand awareness, brand image, brand loyalty, and perceived quality. They confirmed that brand equity is a multi-dimensional concept comprised of the four elements. They investigated how the four dimensions influence quick-service restaurant (QSR) chains' financial performance. Brand loyalty, which was proposed to be an important element in QSR chains, did not show any significant impact on firms' performance. Brand awareness, perceived quality, and brand image were found to be important dimensions that have significant influence on financial performance of QSR firms.

Atilgan et al. (2005) generalized the customer-based brand equity scale suggested by Yoo et al. (2000), in the context of the beverage industry in Turkey. They operationalized the brand equity as the four dimensions: perceived quality, brand loyalty, brand awareness, and brand associations. Their findings indicated that brand loyalty was the most powerful dimension affecting brand equity. However, the other three dimensions including perceived quality, brand awareness, and brand association did not have a significant effect on brand equity.

Application

Implementation of branding, brand extension, and co-branding strategies

The Websites of tourism destinations have developed into important branding distribution channels. However, in the area of tourism destination marketing, electronic branding has not received much attention (Lee et al., 2006). Furthermore, most US State Tourism Websites do not fully take advantage of the Web for building brand and enhancing their brand image as an attractive destination. Lee et al. (2006) analyzed official tourism Websites of 50 states and summarized the unique selling propositions (USPs) and positioning strategies of state tourism organizations via a content analysis of slogans and the sites' Web-based brand-building features. Their findings revealed that almost all the states highlighted nature and culture/heritage. They also found that many of the states' tourism bureaus were not fully taking advantage of their Web sites as promotional vehicles, owing to lack of consistency among the Web site elements. These findings could help develop strategies for web-based destination marketing and destination branding.

Previous research has confirmed that tourism destination branding improves destination image among tourists (Blain et al., 2005). The 1998 Annual Travel and Tourism Research Association (TTRA) conference presented destination branding success cases: New York, Florida, Australia, Canada, Louisiana, Missouri, Texas, and Oregon. Blain et al. (2005) conducted a survey of 409 senior executives of destination management organizations (DMOs) who were the members of IACVB (International Association Convention and Visitor Bureau). The primary purpose of this study was to explore the current destination branding practices among DMOs. They found that the destination image and message resonated from the Web should be consistent and be incorporated throughout different DMO members and activities.

DMOs should make sure that the logo delivers a distinct destination image to offer a USP. Their findings show that top managers of DMO have a good conceptual understanding of destination branding and have practiced the concept to a certain degree. However, their applications were limited to selective perspectives of the concept such as logo design and development.

During the 1980s and 1990s, brand extensions have been the primary expansion strategies for both hotel and restaurant firms. Brand extension refers to using the leverage of a successful brand name in one category to initiate new or modified products in different categories within the same market. The two most popular methods to leverage brand equity are line extensions and category extensions. Line extension is the usage of a well-known brand for a new product offered in the same product category. Category extension is to extend an established brand into a new product category or class (Aaker and Keller, 1990). A successful brand assists a company in introducing new product categories. Since brand extension could decrease the risk perceived by consumers and reduce promotion costs, hotel companies have adopted it as their expansion vehicle during the 1980s and 1990s. For example, Marriott and Hilton have successfully adopted a line extension strategy to endorse the power of well-accepted brand identity to a number of new concepts differentiated by market segment (Jiang et al., 2002). Aaker (1990) argued that the general perception of quality associated with a name was a primary element for a brand's successful extension.

Hotel brand managers may wonder whether many brands really resonate in the minds of consumers. US hotel groups have adopted brand extensions as a vehicle to avoid loss of customers to competitive hotels and increase their market influence (Jiang et al., 2002). Global hotel firms have a large number of multi-brand portfolios to cater to highly fragmented market segments. Some hotel chains were successful in positioning their brands distinctly from their competition. Marriott's aggressive expansion in the number of properties and sales revenue originated from its brand extension strategies that introduced eight different brands from its four core brands. For example, adding the 'by Marriott' name tag on affiliated brand names aided Marriott in maintaining differentiation, reducing operational risks, limiting new-product introduction costs, and enhancing financial performance (Muller, 1998). Other major hotel companies have jumped on the same bandwagon. A recent proliferation of newly introduced hotel brands has created confusion amongst travelers. For example, travelers now have more than 25 different brand choices when they want to stay at an extended-stay property. Thus, it is important for the hotel development team to thoroughly assess whether a brand extension will create new demands or erode existing demands for other brands.

Starwood was the first hotel company to launch a category extension strategy by focusing on pillow and bed. Westin has developed its innovative bed called 'Heavenly Bed.' Its channel of distribution includes its own catalogue on the Internet and At Home departments of 48 Nordstrom stores nationwide, and it is available by special order at other stores. Its brand extension strategy turned out to be a great success boosting the hotel's retail business (Lee and Widdows, 2007).

The Pappas restaurant group originally built its reputation as the best seafood supplier in the limited market areas of Houston, Dallas, Atlanta, Chicago, Denver and Phoenix. The Pappas' concept now extends into a variety of food concepts: seafood, steakhouse, Mexican, and Greek. The Pappas has adopted product extension strategies and their baby brands embedded with the Pappas name include Pappadeaux Seafood Kitchen, Pappas Seafood House, Pappas Bros. Steakhouse, Pappas Burger, Pappas Grill & Steakhouse, Pappas Bar-B-Q, Pappasito's Cantina with Mexican cuisine, and Yia Yia Mary's Pappas Greek Kitchen.

The Virgin Group, one of the most respected brands in the United Kingdom, has become a global brand by successfully implementing a category extension strategy. Originally focused on the music, movie, and game sectors, the Virgin Group has effectively extended into the travel and tourism business. Its travel and tourism business now includes Virgin Atlantic Airways, Virgin Vacations, Virgin Holidays, Virgin Limited Edition (a luxury resort business), and Virgin Galactic (space tourism). Virgin is also involved in trains, finance, soft drinks, mobile phones, wines, publishing, and the cosmetics business, generating approximately US$7.2 billion in total revenues in 2002.

Berry (2000) suggests that brand developers rely on invention rather than imitation to create a new brand concept:

Firms such as Starbucks and Midwest Express Airlines employ all of the tools at their disposal to build a unique, integrated identity, including facilities design, service provider appearance, core service augmentation, advertising content and style, and media selection. Starbucks could compress more tables and chairs into their restaurants, but doing so would damage what they are selling: a respite and a social experience. Because of its two-by-two configuration of leather seats (instead of the more common three-by-three seating), Midwest Express Airline's economy service appears to be first class. Meal service with china plates, cloth napkins, free wine or champagne, and freshly baked chocolate cookies reinforces the perception. The leather seats, meal service, and cookies are signature clues that enhance the core service and differentiate the brand from others.

(p. 131)

Recently, hospitality and tourism firms have begun to understand the importance of co-branding strategies (Lee et al., 2006). Increasing numbers of restaurants, lodging firms, and theme parks have jointly adopted co-branding strategies to achieve synergy (Young et al., 2001). These business partners often operate in the same space, share the customer's information, and accomplish cross promotion of the brands (Boone, 1997). Many hotels faced deteriorating profit margin from food and beverage operation. To overcome this challenge, some hotels and restaurants initiated co-branding strategies. Country Inns' co-branding alliance with T.G.I. Friday's was a win–win strategy for both brands. T.G.I. Friday's achieved significant additional sales (15–20%) from hotel guests during their lunch and dinner business. Ramada partnered with Bennigan's, which allowed Bennigan's to operate in Ramada hotels. Casper (1995) reported that the alliance of T.G.I. Friday's with Holiday Inn was successful, resulting in a significant revenue increase for both brands. Upper upscale hotel brands such as Marriott and Hyatt also joined as co-branding partners with restaurant chains. Starbucks decided to make a strategic alliance with Marriott and Hyatt to place a coffee shop inside the hotel by signing a long-term contract (Kotler et al., 2005). Pizza Hut signed a license agreement with Marriott in 1989 which allowed Pizza Hut's kiosk operations in lobbies of Marriott hotels (Littman, 1996).

Sometimes hotel companies have formed strategic alliances with companies that are engaged in totally unrelated businesses. For example, Econo Lodge partnered with Procter & Gamble's Mr. Clean. With special marketing efforts promoting this partnership, Econo Lodge reached out to hotel guests to deliver the message that the brand really cared about cleanliness (Yip, 2005). According to Jensen and Pollack (1996), McDonald's has made an agreement with Walt Disney to promote Happy Meals that feature Disney movie characters.

Howard Schultz, the founder of Starbucks, advises caution in leveraging brand equity in alliance with other companies. He states that 'there are significant opportunities to leverage the equity of the Starbucks brand on all sorts of products and services, but we turn down 99 percent of them even though they would create substantial short-term revenues and profits. These are matters that are not in the textbook, but that are in your heart, about what we feel is right for Starbucks to be doing' (Lippincott Mercer, 2007).

Global hospitality brands ranked

Interbrand, a British consulting group, annually ranks and provides the values of the top 100 global brands. Interbrand's formula is based on the sum of the present value of future cash flows or earnings that the specific brand is expected to generate in the future. Among the top 100 companies, the brand rankings and values of top hospitality and tourism firms in 2005 are, in the descending order, Walt Disney ranked 7th with $26.4 billion, McDonald's 8th with $26.0 billions, KFC 61st with $5.1 billion, Pizza Hut 63rd with $4.9 billion, and Starbucks 99th with $2.5 billion. Surprisingly, only three restaurant brands, but no lodging brands, were ranked within the top 100 global brands. Given the fact that hotel chains' multiple brands have had global presence for a long time, the disappointing fact clearly indicates that global hotel firms need to manage their brands better to create higher brand equity values. One of the reasons why many hospitality brands are not listed under top 100 brands is that some lodging firms like Marriott and Hilton were not big enough and did not reach the brand value threshold of $2.7 billion. Interbrand also explained why no airline companies were included in the list in spite of their large revenue:

There has evidently been large investment in airline brands and many of them are international brands too, but they are still operating in situations where the brand plays only a marginal role. In most cases, the customer decides based on airfare, route, schedule, corporate policy or frequent flyer points. The brand may often have a significant influence when all these factors are at parity. We have assessed the brand value for airlines by using internal data to strip out the impact of these other factors. However, it is difficult to assess the value reliably from purely public information. The exception to this would be Virgin Airline, which is clearly a brand-driven proposition. However, as a private company, it is not possible to value that brand from public information.

(Interbrand, 2006)

Case examples

Lodging success story: Marriott international in brand portfolio management

Lewis and Chambers (2000) report that Marriott International is one of the most successful hotel firms in extending their brands to adjacent markets or completely new markets. Marriott was able to distinguish its brands from those of competitors. They use Marriott as a success story of brand extension and underscore the importance of positioning each brand rather than the name. Pierce et al. (2002) described the success story of Marriott in managing brands successfully. According to them, Marriott has excelled in brand extension with its 2,741 lodging properties boasting approximately 500,000 rooms in 68 countries as of year end 2005. While the hotel industry grew at less than 6% per annum during the 1990s, Marriott grew at more than 10%. In Addition, Marriott's bottom line profitability grew at 18.4%, three points higher than the average of the whole industry. Marriott's success could be attributed to its sophisticated revenue management system and centralization of purchasing (Pierce et al., 2002).

There is no doubt that Marriott's success originated from smart brand portfolio managers who have successfully developed differentiated brands. During the early 1980s, the mid-priced hotel segment was populated by regional brands that many customers were unfamiliar with. Marriott saw an opportunity to introduce a unique and appealing hotel concept named 'Courtyard by Marriott.' The new hotel brand was developed by conducting a large-scale consumer survey among business travelers who were their primary target market. The brand extension allowed Marriott to leverage on its famous brand name without creating expectations of the same product/service (Lewis and Chambers, 2000). The newly designed hotel concept was a great example of delivering effective product messages to its target market segment, business customers, in the late 1980s (Cai and Hobson, 2004). However, Cai and Hobson (2004) also report that as the mid-priced hotel segment has become crowded with new brands, it has become more difficult for Courtyard by Marriott to differentiate itself from competitive brands. The standards associated with Marriott attracted travelers who were concerned about the quality of unknown local chains or independent operations. Since its launching in 1985, Courtyard by Marriott dominated the mid-scale segment, with more than 500 units in the United States. The same was done with the Fairfield Inn brand within the economy segment. At the upper end of the lodging spectrum, however, Marriott realized that its brand portfolio could not offer an image to entice affluent clienteles. Thus, Marriott acquired the Ritz-Carlton chain in 1995. The brand enjoyed a sparkling image among wealthy customers with its service messages driven by its Golden Standards and the well-known motto, 'We are ladies and gentlemen serving ladies and gentlemen' (Cai and Hobson, 2004). Marriott continued to add eight distinct lodging brands to its four core brands. For example, TownePlace Suites by Marriott is linked through its identity to the core brand, while others, such as Ritz-Carlton, are not. Marriott was able to realize the value from the brand acquisitions by applying its operating expertise to improve the financial bottom line and using its substantial cash flow to fund international expansion. Furthermore, Marriott was successful in leveraging its existing strong brand equities in each newly developed or adopted brand. For example, Marriott groups have three select-service brands (Fairfield Inn, SpringHill Suites, and Courtyard), two full-service (i.e., luxury) brands (Marriott hotels and Renaissance Residence), two deluxe brands (Ritz-Carlton and JW Marriott), four extended-stay brands (Residence Inn, TownePlace Suite, Marriott ExecuStay, Marriott Executive Apartments), and four time-share brands (Marriott Vacation Club, Grand Residences, Horizons, The Ritz-Carlton Club).

Restaurant success story: Chick-fil-A restaurant with a distinct brand personality

Berry (2000) also recommends that service firms can build strong brands through conscious efforts to be differentiated from competitors and provide a unique brand personality. He offered Chick-fil-A as a success story in developing a QSR chain's distinct brand personality:

> Chick-fil-A has developed a distinctive brand personality to differentiate from major quick-service chicken fast food chains such as Kentucky Fried Chicken, Church's Fried Chicken, and Popeye's Chicken. Chick-fil-A's creative promotional efforts created cows that recommended customers to consume more chicken than beef. The Chick-fil-A cows remind customers that they do not have to select McDonald's or Burger King and they can choose Chick-fil-A as another option. The brand personality of Chick-fil-A is perceived as fun, humorous, and differentiated. The cows allow Chick-fil-A to establish a unique and personable identity. Chick-fil-A's branding originated from shopping mall food courts, the company's unique distribution channel strategy. Inside the shopping mall, the company's primary promotional strategy is to provide food-court customers visually compelling options to a variety of fast-food eateries.

> Chick-fil-A adopts inside-out marketing in its mall units. The independent Chick-fil-A operator is the principal marketer with the mandate to bring the store to life as an advertising medium in order to leverage the latent marketing power of the store front, counter area and menu boards, point-of sale (POS) displays, store layout, and the appearance and attitude of employees. McDonald's, KFC, Burger King, Hardee's, Pizza Hut, and Taco Bell have convincing reasons to spend a large portion of their budget on advertising. Chick-fil-A, with fewer units, regional distribution, and a network of independent owners who finance the advertising, cannot afford to spend a lot of money on advertising like other leading QSR chains. Establishing a unique, charming brand identity is one of the ways to compete effectively against competitive advertising.

> (pp. 131–132)

Directions for future research

Due to the brand proliferation witnessed especially in the lodging industry, there is a growing importance of branding, brand equity, and brand extension in the hospitality and tourism business. To address these issues, more theory development and empirical research are necessary for a better understanding of consumer-based brand equity in a variety of hospitality businesses. It is important for hospitality marketers to design a practical measurement of concepts. Despite the recent advances in measuring customer-based brand equity, hospitality researchers need to develop reliable multiple measures of brand awareness, brand association (i.e., image), brand loyalty, and perceived quality. Different measures may be necessary to capture different characteristics of different segments of the hospitality industry. For example, a brand loyalty measure for luxury hotels may not be the same as that for budget hotels.

Besides measurement issues, further research is needed to examine how brand equity as a whole or which components of brand equity are related to a company's long-term relationships (e.g., trust, commitment, reputation, and loyalty) with customers and eventually with the firm's financial performance. Brand's trust and commitment are known to exert a significant influence on the success of brand extension (Park and Srinivasan, 1994). It is important for hospitality researchers to prove the clear linkage among brand equity, long-term customer relationships, and the firm's financial performance such as return on asset (ROA), return on equity (ROE), and stock returns. These findings will help the hospitality brand management team evaluate brand performance and develop effective branding strategies.

Hitherto, most research has treated brands as operating in isolation (Durme et al., 2003). Despite the claim that the customer's attitude toward a brand spills over to a partner's brand (Simonin and Ruth, 1998), little research has examined the influence of alliance partners on value creation of hospitality firms. Since there are so many alliances among hotels, restaurants, theme parks, airlines, and consumer products, additional research on these topics is needed.

O'Neil and Xiao (2006) reported that differences among parent companies' branding strategies may exert different effects on baby brands. They suggest that researchers examine how the branding strategies of parent companies influence the baby brands' market values. The Wall Street has started witnessing the evidence that brand may have an impact on the share value.

Due to the explosion of new brands by chain hotels, future research needs to address possible threats of cannibalization and brand equity dilution issues among baby brands. Brand management teams need to ask whether frequent business travelers are able to recognize so many different brand choices and differentiate one from another brand. Brand proliferation surely poses a serious issue of brand equity dilution. Research is needed to conduct the cost–benefit analysis of adding additional baby brands under the parent brand. Hotel development management should ensure that the introduction of a new brand is justified only if the benefits (e.g., attracting new customer groups and creating new market niches) outweigh the costs (i.e., brand dilution and cannibalization among baby brands) of launching a new brand.

Destination branding has become a hot research topic in the tourism literature. Blain et al. (2005) suggest that future research examine the relationship between the relationship management activities adopted by DMOs and their outcomes: visitors' revisit intention and their travel expenditure. In addition, they suggest that future research compare general tourism destination branding to branding in other hospitality segments (e.g., hotel, restaurant, and club). Further studies should also develop a clear evaluation method to monitor the relationship between DMOs' promotional efforts and the performance outcome of their marketing activities.

The research on branding in the hospitality industry is in its infancy stage. More research is needed to answer many remaining questions regarding branding, brand equity, and brand extension. Some of the questions awaiting research are:

- How can we measure brand equity of hospitality and tourism firms?
- Do hospitality firms need to adopt measuring and monitoring brand equity as a core business strategy?
- Do customers and brand management teams in the hospitality industry perceive the exploding brand extension strategy as a threat cannibalizing the parent brand or as an opportunity to grow and diversify into different market segments?
- Does brand extension generate customer confusion concerning the quality of the new concept?
- What are the primary drivers of proliferating brand extension in the hospitality industry?
- How many travelers can recognize the difference of each lodging brand?
- How many hospitality brands face brand dilution problems?
- Are continued brand extension strategies going to work in the lodging industry?
- Do loyal customers for a specific parent brand prefer patronizing extended brands to choosing different brands?
- Does travelers' hotel choice predominantly depend on the reputation of the brand or price/value perceptions?
- Is any specific segment (e.g., the extended-stay, mid-price) in the lodging industry already saturated with so many different brands and how do we determine the point of saturation?

Future research in the travel and tourism area needs to explore the main drivers of tourism destination branding process. It is important for DMOs to understand the primary destination branding activities affecting the enhancement of visitor loyalty and destination image.

Summary and conclusion

This chapter addressed the growing interest in branding, brand equity, and brand extension in the hospitality industry. The pros and cons of leveraging brand equity of the parent brand were discussed. A successful brand extension is directly related to expansion and long-term success of a hospitality firm. Brand managers should conduct a thorough cost–benefit analysis before making a brand extension decision. A growing number of foodservice, hotel chain, and tourism companies are partnering with each other to accomplish synergy effects in marketing. Strategic alliance decisions should be carefully made to maximize the synergy. The definitions of the popular branding terms were provided. The chapter also identified four important dimensions of customer-based brand equity: brand awareness, brand loyalty, perceived quality, and brand image. These four dimensions of brand equity were fully explained. It was shown that brand equity could be measured numerically as well as from customers' perceptions and attitudes. The previous literature related to measuring brand equity in the hospitality and tourism industry was thoroughly reviewed and summarized, with actual examples. Extant research in the area of branding, brand equity, and brand extension in general was thoroughly reviewed as well.

Branding remains one of the hottest research topics in the hospitality and tourism industry. Numerous hospitality firms have adopted brand extension as one of their expansion strategies. This topic is of utmost importance to both hospitality practitioners and academicians, since they need additional insights into the issue. More conceptual research identifying brand equity, brand extension, and co-branding is necessary to advance the knowledge base on branding, especially in the hospitality and tourism discipline. It would not be surprising to see that most hospitality programs add a new course on brand management in their curriculum in the next decade. In addition, more practical applications in the areas of hotel, restaurant, theme park, club, convention center, and tourism organizations need to be reported in the brand literature. Many tourism organizations such as convention and visitors bureaus (CVBs) and state DMOs urgently need to know best practices and more innovative applications regarding destination branding.

References

Aaker, D. A. (1990). Brand extensions: The good, the bad, and the ugly. *Sloan Management Review*, 31(4), 47–56.

Aaker, D. A. (1991). *Managing Brand Equity*. New York: The Free Press.

Aaker, D. A. (1996a). *Building Strong Brands*. New York: The Free Press.

Aaker, D. A. (1996b). Measuring brand equity across products and markets. *California Management Review*, 38(3), 102–120.

Aaker, D. A. and Keller, K. L. (1990). Consumer evaluation of brand extensions. *Journal of Marketing*, 54, 27–41.

Aaker, D. and Stayman, D. (1990). Measuring audience perceptions of commercials and relating them to ad impact. *Journal of Advertising Research*, 30, 7–17.

Agarwal, M. K. and Rao, V. R. (1996). An empirical comparison of consumer-based measures of brand equity. *Marketing Letters*, 7(3), 237–247.

Atilgan, E., Aksoy, S. and Akinci, S. (2005). Determinants of the brand equity – a verification approach in the beverage industry in Turkey. *Marketing Intelligence & Planning*, 23(3), 237–248.

Berry, L. L. (2000). Cultivating service brand equity. *Journal of the Academy of Marketing Science*, 28(1), 128–137.

Blackston, M. (1995). The qualitative dimension of brand equity. *Journal of Advertising Research*, 35(4), RC2–RC7.

Blain, C., Levy, S. E., and Ritchie, B. (2005). Destination branding: Insights and practices from destination management organizations. *Journal of Travel Research*, 43, 328–338.

Boone, J. M. (1997). Hotel-restaurant co-branding – a preliminary study. *Cornell Hotel and Restaurant Administration Quarterly*, 38(5), 34–43.

Casper, C. (1995). Confirmed reservations. *Restaurant Business*, 94(17), 104–118.

Cai, L. A. and Hobson, J. S. P. (2004). Making hotel brands work in a competitive environment. *Journal of Vacation Marketing*, 10(3), 197–208.

Cobb-Walgren, C. J., Ruble, C. A., and Donthu, N. (1995). Brand equity, brand preference, and purchase intent. *Journal of Advertising*, 24(3), 25–40.

Davis, S. M. (1995). Brand Asset Management for the 21st Century. Chicago: Kuczmarski & Associates.

Dorsey, J. (1994). Carlson, wagonlit ink merger, aim for a natural evolution. *Travel Weekly*, 53(55), 6.

Durme, J. V., Brodie, R. J., and Redmore, D. (2003). Brand equity in cooperative business relationships: Exploring the development of a conceptual model. *Marketing Theory*, 3(1), 37–57.

Dyson, P., Farr, A., and Hollis, N. S. (1996). Understanding, measuring, and using brand equity. *Journal of Advertising Research*, 36(6), 9–21.

Farquhar, P. H. (1989). Managing brand equity. *Marketing Research*, 1(1), 24–33.

Forgacs, G. (2003). Brand asset equilibrium in hotel management. *International Journal of Contemporary Hospitality Management*, 15(6), 340–342.

Francois, P. and MacLachlan, D. L. (1995). Ecological validation of alternative consumer-based brand strength measures. *International Journal of Research in Marketing*, 12(4), 321–332.

Goeldner, C. R., Ritchie, J. R. B., and McIntosh, R. W. (2000). *Tourism: Principles, Practices, Philosophies*, 8th ed., New York: John Wiley & Sons, Inc.

Hotel & Motel Management. (2004). Extended-stay hotel brands survey. October 4.

Interbrand (2006). Best global brands 2006. *Retrieved from the World Wide Web*, 01.10.07, <http://www.interbrand.com/best_brands_2006_FAQ.asp>.

Jaffe Associates (2006). Branding glossary. *Retrieved from the World Wide Web*, 12.10.06, </http://www.jaffeassociates.com/Jaffe/Glossary-Branding.php>.

Jiang, W., Dev, C., and Rao, V. R. (2002). Brand extension and customer loyalty: Evidence from the lodging industry. *Cornell Hotel and Restaurant Administration Quarterly*, 43(4), 5–16.

Jensen, J. and Pollack, J. (1996). BK pursuing new entertainmentally. Advertising Age 67(16), 1–2.

Kamakura, W. A. and Russell, G. J. (1993). Measuring brand value with scanner data. *International Journal of Research in Marketing*, 10(1), 9–22.

Keeling, J. M. (2001). Brands have the financing edge. *Hotel and Motel Management*, 216(8), 26.

Keller, K. L. (1993). Conceptualizing, measuring, and managing consumer-based brand equity. *Journal of Marketing*, 57(1), 1–22.

Keller, K. L. (1998), *Strategic Brand Management: Building, Measuring and Managing Brand Equity*, Englewood Cliffs, NJ: Prentice-Hall.

Keller, K. L. (2001). Building customer-based brand equity. *Marketing Management*, 10(2), 14–19.

Keller, K. L. and Aaker, D. A. (1992). The effects of sequential introduction of brand extensions. *Journal of Marketing*, 59(1), 35–50.

Keller, K. L. and Sood, S. (2003). Brand equity dilution. *MIT Sloan Management Review*, 45(1), 12–15.

Khan, M. A. (1999). Restaurant Franchising (2nd ed.). New York, NY: John Wiley & Sons, Inc.

Kim, W. G. and Kim, H. B. (2004). Measuring customer-based restaurant brand equity: Investigating the relationship between brand equity and firms' performance. *Cornell H. R. A. Quarterly*, 45(2), 115–131.

Kim, H. B. and Kim, W. G. (2005). The relationship between brand equity and firms' performance in luxury hotels and chain restaurants. *Tourism Management*, 26, 549–560.

Kotler, P., Bowen, J., and Makens, J. (2005). *Marketing for Hospitality and Tourism* (4th ed.). Upper Saddle River, NJ: Prentice-Hall.

Lassar, W., Mittal, B., and Sharma, A. (1995). Measuring consumer-based brand equity. *Journal of Consumer Marketing*, 12(4), 11–19.

Lee, G., Cai. L. A., and O'Leary, J. T. (2006). WWW.Branding.States. US: An analysis of brand-building elements in the US state tourism websites. *Tourism Management*, 27(5), 815–828.

Lee, J. and Widdows, R. (2007). The battle over beds: View from the industry towards brand extension. 12th Annual Graduate Education and Graduate Student Research Conference in Hospitality and Tourism, 1603–1605.

Lee, S., Kim, W. G., and Kim, H. J. (2006). The impact of co-branding on post-purchase behaviors in family restaurants. *International Journal of Hospitality Management*, 25(2), 245–261.

Leiser, M. (2003). Strategic brand value: Advancing use of brand equity to grow your brand and business. *Interactive Marketing*, 5(1), 33–39.

Lewis, R. C. and Chambers, R. E. (2000). Marketing leadership in hospitality: Foundations and practices (3rd ed.). New York: John Wiley & Sons Inc.

Lippincott Mercer (2007). Sense Magazine. Global coffee to go. *Retrieved from the World Wide Web, 02.23.07,* < http://www. lippincottmercer.com/insights/s95_starbucks.shtml>.

Littman, M. (1996). Hotels try to hold 'em in. *Restaurants & Institutions,* 106(17), 44–47.

Low, G. S. and Lamb Jr., C. W. (2000). The measurement and dimensionality of brand associations. Journal of Product and Brand Management, 9(6), 350–368.

Morrison, A. M. (1996). Hospitality and travel marketing (2nd ed.). Albany, New York: Delmar.

Motameni, R. and Shahrokhi, M. (1998). Brand equity valuation: A global perspective. *Journal of Product and Brand Management,* 7(4), 275–290.

MSH Marketing Group, Inc. (2006). Glossary of marketing communications terminology. *Retrieved from the World Wide Web, 12.10.06,* </http://www.mshmgi.com/glossary,B,Branding.html>.

Muller, C. C. (1998). Endorsed branding. *Cornell Hotel and Restaurant Administration Quarterly,* 39(3), 90–96.

Muller, C. C. and Woods, R. H. (1994). An expected restaurant typology. *Cornell Hotel and Restaurant Administration Quarterly,* 35(3), 27–37.

Njite, D., Dunn, G., and Kim, L. H. (in press) Beyond good food: What other attributes influence consumer preference and selection of fine dining restaurants? *Journal of Foodservice Business Research,* 11(2).

Nylohotels (2007). NYLO Hotels fact sheet. *Retrieved from the World Wide Web, 01.22.07,* < http://www.nylohotels.com/releases/ 02_Fact_sheet.htm>.

Odin, Y., Odin, N., and Valette-Florence, P. (2001). Conceptual and operational aspects of brand loyalty: An empirical investigation. *Journal of Business Research,* 53(2), 75–84.

O'Neil, J. W. and Xiao, Q. (2006). The role of brand affiliation in hotel market value. *Cornell Hotel and Restaurant Administration Quarterly,* 47(3), 210–223.

Ourusoff, A. (1993). Who said brands are dead? *Brandweek,* 34(32), 20–33.

Park, C. and Srinivasan, V. (1994). A survey-based method for measuring and understanding brand equity and its extendibility. *Journal of Marketing Research,* 31(2), 271–288.

Pierce, A., Moukanas, H., and Wise, R. (2002). Hard metrics can clarify the 'fuzzy' value of a brand. *Marketing Management,* 11(4), 22–26.

Prasad, K. and Dev, C. S. (2000). Managing hotel brand equity: A customer-centric framework for assessing performance. *Cornell Hotel and Restaurant Administration Quarterly,* 41(3), 22–31.

Ries, A. and Ries, L. (1998). *22 Immutable Laws of Branding.* New York: Harper Business.

Ritchie, J. R. B. and Ritchie, R. J. B. (1998). The branding of tourism destinations: Past achievements and future challenges. *Proceedings of the Annual Congress of the International Association of Scientific Experts in Tourism (AIEST)*, Marrakesh, MOROCCO, September 1, 1998, pp. 89–116.

Siguaw, J. A., Mattila, A., and Austin, J. R. (1999). The brand – personality scale: an application for restaurants. *Cornell H. R. A. Quarterly*, 40(3), 48–56.

Simon, C. J. and Sullivan, M. W. (1993). The measurement and determinants of brand equity: A financial approach. *Marketing Science*, 12(1), 28–52.

Simonin, B. L. and Ruth, J. A. (1998). Is a company known by the company it keeps? Assessing the spillover effects of brand alliances on consumer brand attitudes. *Journal of Marketing Research*, 35(1), 30–42.

Smith, J. W. (1991). Thinking about brand equity and the analysis of customer transactions. In E. Maltz (Ed.), *Managing Brand Equity: A Conference Summary* (pp. 17–18). Cambridge, MA: Marketing Science Institute.

Srivastava, R. K. and Shocker, A. D. (1991). *Brand equity: A perspective on its meaning and measurement*. Cambridge, MA: Marketing Science Institute.

Stewart, A. L. (1995). Co-branding just starting in Europe. *Marketing News*, 29(4), 5–6.

Swait, J., Erdem, T., Louviere, J., and Dubelaar, C. (1993). The equalization price: A measure of consumer-perceived brand equity. *International Journal of Research in Marketing*, 10(1), 23–45.

VentureRepublic (2006). Resources: Brand glossary. *Retrieved from the World Wide Web, 10.10.06*, <http://www.venturerepublic.com/resources/brand_glossary.asp>.

Weinstein, J. (2005). What does your brand stand for? *Hotels*, 39(7), 7.

Yesawich, P. C. (1996). So many brands, so little time. *Lodging Hospitality*, 52(9), 16.

Yip, P. (2005). Basic concepts of co-branding, with examples from the hospitality industry: could co-branding improve your bottom line? Hotel Online Special Report, September. *Retrieved from the World Wide Web, 10.10.06*, <http://www.hotel-online.com/News/PR2005_3rd/Sep05_CoBranding.html>.

Yoo, B. and Donthu, N. (2001). Developing and validating a multi-dimensional consumer-based brand equity scale. *Journal of Business Research*, 52(1), 1–14.

Yoo, B., Donthu, N., and Lee, S. (2000). An examination of selected marketing mix elements and brand equity. *Journal of the Academy of Marketing Science*, 28(2), 195–211.

Young, J. A., Hoggatt, C. D., and Paswan, A. K. 2001. Food service franchisors and their cobranding methods. *Journal of Product and Brand Management*, 10(4), 218–227.

Zeithaml, V. A. (1988). Consumer perceptions of price, quality and value: a means-end model and synthesis of evidence. *Journal of Marketing*, 52, 2–22.

Zeithaml, V. A. and Bitner, M. J. (2002). Service Marketing: Integrating Customer Focus Across the Firm (3rd ed.). New York, NY: McGraw-Hill.

Relationship and loyalty marketing

Stowe Shoemaker and Camille Kapoor

Introduction

Amidst the launch of thousands of new products each year, the costs associated with marketing and promoting a new product can top $50 million (Ball et al., 2004). One of the marketing strategies that companies utilize to maximize the return on their marketing spending is a technique known as relationship/loyalty marketing. Relationship marketing creates both customer bonding and customer understanding, which is integral to the company's sustenance and growth.

Relationships must be developed and sustained because as loyalty increases, the lifetime value of a customer also increases. Frequent-guest programs (sometimes mistakenly called loyalty programs) can help sustain and even increase loyalty, but only if they are designed properly and help to communicate the brand promise. This chapter first introduces different definitions of loyalty, shows why customer loyalty is important, reviews much of the hospitality literature on relationship/loyalty marketing, details how to effectively create a frequent-guest program that encourages customer loyalty, and discusses how to use each of the components of the Loyalty Circle to create loyalty.

Background

Customers are assets. They are the most important assets a company can have. Firms spend large amounts of money on such things as insurance and elaborate alarm systems to protect their assets such as buildings and warehouses. In the same way, firms need to spend money to 'protect' their customers. One way to define relationship/loyalty marketing is marketing that protects the customer base. (We will define it in other ways later on.) Relationship marketing sees the customer as an asset. Its function is to attract, maintain, and enhance customer relationships.

This is essentially what marketing is all about. But relationship/loyalty marketing adds a new dimension. Specifically, the goal is not only to encourage guests to return, but also to get them to tell their friends how wonderful the property or organization is. The goals of loyalty marketing also include two more items:

1. To have customers spend more money while on the property;
2. To have customers tell management when things go wrong, instead of just walking away and never coming back.

Definitions of relationship/loyalty marketing

It is important to understand what we mean by loyalty. One definition suggested by Shoemaker and Lewis (1999) is illustrative of the emotional side of loyalty, as compared to the frequency side. They stated that loyalty occurs when:

The customer feels so strongly that you can best meet his or her relevant needs that your competition is virtually excluded from the consideration set and the customer buys almost exclusively from you – referring to you as their restaurant or their hotel. The customer focuses on your brand, offers and messages to the exclusion of others. The price of the product or service is not a dominant consideration in the purchase decision, but only one component in the larger value proposition.

(Shoemaker and Lewis, 1999, p. 349)

Reichheld (2002) proposes a second definition of loyalty:

A loyal customer is one who values the relationship with the company enough to make the company a preferred supplier. Loyal customers don't switch for small variations in price or service, they provide honest and constructive feedback, they consolidate the bulk of their category purchasers with the company, they never abuse company personnel and they provide enthusiastic referrals.

(p. 126)

Relationship/loyalty marketing can also be defined as an ongoing process of identifying and creating new value for individual customers for mutual value benefits and then sharing the benefits from this over a lifetime of association. In this sense, it differs from our usual definition of marketing, although it is certainly part of it, in the following ways.

- It seeks to create *new* value for customers and *share* the value so created.
- It recognizes the key role of *individual* customers in defining the value they want (i.e., value is created *with* customers, *for* customers).
- It recommends that a company define its organization to support the value that individual customers want.
- It is a continuously cooperative effort between buyer and seller.
- It recognizes the value of customers over their purchasing *lifetimes*.
- It seeks to build a chain of relationships between the organization and its main stakeholders to create the value that customers want.

Relationship/loyalty marketing focuses on the processes and whatever else is needed to advance the customer relationship (Gordon, 1998). The fundamental reason why loyalty marketing is important is the lifetime value of the customer, which is discussed shortly.

Relationship/loyalty marketing is not, contrary to some beliefs, database marketing, frequent traveler programs, partnerships or relationship selling. While some of these may be used to enhance relationships, they are not, in themselves, the bases of relationships. The true sense and purpose of relationship/loyalty marketing is to maintain customer relationships and build loyalty with the expectation that both parties will continue in the relationship long after the formal production/consumption process has ended, seeking not only to keep customers but to bring them back as well. Levitt (1981) compares the relationship to something like a marriage.

The sale merely consummates the courtship. Then the marriage begins. How good the marriage is depends on how well the relationship is managed by the seller. That determines whether there will be continued or expanded business or troubles and divorce and whether costs or profits increase.... It is not just that once you get a customer you want to keep him. It is more a matter of what the buyer wants. He wants a vendor who will keep his promises, who'll keep supplying and stand behind what he promised. The age of the blind date or the one-night stand is gone. Marriage is both more convenient and more necessary.... In these conditions, success in marketing, like success in marriage, is transformed into the inescapability of a relationship.

(p. 96)

As in a good marriage or a good relationship, both parties have to 'get something.' For the firm, it is repeat patronage, expectation that the guest will spread positive word of mouth, and belief that the guest will tell management when things go wrong. These are just a few of the firm's expectations. For the guest, the expectation is that the firm will do everything in its power to ensure an error-free purchase experience, a customized experience, and that the firm will look after the guests' best interest.

Good relationships involve commitment and trust and, as in our personal lives, there are numerous antecedents that bring this about. There are also numerous consequences when they do not exist. Trust is the belief that an individual or exchange partner can be relied on to keep its word and promise. Trust is an antecedent of loyalty because the customer trusts the organization to do the things that it is supposed to do, implicitly or explicitly. Any actions taken to increase feelings of trust will lead to commitment. Conversely, any action taken that decreases trust will lead to a lack of commitment. Commitment is the belief that an ongoing relationship is so important that the partners are willing to work at maintaining it and are willing to make short-term sacrifices to realize long-term benefits.

Oliver (1999) presents excellent definitions of cognitive, affective, conative, and action loyalty. He sees each type of loyalty as a phase consumers go through, with action loyalty being the final, desired phase. Cognitive loyalty is based on available information about the brand that convinces a customer that a brand is better than alternatives. However, cognitive loyalty is shallow and runs no deeper than whether or not a customer was satisfied with the service provided. If satisfaction continues, a customer moves into the next phase, affective loyalty. Although customers are less easily persuaded to switch in this phase, data shows that people switch brands despite having been previously satisfied with their original brand. The next phase, conative loyalty, is when a customer desires to repurchase the brand. However, it is not until the final phase – action loyalty – that they engage in actively repurchasing the brand. If repurchase action begins, an action inertia develops, which facilitates further repurchasing.

Chaudhuri and Holbrook (2001) discuss the differences between behavioral loyalty and attitudinal loyalty:

Brand trust and brand affect are separate constructs that combine to determine two different types of brand loyalty—purchase loyalty and attitudinal loyalty—which in turn influence such outcome-related aspects of brand equity as market share and relative price, respectively. . . .From this, it follows that brand loyalty may be viewed as a link in the chain of effects that indirectly connects brand trust and brand affect with the market performance aspects of brand equity.

(p. 81)

They found that behavioral loyalty consists of repeat brand purchases, while attitudinal loyalty indicates a degree of commitment with the brand.

The lifetime value of a customer

The lifetime value of a customer, in short, is the net profit received from doing business with a given customer during the time the customer continues to buy from the company. As stated by members of the Harvard Business School faculty, 'the lifetime value of a loyal customer can be astronomical – especially when referrals are considered.' These researchers calculate that the lifetime revenue from a loyal pizza customer can be greater than $8,000. (Heskett et al., 1994)

Others estimate that a 5% increase in customer loyalty can produce *profit* increases from 25% to 85%. These authors conclude that *quality* of market share, measured in terms of customer loyalty, deserves as much attention as *quantity* of market share. Taco Bell, in fact, measures 'share of stomach' to compare the company's sales against all other food purchases a customer can potentially make. As a result, Taco Bell tries to reach customers through kiosks, carts, trucks, and the shelves of supermarkets.

Worksheets can be developed for calculating the lifetime value of customers. What one needs to know are the retention rate, the spending rate, the variable costs and the discount rate to compute net present value (i.e., the value today of the customer over a period of time). For instance, consider Exhibit 5.1 (Lowder, 1997). This table shows that in the first year, the customer is worth $75 to the firm. If, however, the customer stays 5 years with the firm, the actual profitability of the

Handbook of Hospitality Marketing Management

Exhibit 5.1   Lifetime value calculation work sheet

		Year 1	Year 2	Year 3	Year 4	Year 5
Revenue						
A	Customers (same customers tracked one year to the next)	1000	400	180	90	50 (at the end of five years, only 50 of the initial 1,000 are still customers)
B	Retention rate (% of those who return from one year to the next)	40% (400/1000)	45% (180/400)	50% (90/180)	55%	60%
C	Average yearly sale	(total sales/total customers) $150	$150	$150	$150	$150
D	Total revenue of customers from original group) A × C	$150,000	$60,000	$27,000	$13,500	$7,500
Costs						
E	Cost percent (or calculate any way that makes sense for your company)	50%	50%	50%	50%	50%
F	Total costs (D × E)	$75,000	$30,000	$13,500	$6,750	$3,750
Profits						
G	Gross profit (D–F)	$75,000	$30,000	$13,500	$6,750	$3,750
H	Discount rate $D = (1 + i)^n$	$1\ D = (1+.20)^0$	$1.2\ D = (1+.20)^1$	$1.44\ D = (1+.20)^2$	$1.73\ D = (1+.20)^3$	$2.07\ D = (1+.20)^4$
I	NVP Profit = profits/discount rate	$75,000	$25,000 ($30,000/1.2)	$9,375 ($13,500/1.44)	$3,902 ($6,750/1.73)	$1,812 ($3,750/2.07)
J	Cumulative NPV (Y1+Y2+···+Y5)	$75,000	$100,000 ($75,000+$25,000)	$109,375	$113,277	$115,088
K	Lifetime value (NPV) (J/1000 (i.e., present no. of customers))	$75	$100	$109.38	$113.28	$115.09

Source: Lowder, J. (1997). The Relationship Marketing Report (May), Relationship Marketing Report, Occoquan, Va.

customer is $115.09. This $115.09 includes future profits the firm will earn from this customer discounted backwards to current dollars. What this means is that if the guest had a problem that would cost $80 to solve, the firm should solve it, as the profitability of the guest's lifetime will still be positive. Without the understanding of lifetime value, it might be tempting to let the guest leave unhappy.

In addition to the financial aspect of loyalty, loyalty is important because it provides critical inoculation across multiple areas. For instance, loyal customers are less likely to ask about price when making a reservation. They are also less likely to shop around; hence, competitive offers face a higher hurdle. The customer becomes more forgiving when you make a mistake because there is good will equity. In fact, loyal customers are more likely to report service failures.Further, marketing and sales costs are lower, as are transaction costs. Bowen and Shoemaker (2003) argue that:

The reduction in marketing costs is a result of the facts that it takes fewer marketing dollars to maintain a customer than to create one and that loyal customers help create new customers through positive word of mouth. Loyal customers are less likely to switch to a competitor solely because of price, and loyal customers also make more purchases than do comparable non-loyal customers.

(p. 32)

Other authors have made similar findings. For instance, Youjae and Suna (2004) found that 'loyal customers tend to maintain their positive expectations relatively longer than low-loyalty consumers, so they are not likely to adjust expectations based on episodic factors' (p. 359). They also discovered that 'loyal customers tend to show a special preference, attachment, commitment, positive WOM, low switching to competitive brands, and willingness to pay premium price' (Youjae and Suna, 2004, p. 354). This, in particular, can have a tremendous impact on service firms, which often struggle with variation in their product and service offerings.

Chaudhuri and Holbrook (2001) found that 'superior brand performance outcomes such as greater market share and a premium price (relative to the leading competitor) may result from greater customer loyalty' (p. 81). In a study about cruise ships, Petrick (2005) proposes that 'errors made in the provision of a service are more apt to be given a second chance if the consumer has loyalty to the provider' (p. 200). Uncles et al.'s study discovered that 'attitudinally-loyal customers are much less susceptible to negative information about the brand than non-loyal customers. Also, where loyalty to a brand is increased, the revenue-stream from loyal customers becomes more predictable and can become considerable over time' (p. 296).

Shoemaker et al. (2006) discuss the three levels that can categorize a relationship:

In the first level, the bond is financial reward. Frequent-purchaser awards are an example of this first bond. In the second level, the primary bond between the buyer and the seller is social. The idea here is that buyers and sellers will stay together because of the social relationships developed between both parties. Mattila (2001) points out that "social bonding might be one of the key drivers behind loyalty in high-contact services such as restaurants" (p. 78). In the third level, the bond between buyers and sellers is structural; that is, solutions to the customer's problems are designed into the service-delivery system.

The first two levels describe the relationships that many service companies currently have with their customers. The problem with these levels is that they do not create sustainable competitive advantages. If a company offers a frequent-guest award, it is easy for their competitors to develop a similar program. The airline and hotel programs are evidence of this. Companies can hire competitors' employees to acquire their customer base and the relationship the employee has built with their customers. In contrast, the third level can create a competitive advantage because structural changes are difficult to copy and ensure that the buyer is bound to the company and not to an individual staff member of the company (Shoemaker et al., 2006).

Roberts et al. (2003) describe a relationship as a bond between a company and its customers. These bonds can be divided into social bonds, knowledge bonds, psychological bonds, and ideological bonds. They also stress the importance of voluntary as opposed to forced participation in these relationships.

Salanova et al. (2005) also realize the importance of making structural changes, noticing, in particular, the positive reciprocal relationship between service climate and customer loyalty. They propose that 'the greater the customers' intention to return to this specific hotel or restaurant for future service, the higher the climate for service among employees, which in turn influences customers' appraisal of employee performance' (Salanova et al., 2005, p. 1224). As put forth by Schneider's study (as cited in Salanova et.al., 2005) 'service climate refers to employees' shared perceptions of the practices, procedures, and behaviors that are rewarded, supported, and expected by the organization with regard to customer service and customer service quality'(p. 1217).

Morais et al. (2005) confirm this by discussing ways in which customers and providers exchange resources in their relationship. For example, customers can provide feedback about the company's performance, while companies can treat customers in a personalized and special way (Morais et al., 2005). Morais et al. (2005) therefore propose that companies make intangible investments in their customers (i.e., personalized and special treatment) and 'create opportunities for the customers to invest similar resources in them' (p. 53). Garbarino and

Johnson (1999) also discuss relational exchanges, 'which are character-ized by cooperative actions and mutual adjustment of both parties, a sharing of the benefits and burdens of the exchange, and planning for future exchanges' (p. 70). Gundlach and Achrol (1995) point out that 'influence strategies that are compatible with relational exchange are likely to rely on expert and referent bases of power rather than the instrumental kinds such as reward and coercion' (p. 79).

How loyalty marketing may backfire

Unfortunately, many companies have not avoided coercions, leading customers to become 'cynical of what they perceive to be the rhetoric of RM (sic relationship marketing)' (O'Malley and Prothero, 2004, p. 1292). Morais et al. (2005) bring up an interesting point:

When customers invest their allegiance in a provider they expect later retribution in the form of similar types of resources. Moreover, the literature also suggests that if customers perceive they have received a certain type of resource from the provider, they will be more satisfied with the relationship if they are given the opportunity to give back similar resources. Consequently, it appears that providers committed to building satisfying relationships with customers need to monitor the types of investments that occur and must create venues for their customers to invest all types of resources in them.

(p. 51)

Customers believe that companies are not truly committed to form-ing relationships with them, but rather are encouraging them to '[buy] into "this customer relationship lark"' and are 'trying to *sell* relation-ships to consumers through their marketing communications strate-gies' (O'Malley and Prothero, 2004, p. 1292). O'Malley and Prothero (2004) project that trust in organizations may have actually dimin-ished because customers view RM programs as efforts designed only to increase consumption, which potentially increases consumer debt and therefore 'recognize relational strategies as shallow and potentially divisive in nature' (p. 1293).

Fournier et al. (1998) were also concerned with some of the prob-lems facing RM; in particular, the untenable amount of one-on-one relationships consumers are asked to maintain with different compa-nies. She proposes that this diminishes the uniqueness and value of many marketing initiatives, in part because although 'companies ask their customers for friendship, loyalty, and respect, too often they don't give those customers friendship, loyalty, and respect in return' (p. 44). Fournier et al., (1998) discuss the dissatisfaction some customers have with relationship marketing tactics:

When we talk to people about their lives as consumers, we do not hear praise for their so-called corporate partners. Instead, we hear about the confusing, stressful, insensitive, and manipulative marketplace in which they feel trapped and victimized... 'The flood of advances from companies undermines any one overture so that it doesn't matter which company you end up doing business with,' said [a] disillusioned customer.

(pp. 43–44)

They also argue that 'companies' claims that customer relationships are valued don't hold water. Sometimes people feel put at a disadvantage by their loyalty. And sometimes a company's preoccupation with its so-called best customers leaves other revenue-generating customers feeling left out and underappreciated' (Fournier et al., 1998, p. 46). Fournier et al. (1998) also suggest that 'companies are trying to satisfy – and log a sale on – customers' every desire or fleeting whim. But customers view the scene differently. They see a bewildering array of seemingly undifferentiated product offerings' (Fournier et al., 1998, p. 46).

The evolution of customer loyalty

Exhibit 5.2 shows the evolution of building loyalty. Initially, the focus of marketing was purely on sales, not loyalty. The goal was to get as many new customers as possible. In this phase, there was little targeting, little measurement, and lots of discounts. As marketing developed, marketing managers began to focus on specific market segments, but the mentality was still on pushing traffic to the property.

Exhibit 5.2   Interview with Adam Burke, Senior Vice President and Managing Director, Hilton HHonors Worldwide

It is often said that if hotels could get rid of these frequency programs, they would, because they are a waste of time, cost the company money, etc. How would you respond to that?

I think experience has taught us [at Hilton] that even if others were to get rid of their program, we likely would not. When we talk about the program today, it has been that move from frequency to true loyalty. In the early genesis of programs – if you were to go back 20 years – you could argue that they really were nothing more than glorified frequency programs. Over the past 5 or 10 years, the focus has really been on cultivating a one-to-one relationship with the customer based on their individual preferences. As a result, whether you call it a program or not, that type of initiative is exactly what allows you to engender true long-term loyalty from your customers. I don't think we would get rid of it because the reality is we've been able to demonstrate, one, that there is a significant amount of incrementality associated with the program if it's properly implemented – meaning business that we are able to capture that we wouldn't if customers weren't part of the program. And, two, while we would likely make some modifications to our cost structures if competitors did away with their programs, having a long-term relationship with our customers and being able to utilize their preferences to differentiate their experience is at the core of what we do as a hotelier. In an era of consolidation where you have literally tens of millions of customers, technology enables you to really deliver the core of being a hotelier, which is providing a personalized stay experience based on what an individual customer is looking for.

We've learned over time that true program loyalists have a very different profile in terms of how they interact with us, and that is really one of the key metrics for demonstrating how viable loyalty programs are. It's not just about program incrementality – it's also about how members transact with us. For example, our members tend to book online more than nonmembers, which is a lower distribution cost. They tend to have a higher conversion rate for our reservations offices, which means that you have a greater return on the investment for the cost of that booking. They tend to have a higher incidence of problem reporting, which may seem a little counterintuitive at first, but the biggest problem you can have is the one you don't know about. Across the industry, most problems go unreported. Honors members, however, want to raise their hand and say, 'I had a problem,' because they want and expect us to fix the problem. And if we're able to do so, they are still going to be very satisfied with the program and with the Hilton Family of Hotels. The higher incidence of problem reporting actually gives us the insulation to ensure that service recovery issues don't create defection.

Frequency programs were the next element of the evolution of loyalty. We discuss frequency programs in more detail later in the chapter, but these programs initially were used to reward frequent purchasers. Exhibit 5.2 presents excerpts of an interview with Adam Burke, who is the executive in charge of the Hilton HHonors program for Hilton.

The next phase is the creation of the relationship between the consumer and the brand. We examine brands in the next section.

In the final phase of the evolution of relationship marketing, the firm fully understands the customer. The focus is on knowing the customer and using that knowledge to augment the product to better serve the customer. Service augmentation means building extras into the service that help improve the customer's stay. We call this final phase *knowledge relationships.* This is the one-to-one marketing popularized by Peppers and Rogers. An example of one hospitality firm that is beginning to move in this direction is Wyndham Hotels with their Wyndham By Request program. This program is not a point or mileage-based program, as are many hotel programs found to be. Rather, guests customize their hotel stay by providing Wyndham with information on their room preferences (e.g., smoking versus nonsmoking, bed type, and the like) and the types of snacks they would like to see in the honor bar. The information provided by the customer is then stored in a central database so that the room will be customized in any Wyndham location the customer chooses.

A second example of this move toward knowledge relationships is Hilton Hotel Corporation's OnQ, which was launched in May 2003 across all Hilton brands (e.g., Double Tree, Hampton Inns, and Hilton Garden Inns). This system is billed as the first and only system of its kind that gives front desk personnel real-time information on every HHonors member who checks into any one of the Hilton brands worldwide. Unlike the Wyndham system, information comes from two sources: information provided by the guest and information provided by the individual property that observes the guest's behavior. Clearly, the more one stays at a Hilton, the more information Hilton collects. And, the more information collected, the more the stay can be customized to meet the guest's needs. This customization makes it harder for the guest to switch to another brand.

Branding and relationships

This section delves further into customers' relationships with companies; in particular, the way in which they form relationships with brands and the benefits these brand–customer relationships have for the brand. Aggarwal (2004) suggests that 'people sometimes form relationships with brands in much the same way in which they form relationships with each other in a social context' (p. 87). He continues, 'people sometimes form a very intimate bond with brands and, in some extreme cases, a passion that is often associated only with a close circle of friends and family' (Aggarwal, 2004, p. 87). Ambler (1997) agrees writing that 'brands are, in the relational paradigm, anthropomorphized to the extent that people have 'relationships' with them' (p. 283). Cooper (1999) discusses how brands themselves have changed from lifeless, manipulatable artifacts to living entities with personalities, which allows customers to form relationships with the brand and allows the brand to change and evolve over time.

However, it is important to realize that customers do not distinguish brands from brand manufacturers (Aggarwal, 2004). Aggarwal (2004) agues that 'this perception is more likely for service brands (e.g., hotels and airlines) and for brands that have a combination of products and services (e.g., many online stores)' (p. 88). Earlier, Kim et al. (2003) also found that 'in the service industry, customers generally choose or reject based on the company brand . . . .That is, customers develop company brand associations rather than the brand association of product items' (p. 336). Aggarwal (2004) proposes that when 'brands behave like socialized members of a culture then they are evaluated by the rules that govern the society and have to act in accordance to these rules' (p. 88). These actions have other negative or positive evaluations, depending on whether they violate or conform to the norms of a relationship (Aggarwal, 2004). It is critical for companies to recognize that, while customer–brand relationships have many benefits for the brand, these relationships must be treated with respect.

Unlike personal social relationships, 'relationships with brands almost always involve some degree of monetary exchange. In addition, the relationship with the brand is a mix of personal and impersonal, more like a celebrity and a fan than like two people who know each other intimately' (Aggarwal, 2004, p. 89). Because of this, brand relationships are very similar to exchange relationships. This means that:

The relationship norms in a commercial context are likely to be somewhat moderated by this underpinning of exchange-ness even in a communal relationship. In other words, it is likely that the commercial context creates its own norms of behavior that lay on top of the social relationship norms that ultimately determine consumers' attitudes and behavior.

(Aggarwal, 2004, p. 99)

Earlier, O'Reilly's and Chatman's study (as cited in Gundlach and Achrol, 1995) had pointed out the instability of exchange relationships because of the requirement of more costly and sophisticated control systems. However, 'where parties share goals, values, and an affective attachment, they can be expected to act instinctively for the benefit of one another' (Gundlach and Achrol, 1995, p. 80).

Despite the 'exchange-ness' of these brand relationships, Ambler (1997) points out the difficulty of measuring and financially valuing the brand–customer relationships. One way to value brands is by measuring brand equity. Ogilvy's study (as cited in Blackston, 2000) defines brand equity as the 'consumer's idea of a product' (p. 101). According to Ambler (1997), 'brand equity is made up of memories of different kinds . . . . Declarative memory can be cognitive (thinking-related) and affective (feeling-related). Awareness is cognitive, as is our knowledge of a brand's functional performance characteristics and price. Attitudes towards the brand are primarily affective' (p. 284). Ambler (1997) explains that 'the perceived quality of the brand will be a mix of actual quality facts we may know, e.g., from consumer reports, image characteristics from advertising, packaging, word of mouth and usage experience' (p. 285). Muller's study (as cited in Kim et al., 2003) presents three main areas that service brands should focus on to build brand equity: '(1) quality products and services; (2) execution of service delivery; and (3) establishment of a symbolic and evocative image'(p. 338). Blackston (2000) proposes that in order to directly manage and understand some of the intangible elements of brand equities, companies need to rely on their customers. Understanding the brand's attitudes and behaviors toward its customers means 'acknowledging that the individual is *more* than just a statistic or a client code' (p. 104). Blackston (2000) warns that if a corporate brand 'does not act as if it *knows* who its customers are,' it 'will not earn their trust, regardless of its credibility and reliability' (p. 104). Blackston (2000) summarizes the brand–customer relationship by recognizing that first companies must understand customers' attitudes and behaviors toward the brand and then consider the brand's attitude and behaviors toward the customers purchasing the brand.

Although customers often purchase a variety of brands, understanding how people form relationships with brands can assist companies in developing relationship marketing directives. Escalas and Bettman (2003) propose that 'consumers use brands to meet self-needs such as self-verification or self-enhancement' (p. 339). People form connections with brands when their associations with brands are used to construct or communicate their self-concept (Escalas and Bettman, 2003). According to McCraken's study (as cited in Escalas and Bettman, 2003), when consumers form connections with brands, these connections help consumers create and build their self-identities. Therefore, people choose brands because of a need for self-consistency and for matching themselves to prototypical users of the brand offering (Escalas and Bettman, 2003).

Fournier (1998) agrees, arguing that 'meaningful relationships are qualified not along symbolic versus functional product category lines, or in terms of high versus low involvement classes, but by the perceived ego significance of the chosen brands' and proposes that 'individual consumer-brand relationships make the most sense when considered at the aggregate level of the personal brandscape' or the totality of brands that each customer utilizes and identifies with (p. 366). As she summarizes, 'consumers do not choose *brands*, they choose *lives*' (Fournier, 1998, p. 367). Fournier (1998) discusses customer–brand relationships:

For the brand to serve as legitimate relationship partner, it must surpass the personification qualification and actually behave as an active, contributing member of the dyad. Marketing actions conducted under the rubric of interactive and addressable communications qualify the brand as a reciprocating partner. Animated brand characters also satisfy the activity criterion through their performances. It is argued, however, that the brand need not engage these blatant strategies to qualify as active relationship partner. At a broad level of abstraction, the everyday execution of marketing plans and tactics can be construed as behaviors performed by the brand acting in its relationship role.

(p. 345)

Gundlach and Achrol (1995) found that one benefit for companies of forming long-term relationship with their customers is the reduction in customer turnover and the resulting decrease in the search and startup costs of finding new customers. They also propose that long-term customers 'require simpler governance structures and monitoring systems and provide a host of efficiencies stemming from flexibility, adaptability, and reduced role ambiguity' (Gundlach and Achrol, 1995, p. 80). However, they warn that 'disproportionate commitments can result in conflict, dissatisfaction, and opportunistic tendencies, and erode the governing properties of relational norms leading to the eventual decline of an exchange relationship' (p. 80).

Escalas and Bettman (2003) go on to point out that brand connections are psychological manifestations of brand equity. These 'self-brand' connections may lead consumers to form attitudes about the brand that are not very susceptible to change (Escalas and Bettman, 2003). In fact, they found that 'when consumers' self-concepts are linked to a brand, then the company behind the brand may be able to gain an enduring competitive advantage because this type of connection is difficult for competitors to imitate' (Escalas and Bettman, 2003, p.347). Some of the aspects of this competitive advantage may include: customer being more forgiving of marketer blunders (i.e., poor advertising campaigns) or a temporary product quality problem; being more loyal to the brand; and being less likely to switch brands owing to price cuts, coupons, etc. offered by competitors (Escalas and Bettman, 2003).

Before customers can form relationships with brands, however, they must have a positive brand experience. Dunne (2004) presents the four domains inherent in brand experiences: physical, emotional, intellectual, and spiritual. According to Dunne (2004), each of these domains 'can provide a company with new ways of connecting with its consumers on a much more intimate level' (p. 11). Lozito (2004) argues that the 'restaurant emotional brand experience starts creating a bond from the minute the patron sees an ad, a name or a logo and doesn't end until the music, lights and aroma are only a recent memory. Every touch point in between is an opportunity to differentiate and reinforce the brand promise . . . what you want the consumer to think about your business' (p. 58). Nevertheless, Luvy (2002) cautions that brands cannot appeal to every person all of the time, but suggests that brands can be hated as long as they are also loved. As he puts it, 'a brand that appeals strongly to one group while alienating another is nearly always going to be more successful than a brand that neither inspires nor irritates anyone' (Luvy, 2002, p. 7).

Along the same lines, Muniz and O'Guinn (2001) propose the idea of brand communities, which 'may form around any brand, but are probably most likely to form around brands with a strong image, a rich and lengthy history, and threatening competition' (p. 415). They describe brand communities:

A brand community is a specialized, non-geographically bound community, based on a structured set of social relationships among admirers of a brand. It is specialized because at its center is a branded good or service. Like other communities, it is marked by a shared consciousness, rituals and traditions, and a sense of moral responsibility.

(Muniz and O'Guinn, 2001, p. 412)

These communities transcend geographical boundaries because mass media transcends geographical boundaries (Muniz and O'Guinn, 2001). According to Muniz and O'Guinn (2001), 'things that are publicly consumed may stand a better chance of producing communities than those consumed in private' (p. 415).

Three positive aspects of brand communities are 'first, brand communities . . . represent a form of consumer agency. . . . Second, brand communities represent an important information resource for consumers . . . . Third, to the extent that communal interaction generally provides wider social benefits to its members . . . brand communities likewise provide these' (Muniz and O'Guinn, 2001, p. 426). Bagozzi and Dholakia (2006) point out that brand communities are 'venues where intense brand loyalty is expressed and fostered and emotional connections with the brand forged in customers' (p. 45). Muniz and O'Guinn (2001) not only showed that brands were social objects that were socially constructed, but they also found that brand community affected brand equity. They argue that 'developing a strong brand community could be a critical step in truly actualizing the concept of relationship marketing. A strong brand community can lead to a socially embedded and entrenched loyalty, brand commitment, and even hyper-loyalty' (McAlexander and Schouten's study as cited in Muniz and O'Guinn, 2001, p. 427). It is clear, therefore, that brand–customer relationships, whether as part of brand communities or in other contexts, are a critical step towards developing commitment and eventual loyalty.

Making loyalty marketing work

In a response to Fournier's (1998) article, Williams (1998) proposed that RM (relationship marketing) should be 'less about "getting as much information as we can so we know what consumers will buy" and more about 'giving them as much information as they need so they'll know what to buy.' (p. 178). Although effective RM programs can have strong benefits for companies, they must take care not to treat these relationships lightly or offer products that customers do not want or need, just for the sake of selling something.

Earlier, Sheth et al.'s study (as cited in Orth et al., 2004) acknowledged that 'effective marketing communications must recognize the relationship between a product/brand and the consumption values or benefits consumers seek' (p. 97). Rust et al. (2004) realize that firms must maximize customer lifetime value – 'the net profit a company accrues from transactions with a given customer during the time that the customer has a relationship with the company' – in order to be successful in the long term (p. 113). To do this, they propose that 'companies must focus on *customer equity* (the sum of the lifetime values of all the firm's customers, across all the firm's brands) rather than *brand equity* (the sum of customers' assessments of a brand's intangible qualities, positive or negative)' and recognize that 'acting in the best interests of brand equity isn't necessarily the same as acting in the best interests of customer equity' (Rust et al., 2004, p. 113).

Another way to think about creating customer loyalty is The Loyalty Circle©, as shown in Exhibit 5.3. The three main functions on the circle are Process, Value, and Communication. The reader will notice that at different points along the circle, there are places where the customer might exit the circle and hence the relationship. The goal of a company is to keep the customer in the circle by executing the three functions of the circle equally well. Equality is the key to the loyalty circle. If hoteliers are great on creating value, for instance, but do not effectively communicate with the customer, then that customer may leave the relationship.

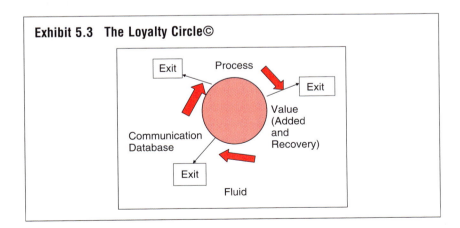

Exhibit 5.3   The Loyalty Circle©

On one side of The Loyalty Circle©is the Process, which can be defined as 'how the service works.' It involves all activities from both the guest's perspective and the hotelier's perspective. Ideally, there should be no gaps in this process. For the guest, the process includes everything that happens from the time he or she begins buying the service (e.g., calling to make a reservation) to the time that he or she leaves the property (e.g., picking up his or her car from a valet). All interactions with employees are part of this process.

For the hotel, the process includes all interactions between the employees and the guests, the design of the service operations, the hiring and training of service personnel, and the collection of information to understand customers' needs, wants, and expectations. One way to monitor the *Process* is through the use of consumer research and intelligence techniques. One such technique is mystery shopping. In this technique, people hired by the service organization or by a third party pretend as customers and report everything that occurred during the purchase of the service. Another way is to conduct 'focus group' discussions with participation of customers. Focus groups consist of 10–12 customers (or non customers) who are asked to focus on one or two topics of interest to the service organization. A moderator leads the discussion and keeps participants focused on the topics of interest to management. A third way is to undertake large-scale survey research with current customers as well as past customers.

The second component of The Loyalty Circle© is Value Creation. Value creation is subdivided into two parts: value-added and value-recovery. Value-added strategies increase loyalty by providing guests more than just the core product, that is, for hotels, offering more than just a place to sleep. Value-added strategies increase the long-term value of the relationship with the service firm by offering greater benefits to customers than can be found at competing firms who charge a comparable price. Features that pertain to value-added are of six types: *financial* (e.g., saving money); *temporal* (e.g., saving time); *functional* (e.g., the product does what it was designed to do); *experiential* (e.g., enhancing the experience such as by getting an upgrade); *emotional* (e.g., more recognition and/or more pleasurable service experience); and/or *social* (e.g., interpersonal link with a service provider). Temporal value is important because business travellers have stated that they value their time at $100 per hour and anything that saves them time saves them money.

Consider, for instance, the check-in process of a hotel. Research reveals that many frequent business travelers want to go immediately to their room and do not want to wait in line to check-in. If they have to wait in line for 15 minutes, they mentally figure they have spent $25 to check-in. Waiting in line is especially annoying if the guest is a member of the hotel's frequent-guest program and all guest's information is already stored on file. Certain technologies (e.g., blue-tooth software that works with one's PDA – personal digital assistant) allow guests to check-in, receive their room number, unlock their room, and have charges automatically billed to their credit card, without having to check-in with the front desk. Moving these guests to this form of check-in would have the benefit of shortening the line for those guests who want to speak with a front desk clerk. This new check-in procedure speeds up and improves the process (*functional value*) and adds value because it saves the guests' time (*temporal value*).

The importance of value-added strategies in creating customer loyalty is illustrated in a study conducted by one of the authors on business travelers who both spend more than $120 per night for a hotel room and take six or more business trips per year. The study revealed that 28% of the 344 who spent more than 75 nights per year in hotels claimed that the feature 'was a good value for the price paid' and was important in the decision to stay in the same hotel chain when traveling on business. A similar percentage rated the features 'collects your preferences and uses that information to customize your current and future stays' and 'accommodates early morning check-in and late afternoon checkout' important in the decision to stay with the same chain. Both these tactics are examples of features that add value to the core product offering.

Value-recovery strategies are designed to rectify a lapse in service delivery. The goal is to ensure that the guest's needs are taken care of without further inconveniences. Empowering employees to solve problems and offering 100% guarantee are examples of value-recovery strategies. The key to value-recovery strategies is that the complaints be taken seriously by the hotel and processes be put in place so that the same mistakes do not happen over and over again. We discuss complaints later in this chapter.

The final component of The Loyalty Circle©is Communication. This side of the circle incorporates database marketing, newsletters and general advertising. It involves all areas of how the hotel communicates with its customers. When communicating with guests, it is critical that external communications do not promise what the service cannot deliver. It is also critical that the communiqué reflect the needs of the customer and that the customers do not receive offers in which they have no interest.

If marketers can make the organization focus on these components they will create loyal customers who will return over and over again. If they do not focus on the components of the circle, they will be forced to focus on getting more and more customers to replace those who have left the circle.

Database marketing as part of communication

Database marketing used to be known as direct marketing, but it is much more than that. Direct marketing implies a one-way communication: the firm to the customer. Database marketing, however, involves two way communications. It is both part of the communications mix and also part of interactive marketing. Its most important usage is that of managing relevant data on customers to identify them for the purpose of developing a long-standing relationship of repeat business, to send desired messages at the right time, in the right form, and to the right people, and to develop the right product that satisfies their needs and wants. Essentially, databases are decision-support systems.

The information in the systems typically includes internally collected data on customers and purchased data (list sources) on both customers and prospects. The information can be used to generate mailing lists and prospect lists for salespeople and to identify market segments. A direct communications channel with customers and prospects is provided through a computerized customer database. Database marketing augments more traditional communications vehicles such as advertising and personal selling. Before the late 1990s, database marketing was generally limited to the use of brochures and letters with offers, sent by mail. Today's marketing environment includes e-mail marketing, which has become an integral component of a comprehensive database marketing strategy.

Database marketing works well with certain market segments of the hospitality industry. Restaurant customers respond well to database marketing, as do weekend package customers for hotels. Individuals tend to respond to database marketing better than organizational customers. There appears to be a correlation between the size of the purchase and the response to database marketing. Dinner for two, which may cost $100, brings a better response than offers targeted at a group that may spend $100,000 in a hotel.

Database information enables companies to target individuals or small segments of like customers. This is very useful for sales and sales management support and for direct marketing programs. Database marketing has three main benefits:

1. It provides a strategic advantage through the more effective use of marketing information collected internally
2. It improves the use of customer and market information
3. It forms a basis for developing long-term customer relationships, especially with those customers who account for a large portion of a firm's business.

E-mail allows a degree, that was not available in the past, of tracking consumer behavior. In the past, a hotel company would send a direct mail solicitation to customers to come to the hotel. A redemption offer would be enclosed to encourage the customer to buy a hotel room. Elaborate mechanisms and standard operating procedures were established to collect the coupons at the front desk to track the results.

E-mails can now be tracked by 'click through' rates (how many customers opened the e-mail), by the number of unique visitors to the landing page on a website (how many customers actually viewed the offer) or by actual bookings (how many customers made a reservation). A return on investment for each campaign can be viewed by the marketer.

An additional way to use one's database is telemarketing. This technique, however, has its limits. In some industries, its usage is so frequent that it becomes annoying to those who are contacted and hence counterproductive. The US government responded to the numerous complaints by citizens tired of receiving unsolicited sales calls at home. A website was established to allow citizens to register their telephone numbers as part of a government mandated 'do not call' list (www.donotcall.gov). The response was overwhelming, with over 50 million Americans voting with their mouse to remove their names from telemarketers' lists. However, once the customer gives permission, his name can go into the database. In this way, databases complement advertising and personal selling. From either of these sources information may be obtained to set up the database, which is then used for further contact.

Proprietary marketing databases are those developed by an individual company for its own use. They provide a competitive advantage in enabling a company to focus on a particular market segment. Examples in the hotel industry include databases that contain guest history information or information on the participants in frequent-guest programs. Preferred room type, pillows, amenities, and other preferences may be loaded into these databases to enable a hotel to be more responsive to each customer's personal requests upon arrival and without hassle. This is a powerful aspect of relationship marketing. Some systems, such as Ritz-Carlton's, enable any Ritz-Carlton in the world to tap into these preferences once a customer has stayed at any Ritz-Carlton at any location. As previously discussed, a similar program, introduced by Wyndham International, invites guests to populate a database with their personal preferences (Wyndham By Request) so that these may be arranged prior to the guest's stay at any property in their system. E-mail confirmations now allow hotels to thank the customers for making the booking, ask if they would like a spa treatment or tee time during their stay and later send a thank-you note upon their departure.

Customized marketing databases are used to profile prospective customers. Data obtained from outside sources are customized to fit the property's customer profile. Customer information is obtained before the customer is actually contacted so that product information can be filtered appropriately in advance. Also, contacts can be made with potential customers who have profiles similar to present customers. These prospects have a greater probability of becoming future customers.

Database marketing components

Database marketing has four fundamental components – strategy, data, information, and knowledge. Strategy begins with the development of objectives for the marketing program: Who is the target customer? where do they live? what do they buy? where else do they go? etc. Once the strategy is conceived and integrated with the other marketing vehicles such as advertising and public relations, the data are assembled.

Data collection starts with the actual names, addresses, telephone numbers, dates of arrival and departure, room preferences, purchase habits, credit card usage, etc. The initial database should contain data on past customers. New customer prospects, obtained from list sources, can then be added. As discussed earlier, to be meaningful, the data has to be accurate (easier said than done!). The advantage of loyalty programs is that it helps ensure the accuracy of the data. One way to ensure both the accuracy of the database and the avoidance of breaking any database marketing rules is to gain customers' permission to communicate with them. Permission means giving the customer the ability to easily change their information on-line, opt-in (sign up for the mailing), provide preferences (e.g., the type of information they would like to receive and the frequency with which these e-mails arrive) and easily opt-out (cancel membership or mailings.)

The information portion of database marketing consists of the analysis of the data. The demography and psychographics of customers need to be analyzed. Other factors, such as why they use a particular hotel or restaurant, can be added.

The knowledge stage of a database program includes segmentation, clustering, and modeling. Segmentation includes gathering 'like' customers together. For example, a hotel might have a list of customers who buy weekend packages segmented under a 'leisure' code. A restaurant might have a list of customers who attend Sunday Brunch. These segments are then clustered. It is important to realize that the leisure traveler may also eat brunch at the same property. Or, the leisure customer might live in Northern New Jersey and come to New York City, another cluster, on weekends in April. Once customers are clustered, the search for new lists (and potentially new customers) begins through modeling. The assumption is that non-customers will cluster in a manner similar to that of current customers and list sources screened in this manner will have a higher yield than those with no known similarity to current customers.

Ways to use the database

One way to use the database is customer segmentation. Not all customers are equal. Some are more valuable to the firm than others.

A way to determine the value of an individual customer is to look at his or her recency, frequency, and monetary value. This is known as RFM analysis. The basic idea is that customers have a three digit code attached to their records: one code for recency, one for frequency, and one for monetary value. While there are different ways to assign a code number, traditionally each code ranges in value from 5 to 1, with 5 being the most recent, frequent, or highest monetary value and 1 being the least. The actual value is determined by sorting the database on one code at a time. The sorted database is then divided into quintiles. This is done for each of the three codes. So, a customer with a code of 555 would be in the most recent customer grouping, the most frequent customer grouping, and the largest monetary value grouping. This customer would clearly be one of the 'best' customers. A customer with a value of 111, however, would be one of the 'worst'.

Different communication strategies can then easily be developed based on this coding scheme. For instance, a customer with a 335 would clearly be targeted for a 'come see us again' type promotion, while a customer with a 551 might not receive anything. Although this customer has been with the firm recently and comes frequently, he or she spends very little money with the firm. It would be recommended that research be undertaken to find out why this customer spends so little money on the property.

A second way to use the database is to communicate with the customer, as was detailed above in the context of e-mail marketing. The most important tactic for this strategy is to deliver a message consistent with product usage. For instance, once a week, airlines usually send special web fares to their most valuable customers. However, if one customer lives in Dallas, he or she should not be getting special web fares for flying from Boston. If the message is not targeted based upon buying behavior, the message becomes SPAM, and, after a while, is automatically deleted without ever being opened. Thus, when a Dallas fare does become available, it will most likely be missed.

A third way to use the database is for customer management. That is, giving the customers what they want before they have to ask for it. This is the hallmark of Four Seasons and Ritz Carlton. Customer management also involves providing the customer with choices.

A fourth way to use the database is to improve the delivery of sales promotions. This improvement comes in two ways. One, because it is sent directly to specific customers, the competition may never know about it and hence be unable to offer a similar type of promotion; this is called stealth communication. Two, promotions can be sent at a time when the customer is most likely to buy, but needs some sort of reminder or inducement. Harrah's Entertainment is a world leader in knowing this type of information. An example of this would be that when the customer is close to moving to his or her next tier of reward benefits, he or she will be more likely to respond to a targeted promotion than someone a long way away.

The final way databases can be used is to increase the channels of distribution. The least expensive way to make a reservation is for the guests to book it themselves through the firm's own website. The database can aid in this by reminding the customer to always book directly.

Frequency programs

One way that many companies have sought to form and/or build customer–brand relationships is through the creation and support of frequency programs. There are two questions that are often asked: One, are frequency programs the same as loyalty programs? and two, do frequent-guest programs build loyalty? The answer to the first question is, No, frequency programs are not the same as loyalty programs, even though many firms call their frequent guest program a loyalty program. In this chapter, loyalty program is defined as a strategy undertaken by a firm to manage the three components of The Loyalty Circle© in order to create an emotional bond with the customer so that the customer gives the company a majority of his or her business, provides positive word of mouth, acts in partnership with the firm, and spends more with the firm than would a non-loyal customer.

In contrast, a frequency program is any program that rewards the customer with points, miles, stamps or 'punches' and that enables the buyer to redeem such rewards for free or discounted merchandise. The potential trap is to confuse purchase frequency with customer loyalty; that is, to confuse the ends with the means. Frequency in itself does not build loyalty as we define it; it is loyalty that builds frequency. Frequency can create loyalty if the firm uses the information gathered on frequent visits to focus on the components of The Loyalty Circle©; however, if the firm ignores this opportunity, then it ignores the emotional and psychological factors that build real commitment. Without that commitment, customers focus on the 'deal,' not on the brand or product relevance. If there is no mechanism in place to track specific customer requests or identify the customer, the customer focuses only on the deal.

With frequency-only programs, sales may increase, as they would with price discounts. Repeat purchase may also increase, but the focus is on the rewards, not on product superiority or brand relevance. Thus, awards programs are tactical solutions to a strategic problem – an awards program for unprofitable customers, parity instead of differentiation. This behavior focus makes bribing the customer the line of reasoning. Over time, the economics of bribery begin to collapse with greater and greater bribes, eventually eroding the brand image and diminishing product/service differentiation. The differences between frequency and loyalty programs are shown in Exhibit 5.4.

Exhibit 5.4   Frequency program versus loyalty program

	Frequency program	**Loyalty program**
Objectives	Build traffic, sales, profit	Build sales, profits, brand desirability
Strategy	To incentivize repeat transactions	Build personal brand relationship
Focus	Segment behavior and profitability	An individual's emotional and rational needs and their value
Tactics	Freebies/discounts/ rewards, profitability	Individual value, tenure, preferred status, 'insider', value-added upgrades, add-ons, tailored offers/messages, emotional rewards
Measurement	Transactions, sales growth	Individual lifetime value, attitudinal change, emotional response

Note: From *'Turning Lost Customers Into Gold and the Art of Achieving Zero Defections,'* by J.K. Cannie, 1994, New York: AMACOM Books.

Mattila (2001) argues that:

True loyalty cannot be assured by promises of free items and gift certificates, because there is more to loyalty than frequent patronage. Loyalty goes beyond racking up points and even beyond repeated purchases. The loyalty that restaurateurs really seek involves attitudinal, behavioral, and emotional commitment to the restaurant. If a patron has developed strong emotional ties with a restaurant or its employees, then that affective bond leads to greater commitment than any loyalty program can create. Such a patron is willing not only to return to the restaurant but also to recommend the place to others.

(pp. 73–74)

She also points out the importance of understanding psychological commitment (Mattila, 2001). Without strong brands, emotional bonding cannot occur because there exists no disincentive to prevent customers from switching brands. Mattila (2001) argues that 'frequency programs ... are not only easy to copy, but they encourage deal-induced responses by customers who are in pursuit of the best prices or rich-est rewards' (p. 74). Hence, an improperly set up loyalty program can potentially damage a strong brand and provide an incentive for customers to switch brands. An example is the deal-induced behavior engendered by cell phone companies, who offer free or steeply dis-counted phones to new customers, but not to their existing customers, which encourages existing customers to find a new company once their contract expires.

In order to understand how frequency programs can best be lever-aged, it is important to understand how consumers relate to behavioral reinforcement strategies. Rothschild and Gaidis (1981) found that 'a delayed reinforcement is worth less than immediate reinforcement dur-ing acquisition of a behavior; delayed reinforcement inhibits learning and will lead to a lower probability of a future occurrence' (p. 73). They point out that 'primary reinforcers . . . have intrinsic utility (the product) while secondary reinforcers (tokens, coupons, trading stamps) have no such utility and must be converted' (Rothschild and Gaidis, 1981, p. 73). For example, coupons or points must be collected before they can be redeemed, which results in a delayed reinforcement and may erode the success of the promotion (Rothschild and Gaidis, 1981). Therefore, it is critical that frequency programs incorporate some pri-mary reinforcers in order to be successful. In addition to the five ele-ments that combine to determine a program's value as presented by O'Brien and Jones (1995) – cash value, choice of redemption options, aspirational value, relevance, and convenience – Dowling and Uncles (1997) add the psychological benefits of belonging and accumulating points.

Regardless, according to Solomon's research, consumers 'purchase products to achieve value-related goals' (as cited in Baker et al., 2004, p. 997). According to Morais et al. (2005):

When customers feel that they are receiving special treatment, they tend to feel indebted to the provider and may reciprocate by recommending the provider or by giving that provider valuable feedback and personal information . . . .Then, as the value of the investments they made in the provider increases, they begin to feel dependent on the relationship with the provider because they want to protect their equity.

(p. 53)

It can therefore be suggested that the value-related goals customers pursue can be achieved by engaging in a reciprocal relationship with a company – a relationship that the company began by providing special treatment to its customers. According to Rothschild and Gaidis (1981), providing positive reinforcement for desired behavior (i.e., purchasing) is critical due to the close tie between repeat purchase behavior and successful marketing.

Dowling and Uncles (1997) discuss the efficacy of frequency programs in high- and low-customer-involvement purchases:

For frequent-buyer programs, the level of customer involvement is an important consideration. For a high-involvement purchase, the consumer is likely to be involved with both the category purchase decision (Will I fly or go by train from London to Paris?) and the brand choice (Will I fly British Airways or Air France?). For low-involvement decisions, the level of involvement is likely to be low for both decisions, although somewhat higher for the category purchase decision. We suggest that frequency programs will be more effective for high- rather than low-involvement products and services, primarily because low-involvement products are often bought by consumers out of habit, while, for high-involvement products, consumers might form a relationship with the supplier (the difference between the habitual purchase of Nescafe, say, and joining Club-Med).

(p. 79)

They also suggest that frequency programs that provide incentives to bond customers to their products *might* help protect existing customers, but at the cost of increasing marketing expenditures (Dowling and Uncles, 1997). Dowling and Uncles (1997) agree that frequency programs can be effective in the long term by building presence in the marketplace. Rothschild's and Gaidis' (1998) research on behavioral learning theory suggests that customers might become loyal to the program rather than to the brand. However, Dowling and Uncles (1997) propose that program rewards that directly support the value proposition of the product or service will more directly influence brand loyalty than if the rewards indirectly support the value proposition, such as receiving airline miles for restaurant visits.

Hausfater (2005) cautions that the best restaurant tool for building loyalty is the experience customers have while dining. Shoemaker and Lewis (1999) stress that if customers are not satisfied, they will never build loyalty towards the brand. However, Hausfater (2005) suggests that 'against a background of strong customer satisfaction, frequent card programs can be effective for retaining high-value patrons and gaining a larger share of their out-of-home eating dollars' (p. 70). Jang and Matilla (2005) explore customers' reward preferences and reasons for joining a rewards program:

Since people typically prefer immediate rewards to delayed gratification, we expect that most restaurant customers, if given a choice, prefer immediate rewards to point-system rewards even if accumulated rewards carry higher values. Another factor driving customer preferences is the amount of effort needed to reach the requirements of a particular reward. In general, the consumption of luxury items is hard for consumers to justify because such experiences tend to result in feelings of guilt (Berry, 1994; Kivetz & Simonson, 2002;

Prelec & Loewenstein, 1998). Yet, Kivetz and Simonson (2002) found that when the reward requirement is high, customers seem to prefer luxury rewards (e.g. expensive wine) to necessary rewards (e.g. gas coupons).

(p. 403)

In addition to receiving monetary rewards, people also join frequency programs for quality, convenience, value expression, exploration, and entertainment (Jang and Mattila, 2005). Jang and Mattila (2005) found that fast-food and casual dining customers preferred immediate, necessary, and monetary rewards over points-system, luxury, and non-monetary rewards. According to Frequency Marketing's research (as cited in Jang and Mattila 2005), 'Subway's Electronic Sub Club Card program, for instance, shows that the average reward member spends $7.85 per visit, almost 50% more per transaction compared to the average non-member, who spends $5.25 per visit'(p. 402). However, Subway's Sub Club Card program ended in 2005. Lockyer (2004) confirms, despite the lack of empirical data, that loyalty programs for restaurants seem to have success. According to her, restaurateurs 'note that such customers return more often and tend to spend more while dining, perhaps because the diners enjoy being part of a club and receiving the special recognition from the hostess or manager that goes with it' (Lockyer, 2004, p. 66).

However, O'Brien and Jones (1995) caution against programs that include discount cards that seem similar to coupons in that they are given regardless of a customer's RFM. Rather, successful frequency programs should maintain rewards that are similar to traditional perks, which are only offered by restaurateurs to their regular customers. They also suggest that 'customers are so inured to offers promising everything from a free vacation in Florida to a free credit card that they either yawn when they see a new one or become experts at getting something for nothing' (O'Brien and Jones, 1995, p. 77).

O'Brien and Jones (1995) argue that customers may be polygamously loyal, recognizing that customers 'don't want to play in 20 different games or wait 20 years to accumulate airline tickets . . . . If they were to spread their purchases out evenly, it would take them ten times as long to attain rewards. That's too long to wait' (p. 80). Nevertheless, O'Brien and Jones (1995) found that 'a rewards program can accelerate the loyalty life cycle, encouraging first- or second-year customers to behave like a company's most profitable tenth-year customers—but only if it is planned and implemented as part of a larger loyalty-management strategy' (p. 75). They argue that a critical component of developing a successful frequency program is whether the company is able to communicate the value of the program to their customers (O'Brien and Jones, 1995). Dowling and Uncles (1997) agree that for frequency programs to be as effective as possible, they must leverage the brand's perceived value by communicating the program's benefits to customers. Frequency programs can thus be very beneficial to companies, if they effectively communicate the value to their customers and support the brand promise and company's mission and values.

What frequency programs do not do

Sometimes the wrong things are expected from loyalty programs. These programs are not 'quick fixes.' They will not fix an essential problem in the operation that may be costing customers. They won't show a profit in the short run – these are dedicated long-term efforts. They are not a promotion that is temporary or, worse, becomes part of the product that only becomes a cost. And they won't bring in new customers. The brand has to overcome the barriers to first trial before the loyalty program can kick in.

What makes frequency programs work

According to Richard Dunn at Loyaltyworks, the following elements are essential to a successful frequency program:

- A vital database – the relationship foundation
- Targeted communications – the relationship dialogue
- Meaningful rewards – the relationship recognition
- Simplicity – easy to participate and understand
- Attainability – motivational rewards must be attainable (e.g., upgrades)
- Sustainability – do not let it lapse, keep it active
- Measurability – make sure it is working in the right ways
- Management – full commitment and behind it all the way
- Manageability – do not let it get out of hand
- Profitability – is it really working in the long term?

Further caveats from Dunn are these:

- Do not treat the program like a promotion.
- Do not focus excessively on rewards, but on the relationship.
- Do not short-change the communications component.
- Do not underestimate the importance of internal support.
- Do not pretend to care more than you really do.
- Tailor the value of benefits to specific customers based on their achieved or expected value.

The past and future of relationship/customer loyalty marketing

Although everyone talks about the customer and relationship marketing, that isn't the way it necessarily works in the organization. In fact, the way that many organizations work is as follows:

1. Some organizations talk only about treating customers better. Management does not always understand what outstanding service is like and is not ready to turn its organization upside down to provide it. They paint happy faces on frontline people. Or, they conduct a service program for employees, but do not make it a part of their core strategy. Rhetoric does not become reality.
2. The organization tries to be everything to everybody. Customers are lumped together as one big mass. Their separate expectations are not known or are not weighted and prioritized.
3. Customer surveys are acknowledged when they are positive, but negative data are often denied. Budget priorities are set and resources allocated with little, if any, connection to customer expectations. Priority is on what management or the company thinks is important.
4. Customers are not part of research and development of new services and products.
5. Employees are seen as the cause of service breakdowns, even if research shows that a large majority of service breakdowns are caused by the system, the process, or the structure, and only a few by the people in the trenches.
6. Focus is on customer acquisition rather than customer retention. Sales and marketing efforts are aimed more at bringing in new customers than keeping or expanding the business of old customers.

The future promises something different for those companies that deal with these negatives and focus on the positives. In today's technological world, there is little reason for not understanding the customer and what they expect. But technology only provides the means; it does not by itself change attitudes or behavior, and, if it is not paid attention to, it becomes no more than a costly, fruitless expense.

Innovative leaders in the hospitality marketplace are not only translating guest experience and expectation data into operational changes, but are also forging links between data acquisition, analysis, and delivery. They are rethinking customer and service strategy and improving customer services and value by providing frontline employees with the information they need to provide higher quality customer service and retain more customers. These will be the companies of the future, with the sustainable competitive advantage.

Summary

A technique of non-traditional marketing is relationship marketing. RM creates customer bonding and understanding that is an integral part of any company's sustenance and growth. One way to understand RM is to use The Loyalty Circle©, which includes Process, Value and Communication. Relationships must be developed and sustained so that they build loyalty and increase the lifetime value of a customer. Frequency programs can help to sustain and even increase loyalty, but only if they are properly set up and help to communicate the brand promise. Communication with the customer can best be leveraged when effective database marketing strategies are used.

Despite every company's desire to have customers that are loyal only to their product/service offerings, Dowling and Uncles (1997) contend that most heavy users are multi-brand loyal and that a company's most profitable customers will probably be the competitors' most profitable customers as well. Uncles, Dowling, and Hammond (2003) argue:

If consumers have good reasons for being multi-brand loyal, then it is unrealistic for brand managers to expect them suddenly to become single-brand loyal. Empirically, consumers appear not to want to watch one television station, eat at one restaurant, patronize one hotel chain, drink one brand of wine, get all their business news from one magazine, go to one holiday destination, buy one brand of petrol, only attend one theatre, always shop at the same bookstore, etc. Hence, it is a major challenge for brand managers to convince enough people to reduce their repertoire of brands such that the propensity to buy their particular brand increases enough to cover the full costs of the program. In these circumstances, the best way for customers to reallocate some of their category purchasing to a particular brand is for a program to address the underlying reasons for polygamy. Thus, program members might be given greater access to the brand, offered more variety, or helped to consolidate their purchases with fewer business providers/brands.

(p. 294)

Although there are clear costs associated with serving new customers that are higher than serving repeat customers, Dowling and Uncles (1997) suggest that there is no clear reason why the cost of servicing a loyal repeat customer should be any higher than serving any other type of repeat customer. O'Brien and Jones (1995) propose that companies consider offering special prices to loyal customers, similar to the lower interest rates offered by credit card companies to customers with better credit history. In fact, they argue that companies must differentiate between their loyal and non-loyal customers in order to maximize loyalty and profitability. They go on to argue that customers will not become sustainable in their loyalty unless a company has developed and effectively communicated long-term benefits for their customer.

References

Aggarwal, P. (2004). The effects of brand relationship norms on consumer attitudes and behavior. *Journal of Consumer Research*, 31(1), 87–89.

Ambler, T. (1997). How much of brand equity is explained by trust? *Management Decision*, 35(3/4), 283–285.

Bagozzi, R. and Dholakia, U. (2006). Antecedents and purchase consequences of customer participation in small group brand communities. *International Journal of Research in Marketing*, 23(1), 45.

Baker, S., Thompson, K.,and Engelken, J. (2004). Mapping the values driving organic food choice: Germany vs. the UK. *European Journal of Marketing*, 38(8), 997.

Ball, D., Ellison, S., and Adamy, J. (2004) Just what you need!. *Wall Street Journal* – Eastern Edition, pp. B1, B8.

Berry, C. J. (1994). *The Idea of Luxury*. Cambridge: Cambridge University Press.

Blackston, M. (2000). Observations: Building brand equity by managing the brand's relationships. *Journal of Advertising Research*, 40(6), 101–104.

Bowen, J. T. and Shoemaker, S. (2003). Loyalty: A strategic commitment. *Cornell Hotel and Restaurant Administration Quarterly*, 44(5/6), 32.

Cannie, J. K. (1994). *Turning Lost Customers into Gold and the Art of Achieving Zero Defections*. New York: AMACOM Books.

Chaudhuri, A. and Holbrook, M. (2001). The chain of effects from brand trust and brand affect to brand. *Journal of Marketing*, 65(2), 81–93.

Cooper, P. (1999). Consumer understanding, change, and qualitative research. *Journal of the Market Research Society*, 41(1), 259–268 .

Dowling, G. and Uncles, M. (1997, Summer). Do customer loyalty programs really work? *Slogan Management Review*, 38(4), 71–82.

Dunne, D. (2004, May 10). Branding the experience. *Marketing Magazine*, 109, 11.

Escalas, J. and Bettman, J. (2003).You are what they eat: The influence of reference groups on consumers' connections to brands. *Journal of Consumer Psychology*, 13(3), 339–347.

Fournier, S. (1998). Consumers and their brands: Developing relationships theory in consumer research. *Journal of Consumer Research*, 24(4), 345, 366–367.

Fournier, S., Dobscha, S., and Mick, D. (1998). Preventing the premature death of relationship marketing. *Harvard Business Review*, 76(1), 43–46.

Garbarino, E. and Johnson, M. (1999). The different roles of satisfaction, trust and commitment in customer relationships. *Journal of Marketing*, 63(2), 73.

Gordon, I. (1998). *Relationship Marketing*. Toronto, Canada: John Wiley & Sons.

Gundlach, G. and Achrol, R. (1995). The structure of commitment in exchange. *Journal of Marketing*, 59(1), 79–80.

Hausfater, G. (2005). A loyal subject: Card programs inspire brand devotion among hungry customers. *Nation's Restaurant News*, 39(1), 70.

Heskett, J. L., Jones, T. O., Loveman, G. W.et al. (1994). Putting the service-profit chain to work. *Harvard Business Review*, 72(2), 164–170.

Jang, D. and Mattila, A. S. (2005). An examination of restaurant loyalty programs: What kinds of rewards do customers prefer? *International Journal of Contemporary Hospitality Management*, 17(5), 403.

Kim, H., Kim, W., and An, J. (2003). The effect of consumer-based equity on firms' financial performance. *Journal of Consumer Marketing*, 20(4), 336–338.

Kivetz, R. and Simonson, I. (2002). Earning the right to indulge: Efforts as a determinant of customer preferences toward frequency program rewards. *Journal of Marketing Research*, 39(2), 55–70.

Levitt, T. (1981). Marketing intangible products and product intangibles. *Harvard Business Review*, 53(2), 94–102.

Lockyer, S. (2004). Keep 'em coming back for more. *Nation's Restaurant News*, 38(33), 63–72.

Lowder, J. (1997). The Relationship Marketing Report (May), Relationship Marketing Report, Occoquan, Va.

Lozito, W. (2004). Brands: More than a name. *Restaurant Hospitality*, 88(9), 58.

Luvy, G. (2002). Love and loathing in the brand world. *Brand strategy*, 7.

Mattila, A. (2001). Emotional bonding and restaurant loyalty. *Cornell Hotel and Restaurant Administration Quarterly*, 42(6), 73–74.

Morais, D., Dorsch, M., and Backman, S. (2005). Building loyal relationships between customers and providers: A focus on resource investments. *Journal of Travel & Tourism Marketing*, 18(1), 51–53.

Muniz A., Jr. and O'Guinn, T. (2001). Brand community. *Journal of Consumer Research*, 27(4), 412–427.

O'Brien, L. and Jones, C. (1995). Do rewards really create loyalty?. *Harvard Business Review*, 73(3), 75–82.

Oliver, R. (1999). Whence consumer loyalty? *Journal of Marketing*, 63(4), 33–44.

O'Malley, L. and Prothero, A. (2004). Beyond the frills of relationship marketing. *Journal of Business Research*, 57(11), 1292–1293.

Orth, U., McDaniel, M., Shelhammer, T., and Lopetcharat, K. (2004). Promoting brand benefits: The role of consumer the role of consumer psychographics and lifestyle. *Journal of Consumer Marketing*, 21(2), 97.

Petrick, J. (2005). Reoperationalising the loyalty framework. *Tourism & Hospitality Research*, 5(3), 199–212.

Prelec, D. and Loewenstein, G. (1998). The red and the black: Mental accounting of savings and debt. *Marketing Science*, 17(1), 4–28.

Reichheld, K. (2002). Letter to the editor. *Harvard Business Review*, 80(11), 126.

Roberts, K., Varki, S., and Brodie, R. (2003). Measuring the quality of relationships in customer services: an empirical study. *European Journal of Marketing*, 37(1/2), 169–196.

Rothschild, M. and Gaidis, W. (1981). Behavioral learning theory: Its relevance to marketing and promotions. *Journal of Marketing*, 45(2), 73.

Rust, R., Zeithaml, V., and Lemon, K. (2004). Customer-centered brand management. *Harvard Business Review*, 82(9), 113.

Salanova, M., Agust, S., and Peiró, J. (2005). Linking organizational resources and work engagement to employee performance and customer loyalty: The mediation of service climate. *Journal of Applied Psychology*, 90(6), 1217–1224.

Shoemaker et al., (2006). Affective commitment. *Working paper*. University of Houston, 3–4.

Shoemaker, S. and Lewis, R. (1999). Customer loyalty: The future of hospitality marketing. *Hospitality Management*, 18, 349.

Uncles, M., Dowling, G., and Hammond, K. (2003). Customer loyalty and customer loyalty programs. *Journal of Consumer Marketing*, 20(4), 294.

Williams, M. R. (1998). The influence of salespersons' customer orientation on buyer-seller relationship development. *Journal of Business & Industrial Marketing*, 13(3), 271–287.

Youjae, Y. and Suna, L. (2004). What influences the relationship between customer satisfaction and repurchase intention? Investigating the effects of adjusted expectations and customer loyalty. *Psychology* & Marketing, 21(5), 351–373.

CHAPTER 6

Advertising, public relations and crisis management

Kathryn LaTour

> *Strategy and timing are the Himalayas of marketing. Everything else is the Catskills.*
>
> —Al Ries and Jack Trout (1986, in Donadio, 1992)

Those in the hospitality and tourism industry can relate to the differences between the Himalayas and Catskills. What the industry is just beginning to embrace is how advertising and public relations (PR) can be used to change customers' image of a destination, hotel, restaurant, or tourist attraction and that having a cohesive strategy can make or break a communication attempt.

The category within the tourism industry that perhaps best understands the importance of advertising is the airline business. For instance, in 2005, despite the fact that both Delta and Northwest Airlines filed Chapter 11 bankruptcy, neither indicated having any plans to cut their advertising budget. In fact, the day after filing, Delta took out a full-page ad in *USA Today* costing roughly $94,000 before discounts, and Northwest Airlines sent its frequent-flier customers an e-mail assuring them it would continue operating as normal during the bankruptcy proceedings. When United went into bankruptcy protection in 2003, its advertising budget actually increased 17.5% from the year before (Thomaselli, 2005).

But not all sectors in the hospitality and tourism industry have embraced the use of advertising (Michael, 2002), and fewer still have successfully incorporated PR into their promotional mix; many cite budgetary constraints as the rationale for their skimpy allocations for advertising (and PR). As the airline example suggests, however, as industries become more competitive, it may be more costly for the organization to *not* advertise. Industry trends indicate more and more sectors of hospitality and tourism are realizing the benefits of such promotional efforts, with travel sites like Travelocity, Expedia, Priceline, and Orbitz developing advertising campaigns. The cruise industry has also recognized the importance of advertising to differentiate its product offerings (Case, 2006).

The academic literature in the area of advertising and PR as it relates to the hospitality industry has been rather sparse. In 2004, Oh, Kim and Shin conducted a review of the articles published during 2002–2003 in the top four hospitality and top four tourism journals and found only three articles on advertising in hospitality journals and one in a tourism journal. There were two articles on PR (both on crisis management) in hospitality journals and three on PR/crisis management in tourism journals. This author employed the same coding scheme for articles appearing in the same journals between the years 2004–2006 and found low article appearances (one) on advertising in hospitality journals , but more interest in the tourism journals with a total of eight advertising-related articles. The trend of publishing more on crisis management was apparent – there was a special issue of *Journal of Hospitality and*

Leisure Marketing on crisis management, leading to seven articles in the hospitality area, and two special issues of *Journal of Travel and Tourism Marketing* leading to a total of 22 articles in the tourism journals. This trend toward more coverage of response during crises follows the more traditional way people tend to view PR, where PR is employed to help a destination or organization restore its image. This is a *reactive PR* strategy, and both researchers and practitioners find that in order to react well, a firm needs to have a continuous *proactive PR* strategy in place. Proactive PR is offensively rather than defensively focused. PR departments can help shape a hospitality company's overall image and presence and should be involved in day-to-day operations. It is noteworthy that while the trend was toward more coverage of PR overall in the last three years, only one hospitality article discussed the more proactive form of PR.

Researchers from many disciplines including psychology, marketing, and communication studies have examined advertising and PR and how these relates to their areas of expertise. The advertising field has also developed two of its own journals – in 1960 introducing the *Journal of Advertising Research* to respond to more practitioner-related concerns and in 1971 developing the *Journal of Advertising* to build on theoretical issues. The PR area has not been as developed, with most of the top research appearing in more general marketing and communication journals, though PR also has a specialty journal.

Thus far, the hospitality and tourism literature has generally built off the findings from these other disciplines and, to greatly simplify things, the main thrust has been to understand advertising's potential to drive tourism/hospitality choice and the role advertising plays with experiential consumption overall. As mentioned, PR has mainly been discussed in terms of crisis resolution. The hospitality and tourism literature therefore has not generally been designed to offer insights into how advertising and PR 'work,' but rather to more specifically address issues related to applied problems within their domain of interest. Therefore, the goal of this chapter is to introduce the major issues found in advertising and PR research and highlight the top hospitality research which addresses the more specific concerns. When appropriate, industry examples and academic research from hospitality and tourism are cited.

The intent of this chapter is to review and put into context the 60-or-so-year old body of research on how advertising works. Some of the terms used throughout this chapter appear in Box 6.1. The traditional model of how advertising or communication was thought to work (AIDA – i.e., awareness, interest, desire, and action) and some newer ways of thinking about communications' influence on the customers' experience at a more subconscious level are discussed. An alternative model – Experience Framing – is introduced, which might be more appropriate for considering the impact of advertising on experience.

Then attention is turned to the major decisions facing advertisers (determining objectives, media choice, creative content, scheduling) and a review is provided of what the advertising research and hospitality/tourism research has to say about these decisions. The research process itself is then discussed, followed by the discussion on ways in which research can add (and is adding) insights into advertising decisions. The focus then turns to PR, demonstrating how PR can help both in good times and bad, with real world examples of each. The chapter ends with a summary and some ideas for future research in hospitality and tourism.

Box 6.1   Basic concepts and definitions

Advertising Any paid form of promotion aimed at a large audience.

Advertorial A paid-for press release that appears within a magazine or newspaper and 'blends into' the content.

CPM Literally, 'cost per thousand' – a way of comparing the cost/reach of various media outlets.

Continuous Strategy A media scheduling strategy that advocates distributing the messages evenly over time.

Event creation Developing and publicizing events to promote a cause or non-profit agency with expectations that the event will result in positive feelings toward the host company.

Flighting A media scheduling strategy that advocates concentrating the ads together in time.

Frequency How often a customer sees a message. Typically an ad may have to be seen several times before it has an impact on customers.

Impact The influence of the communication message on either attitudes or behavior.

Media Non-personal communication channels used to convey messages (TV, radio, newspaper, etc).

Noise Anything that gets in the way of a message being effectively communicated to its target recipient.

Press release Information released to media informing them of activities or services at a location.

Proactive PR Offensive PR, meaning PR activities not done as a reaction to some negative event but rather as an overall strategy to provide the organization visibility, newsworthiness and credibility (Shimp, 2000).

Product placement A paid-for appearance within a TV program or a movie, for a product. In the hospitality sector, this often involves where the characters meet (such as the *Real World* Las Vegas in the Palms). Product placements can also occur within the hospitality experience itself, such as having a certain spa at a hotel and placing its soaps in guest's rooms.

Public relations (PR) The process by which a company creates a positive image and customer preference through third-party endorsement (Kotler et al., 2003).

Reach How many people are potentially exposed to a given message. One of the ways to compare which media outlet is most appropriate for a given campaign.

Reactive Public Relations Defensive PR strategy to respond to unanticipated market developments (i.e. crises).

Recall A dependent measure in most advertising studies, where the researcher assesses either free recall (e.g., *what ads do you remember seeing last night?*), or aided recall (e.g., *what travel ads do you remember seeing last night?*)

Recognition A dependent measure in advertising studies that is less taxing than recall and asking whether or not the respondent remembers seeing the ad when the researcher lists (or shows) it.

The communication process

Figure 6.1 depicts the typical model of communication involving a sender that decodes the communication objective and transmits that message through some sort of media channel to the receiver. Both advertising and PR follow this basic process. Where they differ is in

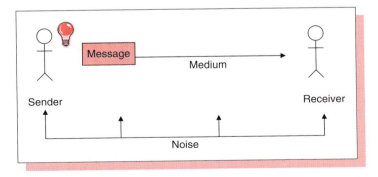

Figure 6.1
Communication model

the manner in which the message is sent out. In the case of advertising, the marketer has control over the development of the message and the media in which it is sent out (because it is paid for). In the case of PR, the marketer has to pay someone on the staff to write and send out a press release to the media (or develop an event), but the actual message that is delivered and the media in which it is sent out is dependent on the third party (such as a travel show or news program). In the case of PR, the message is associated with the third – impartial – party, rather than the hospitality organization that has something to gain by what is said, which increases its potential credibility to the receiver (see Loda et al., 2005, for a comparison of advertising and PR in tourism).

While advertising and PR are two different activities, there has recently been some 'blurring of the lines' between the two, such as in the case of product placements. Placements are paid for (like advertising), but they are associated with the media (such as a TV show) in which they are placed, therefore potentially benefiting from that third-party association. Like advertising, the marketer has to 'buy' the placement opportunity through a media placement agency and, many times, marketers must guarantee a certain level of advertising commitment to secure the placement (see Hudson and Ritchie, 2006, for examples of destinations being promoted in films). Another 'blended' advertising option is the 'advertorial.' These are often grouped together within a magazine with 'Advertisement' written in small letters at the top of the page, but, for the most part, blend into the magazine's content. *The New York Times* Sunday Magazine often has such features. The upside of this technique is that a marketer can write a 'press release' copy that appears to be coming from the magazine and thus increase the potential credibility of the message.

Notice in the figure that 'noise' can occur during the communication process, which diminishes the message's effectiveness. Noise can occur at all stages of the communication process. For instance, the sender (marketer) can incorrectly translate its communication goal into the message. In the case of PR, the marketer may have little control over the message that is ultimately delivered to the customer. Noise can also occur within the media channel where competing messages from other destinations or placement within programs can interfere with recipients' ability to properly decode the message. The media choices and their ability to cut through the noise are discussed in an upcoming section.

Noise can also occur due to receiver issues. For instance, it has been estimated that customers are exposed to over 1,500 advertising messages a day, and that number keeps rising as marketers find new ways to reach customers, i.e. text messaging, iPod, etc. (Rosen, 2000). Not all messages that customers see or hear are likely to be deeply processed and, in most cases, a single message will not even be remembered. Tourism researchers have found that whether or not a person has traveled to a particular destination will influence how he or she processes a related advertising message (Kerstetter and Cho, 2004). Customers tend to notice and pay attention to information that is relevant to them or helps them in upcoming decisions or reinforces past decisions. Therefore, targeting potential tourists, when they are seeking information, may have the biggest payoff because they are less prone to noise effects. For example, media choices like *Travel & Leisure* or travel sections in local papers are likely to result in more engaged recipients.

How advertising works

The traditional model of advertising

Advertising theories and philosophies have changed dramatically over the past six decades of advertising research. It behooves hospitality marketers to understand both the traditional way of thinking about advertising and the new insights that add to that school of thought. An early taxonomy was developed to take thinking into what many call the 'advertising funnel' associated with the AIDA model (Barry, 1987; Strong, 1925) as shown in Figure 6.2. According to this model, customers change their minds about a product, then their attitude, and then they act. According to the model, therefore, cognition precedes affect which precedes behavior. The purpose of advertising, then, is to get the brand into the customer's mind, convince the customer of the brand's superiority, and then from that positive attitude will theoretically come the purchase.

The first stage of the AIDA model focuses on creating 'awareness.' The next stage is creating 'interest,' which in a funnel metaphor implies

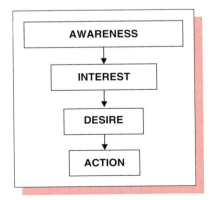

Figure 6.2
The AIDA model

that this applies only to those who are already 'aware' of the message. As the 'funnel' continues, 'desire' is the next stage, where the communication has effectively created a distinction in the customers' minds as well as motivation for a particular destination. Finally, the narrowest point of the funnel corresponds to 'action.' Naturally managers would like 'action' to be as wide as possible so that more people act based on seeing the message. Ideally, it is desirable for advertising to progress 'cleanly' through the 'funnel' without getting 'stuck' in any one of these stages. In other words, move the buyer to patronage via advertising alone. In reality, though, hospitality managers have to rely on a combination of methods, along with advertising, to make all of this happen. Hence, the advertising jargon of focusing on more of an 'integrated approach,' where advertising strategy works as part of an 'arsenal' of promotional methods to achieve a 'clean funnel' effect, has been the traditional way of approaching effectiveness.

Effectiveness of advertising is augmented by the Internet, database technology, PR and, of course, the old 'standby'—personal selling. Key to all of these is the sharing and managing of information about the customer so as to target communications as effectively as possible. From a strategic perspective, it makes sense to think of advertising as part of a greater collection of tools for communication, not a stand-alone alternative. As firms realize that 'building brands' literally takes place 'between the customer's ears,' greater, more intimate knowledge and research about the target market make for the most impact.

Subconscious impacts

While the AIDA model seems straightforward, there is research suggesting that customers do not go through such a hierarchical process – for instance, researchers find that in many cases affect may precede cognition (Holbrook and Batra, 1987). Further, the theory regarding the impact of a communication attempt originally followed the viewpoint of psychologists that for something to have an impact, it needed to be consciously attended to or noticed. Now psychologists and marketers recognize that learning can occur even without conscious recognition of the communication attempt and that the AIDA model might not always represent customer reality in the process of making a choice (Braun, 1999; Hall, 2002; Zaltman, 2003). For instance, some choices might be based on simple awareness of the brand, and familiarity breeds credence enough to guide choice. This creates both some opportunities and barriers for hospitality marketers. Opportunities abound; placing the brand name in numerous outlets to breed familiarity and acceptance is a strategy that works more on the unconscious, and an example of such strategy, with in-flight media, is discussed further in Box 6.2. Barriers also occur, such as in the manner in which communication effectiveness is assessed. The fact that customers are not aware of the communication attempt does not mean it did not impact them on some level. Therefore, indirect measures, or physiological measures, might be better suited than traditional surveys for measuring the impact of a campaign that seeks to change customers through less intrusive means. Later, in the 'Future Research' section, some of these newer measures are discussed.

Box 6.2 In-Flight advertising

One of the unique media opportunities available to hospitality marketers is in-flight options. Most airlines have magazines where restaurants, hotels and attractions can advertise to travelers coming to their destination. While some decisions regarding lodging might have already been made by the time the traveler sees the ad, at times those decisions can be altered or the traveler might remember the hotel/restaurant for a future visit. To be effective, the in-flight magazine has to be read, which may or may not occur. Travelers have a harder time escaping video programs shown to the entire flight (within safety procedures, news programs, etc.). There has not been the proliferation of advertising in this vehicle, perhaps due to airlines limiting their relationships to certain providers. But it remains a fruitful media to investigate, and worldwide sales of in-flight advertising options rose to $15 million in 2004 in Asia, the research agency studying that growth, Emphasis, predicting even more growth. 'The wealthy, brand-conscious, frequent international traveler is one of, if not the most sought after demographic by advertisers,' says Monica Woo, managing direct of Emphasis (Bowman, 2005). And airlines are getting more creative when they sell their advertising space. Europe's low-fare airline Ryanair has Mars-chocolate-bar-branded headrests in flight. Branded cards on meal trays, along with branding on boarding passes, and radio ads on in-flight audio are now being included on some airlines. In order to make sure travelers see and process the in-flight video material, some airlines have added interstitials, which are still-images on screen that require the viewers to push a button before they move on.

Framing the customers' experience: An alternative model

Hospitality products are all about the customer experience and the intangible nature of experiences allow advertising to shape those experiences. One way advertising can exert a more unconscious effect on customers is through altering how they perceive, experience, or remember their vacation or other service encounters. Hospitality researchers have noted the importance of exposing customers to marketing messages in order to set expectations for their coming visit. For instance, Deighton's two-step model (1984; Deighton and Schindler, 1988) posits that advertising raises expectations or induces hypotheses that tend to be confirmed by the experience. Within tourism research, pre-consumption search behavior has been an important component in almost all processing and decision-making models (cf. Gursoy and McCleary, 2004). The main type of tourism advertising research – conversion studies – looks at an advertising campaign's ability to forward influence tourists' decision to visit a particular destination (Woodside and Dubelaar, 2003). In this way, the advertising message is seen as a 'forward frame' whereby those created expectations guide the actual perception of the experience; in other words, customers see and experience what they expect.

This view of advertising as serving as a 'frame' augments research on developing servicescapes that employ atmospheric elements that alter the customers' perception at the time the experience is occurring (Berry et al., 2002; Wall and Berry, 2007). See Figure 6.3 for a model of how advertising can be seen as a frame that alters the customers' experience (adapted from Braun and Zaltman, 1998). In this model, the

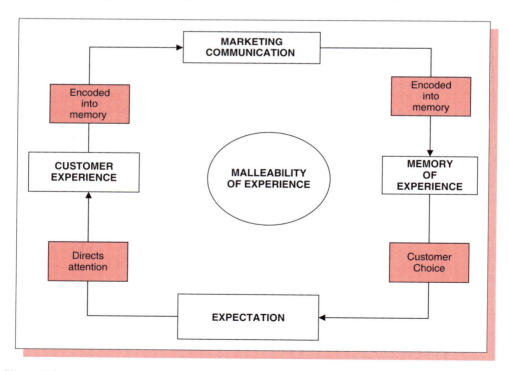

Figure 6.3
Framing of experience

marketing communication is encoded into memory, and the customer combines that information with prior memories of visiting the destination and/or other information. Then the customer acts, makes a choice of where to visit, or eat or stay. The customer's prior knowledge acts as a forward frame that sets certain expectations and influences how he or she attends to or focuses on information during the actual experience. When the experience is over, the customer encodes that into his or her memory and that experience will then influence how subsequent marketing communications are viewed. The process continues over time.

Notice at the center of the figure the term 'malleability of experience.' It had once been believed in both the psychological and marketing arenas that experience was the most important factor when making a decision, and that experience trumped other information. Now it is generally recognized that experiences are malleable and can be influenced by external information (like marketing communications). This malleability in part is due to the reconstructive nature of memory. This view finds that every act of encoding and recalling an experience is reconstructive, meaning that the memory is constructed based on cues in the present environment as well as what had been learned in the past. At times, this reconstructive process can lead to a memory of an experience very different from the actual experience. To illustrate this point, consider a more extreme example of memory alteration from the movie *Total Recall* where Arnold Schwartzenager's character had an entire trip to Mars implanted in his brain. According to the 'travel agent' the benefits were no lost luggage and only favorable associations such as a visit to the sinful Venusville. While that is an extreme case of changing or, in fact, creating a memory of an experience, researchers find that such post-experience management is possible given the malleability of human memory. In fact, neuroscience finds that there is very little difference in brain activity between when one recalls a 'true' memory and when one recalls a 'false' memory (Schacter, 1996).

This reconstructive process allows marketers to frame the customer experience after it has ensued. For example, Braun-LaTour et al. (2006) found that referring to childhood memories in an advertisement can result in overall more favorable memories of the destination. These researchers have also demonstrated in several studies that post-experience advertising can in fact implant memories of things that never happened. In a nostalgic ad for Disney they inserted an image and text referring to Bugs Bunny and found that (in some cases) nearly half of those exposed to the ad had a memory of meeting Bugs at a Disney resort during their childhood (which was impossible because Bugs Bunny was a competing Warner Bros. character). So hospitality marketers can use advertising as a means not only to steer customers to their destination and set expectations that influence the experience, but also as a means to recreate the experience in memory to encourage revisitation (Braun-LaTour, Grinley, and Loftus, 2006; Braun-LaTour et al., 2004). Because these framing effects on experience may occur below customers' conscious awareness, there is a need for indirect measures of effectiveness, like experimental designs, which are again discussed in the 'Future Directions' section later.

Types of advertising decisions

There are four main questions a hospitality manager has to face when deciding on an advertising plan: first, what is the communication goal for the campaign?; second, where is the best place to put the advertising so that the target market will be exposed to the message (media)?; third, what type of message or format is best to communicate to the target market?, and fourth, how often or frequently should the advertising message be scheduled? Note that these decisions might be made in different orders, depending on the organization. Each of these major decisions is discussed below. Research can be used to make all of these decisions more effectively. Also discussed in this section are the types of research methods and measures normally employed within an advertising setting, with several examples of how different hospitality companies have utilized research in their advertising planning.

Decision 1: Communication objectives

Hospitality marketers first have to ask themselves: what is the overall purpose of the campaign? Do you represent a new property that no one knows about? Or is yours a property where research shows that customers know you, but they just do not like or prefer you? Or is yours a property where customers visit, report they have a great time, but yet never revisit? Each situation will warrant a different type of communication objective that will drive how the campaign is created and distributed to customers. There are three main types of goals for a campaign: inform, persuade, and remind (Kotler et al., 2003). New properties or destinations have to work on creating awareness and informing customers of their benefits. Informative campaigns are also employed when a destination has undergone a major renovation or change that might influence customer decision-making. For example, after Katrina, many of the hospitality properties concentrated on informing tourists that they were still open for business. Once a property or destination is well-known, and perhaps is part of the customers' consideration set, there is no need to provide information but rather to persuade customers that the destination or property is more desirable than the competition. For example, W Hotels does this well with its new campaign: 'Whatever, whenever,' where it features situations where employees have gone out of their way for their cus-tomers at all hours (*Lodging Hospitality*, 2006). Reminder campaigns work by reinforcing positive memories of the experience and motivat-ing the customer to return. A hospitality firm's internal data may reveal very low repeat patronage, but high satisfaction scores. In addition to traditional media outlets (TV, radio), a more targeted approach to past customers using the company's database, with perhaps a sales pro-motion, would be an effective reminder campaign. A marketer might have a communication goal that transcends the ones mentioned here and which was illuminated in their research. The important thing is to know where the campaign is going so that the media planning and message execution are on track.

Decision 2: Media selection

Once the communication objective has been set, marketers need to ask: What is the best way to reach my target customers? This decision may supersede the message content decision because it will have a greater impact on the format (i.e., via a static print ad or billboard or through a more dynamic medium like TV or radio). In the past, the main media choices for an advertiser were limited to newspaper, magazine, radio, billboards or television. Now media choices include Internet adver-tising, websites and product placements. Actually, advertising oppor-tunities are only limited by one's imagination. Advertising managers at Northwest Airlines found an unusual way to tell busy Japanese executives in Tokyo about the new lie-down business-class seats. The company secured space on window cleaners' platforms with ads that faced into office windows featuring a picture of the new high-tech seats with the tagline: 'Does your seat recline all the way down to 176 degrees?' (Madden, 2005).

Each media has its own unique strengths and weaknesses. (See Table 6.1) for a summary. Basically there are three types of formats: video, audio, and static visual (print). Video (or film) advertisements are usually the costliest. However, the costs of advertising on broad-cast (i.e. network) television have lessened due to a more fractionalized space; cable advertising might be a good option for mid-sized hospi-tality companies as it reaches targeted audiences at a relatively lower cost. The marketer can also choose between local and national buys for broadcast television, which can provide better geographic targeting at lower costs. For instance, Super Bowl advertising on a national level is often prohibitively expensive for most advertisers (costing millions of dollars per thirty-second spot), but local broadcast stations also have time to sell during the game, usually available at much more reasonable rates. Steve Wynn took advantage of local buys during the 2005 Super Bowl. The NFL does not allow gaming companies to advertise within its programming because of a conflict of interest. Steve Wynn, buying

Table 6.1 Comparison of media choices

Media	Strengths	Weaknesses
Newspaper	Flexible and can target individual or national markets; reasonable cost	Short life, as thrown away at the end of the day; limits on color and other creative choices
Magazine	High targeting opportunity; creative color options; longer life	Position not always guaranteed; pre-purchase time lag; competition likely within highly targeted magazines (such as *Travel & Leisure*)
Network television	Combines visual and auditory elements; large audience base (though shrinking)	High cost; less targeted (paying to reach customers who may have no interest in your destination); short life; repetition needed to make sure message attended and understood
Cable	Lower cost than network television and the same benefits regarding message design; better targeting	Short life; repetition strategy needed to ensure message understood; smaller audience than network TV
Radio	Good targeting; lower cost, more flexible (less production time before air)	No visuals to attract attention; once heard, cannot repeat and no visual image to cue information
In-Flight Video/ Magazines	Captive audience, targeting business and leisure travel market effectively; can focus on certain destination/routes	Video advertising limited to certain partnerships
Billboards	Semi-captive audience; can catch customers in their decision-making; low cost	Limited space to convey message; requires focused attention
Direct mail	Can target customers effectively; lower cost compared to other methods; can be combined with sales promotions to direct behavior	May be thrown away within 'junk mail'; messages have to be very simple and direct to get customers' attention
Internet	Low cost; can direct customer to website for more detailed information	May be seen as annoying or intrusive; some computer systems may block
Product placements	Shows hospitality product in use with attractive celebrity spokespeople; sends a message regarding the cultural desirability of your product	May not have much creative control over the context in which your product is seen (positive/negative); long lead-time needed; May have to promise ad dollars in addition to fee for placement

at the local level in several key markets in the Southwest, was able to go under the NFL radar and launch his Wynn Resorts in grand style. He also benefited from some of the media fall-out over his non-authorized ads, during the following days (Velotta and Simpson, 2005). The downside of video or televised ads is that they are the least flexible because time must be allotted for production. Radio (audio) ads, meanwhile, are extremely flexible and little lead-time is required; but because they have no visual accompaniment, and because humans are primarily visually oriented creatures, the ads need to be repeated more often to have an impact. Print ads don't have the dynamic aspects of either radio or video, but can convey information creatively through images. Print ads, as well as billboards, can also be revisited by customers, either by re-reading a magazine or newspaper ad or driving again by a particular billboard. Marketers should consider which of these formats might best 'sell' their message, when considering media options.

Key to the concepts of media choices are the terms *reach*, *frequency*, and *impact*. The first two are readily measurable and very straight-forward. Reach pertains to how many people can be exposed to a given advertisement. Media kits provided by the various media outlets as well as advertising agencies will indicate the audience size and demographic breakdown. Cost per thousand (CPM) is a term media planners use to compare the cost of different media outlets. Frequency pertains to how many actual exposures on average are scheduled. The frequency is largely determined by the marketer, noting that media outlets will generally make deals with respect to quantity. Thus, long-term planning is advised. However, given how saturated and cluttered our multi-media environment is, there is no guarantee that exposing someone to a message several times is enough to get through, nor is there a guarantee that the message is not getting repeated so much as to be an irritant. These factors need to be considered in making the scheduling decisions (to be discussed later in more detail). Impact refers to the actual consequences of planned communications, with a wealth of variables attached: measurement challenges and individual variance. To that extent much of the recent thinking about advertising has been focused on advertising's impact and the complexity of the human organism as it reacts to our cluttered media environment.

Decision 3: Message execution

The advertising agency's creative staff must translate the advertising's communication objective and message content in an executable style. Some of the more common styles found within hospitality and tourism are discussed in this section. One of the biggest mistakes novice marketers make is trying to say too much – the use of white space in a print ad or silence within a video or radio ad can make an advertising message stand apart. Especially within the cluttered media environment, it is important to keep the message simple. While price or rational ads still dominate some mediums, tourism marketers do recognize the value of pictures in their advertising. Images are especially important in destination marketing, and researchers find that both young and elderly tourists retain memory of communications that contain images (more so than text) (MacKay, 2005).

Equally important, though, is recognizing that travel decisions are often not based on rational thinking, and that appealing to the customers' emotions is effective. In 2005, for example, Club Med decided, rather than focusing on its property improvements, to focus on the emotional bonds that can occur on the properties, such as family or school reunions, honeymoons, and trips with office colleagues. The central theme is that Club Med is a resort where people travel great distances to get closer. This campaign is based on two trends the resort saw occurring in the leisure trip market where value and reuniting are key decision points (Beirne, 2004). Below are some other approaches.

Sexual appeals Sex is certainly one way to get the audience's attention, but it might not be best for all types of destinations (like family resorts). Typically when one thinks of sexual appeal ads, images of women in barely-there clothing come to mind and, from the billboards surrounding Las Vegas Boulevard, that conclusion is certainly warranted. But in the age of enlightenment, sexual appeals are also targeted at women. The Swiss Tourism Board identified a temporary tourist market – 'World Cup Widows' – during the Summer 2006 matches. In order to reach these 'desperate housewives' they employed a television campaign with a sultry voiceover saying 'Dear girls, why not escape this summer's World Cup to a country where men spend less time on football, and more time on you?' The ads featured images of hunky Swiss men – a farmhand, a lumberjack, a ferryman and a mountain climber – doing 'manly' things as they gazed into the camera. The ad ended with Mr. Switzerland 2005 milking a cow. The World Cup was being hosted by Germany, so the Swiss were primarily targeting females in Germany and its neighbors, France and Italy. The campaign got a lot of attention both from the targeted females as well as the press for employing such an innovative approach (Wentz, 2006).

Mood or Image More and more destinations, hotels, and restaurants are recognizing they have to do more than offer the desired product attributes to potential customers – they need to sell them the overall experience offered. For example, Starwood's W Hotel positioned itself as offering a clean, modern, sleek cutting edge environment and its advertising conveys this by featuring images of lobbies that appear lifted from an avant gard decorating guide. The W brand was launched in 1998 as a boutique hotel apart from the mass of comfortable yet similar big-city business hotels. As the brand evolved, so did the advertising. Guy Hensley, W's Vice President of Operations, says regarding the advertising: 'It gives you a sense of what the experience is. And that's what we're selling: the experience.' (Goetzl, 2000a).

Comparative Advertising The traditional comparative advertising directly compares product A to product B. Typically it is employed by the new or lower market share brand, which hopes to create an association as being similar to or better than the leader brand. The Avis campaign 'We try harder' is an implicit comparison to the leader in that category, Hertz. Researchers dispute the effectiveness of using comparatives: On one hand, they can force customers to make an association between brands; on the other hand, featuring the competitor's brand in your advertising provides them free exposure, and some say, any publicity is good publicity (Braun-LaTour and LaTour, 2004).

Iconic or Personality Ads In order to make an intangible brand or product more relatable to customers, some marketers have attempted to humanize their product by creating characters or icons for the brand (and destinations do this as well; see Ekinci and Hosany, 2006). Consider Charlie the Tuna, the Chevron car with the humanized front end, or the Geico gecko. VisitLondon found this to be an effective strategy when launching its advertising campaign in Japan. The character was a white rabbit based loosely on the Mad Hatter in Lewis Carroll's Alice in Wonderland and was nicknamed Usagi – the Japanese word for rabbit. The rabbit is seen in the campaign as acting as a tour guide of London and has the tagline 'Wonder London' (*Marketing Week*, 2006).

Animation Wienerschnitzel is aired an animated TV spot with talking taste buds in a campaign dubbed 'Pushing the Boundaries of Taste,' designed to appeal to 'flavor cravers' and reinforce the chain's positioning as a leader in offering new tastes, according to Vice President of Marketing Tom Amberger. The campaign marks the first time in about 40 years that the 353-unit hot dog chain has aired an entirely animated TV spot. The chain's longstanding ad character, called the Delicious One, is animated but appears in live-action spots. Animation is a great way to differentiate a spot from the rest of the commercials. It is also a great way to appeal to a younger audience (Cebrynski, 2006).

Testimonial There is no better selling point than someone (similar to the customer) reporting back on the positive experience he or she had at a given destination. Word-of-mouth can be a powerful influence for hospitality marketers. Testimonial ads try to work off this positive effect by featuring customers describing their stay or experience, 'in their own words'. (Reinartz, 1996).

Rational or informative advertising This often takes the role of educating customers about the product offering. Culver's frozen custard felt it needed to educate customers about how its product was different from ice cream and, thus, the company employed an educational advertising campaign. Through research it was found that many people knew about their sandwiches but were unaware of their frozen desserts, and, outside the Midwest, people did not know what frozen custard was. The new ads were designed to position Culver's frozen custard desserts as better tasting than other chains' soft-serve ice cream. One of their ads opens on a driver in an ice cream truck, which is rammed from behind by Culver's concrete mixer truck. 'Ice cream has met its match' is heard in the voiceover narration, and then it describes the product as 'better than ice cream' (Frumkin, 2006).

Reminder A reminder ad is targeted toward customers who have previously had an experience at the establishment and 'reminds' them of why they should revisit. Chik-Fil-A's 'Eat Mor Chikin' is a classic campaign showing cows with signs pleading with customers to eat chicken over meat. Variations of the campaign have been running for over 10 years. Big Boy restaurants is using this type of strategy in its advertising that features the Big Boy statue in a road trip. In one scene the statue is wearing a camera dangling from his neck. In another the statue is standing in front of a sign that reads, 'Bob's Las Vegas.' The various shots are accompanied by a remake of 'He's Sure the Boy I Love,' which The Crystals performed in 1962. It was part of the company's 70th anniversary celebration and celebrates the longevity of the brand (Cebrzynski, 2006).

Nostalgia A nostalgia ad is one that features images or words associated with one's childhood or adolescence. Through these images, advertisers hope to associate their service offering with the positive emotion evoked through activating the customer's childhood memories. This technique might be particularly effective for targeting young parents who want to provide their own children with the same type of experiences they have had as a child. Family destinations or restaurants might find this technique effective.

Slice of life Las Vegas Convention and Visitor Association's (LVCVA) 'What happens in Vegas, stays in Vegas . . . ' is fast becoming a classic 'slice of life' advertisement for sin city. The campaign began in 2003 with several ads featuring the 'darker side' of Vegas such as a Shriner who goes missing. The ads have evolved since then, featuring a variety of scenarios including people returning home on an airplane, some drinking tons of water to compensate for the drinking and others with a permanent smile on their face recollecting their weekend trysts. The 2006 campaign takes the 'What happens . . . ' theme a bit further by providing visitors with 'alibis.' For instance, one ad features a guy running into a woman friend at the supermarket

who asks where he has been. 'You know . . . . . I've been around . . . .
I was in Vegas,' he answers. 'What did you do there?' 'I ate. Went to
restaurants. Bradley Ogden, Delmonico. I'm a . . . bit of a "foodie." '
His delivery is underscored by views of his shopping car full of
soda pop, cheese puffs, spray cheese, cupcakes and Popsicles. Then
the 'Our World-class Dining' appears on-screen followed by 'Can be
your alibi.' The slice-of-life ads can be effective because they show
people in the process of experiencing a destination or showing some
of the product benefits in action. As in the Vegas spot, they also can
be humorous and very catching (Garfield, 2006).

Celebrity Spokespeople Messages delivered by attractive or well-known
celebrity sources achieve higher awareness and recall than other
types of messages. Advertisers often use celebrities as spokespeople
for their brand. For example, Air Canada hoped that Celine Dion's
well-known voice and association to Canada might help the airline.
Air Canada teamed up with the Canadian Tourism Commission
(CTC) to attract US travelers, committing $35.5 million over 3 years.
The campaign features Celine Dion singing 'You and I . . . were
meant to fly.' Dion doesn't appear in the spots, which feature the outline of an airline's windows imposed on scenes of people outdoors
running for a bus or canoeing. CTC Chairman Charles Lapointe said,
'We feel the ad campaign will draw huge attention to Canada and
the airline, because Celine Dion means Canada' (Chiasson, 2004).

Germany meanwhile tried to lure international investors with a
campaign featuring supermodel Claudia Schiffer. Outdoor ads were
placed in London, Tokyo, and New York. One running in London
featured Schiffer with copy: 'Trautman, Hamann and Lehmann –
we are world leaders in export,' a reference to the three German
soccer players who have joined English teams. 'Claudia represents
Germany not only with renowned characteristics like quality and
thoroughness, she also conveys a likable and attractive image of
Germany,' said Gerhar Maier, CEO of Invest in Germany. The full-
size ads appearing in the subway were also likely to be very much
noticed (Mussey and Went, 2006).

Decision 4: Media scheduling

Other than the design of advertising messages themselves, the issue
of how to best schedule advertising delivery is perhaps one of the
most important and practical issues facing advertisers (Longman, 1997).
Research has shown that the same ad campaign can lead to very
different levels of customer memory depending on how it is scheduled (Zielske and Henry, 1980). The two main strategies involve either
flighting (concentrating ads together in a relatively short period of time)

or distributing the ads evenly in a more continuous fashion. Those who support a flighting strategy believe that the ads will receive more attention if grouped together, whereas those who support a more continuous strategy believe that customers need to be continuously reminded of the brand. Both strategies support the view that advertising needs repetition to be effective.

Since the very beginning of advertising practice, a major goal of marketers has been to get customers to remember the brand's name. Repeating advertising exposures is a common strategy to reach that goal. Recall of a brand's name is important because first-remembered brands tend to be the most popular, and customers may infer desirability and even superiority from the ease of recall (Singh et al., 1994). More theoretical research on advertising finds that repeated exposures can improve brand memory, strengthen an association between a brand name and product benefit, enhance attitudinal response, and influence behavior by attempting to make the advertised brand part of the customers' consideration set (Kent and Allen, 1994).

Although the effects of repeating advertising exposures are ubiquitous in both practice and academia, there is relatively little understanding of the process by which the subsequent advertising is processed which leads to the memory enhancement. Herbert Krugman's three-exposure hypothesis, which is based on more intuition than empirical data, remains the driving force in media scheduling (Krugman, 1972). This hypothesis says that the first exposure causes the customer response, 'what is it?' and the second exposure causes the response, 'what of it?' and the third and additional exposures serve as a reminder of the previously learned information. Despite the fact that this hypothesis is neither theoretically grounded nor practically supported, most media schedulers have used Krugman's three exposure hypothesis to provide guidance on how many exposures need to be scheduled during any one advertising period – and usually that results in scheduling at least three exposures during a typical four week period. Advertisers have been told that they are wasting their money if they cannot afford that minimum frequency.

Erwin Ephron, a New York media specialist, has been quite vocal in his opposition to Krugman's hypothesis, saying that following it leads to inappropriate allocations of advertising dollars. He has proposed a 'shelf space' model of advertising. In contrast to Krugman's view that advertising should 'teach' customers about the brand, this model views the role of advertising as reminding, reinforcing, or evoking earlier messages (Ephron, 1995).

Regardless of what theoretical view one happens to take about media scheduling, the bottom line is that advertising needs to be seen more than once to have an effect on customers. The different exposures can work together resulting in creative scheduling; for instance, one could run a long introductory ad for several weeks and then replace it with 15-second spots to reinforce the memory (and cut costs). Or within a magazine, run a short headline ad in the first few pages to provoke interest and, later in the magazine, run a longer ad that results in more attention because of the earlier exposure. In the case of the LVCVA campaign, the advertising agency was able to work off customers' previous knowledge of the 'What happens in Vegas stays in Vegas. . .' campaign with the newer 'alibi' spots, which are thematically similar but introduce new elements (like fine dining) to the messages. Research is needed to determine the optimal scheduling for a given hospitality organization.

Advertising research

Research can help hospitality managers with the four major decisions they will make for their advertising campaign. This research can be both informal and formal. For example, customer feedback cards might indicate an aspect of the hotel that customers really enjoyed, and were not aware of before, and that could be highlighted in a campaign. Or sales data might indicate the best timing for scheduling an advertising campaign. For example, in Las Vegas the Strip properties are normally at 95% or more occupancy except for a few weeks in the summer when temperatures reach 120 °F. During those weeks, the properties generally drop their prices and advertise to the local market as a means to fill their rooms. Scanning what the competitors are doing and finding a unique 'niche' are also important. For example, in a recent *New York Times* travel special issue featuring the United States, the tourism ads for Maine, New Hampshire, etc. all looked strikingly similar: featuring pretty pictures and touting the state's scenery. While these might be selling points for the states, there wasn't a distinctive feel or approach taken. Sometimes, doing the opposite of what everyone else is doing is a way to attract attention.

In advertising research, a lot of attention is given to the measurement of advertising effectiveness and media channel choice. Most advertising agencies will have media planners who are equipped with research regarding the reach and frequency of different media outlets and can assist the hospitality marketer in putting together a media mix that most effectively targets his or her market. Where the hospitality marketer might seek some additional research is with construction of the advertising message. Focus groups or in-depth interviews can be used to assess if the message is well-received by the target market (and if it is communicating the intended message). Research can also be conducted following a new campaign to determine if it is effective. An example would be follow-up calls in the market where the campaign aired, to measure recall and recognition rates among target customers.

Message evaluation and selection

Often, the best advertising message is based on research. In 2000, Hilton Hotel's Doubletree line launched a $15 million print advertising effort to position it as the welcoming, unpretentious option within the upscale tier. This campaign grew out of customer research Doubletree did with agency FCB Worldwide, where the brand was found to have a 'more homey' feel than other brands. One execution grew almost verbatim from the research: one female research participant said Doubletree was the kind of place where she might walk down the hall to get ice from the machine, in her robe, with wet hair, 'that would never happen at a Hilton.' The ad derived from that shows a woman en route, wearing a robe, with a towel wrapped around her head (Goetzl, 2000b).

Sometimes, the advertising can really miss the mark. This is more likely to occur when advertising crosses different cultures. There are many marketing misses that have occurred because of inappropriate knowledge of the language, such as Chevrolet's Nova being marketed in Mexico (no va in Spanish means 'doesn't go') or Pepsi's Come Alive campaign which, when translated into Chinese, became 'bring your ancestors back from the dead' (Linen, 1991).

These cultural differences are sometimes more than language barriers, however. Consider Tourism Australia's campaign with the tagline 'So where the bloody hell are you?' which is a typical Aussie phrase but holds little relevance to its target markets. The Canadian Broadcasting Corporation imposed restrictions on airing the ad in family programming, and family groups in the United States complained about the language. In Japan people were confused about the use of the tagline. In Australia, though, people were adamant over keeping the language as is, arguing it represented their country well. The campaign got a lot of attention and some claim that such publicity speaks of its effectiveness. Others wonder whether the ad effectively communicated Australia's benefits beyond its own country's borders (Murphy, 2006). Testing the message content prior to launching might have avoided some of the problems faced by this Australian campaign.

Measuring effectiveness

After spending money on an advertising campaign, a natural managerial question is, 'Did it work?' Measures of effectiveness depend on the original goal of the campaign. For instance, if the campaign's goal was to increase awareness of the destination, then measuring the target market's awareness before and after the campaign would be appropriate. Other times, managers might be interested in whether or not their advertising is remembered, and they might employ day-after phone calls to the target market to ask them to recall ads seen the previous night and/or recognize the brands that they might have been exposed to. However, most hospitality marketers are interested in changing people's behavior. The marketing literature is full of examples demonstrating that advertising recall and recognition are often not correlated with behavior.

In tourism research, evaluating the effectiveness of a given promotional message has focused largely on the extent to which it 'stimulates' visits to a particular destination. Conversion studies have been a popular approach employed by state and regional tourism organizations. This approach focuses on evaluating potential tourists' response to advertising campaigns by considering their destination awareness, visitation, and visitor expenditure. This approach, however, has been criticized because it does not take into account how the tourist actually makes a decision and does not provide much insight as to how a given campaign will fare, nor does it consider longer-term effects of the advertising (Kim et al., 2005).

Most managers want to see an immediate impact of their advertising dollars. However, such a short-term approach may not capture some of the longer run effects of a campaign (Braun-LaTour and LaTour, 2004). Web campaigns, for instance, have usually been measured by their ability to have click-throughs lead directly to purchase. Continental Airlines found in a study with the ad-serving firm Double-click that, rather than acting right away by clicking through on an ad, customers bought tickets on Continental.com up to a month after they saw an ad. They found that 67.5% of sales conversions were attributed to online ads and that the highest point of sales was two weeks after the ad was seen (Oser, 2004). For campaigns focusing on improving or changing a property's image, the results may be even more long-term. Too often companies change an image strategy before it has an opportunity to reap the desired benefits.

Public relations

Hilton International's definition of PR is: 'The process by which we create a positive image and customer preference through third-party endorsement' (cf. Kotler et al., 2003). Until recently, PR was under-utilized by hospitality marketers. But following the tragic events of 9/11, the SARS epidemic, and the Iraqi war, all of which greatly reduced tourism, the importance of PR has increased, as evidenced by the large number of academic publications addressing this issue in the period 2003–2006. For instance, destination managers found that following such crises travelers respond better to information from third parties because it appears more "genuine" (Kotler et al., 2003). PR is a process rather than a single technique. Managers can either take a proactive or reactive approach to this process (Shimp, 2000). A proactive approach uses the PR tools such as news events, publications, community relations, and other PR techniques as a means to distinguish the organization in the marketplace. A reactive strategy involves waiting for a crisis to happen and then responding to that situation. However, even a crisis, according to some public relation managers, can be thought of as an opportunity, if handled correctly.

The output of a PR campaign, in contrast to an advertising campaign, is not paid for. That does not mean that PR is free. Companies need to employ personnel to handle media relations. That can mean distributing news releases when an event is taking place or after a reconstruction or property change. It can also mean entertaining and covering the costs of media, e.g., travel writers, in order to secure a positive write up or story in their outlet.

Some of the major promotional activities include:

- *Publications* such as brochures or company background-material, which can be made available on the organization's website.
- *Customized events* Free-to-the-press events to promote a new aspect of the organization. For example, the Stratosphere had an invitation-only party for the press with its opening of Valentine Lounge. The event was catered, with top-shelf alcohol and live music, with the purpose of educating the media and press in Las Vegas about the new venue.
- *Cause-related marketing* An event can also be sponsored by an organization for a non-profit or charitable organization in order to build good will toward the sponsoring organization. As example, Dominos Pizza teamed up with Easter Seals in a promotional effort. Twenty-eight million Domino's box tops offered customers a coupon worth up to $10 toward the purchase of a computer game called SimCity. When redeeming the coupons, customers were required to send $5 donations to Easter Seals (Howard, 1999).
- *Publicity* Publicity is a major tool of PR. Like advertising, its goal is to enhance brand awareness and image by forging strong and favorable associations. Companies obtain publicity via news releases, press conferences, and other types of information dissemination. Executive-statement releases are news releases quoting CEOs and other corporate executives that can address issues such as industry trends, views on the economy, company strategies, etc. and can appear as 'news.'
- *Sponsorship marketing* Sponsorship involves assisting, with money, people, or equipment, another organization for the purpose of achieving communication objectives. Sponsorship can involve anything from underwriting an entire event to smaller scale contributions such as paying for tote bags and badge holders, paying for a key note speaker, or covering coffee/refreshment breaks at a conference (Suh et al., 2004).

PR departments are more visible at times of crises. During those times they can either assist in maintaining the destination or property image in the minds of the target customer, or, if mismanaged, cause fear and uneasiness among customers.

Crisis management

A crisis is a major, unpredictable event that threatens to harm the organization. Communication strategies are integral to managing the negative influence of the crisis. Traditionally, crisis management gurus have focused on what companies should do during a crisis, such as being visible to the customer, providing straightforward information, and being internally consistent with that information (*Harvard Business Essentials: Crisis Management*, 2004). For example, a good response to a crisis situation was how the Pepsi company handled the syringe/tampering hoax. Several customers had reported that they had bought a can of Diet Pepsi that contained a syringe. Pepsi officials were confident that the reports were false and responded by showing a video of the Pepsi bottling process, which was seen by 187 million viewers. The video demonstrated that it was nearly impossible for something to be added at the bottling plant, especially something as large as a syringe. The FDA Commissioner was brought on-board and he claimed that Pepsi products were 99.9% safe and warned customers of the penalties for making false claims. Several days later, a woman was caught on a surveillance camera inserting a syringe into her can of Diet Pepsi to make her claim of a tampered product. That video was broadcast immediately, with the FDA Commissioner again stating his belief in the safety of the Pepsi product. But Pepsi did not stop there. Pepsi ran a nationwide full-page print ad to assuage any residual customer fears. That ad read: 'Pepsi is pleased to announce . . . nothing' (Khermouch, 1993; Magiera, 1993).

Sometimes academics and practitioners can learn about crisis management techniques by looking at a situation that went wrong. In 2005, Las Vegas native Anna Ayala reported that she found a fingertip in her chili, at a San Jose Wendy's restaurant. That incident generated national and international media attention, yet Wendy's corporate reaction to the incident was extremely low-key. It is estimated the chain lost over 2.5 million dollars in sales immediately after the incident (and there were probably more sales lost after that). After the incident was resolved, and it was found that Ayala tainted the chili herself, Wendy's attempted a price promotion in order to help its stores rebound. The advertising featured a 'Free Frosty' promotion. Research by Braun-LaTour et al. (2006) looked at whether or not such a rational approach was the best strategy for the chain to take post-crisis. They found that a nostalgic ad resulted in more favorable feelings and customers reporting a likelihood of revisiting (and ordering the chili) than did the price promotion advertising. In fact, some believed that the price promotion meant that the chain was admitting to some mistake. This study underscores the importance of establishing (and re-establishing) an emotional bond with customers (Braun-LaTour et al., 2006).

The Pepsi's handling of its crisis and the Wendy's mismanagement illustrates some basic rules for crisis management:

1. *Define the problem and scope:* In Pepsi's case, what is the likelihood that it was product tampering? How much is at risk? In Pepsi's case, people were beginning to boycott the product, so the risk was huge. How much time do you have to respond? Pepsi acted immediately and was able to save a huge decline in sales (losing only 2% during the crisis), in comparison to Wendy's that did not respond in a timely fashion and eventually lost millions.

Some crises can be averted by proactive management. For instance, consider the case of Popeye's Chicken. This company has prepared a campaign dubbed '360° Safe,' which was developed to allay customers' fears of avian flu in the United States. Popeyes, which franchises 334 restaurants abroad, had some experience addressing fears of avian flu in Jordan and Indonesia, where human cases of the virus were recorded. The message delivered in those two countries was designed to let both customers and employees know that properly cooked chicken is safe to eat. The company's message was that its quality control was not a response to avian flu, but rather something that the company does every day. As with the Pepsi video, Popeye's believed informing customers about its safe food practices would help avert a potential crisis (Spielberg, 2006). The company also demonstrates a best practice of crisis management: using past problems or situations to develop proactive strategies.

2. *Set priorities for action*: Locate the areas of greatest danger or vulnerability and the areas where the most effective steps can be taken. For example, after the tsunami hit Maldives, the Four Seasons staff's first priority was making sure its guests and staff were safe before they began damage control (*Wall Street Journal*, 2004).

3. *Set the crisis team:* In case of a crisis it is appropriate for the top leader of the company to take charge. In Wendy's case a spokesperson for the company reacted to the tampering and did not present the image that Wendy's top personnel were in control of the situation. Such personal leadership during a crisis is also a way of signaling the company's values – that avoiding harm to the public, as in the Pepsi crisis, is the most important thing a leader can do.

4. *Communication during the crisis:* Crises generate feelings of anxiety and uncertainty among the organization's various members and if crisis communication is not handled appropriately, rumors can fly. It is

therefore important that the organization has a means to disseminate accurate and timely information. Such communication is enhanced if a PR strategy is already in place. Communication should address the 'cognitive' needs of the customers, staff, and other stakeholders, such as providing concrete information about the status of the crisis. However, recognizing the emotional side of things is important as well (*Harvard Business Essentials: Crisis Management*, 2004). For example, in a report, following 9/11, on destination managers most recognized the importance of being more sensitive to the emotional and psychological state of travelers, opting for softer, subtler, and less self-promotional messages (Fall, 2004).

5. *Recovery after a crisis:* What happens to a company-in-crisis after the issue has seemingly been resolved can be equally, if not more, important in restoring the brand's reputation. The commonly held view is that it is best not to advertise after a crisis, and give customers time to 'forget' the situation. Northwest Airlines followed this strategy, choosing not to publicly apologize for its 'imprisoning' of airline passengers during a 1999 snowstorm in Detroit, and concentrating on local advertising efforts to restore its image (Hallowell, 1998). However, the Pepsi situation shows that post-crisis reassurance to customers via advertising is an important part of crisis management.

The tourism industry is particularly sensitive to the impact crises can have on it. Hong Kong tried to lure tourists back after the SARS scare, noticing a severe drop in the number of US travelers. Hong Kong launched a $58 million global campaign featuring film star Jackie Chan, using the tagline 'Live it, Love it.' Timing was critical for this campaign; not only had SARS scared many tourists off, but there also were problems with perceptions regarding the Chinese take-over as well as increased competition from places like Beijing (home to the 2008 Summer Olympics). The television ad featured breathtaking shots of Hong Kong, such as the harbor and skyline, interspersed with phrases such as 'See it' and also images of culinary experiences, with phrases like 'Taste it.' The commercial ends by showing Jackie Chan directing a movie, and as a crowd gathers he invites one member to sit in his director's chair (Thomaselli and Madden, 2003). This is an excellent example of timing and strategy put together to solve a tourist destination's crisis situation.

Directions for future research

The majority of research on advertising, PR, and crisis management comes from the more traditional product-marketing literature. The hospitality and tourism industry can learn from this research, but needs to develop research programs to address its own particular needs. Several areas of research offer some exciting opportunities for tourism researchers.

Using newer psycho-physiological approaches to evaluate advertising response. Arousal underlies most response to advertising (including fear, humor, and sexual stimuli) and is a very complex phenomenon that should not be oversimplified. Therefore, as a starting point, hospitality managers need to measure dimensions of arousal response to their sponsored advertising communications as a mechanism of understanding how their message breaks through or fails to break through media clutter. A classic example is Las Vegas McCarran airport where highly arousing sensory stimulation hits arriving passengers from the moment they step off the plane and reaches a crescendo in baggage claim. So, what kind of message is best delivered to a visitor to that state? Are the many video billboards an effective way to gain customer attention, or have they reached a point of overload? But, of course, why should we stop there when modern brain-science has offered managers even deeper insights.

For instance, some advertisers are using PET scans and fMRI to see the customer's mind at work as they view the advertiser's commercials. It is being billed as the ultimate focus group, whereby advertisers can see whether the areas associated with emotion and encoding of new information are activated at the message presentation, or whether areas associated with withdrawal are active (Zaltman, 2003). These techniques bypass customers' rational thought processes and give advertisers an immediate view of their advertisement's potential effectiveness. However, the high costs, and privacy invasion perceived by customers may limit how much these measures are actually used in practice.

Depth interview methods. A more practical and useful method for tourism researchers to consider when designing or evaluating their message strategy may be depth interviews. The Zaltman Metaphor Elicitation Technique (ZMET), developed by Harvard Business Professor emeritus Gerald Zaltman, is based on how the mind works. The one-on-one interviews use pictures to probe customers' unconscious associations with a product or brand. Researchers used this method to better understand the value the Guggenheim museum added to tourists' perceptions of the Venetian casino mega resort. The revenue per square foot and other rational measures of effectiveness indicated that Guggenheim did not add substantial value. The ZMET interview data, however, demonstrated that the Guggenheim was an important part of the opulence of the resort and offered tourists a 'balance' to their indulgent vacation in Las Vegas. The images participants brought in for their interview could be used for the positioning of either the Venetian or Guggenheim in an image-based advertising campaign (Braun-LaTour et al., 2006).

Evaluating the effectiveness of various media and message executions. There are so many new media alternatives available today to the tourism marketer. More research needs to evaluate the effectiveness of these outlets. In addition, as tourism researchers reach beyond the more traditional rational, price, or image advertising approaches to embrace other creative execution opportunities, research needs to assess the effectiveness of their appeals on tourists. Little is known about the most effective scheduling of messages, either within or across different media. The measures used to gauge effectiveness should also broaden beyond the traditional conversion study to embrace newer, more effective methods (Law and Braun, 2000).

Evolving the model of experience framing. How can advertising and PR (and other marketing communications) be used to evolve the customers' experience? Researchers find that narrative communication styles and images are particularly important in setting expectations and encouraging remembering. Future research ought to also investigate the timing of communications (before/after experience) and how the coordination of marketing efforts can work together to enhance the experience offering. How well a communication effort 'frames' the customer experience may be best tested in experimental designs (Braun-LaTour et al., 2006). In this, those who see advertising or PR attempts can assess their experience compared to those who do not receive any information (control group).

Managing crises before they happen. There has been much attention, of late, as to how to best respond to a crisis. It is suggested that hospitality and tourism researchers take that knowledge and use it to explore how tourism can proactively confront future crises. For instance, the Popeye's example in this chapter is one way where a company has taken a past situation and used that knowledge to confront a potential future problem. Theoretical research should be augmented to address these sorts of proactive management issues.

Summary and conclusions

The purpose of this chapter was to discuss two types of non-personal communication: advertising and PR. Both are important in building and maintaining an organization's brand image. Advertising is more costly, but also more controllable by an organization. The traditional model of how advertising works was discussed and a newer Experience Framing model introduced. This chapter reviewed the four main advertising decisions a hospitality marketer has to make: setting communication objectives; evaluating and making a media selection; creating the message execution; and determining the media schedule.

In addition, the various ways advertising effectiveness is currently measured was presented. PR was discussed from both a proactive and reactive perspectives. Crisis management strategies were overviewed, with examples of Pepsi and Wendy's highlighted. The chapter ended with some suggestions for future research, focusing on research intended to provide more depth for hospitality marketers as they embark on devising their advertising and PR strategy in good times and in times of crises.

References

Beirne, M. (2004 December 6). Club Med to travel 'emotional' route. *Brandweek*, 45(44), 9.

Barry, T. E. (1987). The development of the hierarchy of effects: A historical perspective. *Current Issues and Research in Advertising*, 10(2), 251–295.

Berry, L. B., Carbone, L. P., and Haeckel, S. H. (2002). Managing the total customer experience. *MIT Sloan Management Review*, 43, 85+.

Bowman, J. (2005 February 1). Targeting a captive audience in the sky. *Media*, 24–25.

Braun, K. A. (1999). Post-experience advertising effects on consumer memory. *Journal of Consumer Research*, 25, 319–334.

Braun, K. A. and Zaltman, G. (1998). Backward framing: A theory of memory reconstruction. *Marketing Science Institute's Working Paper Series*, 98–109.

Braun-LaTour, K. A., Grinley, M., and Loftus, E. F. (2006), "Tourist Memory Distortion," *Journal of Travel Research*, 44(4), 360–367.

Braun-LaTour, K. A., Hendler, F., and Hendler, R. (2006). Digging deeper: Art museums in Las Vegas? *Annals of Tourism Research*, 33, 265–268.

Braun-LaTour, K. A. and LaTour, M. S. (2004). Assessing the long-term impact of a consistent advertising campaign on consumer memory. *Journal of Advertising*, 33, 49–61.

Braun-LaTour, K. A., LaTour, M. S., and Loftus, E. F. (2006). Is that a finger in my chili? Using affective advertising for post-crisis brand repair. *Cornell Hotel and Restaurant Administration Quarterly*, 47, 106–120.

Braun-LaTour, K. A., LaTour, M. S., Pickrell, J., and Loftus, E. F. (2004). How (and when) advertising can influence memory for consumer experience. *Journal of Advertising*, 33, 7–26

Braun-LaTour, K. A. and Zaltman, G. (2006). Memory change: An intimate measure of persuasion. *Journal of Advertising Research*, 46, 57–83.

Case, T. (2006 May 1). Hotel & travel. *Brandweek*, 47, SR24.

Cebrzynski, G. (2006 July 3). Chipotle, Wienerschnitzel, Culver's change ad strategies. *Nation's Restaurant News*, 40, 4+.

Chiasson, G. (2004 November 1). Celine wants you to fly Air Canada. *Advertising Age*, 75, 15+.

Deighton, J. (1984). The interaction of advertising and evidence. *Journal of Consumer Research*, 11, 763–770.

Deighton, J. and Schindler, R. M. (1988). Can advertising influence experience? *Psychology & Marketing*, 5, 103–115.

Ekinci, Y. and Hosany, S. (2006). Brand personality to tourist destinations. *Journal of Travel Research*, 45, 127–139.

Ephron, E. (1995). More weeks, less weight: The shelf space model of advertising. *Journal of Advertising Research*, 35, 18–23.

Fall, L. T. (2004). The increasing role of public relations as a crisis management function: An empirical examination of communication restrategising efforts among destination organization managers in the wake of 11th September, 2001. *Journal of Vacation Marketing*, 10, 238–252.

Frumkin, P. (2006 July 31). Taking new approach in advertising is not necessarily easy, but it's often necessary. *Nation's Restaurant News*, 40, 25.

Garfield, B. (2006 August 21). This time, Vegas tourism gets the credit it deserves. *Advertising Age*, 77, 25.

Goetzl, D. (2000a September 18). W hotel strategy. *Advertising Age*, 71, 13+.

Goetzl, D. (2000b October 16). Doubletree puts friendly face on upmarket hotel. *Advertising Age*, 71, 83+.

Gursoy, D. and McCleary, K. (2004). An integrative model of tourists' information search behavior. *Annals of Tourism Research*, 31, 353–373.

Hall, B. F. (2002). A new model for measuring advertising effectiveness. *Journal of Advertising Research*, 42, 23–31.

Hallowell, R. (1998). Northwest and the Detroit snowstorm. *Harvard Business School Case*, (July), item # 800053.

Hanlan, J. and Kelly, S. (2005). Image formation, information sources and an iconic Australian tourist destination. *Journal of Vacation Marketing*, 11, 163–177.

Harvard business essentials: Crisis management. (2004), Cambridge, MA: HBS Press.

Holbrook, M. B. and Batra, R. (1987). Assessing the role of emotions as mediators of consumer responses to advertising. *Journal of Consumer Research*, 14, 404–421.

Howard, T. (1999 January 11). Domino's links Easter seals to cd-rom. *Brandweek*, 10.

Hudson, S. and Ritchie, J. R. B. (2006). Promoting destinations via film tourism: An empirical identification of supporting marketing initiatives. *Journal of Travel Research*, 44, 387– 396.

Kent, R. J. and Allen, C. T. (1994). Competitive interference effects in consumer memory for advertising: The role of brand familiarity. *Journal of Marketing*, July, 97–105.

Kerstetter, D. and Cho, M. H. (2004). Prior knowledge, credibility and information search. *Annals of Tourism Research*, 31, 961–985.

Khermouch, G. (1993 June 21). Pepsi flack attack nips hoax in the bud. *Brandweek*, 34, 5.

Kim, D. Y., Hwang, Y. H., and Fesenmaier, D. F. (2005). Modeling tourism advertising effectiveness. *Journal of Travel Research*, 44, 42–49.

Kotler, P., Bowen, J., and Makens, J. (2003). *Marketing for hospitality and tourism* (3rd ed.). Upper Saddle River, NJ: Pearson.

Krugman, H. (1972), "Why Three Exposures May Be Enough," *Journal of Advertising Research*, 12(6), 11–14.

Linen, C. T. (1991). Marketing and the global economy. *Direct Marketing*, 53, 54–57.

Loda, M. D., Norman, W., and Backman, K. (2005). How potential tourists react to mass media marketing: Advertising versus publicity. *Journal of Travel and Tourism Marketing*, 18, 63–70.

Longman, K. A. (1997). If not effective frequency, then what? *Journal of Advertising Research*, 37, 44–51.

MacKay, K. (2005). Destination advertising: Age and format effects on memory. *Annals of Tourism Research*, 33, 7–24.

Madden, N. (2005 August 1). Northwest uses unusual ad platform. *Advertising Age*, 76, 10+.

Magiera, M. (1993 June 19). The Pepsi crisis: What went right. *Advertising Age*, 64, 14–15.

Michael, S. C. (2002 April). Undermarketed! Why some operators short themselves on advertising. *Cornell Hotel and Restaurant Administration Quarterly*, 64–71.

Murphy, J. (2006 May 5). Is 'bloody' push for Aussies or visitors? *Media*, 17.

Mussey, D. and Went, L. (2006 June 26). Germany taps Claudia to lure international investors. *Advertising Age*, 77, 18.

Oh, H., Kim, B. Y., and Shin, J. H. (2004). Hospitality and tourism marketing: Recent developments in research and future directions. *International Journal of Hospitality Management*, 23, 425–447.

Oser, K. (2004 July 26). Web ads get results weeks later. *Advertising Age*, 75, 18+.

Reinartz, R. D. (1996). Testimonial ads win loyalty and attract customers. *Bank Marketing*, 28, 25–30.

Ries, A. and Trout, J. (1986), quoted in Donadio, S. (1992), *The New York public library: Book of twentieth-century American quotations*, New York: Stonesong Press, 71.

Rosen, E. (2000). *The anatomy of buzz: How to create word-of-mouth marketing*. New York: Currency.

Schacter, D. S. (1996). *Searching for memory*. New York: BasicBooks.

Shimp, T. A. (2000). *Advertising promotion: Supplemental aspects of integrated marketing communications* (5th ed.). Orlando: The Dryden Press.

Singh, S. N., Mishra, S., Bendapudi, N., and Linville, D. (1994). Enhancing memory of television commercials through message spacing. *Journal of Marketing Research*, 31, 384–392.

Spielberg, S. (2006 June 5). Popeyes develops campaign to calm bird flu worries. *Nation's Restaurant News*, 40, 4+.

Strong, E. K., Jr. (1925). Theories of selling. *Journal of Applied Psychology*, 9, 75–86.

Suh, E., Love, C., and Bai, B. (2004). An examination of the impact of sponsorship on attendees' recognition of sponsors. *Journal of Convention and Event Tourism*, 6, 27–47.

Thomaselli, R. (2005 September 19). Chapter 11 won't bust airline budgets. *Advertising Age*, 76, 8+.

Thomaselli, R. and Madden, N. (2003 September 22). Hong Kong ads target tourists. *Advertising Age*; 74, 4+.

Tsunami batters Asia, claiming over 11,000 lives; waves hit coastal areas from Sumatra to Somalia; billions in aid needed. (2004 December 27). *Wall Street Journal*, (eastern edition), p. A.1.

Velotta, R. N. and Simpson, J. (2005). Wynn ad a prelude to resort's April opening. *Casino City Times*, accessed October 2006 at: http://www.casinocitytimes.com/news/article.cfm?contentID=148291.

VisitLondon Asian ad push uses rabbit icon. (2006 January 1). *Marketing Week*, p. 7.

Wall, E. A. and Berry, L. L. (2007). The combined effects of the physical environment and employee behavior on customer perception of restaurant service quality. *Cornell Hotel and Restaurant Administration Quarterly*. 48, 59–71.

Wentz, L. (2006 May 22). Switzerland targets 'World cup widows'. *Advertising Age*, 77, 16.

W heightens hip factor. (2006 September 1). *Lodging Hospitality*, 61(12), 10+.

Woodside, A. G. and Dubelaar, C. (2003). Increasing quality in measuring advertising effectiveness: A meta-analysis of question framing in conversion studies. *Journal of Advertising Research*, 43(1), 78–85.

Zaltman, G. (2003). *How customers think*. Cambridge, MA: Harvard Business School Press.

Zielske, H. A. and Henry, W. A. (1980). Remembering and forgetting television ads. *Journal of Advertising Research*, 20(2), 7.

CHAPTER 7

Distribution channels and e-commerce

Peter O'Connor

Introduction

Information technology can fulfill various roles in tourism, acting as 'a creator, protector, enhancer, focal point and/or destroyer of the tourism experience' (Stipanuk, 1993, p. 267). However, many people believe that its greatest impact has been the change it has caused in how tourism products and services are marketed and sold. Developments in technology have driven a revolution in tourism distribution channels, totally changing relationships between suppliers and intermediaries, and even the very structure of the distribution network itself. Suppliers, intermediaries, and consumers have all embraced the electronic world, with the result that tourism, in common with many other aspects of society, increasingly operates in a digital world (Buhalis, 1998).

A variety of different electronic systems have been developed to facilitate tourism distribution and these have dramatically affected the way in which tourism products are marketed, sold, and delivered (Connell and Reynolds, 1999). Before examining these effects, this chapter outlines how electronic distribution has developed within tourism to explain where we find ourselves today. The evolutionary path from manual systems to the closed Global Distribution Systems (GDS)-based systems to the open distribution network enabled by the Internet is explored. Current challenges, such as managing multiple simultaneous distribution channels, working with online intermediaries, and reacting to rapidly changing technology are also examined to help readers understand this highly complex environment. The absence of quality academic research on tourism distribution is highlighted, and suggestions are made as to why and how this deficiency should be addressed.

The importance of information

Information has been described as the lifeblood of the tourism industry, as, without it, the potential customer's incentive and ability to travel is severely limited (Wagner, 1991). In few other activities are the generation, collection, processing, communication, and use of information as important for day-to-day operations as in the tourism sector (Poon, 1993). Potential travelers need appropriate information before departing on a trip to help with planning and help them choose between different options, and also need access to accurate and detailed information during their visit, as the trend toward more independent travel increases (Preston and Trunkfield, 2006).

Certain characteristics of tourism heighten this dependence on information. Foremost among these is the intangibility of the tourism product; unlike manufactured goods, a travel experience cannot be inspected prior to purchase and therefore consumers are almost completely dependent on descriptions or representations when making a purchase decision (Middleton, 1994). Tourism's diversity is also important, as in many cases it is this heterogeneity that makes such a product attractive in the first place. Tourism products are also fixed geographically, meaning that the customer cannot pre-test the product and must travel – in effect, consume the product – in order to experience what they are buying (Lewis et al., 1995). These characteristics combine to make consumers highly dependent upon accurate information to gain an indirect sense of a tourism product's qualities and to help differentiate between competing products (Go and Pine, 1995). In addition, tourism products are rarely bought in isolation, and 'the endless combinations and permutations of alternative travel routes, transportation modes, time and lodging accommodation make travel decisions difficult even for the initiated', further increasing the need for appropriate information to aid in the decision-making process (Kaven, 1994, p.116).

Recent changes in social life heightened the need for information (Vaughan et al., 1999). In today's world, time has become a scarce commodity and thus leisure travel represents an important emotional investment that cannot be easily replaced if something goes wrong. As a result, annual holidays or even weekend breaks have become increasingly associated with risk. Planning the simplest trip means choosing among a bewildering array of options and running a risk of making an inappropriate choice. As Buhalis (1997) points out '*the greater the degree of perceived risk in a pre-purchase context, the greater the consumer propensity to seek information about the product.*'. Therefore, to minimize such risk, consumers seek out appropriate information to minimize the gap between their expectations and their subsequent experience.

Consumers have also become more knowledgeable and demanding. Having grown up comfortably with foreign travel through package holidays in their formative years, and with exposure to broader horizons as a result of television and increased education, many want more than the sun, sea, and sangria experience, and are increasingly comfortable organizing it for themselves (Poon, 1994). Travel frequency has increased, and instead of (or frequently in addition to) an annual summer vacation, these 'new leisure travellers' take multiple short breaks throughout the year, often organized independently and at short lead-times (Preston and Trunkfield, 2006). To facilitate such customers, the fast, efficient exchange of information between the supplier and the customer (or their agent) is essential.

Consumers have traditionally sourced travel information in a variety of ways. These include either directly from tourism suppliers such as hotels, airlines and car hire companies, or through intermediaries such as travel agents and tour operators, who act as information brokers making the connection between customer and supplier (Kotler et al., 1996). The latter have traditionally serviced traveler's information needs in one of two ways: either by distributing print-based promotional materials or through personal contact (Dube and Renaghan, 2000). Print-based materials, such as brochures, catalogues, and travel trade manuals, suffer from several limitations. Print is a static, one-dimensional medium that is limited in its capacity to adequately communicate the intricacies of the multi-sensory tourism experience (Middleton, 1994). In addition, developing print-based media is costly and time consuming, with the resulting material becoming outdated quickly. Space limitations also mean that choices must be made in terms of content, potentially limiting the effectiveness of the selling message.

Communicating information personally is more effective, as the information provided to potential customers can be more closely matched to their needs. However, this approach is also problematic. Tourism is the ultimate dispersed industry, with potential clients coming from everywhere and wanting to go everywhere. Each has very different information needs. With millions of individualistic purchasers and thousands of heterogeneous tourism experiences, the permutations of information expand to a fearsome level – far above the level with which a typical travel advisor could be expected to be familiar, irrespective of their level of training or expertise. Developments in information technology have provided a solution to this 'knowledge gap' (Buhalis, 2000).

The origins of travel e-commerce

Go and Pine (1995, p.307) define a channel of distribution as one that provides 'sufficient information to the right people at the right time and in the right place to allow a purchase decision to be made, and provides a mechanism where the consumer can purchase the required product.'

This viewpoint is supported by a variety of authors (e.g. Bitner and Blooms 1982; Middleton 1994; Buhalis 2000; O'Connor and Frew, 2003) who support the argument that the primary purposes of distribution channels within tourism are to provide information for prospective purchasers (be they end consumers or intermediaries) as well as to establish some mechanism to enable consumers to make, confirm, and pay for reservations.

The highly perishable nature of the tourism product makes efficient and effective distribution particularly important, as any unsold item cannot be stored and subsequently consumed at a later date. Thus, selling every airline seat, hotel room, cruise-berth, or excursion seat every night at an optimum price is key to profitability. As was discussed above, most tourism suppliers make use of intermediaries such as travel agents and tour operators, but increased emphasis is being placed on direct sales using electronic channels (Tse, 2003). Electronic systems have many advantages over their traditional, labor-intensive counterparts. They have few capacity limitations, offer infinitely more geographical reach, have a low marginal cost, and are more easily able to incorporate dynamic data such as room inventory/rates (O'Connor, 1999). Furthermore, while traditional distribution channels have to be used in pairs – i.e., combining an advertising medium (e.g., brochures or guidebooks) with an interactive medium (e.g., a telesales agent or a travel agent) – to complete the transaction, electronic systems can potentially fulfill both roles and allow travelers to make reservations for themselves in a fraction of the time, cost, and inconvenience involved in traditional methods (Chung and Law, 2003). These benefits prompted widespread adoption of electronic systems throughout the tourism value chain, and thus have changed the way in which travel goods and services are sold . . . forever!

Electronic distribution in tourism has its origins in the travel-agent-focused GDSs. Originally conceived by the airlines as internal inventory control systems in the late 1960s, the GDSs subsequently broadened their scope by incorporating travel products, in addition to airline seats, and by providing direct access to travel agents to their systems (Karcher, 1995). From a travel agent perspective, processing reservations manually is a time-consuming, labour-intensive, and, therefore, costly process. Using a computerized system allow them to see real-time availability and pricing information, and to make instant bookings, making the entire searching/booking process faster, cheaper, and more efficient. De-regulation of the airline sector in the United States in the 1970s accelerated GDS adoption, as a computerized system became, to a large extent, essential to help untangle the vastly increased number of flight and fare options (Hitchins, 1991). At the same time, most airline reservation systems began cross-selling complementary travel products, including hotel accommodation, car hire, cruises, rail tickets and virtually every other travel product, both to increase service levels to their travel-agent customers and to help offset the high costs of running the system. This ultimately resulted in the one-stop-travel-shops that we know today as Global Distribution Systems or GDSs (Knowles and Garland, 1994). Subsequent mergers and acquisition have resulted in four main companies (Amadeus, Galileo, WorldSpan, and Sabre) dominating the sector. GDSs today are used by approximately 95% of travel agencies worldwide, and many of the major travel agency chains will no longer make a booking for a client unless it can be processed electronically (HEDNA, 1997). This makes representation on the major GDSs essential for any tourism company wishing to sell through the travel-agent community (Bennett, 1993).

The GDSs are not without their limitations. First, they service a small (although influential) user base – in effect, just travel agents. Although consumers can now access the systems over the Internet, their structure and methods of operations still focus primarily on the needs of travel agents, resulting in complex procedures, cryptic codes, and unintelligible data. A further problem is the lack of flexibility in terms of the data displayed to the user. While less of a problem in the United States where hospitality chains predominate, the majority of tourism products are heterogeneous, not standardized, and relatively complex. Indeed, in many cases it is these characteristics that make them attractive to travelers, in the first place (Bennett, 1996). However, as the GDSs were designed to distribute the more homogeneous airline product, the structure of their databases cannot cope with the depth and diversity of data needed to effectively market such diverse tourism products (Emmer et al., 1993). Given their size, complexity and the fact that they rely on technology that is over 30 years old, changing these databases to incorporate more complex requirements is a nearly impossible task.

In response to this problem, many tourism companies have developed their own reservation systems (known as central reservation systems (CRS)) with more appropriate database structures, and have subsequently linked them electronically to the GDSs for access to the travel agent market (McGuffie, 1994). However, developing and maintaining a reservation system is relatively expensive, with both high upfront capital costs and substantial running and transaction costs. As a result, many companies outsource their electronic distribution to third-party providers. For example, in the hotel sector, representation companies have emerged to provide distribution services to smaller non-chain hotels, providing them with CRS capabilities and connecting them to the GDS market (Morrison et al., 1999). Destination Management Systems, which concentrate on distributing tourism products of particularly smaller and independent tourism suppliers from a distinct geographical region, could be regarded as providing similar services (Pollock, 1995). However, with the exception in a small number of European countries, the impact of destination management systems has been relatively minimal, as most have failed to evolve beyond the experimental stage into full commercial systems (Frew and O'Connor, 1999).

The arrival of the e-commerce

Until the early 1990s, electronic channels of distribution in tourism were as described above – a cozy status quo where the operators of electronic systems cooperated, rather than competed, with each other. Relationships were effectively linear and participants had a mutually beneficial role to play (Anderson Consulting, 1998). From the perspective of the supplier, electronic channels of distribution were effective in that they generated business, but at the same time were unpopular in that they were expensive to develop and use. Between 1993 and 1997, commissions and other reservation costs increased by approximately 117%, prompting many suppliers to seek alternative ways of distributing their product (Waller, 1999). During this period, one of the most revolutionary technological developments of all time – the Internet – became available for public and commercial use. The widespread consumer adoption of the World Wide Web – one of the key services enabled by the Internet – provided an outstanding opportunity for suppliers to bypass the multiple intermediaries controlling electronic distribution and reach out to transact business directly with the customer (Smith and Jenner, 1998).

Tourism suppliers were quick to exploit the opportunity presented by the Web, in part because of the existing high level of computerization in airlines and travel agencies. As a commercial medium the Web is ideal, facilitating direct access to customers with a high propensity to travel, as well as potentially offering major savings, as the cost of processing voice calls and intermediary commission can be eliminated (Jeong and Lambert, 1999). These benefits prompted what Buhalis (2000b) described as 'a radical change in the operation, distribution and structure of the tourism industry.' The majority of tourism suppliers began distributing over the medium (Pusateri and Manno, 1998) and it had a profound effect on the way in which travel products were being marketed, distributed, sold, and delivered (Williams and Palmer, 1999).

Perhaps the most significant effect was the shake up that it prompted in channel structure. While the previous GDS-based network had been linear, closed, and cooperative, Web-based distribution was open, competitive, and extremely confusing! In addition to cooperating with each other as they did in the past, most participants in the travel distribution chain began directly competing with each other by developing consumer-orientated websites with provision of information and booking facilities (Connolly et al., 1998). The situation is well summarized by Dombey (1998, p. 3) as 'little short of a technological stampede. Up and down the traditional distribution chain . . . providers are working feverishly to re-engineer their travel systems . . . to bypass both the GDS and the travel agent and create a direct link with the customer.' In essence, the level of mutual dependence between participants has decreased as each tried to circumnavigate intermediaries lower down on the distribution chain and transact business directly with the customer (Jarvela and Loikkanen, 1999).

Paradoxically, in addition to more competition, there was also more cooperation – a phenomenon which Werthner and Klein (1999) dubbed 'coopetition!' As will be discussed, the more successful online travel sites offer multiple products (air, hotel, car, etc) from multiple vendors, as their key attraction (Preston and Trunkfield, 2006). To be successful, they need to be full-service and provide the ability to research and purchase an entire trip on-line. In order to do this, they need the detailed content and access to reservation facilities that they can only get by cooperating with other distribution providers (Wade and Raffour, 2000). Non-exclusive virtual alliances were thus formed, with companies joining to develop new synergistic relationships (Dale, 2003). Dale maintains that establishing such virtual clusters leads to 'synergistic strategic value', with each partner reciprocally and mutually benefiting from the relationship, generating inimitable and non-substitutable network resources. For example, the GDS, in addition to facilitating travel agent bookings, also began providing the reservation engine behind many of the online travel agency websites – in effect, to their own competitors. However, each partner with the GDS benefited by leveraging their investment, and their virtual partners, by having access to an efficient information and reservation service without having to develop a reservation engine for themselves. Dale (2003) identifies five different levels of relationships: *Channel*, which enables one company to access the distribution channels of another; *Collaborative*, where competitors cooperate with each other to achieve goals that would be difficult in isolation; *Communicative*, where content from 'infomediaries' enriches and adds value to partner websites; *Complementary*, where companies cross-sell products normally bought together (e.g., flights and hotel rooms); and *Converse*, where the partners distribute unrelated products, thus allowing each one to access the distribution channels of the other in a non-threatening manner. He speculates that competition in the future will be dictated more by the network of partners as a whole than by single intermediaries, and advises firms to participate in such networks unless they want to be left at a competitive disadvantage (Dale, 2003).

The arrival of the Web upset the tourism distribution apple cart and prompted major changes in the way tourism products were being sold. Movement toward web-based distribution has been swift, and travel has quickly become the most popular product sold online. While actual dollar estimates vary, most analysts agree that spending on travel is about one third of total online business-to-consumer (B2C) transactions. At the time of publication of their US online travel market report Internet analyst firm PhoCusWright put the size of the US market at over US$50 billion (PhoCusWright, 2006). While both Europe and Asia lag considerably, their pace of growth is higher and, with bigger potential markets, are likely to catch up with and even overtake US penetration rates in the very near future (Carroll and O'Connor, 2005). However revenue figures alone do not demonstrate the importance of e-commerce to the tourism sector. Online statistics effectively ignore bookings influenced by, but not completed, in the online environment. Estimates say that over 40% of travelers who research travel online subsequently make their bookings in some other way. As such revenues are not included in online travel statistics, published figures in reality significantly understated the importance of the web for travel.

Broken promises – direct distribution to the customer

As e-commerce developed during the 1990s, many commentators focused on its ability to facilitate direct communication with, and even direct sales to the customer. Most claimed that travel distribution as we knew it would change forever, and the trade press was packed with predictions of dis-intermediation and the death of the travel agent. Tourism suppliers were naturally enthusiastic about this potential, as fewer (or ideally no) middlemen meant fewer commissions and no transaction charges (Heung, 2003). Web distribution was also called the 'great leveler,' potentially offering smaller and independent suppliers the opportunity to compete effectively on an equal footing with bigger companies by selling directly to the customer (Buhalis, 1999). Yet over 10 years later, intermediaries are stronger than ever, and online travel distribution is controlled by a handful of companies – all of them intermediaries! Precisely, how did this occur?

The adoption of the Web as a mainstream consumer research and commerce tool certainly prompted major change in the way tourism products and services were being sold. In addition to bringing together a vast network of suppliers and a widely dispersed customer pool into a centralized electronic market place, in contrast to earlier electronic channels, the Web allowed for a much richer consumer experience. Developing web technology allowed both suppliers and intermediaries to place a full color, interactive multi-media brochure directly into the hands of potential customers at a relatively low cost (Murphy et al., 1996). Furthermore, it permitted two-way communications, allowing transactions to be carried out directly and instantly with the customer. And unlike with physical products, fulfillment of transaction was not a problem with travel services, particularly as the use of electronic ticketing grew.

Tourism suppliers were quick to take advantage of the direct distribution potent of the Web. For example, a 2002 survey published in the *Cornell Quarterly* shows how the majority of major hotel chains provided both detailed product information and reservation facilities directly to consumers on their brand websites. Similar studies of Aragonese hotels (Garcés et al., 2004), Balearic hotels (Vich-i-Martorell, 2003), Scottish hotels (Buick, 2003), and Italian hotels (Minghetti, 2003) indicate that usage of the Internet as a distribution channel had also diffused into smaller unbranded hotels, typically producing between 2 and 5% of revenues for such properties. Unfortunately, brand-direct websites typically provide limited utility in that shoppers can only view and purchase the products of that particular supplier. Even the largest operators (for example, the airlines) essentially limited themselves to distributing just their core product. However, research has shown that consumers do not purchase travel in this way. A traveler booking an airline ticket also usually needs a hotel (or vice versa), or to find out something about the destination, and would like to know about visas and health requirements (Poon, 1994). To satisfy these complex and diverse information needs, consumers increasingly turned to online travel agencies, whose key differentiating point was broad choice, not only in terms of offering products from multiple competing brands, but also by providing a full product range and thus offering a one-stop-travel-shop for the 'harassed' consumer (Preston and Trunkfield, 2006).

Offering 'full-service' has become a key aspect of online travel agent strategy (Preston, 2005). Driven by falling (or even eliminated) airline commission, most began placing great emphasis on cross-selling hotel, car hire and destination services – products that are attractive because of their relatively high profit margins. By encouraging consumers to buy all their travel needs from the same site, they can both increase average spending and generate higher profits. This strategy is reinforced by the promotion of dynamic packaging services, which leverage the online intermediary's product portfolio and technological expertise to provide customers with the facilities to interactively assemble their own made-to-measure travel packages (Cai et al., 2004). Brand-direct supplier sites simply cannot compete in terms of breadth of service or depth of functionality. The mega agencies have also been investing millions in offline and online advertising to build brand awareness and have, to a large extent, succeeded in convincing the consumer that the best bargains and best service can be found on their sites. Thus, despite efforts by tourism suppliers, the combination of features, i.e., brand and pricing, is accelerating a trend toward re-intermediation, with the big winners in the growth of the sale of travel online being the mega agencies rather than the travel supplier.

It is interesting to note that many of the online travel agencies have their origins outside the travel sector. Thus, while traditional travel agents hesitate to change their archaic methods of operations (Ozturan and Akis-Roney, 2003), online companies are not conceptually limited by pre-existing relationships or traditional notions of how to do business, which has allowed them to challenge the status quo and introduce new and innovative business practices. For example, the business model that most online intermediaries use to work with travel suppliers has come to be known as the *merchant model* (Carroll and Siguaw, 2003). In contrast to the traditional commission-based agent relationship (where suppliers paid intermediaries a commission each time they sold a product), with the merchant model the intermediary negotiates fixed allocations of inventory at highly discounted net rates and subsequently sells these products at a mark up, taking as profit the difference between the rate negotiated and the price at which they manage to sell the product online (O'Connor, 2003). While this might look like a good deal for the supplier (no commissions or other transaction costs, and the ability to set net rates to reflect the minimum amount they are prepared to accept for their product), the stronger negotiating power of the online merchants means they can demand rates significantly lower than what the supplier might freely wish to give. In addition, by careful management of their margin, they can then sell onward such rooms at highly competitive prices – in many cases cheaper than the rates being offered on the supplier's own website! For example, O'Connor's (2002) study of online hotel chain pricing found that online travel agencies frequently offered the cheapest prices for hotel rooms, particularly at the upper end of the market. Of course suppliers are always free to refuse to participate, but, in classic fashion, nobody wants to be the first to leave the online agencies, as to do so risks losing out on large volumes of potential (even if low yield) bookings.

Managing multiple channels of distribution

With electronic distribution in tourism growing more complex, a variety of issues associated with the management of the area have developed. As Sigala and Buhalis (2002) note, hoteliers who successfully manage their electronic distribution add value, develop their brand, and build customer loyalty; those who fail risk losing customers to intermediaries. This section examines four of the most topical issues in tourism distribution channel management identified from the literature – channel choice, pricing over multiple channels, managing distribution cost, and ownership of the customer.

Channel choice

One effect of the growth in tourism e-commerce is an exponential growth in the number of distribution channels through which the tourism product can be sold. As has been discussed, a large variety of electronic channels have developed to supplement, but never quite completely replace, traditional offline intermediaries. GDS-based channels continue to thrive and, at the same time, Internet-based channels have also grown into an important source of business for most tourism suppliers.

However, the set of channels used cannot be increased infinitum. As the number of channels increases, so too does the complexity of the supporting infrastructure and, in turn, the cost of running the overall distribution system (O'Connor and Picolli, 2003). For example, working with multiple distribution channels implies maintaining both price and inventory in multiple distribution databases. If the supplier works with online travel agencies, this can be cumbersome, labor-intensive, and therefore costly as most require suppliers to perform these tasks manually on an extranet-based system. Suppliers have to log into each system in turn, process reservations or cancellations, and manually change pricing/availability data to reflect updated market conditions.

Obviously, developing interfaces between the online travel agency systems and the reservation systems of tourism suppliers would greatly simplify this process. Such developments would not only allow availability and prices to be updated automatically, but would also allow suppliers' yield management modules to work more effectively, as they would have more complete and accurate historical data on allocation take-up and could therefore forecast more accurately. And while theoretically the technology exists to automate this process (in particular using the Open Travel Alliance's XML standard), online travel agents have little motivation to facilitate such connectivity, as they effectively profit from the market disequilibria created by suppliers who have to manually perform updates. Faced with a cumbersome, time-consuming task, many suppliers simply do not make updates as frequently as they should, allowing the online agents to make higher margins by exploiting the differences between the prices charged and actual demand. Automation of the process would eliminate these differences as prices and availability would be instantaneously updated whenever market conditions changed. Thus, despite promises to the contrary, only the largest tourism companies have been successful at convincing online travel agencies to provide such direct connect facilities.

How then can suppliers decide which of the growing range of channels to include in their portfolio of distribution channels? As O'Connor and Frew (2004, p.180) point out, 'the decision as to which channel to use has become increasingly complex, and hotel managers currently have little guidance to help them determine which best match their needs.' In their paper, they propose an evaluation methodology for electronic channels of distribution to help practitioners make this decision. In contrast to contemporary literature, which stresses evaluating projects on financial or marketing criteria, O'Connor and Frew suggest that technical and operational factors should instead drive the evaluation and decision process. The study highlights the complex nature of such evaluations, as well as demonstrates how the increasingly complex environment makes the use of a formal methodology more important. However, as Enz (2003) points out, in reality most suppliers are using multiple simultaneous electronic channels without a clear understanding of their impact and the effect this has on their overall profitability, as will be discussed below.

Pricing in an online world

Yield management is a set of techniques frequently used by airlines, hotels, and other service firms with fixed capacity to try to balance supply of their perishable product with forecasted demand in such a way as to maximize revenue in the long term (Kimes and Wagner, 2001). Being already a complex process, yield management has become more difficult to implement because of the growth in the use and variety of electronic distribution channels discussed above. In addition to providing suppliers with more distribution options, each channel has different revenue characteristics, costs, and levels of control (Helsel and Cullen, 2005), making the manipulation of the channel over which the customer makes a reservation an important issue (O'Connor and Frew, 2002).

In the past, suppliers achieved this by segmenting customers and offering different prices/conditions for each segment over different channels (Choi and Kimes, 2002). Inefficiencies in information distribution effectively prevented rates destined for one market segment from being seen or booked by the others (Lehmann, 2003). However, the adoption of the Internet as an information medium has greatly increased price and rate transparency (O'Connor, 2003). Consumers can quickly and easily search multiple online channels before committing to making a reservation (PriceWaterhouseCoopers, 1999). In addition, a new type of online tool (known as meta-search) has developed that allows travelers to comparison shop a large number of sites in practically a single click (well known examples include Kayak, Sidestep, TravelAxe and Kelkoo). As a result, it has become increasingly difficult to use differential pricing, either by market segment or by point of sale. In practice, any rate, given to any distributor, can potentially end up on the Web and thus be seen and booked by all customers.

Thus managing price has become both more important and, at the same time, more difficult. One widely adopted strategy is price consistency – having the same rate for each customer on all distribution channels and at all points-of-sale (Santoma and O'Connor, 2006). An alternative is to offer cheaper prices on direct websites – a strategy that is often used to try to encourage customers to book directly, rather than through intermediaries. In a 2003 study, O'Connor analyzed the online hotel market to establish which pricing strategy had become the norm. His findings show that hotel companies typically use multiple simultaneous distribution channels, but that no one channel was consistently cheapest. Analyses reveals differences based on market segment, with consumers more likely to find cheaper prices on direct channels (chain website and call center) at the lower end of the market, and through intermediaries, at the upper end. Highlighting how up-market and luxury hotels appear to be offering their cheapest prices though channels with the highest cost of distribution, O'Connor concludes that hotels, in general, do a poor job of managing prices over multiple distribution channels and urges them to develop well-thought-out pricing policies that would encourage consumers to book directly through brand websites. Anecdotal evidence would seem to suggest that operators have followed this advice, as evidenced by the recent growth in the inclusion of 'Best Rate Guarantees' on many supplier websites (Chin-Chien and Schwartz, 2006).

However a worrying effect of such guarantees is the downward pressure they appear to place on rates. With everyone promising the 'best' rate, suppliers and intermediaries are in effect engaged in a price war that, while beneficial for the consumer, has resulted in lower and lower margins for suppliers (PriceWaterHouseCoopers, 2005). This downward spiral is being amplified by the online intermediaries, who employ market managers to encourage suppliers to further reduce their negotiated rate in return for better placement on search results listings. Consumers are also learning that they can often find better prices by waiting until the last minute to make their booking (Thompson and Failmezger, 2005). Thus, while the Web promised incremental business by allowing suppliers to reach customers that they could otherwise not have attracted, in practice many of the customers that actually book online are ones who would have booked through some other channel, in any case. The difference is, however, that the prices that are paid results in a far lower yield for the hotel than had the booking been made in the 'normal' fashion. Some more street-smart customers are booking far in advance, monitoring online channels for better prices and wherever possible canceling their original reservation to re-book at a cheaper rate, closer to the arrival date. Failure to include appropriate restrictions or fences to prevent such practices can potentially have a drastic effect on profitability (Enz, 2003).

Managing distribution cost

As can be seen from the above discussion, Internet-based distribution has created both opportunities and problems for revenue managers (Choi and Kimes, 2002). More channels generally mean increased reach, potentially allowing hotels to sell more rooms. However the cost of using such channels can vary greatly. Considering only transaction costs, direct Internet channels (e.g., the hotel's own website) tend to be cheaper than indirect channels (Helsel and Cullen, 2005). Yet, more than half of all online bookings come through intermediaries, whose transaction costs vary from around 10% to substantially higher (PhoCusWright, 2006). Informal discussions with industry practitioners indicate that most online intermediaries demand (and frequently receive) mark-ups of between 17 and 30%. In addition, other administrative, technical, and organizational costs mean that working with certain online intermediaries can be between two to three times more expensive than using traditional methods.

Thus, in order to maximize profitability rather than just sales, distribution managers need to shift their focus from what rate can be achieved through a channel to the incremental cost of using that channel (Choi and Kimes, 2002). However, little empirical research has focused on how to manage distribution costs across multiple electronic channels. In a 1999 paper, Noone and Griffin propose combining *Activity Based Costing* with yield management principles in what they call *Customer Profitability Analysis*, while in a 2002 paper Choi and

Kimes use a simulation to demonstrate the application of yield management techniques to multi-channel problems. No study provides practical advice on how to implement yield management in such situations, or to help yield managers decide what rate to charge on what channel.

Ownership of the customer

The growth in the number and diversity of tourism distribution channels has also lead to another problem – ownership of the customer. Travelers now have the ability to search for and book travel products in many different ways. As has been discussed above, online travel agencies are particularly attractive to consumers because of their convenience, their rich feature set, and their competitive prices (Preston, 2005). Consumers searching and booking on such sites practically always find a product that meets their needs and, in most cases, the site will propose several alternatives, in direct contrast to supplier sites that may not have a suitable product available or may be booked out for the dates requested. As has also been discussed above, in many cases the prices offered by the online intermediary will frequently be as good as, if not better than, those available on supplier-direct sites. Given such levels of service, where is the customer likely to go the next time he or she wants to make a travel booking? Few studies provide concrete guidelines about how to develop and maintain effective lodging websites, making it difficult for suppliers to know how to compete (Jeong et al., 2003). Chung and Law (2003) do provide some guidelines as to the type of information that should be included to help develop better sites. More guidance on best practice is needed as the majority of online agencies have started to put more emphasis on building customer loyalty, by developing reward programs that recognize frequent and high value customers and use electronic marketing techniques to develop a closer relationship with them (Preston and Trunkfield, 2006).

O'Connor and Picolli (2003) highlight this threat and stress the need for suppliers to drive customers to direct websites to help regain ownership of the shopping experience and gather valuable customer data. They council hoteliers to rethink their approach to distribution and to move away from a *shelf space approach* – being present on as many channels as possible – toward being more selective in terms of the channels with which they work (Castleberry et al., 1998). O'Connor and Frew (2004) similarly stress the need to drive customers to the direct websites. They suggest that by using sophisticated customer relationship management (CRM) techniques based on their personal contact with the customer, they can build customer loyalty and in this way combat the growing power of the online intermediaries. Only by developing such close relationships with the customer can they reduce the danger of substitution, thus helping to ensure long-term profitability (Piccoli et al., 2003).

Suppliers have begun to give customers increased incentives to book directly on branded websites, with trends indicating that the promise of the Web as a facilitator of direct distribution may finally be about to happen. Rewards for booking directly include extra frequent-flyer miles, tiered benefits and special prices. Suppliers are also becoming more aggressive in their pricing strategies, want everyone to know that the best deals are available on their own websites, and thus are unwilling to allow any intermediaries to have a noticeable advantage in pricing. Many are also increasing the range of products sold through their brand-direct sites. As was discussed above, one of the primary reasons that suppliers have not been successful at driving significant amount of business to their sites is that consumers often want a one-stop-shop offering both brand choice and the ability to cater for all their travel booking requirements – something that is clearly not available on a single company's branded website. This has not stopped some suppliers from trying; for example, SouthWest.com now offers hotel and car rentals, Hyatt.com provides air and car booking facilities as well as packaged vacations, and Dollar.com, air and hotel reservation capabilities (Buhalis and O'Connor, 2006).

Are suppliers winning the battle? PhoCusWright estimates that direct to supplier sales comprised 51% of the total online market in 2005 – a very insignificant increase over prior years (PhoCusWright, 2005). Despite considerable effort, the majority has failed to significantly change their distribution mix. While brand-direct websites are in general quite successful at selling to loyalty club members – in effect to their existing customers – they are less successful at attracting incremental business. The online agencies, with their broader choice and product categories, offer the opportunity both to attract new business and also make a valuable contribution in terms of keeping planes and hotels full. An adaptation of the merchant model discussed above may help to preserve this relationship. With this strategy, both parties win; the supplier gets to set the minimum acceptable rate that they are willing to accept as the net rate offered and the online agency can achieve an acceptable level of profitability by adding their own margin before sale to the customer.

Summary and conclusion

It can be seen that trouble continues to brew in the online travel sector. While suppliers would ideally like consumers to book directly, they face severe competition from online travel agencies. Both parties are engaged in a battle for the hearts and minds of the traveler – a battle that is being fought in the relatively unexplored terrain of Internet commerce.

From the above discussion, it is clear that empirical research in this area could best be described as sparse. At a strategic level, little useful guidance is available to either suppliers or intermediaries as to how best to attract, convert, and build loyalty in today's elusive travel consumer. In common with most of the tourism and hospitality research, the little published research that exists in the field of electronic distribution in tourism tends to be relatively weak (Lynn, 2002). As O'Connor and Murphy (2005) point out, the majority of studies display 'an over-reliance on the survey method, unrepresentative and convenience sampling, shallow analyses, misinterpretations of data, and a tendency to draw conclusions and make broad generalizations without providing adequate evidence.' They also point out that there appears to be a lack of meta-knowledge as to what other researchers are doing, with the result that many studies replicated each other with minor difference in focus or geographical area, and that few articles build on each other to extend the pool of available knowledge in any meaningful way.

It is clear that e-commerce and distribution in tourism is a topic that is important, but not well understood. A very large number of research opportunities are self-evident. What has been the effect, financially and strategically, of the move from a commission model to the merchant model? How should suppliers price their products across multiple simultaneous channels to both drive as much business as possible directly, but at the same time benefit from the reach that intermediary channels provide? Research from the consumer perspective is particularly needed to help clarify many issues. What motivates a consumer to use one distribution channel rather than another? How do price, convenience, website design, and website content encourage consumers to change from lookers into bookers? How do consumers react to seeing different prices on different distribution channels? Does the use of restrictions or fences have an effect on their perceptions, or on where they book? How effectively do loyalty or frequent-flyer programs attract, retain, and build customer loyalty? Will current developments in user-generated content result in customers displaying less faith in brands? These suggestions, albeit in no way exhaustive, illustrate the rich and interesting range of potential research questions that could be addressed.

The Chinese have a saying – 'May you live in interesting times' – which may be interpreted as either a blessing or a curse. Its meaning is particularly relevant in the field of electronic distribution in tourism and e-commerce. In this chapter, I have attempted to provide an overview of the current state of play in this rapidly evolving arena. Intellectually, I find this segment of the tourism industry to be particularly fascinating. Technology continues to develop at a rapid pace, and in fact has been identified as one of the top five most volatile factors affecting tourism (Olsen, M. 1995). Each change presents new challenges and opportunities, making the distribution arena both difficult to understand and at the same time highly exciting. To be successful, tourism suppliers and intermediaries must continually assess the likely impact of new developments and examine how to integrate them into their methods of operation. Doing so presents tremendous opportunities, yet is risky as technology may move on even before implementation is complete. Yet, not to do so risks being left behind in a state of competitive disadvantage. Such choices are faced by tourism companies every day, and it's only by having a thorough understanding of the electronic distribution environment that they can succeed in the long run.

References

Anderson Consulting. (1998). *The future of travel distribution: Securing loyalty in an efficient travel market*. New York: Anderson Consulting.

Bennett, M. (1993). Information technology and travel agency – A customer service perspective. *Tourism Management, 14*, 259–266.

Bennett, M. (1996). Information technology and databases for tourism. In A. Seaton and M. Bennett (Eds.), *The Marketing of tourism products: Concepts issues and cases* (pp. 423–450). London: Thomson International Business Press.

Bitner, M. and Blooms, B. (1982). Trends in travel and tourism marketing: The changing structure of distribution channels. *Journal of Travel Research, 20*, 39–44.

Buhalis, D. (1997). Information technology as a strategic tool for economic, social, cultural and environmental benefits enhancement of tourism at destination regions. *Progress in Tourism and Hospitality Research, 1*, 71–93.

Buhalis, D. (1998). Strategic use of information technologies in the tourism industry. *Tourism Management, 19*, 409–421.

Buhalis, D. (1999). Information technology for small and medium sized tourism enterprises: adaptation and benefits. *Information Technology & Tourism, 2(2)*, 79–95.

Buhalis, D. (2000). Relationships in the distribution channels of tourism: Conflicts between hoteliers and tour operators in the Mediterranean region. *International Journal of Hospitality and Tourism Administration, 1(1)*, 113–139.

Buhalis, D. (2000b). Tourism and information technologies: Past, present and future. *Tourism Recreation Research, 25(1)*, 41–58.

Buhalis, D. and O'Connor, P. (2006). Information and communications technology – revolutionizing tourism in D. Buhalis and C. Costa (Eds.), *Tourism Management Dynamics – trends, management and tools* (pp. 196–210). Burlington, MA: Elsevier.

Buick, I. (2003). Information technology in small Scottish hotels: Is it working. *International Journal of Contemporary Hospitality Management, 15*, 243–247.

Cai, L., Card, J., and Cole, S. (2004). Content delivery performance of world wide web sites of US tour operators focusing on destinations in China. *Tourism Management, 25,* 219–227.

Carroll, B. and O'Connor, P. (2005). *European Hotels: Managing Hospitality Distribution.* Sherman, CT: PhoCusWright.

Carroll, B. and Siguaw, J. (2003). The evolution of electronic distribution: Effects on hotels and intermediaries. *Cornell Hotel and Restaurant Administration Quarterly, 44*(4), 38–50.

Castleberry, J., Hempell, C., and Kaufman, G. (1998). Electronic shelf space on the global distribution network. *Hospitality and Leisure Executive Report, 5,* 19–24.

Chin-Chien, C. and Schwartx, Z. (2006). The importance of information asymmetry in customers' booking decisions. *Cornell Hotel and Restaurant Administration Quarterly, 47*(3), 272–285.

Choi, S. and Kimes, S. (2002). Electronic distribution channels' effect on hotel revenue management. *Cornell Hotel and Restaurant Administration Quarterly, 43*(3), 23–31.

Chung, T. and Law, R. (2003). Developing a performance indicator for hotel websites. *International Journal of Hospitality Management, 22,* 119–125.

Connell, J. and Reynolds, P. (1999). The implications of technological developments on tourism information centers. *Tourism Management, 20,* 501–509.

Connolly, D., Olsen, M., and Moore, R. (1998). The Internet as a distribution channel. *Cornell Hotel and Restaurant Administration Quarterly, 39*(2), 42–54.

Dale, C. (2003). The competitive networks of tourism e-mediaries: New strategies, new advantages. *Journal of Vacation Marketing, 9*(2), 109–118.

Dombey, A. (1998). Separating the emotion from the fact – The effects of new intermediaries on electronic travel distribution. Presentation at ENTER Information Technologies in Tourism Conference, Edinburgh.

Dube, L. and Renaghan, L. (2000). Marketing your hotel to and through intermediaries. *Cornell Hotel and Restaurant Administration Quarterly, 41*(1), 73–83.

Emmer, R., Tauck, C., and Moore, R. (1993). Marketing hotels using Global Distribution Systems. *Cornell Hotel and Restaurant Administration Quarterly, 34*(6), 80–89.

Enz, C. (2003). Hotel pricing in a networked world. *Cornell Hotel and Restaurant Administration Quarterly, 44*(1), 4–5.

Frew, A. and O'Connor, P. (1999). Destination Marketing System Strategies: Refining and extending an assessment framework. *Information Technology and Tourism – Applications, Methodologies, Techniques, 2*(1), 3–13.

Garcés, S. A., Gorgemans, S., Sánchez, A. M., and Pérez, M. P. (2004). Implications of the Internet – An analysis of the Aragonese hospitality industry. *Tourism Management, 25,* 603–613.

Go, F. and Pine, R. (1995). Globalization strategy in the hotel industry. New York: Routledge.

HEDNA. (1997). *Onward Distribution of Hotel Information via the Global Distribution Systems.* London: Partners in Marketing.

Helsel, C. and Cullen, K. (2005). *Hotel distribution nirvana: A multichannel approach,* HEDNA 2005 White Paper Series, Falls Church, VA: Hotel Electronic Distribution Network Association.

Heung, V. (2003). Barriers to implementing E-Commerce in the travel industry: a practical perspective. *International Journal of Hospitality Management, 22,* 111–118.

Hitchins, F. (1991). The influence of technology on UK travel agents. *EIU Travel and Tourism Analyst, 3,* 88–105.

Jarvela, P. and Loikkanen, J. (1999). Business models for electronic commerce in the travel services. *Information Technology & Tourism, 2*(3/4), 185–196.

Jeong, M. and Lambert, C. (1999). Measuring the information quality of lodging web sites. *International Journal of Hospitality Information Technology, 1,* 63–75.

Jeong, M., Oh, H., and Gregoire, M. (2003). Conceptualizing web site quality and its consequences in the lodging industry. *International Journal of Hospitality Management, 22,* 161–175.

Karcher, K. (1995). The emergence of electronic market systems in the European tour operator business. *EM – Electronic Markets,* (13/14), 10–11.

Kaven, W. (1994). Channels of distribution in the hotel industry. In J. Rothmell (Ed.), *Marketing in the Services Sector* (pp. 114–121). Cambridge, Mass: Winthrop Publications.

Kimes, S. and Wagner, P. (2001). Preserving your revenue management system as a trade secret. *Cornell Hotel and Restaurant Administration Quarterly, 42*(5), 8–15.

Knowles, T. and Garland, M. (1994). The strategic importance of CRSs in the airline industry. *EIU Travel and Tourism Analyst,* (4), 4–6.

Kotler, P., Bowen, J., and Makens, J. (1996). *Marketing for Hospitality and Tourism.* New Jersey: Prentice Hall.

Lehmann, E. (2003). Pricing behavior on the Web: Evidence from Online Travel Agencies. *Empirica, 30,* 379–396.

Lewis, R., Chambers, R., and Chacko, H. (1995). *Marketing leadership in hospitality.* New York: Van Nostrad Reinhold.

Lynn, W. M. (2002). The industry needs less descriptive and more causal research. *Cornell Hotel and Restaurant Administration Quarterly, 43*(2), ii.

McGuffie, J. (1994). CRS development in the hotel sector. *EIU Travel & Tourism Analyst, 2,* 53–68.

Middleton, V. (1994). *Marketing in travel and tourism.* London: Butterworth-Heinemann.

Minghetti, V. (2003). Building customer value in the hospitality industry: Towards the definition of a customer-centric information system. *Information Technology & Tourism, 6*(2), 141–153.

Morrison, A., Taylor, S., and Douglas, A. (1999). Marketing small hotels on the World Wide Web. *Information Technology & Tourism, 2*(2), 97–113.

Murphy, J., Forrest, E., Wotring, C., and Brymer, R. (1996). Hotel management and marketing on the Internet: An analysis of sites and features. *Cornell Hotel and Restaurant Administration Quarterly, 6*(37), 70–82.

Noone, B. and Griffin, P. (1999). Managing the long-term profit yield from market segments in a hotel environment: A case study on the implications of customer profitability analysis. *International Journal of Hospitality Management, 18,* 111–128.

O'Connor, P. (1999). *Electronic Information Distribution in Hospitality and Tourism.* London: CAB International.

O'Connor, P. (2002). An analysis of the online pricing strategies of the international hotel chains. In K. Woeber, A. J. Frew and M. Hitz (Eds.), *Information and Communications Technologies in Tourism 2002* (pp. 285–293). New York: Springer-Verlag Wien.

O'Connor, P. and Frew, A. (2002). The future of hotel electronic distribution: expert/industry perspectives. *Cornell Hotel Administration Quarterly, 43*(3), 33–45.

O'Connor, P. and Frew, A. (2004). An evaluation methodology for hotel electronic channels of distribution. *International Journal of Hospitality Management, 23*(2), 179–199.

O'Connor, P. and Murphy, J. (2005). Research on information technology in the hospitality industry. *International Journal of Hospitality Management, 23,* 473–484.

O'Connor, P. (2003). On-line pricing: An analysis of hotel-company practices. *Cornell Hotel and Restaurant Administration Quarterly, 44*(1), 88–96.

O'Connor, P. and Frew, A. (2003). An evaluation methodology for hotel electronic channels of distribution. *International Journal of Hospitality Management, 23,* 179–199.

O'Connor, P. and Piccoli, G. (2003). Marketing hotels using global distribution systems revisited. *Cornell Hotel and Restaurant Administration Quarterly, 44*(5/6), 105–114.

Olsen, M. (1995). *Into the New Millenium: The IHA white paper on the Global Hospitality Industry: The Performance of the Multinational Industry.* pp. 27–49. Paris: International Hotel Association.

Ozturan, M. and Akis-Roney, S. (2003). Internet use among travel agents in Turkey: an exploratory study. *Tourism Management, 25,* 259–266.

PhoCusWright Inc. (2005). *Online travel overview*, Sherman, NY: PhoCusWright.

PhoCusWright Inc. (2006). *Market report – UK*, Sherman, NY: PhoCusWright.

Picolli, G., O'Connor, P., Capaccioli, C., and Alveraz, R. (2003). Customer Relationship Management – A driver for change in the structure of the U.S. lodging industry. *Cornell Hotel and Restaurant Administration Quarterly*, 44(4), 61–73.

Pollock, A. (1995). The impact of Information Technology on destination marketing. *EIU Travel & Tourism Analyst*, (3), 66–83.

Poon, A. (1993). *Technology and competitive advantage*. London: CAB International.

Poon, A. (1994). The New Tourism Revolution. *Tourism Management*, 15, 91–91.

Preston, M. (2005, March). Consumer Loyalty – the next battle ground for hotel distribution? *Hospitality Directions Europe*, 11, London: Price-WaterHouseCoopers.

Preston, M. and Trunkfield, D. (2006, November). How to maintain success in the online travel space. *Hospitality Directions Europe*, 14, London: PriceWaterHouseCoopers.

PriceWaterHouseCoopers. (1999 July). The Internet transforms the traditional hotel distribution system, *Hospitality Directions US Edition*, PriceWaterHouseCoopers, New York, 33–42.

PriceWaterHouseCoopers. (2005 February). Effect of the Internet on lodging demand – update and additional analysis, *Hospitality Directions Europe Edition*, London: PriceWaterHouseCoopers, pp. 31–34.

Pusateri, M. and Manno, J. (1998, June). Travelers take to the 'Net. *Lodging*, 23–24.

Santoma, R. and O'Connor, P. (2006). Estratejias de Precios 'Online' En Hotles de Lujo Europeos: Una perspectiva internacional, *Fourth International Doctoral Tourism & Leisure Colloquium, XV Simposio Internacional de Turismo y Ocio ESADE*, ESADE, Barcelona.

Sigala, M. and Buhalis, D. (2002). Changing distribution channels in the travel industry – New channels, new challenges. *Information Technology & Tourism*, 5(3), 185–186.

Smith, C. and Jenner, P. (1998). Tourism and the Internet. *EIU Travel & Tourism Intelligence* (1), 62–81.

Stipanuk, D. (1993). Tourism and technology, Interactions and implications. *Tourism Management, 14*, 267–278.

Thompson, G. M. and Failmezger, A. (2005). *Why customers shop around: A comparison of hotel room rates and availability across booking channels*. Ithaca, NY: Cornell University School of Hotel Administration Centre for Hospitality Research.

Tse, A. (2003). Disintermediation of travel agents in the hotel industry. *International Journal of Hospitality Management*, 22, 453–460.

Vaughan, D., Jolley, A., and Mehrer, P. (1999). Local Authorities in England and Wales and the development of tourism Internet sites. *Information Technology & Tourism*, 2(2), 115–129.

Vich-i-Martorell, G. (2003) The Internet and tourism principals in the Balearic Islands. *Tourism and Hospitality Research*, 5(5), 25–44.

Wade, P. and Raffour, G. (2000, April). L'Internet, un nouveau canal de distribution. *ESPACES*, 19–21.

Wagner, G. (1991 December). Lodging's Lifeblood. *Hospitality*, 105.

Waller, F. (1999 March). The distribution revolution. *Hotels*, 103.

Werthner, H. and Klein, S. (1999). *Information Technology and Tourism – A Challenging Relationship*. New York: Springer-Verlag Wien.

Williams, A. and Palmer, A. (1999). Tourism destination brands and electronic commerce: Towards synergy? *Journal of Vacation Marketing*, 5(3), 263–275.

Service quality and business performance

Dia Zeglat, Yuksel Ekinci and Andrew Lockwood

Introduction

While it is argued in the literature that product quality is incompatible with profits because of incurring high levels of costs and needing different sets of actions (Philips et al., 1983), significant evidence also suggests that this apparent incompatibility of quality and profits can be false (Smith, 1980; Wheelwright, 1981). Indeed the quality notion emerged in 1980s as a fundamental competitive strategy for organizations (Zeithaml and Bitner, 2003). In other words, quality is considered one of the key methods to attain a differential position and advantage over competitors in order to achieve high levels of revenues and profits (Hall, 1980; Porter, 1980). As a result, the concept of quality has been adopted by researchers and practitioners as a major theme in the service sector (Parasuraman et al., 1988) in order to deliver a positive impact on business performance and profitability (Harrington and Akehurst, 1996).

The service sector plays an important economic role both in terms of its contribution to gross domestic product (GDP) as well as through the percentage of the total workforce employed in service companies (Kotler et al., 2003). The service sector covers a very broad variety of organizations such as banking, hotels, transport, communication, and consultancy firms. In these service organizations, quality management practices have received increasing attention as a way of improving competitiveness (Hasan and Kerr, 2003).

As mentioned, some previous studies have found evidence that an organization's profit is a consequence of service quality. In addition, these studies suggest that the link between service quality and profitability is indirect and complicated. To put it another way, the literature shows that there are a number of variables that mediate the relationship between service quality and profitability, such as customer satisfaction, customer retention, price, costs, and market share (Zeithaml, 2000).

The main purpose of this chapter is to investigate the complex relationship between service quality and profitability in the hotel industry through the development of a conceptual framework. The factors involved in this relationship have emerged from the literature and indicate an indirect relationship between service quality and profitability. The conceptual framework recognizes the importance of customers' perceptions of service quality to determine which aspects or dimensions of service quality have a significant impact on profitability. This chapter consists of three sections. The first section reviews the theoretical background of service quality and business performance measurement. The second section introduces the conceptual framework, and the final section develops the propositions for future studies.

Theoretical background

Service quality

Service quality is an elusive concept that is difficult to define and measure. Accordingly, several conceptualizations have been introduced from different perspectives. Early studies defined quality as conformance to specification, which means that, for a product to be good, its attributes should match with the predetermined standards. This definition of quality is more suitable to goods than to services, because services are more difficult to standardize. Furthermore, these standards are determined from the management perspective rather than the customer perspective (Reeves and Bednar, 1994). To overcome this limitation, three definitions of quality have been introduced to understand the concept from the customer's perspective: (a) quality as excellence; (b) quality as value; and (c) quality as meeting or exceeding expectations.

The first definition of quality displays some inherent weaknesses, because 'excellence' is highly subjective and difficult to measure. Thus, tracking changes between two different assessments may be questionable. The second definition of quality implies that perceived quality is the same as perceived value. This approach introduced the concept of price into the definition of quality, but some scholars argue that perceived value and perceived quality are different (Bolton and Drew, 1991). Perceived value is a ratio between what customers get in exchange for what they sacrifice. The 'sacrifice' components of value are usually seen as monetary costs, whereas the 'get' components of value are the product or service benefits. Thus, quality may appear the same as product benefits when customers compare the quality of goods/services against the paid price in order to assess the perceived value. The final approach views quality as a situation where performance meets or exceeds expectations. This expectation–performance based definition of quality is more generic and customer-friendly than other definitions, because quality is defined from the customer's point of view regardless of being specific to a particular hospitality unit or customer segment. According to this view, quality can be measured from the customer's point of view by either the perceived disconfirmation or inferred disconfirmation scale (perhaps best known as gap scoring). However, empirical studies have shown that disconfirmation-based measurements could fail to produce a valid score to capture customers' perceptions of service quality (Cronin and Taylor, 1992; Teas, 1994); rather, they show that perceived quality is best captured by a performance-only scale. Hence, the findings of recent studies have suggested that service quality should be better defined simply as the customer's subjective assessment of performance (Cronin and Taylor, 1992; Dabholkar et al., 2000).

Models of quality suggest that service quality is multi-dimensional. Acting on this assumption, researchers have investigated the number and nature of the service quality dimensions in a variety of service organizations, such as hotels, restaurants, and banks. However, the outcome of this research is mixed. To date, there has been no clear agreement across service industries on what might constitute the generic and specific dimensions of service quality. The lack of consensus can largely be attributed to the fact that service quality research has been dominated by two separate schools of thought – the North American and the Nordic European – that employ different assumptions.

As Parasuraman et al. point out the North American school initially introduced ten service quality dimensions, best known as the SERVQUAL dimensions (Parasuraman et al., 1985). Following their second study, the ten service quality dimensions were found to be highly correlated, and were therefore reduced to five dimensions: tangibles, assurance, reliability, empathy, and responsiveness (Parasuraman et al., 1988). Applications of the five-dimensional SERVQUAL scale in various service firms have shown that even these dimensions were not distinct (e.g., Carmen 1990; Parasuraman et al., 1991, 1994). These studies supported the view that service quality should be only either three- or four-dimensional. To complicate matters further, applications of the SERVQUAL model using content-specific attributes have produced some new dimensions in different service organizations such as hotels and restaurants (Saleh and Ryan, 1991).

The Nordic European School (e.g., Lehtinen and Lehtinen, 1991) introduced both two- and three-dimensional quality models. For example, Grönroos's (1984) model of service quality is based on two dimensions: first, what customers obtain from a service firm and, second, how customers obtain these services. Although this model is simpler and more generic than the SERVQUAL model, it has been criticized for a number of reasons. First, the study sample used to develop this model was biased because it was specific to only North European nationals (Moore, 1994). Second, the Nordic European model used the perceived disconfirmation (i.e., perceived difference between expected and performed services) scale to measure service quality, without offering any insight into what kind of customer expectations should be measured (Zeithaml, et al., 1988). Although the perceived disconfirmation scale usually produces a better reliability score than the inferred disconfirmation (i.e., the performance–expectation arithmetic) scale when measuring service quality, the outcome of this measurement offers little information for improving quality. For example, managers would like to know the level of service performance in relation to different types of expectations (e.g., whether performance is below the ideal or below the expected minimum tolerable). This would enable managers to better diagnose the deficiency of quality in services and to track changes over time. The final criticism of the Nordic European School in general is that its proponents have produced rather limited empirical evidence to support the validity of their model.

Issues in measuring service quality in the hospitality industry

Although customer behavior studies have been heavily focused on the customer's pre-purchase evaluation and choice behavior (Callan, 1993; Riley and Perogiannis, 1990), in recent years a large number of researchers have focused on customers' post-purchase evaluation, in particular the measurement of service quality from different perspectives (Barrington and Olson, 1987; Brathwaite, 1992; Riley, 1984; Wood, 1994; Wilensky and Buttle, 1988). Ingram (1996) noted that the significance of service quality was being debated energetically in the business community and, therefore, deserves more attention. Oh and Parks (1997) state that, although some studies in the hospitality literature contribute to the understanding of customer behavior, more rigorous theoretical and methodological treatments are needed to improve the underdeveloped approaches to satisfaction and service quality research.

Lewis (1988) and Yesawitch (1987) commented that the hospitality industry had lagged behind many similar service industries in terms of the application of rigorous market research techniques and had tended to rely too much on intuition and past practice to aid its marketing decisions and measurement of customer satisfaction. Furthermore, Lewis and Pizam (1981) argue that most of the customer satisfaction surveys used in the hospitality industry are methodologically biased producing inaccurate results. They recommend that if researchers intend to measure the true components of satisfaction and service quality, multivariate techniques should be applied.

The measurement of service quality in the hospitality industry varies according to the research methods employed. Research designs vary along both qualitative and quantitative paradigms. Thus, depending on the study objectives, some differences have occurred in the selection of research methods. Qualitative studies have been used principally for exploratory purposes and aimed to identify the antecedents and consequences of service quality. The intention of many quantitative studies has been to measure the quality of service from the different perspectives of employees, managers, and customers on the basis of the attributes identified through the exploratory studies. In addition, some researchers have used existing measurement scales to test various models of service quality.

Early service quality scholars in the hospitality industry focused on the understanding and conceptualization of service quality. They, therefore, used mainly exploratory research methods. Lockwood (1994), for example, applied the Critical Incident Technique to record the success and failure of service quality in hospitality firms.

Nightingale (1983) used repertory grid methods with hotel customers to identify the key success factors for hotel operations. He developed a service management model that was similar to the Nordic European models, in which perceived performance was compared against customers' expectations. Nightingale (1983) also recognized the importance of management and employee commitment to achieving high quality service. Oberoi and Hales (1990) attempted to develop a service quality scale in conference hotels by applying a mixed qualitative and quantitative methodology. Martin (1995) investigated the usefulness of 'Importance/Performance Analysis' and the 'Service Gap Technique' for assessing service quality from the management and employee perspectives. Several attempts have been made to develop new methods for the use of existing techniques for measuring and monitoring service quality in the hospitality industry. For example, Johns and Lee-Ross (1995) introduced the 'Profile Accumulation Technique', which built up qualitative and quantitative service profiles. Their approach claimed to make it possible to compare service quality between different hospitality operations, events, and departments.

In a study of service quality in the UK roadside lodge sector, Senior (1992) developed 'Perceptual Blueprinting', which was a combination of three different methods: the principles of soft system methodology (e.g., repertory grid, interview, and questionnaire), service blueprinting, and perceptual gap analysis. Perceptual blueprinting essentially provided a multi-perspective phenomenological systems tool for studying a service delivery system, as perceived by customers and employees. Senior (1992) recommended that the outcome of this survey would assist managers to direct their human resources and re-design the service delivery system to achieve high quality service.

Saleh and Ryan (1991) used a form of Fishbeinian multi-attribute attitude model to assess service performance and its importance. Barsky (1992) introduced the expectancy–disconfirmation paradigm into the hotel industry. He attempted to expand the perceived disconfirmation model by adding attribute-importance weighting. However, Oh and Parks (1997) commented that Barsky's method was deeply biased because there was no standard way of measuring the importance of a service attribute. Referring to similar deficiencies in the attitude literature, it is agreed that the inclusion of importance measurement into service quality measurement continues to remain an unresolved issue worthy of further research.

To assess quality, numerous official and semi-official bodies operate restaurant and hotel rating schemes. Their assessments are usually conducted by skilled inspectors based on a checklist of subjectively determined quality attributes. However, Callan (1993) questioned the validity of these hotel classification schemes. Further, Callan and Lefebve (1997) compared and contrasted the effectiveness of these schemes from the customer's and manager's points of view. They found that these approaches were not customer friendly. Furthermore, the customer's choice of hotels was not significantly influenced by these schemes. The findings of their study indicated that the existing criteria should be redefined and assessed from the customer's point of view. Brotherton (2004) explored the nature of critical success factors (CSFs) in UK budget hotel operations to ascertain the relevance and importance of a range of factors referred to as critical in the extant academic and trade literature. His results showed that budget hotel unit managers from the leading brands largely agreed with the criticality of the factors, as stated in the literature.

Lewis (1987) argued that, rather than developing a new service-quality model, the generic service quality models should be tested and, if necessary, customized to hospitality firms. Accordingly, the SERVQUAL model was tested and three new service quality gaps were identified for the hotel industry. A similar approach was adopted by Saleh and Ryan (1991), who utilized a context-specific scale, based on the SERVQUAL model, to measure service quality in hotels from the customers' and managers' perspectives, respectively. Getty and Thompson (1994) also examined the applicability of SERVQUAL in the hospitality industry. They found that only two of the SERVQUAL dimensions were generic. Getty and Thompson's (1994) approach made an important contribution to the measurement of service quality in the hospitality industry, for a number of reasons. First, the assessment of service quality was defined from the customer's point of view. Second, the reliability and validity of a service quality instrument was recognized as critical in measuring quality. Third, service quality was seen as a multi-dimensional construct that was consistent with the developing marketing literature on perceived quality.

Other techniques and methods (e.g., internal auditing, focus group interviews) are also used for measuring service quality in various sectors of the industry. Sulek (2004) reports that statistical process-control techniques are widely implemented in the manufacturing industry, requiring the collection of detailed operational data and the application of sophisticated analytical techniques such as control charts. After testing the usefulness of this technique in a restaurant setting, Jones and Dent (1994) suggest that this should be of substantial interest to hospitality managers who wish to achieve reliable service performance in the hospitality industry.

Service quality dimensions in the hospitality industry

Zeithaml et al. (1990) argue that, regardless of the type of organization being studied, reliability is the most important dimension, followed by responsiveness, assurance, empathy, and tangibles. However, Fick and Ritchie (1991) demonstrated that tangibles and assurance were the two most important service quality dimensions in hotels. Farsad and LeBruto (1994) reported that customers were usually interested in the physical environment of hotels, the condition of the rooms, the degree of caring, and the consistency of attention paid by employees. Nightingale (1983) also suggested that the customers' expectations of physical attributes were key components of service quality in the hospitality industry. Accordingly, he identified five service quality dimensions from the customer's point of view: spaciousness, efficiency, guest control, ease of use, and availability.

Clow et al. (1994) identified that leisure travelers' selections of hotels were mainly based on security and brand name. Although it is difficult to suggest that these same attributes would necessarily be used to evaluate service quality after purchasing, security has always been recognized by managers as an important factor in both pre- and post-purchase evaluation (Duncan, 1993; Wolf, 1993). Zeithaml (1981) stated that the physical aspects of services were used in both pre- and post-purchase evaluations. Saleh and Ryan (1991) found that the aesthetics of the interior and exterior significantly contributed to the perception of service quality in hotels. Lewis (1984a,b) analyzed 66 hotel attributes to determine how business and leisure travelers selected hotels and evaluated quality of service after purchasing. His studies suggested that hotel attributes could be classified into 16 factors, based on travelers' post-purchase evaluation: overall feeling, beverage service quality, security, service quality, restaurant quality–price options, amenities and special conveniences, reputation and image, room–bath furnishings and their condition, quietness, building and aesthetics, contemporary and modern conveniences, health facilities, VIP treatment and extra luxury, location, price and value, and the check in and checkout process.

Choi and Chu (2001) examined the relative importance of various hotel factors in relation to travelers' overall satisfaction with their hotel stays in Hong Kong and the likelihood of their returning to the same hotels on subsequent trips. They identified seven factors that were likely to influence customers' intention to return: staff service quality, room quality, general amenities, business services, value, security, and internal direct-dial facilities. Cadotte and Turgeon (1988) categorized trends in the compliments and complaints on hotel services into four categories: satisfiers, dissatisfiers, criticals, and neutrals. The most frequently mentioned attributes were (1) employee attitudes and knowledge, (2) availability of services, (3) cleanliness and quietness of hotel environment, and (4) price. Nikolich and Sparks (1995) found that good communication skills were an essential element of encounter satisfaction.

Lockwood et al. (1992) investigated the key criteria of service quality in low-tariff roadside and budget hotels. They found that value for money, cleanliness, and employee friendliness were the most frequently quoted dimensions of service quality from the customer's point of view. They recommended that cleanliness of the hotel and the friendliness of employees should be seen as generic dimensions for the hospitality industry. Oberoi and Hales (1990) showed that, although service quality attributes of conference hotels were closely related to the five SERVQUAL dimensions (tangibles, understanding, competence, responsiveness, and reliability), these attributes were grouped into two dimensions: tangibles and intangibles.

Haywood (1983) suggested that hotels should be designed according to the purpose of stay. Therefore, hotel service quality should be measured based on Juran's (1979) fitness-for-use principle, which has three dimensions: availability, reliability, and maintainability. Availability is concerned with the timeliness of service and the convenience of location. Reliability refers to the security and the consistency of the delivery process. The maintainability dimension is the ability to provide services according to the market needs.

Barsky and Labacgh (1992) commented that customer satisfaction had neither been integrated directly into business plans nor truly accepted as a strategic dimension. Their study indicated that customer satisfaction was based on the following quality dimensions: employee attitude, location, room, price, facilities, reception, service, parking, and food and beverage. Their findings were supported by similar studies also in the hospitality industry (Atkinson, 1988; Knutson, 1988a).

Lewis and Owtram's (1986) study suggested that facilities, location, and comfort were the most important contributors to travelers' overall satisfaction. The most successful hoteliers reported that their quality reputation was based on the courtesy of their employees, physical environment, home-type atmosphere and consistency of service delivery (Carper, 1991). In a study investigating the pattern of frequent travelers' loyalty behavior, Knutson (1988b) identified five important components: cleanliness and convertibility of room, safety and security of establishment, location, friendliness and courtesy of employees, and price.

Studies in the hospitality industry have also referred to the SERVQUAL model as a 'skeleton' for measuring service quality. In line with this trend, hospitality management researchers have either adapted the SERVQUAL model (e.g., LODGSERV, LODGQUAL) or developed a content-specific scale for measuring service quality in various sectors of the hospitality industry, across different countries (Getty and Thompson, 1994). Lee and Hing (1995) assessed the applicability of SERVQUAL within the fine dining segment of the restaurant industry. Richard and Sundaram (1993) studied the 'Gap 5' of service quality. They focused on the home-delivery pizza market and compared Domino's against Pizza Hut. In their study, they used the original SERVQUAL scale to measure the difference between the expected and perceived service quality. Ooi et al. (1999) tested a revised version of the SERVQUAL scale in mid-luxury hotels in Australia. The findings of this study confirmed the validity of a three-dimensional model for the hospitality setting, including employee behavior and appearance, tangibles, and reliability. Moreover, their study showed that the employee dimension was the best predictor of overall service quality. As a result, a 27-item instrument, called HOLSERV, was produced to measure service quality in hotels.

Oberoi and Hales (1990) investigated the perceived quality of service in conference hotels in the UK. To do this, the researchers interviewed hotel managers to identify the attributes and context-specific dimensions of service quality. Initially, 54 attributes were identified. These attributes were organized into four groups: facilities, catering, pricing, and activities. After testing the validity of these attributes with a customer survey, only 23 attributes were retained. Following Gronroos' approach, these attributes were later classified simply into two groups: functional quality (12 attributes) and technical quality (11 attributes). Accordingly, Oberoi and Hales (1990) developed a content-specific instrument (23-item) for measuring service quality of conference hotels. Moreover, their study showed that the functional aspects of service quality made more contribution to overall service quality, than technical quality.

Brotherton and Booth (1997) applied the SERVQUAL instrument as a vehicle to assess customer perceptions of service quality within a 4-star hotel leisure club environment in the United Kingdom. Their study suggested that the 'tangibles' dimension was not a single entity but that leisure club customers viewed the tangible elements of the product as comprising two distinct dimensions: hygiene/cleanliness and resource appropriateness. Similarly, these same customers also appeared to differentiate between two aspects of the SERVQUAL's 'reliability' dimension: reservations and facilities/opening hours. Again this suggested that the homogeneity of this SERVQUAL dimension may not be sustainable in this type of environment. Ekinci et al. (2003) found that, when the SERVQUAL scale was applied to resort hotels, perceived quality could be captured by two global dimensions: tangibles and intangibles. Thus, four of the SERVQUAL dimensions – assurance, reliability, empathy, and responsiveness – were loaded into a dimension called intangibles, while the tangibles dimension remained distinct. Another stream of research developed new scales that were specific to niche markets of the hospitality industry. For instance, Knutson et al. (1990) developed LODGSERV for measuring service quality in the US lodging industry. Mackay and Crompton (1990) designed REQUAL for assessing service quality in recreation centers. Stevens et al. (1995) introduced DINESERV for service quality measurement in restaurants.

In conclusion, the empirical studies have confirmed a few generic service quality dimensions and identified some unique service quality dimensions in the hospitality industry. In particular, the two service quality dimensions – physical and interaction quality – offered by the Nordic school (e.g., Grönroos, 1984; Lehtinen and Lehtinen, 1991) were found to be more generic than the other service quality models (Ekinci, 2001; Mells et al., 1997). In a recent study, Brady and Cronin (2001) suggested that service quality should be measured with fewer dimensions than those suggested by the SERVQUAL model. Furthermore, it is suggested that service quality may be split into primary and secondary dimensions at various levels of abstraction. The primary dimensions (e.g., physical environment quality, interactions quality) are generic and therefore applicable to all hospitality units, whereas the secondary dimensions are specific and only applicable to a particular hospitality unit (e.g., restaurant, café, or resort hotel) or customer market (e.g., leisure or business travelers).

Business performance

Business performance (BP) measurement represents an essential tool to enable managers to achieve and to control their desired objectives as well as their strategies (Simons, 2000). Accordingly, such tool sets include metric and non-metric measures that can be used to quantify both the efficiency and effectiveness of the firm's performance. To put it more simply, BP measurements can help a company to assess its ability to exploit resources and to make sure that the company meets the requirements of its customers (Neely et al., 1995).

This part of the chapter introduces some commonly used BP measures from a number of alternative approaches as follows:

- The Balanced Scorecard was developed by Kaplan and Norton (1992) to measure business performance by using a set of different perspectives: the financial perspective, the customer perspective, the innovation and learning perspective, and the internal business perspective. This approach uses both financial and non-financial measures of BP.
- The Performance Pyramid System (PPS) was developed by Cross and Lynch (1988–1989) to measure BP through linking the overall company strategy to its operations after developing suitable measures for all levels in the company.
- The Performance Measurement System for Service Industries (PMSSI) was developed by Fitzgerald et al. (1991) to measure BP in service companies based on the unique characteristics and features of such businesses. As a result, the PMSSI includes dimensions to measure service performance such as: competitiveness, financial performance, quality of service, flexibility, resource utilization, and innovation.
- The Integrated Performance Measurement System (IPMS) measures BP through using seven financial and non-financial factors grouped into internal and external factors. As a result, the causal relationships between these factors can follow the use of resources from the point of allocation to the point of receiving revenues (Laitinen, 2002).

In contrast to the diversity of business performance measurement systems, financial performance has been traditionally measured by using ratio analysis calculated directly from a company's financial statements. These ratios can be categorized into five main groups:

1. Profitability ratios, which indicate the ability of a company to generate profits from its capital employed or assets (Mclaney, 2000).
2. Investment ratios, which evaluate business performance from the viewpoint of shareholders and investors (Adams, 1997).
3. Activity ratios, which show how efficient a company is in using and managing its assets to make sales and profits (Brigham and Houston, 2004).
4. Liquidity ratios, which indicate a firm's ability to pay off its short-term obligations (Brealey et al., 2001).
5. Leverage ratios, which determine the proportionate contributions of owners and creditors to a business structure, i.e., the extent to which debt is used in a company's capital structure (Brigham and Houston, 2004).

Issues in Measuring BP in the Hospitality Industry

Given the huge surge in academic interest in recent years in the area of performance measurement, it is surprising that few researchers have, as yet, turned their attention to measuring BP the hospitality industry, which displays a number of characteristics of variety, variability, and volatility that would seem to give it rich potential. There are, however, a small number of authors who have approached this area directly and some others who have considered it as part of a broader study with a direct focus elsewhere.

In reviewing hospitality research published in 1995, Teare (1996) highlights BP as one of his key themes. Although it would be true to say that his definition of BP is rather less focused than the position taken in this paper, he does identify papers on the use of the balanced scorecard in hotels and the contribution of yield management to profit performance, as well as broader aspects of business excellence, benchmarking, and the impact of technology. It is interesting, however, that he does not view BP as an area that emerges from his analysis of publications between 1989 and 1994 and, as can be seen here, only limited attention has, surprisingly, been given to this important area, since 1995.

The next work to emerge is by Hepworth (1998) who conducts a review of the literature on the balanced scorecard. His review, following from his dissertation work, finds limited evidence of the application of the concept in the hospitality industry, other than Brander-Brown's and McDonnell's (1995) work already mentioned in Teare's review and indeed his own work in the Food Services branch of the Royal Logistics Corps within the British Army. He highlights some concerns about the problems of implementing the 'softer' dimensions of the approach and whether this US management approach would sit well with the British culture.

Harris and Mongiello (2001) acknowledge changes in the field of performance measurement, based on criticisms of narrowness and profit centric approaches, toward more balanced and success-oriented views. Drawing on the views of hotel general managers working in chain-affiliated European properties, their study considers three key dimensions of balance, orientation, and coherence as evident in a manager's decision-making process through the selection, interpretation, and application of their performance measures. Their research first established what performance indicators managers used regularly to determine their business progress and then tried to establish what these measures actually meant to the managers concerned, before progressing to the decisions these measures allowed managers to take. They found that the most important perspectives concerned human resources, operations, and the customer, while, in practice, it is the financial and customer related indicators that are used as the basis for management decisions and consequent action. It would appear that human resources, operations, and customer measures are used to inform the decisions taken that are then checked against their impact on financial performance.

In the small- and medium-sized UK hospitality industry units, Phillips and Louvieris (2005) investigated ten best-practice organizations and the performance measures by using a theoretical framework derived from the balanced scorecard approach. Results revealed that four key concepts drove measurement systems across these businesses. These were concerned with (1) budgetary control, particularly to ensure the achievement and improvement of revenue targets, (2) customer relationship management as a way of improving quality of service and customer retention, (3) strategic management in managing internal business processes, and (4) collaboration both inside and outside the business to drive innovation and learning. Based on this work, they also propose a balanced scorecard approach identifying critical success factors and key performance indicators that would be suitable for hotel businesses as an exemplar for further development.

Others studies which consider aspects of BP and its measurement in the hospitality industry are limited. Phillips et al. (1999) used neural network analysis to explore the effect of strategic planning on BP in hotels. They distinguished between aspects of thoroughness and sophistication of the strategic planning process and its market-led formality. While the degree of thoroughness and sophistication of the strategic planning process had a direct positive effect on overall performance, the degree of formality and rigidity of the process could be seen to hamper overall performance. Gray et al. (2000), working in New Zealand, isolated the results of 21 hospitality companies from a larger multi-industry sample of over one thousand firms. Comparing the results of the hospitality firms and the top performing service firms, they found some interesting differences. They found the top performing firms were more market-oriented and that these firms also encounter greater technological turbulence and have to deal with more powerful suppliers. While there were few performance differences between the two groups, they suggest that hospitality firms should improve their market orientation to be able to cope with future market turbulence, where forming closer relationships with customers will be more important. They also suggest developing a corporate culture which emphasizes innovation and the development of new, efficient service development processes.

Drawing on a sample of 189 hospitality firms in Spain, Garrigós-Simón et al. (2005) link the Miles and Snow strategy typologies to BP. Their analysis revealed four dimensions of performance: profitability, growth, stakeholder satisfaction, and competitive position, which they subsequently merged into a single overall performance measure. Their findings reinforced the existing literature in that the prospector, defenders, and analyzer types had significantly better performance across all variables than the reactors. Within the successful types, prospectors were almost always associated with superior performance, although analyzers scored better in the area of profitability.

This review shows only limited interest from the academic community in aspects of BP in the hospitality industry, whereas outside the industry this area of academic interest has shown substantial growth. This is especially surprising because BP is fundamentally important to the commercial success and continuation of this industry where the separation of management and ownership places particular demands on managing and measuring performance.

Developing a model linking service quality with BP

There is little agreement from previous research on the link between service quality and performance. Some previous empirical studies have investigated the relationship between service quality and profitability by adopting both direct and indirect relationship perspectives. Some of these studies have found that quality has a positive impact on BP that could be measured by profitability ratios such as return on investment (ROI) and return on equity (ROE) (Duncan and Elliott, 2002; Garuana and Pit, 1997; Hendricks and Singhal, 1997; Kimes, 2001; Hasan and Kerr, 2003; Nelson et al., 1992; Philips et al., 1983; Raju and Lonial, 2002; Schoeffler et al., 1974; Zhang, 2000). On the other hand, some other studies have indicated that the nature of the relationship between service quality and profitability is negative, i.e., increasing the quality of service may decrease the profitability of firms in the short term (Easton 1993; Harrington and Akehurst, 1996; Sterman, et al., 1997; Reger, et al., 1994). A further set of studies has suggested that improving quality may have a minimal or at best a weak effect on BP (Adam, 1994).

As mentioned above, despite a long-term interest in investigating the relationship between service quality and profitability, there is still debate concerning the exact nature of the relationship between these two concepts. Previous studies have been carried out in industries including finance, healthcare, and retail by investigating the common variables related to the service quality–profitability relationship, such as customer satisfaction, customer retention, market share, price, cost, and productivity. Only a few of these studies have used sophisticated statistical methods, such as structural equation modeling, to explore the nature of the relationship between all the variables. Thus, 'despite nearly two decades of research on quality improvements efforts, the relationships between customer perceptions of quality and financial outcomes are still being debated' (Babakus et al., 2004, p. 714).

In most cases, the literature shows a positive effect of service quality on BP. However, there are very few studies available that have addressed these issues in the hotel industry. Of those studies that have looked at hotels, the majority has not examined the quality/ performance relationship and included all the probable mediating variables; most studies in the hotel industry have investigated the relationship by using only a direct perspective.

There is an obvious deficiency of research in this area. For that reason, this chapter addresses the relationship between service quality and profitability by including a set of mediating variables in order to explore the direction of the relationship between the variables. A conceptual framework is developed to uncover the structural relationships and the expected effects between all variables. Service quality commonly affects a firm's profitability through indirect mechanisms and relationships. A high level of service quality affects the intermediate variables which in turn will have an impact on a firm's performance and profitability (Hardie, 1998).

The conceptual framework in Figure 8.1 suggests that service quality has a positive indirect effect on hotels' profitability via two scenarios. The first scenario involves increasing revenues through improving customer satisfaction and retention, while the second scenario involves lowering costs through process improvements (Hardie, 1998; Rust et al., 2002). The main variables in this conceptual framework are the results of previous case studies, opinion surveys, experiments and correlation studies that support a number of causal relationships. The signs (+ or –) signify the expected direction of the relationship between the variables.

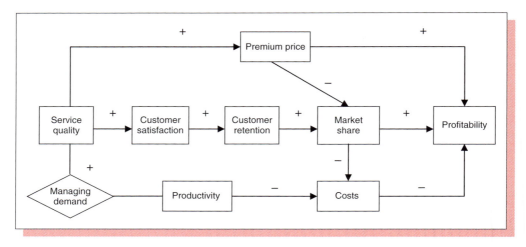

Figure 8.1
A conceptual framework of the service quality–profitability relationship (*Source*: Zeglat et al. (2005)).

The link between service quality, premium price, and profitability

The literature indicates that premium price can be used as an indicator of perceived high quality (Dodds et al., 1991; Lichtenstein and
Burton, 1989; Rao and Monroe, 1989; Zeithaml, 1988). Perceived high
levels of quality allow a company to charge higher prices. Producing
high-quality products gives a company the option to charge premium
prices above competitors' due to perceived superior quality performance. The premium price will be translated into higher bottom line
profits. Charging premium prices allows a company to invest more
than competitors in R&D and in new products to achieve higher perceived quality and market share in the future. Thus, offering superior
service quality gives a company the ability to command higher prices
which in turn increases profitability (Buzzell and Gale, 1987).

Service quality and customer satisfaction

Service quality is a cognitive evaluation of a service provider's performance whereas customer satisfaction is a short-term emotional reaction to a specific service performance, i.e., the evaluation of specific
transactions that follows a purchase event or a series of customer–
supplier interactions (Lovelock and Wright, 2001). The literature indicates that perceived service quality leads to an affective response in
the form of customer satisfaction. In other words, perceived high levels of service quality in the target service produced by comparisons
between customers' expectations and perceptions leads to a psychological state called customer satisfaction. Therefore, customer satisfaction

can be said to be an outcome of the customer's perceptions of service quality (Anderson et al., 1994; Brady and Robertson, 2001; Churchill and Surprenant, 1982; Cronin et al., 2000; Dabholkar et al., 2000; Fornell et al., 1996).

Service quality, productivity, costs, and profitability

In the service sector, the management of quality cannot be separated from the management of productivity (Filiatrault et al., 1996). Quality improvement must embrace both productivity and profitability (Gummesson, 1998). Improving quality will lead to increased productivity through reducing defects and wastage as well as improvements in worker productivity that could lead to a reduced workforce (Garvin, 1984). That is, quality should reduce costs through better productivity by reducing the inputs of labor and/or materials required to produce a unit of output (Rust et al., 2002).

When demand patterns are understood and actively managed, higher quality can lead to increased productivity, which in turn leads to lower costs (Harkey and Varciu, 1992). Excess demand may mean higher costs of labor and materials, which would in turn decrease profits. Low levels of demand may mean an underutilization of resources. Thus, the relationship between service quality and productivity will be positively correlated only when the company can manage and control patterns of demand for their services.

Customer satisfaction and customer retention

Achieving a high level of customer satisfaction brings some offensive and defensive advantages at the macro and micro levels such as increased customer loyalty for the current customers, reduced price elasticity (more tolerance of increases in price), insulation of current customers from other competitors' campaigns, reduced costs in attracting new customers (by positive word-of-mouth), reduced costs of future transactions, and enhanced reputation for the company. Thus, customer satisfaction also represents an economic indicator for the individual business (Anderson et al., 1994; Fornell, 1992). Increasing customer satisfaction means increasing customer loyalty and the intention to buy from the same supplier. The literature indicates that customer satisfaction is an antecedent of customer retention and that customer satisfaction mediates the relationship between service quality and the customer's behavioral intentions (Anderson and Sullivan, 1993; Dabholkar et al., 2000; Oliver, 1980; Olsen, 2002; Mittal and Kamakura, 2001). These behavioral intentions imply favorable customer habits such as saying positive things about the company, recommending it to other potential customers, remaining loyal, and spending more with the company (Cronin et al., 2000).

Customer retention and market share

Retaining the current customers is an important policy in that it brings advantages such as increased revenues, reduced marketing and operational costs of acquiring new customers, and reduced problems and questions (Bateson, 1995). Customers who maintain a long-term relationship with a firm are more likely to purchase additional services than new customers and spread favorable word-of-mouth (Zeithaml et al., 1996). Increasing customer retention leads to increased market share and revenues (Rust et al., 1995). The literature indicates that customer retention results from customer satisfaction, which in turn represents an important component of market share. Thus, customer satisfaction represents a central issue in the financial impact of service quality. To put it more simply, customer satisfaction is connected sequentially to customer loyalty, retention rate, market share, and, hence, profits (Rust and Zahorik, 1993).

Market share and profitability

Increasing market share may result in financial benefits for a company for several reasons such as economies of scale from different aspects of operations including procurement, manufacturing, marketing, R&D, etc., owing to the 'experience curve' leading to reduced unit production costs. A higher market share also leads to increased customer volumes and in turn to greater bargaining power in the market with customers and suppliers (Aaker, 1995). Economies of scale will lead to reduced unit costs over time, which in turn should be translated into higher profits (Buzzell and Gale, 1987). Although there are some inconsistencies in the literature about the direction of such a relationship, researchers have found positive relationships between market share and profitability. That is, companies with a high market share tend to have higher earnings (Buzzell and Gale, 1987; Schoeffler et al., 1974; Szymanski et al., 1993).

Directions for future research

Service quality and performance measurement models are the focus of considerable attention in academic and practitioner communities. Service quality models and performance measurement systems make significant contributions to the management of hospitality firms. However, the relationship between the two constructs is still not clearly understood. Although this chapter has addressed this issue by introducing a conceptual model, the hypothesized relationships between service quality and BP need to be subjected to empirical testing within the specific context of the hospitality industry. Thus, future research needs to answer the questions: *What is the nature of the relationship between service quality and BP in the hospitality industry? Are they directly or indirectly related? Is it a positive or negative relationship? What variables, if any, mediate the relationship between service quality and BP in the hospitality industry?*

For the contribution of this research to be realized, it is essential that the measurement models used be relevant and appropriate for the environment and strategies of hospitality firms. Given the dynamic and rapidly changing environment in which most hospitality firms compete, it is important that hospitality firms effectively manage their service quality and performance measurement systems so that the company's decisions are based on the information that is relevant to the issues of current importance.

The service quality literature asserts that perceived quality is generic but empirical tests of the current service quality models have produced inconsistent results regarding the validity of the generic nature of service quality dimensions in the hospitality industry. To date, studies have failed to determine the exact nature and number of dimensions that are applicable to all hospitality firms. It seems that a two-dimensional model of service quality – physical quality and interaction quality – is most suited to measuring service quality in the hospitality industry. However, future research testing the relationship between service quality and BP should address this issue. Furthermore, when testing the relationship between service quality and financial BP, researchers should consider adopting cross-sectional and longitudinal studies in order to expand our understanding of the relationship between these two concepts across various hospitality firms. Because firms in the hospitality industry are highly fragmented and service-oriented, testing this relationship may require different research designs and measurements.

Finally, some specific questions that need to be answered are: What levels of service provision are needed to retain customers? What aspects of service quality are most important for customer retention? Where should companies invest in service quality to have the greatest impact on customer satisfaction, customer retention, and financial outcomes? How can existing customers be identified and segmented in terms of profitability? How can potential customer be identified in terms of profitability? Questions can go on.

Conclusions

Quality of service represents a critical factor for business success due to its marketing and financial implications. Customer behavior, market share, price, productivity, and costs are all related to quality improvements. As a result, the relationship between service quality and profitability is complex and multi-directional. To simplify this complexity, two scenarios or routes for quality efforts are suggested to improve profitability: (1) increasing revenues by increasing customer satisfaction and customer retention and (2) reducing costs by increasing productivity. Future research should investigate the relationship between the quality of service and profitability in the hospitality industry in order to determine which of the above scenarios will make the most significant contribution to the financial performance of hospitality firms.

References

Aaker, D. (1995). *Strategic Marketing Management* (4th ed.) John Wiley and Sons, USA.

Adam, E. (1994). Alternative quality improvement practices and organization performance. *Journal of Operations Management*, 12 (1), 27–44.

Adams, D. (1997). *Management Accounting for the Hospitality Industry: A Strategic Approach* (1st ed.) Cassell, London.

Anderson, E., and Sullivan, M. (1993). The antecedents and consequence of customer satisfaction. *Marketing Science*, 12 (2), 125–143.

Anderson, E., Fornell, C., and Lehmann, D. (1994). Customer satisfaction, market share, and profitability: Findings from Sweden. *Journal of Marketing*, 58 (3), 53–66.

Atkinson, A. (1988). Answering the eternal question: what does the customer want? *The Cornell Hotel and Restaurant Administration Quarterly*, 30 (2), 12–14.

Babakus, E., Bienstock, C., and Scotter, J. (2004). Linking perceived quality and customer satisfaction to store traffic and revenue growth. *Decision Science*, 35 (4), 713–737.

Barrington, M.N. and Olson, M.D. (1987). The concept of service in the hospitality industry. *International Journal of Hospitality Management*, 6 (3), 131–138.

Barsky, J.D. (1992). Customer satisfaction in the hotel industry: Meaning and measurement. *Hospitality Research Journal*, 16 (1), 51–73.

Barsky, J.D., and Labacgh, R. (1992). A strategy for customer satisfaction. *The Cornell Hotel and Restaurant Administration Quarterly*, 33 (5), 32–40.

Bateson, J. (1995). *Management Services Marketing: Text and Readings* (3rd ed.) The Dryden Press, USA.

Bolton, R.N. and Drew, J.H. (1991). A multistage model of customers' assessment of service and value. *Journal of Consumer Research*, 17 (4), 375–384.

Brady, M. and Roberson, C. (2001). Searching for consensus on the antecedent role of service quality and satisfaction: An exploratory cross-national study. *Journal of Business Research*, 51 (1), 53–60.

Brady, M.K., and Cronin, J.J. (2001). Some new thoughts on conceptualizing perceived service quality: A hierarchical approach. *Journal of Marketing*, 65 (3), 34–39.

Brander-Brown, J. and McDonnell, B. (1995). The balanced scorecard: short term guest or long term resident? *International Journal of Contemporary Hospitality Management*, 7 (2/3), 7–11.

Brathwaite, R. (1992). Value-chain assessment of the travel experience. *The Cornell Hotel and Restaurant Administration Quarterly*, 33 (5), 41–49.

Brealey, R.A., Myers, S.C., and Marcus, A.J. (2001). *Fundamentals of corporate finance* (3rd ed.) McGraw-Hill Irwin, Boston.

Brigham, E.F., and Houston, J.F. (2004). *Fundamentals of Financial Management* (10th ed.). Thomson South-Western, USA.

Brotherton, B. (2004). Critical success factors in UK budget hotel operations. *International Journal of Operations and Production Management*, 24 (9), 944–969.

Brotherton, B. and Booth, W. (1997). An application of SERVQUAL to a hotel leisure club environment. *The Proceedings of the Euro CHRIE/IAHMS Autumn Conference*, ISBN: 086–339–762 X, Sheffield Hallam University, pp. 117–121.

Buzzell, R. and Gale, B. (1987). The PIMS principles: Linking strategy to performance. Free Press, USA.

Cadotte, E.R. and Turgeon, U. (1988). Dissatisfiers and satisfiers suggestions for consumer complaints and compliments. *Journal of Consumer Satisfaction, Dissatisfaction and Complaining Behavior*. 1, 74–79.

Callan, R. (1993). An appraisal of UK hotel quality grading schemes. *International Journal of Contemporary Hospitality Management*, 5 (5), 10–18.

Callan, R. and Lefebve, C. (1997). Classification and grading of UK lodges: Do they adequate to managers' and customers' perception? *Tourism Management*, 18 (7), 417–424.

Carmen, J.M. (1990). Consumer perceptions of service quality: An assessment of the SERVQUAL dimensions. *Journal of Retailing*, 66 (1), 33–55.

Carper, J. (1991). Hoteliers of the world: Southern hospitality the right way, *Hotels*, 25 (11), 44–45.

Choi, T.Y. and Chu, R. (2001). Determinants of hotel guests' satisfaction and repeat patronage in the Hong Kong hotel industry. *International Journal of Hospitality Management*, 20, 277–297.

Churchill, G. and Surprenant, C. (1982). An investigation into the determinants of customer satisfaction. *Journal of Marketing Research*, 19 (4), 491–504.

Clow, K. E., Garretson, J.A., and Kurtz, D.L., (1994). An exploratory study into the purchase decision process used by leisure travelers in hotel selection. *Journal of Hospitality and Leisure Marketing*, 2 (4), 53–72.

Cronin, J., Brady, M., and Hult, G. (2000). Assessing the effects of quality, value, and customer satisfaction on behavioral intentions in service environment. *Journal of Retailing*, 67 (2), 193–218.

Cronin, J.J. and Taylor, S.A. (1992). Measuring service quality: A re-examination and extension. *Journal of Marketing*, 56 (3), 55–65.

Cross, K. F. and Lynch, R. L. (1988–1989). The SMART Way to Define and Sustain Success. *National Productivity Review*, 8 (1), 23–33.

Dabholkar, P.A., Shepherd, D.A., Thorpe, D.I. (2000). A comprehensive framework for service quality: an investigation of critical conceptual and measurement issues through a longitudinal study. *Journal of Retailing*, 76 (2), 139–173.

Dodds, W., Monroe, K., and Grewal, D. (1991). Effects of price, brand, and store information on buyers' product evaluations. *Journal of Marketing Research*, 28 (3), 307–319.

Duncan, E. and Elliott, G. (2002). Customer service quality and financial performance among Australian retail financial institutions. *Journal of Financial Service Marketing*, 7 (1), 25–41.

Duncan, V. (1993). Fewer chocolates, greater safety. *Lodging Hospitality*, 49 (12), 12–13.

Easton, G.S. (1993). The 1993 state of U.S total quality management: A Baldridge examiner's perspective. *California Management Review*, 35 (3), 32–54.

Ekinci, Y. (2001). The validation of the generic service quality dimensions: An alternative approach. *Journal of Retailing and Consumer Services*, 8 (6), 311–24.

Ekinci, Y., Prokopaki, K., and Cobanoglu, C. (2003). Service quality in certain accommodations: Marketing strategies for the UK holiday market. *International Journal of Hospitality Management*, 22 (1), 47–66.

Farsad, B. and LeBurto, S. (1994). Managing quality in the hospitality industry. *Hospitality Tourism Education*, 6 (2), 49–42.

Fick, G.R. and Ritchie, J.R.B. (1991). Measuring service quality in the travel and tourism industry. *Journal of Travel Research*, 30 (2), 2–9.

Filiatrault, P., Harvey, J., and Chebat, J. (1996). Service quality and service productivity management practices. *Industrial Marketing Management*, 25 (3), 243–255.

Fitzgerald, L., Johnston, R., Brignall, S., Silvestro, R., and Voss, C. (1991). *Performance Measurement in Service Industries* (1st ed.) CIMA, UK.

Fornell, C. (1992). A national customer satisfaction barometer: The Swedish experience. *Journal of Marketing*, 56 (1), 6–21.

Fornell, C., Johnson, M., Anderson, E., Cha, J., and Bryant, B. (1996). The American customer satisfaction index: Nature, purpose and findings. *Journal of Marketing*, 60 (4), 7–18.

Garrigós-Simón, FJ., Marqués, DP., and Narangajavana, Y (2005). Competitive strategies and performance in Spanish hospitality firms. *International Journal of Contemporary Hospitality Management*, 17 (1), 22–38.

Garuana, A. and Pit, L. (1997). INTQUAL-an internal measure of service and the link between service quality and business performance. *European Journal of Marketing*, 3 (8), 604–616.

Garvin, D. (1984). What does product quality really mean? *Sloan Management Review*, 26 (1), 25–43.

Getty, J.M. and Thompson, K.N. (1994). A procedure for scaling perceptions of lodging quality. *Hospitality Research Journal*, 18 (2), 75–96.

Gray, B.J., Matear, S.M., and Matheson, P.K. (2000). Improving the performance of hospitality firms. *International Journal of Contemporary Hospitality*, 12 (3), 149–155.

Grönroos, C. (1984). A service quality model and its marketing implications. *European Journal of Marketing*, 18 (4), 36–44.

Gummesson, E. (1998). Productivity, quality and relationship marketing in service operations. *International Journal of Contemporary Hospitality Management*, 10 (1), 4–15.

Hall, W.K. (1980). Survival strategies in a hostile environment. *Harvard Business Review*, 58 (5), 75–92.

Hardie, N. (1998). The effects of quality on business performance. *Quality Management Journal*, 5 (3), 65–83.

Harkey, J. and Varciu, R. (1992). Quality of health care and financial performance: Is there a link. *Health Care Management Review*, 17 (4), 55–63.

Harrington, D. and Akehurst, G. (1996). Service quality and business performance in the UK hotel industry. *International Journal of Hospitality Management*, 15 (3), 283–286.

Harris, P.J. and Mongiello, M. (2001). Key performance indicators in European hotel properties: General managers' choices and company profiles. *International Journal of Contemporary Hospitality Management*, 13 (3), 120–128.

Hasan, M. and Kerr, R. (2003). The relationship between total quality management practices and organizational performance in service organizations. *The TQM Magazine*, 15 (4), 286–291.

Haywood, K.M. (1983). Assessing the quality of hospitality services. *International Journal of Hospitality Management*, 2 (4), 165–177.

Hendricks, K.B. and Singhal, V.R. (1997). Does implementing an effective TQM program actually improve operating performance?; Empirical evidence from firms that have won quality awards. *Management Science*, 43 (9), 1258–1274.

Hepworth, P. (1998). Weighing it up – a literature review for the balanced scorecard. *Journal of Management Development*, 17 (8), 559–563

Ingram, H. (1996). Clusters and gaps in hospitality and tourism academic research. *International Journal of Contemporary Hospitality Management*, 8 (7), 91–95.

Jones, P. and Dent, M. (1994). Lessons in consistency: Statistical process control in Forte plc. *The TQM Magazine*, 6 (1), 18–23.

Johns, N. and Lee-Ross, D. (1995). Profile accumulation: A quality assessment technique for hospitality SMSs. In Teare, R. and Armistead, C. (eds.), *Service Management: New Directions and Perspectives*, Cassell, London.

Juran, J.M. (1979).*Quality Control Handbook* (3rd ed.). Mac-Graw Hill, New York.

Kaplan, R.S. and Norton, D.P. (1992). The balanced scorecard-measures that drive performance. *Harvard Business Review*, 70 (1), 71–79.

Kimes, S.E. (2001). How product quality drives profitability. *Cornell Hotel and Restaurant Administration Quarterly*, 42 (3), 25–28.

Knutson, B. (1988a). Ten laws of customer satisfaction. *The Cornell Hotel and Restaurant Administration Quarterly*, 29 (3), 14–17.

Knutson, B. (1988b). Frequent travelers: Making them happy and bringing them back. *The Cornell Hotel and Restaurant Administration Quarterly*, 29 (1), 82–87.

Knutson, B., Stevens, P., Wullaert, C., and Yokoyoma, F. (1990). LODGSERV: A service quality index for the lodging industry.*Hospitality Research Journal*, 14 (2), 227–284.

Kotler, P., Bowen, J., and Makens, J. (2003). *Marketing for Hospitality and Tourism* (3rd ed.) Prentice Hall, USA.

Laitinen, E.K. (2002). A dynamic performance measurement system: Evidence from small finish technology companies. *Scandinavian Journal of Management*, 18 (1), 65–99.

Lee, Y.L. and Hing, N. (1995). Measuring quality in restaurant operations: An application of the SERVQUAL instrument. *International Journal of Hospitality Management*, 14 (3/4), 293–310.

Lehtinen, U. and Lehtinen, J.R. (1991). Two approaches to service quality dimensions. *The Service Industries Journal*, 11 (3), 287–303.

Lewis, B.R. and Owtram, M. (1986). Customer satisfaction with the package holidays. In Moores, B. (ed.) *Are they Being Served?* (pp. 201–213). Oxford: Philip Allan Publisher Limited.

Lewis, R.C. (1984a). Theoretical and practical considerations in research design. *The Cornell Hotel and Restaurant Administration Quarterly*, 25 (1), 25–35.

Lewis, R.C. (1984b). Isolating differences in hotel attributes. *The Cornell Hotel and Restaurant Administration Quarterly*, 25 (3), 64–77.

Lewis, R.C. (1987). The measurement of gaps in the quality of hotel services. *International Hospitality Management*, 6 (2), 83–88.

Lewis, R.C. (1988). Uses and abuses of hospitality research. *The Cornell Hotel and Restaurant Administration Quarterly*, 29 (3), 11–12.

Lewis, R.C. and Pizam, A (1981). Guest survey: A missed opportunity. *The Cornell Hotel and Restaurant Administration Quarterly*, 22 (3), 37–44.

Lichtenstein, D. and Burton, S. (1989). The relationship between perceived and objective price-quality. *Journal of Marketing Research*, 26 (4), 429–443.

Lockwood, A. (1994). Using service incidents to identify quality improvement points. *International Journal of Contemporary Hospitality Management*, 6(1/2), 75–80.

Lockwood, A., Gummesson, A., Hubrecht, J., and Senior, M., (1992). Developing and maintaining a strategy for service quality. In Teare, R. and Olsen, M. (eds.) *International Hospitality Management Corporate Strategy in Practice* (pp. 312–339). Pitman Pub, London.

Lovelock, C. and Wright, L. (2001). *Principles of Service Marketing and Management* (2nd ed.). Prentice Hall, USA.

MacKay, K. and Crompton, J. (1990). Measuring the quality of recreation services. *Journal of Park Recreation Administration*, 8 (3), 47–56.

Martin, D.W. (1995). An importance/performance analysis of service providers' perception of service quality service in the hotel industry. *Journal of Hospitality and Leisure Marketing*, 3 (1), 5–17.

Mclaney, E.J. (2000). *Business Finance: Theory and Practice* (5th ed.) Financial Times Prentice Hall, Britain.

Mells, G., Boshoff, C., and Deon, N. (1997). The dimensions of service quality: The original European perspective revisited. *The Service Industries Journal*, 17(1), 173–189.

Mittal, V. and Kamakura, W. (2001). Satisfaction, repurchase intent, and repurchase behavior: Investigating the moderating effect of customer characteristics. *Journal of Marketing Research*, 38(1), 131–142.

Moore, S.A. (1994). *Perceptions of Service Quality: An Empirical Analysis in the Freight Sector*. Unpublished Ph.D. thesis, University of Wales.

Neely, A., Gregory, M., and Platts, K. (1995). Performance measurement system design: A literature review and research agenda. *International Journal of Operations and Production Management*, 15 (4), 80–116.

Nelson, E., Rust, R., Zahorik, A., et al. (1992). Do patient perceptions of quality relate to hospital financial performance? *Journal of Health Care Marketing*, 12 (4), 6–13.

Nightingale, M. (1983). Determination and control of quality standards in hospitality services, Unpublished M.Phil. Thesis, University of Surrey.

Nikolich, M.A. and Sparks, B.A. (1995). The hospitality service encounter: The role of communication. *The Hospitality Research Journal*, 19(2), 43–56.

Oberoi, U. and Hales, C. (1990). Assessing the quality of the conference hotel service product: Towards an empirically based model. *Service Industries Journal*, 10 (4), 700–721.

Oh, H. and Parks, S. (1997). Customer satisfaction and service quality: Critical review of the literature and research implications for the hotel industry. *Hospitality Research Journal*, 20 (3), 35–64.

Oliver, R. (1980). A cognitive model of the antecedents and consequences of satisfaction decisions. *Journal of Marketing Research*, 17 (4), 460–469.

Olsen, S. (2002). Comparative evaluation and the relationship between quality, satisfaction, and repurchase loyalty. *Journal of the Academy of the Marketing Science*, 30 (3), 240–249.

Ooi, A., Dean, A., and White, C (1999). Analyzing service quality in the hospitality industry. *Managing Service Quality*, 9 (2), 146–143.

Parasuraman, A., Berry, L.L., and Zeithaml, V.A. (1991). Refinement and reassessment of the SERVQUAL scale. *Journal of Retailing*, 67, 421–450.

Parasuraman, A., Zeithaml, V.A., and Berry, L.L. (1985). A conceptual model of service quality and its implications for future research. *Journal of Marketing*, 49 (3), 41–50.

Parasuraman, A., Zeithaml, V.A., and Berry, L.L. (1988). SERVQUAL a multiple-item scale for measuring consumer perception of service quality. *Journal of Retailing*, 64 (1), 13–40.

Parasuraman, A., Zeithaml, V.A., and Berry, L.L. (1994). Alternative scales for measuring service quality: a comparative assessment based on psychometric and diagnostic criteria. *Journal of Retailing*, 70 (3), 193–199.

Parasuraman, A., Zeithaml, V., and Berry, L. (1985). A conceptual model of service quality and its implications for future research. *Journal of Marketing*, 49 (4), 41–50.

Philips, L.W., Change, D.R., and Buzzell, R.D. (1983). Product quality, cost position and business performance: A test of some key hypotheses. *Journal of Marketing*, 47 (2), 26–43.

Phillips, P. and Louvieris, P. (2005). Performance measurement systems in tourism, hospitality, and leisure small medium-sized enterprises: A balanced scorecard perspective. *Journal of Travel Research*, 44 (2), 201–11.

Phillips, P., Davies, F, and Mountinho, L. (1999). The interactive effects of strategic planning on hotel performance: A neural network analysis. *Management Decision*, 37 (3), 279–288.

Porter, M.E. (1980). *Competitive Strategy*. New York: The Free Press.

Raju, P.S. and Lonial, S.C. (2002). The impact of service quality and marketing on financial performance in the hospital industry: An empirical examination. *Retailing and Consumer Services*, 9 (6), 335–348.

Rao, A. and Monroe, K. (1989). The effect of price, brand name, and store name on buyers' perceptions of product quality: An integrative review. *Journal of Marketing Research*, 26 (3), 351–357.

Reeves, C.A. and Bednar, D.A. (1994). Defining quality: Alternatives and implications. *Academy of Management Review*, 19 (3), 419–445.

Reger, R., Gustafson, L., Demarie, S., and Mullane, J. (1994). Reframing the organization: Why implementing total quality is easier said than done. *Academy of Management Review*, 19 (3), 565–584.

Richard, M. and Sundaram, D. (1993). Lodging choice intentions: A casual modeling approach. *Journal of Hospitality and Leisure Marketing*, 1 (4), 81–98.

Riley, M. (1984). Hotels and group identity. *International Journal of Tourism Management*, 5 (2), 102–109.

Riley, M. and Perogiannis, N. (1990). The influence of hotel attributes on the selection of a conference venue. *International Journal of Contemporary Hospitality Management*, 2 (1), 17–22.

Rust, R. and Zahorik, A. (1993). Customer satisfaction, customer retention, and market share. *Journal of Retailing*, 69 (2), 193–215.

Rust, R., Moorman, M., and Dickson, P. (2002). Getting return on quality: Revenue expansion, cost reduction, or both? *Journal of Marketing*, 66 (4), 7–24.

Rust, R., Zahorik, A., and Keiningham, T. (1995). Return on quality (ROQ): Making service quality financially accountable. *Journal of Marketing*, 58 (2), 58–70.

Saleh, F. and Ryan, C. (1991). Utilizing the SERVQUAL model: An analysis of service quality. *The Service Industries Journal*, 11 (3), 324–345.

Schoeffler, S., Buzzel, R., and Heany, D. (1974). Impact of strategic planning on profit performance. *Harvard Business Review*, 52 (2), 137–145.

Senior, M.C. (1992). Managing service quality: A study in The UK roadside lodge sector, An unpublished Ph.D. thesis, Dorset Institute: University of Bournemouth.

Sterman, J., Repenning, N., and Kofman, F. (1997). Unanticipated side effects of successful quality programs: Exploring a paradox of organizational improvement. *Management Science*, 43 (4), 503–521.

Simons, R. (2000). *Performance Measurement and Control Systems for Implementing Strategy*. Prentice-Hall, USA.

Sulek, J. (2004). Statistical quality control in services. *International Journal Services Technology and Management*, 5 (5/6), 522–531.

Smith, W.C. (1980). Finding new opportunities for profitability in manufacturing. *Management Review*, 69 (3), 60–62.

Stevens, P., Knutson, B., and Patton, M. (1995). DINESERV: A tool for measuring service quality in restaurants. *The Cornell Hotel and Restaurant Administration Quarterly*, 36 (2), 56–60.

Szymanski, D., Bharadwaj, S., and Varadarajan, R. (1993). An analysis of the market share-profitability relationship. *Journal of Marketing*, 57 (3), 1–18.

Teare, R. (1996). Hospitality operations: Patterns in management, service improvement and business performance. *International Journal of Contemporary Hospitality Management*, 8 (7), 63–74.

Teas, R.K. (1994). Expectations as a comparison standard in measuring service quality. *Journal of Marketing*, 58 (1), 132–139.

Wheelwright, S.C. (1981). Japan – where operations really are strategic. *Harvard Business Review*, 59 (4), 67–74.

Wilensky, L. and Buttle, F. (1988). A multivariate analysis of hotel benefit bundles and choice trade-offs. *International Journal of Hospitality Management*, 7 (1), 29–41.

Wolf, C. (1993). Setting security. *Lodging Hospitality*, 49(3), 30–32.

Wood, R.C. (1994). Hotel culture and social control. *Annals of Tourism Research*, 21 (1), 65–80.

Yesawitch, P.C. (1987 May). Hospitality marketing for the 90's: Effective marketing Research. *The Cornell Hotel and Restaurant Administration Quarterly*, 28, 49–57.

Zeglat, D., Lockwood, A., and Ekinci, Y. (2005). An investigation of the relationship between service quality and profitability in the hotel industry. *EuroCHRIE Conference 2005*, October 26–28, Paris, France.

Zeithaml, V. (1988). Consumer perceptions of price, quality, and value: A means-end model and synthesis evidence. *Journal of Marketing*, 52 (3), 2–22.

Zeithaml, V., Berry, L., and Parasuraman, A. (1996). The behavioral consequences of service quality. *Journal of Marketing*, 60 (2), 31–46.

Zeithaml, V.A. (2000). service quality, profitability, and the economic worth of customers: What we know and what we need to learn. *Journal of the Academy of Marketing Science*, 28 (1), 67–85.

Zeithaml, V.A. and Bitner, M.J. (2003). *Service Marketing: Integrated Customer Focus Across the Firm* (3rd ed.). McGraw-Hill, Boston.

Zeithaml, V.A. (1981). How consumer evaluation processes differ between goods and services, In Donnelly, J.H. and George, W.R. (eds.), *Marketing Services* (pp. 186–190). Chicago, IL, American Marketing Association.

Zeithaml, V.A., Berry, L.L., and Parasuraman, A. (1988). Communication and control processes in the delivery of service quality. *Journal of Marketing*, 52 (2), 35–48.

Zeithaml, V.A., Parasuraman, A., and Berry, L.L. (1990). *Delivering Quality Service: Balancing Customer Perceptions and Expectations*. The Free Press, New York.

Zhang, Z. (2000). Developing a model of quality management methods and evaluating their effects on business performance. *Total Quality Management*, 11 (1), 129–137.

Part Three

Hospitality Consumer Behavior

CHAPTER 9

Motivations, attitudes, and beliefs

Alan D. Bright

Consumer behavior is 'the psychological and social processes people undergo in the acquisition, use and disposal of products, services, ideas, and practices' (Bagozzi et al., 2002, p. 1). Several models of consumer behavior apply to travel and tourism. While the models posit different paths to travel behavior, similarities exist. Each model posits an effect of external and internal variables on behavior/destination choice by affecting the decision process. Among the most important external variables are *communications about travel and travel destinations* (Schmoll, 1977; Woodside and Lysonski, 1989; Um and Crompton, 1990), *significant referents* (Schmoll, 1977; Mayo and Jarvis, 1981; Moutinho, 1987; Um and Crompton, 1990), and *attributes of travel destinations and providers* (Schmoll, 1977). External variables affect travel decisions and behavior by influencing psychological constructs internal to the traveler. Common internal factors include *personality* (Schmoll, 1977; Mayo and Jarvis, 1981; Moutinho, 1987), *attitudes and beliefs* (Schmoll, 1977; Mayo and Jarvis, 1981; Moutinho, 1987; Middleton, 1988; Woodside and Lysonski, 1989; Um and Crompton, 1990; Gilbert, 1991), and *motivations* (Schmoll, 1977; Mayo and Jarvis, 1981; Moutinho, 1987; Um and Crompton, 1990; Gilbert, 1991). This chapter discusses the impacts of motivations, attitudes, and beliefs on travel behavior and decision-making, with a focus on travel motivation frameworks and social psychological theories of attitudes and beliefs. Though presented separately in this chapter, their close proximity in most models of consumer behavior suggests that these factors are related. While motivations 'energize' actions (March and Woodside, 2005) related to travel, their relationship to behavior depends upon attitudes and beliefs about travel destinations and behavior within specific contexts (Baloglu, 2000). That is, attitudes and beliefs about specific travel behavior mediate the relationship between one's travel motivations and behavior.

Travel motivations

Fundamental to travel motivation research is the fact that people have *needs*. For example, on April 16, after a busy tax season, a certified public accountant (CPA) feels tired and listless. After a busy 3 months preparing tax returns, she needs rest, relaxation, and diversion. For the CPA, these needs translate into a *want*, a 2 week beach vacation in Florida. When the CPA identifies the *wants* to satisfy a *need*, motivation occurs, and the travel process begins (Morrison, 2002; Witt and Wright, 1993). Travel motivation is 'the set of needs and attitudes which predisposes a person to act in a specific touristic goal-directed way' (Pearce, 1991, p. 113). An internal state, motivation energizes and directs travel behavior for achieving personal goals. *Motivation* for travel is more fundamental to an individual than the *purpose* or *objective* of a trip.

Pizam, Neumann, and Reichel (1979) made this distinction nearly three decades ago:

A tourist may be motivated to travel to attend a family function in order to satisfy any of his needs of belonging, status, or recognition, though his stated objective for such travel may be to visit friends and relatives. The difference between these two – motivation and objective – is that while the objective is a conscious and overt reason for acting in a certain way, motivation may be an unconscious or covert reason for doing so.

(p. 195)

Studying tourism motivations advances theoretical exploration of the travel phenomenon (Poria et al., 2004). Tourism motivation has been, since the early days of tourism research, a predominant theme in attempting to understand what drives people to travel. (Todd, 1999). In addition to theoretical advances, exploring tourist motivations informs tourism planning and management efforts. Many studies have identified relationships between tourist motivations and management-relevant behaviors such as destination choice, information search, and experience expectations. Tourist motivations correlate with socio-demographic characteristics of travelers, enhancing tourism-marketing tasks such as product and service development, target marketing, and promotion (Decrop, 1999; Hanqin and Lam, 1999; Poria et al., 2004).

Early theories of motivation

Early research on motivations addressed issues in clinical psychology and employee satisfaction and behavior. Murray (1938) identified 30 psychological (e.g., autonomy, recognition, achievement, affiliation, cognizance, etc.) and 14 physiological (e.g., sex, sentience, heat and cold avoidance, passivity, etc.) needs. Murray's classification provides a valuable point of departure in examining the needs people have in connection with their travel and tourism choices (Witt and Wright, 1993).

In his *need hierarchy*, Maslow (1943) identified eight human need categories and hypothesized that people address basic needs prior to attending to higher order needs. The most basic needs are *physiological needs*, (e.g., hunger and thirst), after which the individual focuses on *safety needs* (e.g., security, a predictable environment). These are followed by *love*, or *social needs* (e.g., feelings of belonging, friendship), *esteem needs* (e.g., self-respect, status), *cognitive needs* (e.g., to know, understand) and *aesthetic needs* (e.g., symmetry, beauty). The last two classes are *self-actualization needs* (e.g., self-fulfillment, reaching one's potential) and *transcendence needs* (e.g., help others achieve self-actualization). While being a popular model for describing human needs, Maslow's hierarchy has received little empirical validation from scientific research. Regardless, this theory has generated interest in understanding human motivation through out a variety of applied fields, including travel and tourism behavior.

Herzberg (1959) proposed a *motivator–hygiene* model of job satisfaction. Job characteristics called *motivators* (e.g., achievement and opportunity for advancement) are associated with the content of one's job and encourage strong effort and good performance. *Hygiene factors* (e.g., working conditions and salary) drive job dissatisfaction, are associated with the work environment, but are not motivational (Kreitner and Kinicki, 1998). Applied to travel behavior, a hygiene factor for a hotel near an airport (e.g., a swimming pool for kids) may not sell a room in that hotel for the night, given that nearby hotels have a pool, but the absence of a pool may eliminate any chance at a sale.

Vroom's (1964) and Lawler's (1973) versions of *expectancy theory* explore why people choose courses of actions in the workplace using three factors: valence, expectancy, and instrumentality. *Expectancy* is the belief that one's output or effort will lead to success in a task. *Instrumentality* is the belief that success will result in a certain outcome, such as praise or increased remuneration. *Valence* is the value the individual places on that outcome. Expectancy theory has received empirical support in the area of occupational preference and choice, as well as in a number of disciplines including travel preferences and outdoor recreation.

McClelland's (1988) *motivational needs theory* suggests individuals have three needs that exist at different levels. The strength of these needs influence both how people are motivated and attempt to motivate others. These fundamental needs are *need for achievement* (e.g., seeking achievement and sense of accomplishment/progress), *need for affiliation* (e.g., need for friendships and interactions), and *need for power* (e.g., need to influence others).

While different in many ways, examination of traditional motivation theories brings out similar themes. People do things when they believe that action will result in the fulfillment of a need. In addition, individuals express different needs at different times and in different ways. Furthermore, need fulfillment does not always encourage a behavior, but may prevent a behavior. Many disciplines have adopted these and other theories to understand motivated behavior. Such is the case with travel and tourism, where exploration of need fulfillment and motivation has been a primary area of research.

Travel motivation frameworks

This section of the chapter focuses on four categories of travel motivation frameworks. These include frameworks based on (1) identifying travel motivations, (2) developing tourist typologies,

(3) expectancy theories of motivation, and (4) a functional approach to understanding travel motivations.

Identifying travel motivations

Much of the early research on travel motivations was content-oriented, identifying what factors drive people to travel to certain places to engage in certain travel activities. Discussion of these factors center on the identification of push and pull factors. Push factors refer to intrinsic motivators and needs (e.g., desire for escape and relaxation) that lead to a desire to travel. Pull factors are attributes of a destination that attract an individual once he or she makes the decision to travel, and includes tangible resources as well as traveler perceptions and expectations about a destination. Chapter 15 of this text describes more specifically the background, evolution, and empirical evidence for the notion of push and pull factors. This section describes specific reasons for people's travel and activity decisions. A review of travel motivation literature reveals many different travel experiences. However, broader analyses of these suggest two very basic reasons people leave their home environment: to escape, if only temporarily, from that environment, and/or to have experiences the home environment does not provide.

Dann (1977) identified two factors that influence why people travel, *anomie* and *ego-enhancement*. An anomic society is one where 'norms governing interaction have lost their integrative force, and where lawlessness and meaningless prevail'. While often connected with nineteenth-century Europe, Dann (1981) suggests that modern issues surrounding war, crime, and other stressful circumstances contribute to this societal condition. *Anomie* is an individual condition that arises from a response to the social situation a person finds himself or herself in. It is a person's need to 'get away' from the isolation of his or her normal life to enhance social interaction. A second push factor, *ego-enhancement*, is the need for positive recognition and enhanced status from others. A person can step out of his normal social position and, while traveling, engage in activities that boost his or her ego. Dann's identification of anomie is a restatement of Maslow's *love* or *social needs* while ego-enhancement is consistent with *esteem needs*. A subset of this approach by Dann is the concentration on fantasy (Dann, 1981). The behavioral norms of one's home are, to a degree, absent at the destination. Engaging in 'taboo' behavior is easier to justify at a travel destination than at home. His view of what motivates travelers is as follows:

Related to anomie, the fantasy world of travel seeks to overcome the humdrum, the normlessness and meaninglessness of life, with more satisfying experiences. As regards ego-enhancement, travel presents the tourist with the opportunity to boost his or her ego in acting out an alien personally.

(Dann, 1977, p. 188)

Crompton (1979) emphasized the importance of a 'break from routine' as the primary essence of travel. He suggested that people experience short- and long-term states of disequilibrium, or 'temporal disruptions to homeostasis' (p. 414). Short-term disequilibrium demands immediate attention. A 'break from routine' is a necessary and sufficient condition to restore homeostasis, achievable through a single pleasure vacation. Long-term disequilibrium, though ever-present in an individual, is postponable through a series of pleasure vacations. The 'break from routine' is necessary, but not sufficient to restore long-term equilibrium; satisfaction of other motivations is required as well. After a person identifies a need for a break in routine (the primary push factor), more specific motivations arise, ultimately directing a person to a specific type of vacation or destination.

Gray (1970) called motivation to travel *wanderlust*, a human trait that causes people to want to leave things with which they are familiar in order to experience, first-hand, different cultures and places. Gray also identified a factor described as *sunlust*; travel that depends on the existence of different amenities or experiences than are available in one's home environment.

Iso-Ahola (1982; Mannell and Iso-Ahola, 1987) identified two forces that simultaneously motivate leisure behavior. People seek activities that provide *novel experiences*, allowing a person to escape personal problems/issues in his interpersonal world (e.g., friends and family). People also seek *psychological rewards* from participation in leisure activities. These rewards are personal (e.g., self-determination, achievement, exploration, and learning) and inter-personal (e.g., positive social interactions).

Applying Maslow's hierarchy, Pearce and Caltabiano (1983) presented a five-tier travel-career tapestry that connected needs important to people as they travel to their experience level. This dynamic model suggests people change motivations over time across travel situations and allows travelers multiple motives (Pearce, 1993). The five motivational needs are concern for *biological needs, safety and security, relationship development and extension, special interest and self-development,* and *fulfillment or self-actualization*. People (1) have a 'career' in their tourist behavior, (2) ascend the ladder as they become more experienced in travel settings, (3) sometimes fail to move up the ladder due to external factors such as finances and health, and (4) retire from their 'travel career'. The travel career tapestry successfully described visitors to historic theme parks (Moscardo and Pearce, 1986) and ski resorts (Holden, 1999).

To Gottlieb (1982) and Graburn (1983), travel motivation was a reversal of normal routines and situations. Gottlieb (1982) suggested that in travel, aspects of American socio-economic ideology and experience are 'inverted', creating two-cultural ideals for vacation styles. Upper- and upper-middle class people, desiring relaxation of social constraints in their home environment, actively seek to mix with lower class residents of the host society. They take on a 'peasant for a day' vacation style, participating in activities and events avoided at home. Lower- and lower-middle class people invert the social order of their home environment by elevating their position in their vacation environment, adopting a 'queen for a day' vacation. Behavior becomes extravagant, attitudes of social-superiority are adopted, interests in high culture, though temporary, are enhanced, and encounters with lower-class residents are avoided. Inversions imply that 'certain meanings and rules of ordinary behavior are changed, held in abeyance or even reversed' (Graburn, 1983, p. 24). Graburn proposed several travel inversion dimensions and provided a series of continua that represent polar opposite conditions that occur within those dimensions. These included *the environment* (e.g., familiar vs. exotic; crowds vs. isolation; modernity vs. history), *class/lifestyle* (e.g., thrift vs. self-indulgence; affluence vs. simplicity; superficiality vs. self-enlightenment), *civilization* (e.g., urbanism vs. nature; security vs. risk; fast pace vs. slow pace), *formality* (e.g., rigid schedules vs. flexibility; formal clothing vs. informal; sexual restriction vs. license), and *health and person* (e.g., gluttony vs. diet; sloth vs. exercise; ageing vs. rejuvenation). Graburn suggested that (a) these inversions can be bi-directional, (b) polarities are inter-related such as familiarity–exotic and security–risk, and (c) while travelers are motivated by more than one reversal, they invert only a few aspects of their behavior at a time.

Lett (1983) described similar *liminoid* (threshold) experiences during vacation travel. Here, the traveler expresses needs he or she lacks at home. 'Liminoid activities' are socially accepted and approved activities which seem to deny or ignore the legitimacy of the institutionalized statuses, roles, norms, values, and rules of everyday, ordinary life (Lett, 1983, p. 45). Jafari (1987) suggested that breaking cultural norms is not limited to those experienced at home, but also destination norms, since 'breaking the rules is one of the principles of touristhood' (p. 153). Currie (1997) adopted the concept of liminoid behaviors in his Liminoidal, Inversionary, and Prosaic (LIP) Behaviors Framework. This framework predicts pleasure travelers' behaviors that are similar (prosaic) to and opposite (inversionary) of those found in the home environment. To experience prosaic and inversionary behaviors, travelers must disconnect from their home environment. Once done, they traverse the *limen*, or threshold, into the liminoidal state. Their ability to separate from their home environment determines when travelers cross the *limen*. According to Currie and Gagnon (1999):

Once across the limen, pleasure travelers are able to enjoy the feeling of being liberated from the social norms and values of their home environment. While in the liminoid state, pleasure travelers can temporarily create their personal rules of behavior different from those found within the home environment.

(p. 119)

Tourist typologies

In widely cited tourist typologies, Plog (1974) suggested that people fall along two continua based on their travel preferences: a psychocetric-midcentric-allocentric continuum and an energy continuum. People high on allocentrism prefer unstructured vacations in exotic destinations away from what they are accustomed to at home. Psychocentric people prefer packaged tours and familiar destinations, visiting destinations similar to their home with many tourist amenities. The energy dimension describes people on their preference for fast-paced versus slower-paced activities. Criticisms of Plog's framework imply that it is difficult to apply since travelers have different motivations on different occasions (Gilbert, 1991). Researchers have been unable to support, in empirical research, hypothesized relationships between personality types and destination (Smith, 1990).

Cohen (1974) proposed four classes of tourists: the *organized mass tourist* who is dependent on all-inclusive tours or packages; *the individual mass tourist* who is likely to travel alone or with very few people; *the explorer* who seeks novel experiences but occasionally opts for familiar and comfortable accommodations; and *the drifter* who avoids tourist establishments. Others have made similar attempts at developing tourist typologies (e.g., Perreault et al., 1977; Yiannakis and Gibson, 1992).

Plog's typology linked travel orientation to destinations while Cohen's (and others') focused on psychographics to identify tourist types, all representing a classification of tourists based on motivations for travel to specific destinations. Lowyk et al. (1992) suggested that tourist typologies would be more effective if based on how people experience tourist settings. Cohen (1979) provided a theoretical and conceptual classification of visitors based on their experiences, identifying five distinct forms of experience including *recreational, diversional, experiential, experimental,* and *existential.* Based on Cohen's experience domains, Elands and Lengkeek (2000) identified five modes of experiences with specific experiential and motivational characteristics. These included (1) *amusement* (fun, familiar environment of short duration), (2) *change* (escape from boredom and everyday life, relaxation, and recovery), (3) *interest* (search for interesting vistas and stories, variation, and stimulation of the imagination), (4) *rapture* (self-discovery, unexpectedness, and discovery of physical boundaries), and (5) *dedication* (authenticity, devotion, and timelessness). Cottrell et al. (2005) successfully applied the dimensions developed by Elands and Lengkeek in a study of Dutch forest service visitors.

Expectancy theory

The emergence of expectancy theory in outdoor recreation and tourism addressed a key drawback of content-based theories of motivation.

Needs are a source of behavior driven by motivations; however, knowing what the need is does not automatically inform us of what the behavior will be, or if there will be any behavior (Witt and Wright, 1993). Knowing that someone has experienced a difficult business trip and developed a need for rest and relaxation does not tell us how it will influence his behavior. He may go to bed early for several nights in a row, stay home all day on the upcoming weekend, or plan a weeklong fishing trip at his mountain cabin. What he does depends on more than his need for rest and relaxation. Can he get the time off work? Is his fishing gear organized and ready to go? Is there a weekend football game on TV he wants to see? Does his daughter have a volleyball tournament next weekend? Understanding the impact of motivations on human behavior requires more than knowing a person's needs. It requires understanding the process by which these needs drive behavior.

Drawing from Vroom's (1964) theory of work motivation, Witt and Wright (1993) described expectancy theory's application to motivations and travel behavior. Vroom's model has two equations, the first of which suggests that some outcomes to travel behavior are attractive to a person, not for their own sake, but in their ability to generate other attractive outcomes. This equation states:

$$V_j = f\left[\sum_{k=1}^{n}(V_k I_{jk})\right]$$

V_j represents the value of an outcome j; I_{jk} is the extent to which outcome j results in outcome k; V_k is the value of outcome k; and n is the number of outcomes. The value of an outcome (j) depends upon an individual's belief that it will result in other outcomes (k) and the value of those outcomes to the individual. Applied to travel, this equation suggests that the attractiveness of a destination/activity depends on how attractive specific attributes of that destination/activity are and whether that destination/activity provides positive, and avoids negative, outcomes. This equation can explain why people prefer to go to a destination or do an activity and whether they would do so, as long as the outcomes of not going at all were included in the model (Witt and Wright, 1993). The second equation considers that an individual may not be able to go to his or her preferred destination or do his or her preferred activity.

$$F_i = f\left[\sum_{j=1}^{n}(E_{ij} V_j)\right]$$

F_i is the force on an individual to do an act i; E_{ij} is the strength of the expectancy that doing i will result in outcome j; V_j is the value of outcome j; and n is the number of outcomes. The force on a person to do act i will be determined by the strength of that person's expectancy that outcome j will result and the value of that outcome. Applied to travel, this describes how and why an individual selects a destination connecting the value outcomes of traveling to a destination to the ability to go to that destination, considering such factors as cost, access, or available time. The destination or activity chosen is the one with the highest force, or strongest interaction between value and expectancy of action. This equation describes where an individual will go on vacation and/or what he or she will do there, but only partially impacted by their preference for a destination or activity. Driver et al. (1991) conducted psychometric analysis over several years (more than 35 studies and 30,000 subjects) to identify motivations, or 'desired psychological outcomes' behind outdoor recreation. The focus of this research was to develop quantitative measures of the motivational dimensions of people's outdoor experiences.

A drawback of expectancy theory is its complexity. Predicting a specific behavior requires identification of all salient outcomes of a behavior (and their value) and implies that the salient outcomes are similar across populations. However, the theory allows many of the concepts (needs, motives, and cognitions) that have arisen from research on tourism motivation to be included in a single theoretical framework. In addition, both push and pull factors can be included without the futile discussion of the temporal relationship between them. Furthermore, expectancy theory examines the process by which tourists make decisions from motivations, rather than simply listing them.

A functional perspective of travel motivations

Fodness (1994) suggested that motivations in content-based frameworks are (1) not motivations, but reasons for benefits sought in travel, (2) *strategies* for meeting goals and needs, and (3) resistant to valid and reliable measurement and application. To address these issues, he conceptualized and developed scales of tourist motivation based on the functional theory of attitudes, an approach that suggests attitudes serve needs (Katz, 1960; Smith et al., 1956). Applying this theory to motivations, the reasons people give for travel behavior represent psychological functions of their vacation. Using qualitative and quantitative survey techniques, Fodness identified four dimensions of motivations for travel, consistent with the attitude function dimensions identified by Katz (1960) and Smith et al. (1956). Consistent with Katz's (1960) *object-appraisal function* of attitudes, Fodness identified a motivation dimension that contained two functional sub-dimensions. The *knowledge function* in Fodness' framework includes traveler motivations for knowledge, organization, and consistency in the world, for example, seeing how others live and visiting sites of cultural and historical significance. The *utilitarian minimization of punishment* function reflects an escape-*from* travel motivation, for example, to rest and get away from the pressures of everyday life. The *utilitarian reward maximization* function reflects an escape-*to* motivation for 'fun' recreational activities that allow a person to live life fully. The *social-adjustive* function emphasizes social interaction with family, friends, and others.

Conceptual and methodological issues for travel motivations

Scholars have suggested that most motivation frameworks are classifications of reasons people travel rather than theories of travel motivation (Pearce, 1982, 1993; McCabe, 2000; Poria et al., 2004) and questioned whether researchers are investigating the same concept (Dann, 1981; Jafar, 1987; Poria et al., 2004). While similarities among travel motivation frameworks exist, unresolved differences in what motivations are suggest much work is still required. As a psychological construct, tourism motivation addresses, among others, why people travel, why they choose the destinations they do, what attributes of destinations and activities they demand, how travel market segments differ, and what influences visitor satisfaction. However, it competes with related concepts such as attitudes, values, beliefs, needs, behavior intentions, and goals in attempting to predict visitor behavior. McCabe (2000) saw the problem of motivation as epistemological:

It is a question about what we can reasonably expect to know about individuals' drives by asking them about their motivations and needs. Are these drives available to us as part of our consciousness? Or do we simply repeat the needs that have been suggested to us as needs through our immediate social peers, the wider contexts of our particular social realties in this place at this time and, the influence of the media?

(p. 109–110)

It has been suggested that motivation for travel, within the context of psychological theories, is an extremely complex process, so complex that the traditional content-oriented theories of travel motivation are inadequate and irrelevant (Parrinello, 1993). Addressing conceptual and methodological issues can help lead the field to a cogent theory of travel motivations.

Conceptual issues related to travel motivations

Conceptual issues have been raised that may push us closer to an organized theory of travel motivations. First, travel motivation theory must be dynamic and flexible across situations and incorporate individual changes across the lifespan (Pearce, 1993). Recognizing a lack of dynamism in many travel motivational frameworks, Gnoth, (1997; Gnoth et al., 2000) suggested, and empirically supported, incorporating mood into a 'static versus dynamic model' of motivations. In this model, an individual with a 'static-orientation' in a situation is one who may be tired, lack energy and concentration, and/or feel introverted about travel choices he or she may have. This person's choice of travel destinations or activities would likely represent a need to escape. The same person with a 'dynamic-orientation' in another situation would feel more open-minded, seek challenges, and choose travel destinations that represent a need for new and challenging experiences. It is reasonable to suspect that some people favor one of these orientations over their life course; however, it is also reasonable that an individual could take both a static and a dynamic orientation across different situations.

Second, not only might travelers have different motivations for travel across different situations, but multiple motivations also are likely, within a single travel situation, to describe why people travel (Harre et al., 1985). Many people will have more than one motive operating in a social setting such as travel, and a dynamic theory of travel motivation should adequately represent 'this interlocking pattern of shifting and fluctuating motivations represented and treated within the theoretical formulation' (Pearce, 1993, pg. 120).

Third, there is an interaction between intrinsic and extrinsic travel motivations. Intrinsic motivation relates to travel behavior done for its own sake, or for the internal benefits gained from doing that behavior. Leisure theorists (e.g., Csikzentmihalyi, 1977) have long espoused the importance of this type of motivation in driving peoples' behavior. Traditionally, discussion of intrinsic motivation has focused on the immediate internal benefits from doing the behavior; however, leisure researchers have also espoused the importance of future intrinsic benefits tied, in our case, to the recollection of and reflection on past travel experiences. Extrinsic motivation relates to behavior done for purposes related to one's social environment such as outside rewards or recognition by others. Harre et al. (1985) claimed that extrinsic motivation is predominant in why we choose to do the things we do. Developing a theory of motivation requires examining the roles of intrinsic and extrinsic motivations in leisure, and more specifically, travel behavior.

Methodological issues related to travel motivation research

Methodological issues regarding travel motivation research also exist. First, researchers use different methods and items to measure motivations, making it difficult to compare results across studies and to develop an empirically tested theory of travel motivation. Todd

(1999) compared three common methods for measuring motivations; (1) a respondent rating of the importance of various reasons for travel (a quantitative method), (2) a respondent rating of the importance of destination attributes (a quantitative method), and (3) a respondent narrative description of positive and negative holiday experiences (a qualitative method). Todd found very low association between the methods, regarding the nature of motivations identified as important by respondents.

Second, quantitative research is often limited in its usefulness as a stand-alone approach. For example, development of fixed items for surveys is often ad hoc – not based on a specific conceptualization of human behavior. In addition, the content underlying fixed items in surveys are often researcher-generated instead of respondent-driven. Dimensions tested in this way reflect more what the researcher believes should exist, and less what may actually exist for the traveler. This etic-based approach (i.e., from the mind of the researcher) is not limited to quantitative approaches; qualitative approaches that depend on participant observation and interviews conducted by researchers also often take an etic-based approach to data interpretation (e.g., Arnould and Price, 1993; Belk and Costa, 1998). Etic-based approaches should complement research that provides thick descriptions of traveler thoughts and actions (Woodside and Dubelaar, 2002). An emic-based approach (i.e., from the mind of the tourist) captures the complexity of how and why people make decisions about pleasure travel and allows many motivations to arise from tourists' description of their experience rather than when being asked to 'pick the best one'. There are several reasons that such a holistic approach to travel research is beneficial. This approach draws upon episodic memory that dominates most of the conscious and unconscious thinking of individuals. Also, most positivist approaches collect data long after the travel experience, by which time thoughts and behaviors a traveler had during his experience are relegated to the unconscious and, therefore, inaccessible. Furthermore, pleasure travelers prefer narrative forms of describing events at a destination instead of a list of researcher-generated attributes and benefits (Wyer and Adaval, 2002; Woodside et al., 2004). Illustrating grounded theory and travel behavior of tourists to Prince Edward Island, Canada, Woodside et al. (2004) concluded that collecting data emically provided a 'rich, deep and nuance-filled understanding of the causes and consequences of such behaviors' (p. 7).

The timing of measurement of motivations affects their meaning (Manfredo et al., 1996). Measured long before a destination decision, the importance of desired outcomes reflects motivations for travel. Measured just prior to the travel experience, but after destination choice has been made, these desired outcomes reflect beliefs, experience preferences, and expectations. Measured after the travel experience, these outcomes reflect a level of satisfaction for the trip.

A caution for such research relates to the veracity of tourists' vacation descriptions. In a review of research, Pearce (1982) noted that responses to qualitative questions about a person's reason for travel related to the choice of a destination and not to why that individual traveled in the first place. It is possible that people are either reluctant or unable to reveal deeply personal or intimate reasons for travel (Witt and Wright, 1993), although the existence of such an *esteem* need related to travel is common.

Attitudes and beliefs

Attitudes and beliefs are among the most oft-examined constructs in the social sciences. Beyond the theoretical concerns of social and cognitive psychologists, applied disciplines such as health, political science, organizational behavior, natural resources, and many others apply the concepts of attitudes and beliefs to understanding how and why people do the things they do. Attitudes and beliefs describe perceptions and behavior about many issues, including perceptions of tourism impacts (e.g., Ap, 1992), support for tourism development (e.g., Perdue et al., 1990; Andereck and Vogt, 2000), destination choice (e.g., Mohsin, 2004), destination pricing and value (e.g., Kerr and Manfredo, 1991; Murphy and Pritchard, 1997), adoption of e-shopping for travel services (Christou and Kassianidis, 2002), and others.

Definition of attitude

Attitudes are *'a psychological tendency that is expressed by evaluating a particular entity with some degree of favor or disfavor'* (Eagly and Chaiken, 1993, p. 1). The most evident component of this definition is *evaluation*. Holding an attitude toward an entity suggests that a person characterizes it as positive or negative. Two aspects of evaluation are *valence* (whether an evaluation of an attitude-object is positive or negative) and *extremity* (how positive or negative that evaluation is). Two individuals may both think an Alaskan cruise is a good way to enjoy rest and relaxation. For individual A the cruise is a great option for a vacation and puts it on top of his choice set, while individual B sees it as okay if she cannot find anything better, reflecting a different extremity of a positive attitude. *Entity*, or attitude-object, is a component of the definition also. Attitude-objects can be abstract (e.g., environmentalism) or concrete (e.g., a travel destination). They can reflect active (e.g., a decision to travel to a destination) or passive (e.g., support for enhanced security policies at an international airport) behaviors. A third component of an attitude is as a *psychological tendency*. When a person engages an attitude-object, he or she internally evaluates that object. That evaluation is present for at least a short time but may endure for a longer period. An individual's attitude is not directly observed, but deduced from how he or she cognitively, affectively, or behaviorally reacts to the object.

The components of attitude

If attitudes represent evaluative meaning of objects and behaviors, how do they form and, once formed, what is their structure? To answer this we focus on social psychological factors that come together to form summary evaluations of an object or behavior. Social psychological literature suggests attitudes contain cognitive, affective, and behavioral components.

The *cognitive component* of an attitude is the beliefs (perceptions and knowledge) people have about an attitude-object. Each belief attaches an attribute to an object or an outcome to a behavior, and reflects the subjective value that people place on each attribute or outcome. For example, an individual's attitude toward a resort destination is likely to arise from several beliefs. He may believe that going to the resort would (1) be expensive; (2) provide opportunities to meet and socialize with other people; (3) be a good way to escape the city; but (4) present potential health dangers. These beliefs form the traveler's summary evaluation or attitude toward the resort. Several factors influence how beliefs affect the individual's decision to travel to the resort. First, beliefs might arise from several sources. A direct source is personal experience; perhaps he has been to the resort before. Indirect sources include conversations with friends who have been there, or travel literature. When a person acquires beliefs through direct personal experience, the resultant attitude is more likely to impact behavior (Fazio, 1995). Second, the traveler views each of the attributes as positive or negative. For some, that the resort caters to singles is a positive attribute, but for others this is a negative attribute. Third, the salience, or personal importance, of each belief contributes to its effect on the overall attitude (Ajzen and Fishbein, 1980). To the wealthy traveler, that the resort is expensive may not affect his or her attitude toward visiting the resort. Alternatively, if the person had been scrimping and saving for years for this vacation, the cost may be particularly important in his or her decision on what to do and where to go.

The *affective component* of attitudes is the 'feelings, moods, emotions, and sympathetic nervous-system activity that people experience in relation to an attitude-object and subsequently associate with it' (Eagly and Chaiken, 1998, p. 272). For example, a travelogue on television about exotic beach resorts in the Caribbean may elicit cognitive and affective responses from viewers. The show may provide several facts about what resorts exist, what airlines serve the region, what activities are available, and the best times to go, all cognitive information. At the same time, the show uses music as well as video of people enjoying the resorts and beaches to elicit positive, excited feelings. The viewer's affective state reflects positive feelings toward visiting a resort, which translates to a positive attitude toward booking a vacation trip.

The *behavioral component* of an attitude is the actual behavior or behavior intention toward the attitude-object. For example, an individual preparing to visit a beach resort or expressing his intention to do so implies a positive attitude toward visiting the resort. Past behavior is also a behavioral component of attitudes. For example, an individual who has taken ski vacations in the past to Colorado with family and friends will form a positive attitude toward taking similar vacations in the future, given the assumption that his/her attitude toward the previous trip to Colorado remains stable.

Attitudes and behavior

As noted earlier in the chapter, attitudes and their underlying beliefs likely mediate the relationship between motivations and travel behavior. Among the most often-studied aspects of attitudes is the extent to which they predict behavior. Attitudes have predicted travel-related behaviors such as where to go, with whom to go, how to get there, what to do once there, how long to stay, and many others. If an individual has a positive attitude toward vacationing in Belize to fish for tarpon, will that person actually go on this trip? In the 1960s and 1970s, doubts regarding the ability of attitudes to predict behavior prevailed; however, systematic research has since changed the overriding question from *do attitudes predict behavior?* to *what circumstances or factors affect the ability of attitudes to predict behavior?* Internal factors such as characteristics of a person's attitude influence attitude–behavior correspondence. For example, the stronger one's attitude toward an attitude-object, the more likely that attitude will predict behavior. External or situational factors affect attitude–behavior correspondence as well. A rock climber may feel positively toward drilling bolts into the rock for protection in just-discovered unclimbed areas; however, social norms against this activity would preclude him from doing so at an established climbing area. An important advancement in attitude–behavior research is the recognition of two types of attitude: *attitude toward a behavior* and *attitude toward the target of a behavior*. A person may have a positive attitude toward New York City as a place to get away, enjoy fine dining, and attend Broadway shows (attitude toward a target). However, he or she may negatively evaluate taking a trip to New York City because it is beyond the financial means of the family and not a good place to take his or her young children (attitude toward a behavior), deciding instead to visit a child-friendly beach resort closer to home.

Attitude toward the target of behavior

Research on attitude toward the target of a behavior has received a great deal of attention in the tourism field through exploration of several factors such as destination image. Although conceptual differences may exist between destination image and attitude toward the destination (Sussman and Unel, 1999), the factors are similar in that they both represent beliefs, expectations, feelings, and evaluations of attributes of a potential target of a behavior. That is, a person's perception of the state of Colorado as a place to experience adventure, get away from the city, enjoy outdoor recreation, yet expensive to get to not only says something of the image he or she holds about the state, but also represents his or her general attitude toward Colorado as a destination. One model that considers the relationship between attitudes toward a target and behavior is the *automatic activation model of attitudes* (Fazio, 1995).

The automatic activation model defines *attitude-accessibility* as the 'likelihood that the attitude will be activated from memory automatically when an attitude-object is encountered' (Fazio, 1995, p. 248). In addition, the more an attitude forms through direct experience with or repeated expression about an object, the more accessible the attitude when a person encounters that object. An attitude that automatically activates without conscious thought by the individual will result in a biased perception of the object in the immediate situation, and behavior follows from these biased perceptions without a conscious reasoning process. For example, consider a proposal to expand a local airport in a region going through an economical depression that will result in greater numbers of arrivals by larger aircrafts. The region's economy depends heavily on the tourism industry. The airport expansion will bring in more tourists and business development in a way as to not negatively affect the 'rural' nature of the region, which attracts tourists and is the reason many locals moved there. An individual who has lived in the region for years may vote against airport expansion without considering the economic benefits of doing so. In this case, his anti-development attitude would automatically activate when presented with the proposal to expand the airport. This previously held attitude would influence his voting behavior on this issue.

Attitude toward a behavior

Much of the success researchers have had in predicting behavior with attitudes is due to the conceptualization of an *attitude toward a behavior* regarding that object. Two models of attitudes and behavior are the *theory of reasoned action* (TRA) (Fishbein and Ajzen, 1975) and its derivative, the *theory of planned behavior* (TPB) (Ajzen, 2001). These theories suggest that in making decisions about behavior, people consider the outcomes of their actions, prior to acting. Taking an *expectancy–value* approach, these models incorporate the *principle of compatibility* with the process in which attitudes toward a behavior form and predict that behavior. According to the *principle of compatibility*, the measured attitude and behavior must be at the same specificity regarding the *action* (taking a weekend trip), the *target* (to Yellowstone National Park), the *context* (with family), and *time* (Labor Day weekend) (Ajzen and Fishbein, 1980).

According to TRA, the best predictor of a person's behavior is his or her intention. That is, the most important and only direct predictor of whether an individual will travel to Colorado this fall to go elk hunting is his intention to do so. In this model, *attitude toward the behavior* influences behavior through its direct effect on behavior intention. For example, an individual's attitude toward going elk hunting in Colorado this fall will influence his intention to do so. Attitude toward the behavior arises from the evaluation of perceived consequences of, or salient *outcome beliefs* about, the behavior in question. The hunter's attitude toward going to Colorado this fall to hunt elk might form from his beliefs that he would bag an elk, spend time with his friends, and camp in cold weather, and the extent to which he evaluates these outcomes as good or bad. *Subjective norms*, the desires of other people and groups, may affect behavioral intention. Here, the hunter's intention to go elk hunting in Colorado depends on *normative beliefs*, that is, what his wife and his hunting partners want him to do, and his *motivation to comply* with his normative beliefs. Young and Kent (1985) explored the relative effects of attitudes and subjective norms within the context of going camping. Since then, this theory has enjoyed much popularity in explanations of behavior across many areas of society, including tourism and recreation.

An important requirement of TRA is that the behavior must be volitional. However, for most behaviors, factors outside one's control influence behavior, regardless of intention. Ajzen (2001) addressed this issue in TPB by including a factor, *perceived behavioral control,* that predicts both the intention to behave and the behavior. This factor includes *control beliefs* about the perceived difficulty of and the extent to which the individual believes he or she has control over doing the behavior. In the elk-hunting example, behavioral control factors such as monetary cost, hunting access, availability of a license, and game availability could influence the hunter's intention to go elk hunting in Colorado this fall over and above attitude and subjective norms. Ajzen and Driver (1992) found TPB useful in understanding the influence of factors on college students' choices of leisure behavior. Notani (1998) conducted a meta-analysis of TPB and found that the additional factor, perceived behavioral control, is a strong predictor of behavior when it is (1) a belief-based measure, (2) conceptualized as being control over factors internal to a person, and (3) based on familiar behaviors. Notani concluded that including perceived behavioral control as a predictor of behavioral intention and behavior was sound.

Conceptual and methodological issues for attitudes and beliefs

Applications of TRA and TPB exist across many social science disciplines to understand attitudes and predict behaviors. However, scholars have identified several limitations to these models. For a more complete discussion of these limitations within the contexts of consumer and travel behavior, see Bagozzi et al. (2002) and March and Woodside (2005).

The connection between planned behavior and actual behavior

Attitudinal research in consumer behavior usually takes a pre-purchase approach, connecting attitudes, subjective norms, and behavioral control to intention, and then inferring actual purchase behavior. This ignores intervening factors that exist at the point of purchase, and may result in realized or actual behavior different from one originally planned. When actual purchase behavior is considered, the correlation between intention and actual purchase differs across diverse products, travel services, and experiences (Morwitz, 1997). These models, applied to travel behavior, do not conceptualize behaviors that are 'unplanned', yet done. March and Woodside (2005), noting past research in marketing on unplanned and impulse purchasing, adapted this concept to TPB and travel behavior. In this model, antecedent attitudes, subjective norms, and perceived behavioral control influence behavioral intention and planned behavior, as mentioned before. However, these researchers also hypothesized that these antecedents would directly predict 'unplanned and not done behavior' and 'unplanned and done behavior'. Behavioral intention would also predict 'planned and not done behavior' along with 'planned and done behavior'. In a study of travelers to Prince Edward Island, March and Woodside (2005) found that actual money spent, length of stay, activities done, and attractions visited were significantly greater than planned prior to the trip. Within the frameworks of TRA and TPB, unforeseen events during a vacation influence whether the traveler actually does the activities he or she planned to do. This affects the volitional nature of the planned activities, a required characteristic of behavior studies using TRA as a framework and recognized within the tenets of March's and Woodside's expanded TPB.

Attitudes regarding multiple travel behaviors

A common approach used in models such as TRA and TPB is to predict single travel behaviors instead of recognizing that, in most situations, people have choices among several alternative behaviors and destinations. Consumer behavior research has found that models of multiple-item choice decision that include concomitant attitudes and beliefs about several alternatives are more predictive of final purchase decisions than are models of single-item choice and suggests that the underlying processes in multiple-alternative decisions are different than in single-option frameworks. Studies in travel behavior have recognized this multiple-alternative phenomenon through the identification of choice sets (Woodside and Lysonski, 1989; Um and Crompton, 1990; Ankomah et al., 1996). These frameworks suggest that travel destination choice is a multi-stage process. In the first stage, people have an 'initial' or 'awareness' set of potential destinations available to them. After deciding to travel, individuals actively search for information about destinations, consider situational constraints, and form attitudes toward the attributes of different destinations. This leads to a 'choice' set of potential destinations, those destinations the traveler considers reasonable alternatives for selection. Finally, evaluation of situational constraints and attitudes toward destinations in the evoked set results in a final destination choice.

The functional structure of beliefs

Models like TRA and TPB explain how attitudes develop from the existence and evaluation of outcome, normative, and control (in the case of TPB) beliefs about behavior. However, they fail to capture underlying causal and functional relationships among beliefs and other psychological constructs. An approach for doing this is *means–end theory*. Developed to describe the structure of consumers' knowledge and beliefs about products, means–end theory views product features as having meaning through consequences they provide or help to avoid (Klenosky, 2002). The hierarchical structure described by this model can explain attitudes and subjective norms by linking them to broader goals. Concrete knowledge about product attributes connects to abstract beliefs about psychological and social consequences of those attributes. In turn, abstract beliefs associate with even more abstract values. Klenosky (2002) described a means–end chain based on students' choices of spring-break destinations. To illustrate, spring-break destinations with a warm climate and beaches (concrete attributes) connect to abstract consequences like enjoying nature, getting sun, looking healthy, and resting. These abstract consequences connect to abstract values like accomplishment, fun/enjoyment, and self-esteem (Harlam and Lodish, 1995).

Conclusions

The connection between motivations, attitudes, and beliefs

Tourist motivations can be considered within the context of two broad reasons for traveling: to escape or leave one's home environment and/or to enjoy experiences not available at home. Beyond these general reasons for travel, the motivational connection between needs and travel destinations is complex. On one hand, many different kinds of destinations can serve to satisfy a specific type of need. On the other hand, many people may travel to a particular destination, yet have very different needs and motivations for traveling there. As a result of this complexity, more situation-specific factors must be considered to understand why a person travels to a certain destination to do a certain activity that satisfies a certain need. Attitudes, beliefs, and related constructs regarding a destination's ability to provided desired experiences are (a) situation-specific, and (b) more effective at predicting a person's destination or activity choice than more general needs and motivations.

Research on motivation, attitudes, and beliefs helps tourism professionals and researchers understand why and how people make decisions about travel. This enhances the ability of the travel industry to effectively market their products and services to consumers. Figure 9.1 reflects the relationship between motivations (as needs and wants) and situation-specific attitudes, beliefs, etc. That is, identification of a basic need, such as 'excitement,' begins an individual's consideration of specific destinations or activities (wants) that will satisfy that need. Motivations emanate from the push of need factors and the pull of destination factors or wants. However, the extent to which these motivations drive destination choice depends upon, or is mediated by, attitudes toward the destination and its ability to provide experiences

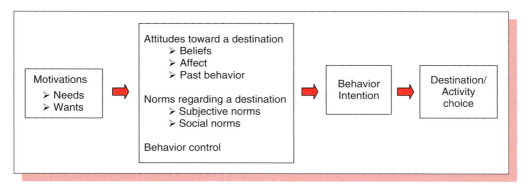

Figure 9.1
Model of motivation–destination choice relationship

(informed by beliefs, affect, and past behavior), norms regarding specific behaviors (both subjective and social), and control over behaviors.

Application of travel motivations, attitudes, and beliefs

Several areas of marketing depend on knowledge of traveler motivations, needs, attitudes, and beliefs. The marketing areas for which motivations, attitudes, and beliefs have important implications are *market segmentation, targeting*, and *positioning. Market segmentation* involves identifying specific bases for segmenting the market and developing profiles of the segments identified. Regardless of the primary basis of segmentation (i.e., demographics, geography, psychographics, or behavior), motivations, attitudes, and beliefs are important factors that identify and distinguish between market segments. *Targeting* market segments requires the travel provider determine which segments to serve and which to ignore. For example, are travelers who desire risk and adventure experiences a large enough market for the travel provider to target? Do travelers who want these experiences require unique attention regarding services demanded? Can the travel provider be competitive at providing experiences consistent with motivations of risk and adventure? What attitudes and beliefs do members of this segment have regarding the provider's ability to provide these experiences? Do market segments with different motivations for and attitudes/beliefs regarding travel require different kinds of activities or promotions? Once market segments are targeted, the travel organization must ensure that the *position* it holds in the minds of its potential customers coincides with what the organization provides. This position is often based on the benefits and experiences that people desire when they travel, factors closely connected with what drives people to travel (motivations), and people's assessment of the organization's ability to provide for those (attitudes and beliefs).

The final step of the marketing process is to bring together the different components of the marketing mix in a way as to encourage the selected target segments to visit the travel destination or engage in a tourism activity. Motivations, attitudes, and beliefs have an important role in this *implementation of the travel product/service marketing mix*. This involves designing marketing strategies in ways that connect a travel product or service to targeted travel segments. Research on motivations, attitudes, and beliefs can identify the salient attributes, in the consumer's perspective, of the travel destination or activity. The travel provider can develop or modify products and services consistent with the attributes that a segment of travel consumers demands, at a price that they are willing to pay. Travel advertising can focus on those attributes in order to persuade the potential traveler toward specific destinations or activity choices.

References

Ajzen, I. (2001). Nature and operation of attitudes. *Annual Review of Psychology*, *52*: 27–58.

Ajzen, I. and Driver, B.L. (1992). Application of the theory of planned behavior to leisure choice. *Journal of Leisure Research*, *24*(3): 207–224.

Ajzen, I. and Fishbein, M. (1980). *Understanding Attitudes and Predicting Social Behavior*. Englewood Cliffs, NJ: Prentice-Hall.

Andereck and Vogt, C.A. (2000). The relationship between residents' attitudes toward toursim development options, *Journal of Travel Research*, *39*, 27–36.

Ankomah, P.K., Crompton, J.L., and Baker, D. (1996). Influence of cognitive distance in vacation choice. *Annals of Tourism Research*, *23*, 1, 138–150.

Ap, J. (1992). Residents' perceptions of toursim impacts. *Annals of Toursim Research*, *19*(4), 665–690.

Arnould, E.J. and Price, L.L. (1993 June). River magic: Extraordinary experience and the extended service encounter. *Journal of Consumer Research*, *20*: 1–23.

Bagozzi, R.P., Gurhan-Canli, Z., and Priester, J.R. (2002). *The Social Psychology of Consumer Behavior*. 222 pages. Buckingham, England: Open University Press.

Baloglu, S. (2000). A path analytical model of visitation intention involving information sources, socio-psychological motivations and destination images. In Woodside, A.G., Crouch, G.I., Mazanec, J.A., Oppermann, M., and Sakai, M.Y. (eds.), *Consumer Psychology of Tourism, Hospitality, and Leisure* (pp. 63–90). New York: CABI Publishing.

Belk, R.W. and Costa, J.A. (1998 December). The mountain man myth: A contemporary consuming fantasy. *Journal of Consumer Research*, *25*: 218–240.

Christou, E. and Kassianidis, P. (2002). Examining the adoption of e-shopping for travel services: Determinants of consumers' perceptions (pp. 187–196). In Wober, K.W., Frew, A.J., and Hitz M. (eds.), Information and communication technologies in Tourism 2002, Proceedings of the International Conference, Innsbruk, Austria. New York: Springer-Verlag, Wien.

Cohen, E. (1974). Who is a tourist? A conceptual classification, *Sociological Review*, *22*: 527–555.

Cohen, E. (1979). A phenomenology of tourist experiences, *The Journal of the British Sociological Association*, *13*: 179–201.

Cottrell, S.P., Lengkeek, J., and van Marwijk, R. (2005). Typology of recreation experiences: Application in a Dutch forest service visitor monitoring survey. *Managing Leisure*, *10*: 54–72.

Crompton, J.L. (1979). Motivations for pleasure vacation. *Annals of Toursim Research*, *6*, 408–424.

Csikzentmihalyi, M. (1977). *Beyond Boredom and Anxiety.* San Francisco: Jossey-Bass.

Currie, R.R. (1997). A pleasure-tourism behaviors framework. *Annals of Tourism Research, 24*(4): 884–897.

Currie, R.R. and Gagnon, M. (1999). When do individuals become pleasure travelers? An exploratory study into the relationship between the fulfillment of primary expectations and the liminoidal state. *Journal of Travel & Tourism Marketing, 8*(2): 115–128.

Dann, G.M.S. (1977). Anomie, ego-enhancement and tourism. *Annals of Tourism Research, 4*(4): 184–194.

Dann, G.M.S. (1981). Tourist motivation: An appraisal. *Annals of Tourism Research, 8*(2): 187–219.

Decrop, A. (1999). Personal aspects of vacationers' decision-making processes: An interpretivist approach. *Journal of Travel and Tourism Marketing, 8*(4): 59–68.

Driver, B.L., Tinsley, H.E., and Manfredo, M.J. (1991). Leisure and recreation experience preference scales: Results from two inventories designed to assess the breath of the perceived benefits of leisure (pp. 263–287) in B.L. Driver, P.J., Brown, and G.L. Peterson, (eds.). *The Benefits of Leisure.* State College, PA: Venture Publ.

Eagly, A.H. and S. Chaiken. (1993). *The Psychology of Attitudes.* Fort Worth, TX: Harcourt Brace.

Eagly, A.H. and S. Chaiken. (1998). *Attitude structure and function.* In D.T. Gilbert, S.T. Fiske, and G. Lindzey. (eds.), *The Handbook of Social Psychology* (Vol. 1, 4th ed., pp. 269–322). Boston: McGraw-Hill.

Elands, B.H.M. and Lengkeek, J. (2000). *Typical tourists: Research into the theoretical and methodological foundations of a typology of tourism and recreation experiences,* Leiden: Backhuys Publishers.

Fazio, R.H. (1995). Attitudes as object-evaluation associations: Determinants, consequences, and correlates of attitude-accessibility. In R.E. Petty and J.A. Krosnick (Eds.), *Attitude strength: Antecedents and consequences* (pp. 247–283). Mahwah: Erlbaum.

Fishbein, M. and Ajzen, I. (1975). *Beliefs, Attitude, Intention and Behavior: An Introduction to Theory and Research.* Reading, MA: Addison-Wesley.

Fodness, D. (1994). Measuring tourist motivation. *Annals of Tourism Research, 21*(3): 555–581.

Gilbert, G.C. (1991). An examination of the consumer behavior process related to tourism. in Cooper, C. (ed.), *Progress in Tourism, 3*: 78–105.

Gnoth, J. (1997). Tourism motivation and expectation formation. *Annals of Tourism Research, 24*(2): 283–304.

Gnoth, J., Zins, A.H., Lengmueller, R. and Boshoff, C. (2000). Emotions, mood, flow, and motivations to travel. *Journal of Travel & Tourism Marketing, 9*(3): 23–34.

Gottlieb, A. (1982). Americans' vacations. *Annals of Tourism Research, 9*(2): 165–187.

Graburn, N.H.H. (1983). The anthropology of tourism. *Annals of Tourism Research*, *10*(1): 9–33.

Gray, H.P. (1970). *International Travel – International Trade*, D.C. Heath and Company, Lexington.

Hanqin, Z.Q. and Lam, T. (1999). An analysis of Mainland Chinese visitors' motivation to visit Hong Kong. *Tourism Management*, *20*: 587–594.

Harlam, B.A. and Lodish, L.M. (1995). Modeling consumers' choices of multiple items. *Journal of Marketing Research*, *22*: 404–418.

Harre, R., Clarke, D., and DeCarlo, N. (1985). *Motives and mechanisms*, London: Methuen.

Herzberg, F. (1959). *The Motivation to Work*. New York: John Wiley and Sons.

Holden, A. (1999). Understanding skiers' motivation using Pearce's 'Travel Career' construct. *Annals of Tourism Research*, *26*(2): 43–438.

Iso-Ahola, S.E. (1982). Toward a social psychological theory of tourism motivation: A rejoinder. *Annals of Tourism Research*, *12*: 256–262.

Jafari, J. (1987 June). Tourism models: The sociocultural aspects. *Tourism Management*, 151–159.

Katz, D. (1960). The functional approach to the study of attitudes. *Public Opinion Quarterly*, *24*, 163–204.

Kerr, G. and Manfredo, M.J. (1991). An attitudinal based pricing model of pricing recreation services. *Journal of Leisure Research*, *20*(1): 137–150.

Klenosky, D.B. (2002). The 'pull' of tourism destinations: A means-ends investigation. *Journal of Travel Research*, *40*: 385–395.

Kreitner, R. and Kinicki, A. (1998). *Organizational Behavior* (4th ed.). Boston: Irwin/McGraw-Hill.

Lawler, E.E. (1973). *Motivation in Work Organizations*. Monterey, CA: Brooks/Cole.

Lett J.W., Jr., (1983). Ludic and liminoid aspects of the charter yacht tourism in the Caribbean. *Annals of Tourism Research*, *10*: 35–56.

Lowyk, E., Van Langenhove, L., and Bollaert, L. (1992). Typologies of Tourist Roles. In Johnson, P. and Thomas, B. (eds.), *Perspectives on Tourism Policy*, 13–32. London: Mansell.

Manfredo, M.J., Driver, B.L., and Tarrant, M.A. (1996). Measuring leisure motivation: A meta-analysis of the recreation experience preference scales. *Journal of Leisure Research*, *28*(3): 188–213.

Mannell, R.C. and Iso-Ahola, S.E. (1987). Psychological nature of leisure and tourism experience. *Annals of Tourism Research*, *14*: 314–331.

March, R. and Woodside, A.G. (2005). *Tourism Behaviour: Travellers' Decisions and Actions*. Wallingfor, UK: CABI Publishing.

Maslow, A.H. (1943). A theory of human motivation. *Psychological Review*, *50*: 370–396.

Mayo, E. and Jarvis, L. (1981). *The psychology of leisure travel*. Boston: CBI Publishing.

McCabe, S. (2000). The problem of motivation in understanding the demand for leisure day visits. In A.G. Woodside, Crouch, G.I., Mazanec, J.A., Oppermann, M., and Sakai, M.Y. (eds.), *Consumer Psychology of Tourism,Hospitality, and Leisure* (pp. 211–225). New York: CABI Publishing.

McClelland, D.C. (1988). *Human Motivation*. New York: Scot Foresman and Company.

Middleton, V.T.C. (1988). *Marketing and Travel and Toursim*. Oxford, UK: Heinemann.

Mohsin, A. (2004). Tourist attitudes and destination marketing: The case of Australia's Northern Territory and Malaysia. *Tourism Management, 26*, 723–732.

Morrison, A.M. (2002). *Hospitality and Travel Marketing* (3rd ed.). Albany, NY: Delmar.

Morwitz, V.G. (1997). Why consumers don't always accurately predict their own future behavior. *Marketing Letters, 8*(1): 57–70.

Moscardo, G.M. and Pearce, P.L. (1986). Historical them parks: An Australian experience in authenticity, *Annals of Tourism Research, 13*(3): 467–479.

Moutinho, L. (1987). Consumer behavior in tourism. *European Journal of Marketing 21*(10): 1–44.

Murphy, P.E. and Pritchard, M. (1997). Destination price-value perceptions and attitudes. *Journal of Travel Research, 36*(1): 17–22.

Murray, H.A. (1938) *Explorations in Personality*. New York: Oxford University Press.

Notani, A.S. (1998). Moderators of perceived behavioral control's predictiveness in the theory of planned behavior: A meta-analysis. *Journal of Consumer Psychology, 7*, 247–271.

Parrinello, G.L. (1993). Motivation and anticipation in post-industrial tourism. *Annals of Tourism Research, 20*(2): 232–248.

Pearce, P.L. and Caltabiano, M.L. (1983). Inferring travel motivation from travelers' experiences. *Journal of Travel Research, 17*: 16–20.

Pearce, D. (1991). *Tourism Development* (2nd ed.). New York: John Wiley & Sons.

Pearce, P.L. (1982). *The Social Psychology of Tourist Behavior*, Oxford: Pergamon Press.

Pearce, P.L. (1993). Fundamental of tourist motivation. In D.G. Pearce and R.W. Butler (eds), *Tourism research: Critiques and Challenges* (p. 113–134). London: Routledge.

Perdue, R.R., Long, P.T., and Allen, L. (1990). Resident support for tourism development. *Annals of Tourism Research, 17*(4): 586–599.

Perreault, W.D., Darden, D.K., and Darden, W.R. (1977). A psychological classification of vacation life styles. *Journal of Leisure Research, 9*: 208–224.

Pizam, A., Neumann, Y., and Reichel, A. (1979). Tourist satisfaction: uses and misuses. *Annals of Tourism Research, 6*(2): 195–197.

Plog, S.C. (1974). Why destination areas rise and fall in popularity. *Cornell Hotel and Restaurant Quarterly, 14*(4): 55–58.

Poria, Y., Butler, R., and Airey, D. (2004). Links between tourists, heritage, and reasons for visiting heritage sites. *Journal of Travel Research, 43*(1): 19–28.

Schmoll, G.A. (1977). *Tourism Promotion*. London: Tourism International Press.

Smith, M.B., Bruner, J.S., and White, R.W. (1956). *Opinions and Personality*. New York: Wiley.

Smith, S.L.J. (1990). A test of Plog's allocentric/psychocentric model: Evidence from seven nations. *Journal of Travel Research, 28*(4): 40–43.

Sussman, S. and Unel, A. (1999). Destination image and its modification after travel: An empirical study on Turkey (pp. 207–226) In A. Pizam and Mansfield, Y. (eds), *Consumer Behavior in Travel and Tourism*. New York: Haworth Press.

Todd, S. (1999). Examining tourism motivation methodologies. *Annals of Tourism Research, 26*(4): 1022–1024.

Um, S. and Crompton, J.L. (1990). Attitude determinants in tourism destination choice. *Annals of Tourism Research, 17*, 432–448.

Vroom, V.H. (1964). *Work and Motivation*. New York: Wiley.

Witt, C. and Wright, P. (1993). Tourist motivation: Life after Maslow. In P. Johnson and B. Thomas, (eds.), *Choice and Demand in Tourism* (pp. 33–55). London: Mansell Publishing Ltd.

Woodside, A.G. and Dubelaar, C. (2002 November). A general theory of tourism consumption systems: A conceptual framework and an empirical exploration. *Journal of Travel Research, 29*: 120–132.

Woodside, A.G. and Lysonski, S. (1989). A general model of traveler destination. *Journal of Travel Research, 27*(4): 7–14.

Woodside, A.G., MacDonald, R., and Buford, M. (2004). Grounded theory of leisure travel. *Journal of Travel & Tourism Marketing, 17*(1), 7–39.

Wyer, R.S. and Adaval, R. (2002). Narrative-based representations of social knowledge: Their construction and use in comprehension, memory, and judgment. *Advances in Experimental Social Psychology, 34*: 131–197.

Yiannakis, A. and Gibson, H. (1992). Roles tourists play. *Annals of Tourism Research, 19*, 287–303.

Young, R. and Kent, A. (1985). Using the theory of reasoned action to improve the understanding of recreation behavior. *Journal of Leisure Research, 17*(2): 90–106.

CHAPTER 10

Travelers' information search behavior

Dogan Gursoy and Christina G. Chi

Introduction

In today's dynamic global environment, understanding how travelers acquire information is important for marketing management decisions and designing effective marketing communication campaigns and service delivery (Gursoy and McCleary, 2004a, 2004b). Understanding the information search behavior of key current and prospective markets can help destination managers and marketers develop target-marketing communications more effectively, because information search represents the primary stage in which marketers can provide information and influence travelers' decisions (Gursoy, 2001; Schmidt and Spreng, 1996). Application of basic market segmentation techniques, using travelers' information source utilization patterns as either a segmentation base or descriptor, enables focused positioning and media selection. Certainly, understanding external information source utilization can help marketers effectively tailor the promotional mix. Therefore, it is not surprising that consumer's information search has been one of the most examined subjects and one of the most enduring literature streams in consumer research (Schmidt and Spreng, 1996). Marketing and consumer behavior researchers have been examining the consumer's pre-purchase information seeking behavior at least since 1917 (e.g., Copeland, 1917), and even today most consumer information-processing and decision-making models include pre-purchase information search as one of the key components (e.g., Engel et al., 1993; Howard and Sheth, 1969).

There have been three major theoretical streams of the consumer information search literature (Gursoy 2001; Gursoy and McCleary, 2004a; Schmidt and Spreng, 1996; Srinivasan, 1990). The first is the psychological/motivational approach, which combines the individual, the product class, and the task-related variables such as beliefs and attitudes and involvement (Beatty and Smith, 1987). The second is the economics approach, which uses the cost–benefit framework and the economics of information theory (Stigler, 1961) to study information search (e.g., Avery, 1996). The third stream is the consumer information processing approach, which focuses on memory and cognitive information processing theory (e.g., Coupey et al., 1998; Johnson and Russo, 1984).

Like the consumer behavior and marketing fields, conceptual and empirical examinations of the information search behavior have a long tradition in the hospitality and tourism literature (e.g., Etzel and Wahlers, 1985; Fodness and Murray, 1997, 1998, 1999; Gursoy, 2001, 2003, Gursoy and McCleary, 2004a, 2004b, Perdue, 1985; Raitz and Dakhil, 1989; Schul and Crompton, 1983; Snepenger and Snepenger, 1993; Woodside and Ronkainen, 1980). Past research has identified a large number of factors that are likely to influence travelers' information search behavior. Previous studies in the area has focused on developing typologies of consumers' information search strategies, using nearly 60 variables that are likely to influence external information search (Srinivasan and Ratchford, 1991). As noted by Schmidt and Spreng (1996), these typologies included several aspects of the environment (e.g., difficulty of the choice task, number of alternatives, complexity of the alternatives), situational variables (e.g., previous satisfaction, time constraints, perceived risk, composition of traveling party), consumer characteristics (e.g., education, prior product knowledge, involvement, family life cycle, socio-economic status) (Gursoy, 2001, 2003; Gursoy and McCleary, 2004a, 2004b) and product characteristics (e.g., purpose of the trip, mode of travel) (Fodness and Murray, 1998, 1999). Even though several researchers concluded that information search behavior could be conceptualized as a series of interrelated behaviors, there have been only a few attempts to model the interrelationships among these factors. Notable exceptions are Maute and Foresster (1991), Moorthy et al. (1997), Punj and Staelin (1983) and Srinivasan and Ratchford (1991) in the field of consumer behavior and marketing and Gursoy (2001), Gursoy and McCleary (2004a, 2004b), Vogt and Fesenmaier (1998) and Fodness and Murray (1999) in the field of hospitality and tourism.

Most studies on travelers' information search behavior followed one of the two most influential theoretical frameworks proposed to enhance the understanding of tourists' information search behavior (Gursoy, 2001, 2003). The first theoretical framework, the *strategic model*, was proposed by Snepenger et al. (1990) and defines information search strategies as the combination of information sources used. The second theoretical framework, the *contingency model*, defines information search in terms of individual characteristics, effort, the number of sources used, situational influences, product characteristics, and search outcomes (Fodness and Murray, 1999; Gursoy, 2001, 2003; Schul and Crompton, 1983).

The strategic model

Snepenger et al. (1990) define search strategy as the combination of information sources used by a travel party to plan trips. Several studies examined information search strategies utilized by travelers. The findings of these studies suggested that travelers tend to use four broad external information sources when planning their trips. These are: (1) family and friends, (2) destination specific literature, (3) media, and (4) travel consultants (Snepenger and Snepenger, 1993; Woodside and Ronkainen, 1980). However, much of the work that has operationalized information search using the strategic model has considered only those travelers who used a single, specific source, such as travel agents, to plan their trips (Fodness and Murray, 1997; Gitelson and Purdue, 1987; Howard and Gitelson, 1989; Kendall and Booms, 1989).

The findings from previous studies indicate the strategic model that deals with the influence of socio-demographic characteristics of travelers and their utilization of available external information sources (Snepenger et al., 1990). The main focus of the strategic model is the number and combination of information sources utilized by travelers. The strategic model does not help us understand *why* travelers utilize those external information sources and ignore the others. The strategic model is not concerned with the factors (except for socio-demographics) that may affect the traveler's utilization of available external information sources. Some of the studies attempted to differentiate travelers who utilized different external information sources. However, differentiation was only based on socio-demographics (Gitelson and Perdue, 1987; Howard and Gitelson, 1989; Kendall and Booms, 1989; Snepenger et al., 1990; Woodside and Ronkainen, 1980).

The contingency model

Unlike the strategic model, the 'contingency' model defines information search in terms of individual characteristics such as travel-specific lifestyles, efforts such as amount of time spent, previous trip experiences, the number of sources used, situational influences, product characteristics, and search outcomes (Gursoy, 2001, 2003; Schul and Crompton, 1983).

The contingency model was first proposed by Schul and Crompton (1983). They proposed that travel-specific lifestyles and individual differences were better predictors of external search behavior of travelers than socio-demographic variables. They operationalized travel-specific lifestyle by factor-analyzing 16 psychographic variables. Their findings supported their proposition that an individual's travel-specific lifestyle (psychographics) explains his/her search behaviors, better than demographic differences. The contingency model was later expanded by Fodness and Murray (1999) to include situational factors and product characteristics. They examined the influence of situational factors, product characteristics, tourist characteristics, and search outcomes on external information search behavior. They identified the type of decision-making (routine, limited or extended) and composition of travel party as situational influences. Product characteristic included purpose of trip and mode of travel. Tourist characteristics were identified as family life cycle and socio-economic status. Search outcomes were measured as length of stay, number of destinations visited, number of attractions visited, and travel-related expenditures. Their results converged to support the model and its underlying proposition that tourist information search strategies were the result of a dynamic process in which travelers used various types and amounts of information sources to respond to internal and external contingencies.

Both models, strategic and contingency, have certain similarities and differences. Both models examine the influence of the composition of travel party, prior visits to the destination, and the degree of familiarity associated with the destination on external information search behavior. However, the contingency model examines several other factors that are likely to influence the information search behavior of travelers. Even though the contingency model seems superior to the strategic model for understanding travelers' external information search behavior, it has several shortcomings such as the unclear definition of prior product knowledge and ignorance of motivational and psychological factors.

The contingency model assumes that travelers who are familiar with, and/or are experts on, the destination will approach a product decision through a routine or limited problem-solving process so that they are not likely to search for additional information. Their travel decisions are likely to be based on their internal search (Fodness and Murray, 1999). In addition, in the contingency model, prior product knowledge and expertise are measured by a single indicator: previous visits to a destination. However, review of the consumer behavior literature suggests that prior product knowledge is not a uni-dimensional construct (Gursoy and McCleary, 2004a, 2004b). Alba and Hutchinson (1987) propose that prior knowledge has two major components, familiarity and expertise, and cannot be measured with a single indicator. Contrary to Fodness's and Murray's (1999) conclusions, the consumer behavior literature also suggests that prior product knowledge may influence the selective search behavior and the depth of analysis (Alba and Huchinson, 1987; Gursoy, 2001, 2003). Knowledgeable consumers are more likely to search for new information prior to making a decision because they are better equipped to understand the meaning of product information than novices (Alba and Hutchinson, 1987; Duncan and Olshavsky, 1982; Gursoy and McCleary, 2004a, 2004b; Johnson and Russo, 1984; Punj and Staelin, 1983). In addition, knowledgeable consumers are likely to focus on particular product attributes simply because they are aware of the existence of those attributes (Brucks, 1985). On the other hand, novice consumers may have a hard time comprehending and evaluating product-related information because of their inferior ability to comprehend and evaluate the product-related facts (Anderson and Jolson, 1980; Gursoy, 2001). Because of their limited ability to process the product-related information, novices are more likely to sample the opinions of others (Brucks, 1985; Furse et al., 1984; Gursoy, 2003; Gursoy and McCleary, 2004a, 2004b).

The contingency model also ignores the motivational factors that are likely to influence travelers' information search behavior. The direction and intensity of all consumers' actions are affected by motivations of individuals, because the function of an individual's motives is to protect, satisfy, and enhance him/her (Kassarjian and Robertson, 1968). Consumers acquire information as a strategy to reduce certain risks regarding the outcome of an action so as to protect them and to maximize their satisfaction (Gursoy, 2003; Murray, 1991; Urbany et al., 1989). Therefore, the traveler's motivations are suspected to influence the intensity and direction of his/her external information search behavior.

An integrated model of information search behavior

Recently, Gursoy (2001) and Gursoy and McCleary (2004a) proposed a new approach to further advance the understanding of travelers' information search behavior. In this integrated model, they viewed all three theoretical approaches on consumer's information search (i.e., psychological/motivational, economics, and information processing) and the two theoretical frameworks of travelers' information search behavior (i.e., strategic and contingency) as complementary, rather than opposite, to each other. Based on the new approach, Gursoy (2001) proposed a comprehensive model of travelers' information search behavior (see Figure 10.1). In the model, the previous visits, involvement, and learning constructs represent the psychological/motivational approach. The cost of the information search construct was included based on the cost–benefit framework. Finally, the prior product knowledge construct represents the consumer's information processing approach.

The model presented in Figure 10.1 focuses on the pre-purchase information search behavior of travelers. Pre-purchase information search represents the functional approach to explaining the nature of information sought and is defined as information search activities that are related to a recognized and immediate purchase intension. For immediate pre-purchase information needs, the consumer is likely to utilize either internal or external information sources, or both. Studies suggest that the type of pre-purchase information search (internal and/or external) that is likely to be utilized is influenced directly by the perceived cost of internal information search, the perceived cost of external information search, and the level of travelers' involvement. Travelers' familiarity and expertise (prior product knowledge), learning, and previous visits are proposed to influence a traveler's information search indirectly. The influence of travelers' familiarity and expertise is likely to be mediated by the perceived costs of internal and external information search (Gursoy, 2001; Gursoy and McCleary, 2004a).

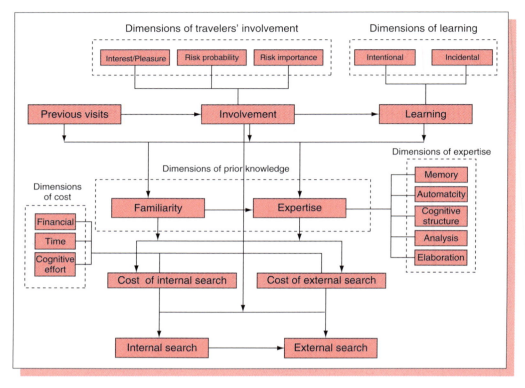

Figure 10.1
A comprehensive model of travelers' information search behavior

Cost of information search

Studies suggest that perceived cost of information search plays a significant role in determining the length and the extent of external information search conducted by travelers (Gursoy, 2001; Gursoy and McCleary, 2004a; Vogt and Fesenmaier, 1998). Travelers tend to keep searching for information as long as they believe that the benefits of acquiring information outweigh the cost of information search as indicated in 'the economics of information' theory (Stigler, 1961). The total cost associated with the utilization of a given information search strategy can be partitioned into three separate components; time spent, financial cost and effort required (Gursoy, 2001; Vogt and Fesenmaier, 1998). While time spent and financial costs are closely associated with the level of external information search utilized by travelers (Marmorstein et al., 1992), the effort required and the expected outcomes determine the extent and depth of the internal information search as suggested by the cost–benefit framework (Beach and Mitchell,

1978; Bettman et al., 1991; Gursoy, 2001). Therefore, when searching for information, travelers have to consider, consciously or unconsciously, the costs associated and benefits gained from utilizing an external information search and/or an internal information search. An increase in the cost of external information search is likely to decrease the level of external search activities and an increase in the cost of internal information search is likely to decrease internal search. The costs of both external and internal information searches are likely to mediate the effects of the traveler's familiarity and expertise, which represent the traveler's prior knowledge.

Cost of external information search

The cost of external information search represents financial and time costs involved in external search activities while the cost of internal search represents the cognitive effort required and the expected outcome of the internal search. Time spent (invested) in search is often considered to be the single most important cost of external information search (Gursoy and McCleary, 2004a; Stigler, 1961). Therefore, it is commonly accepted that the cost of time affects the extent of the traveler's external information search behavior (Avery, 1996; Stigler, 1961). The cost of external search is not likely to be equal for all travelers because time is more costly for travelers with a higher opportunity cost of time (income or wage rate) (Bryant, 1988; Stigler, 1961). However, Marmorstein et al. (1992) argue that wages or income alone may not measure opportunity cost correctly if a person receives satisfaction or other benefits from information search. Some people derive satisfaction and pleasure from the search process itself, that is, enjoy reading and watching programs about destinations without a particular need to make decisions about a specific destination or a travel plan. Many travelers value the information acquired because it enables them to reduce uncertainty if they are planning a vacation (McCleary and Whitney, 1994; Roehl and Fesenmaier, 1992), and it enables them to serve as both opinion leaders and sources of information for their acquaintances (Bloch et al., 1986; Gursoy and McCleary, 2004a; Marmorstein et al., 1992). Therefore, the time spent on collecting information may not be viewed as a pure loss of leisure time, and the traveler's wage rate may be an incomplete proxy for the opportunity cost of continued search. In estimating the opportunity cost of time the 'subjective value of time' rather than the 'objective value of time' should be utilized as suggested by Marmorstein et al. (1992).

Availability of time or time-pressure is also likely to influence the cost of time. The perceived value of time for a traveler under time-pressure is likely to be higher than that for a traveler with no time-pressure and, therefore, will shorten the external search process. Because the cost of time decreases with time availability, the external search activity is likely to increase with greater availability of time (Beatty and Smith, 1987; Schmidt and Spreng, 1996).

Another element of cost of external information search is monetary outlay on search activity such as transportation or phone calls (Avery, 1996; Stigler, 1961). As suggested by Snepenger and Snepenger (1993), travelers are likely to use four broad external information sources when planning their trips: family and friends, destination specific literature, media, and travel consultants. The cost of phone calls, transportation, fax, and mailing to gather information from these sources constitutes the financial or monetary costs of search activity. It is likely that as the monetary cost of information search increases, consumers will search less and less, if they believe that the benefits they will gain from the information search will not exceed the monetary cost of information.

One external information source not mentioned by Snepenger and Snepenger (1993) is the Internet. More and more travelers are utilizing Internet and online resources for their information needs. The rise of the Internet and online information search has had a strong impact on the cost–benefit ratio between internal and external search. It is becoming easier for travelers, even for people highly familiar with the destination, to conduct external information search by utilizing the Internet and online resources rather than trying to remember past experiences. Even though the monetary cost of online search is relatively low and it is easy to retrieve information, travelers still have to spend some time to find the information, pay for the Internet service, and invest a significant amount of effort in processing the information found online. The Internet lowers the cost of information search, but it does not make it free. However, because of low cost and ease of retrieving the information from online sources, more and more travelers are utilizing the Internet to find the information they need for destination selection and trip planning decisions (Gursoy and McCleary, 2004a).

In summary, an increase in financial and/or time costs associated with external information search is expected to lead to a decrease in the effort invested in the execution of an external-search-based decision. Therefore, as financial and/or time costs of external information search increase, internal information should become relatively more attractive to the decision maker, leading to an increase in the amount of internal search effort. Simultaneously, the utilization of external information search is likely to decline with an increase in the cost associated with it (Gursoy and McCleary, 2004a).

The cost of internal information search

The cost of internal information search is determined by the cognitive effort required and the expected outcome. Effort includes cognitive processes such as the evaluation of information, the integration of various pieces of information and the effort devoted to the retrieval of internally available information (i.e. global evaluations and individual pieces of attribute information) (Bettman et al., 1991). Researchers argue that the cost–benefit framework is more useful in determining the level of cognitive cost, and it has been used by a variety of researchers to explain how decision-makers select a choice strategy utilizing internal information sources (Beach and Mitchell, 1978; Bettman et al., 1991; Gursoy, 2001; Gursoy and McCleary, 2004a; Shugan, 1980). The cost–benefit framework suggests that travelers are likely to make better choices by expending cognitive effort used in the selection and application of information search strategy (Avery, 1996; Payne, 1982). Conversely, a traveler who is unwilling or unable to expend considerable cognitive effort in the selection and application of information search strategies may decide that the anticipated additional cognitive cost is greater than the anticipated gain. Therefore, the traveler's internal search activity is likely to be driven by both cognitive cost and benefit factors (Gursoy and McCleary, 2004a). Beach and Mitchell (1978) argued that the strategy selected by an individual would be the strategy that optimally trades off the benefits and the cognitive cost.

Another factor that is likely to influence the cost of internal information search is the outcome of the decision made based on the internal sources. Generally, it is believed that travelers tend to acquire information as a strategy of certain risk reduction efforts in the event of identified uncertainty regarding the outcome of an action (McCleary and Whitney, 1994) and in the event of identified discrepancy between external information and internal information, to protect themselves and to maximize their satisfaction (Locander and Hermann, 1979; Roehl and Fesenmaier, 1992; Urbany et al., 1989). If there is a discrepancy between the internal and external information, or if the traveler does not have sufficient internal information to make the best destination selection decision, the traveler may believe that reliance on internal information would be too costly as suggested by the cost–benefit framework (Gursoy and McCleary, 2004a). Therefore, the traveler may decide to search for additional information from external sources as long as he/she feels that the benefits of acquiring external information outweigh the cost of the same.

In summary, the willingness to expend cognitive effort is likely to have a direct impact on the total amount of cognitive effort that the individual employs in making the required decision. An individual's willingness to expend cognitive effort is likely to be determined by the cognitive cost of information search. If the cognitive cost of information search is high because of low expected benefits, a consumer's willingness to expend cognitive effort is likely to be low and, as a result, internal information search is likely to be low.

Prior knowledge

Prior knowledge with a product category has been recognized as an important factor in consumer decision-making (Park and Lessing, 1981). Consumers' prior knowledge with a product category is measured as a continuous variable that reflects their direct and indirect knowledge of the product category (Alba and Hutchinson, 1987). Researchers suggest that familiarity represents the early stages of prior knowledge while expertise represents the later stage. (Alba and Hutchinson, 1987; Gursoy, 2001).

Familiarity

Since familiarity represents early stages of learning, consumers are likely to gain knowledge and, therefore, familiarity through an ongoing information search such as reading guidebooks, other related books, advertising, and write-ups in newspapers and magazines, watching advertisements on TV, listening to advertising on radio, and talking to friends and relatives, to name a few (Gursoy, 2001; Kent and Allen, 1993). Several researchers argue that the level of familiarity is determined by the consumer's perception of how much he/she knows about the attributes of various choice alternatives being considered (Moorthy et al., 1997). However, Park et al. (1994) suggest that what people think they know and what they actually know often do not correspond. Consumers' familiarity with a product may be a result of their subjective knowledge (Roa and Sieben, 1992). Studies show that product familiarity has a direct impact on consumers' information search behavior (Etzel and Wahlers, 1985; Fodness and Murray, 1997, 1998, 1999; Gursoy, 2001, 2003; Gursoy and McCleary, 2004a, 2004b; Perdue, 1985; Schul and Crompton, 1983; Snepenger and Snepenger, 1993; Woodside and Ronkainen, 1980; Vogt and Fesenmaier, 1998). In both familiar and unfamiliar product categories, consumers first search their memory for some information to help guide them to make decisions. Consumers' familiarity with a product category is likely to lead them to direct access to already available information from their memory (Brucks, 1985; Coupey et al., 1998; Gursoy, 2003). If the consumer has sufficient information in his/her memory, he/she may not need to search for additional information and may make a decision based on internal information (Brucks, 1985; Gursoy, 2003). Researchers agree that if travelers are highly familiar with a destination, they may not need to collect any additional information from external sources because they are likely to make their decisions based on their familiarity with the destination. For example, Milman and Pizam (1995) suggest that the traveler's familiarity with a destination has a significant impact on future travel intentions and it is likely to forward the traveler into a more advanced stage in the purchase decision process. However, travelers who are low in familiarity are more likely to rely on external information sources to make their vacation decisions than those who are high in familiarity (Sheldon and Mak, 1987; Snepenger et al., 1990; Woodside and Ronkainen, 1980).

Expertise

Expertise can be defined as product-related experiences such as advertising exposures, information search, interactions with salespersons, choice and decision-making, purchasing, and product usage in various situations. The term consumer expertise was also used in a very broad sense to include both cognitive structures (e.g., beliefs about product attributes) and cognitive processes (decision rules for acting on those beliefs) required to perform product-related tasks successfully. However, the type of expertise required to perform a product-related task will vary based on the type of such task. Moreover, more than one type of knowledge is generally required for the successful performance of a particular task (Alba and Hutchinson, 1987).

At the most basic level, mere exposure to a brand name may result in perceptual enhancement of the brand during a visual search (Jacoby, 1983). Repeated exposure to a single brand or attribute may lead to an easy retrieval of information about that single brand or attribute (Moorthy et al., 1997). Wider experience results in the accumulation of more information, which enables consumers to include more brands in their memory-based evoked sets and to recall and use more attributes during the internal information-based decision-making (Desai and Hoyer, 2000). When decisions are based on internal information, knowledge may offer an expert consumer an opportunity to use processing decision strategies that are very different from the ones a consumer who is low in expertise may use (Moorthy et al., 1997). When a consumer who is high in expertise and another who is low in expertise learn the same information and later have to make a decision, the expert consumer may be able to rely on memory, whereas the consumer who is low in expertise may again need to engage in an external search or else make an ill-informed decision.

Alba and Hutchinson (1987) propose that there are at least five qualitatively distinct aspects of expertise that can be improved as product familiarity increases. These aspects are automaticity, expertise in utilizing memory, expertise in building cognitive structures, expertise in analysis, and expertise in elaboration. They argue that task performance may be improved by simple repetition because repetition reduces the cognitive effort required to perform the task and increases product knowledge. Further, repetition and increased product knowledge may lead to performance that is automatic. An increase in product knowledge is also likely to lead to more refined and more complete cognitive structures that are used to differentiate products. The ability to analyze information is likely to improve as a result of an increase in product knowledge owing to the fact that consumers may be able to isolate the information that is most important and task-relevant. An increase in product knowledge is also likely to improve the ability to elaborate on the given information that may lead to the generation of more accurate knowledge that goes beyond what is given and to remember product information. Fodness and Murray (1997) suggest that travelers who are highly knowledgeable (experts) are likely to make their travel decisions automatically based on what they already know. A number of studies also support the conclusion that travelers who are high in prior knowledge (experts) are not likely to collect additional information to make their travel decisions and they are likely to make their travel decisions based on their internal knowledge (Etzel and Wahlers, 1985; Snepenger and Snepenger, 1993). However, Gursoy (2001; 2003) suggest that there is a U-shaped relationship between travelers' prior product knowledge and their external information search behavior. He argues that at early stages of learning (low familiarity) travelers are likely to rely on external information sources to make their vacation decisions. However, as their prior product knowledge (familiarity) increases, they tend to make their vacation decisions based on what is in their memory. Therefore, reliance on external information sources decreases in this stage. Again, as they learn more (become experts), they realize that they need more detailed information to make their vacation decision. As a result, they start searching for additional external information to make their vacation decisions.

In general, an increase in familiarity is likely to decrease the cost of internal search and increase the cost of external search, while an increase in expertise is likely to decrease the costs of both external and internal information search. The traveler's familiarity and expertise are likely to be influenced by previous visits to the destination, involvement, and learning.

Involvement

Another factor that is likely to influence information search behavior is the level of involvement with the product/destination. The involvement literature suggests that the degree of the consumer's involvement is likely to have an impact on information search, information processing, and decision-making (Broderic and Mueller, 1999; Celsi and Olson, 1988; Foxall and Bhate, 1993; Gursoy and Gavcar, 2003; Maheswaren and Meyers-Levy, 1990; Mitchell, 1980). The general view of involvement has been one of 'personal relevance' (Zaichkowsky, 1985). That is, the consumer's level of involvement with an object, situation, or actions is determined by the degree to which he/she perceives the target concept to be personally relevant. The personal relevance of a product is represented by the perceived linkage between an individual's needs, goals, and values and his/her product knowledge. To the extent product characteristics are associated with personal goals and values, the consumer will experience strong feelings of personal relevance or involvement with the product (Celsi and Olson, 1988).

However, opinions about the number of dimensions of involvement are mixed. While some leisure and tourism researchers argue that involvement consists of four dimensions: (1) importance/pleasure; (2) sign; (3) risk consequences; (4) risk probability (Dimanche et al., 1991; Jamrozy et al., 1996), others suggest that travelers' involvement consist of three dimensions: (1) importance/pleasure; (2) risk consequences; (3) risk probability (Gursoy and Gavcar, 2003). Leisure and tourism researchers argue that for recreation and tourist activities interest/importance and hedonic (pleasure) dimensions are a single construct (Dimanche et al., 1991; Gursoy and Gavcar, 2003; Havitz et al., 1990; Jamrozy et al., 1996).

Even though there is disagreement regarding the number of dimensions of 'involvement', researchers agree that the direction and intensity of all consumer decisions and information search behavior are affected by their 'involvement' (Kassarjian and Robertson, 1968). Previous research suggests that a travel decision to go to an international destination or even to a domestic destination will be a highly involved decision for most leisure travelers because of personal relevance (Laurent and Kapferer, 1985; McQuarrie and Munson, 1987), the distance traveled (Vogt and Fesenmaier, 1998), perceived risk (Roehl and Fesenmaier, 1992), and the amount of money involved and effort spent (Teare, 1992; Vogt and Fesenmaier, 1998). Research shows that most leisure travelers to international and domestic destinations spend a considerable amount of time to plan their vacations (Fodness and Murray, 1997) and some of them start collecting information even before they select a destination. Generally, it is believed that consumers tend to acquire information as a strategy of risk reduction in the event of identified uncertainty regarding the outcome of an action (McCleary and Whitney, 1994; Roehl and Fesenmaier, 1992) and identified discrepancy between external information and prior knowledge to protect themselves and to maximize their satisfaction (Bettman, 1979; Locander and Hermann, 1979; Mayo and Jarvis, 1981; Roehl and Fesenmaier, 1992; Urbany et al., 1989). Therefore, as perceived risk and its consequences increase, travelers' involvement with the vacation decision is also likely to increase.

Generally, there is strong support for the relationship between involvement and information search behavior (Gursoy and Gavcar, 2003; Havitz and Dimanche, 1999). Literature suggests that when making decisions, highly involved individuals will go through an extended problem solving process: recognizing the problem, actively searching for information, evaluating the alternatives, and making the purchase decision (Clarke and Russell, 1978). Highly involved individuals are likely to use more criteria (Mitchell, 1980), search for more information using available external information sources (Beatty and Smith, 1987; Gursoy and Gavcar, 2003), use more information sources (Jamrozy et al., 1996), accept fewer alternatives (Petty and Cacioppo, 1981), examine the importance of information (Perdue, 1993), process relevant information in detail (Celsi and Olson, 1988; Chaiken, 1980), produce more product-related thoughts and make more product inferences (Celsi and Olson, 1988), want to know the strengths and weaknesses of possible alternatives in more detail (Kim et al., 1997; Maheswaren and Meyers-Levy, 1990), and form attitudes that are more resistant to change (Petty et al., 1983). In low involvement situations, the consumer does not extensively search for information and rarely evaluates alternatives or choices before making the purchase decision (Engel and Blackwell, 1982). The degree of the consumer's involvement, therefore, has an important impact on information processing and decision-making (Celsi and Olsen, 1988; Foxall and Bhate, 1993; Maheswaren and Meyers-Levy, 1990; Mitchell, 1980). In short, as travelers' involvement increases, they are likely to utilize more external information sources to gather additional information about important attributes and strengths and weaknesses of each destination to answer the questions they generated.

A traveler who is high in involvement is likely to utilize both external and internal information search (Gursoy and Gavcar, 2003). A traveler's involvement is also likely to have a positive effect on familiarity and expertise due to the fact that, if the traveler is high in involvement, he/she is likely to be more familiar with the product and is more likely to remember the product information, develop better category structures, analyze the information in more detail, elaborate on it, and make automatic decisions. A traveler's involvement may also positively influence intentional learning. If a traveler is high in involvement, the traveler is likely to pay more attention to the incoming information such as commercials about the destination and, therefore, learn better.

Previous visits are likely to have a positive influence on the traveler's familiarity and expertise. The logic behind this is that if a traveler has been to a destination before, he/she is likely to be more familiar with and develop expertise on the destination than a traveler who has never been to the destination. Previous visits may also have a positive influence on the traveler's involvement. Previous studies suggest that as the number of previous visits to a specific destination increases, the traveler's involvement is likely to increase as well (Gursoy and McCleary, 2004a; Kim et al., 1997). As the level of involvement increases with more visitations, a tourist is more likely to pay attention to any incoming information about the destination because high involvement means (or implies) personal relevance and importance. People tend to pay more attention to incoming information about something that has personal relevance and high importance (Kim et al., 1997).

Learning

Learning is also likely to influence the traveler's information search behavior. Learning can be defined as the process by which experience leads to changes in knowledge, attitudes, and/or behavior (Ormrod, 1999). Studies suggest that travelers' learning has two dimensions: intentional learning and incidental learning (Gursoy, 2001; Gursoy and McCleary, 2004a; Ormrod, 1999). Intentional learning is likely to increase the traveler' expertise and familiarity, while incidental learning is likely to increase the traveler's familiarity. If a traveler acquires the information through intentional learning, he/she is likely to pay more attention to incoming information and process the information thoroughly and, therefore, increase his/her objective knowledge and expertise. On the other hand, a traveler who learns through incidental learning is not likely to process the information thoroughly. However, since the traveler thinks that he/she has some information about the destination and its attractions, incidental learning is likely to increase his/her subjective knowledge and, therefore, his/her familiarity with the destination and its attractions.

Previous visits

Previous visits to a destination is one of the most commonly examined factors that are assumed to influence travelers' prior knowledge of the destination and their information search behavior and decision-making process (Fodness and Murray, 1999; Gursoy, 2003; Gursoy and McCleary, 2004a; Vogt and Fesenmaier, 1998). Even though it is closely correlated with prior knowledge, namely familiarity and expertise, the previous visits construct is only one of the factors that determine the level of knowledge about a destination. Influences of previous visits to a destination on a traveler's information search behavior, preferences, and recreation choice behavior can be explained by cognitive development theory, which suggests that as consumers gain experience through previous visits, they also gain knowledge about a given destination or activities and their internal cognitive representations of the destinations or settings become more complex (Williams et al., 1990). Therefore, a traveler's familiarity and expertise with a destination are likely to increase as the number of visits to a destination increases (Gursoy, 2001). Previous visits are also likely to influence the utilization of memory because, to a certain degree, they are likely to determine the amount and type of internal information available to an individual when making destination choices (Gursoy,

2003; Vogt and Fesemaier, 1998). Also, as the number of visits and experiences increases, the traveler is likely to develop more complex cognitive structures of the product/destination (Spence and Brucks, 1997). For example, a traveler who has been to a certain destination several times is likely to use more attributes to make site choice decisions and is more likely to describe site attributes in more specificity than a traveler who has never been to the destination (Gursoy and McCleary, 2004a; McFarlane et al., 1998). Studies also suggest that previous visits are likely to influence the level of involvement with the product category and activities (Kim et al., 1997). As the number of visits of a traveler to a specific destination increases, the traveler is likely to get more involved with that destination than a traveler with fewer or no previous visits (Gursoy and McClery, 2004a).

Impact of culture on information search

Culture is one of the most important factors that are likely to influence the way travelers make decisions and the sources of information they utilize in decision-making. Several researchers suggest that culture determines what forms of communications are acceptable and the nature and the degree of external search a traveler utilizes (Chen and Gursoy, 2001; Engel et al., 1995; Gursoy and Umbreit, 2004). The culture of a society can be defined at different levels such as national, regional, corporate, and professional. (Trompenaars, 1998). Even though it is well accepted that culture plays a significant role on travelers' information search behavior, only a small number of studies have examined the impact of culture on travelers' external information search behavior in cross-cultural settings (see Gursoy and Umbreit, 2004).

Studies that examined the impact of national culture on travelers' external information search concluded that national culture plays a significant role on what external information sources travelers from specific culture are likely to use for pre-purchase information search (Gursoy and Umbreit, 2004; Schul and Crompton, 1983; Uysal et al., 1990). For example, Uysal et al. (1990) reported that British travelers are likely to use travel agents as the main source of external information, followed by family and friends, brochures and pamphlets, and magazine and newspaper articles while German travelers are more likely to utilize family and friends as the main information source followed by travel agents, brochures and pamphlets, and books and library materials. Their findings also suggested that like Germans, French travelers utilize family and friends as main sources, followed by travel agents, brochures and pamphlets, airlines, and articles in magazines and newspapers. On the other hand, Japanese travelers were found to utilize books and other library materials as main sources, followed by brochures and pamphlets, family and friends, and travel agents.

Studies that examined the information search patterns of travelers from different national cultures also reported significant differences due to the moderating role culture plays. For example, Gursoy and Chen (2000) reported that British, French, and German travelers' information search patterns have two dimensions: business/leisure and dependent/independent. They also identified four distinct market segments based on the travelers' information search behavior.

1. German business and convention travel segment;
2. German leisure & VFR and leisure travel segment;
3. French and British business and convention travel segment; and
4. French and British leisure & VFR and leisure (vacation) travel segment.

Chen and Gursoy (2001) examined first-time and repeat British, French, and German travelers' utilization of external information sources. They also identified a two-dimensional external information search pattern: proprietary/public and focused/unfocused.

Communicating with the tourist market

It is crucial for managers and marketers to understand the importance of travelers' prior product knowledge and how it influences their information search behavior. Understanding the information search behavior of key current and prospective markets can help destination managers and marketers develop cost effective and focused target-marketing communications. Application of basic market segmentation techniques, using travelers' information source utilization patterns as either a segmentation basis or descriptor, may enable focused positioning and effective media selection. Certainly, understanding external information source utilization can help marketers effectively tailor the promotional mix.

Findings of recent studies suggest that travelers who are low in familiarity or high in expertise are likely to rely on external information sources to make their vacation decision. However, destination managers and marketers should understand that different travelers have different types of information needs. Travelers who are low in familiarity need simple, understandable and overall information, while travelers who are high in expertise need detailed information about the destination and attributes to make their vacation decisions. This implies that destination managers and marketers can use travelers' level of prior product knowledge (familiarity and expertise) as a segmentation tool to develop communication strategies that are most appropriate for each segment (Gursoy, 2001).

Communication strategies for travelers who are low in familiarity

Since travelers who are low in familiarity are likely to have a hard time examining the information gathered from external sources because of their limited processing ability, they may require a different communication strategy than travelers who are experts. Communication strategies developed for travelers with low familiarity should provide simple overall information about the destination. Those communication materials may also need to include a comparison of the destination against other destinations that target the same market to make it easier for the traveler to digest the information. In other words, communication materials should clearly identify the unique selling propositions of the destination to differentiate the destination from competitors and to make positioning of the destination easier for travelers unfamiliar with the destination. Establishing a good and understandable communication with travelers low in familiarity is critical in convincing them to choose a destination over other destinations because low familiarity is associated with higher perceived importance of, and receptivity to, new information (Park et al., 1988).

Studies also suggest that travelers who are low in familiarity utilize personal external information sources including word-of-mouth communications, which can be used as an effective method for communicating with them (Gursoy, 2001; Gursoy and McCleary, 2004a, 2004b). Because of their limited ability to process the product related information, travelers with low familiarity are more likely to sample the opinions of others such as their friends and family. Because positive word-of-mouth is the result of satisfaction, special attention needs to be given to customer satisfaction and complaint handling. Customer satisfaction should be constantly monitored in order to identify the problem areas and to make necessary modifications (to enhance customer satisfaction). In addition, customers' complaints should be handled delicately and quickly to ensure satisfaction and positive word-of-mouth.

Communicating with travelers' who are high in expertise

While travelers who are low in familiarity utilizes external information sources to gather simple, understandable, and overall information about a destination, travelers who are high in expertise are likely to gather specific and detailed information about the destination and its attributes. Therefore, a separate communication strategy should be developed to reach expert travelers. Communication materials developed for expert travelers should include detailed information about the attributes that are important to the target market. However, those attributes important to the target market should be identified by conducting formal or informal research on travelers and not be based on managers' perceptions of what attributes are important and what are not. Destinations can design a survey or conduct a focus group study to find out and monitor what attributes are the most important ones for expert travelers. Managers may also identify the important attributes by talking to their existing customers. Destination managers need to pay special attention to identification of expert travelers. If destination managers and marketers fail to ask the right questions to the right audience, they may end up making the wrong conclusions and developing a wrong communication strategy.

After the important attributes are identified, destination marketers will need to communicate them to expert travelers. Expert travelers are more likely to search for detailed information compared to others. Studies also suggest that travelers who are high in expertise are more likely to utilize destination-specific external information sources while travelers who are low in familiarity utilize personal external information sources (Gursoy, 2001; Gursoy and McCleary, 2004a, 2004b). Therefore, destination marketers need to develop communication materials (i.e., up-to-date websites, brochures, direct mailing materials, etc.) that provide detailed information about the destination and the important attributes. However, destination marketers should also be aware of the fact that travelers needs, wants, and desires keep changing and these changes are likely to influence the information needs of travelers. Therefore, destination managers also need to monitor changing consumer needs and wants because changing needs and wants are likely to shift the importance placed on attributes. These materials need to be modified as expert travelers' needs and wants change.

It is also crucial for managers and marketers to understand the importance of the perceived cost of information search. Both familiar and expert travelers are likely to utilize external information sources at varying degrees. However, travelers' utilization of external information is likely to be influenced by their perception of the cost of the information search. The inverse relationship between the perceived costs and external information search should cause marketers to take steps to make external search as inexpensive and time-efficient as possible. This is often not the case in hospitality and tourism marketing. For example, a perusal of destination web sites quickly reveals sites that are difficult to navigate, take a long time to load, and are linked to empty sites and incomplete information. This increase in time and cost to acquire information can cause travelers to look elsewhere for information. Another factor that destination marketers should pay attention to is that the more information available about a destination, the more likely travelers are to increase both incidental and intentional learning. These two factors are likely to lead to an increased familiarity and expertise, which, in turn, decrease information search costs, reduce the necessity for extensive external search, and help focus the search on specific attributes rather than on general information.

Marketers should also recognize the value of actual visitation to a site, for improving marketing outcomes, or the use of familiarization (FAM) trips for travel agents or on-site visitation incentives for selling timeshares. Indeed, previous visits are likely to have a positive impact on involvement with a destination while increasing familiarity and expertise, which lead to the outcomes discussed above.

Studies also suggest that travelers with moderate familiarity are more likely to make their vacation decisions based on what they know about the destination (Gursoy, 2003; Gursoy and McCleary, 2004b). This suggests that destination managers and marketers need to know how much prospective as well as existing travelers know about their destinations and how accurate their knowledge is. Studies show that what people think they know and what they actually know often do not correspond (Park et al., 1994). If travelers' perception (image) of the destination is negative due to their subjective knowledge that is not accurate, results may be disastrous. A traveler who has negative perceptions about a destination is not likely to consider visiting that destination. Furthermore, the traveler is not likely to recommend a destination that he/she has negative perceptions of to his/her friends. Therefore, destination managers and marketers may need to examine travelers' perceptions of the destination to make sure that those perceptions reflect reality. If their examinations indicate that travelers' perception of their destination is negative and does not reflect the true nature of the destination, they may need to take corrective actions. In order to take corrective actions, destination marketers first need to identify what causes those negative perceptions and, then, they need to determine the best way to improve the image.

Marketers should also recognize the importance of understanding the cultural values held by travelers. As suggested by the studies reviewed above, travelers' culture plays a significant moderating role in their information search, decision making, and destination selection behavior. For example, a study conducted to examine the external information search behavior of travelers to 15 European Union (EU) member states revealed that national culture played a significant moderating role in travelers' information search behavior (Gursoy and Umbreit, 2004). Based on the moderating effect of national culture on travelers' utilization of external information sources, those 15 EU member states were grouped into five distinct segments. Each segment was found to utilize significantly different groups of external information sources. Findings of this and other studies suggest that destination managers who want to attract international travelers to their destinations should, first, thoroughly study the culture of the target market they are going after in order to develop the most effective and efficient marketing communication strategies. Cultural values of the target market are likely to determine what an acceptable communication strategy is and what is not in that culture. Destination managers should understand that one strategy that may work in one culture may not work in others. Therefore, communication strategies and specific communication tools should be modified in order to fit in the culture of the target market.

Directions for future research

As discussed earlier, studies suggest that perceived cost of external and internal information search is likely to play a significant role in travelers' information search behavior. Travelers are likely to continue searching for information by utilizing external sources as long as they believe that the benefits gained from the search exceed the cost of search. Travelers are also likely to utilize the external information source that has the lowest external and/or internal search cost. Even though understanding the cost of information is vital in developing communication strategies and materials, there is limited research in the area. Most research in the area has focused on the time spent searching for information, and most data were collected through self-instructed survey instruments. There is an urgent need for studies to examine the other aspects of information search. Researchers need to consider utilizing experimental research designs rather than survey methods in order to truly understand the influence of cost on travelers' utilization of information sources.

One area of external information search tools that has been receiving increasing attention in recent years is the Internet. An increasing number of researchers are conducting studies to understand the impact of the Internet on information search behavior and how best to utilize it. The World Wide Web, or the Internet, has become a powerful and ubiquitous means of delivering a range of messages to hundreds of millions of travelers worldwide. As travelers get more familiar with using the Internet, they are learning to use platforms to find information about travel destinations and travel products other than the ones that are built and maintained by the different sectors of the tourism, travel, and hospitality industry. The Internet made it possible for travelers to share their experiences with other travelers through chat rooms, discussion forums, third-party web sites that are designed to allow travelers post their experiences. These developments are moving in the direction of mash-ups of online and offline information sources, the development of information highways with several lanes, and forcing business to be an active part of the online community by providing relevant and up-to-date information. These changes have created a radically different approach to developing and distributing information, disrupting the traditional communication distribution model. It is pushing businesses to develop new types of information-oriented platforms and new kinds of customizable application environments and is forcing businesses to think about massive information distribution in a novel and customized manner. Furthermore, the landscape shifts very quickly, making it difficult to settle on business models and interaction paradigms. Even though the Internet is changing the way companies conduct their businesses and the way consumers search for information and buy products, hospitality researchers are not paying much attention to these changes. It is critical for companies to understand the why, what, when, and how of the Internet and the way travelers utilize it.

Chapter summary

This chapter examined travelers' information search behavior and the factors that are likely to influence external and internal search behavior. Studies reviewed in this chapter revealed that the type of information search (internal and/or external) a traveler conducts is likely to be influenced directly by the perceived cost of internal information search, the perceived cost of external information search, and the level of travelers' involvement. Studies show that travelers' prior product knowledge, the way they learn the information, and previous visits are likely to have indirect effects on travelers' information search behavior.

Studies reviewed in this chapter suggest that travelers' prior product knowledge has two components, familiarity and expertise, as opposed to the general belief among tourism researchers that travelers' knowledge is a unidimensional construct and can be easily measured by counting the number of previous trips taken to the destination in question. Studies also suggest that the influences of familiarity and expertise on travelers' utilization of external and/or internal information sources vary. While travelers with high familiarity rely heavily on internal information search to make their vacation decisions, travelers who are experts are likely to search for information from external information sources even though they have more prior product knowledge about vacation destinations than familiar travelers. The reviewed studies further suggest that the cost of information search is likely to mediate the relationship between prior knowledge and information search behavior. An increase in the cost of external information search is likely to decrease the level of external search activities and an increase in the cost of internal information search is likely to decrease internal search. The costs of both external and internal information searches are suggested to mediate the effects of the traveler's familiarity and expertise, which represent the traveler's prior knowledge.

Studies suggest that as travelers' familiarity increases they are more likely to make their vacation decisions based on what they know about the destination (Gursoy, 2001). Whether a traveler relies solely on internal information search will depend heavily on the perceived adequacy or perceived quality of their existing knowledge. Tourism managers and marketers should remember that familiarity is a measure of subjective knowledge. Subjective knowledge refers to people's perceptions of what or how much they know about a product or product class (Monroe, 1976; Park et al., 1994). Therefore, if a traveler is confident that he/she knows enough about a destination, he/she may not utilize any of the available external information sources. Even if they utilize external information sources, this perceived self-confidence may affect the utilization of external information sources (Brucks, 1985).

Another factor that is likely to moderate the type and level of information search activity is the culture of the traveler in question. Studies suggested that culture plays a significant role in determining which external information sources a traveler utilizes. Therefore, understanding the cultural variations in each market and revising the communication strategy based on those differences may prove to be crucial for destination marketers targeting travelers in international markets.

It is important for destination marketers to have an overall picture of how travelers acquire information. It is also important to know the major components of the search process and how they fit together. With this understanding, marketers can design communication strategies aimed specifically at different stages in the information search process, which will lead to efficient use of resources and more success in attracting tourists to their specific destinations.

References

Alba, J. W. and Hutchinson, J. W. (1987). Dimensions of consumer expertise. *Journal of Consumer Research, 13* (March), 411–453.

Anderson, R. A. and Jolson, M. A. (1980). Technical wording in advertising: Implications for market segmentation. *Journal of Marketing, 44* (Winter), 57–66.

Avery, R. J. (1996). Determinants of search for nondurable goods: An empirical assessment of the economics of information theory. *Journal of Consumer Affairs, 30*(2), 390–420.

Beach, L. R. and Mitchell, T. R. (1978). A contingency model for the selection of decision strategies. *Academy of Management Review, 3*, 439–449.

Beatty, S. E. and Smith, S. M. (1987). External search effort: An investigation across several product categories. *Journal of Consumer Research, 14* (June), 83–95.

Bettman, J. R. (1979). Memory factors in consumer choice: A review. *Journal of Marketing, 43* (Spring), 37–53.

Bettman, J. R., Johnson, E. J., and Payne, J. W. (1991). Consumer decision making. In T. S. Robertson and H. H. Kassarjian (Eds.), *Handbook of Consumer Research* (50–84). Englewood Cliffs, NJ: Prentice Hall.

Bloch, P. H., Sherrell, D. L., and Ridgway, N. M. (1986). Consumer search: An extended framework. *Journal of Consumer Research, 13* (June), 119–126.

Broderic, A. J. and Mueller, R. D. (1999). A theoretical and empirical exegesis of the consumer involvement construct: The psychology of the food shopper. *Journal of Marketing Theory and Practice, 7* (Fall), 97–108.

Brucks, M. (1985). The effects of product class knowledge on information search behavior. *Journal of Consumer Research, 12* (June), 1–16.

Bryant, W. K. (1988). Durables and wives' employment yet again. *Journal of Consumer Research, 15* (June), 37–47.

Celsi, R. L. and Olson, J. C. (1988). The role of involvement in attention and comprehension processes. *Journal of Consumer Research, 15* (September), 210–224.

Chaiken, S. (1980). Heuristic versus systematic information processing and the use of source versus message cues in persuasion. *Journal of Personality and Social Psychology, 39* (November), 752–756.

Chen, J. S. and Gursoy, D. (2001). An investigation of tourists' destination loyalty and preferences. *The International Journal of Contemporary Hospitality Management, 13*(2), 79–85.

Clarke, K. and Russell W. B. (1978). The effects of product involvement and task definition on anticipated consumer effort. In K. H. Hunt, (Ed.), *Advances in Consumer Research,* Vol. 5. Ann Arbor, MI: Association for Consumer Research.

Copeland, M. T. (1917). Relation of consumers buying habits of marketing methods. *Harvard Business Review, 1* (April), 282–289.

Coupey, E., Irwin, R. I., and Payne, J. W. (1998). Product category familiarity and preference construction. *Journal of Consumer Research, 24* (March), 459–468.

Desai, K. K. and Hoyer, W. D. (2000) Descriptive characteristics of memory-based consideration sets: Influence of usage occasion frequency and usage location familiarity. *Journal of Consumer Research, 27*(3), 309–323.

Dimanche, F., Havitz, M. E., and Howard, D. R. (1991). Testing the involvement profile (IP) scale in the context of selected recreational and touristic activities. *Journal of Leisure Research, 23*(1), 51–66.

Duncan, C. P. and Olshavsky, R. W. (1982). External search: The role of consumer beliefs. *Journal of Marketing Research, 19* (February), 32–43.

Engel, J. F. and Blackwell, R. W. (1982). *Consumer behavior.* New York: Dryden Press.

Engel, J. F., Blackwell, R. W., and Miniard, P. W. (1993). *Understanding the consumer* (7th ed.). Forth Worth, TX: Dryden.

Engel, J., Blackwell, R. D., and Miniard, P. (1995). *Consumer behavior* (8th ed.). Fort Worth, TX: Dryden.

Etzel, M. J. and Wahlers, R. G. (1985) The use of requested promotional material by pleasure travelers. *Journal of Travel Research, 23*(4), 2–6.

Fodness, D. and Murray, B. (1997). Tourist information search. *Annals of Tourism Research, 24*(3), 503–523.

Fodness, D. and Murray, B. (1998). A typology of tourist information search strategies. *Journal of Travel Research, 37* (November), 108–119.

Fodness, D. and Murray, B. (1999). A model of tourist information search behavior. *Journal of Travel Research*, *37* (February), 220–230.

Foxall, G. R. and Bhate, S. (1993). Cognitive styles and personal involvement as explicators of innovative purchasing of 'healthy food brands'. *European Journal of Marketing*, *27*(2), 5–16.

Furse, D. H., Punj, G. N., and Steward, D. W. (1984). A typology of individual search strategies among purchasers of new automobiles. *Journal of Consumer Research*, *10* (March), 417–431.

Gitelson, R. J. and Perdue, R. R. (1987). Evaluating the role of state welcome centers in disseminating travel related information in North Caroline. *Journal of Travel Research*, *25*, 15–19.

Gursoy, D. (2001). *Development of travelers' information search behavior model*. Unpublished doctoral dissertation. Blacksburg, VA: Virginia Polytechnic Institute and State University.

Gursoy, D. (2003). Prior product knowledge and its influence on the traveler's information search behavior. *Journal of Hospitality and Leisure Marketing*, *10*(3/4), 113–131.

Gursoy, D. and Chen, J. S. (2000). Competitive analysis of cross cultural information search behavior. *Tourism Management*, *21*(6), 583–590.

Gursoy, D. and Gavcar, E. (2003). International leisure tourist's involvement profile. *Annals of Tourism Research*, *30*(4), 906–926.

Gursoy, D. and McCleary, K. W. (2004a). An integrative model of tourist's information search behavior. *Annals of Tourism Research*, *31*(2), 353–373.

Gursoy, D. and McCleary, K. W. (2004b). Travelers' prior knowledge and its impact on their information search behavior. *Journal of Hospitality and Tourism Research*, *28*(1), 66–94.

Gursoy, D. and Umbreit, W. T. (2004). Tourist information search behavior: Cross-cultural comparison of European Union Member States. *International Journal of Hospitality Management*, *23*(1), 55–70

Havitz, M. E. and Dimanche, F. (1999). Leisure involvement revisited: Drive properties and Paradoxes. *Journal of Leisure Research*, *31*(2), 122–149.

Havitz, M. E., Dimanche, F., and Howard, D. (1990). Consumer involvement profiles. *Journal of Travel & Tourism Marketing*, *1*(4), 33–52.

Howard, D. R. and Gitelson, R. (1989). An analysis of differences between state welcome center users and nonusers: A profile of Oregon vacationers. *Journal of Travel Research*, *27*(1), 38–40.

Howard, J. A. and Sheth, J. N. (1969). *The theory of buyer behavior*. New York: John Wiley.

Jacoby, L. L. (1983). Perceptual enhancement: Persistent effects of an experience. *Journal of Experimental Psychology: Learning, Memory, and Cognition*, *9* (January), 21–38.

Jamrozy, U., Backman, S. J., and Backman, K. F. (1996) Involvement and opinion leadership in tourism. *Annals of Tourism Research*, *23*(4), 908–924.

Johnson, E. J. and Russo, J. E. (1984). Product familiarity and learning new information. *Journal of Consumer Research, 11* (June), 542–550.

Kassarjian, H. H. and Robertson, T. S. (1968). *Perspectives in consumer behavior*. Glenview, IL: Scott, Foresman Company.

Kendall, K. W. and Booms, B. H. (1989). Consumer perceptions of travel agencies: Communications, images, needs, and expectations. *Journal of Travel Research, 27*, 29–37.

Kent, R. J. and Allen, C. T. (1993). Does competitive clutter in television advertising 'interfere' with the recall and recognition of brand names and ad claims? *Marketing Letters, 4*(2), 175–84.

Kim, S. S., Scott, D., and Crompton, J. L. (1997). An exploration of the relationships among social psychological involvement, behavioral involvement, commitment, and future intensions in the context of Birdwatching. *Journal of Leisure Research, 29*(3), 320–341.

Laurent, G. and Kapferer, J. N. (1985). Measuring consumer involvement profiles. *Journal of Marketing Research, 22* (February), 41–53.

Locander, W. B. and Hermann, P. W. (1979). The effects of self-confidence and anxiety on information seeking in consumer risk reduction. *Journal of Marketing Research, 16*, 268–274.

Maheswaren, D. and Meyers-Levy, J. (1990). The influence of message framing and involvement. *Journal of Marketing Research, 27* (August), 361–367.

Marmorstein, H., Grewal, D.,and Fishe, R. P. H. (1992). The value of time spent in price-comparison shopping: Survey and experimental evidence. *Journal of Consumer Research, 9* (June), 52–61.

Maute, M. F. and Foresster, Jr. W. R. (1991). The effects of attribute qualities on consumer decision making: A causal model of external information search. *Journal of Economic Psychology, 12* (December), 643–666.

Mayo, E. J. and Jarvis, L. P. (1981). *The psychology of leisure travel: Effective marketing and selling of travel services*. Boston: CBI.

McCleary, K. W. and Whitney, D. L. (1994). Projecting western consumer attitudes toward travel to six Eastern European countries. *Journal of International Consumer Marketing, 6*(3/4), 239–256.

McFarlane, B. L., Boxall, P. C. and Watson, D. O. (1998). Past experience and behavioral choice among wilderness users. *Journal of Leisure Research, 30*(2), 195–213.

McQuarrie, E. F. and Munson, M. (1987). The Zaichkowsky personal involvement inventory: Modification and extension. In M. Wallendorf and P. F. Anderson (Eds.), *Advances in Consumer Research*, Vol. 14, (pp. 36–40). Provo, UT: Association for Consumer Research.

Milman, A. and Pizam, A. (1995). The role of awareness and familiarity with a destination. *Journal of Travel Research, 33*(3): 21–27.

Mitchell, A. A. (1980). Involvement: A potentially important mediator of consumer behavior. In W. L. Wilkie (Ed.), *Advances in Consumer*

Research, Vol. 6, (pp. 191–196). Association for Consumer Research, MI: Ann Arbor.

Monroe, K. B. (1976). The influence of price differences and brand familiarity on brand preferences. *Journal of Consumer Research, 3* (June), 42–49.

Moorthy, S., Ratchford, B. T., and Talukdar, D. (1997). Consumer information search revisited: Theory and empirical analysis. *Journal of Consumer Research, 23* (March), 263–277.

Murray, K. B. (1991). A test of services marketing theory: Consumer information acquisition activities. *Journal of Marketing, 55* (January), 10–23.

Ormrod, J. E. (1999). *Human Learning* (3rd ed.). Upper Saddle River, NJ: Prentice-Hall, Inc.

Park, C. W., Gardner, M. P., and Thukral, V. K. (1988). Self-perceived knowledge: Some effects on information processing for a choice task. *American Journal of Psychology, 101* (Fall), 401–424.

Park, C. W. and Lessing, V. P. (1981). Familiarity and its impact on consumer decision biases and heuristics. *Journal of Consumer Research, 8* (September), 223–230.

Park, C. W., Mothersbaugh, D. L., and Feick, L. (1994). Consumer knowledge assessment. *Journal of Consumer Research, 21* (June), 71–82.

Payne, J. W. (1982). Contingent decision behavior. *Psychological Bulletin, 92*(2), 382–402.

Perdue, R. R. (1985). Segmenting state information inquirers by timing of destination decision and previous experience. *Journal of Travel Research, 23* (Spring), 6–11.

Perdue, R. R. (1993). External information search in marine recreational fishing. *Leisure Sciences, 15*, 169–187.

Petty, R. E. and Cacioppo, J. T. (1981), *Attitudes and persuasion: Classic and contemporary approaches*, Dubuque: Wrn C. Brown Company Publishers.

Petty, R. E., Cacioppo, J. T., and Schumann, D. (1983). Central and peripheral routes to advertising effectiveness: The moderating role of involvement. *Journal of Consumer Research, 10* (September) 135–146.

Punj, G. and Staelin, R. (1983). A model of consumer information search behavior for new automobiles. *Journal of Consumer Research, 9* (March), 366–380.

Raitz, K. and Dakhil, M. (1989). A note about information sources for preferred recreational environments. *Journal of Travel Research, 27*(1), 45–49.

Roa, A. R. and Sieben, W. A. (1992). The effect of prior knowledge on price acceptability and the type of information examined. *Journal of Consumer Research, 19* (September), 256–270.

Roehl, W. S. and Fesenmaier, D. R. (1992). Risk perceptions and pleasure travel: An exploratory analysis. *Journal of Travel Research, 30*(4), 17–26.

Schmidt, J. B. and Spreng, R. A. (1996). A proposed model of external consumer information search. *Journal of the Academy of Marketing Science, 24*(3), 246–256.

Schul, P. and Crompton J. L. (1983). Search behavior of international vacationers: Travel-specific lifestyle and sociodemographic variables. *Journal of Travel Research, 22*(3), 25–31.

Sheldon, P. J. and Mak, J. (1987). The demand for package tours: A mode choice model. Journal of *Travel Research, 26*(2), 8–14.

Shugan, S. M. (1980). The cost of thinking. *Journal of Consumer Research, 7* (September), 99–111.

Snepenger, D., Meged, K., Snelling, M., and Worrall, K. (1990). Information search strategies by destination-naïve tourists. *Journal Travel Research, 29*(1), 13–16.

Snepenger, D. and Snepenger, M. (1993). Information search by pleasure travelers. In M. A. Kahn, M. D. Olsen and T. Var (Eds.), *Encyclopedia of Hospitality and Tourism* (pp. 830–835). New York, NY: Van Nostrand Reinhold.

Spence, M. T. and Brucks, M. (1997). The moderating effects of problem characteristics on experts and novices' judgements. *Journal of Marketing Research, 34*(2), 233–247.

Srinivasan, N. (1990). Pre-purchase external information search for information. In V. E. Zeithaml (Ed.). *Review of Marketing* (pp. 153–189). Chicago: American Marketing Association.

Srinivasan, N. and Ratchford, B. T. (1991). An empirical test of a model of external search for automobiles. *Journal of Consumer Research, 18* (September), 233–242.

Stigler, G. (1961). The economics of information. *The Journal of Political Economy, 19*, 213–225.

Teare, R. (1992). An exploration of the consumer decision process for hospitality services. In Teare, R., Moutinho, L. and Morgan, N. J. (Eds.), *Managing and Marketing Services in the 1990s* (pp. 233–248). London, UK: Cassell Educational.

Trompenaars, A., (1998). *Riding the waves of culture: Understanding diversity in global business*. Burr Ridge: Irwin Professional Pub.

Urbany, J. E., Dickson, P. R., and Wilkie, W. L. (1989). Buyer uncertainty and information search. *Journal of Consumer Research, 16* (September), 208–215.

Uysal, M., McDonald, C. D., and Reid, L. J. (1990). Sources of information used by international visitors to U.S. parks and natural areas. *Journal of Park and Recreation Administration, 8*(1), 51–59.

Vogt, C. A. and Fesenmaier, D. R. (1998). Expanding the functional information search. *Annals of Tourism Research, 25*(3), 551–578.

Williams, D. R., Schreyer, R., and Knopf, R. C. (1990). The effect of experience use history on the multidimensional structure of motivations to participate in leisure activities. *Journal of Leisure Research, 22*, 36–54.

Woodside, A. G. and Ronkainen, I. A. (1980). Vacation planning segments: Self planning vs. users of motor club and travel agents. *Annals of Tourism Research*, *7*, 385–393.

Zaichkowsky, J. L. (1985). Measuring the involvement concept. *Journal of Consumer Research*, *12* (December), 341–352.

CHAPTER 11

Customer satisfaction, service failure, and service recovery

Anna S. Mattila and Heejung Ro

Introduction

This chapter critically reviews conceptualizations and empirical evidence in support of customer satisfaction, service failure, and service recovery and their role in hospitality and tourism management. One of the most basic principles in hospitality marketing is that organizational performance is enhanced by satisfying customers. Satisfaction is a major outcome of marketing activity and it links decision-making processes and consumption with post-purchase phenomena, such as attitude change, complaining behavior, word-of-mouth, repeat purchase and brand loyalty (e.g., Oliver, 1980). Although hospitality and tourism organizations may consider customer satisfaction as a major goal, not all service experiences are satisfactory from the customer's perspective (Ennew and Shoefer, 2003). Service failures can, and often do, occur. One reason for these failures is the labor-intensive nature of the hospitality industry, which inevitably leads to more heterogeneous outcomes compared to goods production processes (Kotler et al., 2006). Service performance variability and failures also arise from the inseparability of service production and consumption. Given the relatively high frequency of service failures, service recovery has been identified as one of the key ingredients for achieving customer loyalty (e.g., Tax and Brown, 2000). As a result, developing an effective service recovery policy has become an important focus of many customer retention strategies (Smith et al., 1999). Service recovery strategies involve actions taken by service providers to respond to service failures (Grönroos, 2000). Both what is done (compensation) and how it is done (employee interaction with the customer) influence customer perceptions of service recovery (e.g., Levesque and McDougall, 2000).

This chapter provides a critical analysis of the literature on customer satisfaction, service failure, and service recovery in the field of hospitality and tourism management and identifies several strategies that hospitality organizations can implement in response to dissatisfying service experiences. Following a brief overview of the conceptualization and measurement of the constructs of interest, an attempt is made to bring to the reader's attention the importance of broadening the scope of research in this field. This approach naturally indicates avenues that future research might fruitfully explore. The chapter concludes by presenting a comprehensive framework for the customer's post-purchase evaluation processes.

Background

Customer satisfaction

What is customer satisfaction?

Despite extensive research on satisfaction, researchers cannot agree on a common definition for the concept. Oliver (1997) addresses this definitional issue by noting that "everyone knows what satisfaction is until asked to give a definition. Then it seems, nobody knows" (p. 13). Due to its elusive nature, the literature is replete with different conceptual and operational definitions of consumer satisfaction.

Most definitions favor the notion of consumer satisfaction as an evaluative process. Specifically, there is an overriding theme of consumer satisfaction as a summary concept [i.e., a fulfillment response (Oliver, 1997); overall evaluation (Fornell, 1992); summary attribute phenomenon (Oliver, 1992)]. Satisfaction is also often viewed as an attitude-like judgment based on a series of consumer–product interactions (Yi, 1990). However, there is disagreement concerning the nature of this summary concept.

Researchers portray consumer satisfaction as either a cognitive or an affective response. For example, Westbrook and Reilly (1983, p. 256) refer to satisfaction as 'an emotional response,' while Howard and Sheth (1969, p. 145) consider satisfaction as 'a buyer's cognitive state.' More recent definitions seem to incorporate emotions (Giese and Cote, 2000), and there are several conceptual and operational definitions indicating that satisfaction is a mixed response comprised of both cognitive and affective dimensions (e.g., Oliver, 1997). Recent research indicates that the relative importance of affect versus cognition on satisfaction judgments might be time-dependent (Cote et al., 1989). For example, Homburg et al. (2006) show that the impact of cognition on satisfaction evaluations increases over time while the role of affect diminishes.

Although satisfaction has been conceptualized in terms of either a single transaction (i.e., an evaluative judgment following the purchase occasion) or a series of interactions with a product over time, Anderson and Fornell (1994) note that nearly all satisfaction research has adopted the former, transaction-specific view. Indeed, several scholars have criticized the marketing field for treating satisfaction as a static evaluation derived from a single trial event.

The single-transaction view is particularly problematic for hospitality and tourism services that typically are composed of a series of service encounters within a single consumption experience. For example, tourism is a high-involvement, high-risk purchase, thus leading to a complex evaluation process with no predictable critical evaluation point (Bowen and Clarke, 2002). While some researchers focus on a single aspect of the travel experience such as shopping satisfaction (Heung and Cheng, 2000; Reisinger and Turner, 2002), others include multiple attribute dimensions such as tourist attractions, facilities, services, and prices (Yu and Goulden, 2006) and satisfaction with the tour provider and tour package (Hsu, 2000). Middleton and Clarke (2001), for instance, demonstrate the interdependence of various components of the travel package in driving overall satisfaction (i.e., a medley of products). Tourists are thus likely to evaluate their travel experiences holistically rather than decomposing them to isolated attribute-level components.

Hospitality experiences typically involve a series of service encounters. Satisfaction occurs at each encounter, and each encounter contributes to overall satisfaction. For example, Lemmink et al. (1998) examined the dining service delivery process by breaking it down into four distinct stages: (a) reception, (b) ordering, (c) meal consumption, and (d) check-out. Satisfaction scores were gathered at each stage as well as at the global level. The carry-over effects from previous stages support the notion of satisfaction as a cumulative concept.

In tourism and hospitality research, satisfaction is often used as an independent variable to predict behavioral intentions such as revisit to the destination (e.g., Petrick et al., 2001; Petrick and Backman, 2002; Alegre and Cladera, 2006); return to the hotel or casino (Kandampully and Suhartanto, 2000; Lucas, 2003); or engaging in positive word-of-mouth (e.g., Petrick, 2004; Petrick et al., 2006). Moreover, the relative importance of various attributes in driving these outcomes has been a topic of numerous studies in the hospitality and tourism literature (e.g., Barsky, 1992; Yüksel and Rimmington, 1998).

Dissatisfaction

Compared to satisfaction, conceptualizing dissatisfaction has received relatively little attention in consumer research. In general, dissatisfaction responses are relatively strong reactions to consumption episodes. Dissatisfaction is often accompanied with intense emotions (e.g., anger, frustration) and perceptions of unfairness. Most research on dissatisfaction has focused on understanding consumers' behavioral responses such as complaining behaviors and negative word-of-mouth communication (e.g., Tax, Brown, and Chandrashekaran, 1998). As such, extant literature is relatively silent in terms of defining dissatisfaction (Giese and Cote, 2000). Satisfaction research has, however, examined the unidimensionality of the satisfaction/dissatisfaction construct (Maddox, 1981). Consumer dissatisfaction is typically portrayed as a bipolar opposite of satisfaction (e.g., Spreng et al., 1996; Mittal et al., 1999;). Alternatively, satisfaction and dissatisfaction are sometimes viewed as two different dimensions (e.g., Mano and Oliver, 1993). While the former approach involves well-known scales (e.g., very satisfied vs. very dissatisfied), unipolar satisfaction and unipolar dissatisfaction measures are employed with the latter conceptualization. To illustrate this measurement issue, consumers can have mixed reactions to a consumption episode. A restaurant patron might be satisfied with good food but dissatisfied with a rude server. Under these conditions, satisfaction and dissatisfaction should be viewed as separate dimensions. Having defined satisfaction and dissatisfaction, the next section will briefly discuss the theoretical frameworks underlying consumers' post-purchase evaluation processes.

The expectancy disconfirmation with performance model

The dominant conceptual model in the customer satisfaction literature is the disconfirmation of expectations paradigm (Oliver, 1977; Wirtz and Mattila, 2001). Later, the paradigm has evolved considering the role of performance in the process (Oliver, 1980; Churchill and Surprenant, 1982), and then it has been named the expectancy disconfirmation with performance model (Oliver, 1997). This model posits that customer satisfaction is related to the degree and direction of the disconfirmation experience, where disconfirmation is defined as the gap or difference between an individual's pre-purchase expectations and perceived performance of the product/service (Oliver, 1980). Consumers' expectations are (a) confirmed when the product/service conforms to expectations; (b) negatively disconfirmed when performance is less than expected, and (c) positively disconfirmed when performance is better than expected (Patterson and Johnson, 1993). The disconfirmation model is parsimonious and intuitively appealing (Iacobucci et al., 1994) and it has received strong empirical support (e.g., Boulding et al., 1993). Figure 11.1 is a simplified version of the expectancy disconfirmation with performance model.

Despite robust support for the intervening role of disconfirmation in the satisfaction formation process, research also suggests that perceived performance might directly influence satisfaction (e.g., Anderson and Sullivan, 1993; Oliver, 1993; Oliver, 1994). It has been empirically shown

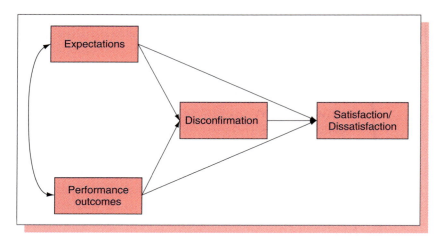

Figure 11.1
A general model of expectancy disconfirmation with performance (based on Churchill and Surprenant, 1982; Oliver, 1997)

that direct causal links from perceived performance to satisfaction can significantly increase the proportion of explained variance in satisfaction, and that sometimes perceived performance can be an even better predictor of satisfaction than the disconfirmation-of-expectations variable (Churchill and Surprenant, 1982; Tse and Wilton, 1988).

The most controversial variable in the disconfirmation paradigm, however, is the comparison standard (e.g., Wirtz and Mattila, 2001). A large amount of theoretical debate and empirical research has revolved around the question on what standard(s) people use in the comparison process. This line of research has resulted in six broad classes of pre-experience standards. They are (1) predictive expectations (e.g., Oliver, 1980), (2) ideal performance (e.g., Sirgy, 1984), (3) needs and wants coined as value-percept (Westbrook and Reilly, 1983) or desires (Spreng and Olshavsky, 1993), (4) experience-based standards (Cadotte, Woodruff, and Jenkins, 1987), (5) comparisons with social norms (Swan, 1983), and (6) multiple standards (e.g., Sirgy, 1984; Spreng et al., 1996). Discussions on these standards are provided elsewhere (e.g., Yi, 1990; Spreng and Olshavsky, 1993), and this review will now move on to consequences of satisfaction and dissatisfaction.

Consequences of consumer satisfaction and dissatisfaction

Most satisfaction models link satisfaction with positive outcomes such as loyalty and positive word-of-mouth. Overall satisfaction has been shown to mediate the effects of quality and price on loyalty intent across various service categories (Fornell et al., 1996; Bolton and Lemon, 1999; Gallarza and Saura, 2006). Given its close linkage to loyalty, consumer satisfaction is believed to drive the firm's profitability (Oliver, 1997). The basic idea is that satisfaction improves profitability by expanding the business by gaining market share, earning customer loyalty, improving a brand's reputation, selling more to current markets, increasing margins, and other strategies (Barsky and Nash, 2003). Yet some recent studies report only a weak connection between satisfaction and loyalty (e.g., Skogland and Siguaw, 2004).

Consumer complaining behavior research has attempted to understand how dissatisfaction influences consumers' post-failure responses. This stream of research has identified two types of response categories: behavioral responses and response styles. The former examines consumers' behavioral responses to dissatisfaction using dissatisfaction level, switching costs, and perceived responsiveness as predictor variables. In contrast, the latter category examines consumers' response styles to dissatisfaction based on personal characteristics and socio-demographics.

Day and Landon (1977) introduced the generally well-received public–private distinction in complaint behaviors. Under their taxonomy, dissatisfied consumers would either 'take some action' or 'take no action.' If action was taken, it was labeled as either public (e.g., redress sought from the seller, legal action, or third-party complaint) or private action (e.g., personal boycott or negative word-of-mouth). While, the 'take no action' response is described as 'forget about the incident and do nothing,' customers may return to the same service provider. This description is consistent with the notion of 'loyalty' in Hirschman's (1970) framework. Based on Day and Landon's taxonomy and Hirschman's framework, Singh (1988) specifies three categories of consumer complaining behavior: (1) *voice*, reflecting actions directed toward the seller; (2) *private*, involving negative word-of-mouth and exit; (3) *third party*, relating to actions directed toward external agencies such as the Better Business Bureau and legal options. In consumer behavior, negative word-of-mouth is considered as a distinct construct (Richins, 1983; Singh, 1990), and four responses (exit, voice, negative word-of-mouth and third-party action) are commonly used in consumer complaining studies (e.g., Blodgett and Granbois, 1992).

In a restaurant context, Jones et al. (2002) found that consumers can be classified into three types: those not likely to complain, those who complain to anyone, and those who complain via word-of-mouth. They further suggest that word-of-mouth complainers are under greater amount of psychological stress than those in the other two groups and that they tend to be less price-conscious and less susceptible to interpersonal influence than complain-to-anyone complainers. The next section of this chapter will briefly review research on service failures and service recovery.

Service failure

Service failures are viewed as a significant determinant of customer dissatisfaction and switching behaviors (Fornell and Wernerfelt, 1987; Keaveney, 1995; Smith and Bolton, 1998; Tax and Brown, 1998). As a result, stabilizing the endangered relationship with dissatisfied customers by utilizing an effective service recovery policy has become the main focus of many customer retention strategies (Stauss and Friege, 1999). In fact, most service organizations are forced to pay attention to service recovery since lingering dissatisfaction is not limited to the incident or customer at hand (Brown, 1997). Various studies indicate that upset customers may tell 10–20 people about their bad experience with a service company (Zemke, 1999). Because every service encounter is the 'Moment of Truth' from the customer's perspective, we will first define the term service encounter.

Service encounters

Surprenant and Solomon (1987) define the service encounter as 'a dyadic interaction between a customer and a service provider.' This definition focuses on the interpersonal element of the service delivery process. From a broader perspective, Shostack (1985) defines the service encounter as 'a period of time during which a consumer directly inter-acts with a service firm.' Her definition encompasses all aspects of the service, including contact with the firm's personnel, its physical facil-ities, and other visible elements. Moreover, Shostack's conceptualiza-tion entertains the idea that service encounters can occur without any human interaction elements. This aspect of the service encounter is par-ticularly relevant in today's high-tech environment where many parts of the service are performed by the consumer via self-service technolo-gies (e.g., self check-in at airports and hotels). Since most hospitality services include a high degree of interaction between employees and customers, therefore, there are plenty of possibilities for service failures.

Service failures

Service failures arise when customers experience dissatisfaction because the service was not delivered as originally planned or expected. It is important to keep in mind that service failures are determined by the customer and not by the service organization (Ennew and Schoefer, 2003). Classifying service failures according to their type is a useful first step in understanding consumer reactions to failure incidents.

The services marking literature recognizes two types of service encounter failures: outcome and process failures (Bitner, et al., 1990). The outcome dimension reflects what customers actually receive from the service (e.g., a clean hotel room), whereas the process dimension involves how they receive the service, that is, the manner in which it is delivered (Parasuraman et al., 1985). Bitner et al. (1990) used a critical-incident technique to identify common themes in service fail-ures. Their analysis involving 700 failure incidents in the airline, hotel, and restaurant industry, resulted in the following three broad service failure categories:

Category 1. Employee Responses to Service Delivery Failure
When the service delivery system fails, contact employees are required to respond to the customer's request and the employee response deter-mines the customer's perceived satisfaction and dissatisfaction. In gen-eral, service delivery system failures consist of three types of failures: (1) unavailable service, (2) unreasonably slow service, and (3) other core service failures. All these incidents are directly linked to the core services (e.g., the hotel room, the restaurant meal service, the airplane flight). Unavailable service refers to services that are normally avail-able,but are lacking or absent in the relevant context, such as cancelled flights or a hotel that is overbooked. Unreasonably slow service relates to services or employees that customers perceive as being inordinately slow in fulfilling their functions (e.g., flight delays and lengthy queues

in a theme park). Other core service failures encompass all other aspects of the service that do not meet basic performance standards for the industry. For example, the hotel room is dirty, the restaurant meal is cold, or the baggage arrives damaged. The latter category is deliberately kept broad to reflect the various core services offered by different industries.

Category 2. Employee Responses to Customer Needs and Requests

The second category relates to employee responses to individual customer needs and special requests. Customer needs can be implicit or explicit (Ennew and Schoefer, 2003). An airline fails to meet an implicit need when a flight schedule is changed without notifying its customers so that alternative connection flights cannot be arranged. Explicit requests, on the other hand, consist of four types: (1) special needs, (2) customer preferences, (3) customer errors, and (4) disruptive others. Special needs involve taking care of individual requests or needs (e.g., medical requests or language requirements). Employee responses to customer preferences typically require some form of customization in the service delivery process. For example, menu item substitutions involve modifications based on customer preferences. Responding to customer errors involves steps taken to correct the problem (e.g., lost theatre tickets or lost hotel keys). Finally, service employees might need to take action against disruptive others (i.e., requesting customers to refrain from smoking in the restaurant's non-smoking sections).

Category 3. Unprompted and Unsolicited Employee Actions

The third category of service failures involves events and employee behaviors that are unexpected from the customers' point of view. These actions are not initiated by the customer, nor are they part of the normal service delivery system. These unprompted employee actions can be sub-divided into five types: (1) lack of attention, (2) unusual actions, (3) cultural norms, (4) gestalt, and (5) adverse circumstances. Lack of attention is common among employees with attitude problems whereas unusual behaviors reflect rudeness, abusiveness, and inappropriate touching. The cultural norms sub-category refers to the actions that violate cultural norms (e.g., lying, stealing, cheating, and other activities considered unfair by the customer). The gestalt sub-category refers to the holistic nature of customer evaluations. Thus, customers are unable to attribute dissatisfaction to any single feature of the event or particular action of the employee. Yet customers evaluate the service experience in a holistic manner such as in 'everything went wrong'. To illustrate, a customer might be highly dissatisfied with his/her vacation but not be able to identify any specific incidents that caused this dissatisfaction. Finally, the adverse circumstances sub-category includes incidents in which the customer is particularly displeased with the way a contact employee handles a stressful situation.

Service recovery

Service recovery can be defined as actions designed to resolve problems, alter negative attitudes of dissatisfied customers, and ultimately retain these customers (Miller et al., 2000). Service recovery is not limited to customers who voice their dissatisfaction (Smith et al., 1999). The purpose of service recovery is to 'seek out and deal with service failures (Johnston, 1995, pp. 53–71).' It is the 'seeking out' part that distinguishes recovery from complaint handling, as a vast majority of dissatisfied customers do not bother to complain. Instead, they vote with their feet and switch to another service provider.

Recovery management is considered to have a significant impact on customer evaluations because customers tend to be more emotionally involved in recovery service than in routine service encounters (Bitner et al., 1990). Justice theory appears to be the dominant theoretical framework applied to service recovery (Tax and Brown, 2000) and, hence, the discussion will now turn to fairness theories.

Fairness of recovery: Justice theory

Literature on customer complaint management shows that consumers expect 'fair' resolutions to product and service failures (e.g., Blodgett et al., 1997). Similar to complaint handling, customers evaluate perception of fairness with the service recovery by three factors: outcomes, procedural fairness, and interactional treatment (Goodwin and Ross, 1992; Tax et al., 1998; Smith et al., 1999). Smith et al. (1999) developed a comprehensive model of customer satisfaction with service failure/recovery encounters and tested it in both a restaurant and a hotel context. Their findings suggest that customers prefer to receive recovery resources that match the type and magnitude of the failure. Also, Blodgett et al. (1977) suggest that consumers' evaluation of the three justice components (distributive, interactional, and procedural justice) in service recovery situations have impact on post-complaint behavior such as re-patronage and negative word-of-mouth. The following diagram (Figure 11.2) illustrates the role of perceived justice in service failure/recovery encounters.

Distributive justice reflects the outcome fairness and focuses on the compensation provided for customers' loss and/or inconvenience suffered (Smith et al., 1999; Tax et al., 1998). As a result, many service organizations offer various combinations of refunds, credits, discounts, and apology to make peace with dissatisfied customers. *Procedural fairness* involves the policies and rules by which recovery effort decisions are made (Smith et al., 1999). The speed with which service failures are corrected or complaints are handled is one of the major determinants of customer perceptions of procedural justice (Blodgett et al., 1997; Tax et al., 1998). *Interactional justice*, in contrast, refers to the manner in

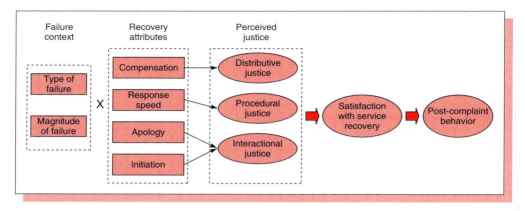

Figure 11.2
Customer evaluation of service failure/recovery encounters: the effect of perceived justice on service recovery satisfaction and post-complaint behavior (based on Blodgett et al., 1997; Smith et al., 1999)

which the customer is treated during the recovery process (Smith et al., 1999). For example, courtesy and empathy (Tax and Brown, 1998) and politeness, and concern and neutrality (Sparks and McColl-Kennedy, 2001) have been shown to influence customers' overall perceptions of justice.

The most recent conceptualization of justice suggests that interactional justice can be analyzed further to present two separate dimensions: interpersonal treatment and informational justice (Colquitt, 2001; Colquitt et al., 2001; Mattila and Cranage, 2005). Informational justice taps into the perceived adequacy and truthfulness of information explaining the causes for unfavorable outcomes (Colquitt, 2001). The role of information in service failure situations has been explored in a restaurant context. Information inadequacy increases consumer frustration (Susskind, 2005) and an informed choice increases loyalty following a service failure, as a result of customers' willingness to share responsibility (Cranage, 2004).

The relationship between the various justice dimensions is complex owing to their interactive effects. Sparks and McColl-Kennedy (2001) examined the various combinations of procedural, interactional, and distributive justice related to service recovery strategies within a hotel setting and found that satisfaction varied significantly depending on the various combinations of recovery measures. Ok et al. (2005) also suggest that all three dimensions of justice had positive effects on recovery satisfaction. Similarly, Wirtz and Mattila (2004) demonstrate that recovery outcome (e.g., compensation), procedures (e.g., speed of recovery), and interactional treatment (e.g., apology) have a joint effect on post-recovery satisfaction in a restaurant setting. Last, Hoffman and Kelley (2000) propose that the evaluation of service recovery efforts depends on six contingencies related to interactional and distributional justice: (1) depth of the relationship, (2) proximity of the relationship, (3) duration of the encounter, (4) degree of customization, (5) criticality of consumption, and (6) switching costs.

The next section of this review will discuss several critical topics in the recent service recovery literature. We will touch on the role of emotions in the service recovery process, the importance of relationship-building in influencing customer perceptions, the myth of service recovery paradox, individual difference factors tangent to customer perceptions of service recovery, and how to build effective service recovery strategies.

The role of emotions in the service failure and recovery encounters

Despite the importance of emotions for service organizations (e.g., Maute and Dubé, 1999), empirical investigations of customers' affective responses to service failures remain scarce (for notable exceptions, see Smith and Bolton, 2002; Yi and Baumgartner, 2004; Chebat and Slusarczyk, 2005). Having a richer understanding of how negative emotions influence customers' satisfaction evaluations and behavioral responses is particularly important, owing to consumers' heightened involvement in the consumption experience, in the context of service failures (Price et al., 1995; Jayanti, 1998).

The common view in satisfaction research is that specific emotions such as anger, sadness, and regret contribute to dissatisfaction (Mano and Oliver, 1993; Oliver, 1997; Smith and Bolton, 2002). The interactions between emotions and (dis)satisfaction (and related post-purchase behaviors) can be modeled by two approaches: the valence-based approach and the specific-emotions approach (Zeelenberg and Pieters, 2004). In the valence-based approach, negative emotions are expected to lead to more serious dissatisfaction, while positive emotions are expected to result in high satisfaction levels. The overall valence (satisfaction – dissatisfaction) then becomes the driving force behind consumers' behavioral responses to service failures. Yet, some researchers argue that important nuances in emotions are not captured in the overall valence approach (Laros and Steenkamp, 2005) and that focusing on specific emotions is more meaningful in understanding consumers' responses to dissatisfying consumption experiences (Zeelenberg and Pieters, 2004). The specific-emotions approach focuses on the idiosyncratic elements of particular emotions (Zeelenberg and Pieters, 2004). Recent studies demonstrate that specific negative emotions have a direct impact on behavior, over and above dissatisfaction (Laros and Steenkamp, 2005; Pieters and Zeelenberg, 2005). Service encounters, especially failed ones, often result in specific negative emotions, and these discrete emotions partly determine subsequent behaviors (Zeelenberg and Pieters, 2004).

The specific-emotions approach relies on attribution theory as a source of negative emotions. The attribution theory suggests that people are rational information processors whose actions are influenced by causal inferences (Folkes, 1984). Previous research has shown that customers' attributions about the failures they experience influence their attitudes and behavioral intentions toward the firm (Folkes, 1984; Bitner, 1990;). For example, attributing responsibility to someone else for what is happening (external attribution) produces anger, disgust, or contempt, whereas blaming one's self (internal attribution) generates emotions of shame and guilt. Conversely, believing that an event cannot be helped and that the situation is to blame (situational attribution) leads to feelings of sadness or fear (Stephens and Gwinner, 1998).

In psychology, anger, sadness, guilt, and anxiety are considered as distinct negative emotions (Lazarus, 1999) and prior research in consumer behavior suggests that these surface as anger, disappointment, regret, and worry in the consumer context (Yi and Baumgartner, 2004). Some of previous findings regarding these four emotions are discussed in the following list.

- *Anger* occurs when another person is blamed for the problem (Smith and Ellsworth, 1985; Lazarus, 1999;). Bougie et al. (2003) suggest that angry customers behave aggressively and complain about the problem.
- *Disappointment* is felt when an outcome is not as good as expected and it is typically associated with blaming others or circumstances (Zeelenberg and Pieters, 2004).
- *Regret* usually involves self-blame and an acknowledgement that one has made a mistake (Zeelenberg et al., 1998).
- *Worry* is related to prospects of undesirable events and uncertainty about what to do (Yi and Baumgartner, 2004). For example, consumers may feel worried when a flight is delayed and might become a cancellation, yet they don't know what to do about the situation.

Recent research in the hospitality and tourism literature has started to uncover the impact of emotions in driving customers' post-failure perceptions (e.g., McColl-Kennedy and Sparks, 2003). Relying on counterfactual thinking and accountability, McColl-Kennedy and Sparks suggest that customers assess whether the service provider could and should have done something more to remedy the problem and how they would have felt had these actions been taken. Moreover, when service providers do not appear to exhibit an appropriate level of effort, consumers interpret the lack of effort as 'not caring'. This lack of caring in turn leads to strong emotional responses such as anger and frustration. Finally, Smith and Bolton (2002) suggest that customers' emotional responses to service failures are context-specific and that the effects of emotions vary across industry settings (e.g., restaurant and hotels). In their study, emotions failed to influence recovery perception in the restaurant setting.

The impact of customer relationships in service failure and recovery encounters

Customer relationship with a service organization can alter their reactions to service failures and recoveries. Some research postulates that strong customer relationships act as a *buffer* when service failures occur, thus resulting in lower levels of dissatisfaction. For example, Berry (1995) suggests that customers may exhibit a greater tolerance for failures when they have cultivated a social bond with the service provider. Similarly, Tax et al. (1998) found that positive prior-service experience mitigated the negative effects of poor complaint handling on customer commitment and trust. Moreover, Hess et al. (2003) show that customers who expect the relationship to continue have lower service recovery expectations, and these lower service recovery expectations, in turn, have a positive impact on post-recovery satisfaction. Scanlan and McPhail (2000) suggest that perceived personalization, social bonding, reliability, and familiarization are the key factors in building relationships with hotel customers.

There is, however, some evidence to suggest that customer loyalty might *magnify* the negative customer responses following service failures. For example, Mattila (2004) suggests that emotionally bonded customers might feel *betrayed* when a service failure occurs, thus resulting in sharp decrease in post-recovery attitudes. Moreover, customers with lower levels of emotional bonding with the service provider might be more *forgiving* when the service recovery is effectively handled.

Recovery paradox and double deviation

'Service recovery paradox' refers to a situation in which secondary satisfaction (i.e., satisfaction after a failure and recovery effort) is higher than pre-failure satisfaction (Smith and Bolton, 1998). 'Double deviation' effect, on the other hand, states that poorly handled service recoveries exacerbate already low customer evaluations following a failure (Bitner et al., 1990).

The evidence for service recovery paradox in the hospitality and tourism literature is inconclusive. McCollough (2000) shows that when the hotel's recovery efforts successfully mitigate the harm caused by the failure, a recovery paradox may be possible. However, this positive outcome may not translate into higher service quality perceptions if the failure is perceived to be stable. Conversely, a successful service recovery might not be sufficient for the recovery paradox in the meeting and convention segment of the industry (Oh, 2003). He argues that successful recoveries do not strengthen customers' original satisfaction. In fact, failures and recoveries – no matter how successful the recoveries might be – collectively undermine the customers' original satisfaction that could have been experienced without any failure. Moreover, Ok et al. (2005) suggest that although a service failure initially hurts customer satisfaction, effective complaint handling through service recovery may reinforce the reliability perception and relationship continuity. They emphasize the notion that recovery efforts should be viewed not only as a strategy to recover immediate satisfaction but also as a relationship-building tool.

Cultural and gender differences in consumers' perceptions of service recovery

Cultural norms and values are likely to influence customers' perceptions of fairness and satisfaction with the service recovery process. Mattila's and Patterson's (2004a) cross-cultural examination of post-recovery satisfaction (East-Asia versus Unites States) suggest that offering compensation can be particularly effective among American consumers while offering an explanation for the failure had a positive impact on customer perceptions regardless of the customer's cultural orientation. Differences due to cultural background were also found in the attribution process for service failures. Mattila and Patterson (2004b) show that the differential sensitivity of East-Asian and American consumers to situational constraints influences consumers' attribution processes, and thus moderates their satisfaction with the service recovery process. More specifically, they suggest that a causal explanation for service failure decreases the likelihood of US consumers falling prey to the fundamental attribution error. Poon and Low (2005) demonstrate that post-recovery satisfaction was higher among Western travelers than their Asian counterparts. Lorenzoni and Lewis (2004) suggest that Italian airline crew members react to service failures with a more emotionally-based strategy than British airline employees. Finally, the findings from Becker's (2000) study with four cultures (Americans, Scandinavians, Asians, and Latinos) suggest that different perceptions of time, different value systems, and different approaches to communication influence customer reactions to service failures. Complaint intentions also seem to vary across cultural boundaries (Yüksel et al., 2006). For instance, Heung and Lam (2003) suggest that Chinese diners tend to be passive in voicing their dissatisfaction to the service provider. Yet they were quick to engage in private complaint behaviors such as word-of-mouth communication and ceasing to patronize the restaurant.

Regarding gender effects, male and female consumers seem to place a differential emphasis on various elements of the service recovery process. Women want their views heard during the service recovery and to be allowed to provide input, while men do not view voice as important (McColl-Kennedy et al., 2003). In a similar vein, Mattila et al. (2003) showed that in service failure situations negative affective displays had a double whammy impact on male participants' satisfaction ratings.

How to develop effective service recovery strategies?

To guide managers in designing an effective strategy, Tax and Brown (1998) suggest a four-stage approach to service recovery. Their service recovery process framework suggests that the first two stages focus on identifying and resolving individual customer problems. The next two stages in the process focus on how recovery data can be classified and integrated with other firm data to identify profitable service-improvement investments. They suggest that companies need to develop a comprehensive service recovery system that encourages dissatisfied customers to voice their complaints and that provides a fair process and outcome. They also stress that service design and investment decisions should be based on understanding of the vital role that recovery plays in contributing to improved performance, customer and employee satisfaction, customer loyalty, and ultimately the firm's profitability.

In the hospitality literature, Hoffman and Chung (1999) identify 11 recovery strategies commonly used by hotel and restaurant operations. They classified these strategies into five separate areas (compensatory responses, managerial responses, corrective responses, empathetic responses, and no action taken). In a restaurant setting, strategies consisting of discounts and free meals were by far the preferred recovery tactic while room upgrades were the most commonly used method in the hotel segment. Prior research further suggests that satisfaction with the recovery effort varies depending on the various combinations of recovery methods (Sparks and McColl-Kennedy, 2001). In the context of theme parks, apology, correction, empathy, compensation, follow-up, acknowledgement, explanation, exceptional treatment, and managerial intervention are the most frequently encountered service recovery methods (Lewis and McCann, 2004). According to Davidow (2000), there are six different dimensions of organizational responses to service failures (timeliness, facilitation, redress, apology, credibility, and attentiveness) that affect post-complaint customer behaviors such as repurchase and word-of-mouth activity. But it is important to bear in mind that service recovery strategies are highly context-specific. The level of post-recovery satisfaction may depend on several factors such as the magnitude of the service failure, the customer's perception of the criticality of the consumption, and whether the service provider or the customer is the first to notice the service failure (Mattila, 1999).

Directions for future research

A number of problems and serious omissions currently plague research on customer satisfaction in the hospitality and tourism literature. Although research in marketing and consumer behavior clearly suggests that consumers' satisfaction judgments are at least partially driven by affect, satisfaction studies in the field of hospitality and tourism continue to focus on cognitive determinants of satisfaction. Most of these studies have employed the disconfirmation paradigm and, hence, little is known about the role of emotions in influencing customer satisfaction with hospitality and tourism services. The reliance on a single paradigm clearly hinders our understanding of the complex satisfaction/dissatisfaction construct.

Service failures and service recovery are topics of great interest to hospitality scholars. Research in this area has resulted in interesting industry-specific applications for complaint handling and service recovery strategies. Clearly, service recovery has an important impact on the company's bottom-line via customer retention. But unfortunately, service recovery is often regarded as an operational concern, rather than a strategic weapon (La and Kandampully, 2004). To that end, there is an urgent need to broaden our understanding of the consequences of dissatisfying service experiences by connecting service recovery to other key concepts such as customer loyalty. One avenue to get there is to systematically conduct a meta-analysis on service recovery studies published in the main hospitality and tourism journals.

There is a dire need for more cross-cultural research in both satisfaction and service recovery. Service encounters and recovery efforts are essentially social exchanges with interaction between the service provider and customer being a crucial component of satisfaction. Given the degree of interpersonal contact and communication involved in most hospitality and tourism services it stands to reason that cultural values are likely to influence the evaluation process. In fact, the field of hospitality and tourism offers an ideal context for studying culture-bound differences in customer perceptions of service encounters.

In terms of methodology, satisfaction research in the field of hospitality and tourism is dominated by survey research and case study (e.g., Gundersen et al. 1996; Lewis and MaCann, 2004; Poria, 2004; Hemmington et al., 2005). Since there is no common instrument to measure satisfaction, the validity of the measures used is somewhat of a concern. Particularly in the area of hospitality and tourism, the literature lacks empirical studies that compare the validity and reliability of various measures across studies (Crompton and Love, 1995; Oh and Parks, 1997). The Critical Incident Method (CIT) has been widely applied to understand hospitality customers' reactions to service failures and service recovery attempts (e.g., Bitner et al., 1990; Hoffman et al., 1995; Mack et al., 2000; Kivelä and Chu, 2001; Lewis and Clacher, 2001; Susskind, 2005;), but it is important to be aware of the limitations of this technique. The CIT is a retrospective research method, thus being subject to memory lapses. Moreover, the qualitative nature of the data sometimes creates problems with category labels (Gremler, 2004). Unfortunately, the use of experimental designs is mainly limited to service recovery research (e.g., Levesque and McDougall, 2000). Moreover, longitudinal studies are rare in the hospitality and tourism literature (for a rare exception see Bernhardt et al., 2000). There undoubtedly is a need to broaden the scope of methodologies used in hospitality inquiry.

Summary and conclusions

Integrating our discussions on customer satisfaction/dissatisfaction, service failure, and service recovery, we developed a conceptual framework shown in Figure 11.3. Our conceptual model proposes that when customers experience a service failure, the initial dissatisfaction turns into more specific negative emotions depending on the customers' appraisal of the responsibility of the problem. By incorporating the specific-emotions approach with causal attribution theories, the current model includes four negative emotions: *anger* arising from controllable failures with others blamed, *disappointment* stemming from uncontrollable causes that can be attributed to the situation, *regret* resulting from self-blame, and *worry* coming from threat with uncertainty (see Yi and Baumgartner, 2004, for detailed discussion on these four emotions). These negative emotions will lead to customer responses to the failure situation (e.g., complain directly on the spot, spread negative Word-of-mouth, or vow to never return to that service provider). If the customers voice their dissatisfaction to the service provider, some form of service recovery is likely to follow. Customers will then evaluate the service recovery efforts based on perceived fairness. An exceptionally successful service recovery may sometimes convert dissatisfied customers into even more satisfied customers (recovery paradox) while an unsuccessful service recovery is bound to lead to a highly negative double deviation effect. According to our model, post-consumption satisfaction may be assessed at three time points, satisfaction with a particular transaction experience (T-satisfaction), satisfaction with service recovery effort by the organization (R-satisfaction), and overall/accumulated satisfaction with the service provider/the company (O-satisfaction).

Our framework offers a starting point for broadening our thinking on consumers' post-consumption evaluation processes. There needs to be an increase in the amount of effort focused on developing theory that can guide hospitality research on these important topics. Systematic, validated research studies, based on the guidelines suggested above, will inform us how to link the important post-purchase constructs

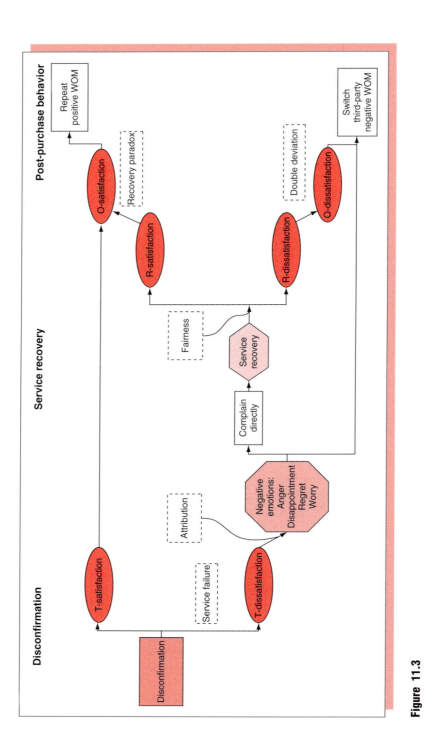

Figure 11.3

A conceptual model of satisfaction, service failure, and service recovery

of satisfaction, service failure, and service recovery with consumers' behavioral responses. We hope that this chapter serves as an impetus for such an effort.

References

Alegre, J., and Cladera, M. (2006). Repeat visitation in mature sun and sand holiday destinations. *Journal of Travel Research, 44*(February), 288–297.

Anderson, E. W. and Sullivan, M. W. (1993). The antecedents and consequences of consumer satisfaction for firms. *Marketing Science, 12*(2), 125–143.

Anderson, E. W. and Fornell, C. (1994). A Customer Satisfaction Research Prospectus. In R. T. Rust and R. L. Oliver (Eds), *Service Quality: New Directions in Theory and Practice* (pp. 241–268). Thousand Oaks, CA: Sage Publications.

Barsky, J. (1992). Customer satisfaction in hotel industry: Meaning and measurement. *Hospitality Research Journal, 16*, 51–73.

Barsky, J. and Nash, L. (2003). Customer satisfaction: Applying concepts to industry-wide measures. *Cornell Hotel and Restaurant Administration Quarterly, 44*(4/5), 173–183.

Becker, C. (2000). Service recovery strategies: The impact of cultural differences. *Journal of Hospitality and Tourism Research, 24*(4), 526–538.

Bernhardt, K., Donthu, N., and Kennett, P. A. (2000). A Longitudinal analysis of satisfaction and profitability. *Journal of Business Research, 47*, 161–171.

Berry, L. L. (1995). Relationship marketing of services – Growing interest, emerging perspectives. *Journal of the Academy of Marketing Science, 23*(4), 236–245.

Bitner, M. J. (1990). Evaluating service encounters: The effects of physical surroundings and employee responses. *Journal of Marketing, 54*(April), 69–82.

Bitner, M. J, Booms, B. H., and Tetreault, M. S. (1990). The service encounter, diagnosing favorable and unfavorable incidents. *Journal of Marketing, 54*, 71–84.

Blodgett , J. G., Hill, D., and Tax, S. S. (1997). The effects of distributive, procedural, and interactional justice on post-complaint behavior. *Journal of Retailing, 73*(2), 185–210.

Blodgett, J. G. and Granbois, D. H. (1992). Toward an integrated conceptual model of consumer complaining behavior. *Journal of Consumer Satisfaction, Dissatisfaction and Complaining Behavior, 5*, 93–103.

Bolton, R., N. and Lemon, K. N. (1999). A dynamic model of customers' usage of services: Usage as an antecedent and consequence of satisfaction. *Journal of Marketing Research, 36*(2), 171–186.

Boulding, W., Kalra, A. Staelin, R., and Zeithaml, V. A. (1993). A dynamic process model of service quality. *Journal of Marketing Research, 30*(February), 7–27.

Bougie, R., Pieters, R., and Zeelenberg, M. (2003). Angry customers don't come back, they get back: The experience and behavioral implications of anger and dissatisfaction in services. *Journal of the Academy of Marketing Science, 31*(4), 377–393.

Bowen, D. and Clarke, J. (2002). reflections on tourist satisfaction research: Past, present, and future. *Journal of Vacation Marketing, 8*(4), 297–308.

Brown, S. (1997). Service recovery through IT: Complaint handling will differentiate firms in the future. *Marketing Management, 6*(3), 25–27.

Cadotte, E. R., Woodruff, R. B., and Jenkins, R. L. (1987). Expectations and norms in models of consumer satisfaction. *Journal of Marketing Research, 24*(August), 305–314.

Chebat, J-C. and Slusarczyk, W. (2005). How emotions mediate the effects of perceived justice on loyalty in service recovery. *Journal of Business Research, 58*(5), 664–675.

Churchill, G. A., Jr. and Surprenant, C. (1982). An investigation into the determinants of customer satisfaction. *Journal of Marketing Research, 19*(November), 491–504.

Cote, J., Foxman, E. R., and Cutler, B. D. (1989). Selecting an appropriate standard of comparison for post purchase evaluations. *Advances in Consumer Research, 16*, 407–422.

Colquitt, J. (2001). On the dimensionality of organizational justice: A construct validation of a measure. *Journal of Applied Psychology, 86*(3), 386–400.

Colquitt, J., Conlon, D., Wesson, M., et al. (2001). Justice at the millennium: a meta-analytic review of 25 years of organizational justice research, *Journal of Applied Psychology, 86*(3), 425–45.

Cranage, D. (2004). Conservative choice, service failure, and customer loyalty: Testing the limits of informed choice. *Journal of Hospitality and Tourism Research, 28*(3), 327–345.

Crompton L. J. and Love, L. L. (1995). The predictive validity of alternative approaches to evaluating quality of a festival. *Journal of Travel Research, 34*(1), 11–25.

Davidow, M. (2000). The bottom line impact of organizational response to consumer complaints. *Journal of Hospitality and Tourism Research, 24*(4), 473–490.

Day, R. L. and Landon, E. L. (1977). Toward a theory of consumer complaining behavior. In A. G. Woodside, J. N. Sheth, and P. D. Bennet (Eds), *Consumer and Industrial Buying Behavior* (pp. 425–437). New York: North Holland Publishing Company.

Ennew, C. and Schoefer, K. (2003). Service Failure and Service Recovery in Tourism: A Review. Retrieved March 1, 2007, from http://www.nottingham.ac.uk/ttri/pdf/2003_6.pdf.

Folkes, V. S. (1984). Consumer reactions to product failure: An attributional approach. *Journal of Consumer Research, 10*(4), 398–409.

Fornell, C. (1992). A national customer satisfaction barometer: The Swedish experience. *Journal of Marketing, 56*(January), 6–21.

Fornell, C., Johnson, M., Anderson, E., et al. (1996). The American customer satisfaction index: Nature, purpose and findings. *Journal of Marketing, 60*(4), 7–19.

Fornell, C. and Wernerfelt, B. (1987). Defensive marketing strategy by customer complaint management: A theoretical analysis. *Journal of Marketing Research, 24*(November), 337–346.

Gallarza, M. G. and Saura, I. G. (2006). Value dimensions, perceived value, satisfaction, and loyalty: An investigation of university students' travel behavior. *Tourism Management, 27*(3), 437–452.

Giese, J. L. and Cote, J. A. (2000). Defining consumer satisfaction. *Academy of Marketing Science Review, 1*. Retrieved March 1, 2007, from http://www.amsreview.org/articles/giese01-2000.pdf.

Goodwin, C. and Ross, I. (1992). Consumer responses to service failures: Influence of procedural and interactional fairness perceptions. *Journal of Business Research, 25*(2), 149–63.

Gremler, D. D. (2004). The critical incident technique in service research. *Journal of Service Research, 7*(1), 65–89.

Grönroos, C. (2000). *Service Management and Strategy: Marketing the Moments of Truth in Service Competition.* 2nd ed., Lexington, MA: Lexington Books.

Gundersen, G. M., Heide, M., and Olsson, H. U. (1996). Hotel guest satisfaction among business travelers. *Cornell Hotel and Restaurant Administration Quarterly, 37*(2), 72–91.

Hemmington, N., Bowen, D., Wickens, E., and Paraskevas, A. (2005). Satisfying the basics: Reflections from consumer perspective of attractions management at the millennium dome, London. *International Journal of Tourism Research, 7*, 1–10.

Hess, R. L., Ganesan, S., and Klein, N. M. (2003). Service failure and recovery: The impact of relationship factors on customer satisfaction. *Journal of the Academy of Marketing Science, 31*(2), 127–145.

Heung, V. C. S. and Cheng, E. (2000). Assessing tourists' satisfaction with shopping in the Hong Kong special administrative region of China. *Journal of Travel Research, 38*(May), 396–404.

Heung, V. C. S. and Lam, T. (2003). Customer complaint behavior towards hotel restaurant services. *International Journal of Contemporary Hospitality Management, 15*(4/5), 283–290.

Hirschman, A. O. (1970). *Exit, Voice and Loyalty: Responses to Decline in Firms, Organizations and State.* Cambridge, MA: Harvard University Press.

Hoffman, D. K., Kelley, S. W., and Rotalsky, H. M. (1995). Tracking service failures and employee recovery efforts. *The Journal of Services Marketing, 9*(2), 49–61.

Hoffman, D. K. and Chung, B. G. (1999). Hospitality recovery strategies: Customer preference versus firm use. *Journal of Hospitality and Tourism Research*, 23, 71–84.

Hoffman, D. K. and Kelley, S. W. (2000). Perceived justice needs and recovery evaluation: A contingency approach. *European Journal of Marketing*, 34(3/4), 418–432.

Homburg, C., Koschate, N., and Hoyer, W. (2006). The role of cognition and affect in the formation of customer satisfaction: A dynamic perspective. *Journal of Marketing*, 70(3), 21–32.

Howard, J. A. and Sheth, J. N. (1969). *The Theory of Buyer Behavior*. New York: John Wiley and Sons.

Hsu, C. H. C. (2000). Mature motorcoach travelers' satisfaction: A preliminary step toward measurement development. *Journal of Hospitality and Tourism Research*, 27(Aug), 291–309.

Iacobucci, D., Grayson, K., and Ostrom, A. (1994). Customer Satisfaction Fables. *Sloan Management Review*, 35(4), 93–96.

Jayanti, R. (1998). Affective responses towards service providers: A categorization theory perspective. *Journal of Consumer Satisfaction, Dissatisfaction and Complaining Behavior*. 11, 51–61.

Johnston, R. (1995). The Determinants of Service Quality: Satisfiers and Dissatisfiers. *International Journal of Service Industry Management*, 6(5), 53–71.

Jones, D. L., McCleary, K. W., and Lepisto, L. R. (2002). Consumer complaint behavior manifestations for table service restaurants: Identifying sociodemographic characteristics, personality, and behavioral factors. *Journal of Hospitality and Tourism Research*, 26(2), 105–123.

Kandampully, J. and Suhartanto, D. (2000). Customer loyalty in the hotel industry: The role of customer satisfaction and image. *International Journal of Contemporary Hospitality*, 12(6), 346–356.

Keaveney, S. (1995). Customer switching behavior in service industries: An exploratory study. *Journal of Marketing*, 59(2), 71–82.

Kotler, P., Bowen, J. T., and Makens, J. C. (2006). *Marketing for Hospitality and Tourism*, 4th ed., New Jersey: Pearson Education Inc.

Kivelä, J. and Chu, C. Y. H. (2001). Delivering quality service: Diagnosing favorable and unfavorable service encounters in restaurants. *Journal of Hospitality and Tourism Research*, 25(3), 251–171.

La, K. V. and Kandampully, J. (2004). Market oriented learning and customer value enhancement through service recovery management. *Managing Service Quality*, 14(5), 390–401.

Laros, F. J. M. and Steenkamp, J. E. M. (2005). Emotions in consumer behavior: A hierarchical approach. *Journal of Business Research*, 58(10), 1437–1445.

Lazarus, R. S. (1999). *Stress and Emotion: A new synthesis*. New York: Springer.

Lemmink, J. G. A. M., de Ruyter, J. C., and Wetzels, M. (1998). The Role of Value in the Delivery Process of Hospitality Services. *Journal of Economic Psychology*, 19(2), 159–177.

Levesque, T. and McDougall, G. (2000), Service problems and recovery strategies: An experiment, *Canadian Journal of Administrative Sciences*, 17(1), 20–37.

Lewis, B. R. and Clacher, E. (2001). Service failure and recovery in UK theme parks: The employee's perspective. *International Journal of Contemporary Hospitality Management*, 13(4), 166–175.

Lewis, B. R. and McCann, P. (2004). Service failure and recovery: Evidence from the hotel industry. *International Journal of Contemporary Hospitality Management*, 16(1), 6–17.

Lorenzoni, N. and Lewis, B. R. (2004). Service recovery in the airline industry: A cross-cultural comparison of the attitudes and behaviors of British and Italian front-line personnel. *Managing Service Quality*, 14(1), 11–25.

Lucas, A. F. (2003). The determinants and effects of slot servicescape satisfaction in a Las Vegas Hotel Casino, *UNLV gaming research*, 7(1), 1–19.

Maddox, R. N. (1981). Two factor theory and consumer satisfaction: Replication and extension. *Journal of Consumer Research*, 8(June), 97–102.

Mack, R., Muleller, R., Crotts, J., and Broderick, A. (2000). Perceptions, corrections and defections: Implications for service recovery in the restaurant industry. *Managing Service Quality*, 10(6), 339–346.

Mano, H. and Oliver, R. (1993). Assessing the dimensionality and structure of the consumption experience: Evaluation, feeling, and satisfaction. *Journal of Consumer Research*, 20(December), 451–466.

Mattila, A. S. (1999). An examination of factors affecting service recovery in a restaurant setting. *Journal of Hospitality and Tourism Research*, 23(3), 184–198.

Mattila, A. S., Grandey, A. A., and Fisk, G. M. (2003). The interplay of gender and affective tone in service encounter satisfaction. *Journal of Service Research*, 6(2), 136–143.

Mattila, A. S. (2004). The impact of service failures on customer loyalty. *International Journal of Service Industry Management*, 15(2), 134–149.

Mattila, A. S. and Patterson, P. G. (2004a). Service recovery and fairness perceptions in collectivist and individualist contexts. *Journal of Service Research*, 6(4), 336–346.

Mattila, A. S. and Patterson, P. G. (2004b). The impact of culture on consumers' perceptions of service recovery efforts. *Journal of Retailing*, 80, 196–206.

Mattila, A. S. and Cranage, D. A. (2005). The impact of choice on fairness in the context of service recovery. *Journal of Services Marketing*, 19(5), 271–279.

Maute, M. F. and Dubé, L. (1999). Patterns of emotional responses and behavioral consequences of dissatisfaction. *Applied Psychology*, 48(3), 219–247.

McColl-Kennedy, J. R. and Sparks, B. A. (2003). Application of fairness theory to service recovery and service recovery. *Journal of Service Research*, 5(3), 251–266.

McColl-Kennedy, J. R., Daus, C. S., and Sparks, B. A. (2003). The role of gender in reactions to service failure and recovery. *Journal of Service Research*, 6(1), 66–82.

McCollough, M. A. (2000). The effect of perceived justice and attributions regarding service failure and recovery on post-recovery customer satisfaction and service quality attitudes. *Journal of Hospitality and Tourism Research*, 24(4), 423–447.

Middleton, V. T. C. and Clarke, J. (2001). *Marketing in Travel and Tourism*, 3rd ed., Oxford: Butterworth-Heinemann.

Miller, J. L., Craighead, C. W., and Karwan, K. R. (2000). Service recovery: A framework and empirical investigation. *Journal of Operations Management*, 18, 387–400.

Mittal, V., Kumar, P., and Tsrios, M. (1999). Attribute-level performance, satisfaction, and behavioral intentions over time: A consumption-system approach, *Journal of Marketing*, 63(April), 88–101.

Oh, H. (2003). Reexamining recovery paradox effects and impact of ranges of service failure and recovery. *Journal of Hospitality and Tourism Research*, 27(4), 402–418.

Oh, H. and Parks, C. S. (1997). Customer satisfaction and service quality: A critical review of the literature and research implications for the hospitality industry. *Hospitality Research Journal*, 20(3), 36–64.

Ok, C., Back, K. and Shanklin, C. W. (2005). Modeling roles of service recovery strategy: A relationship-focused view. *Journal of Hospitality and Tourism Research*, 29(4), 484–507.

Oliver, R. L. (1977). Effect of expectation and disconfirmation on post-exposure product evaluations: An alternative interpretation. *Journal of Applied Psychology*, 62(August), 480–486.

Oliver, R. L. (1980). A cognitive model of the antecedents and consequences of satisfaction decisions. *Journal of Marketing Research*, 16(June), 39–54.

Oliver, R. L. (1992). An investigation of the attribute basis of emotions and related affects in consumption: Suggestions for a stage-specific satisfaction framework. *Advances in Consumer Research*, 19, 237–244.

Oliver, R. L. (1993). Cognitive, affective, and attribute bases of the satisfaction response. *Journal of Consumer Research*, 20(3), 418–430.

Oliver, R. L. (1994). Conceptual issues in the structural analysis of consumption emotion, satisfaction and quality: Evidence in service setting. *Advances in Consumer Research*, 21, 16–22.

Oliver, R. L. (1997). *Satisfaction: A Behavioral Perspective on the Consumer*. New York: McGraw Hill.

Parasuraman, A., Zeithaml, V. A., and Berry, L. L. (1985). A conceptual model of service quality and its implications for future research. *Journal of Marketing*, 49(4), 41–50.

Patterson, P. G. and Johnson, L. W. (1993). Disconfirmation of expectations and the gap model of service quality: An integrated paradigm. *Journal of Consumer Satisfaction, Dissatisfaction and Complaining Behavior, 6*, 90–99.

Pieters, R. and Zeelenberg, M. (2005). On bad decisions and deciding badly: when intention-behavior inconsistency is regrettable. *Organizational Behavior and Human Decision Processes, 97*(1), 18–29.

Petrick, J. F. (2004). The role of quality, value, and satisfaction in predicting cruise passengers' behavioral intentions. *Journal of Travel Research, 42*(May), 397–407.

Petrick, J. F. and Backman, S. J. (2002). An examination of the construct of perceived value for the prediction of golf travelers' intention to revisit. *Journal of Travel Research, 41*(August), 38–45.

Petrick, J. F. Morais, D. D., and Norman, W. C. (2001). An examination of the determinants of entertainment vacationers' intention to revisit. *Journal of Travel Research, 40*(August), 41–48.

Petrick, J. F., Tonner, C., and Quinn, C. (2006). The utilization of critical incident technique to examine cruise passengers' repurchase intentions. *Journal of Travel Research, 44*(February), 273–280.

Poon, W-C. and Low, K. L-T. (2005). Are travelers satisfied with Malaysian hotels?. *International Journal of Contemporary Hospitality Management, 17*(3), 217–227.

Poria, Y. (2004). Employees' interference with the distribution of guest satisfaction questionnaire. *International Journal of Contemporary Hospitality Management, 16*(5), 321–324.

Price, L. L., Arnould, E. J., and Deibler, S. (1995). Consumers' emotional responses to service encounters: The influence of the service provider. *International Journal of Service Industry, 6*(3), 34–63.

Reisinger, Y. and Turner, L. W. (2002). The determination of shopping satisfaction of Japanese tourists visiting Hawaii and the Gold Coast compared. *Journal of Travel Research, 41*(November), 167–176.

Richins, M. L. (1983). Negative word-of-mouth by dissatisfied consumers: A pilot study. *Journal of Marketing, 47*(Winter), 68–78.

Scanlan, L. and McPhail, J. (2000). Forming service relationships with hotel business travelers: The critical attributes to improve retention. *Journal of Hospitality and Tourism Research, 24*(November), 491–513.

Skogland, I. and Siguaw, J. A. (2004). Are your satisfied customers loyal? *Cornell Hotel and Restaurant Administration, 45*(3), 221–234.

Singh, J. (1988). Consumer complaint intentions and behavior: Definitional and taxonomical issues. *Journal of Marketing, 52*(1), 93–107.

Singh, J. (1990). A typology of consumer dissatisfaction response styles. *Journal of Retailing, 66*(1), 57–99.

Sirgy, J. (1984). A social cognition model of consumer satisfaction/dissatisfaction. *Psychology and Marketing, 1*(2), 27–45.

Shostack, L. (1985). Planning the service encounters. In J. Czepiel, M. Solomon, and C. Surprenant (Eds), *The Service Encounters* (pp. 243–254). Lexington, MA: Lexington Books.

Smith, C. A. and Ellsworth, P. C. (1985). Patterns of cognitive appraisal in emotion. *Journal of Personality and Social Psychology, 48*, 813–838.

Smith, A. K. and Bolton, R. N. (1998). An experimental investigation of customer reactions to service failure and recovery encounters: Paradox or peril. *Journal of Service Research, 1*(1), 5–17.

Smith, A. K. and Bolton, R. N. (2002). The effect of customers' emotional responses to service failures on their recovery effort evaluations and satisfaction judgments. *Journal of the Academy of Marketing Science, 30*(1), 5–23.

Smith, A. K., Bolton, R. N., and Wagner, J. (1999). A model of customer satisfaction with service encounters involving failure and recovery. *Journal of Marketing Research, 36*(3), 356–373.

Sparks, B. A. and McColl-Kennedy, J. R. (2001). Justice strategy options for increased customer satisfaction in a services recovery setting. *Journal of Business Research, 54*, 209–218.

Spreng, R. A. and Olshavsky, R. W. (1993). A desires congruency model of consumer satisfaction. *Journal of the Academy of Marketing Science, 21*(Summer), 169–177.

Spreng, R. A., Mackenzie, S. B., and Olshavsky, R. W. (1996). A reexamination of the determinants of consumer satisfaction. *Journal of Marketing, 60*(3), 15–32.

Stauss, B. and Friege, C. (1999). Regaining service customers, costs and benefits of regain management. *Journal of Service Research, 1*(4), 347–361.

Stephens, N. and Gwinner, K. P. (1998). Why don't some people complain? A cognitive-emotive process model of consumer complaint behavior. *Journal of the Academy of Marketing Science, 26*(3), 172–189.

Surprenant, C. and Solomon, M. (1987). Predictability and personalization in the service encounter. *Journal of Marketing, 51*, 86–96.

Susskind, A. M. (2005). A content analysis of consumer complaints, remedies, and repatronage intentions regarding dissatisfying service experience. *Journal of Hospitality and Tourism Research, 29*(2), 150–169.

Swan, J. E. (1983). Consumer satisfaction research and theory: Current status and future directions. In R. L. Day and H. K. Hunt (Eds), *International Fare in Consumer Satisfaction* (pp. 124–129). Bloomington: Indiana School of Business, Indiana University.

Tax, S. S. and Brown, S. W. (1998). Recovering and learning from service failure, *Sloan Management Review, 40*(1), 75–88.

Tax, S. S. and Brown, S. W. (2000). Service recovery: Research insights and practices. In T. Swartz and D. Iacobucci. (Eds), *Handbook of Services Marketing and Management* (pp. 271–286). Thousand Oaks, CA: Sage Publication.

Tax, S. S., Brown, S. W., and Chandrashekaren, M. (1998). Customer evaluations of service complaint experiences: Implications for relationship marketing. *Journal of Marketing, 62*(2), 60–76.

Tse, D. K. and Wilton, P. C. (1988). Models of consumer satisfaction formation: An extension, *Journal of Marketing Research, 25*(May), 204–212.

Westbrook, R. T. and Reilly, M. (1983). Value-percept disparity: An alternative to the disconfirmation of expectations theory of consumer satisfaction. *Advances in Consumer Research, 10,* 256–261.

Wirtz, J. and Mattila, A. S. (2004). Consumer responses to compensation, speed of recovery and apology after a service failure. *International Journal of Service Industry Management, 15*(2), 150–166.

Wirtz, J. and Mattila, A. S, (2001). Exploring the role of alternative performance measures and needs-congruency in the consumer satisfaction process. *Journal of Consumer Psychology, 11*(3), 181–192.

Yi, Y. (1990). A critical review of consumer satisfaction. In A. Zeithaml (Ed.), *Review of Marketing* (pp. 68–123). Chicago: American Marketing Association.

Yi, S. and Baumgartner, H. (2004). Coping with negative emotions in purchase-related situations. *Journal of Consumer Psychology, 14*(3), 303–317.

Yu, L. and Goulden, M. (2006). A comparative analysis of international tourists' satisfaction in Mongolia. *Tourism Management, 27*(4), 1331–1342.

Yüksel, A. and Rimmington, M. (1998). Customer-satisfaction measurement. *Cornell Hotel and Restaurant Administration Quarterly, 39*(6), 60–70.

Yüksel, A., Kilinc, U. K., and Yüksel, F. (2006). Cross-national analysis of hotel customers' attitude toward complaining and their complaining behaviors. *Tourism Management, 27*(1), 11–24.

Zeelenberg, M., van Dijk, W. W., and Manstead, A. S. R. (1998). Reconsidering the relation between regret and responsibility. *Organization Behavior and Human Decision Process, 74*(3), 254–272.

Zeelenberg, M. and Pieters, R. (2004). Beyond valence in customer satisfaction: A review and new findings on behavioral responses to regret and disappointment in failed services. *Journal of Business Research, 57,* 445–455.

Zemke, R. (1999). Service recovery: Turning oops into opportunity. In R. Zemke and J. Woods (Eds), *Best Practices in Customer Service* (pp. 279–288). New York, NY: AMACOM, AMA Publications.

CHAPTER 12

Experiential consumption: Affect – emotions – hedonism

Karl Titz

Introduction

People gravitate to the things that make them feel good. Pleasure and pain are individually defined and lie on a continuum of affective states. Emotions are cognitive linguistic constructs used to give meaning to affective states. Emotional meaning is what differentiates humans from the animal world. We can assess the emotional meanings given to affective states. However, the nature of affect is auto-responsive and instinctual. Thus, while we grasp for individually defined meanings of feelings or affective states, we move toward pleasure and away from pain. One problem or a limiting factor associated with the study of hedonism is the paucity of normative studies. The pathology of hedonism has received attention through the ages and must be examined to understand normative hedonic responses. Pathological hedonism is the extreme of originally normative hedonic response. The alcoholic, the drug addict, the sex addict, the compulsive spender, the food addict, and the gambling addict engage in hedonism carried to the extreme. The pathology, originally used to mask pain, turned to compulsive addictive behavior.

Hirschman and Holbrook (1982) coined the phrase, *hedonic consumption*. They traced the evolution of the concept from product symbolism (Levy, 1959, 1963; Grubb and Grathwohl, 1967). Motivation Research was another footing for experiential consumption (Dichter, 1960). However, the most significant contribution comes from behavioral sciences. Fantasy and absorbing experience (Singer, 1966; Swanson, 1978), culture production systems in sociology (Hirsch, 1972; Becker, 1973; Crane, 1976), aesthetics within philosophy (Jaeger, 1945), and psycholinguistics, i.e., the study of affective response (Osgood et al., 1957) all have contributed to the theoretical development of hedonic consumption. Hirschman and Holbrook (1982, p. 92) defined hedonic consumption, alternatively referred to as experiential consumption, as 'those facets of consumer behavior that relate to the multi-sensory, fantasy and emotive aspects of one's experience with products'.

Given the nature of hospitality, travel, and tourism, hedonism is a natural lens through which to examine the consumption experience. When lounging on a South Sea island or engaged in sumptuous feasting surrounded by beautiful people, what are the underlying experiential states, and what do they tell us about the individual? Some answers to these questions can be found using hedonic constructs, and hedonic scales of likes and dislikes have long been part of the social science methodology.

Hedonic or experiential consumption is central to a comprehensive understanding of consumer behavior in the hospitality and tourism context. The intangibility of the hospitality product must be viewed through a variety of lenses to understand the fullness of the phenomena. The study of hedonic aspects of consumption experiences ties aptly into this intangibility. Examples include an adventure vacation, a memorable meal, or the surroundings of a plush hotel, all of which illustrate the complex nature of consumption experiences. Why does an individual choose one experience over another and what experiential qualities resonate in the individual psyche? The affective emotional states elicited as well as sought in the purchase of these experiences can and will enable developers, marketers, and managers to better understand, design, serve, and market tourism and hospitality experiences.

This chapter begins by defining nomenclature associated with experiential consumption. Particular attention is paid to a variety of conceptual models that may aid in our understanding of the hedonic aspects of the consumption experience. The review includes literatures on atmospherics, tourism, service, food, and lodging. Models and a summary table are presented and discussed for completed studies in each area covering issues on sampling, research design, analysis methods, and key findings. Discussed next are directions for future research, followed by current applications and benefits derived from research on experiential consumption. The reader should be able to grasp both the work completed as well as the wealth of opportunity and potential for the examination of consumer behavior through understanding experiential consumption.

Background

Basic concepts and definitions

This section attempts to define affect, emotion, attitude, and hedonism. Our understanding of these phenomena and their relationship with one another is an evolving process. These concepts have their foundations in psychology and philosophy. Mankind has endeavored to deal with their implications through the ages. Only recently has experiential consumption emerged as a fertile theoretical concept through which to view the consumption experience.

Affect

The definition of affect is not yet agreed upon in the research community. Once considered mental processes characterized by a consciously experienced subjective feeling state that was accompanied by emotions and moods, affect has referred to the evaluative aspects of attitudes based on the tri-partite model of attitudes that includes cognitive, affective, and behavioral dimensions (Eagly and Chaiken, 1993). Attitude can be assessed accordingly. Cognitively, it is the thoughts people have; affectively, it is the emotions or feeling people have; behaviorally, it is the choice-actions people make. According to Cohen et al. (2006, p. 3), this tri-partite model failed:

to adequately differentiate between evaluative measures (e.g., favorable/unfavorable) and antecedent or subsequent processes, which might be feeling-based. Consistent with the most recent scholarly discussion, we reserve the term 'affect' to describe an internal feeling state. One's explicit or implicit 'liking' for some object, person or position is viewed as an evaluative judgment rather than an internal feeling state… separation of affect as a feeling state that is distinct from either liking or purely descriptive cognition. So when we use the term 'affect' to describe stimuli, internal and overt responses, it is only in relation to evoked feeling states.

Emotion

Differentiating between affect, emotion, and attitude is complex. Masters's (2000, p. 32) definition captures the nuance: 'affect is an innately structured, non-cognitive evaluation sensation that may or may not register in consciousness; feeling is affect made conscious, possessing an evaluative capacity that is not only physiologically based, but that is often psychologically (and sometimes relationally) oriented; and emotion is psychosocially constructed, dramatized feeling.' Based on the work of Damasio (1994), Zhu and Thagard (2002, p. 20) explain emotion as follows:

Even though emotions are typically not the result of deliberative, intellectual calculations, they are not *necessarily* irrational or nonrational. Emotions are evaluative and responsive patterns that emerge through the evolution of the species and the development of individuals. They serve the function of providing appraisals about whether what is happening is harmful, threatening, or beneficial to our well-being under certain conditions. In many cases, emotions, rather than deliberate intellectual calculations, supply the most reliable information about the situations and ourselves, and provide the best ways to efficiently achieve our ends. Moreover, emotion may also be integral to the processes of reasoning and decision making.

Hedonism

Root VeenHoven (2003, p. 437) describe hedonism and happiness as:

the term 'hedonism' is used in several contexts. In moral philosophy it denotes the view that a good life should be a pleasurable life. In psychology it stands for the theory that pleasure seeking is a main motivator of human behavior… *a way of life in which pleasure plays an important role*. Hedonists are people who are positive about pleasure and who pluck the fruits of pleasure when possible. The reverse is asceticism, which involves the moral rejection of pleasure and abstinent behavior. There is a longstanding discussion about the merits of this hedonism. Some praise it as natural and healthy, but others equate hedonism with overindulgence and moral decay. The mixed feelings about hedonism are reflected in the connotations surrounding the word. On one hand hedonism is associated with good taste and the art of living well, and on the other hand with addiction, superficiality, irresponsible behavior and short-sighted egoism.

Attitude

Attitudes are historically referenced evaluative judgments about objects that elicit like or dislike judgments and influence approach/avoidance behavior. Fishbein and Ajzen (1972, p. 488) describe attitude as:

A person learns or forms beliefs about an object. These beliefs influence his attitude toward the object... Attitude is viewed as a compound in which the elements are beliefs and the affective value of the compound (i.e., attitude) is some function of the affective value of the constituent beliefs. This attitude constitutes a predisposition to respond in a generally favorable or unfavorable manner with respect to, or in the presence of, the object.

A relationship exists between affective states, emotions, attitudes, and hedonic responses in the consumption experience. Hedonic responses to consumer experience take three forms: Affective response, a pre-linguistic feeling experience which triggers approach or avoidance behaviors; emotions, the name given to the original affective response; attitudes, learned beliefs about an object which elicit behaviors. Accordingly, affect is viewed as the pre-cognitive response that triggers emotions, attitudes, and cognition. As researchers continue to examine the consumptive experience through hedonic lenses, our understanding of affect in the consumption experience will continue to evolve. Affect, emotion, attitude, and cognition act together and separately triggering approach and avoidance behaviors. Thus, existing rational models of consumption can be strengthened by understanding the non-rational dimension of the experience. Researchers in tourism and hospitality have a unique opportunity to examine the relationship between the product and consumer in this context. There is a relatively small body of related work reported or emerging in the hospitality and tourism literature. Much remains to be explored.

Mainstream thoughts and practices

There is an emerging stream of research on experiential consumption in the consumer behavior and marketing literature (see for example Mano and Oliver, 1993; Liljander and Strandvik, 1997; Morris et al., 2002). However, there remains a paucity of related work in the hospitality arena even though significant benefit can be gained from research on experiential consumption. Experiential consumption can be viewed through emotional response, absorbing experiences, pleasure/displeasure, sensation seeking, and cognition. All of these reflect an affective response – the pre-cognitive, pre-linguistic internalized experience of attraction to or avoidance of a particular experience. Much like that of a the child who touches hot iron, our response to experience is predicated on previous experience and the attraction to pleasure and avoidance of pain. This is unique to each individual.

The question for researchers is, *which constructs are appropriate for study?* Hospitality studies using hedonic constructs have focused on atmospherics, service, tourism, and food. Little work has been done in the lodging industry. Although this chapter does not review research on entertainment, which has received attention outside of hospitality research, it is a significant element in the hospitality milieu and experience. Some examples of entertainment include casinos, spectator sports, participatory sports, fairs, movies and theatre, theme parks, music, and recreation. Why does one choose an adventure vacation trekking from one Yosemite High Sierra Camp to the next while another individual chooses the refined elegance of basking on the French Riviera? Experiential consumption may provide a key to this and other phenomena.

The happiness, play, and recreation literature provides some background for the study of experiential consumption. Values, attitudes, and lifestyles (VALs), a proprietary scale developed by Stanford Research Institute International (SRI), divides consumers into eight categories: innovators, thinkers, believers, achievers, strivers, experiencers, makers, and survivors (SRI, 2002). While VALs are not directly related, the concept is informative for the study of experiential consumption and offers useful frameworks for future research.

Topical review of related hospitality research

No single model of experiential consumption has emerged. Rather, models have been tailored to the phenomena under investigation. They have, however, shared common lenses through which the consumption experience is viewed. Common are emotional response, tendency toward absorption, sensations seeking, affective response, and cognition. In a hospitality context these lenses have been used to examine atmospherics, the service experience, the tourism experience, and experiences with food and lodging. While experiential consumption has received limited attention in the general hospitality literature, these studies lay a foundation for further insights. This section reviews each area of investigation followed by an analysis of the various approaches and methodologies.

Atmospherics

Anecdotally, garish room appointments in Casino Hotels drove customers to the casino floor, uncomfortable chairs in restaurants increased table turnover, and the color red was thought to stimulate appetite so that the customer would order more food. Atmospherics refer to layout and design characteristics and include environmental cues such as lighting, color, sound, temperature, textures, and, in some instances, olfactory characteristics. The way atmospherics impact the guest experience has received increasing attention recently in the hospitality literature. In the field of approach or avoidance behavior toward environmental cues, several studies have been conducted in a hospitality context (Bitner, 1992; Lin, 2004).

Bitner's (1992) ground breaking work on 'servicescapes' provided a framework for understanding environment–user relationships in service organizations (see Figure 12.1). The model accounts for both the customer and employee response to environmental cues. In the quick service segment, long plagued with high turnover rates, In-N-Out Burger stands out with large uncluttered production areas flooded with natural light, an information-lean environment characterized by a very limited menu of all freshly prepared ingredients, and bright, clean, spacious customer service areas. When one examines the cognitive, emotional, and physiological impact of store atmospherics on employees and customers, part of the reason for this company's success is evident. Customer and employee behaviors are mediated by their response to environmental cues through cognitive, emotional, and physiological cues elicited in the environment (Bitner, 1992). Bitner proposed that ambient conditions, space and function, and signs, symbols, and artifacts influence customers' and employees' approach and avoidance behaviors to a 'servicescape.' Individual cognitive, emotional, and physiological responses moderate approach or avoidance behaviors. Bitner has integrated both rational and hedonic constructs in the model allowing a fuller understanding of approach/avoidance behaviors in the layout and design of 'servicescapes' (see Figure 12.1).

Lin (2004) examined the effect of cognition and emotion on the 'servicescape'. Lin joined the debate – whether emotion precedes cognition or cognition precedes emotion. In the model, the latter was proposed with a subsequent moderating effect of cognition on approach/avoid behavior. The consumer in Lin's model evaluates the 'servicescape' through a micro (or individual experience) perspective and a macro (environmental) perspective. The micro perspective includes personality traits, expectations, goal behaviors, cognitive style, and involvement. The macro perspective includes socio-cultural aspects, individualism versus. collectivism, demographics, and aesthetics. The model proposes that the elements and attributes of 'servicescapes' are first cognitively processed to organize a perceptual image, second evaluated from an affective/emotional response, and third again cognitively processed resulting in the approach or avoidance behavior.

Reimer and Kuehn (2005) examined the impact of 'servicescape' on quality perception in banking and restaurant environments. The

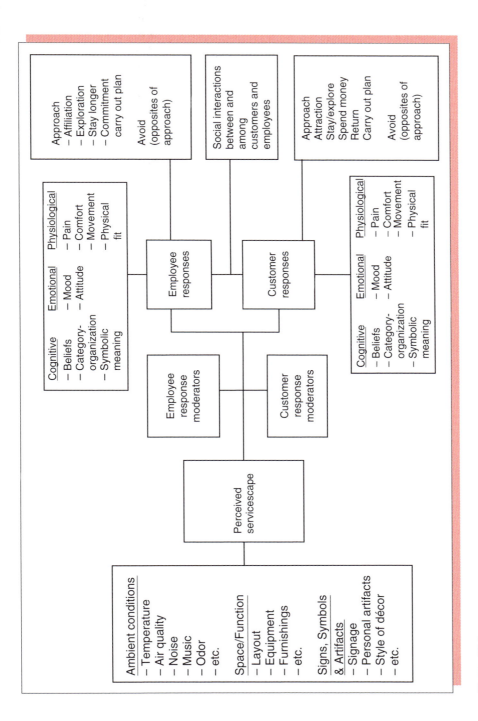

Figure 12.1
Framework for understanding environment/end-user relationships in service organizations (*Adapted from* Bitner (1992). Servicescapes: The impact of physical surroundings on customers and employees. *Journal of Marketing, 56*(April), 60.)

researchers found 'servicescape' was a cue to expected service quality and also an influencer of customers' experience of other quality factors. The 'servicescape' was a more important determinant in a hedonic setting, such as a restaurant, than was in the case of an essentially utilitarian service such as a bank.

Hui and Bateson (1991) examined perceived control and the effects of crowding and consumer choice on the service experience. The model hypothesized consumer choice would be moderated by emotional response to a consumer's perceived control over his/her environment and his/her perception of crowding. The consumer's approach/avoidance behavior was determined by his/her emotional response to the environment. In crowded environments where alternative spaces were available, the consumer could create a greater sense of control. For example in dance bars with quieter, less crowded spaces for relaxation and conversation, customers experienced a greater sense of control over their choices. This experimental study, conducted with a bar and a bank environment, evaluated server pleasantness, perceived customer control based on whether the facility offered an alternative to a crowded space, and approach or avoidance behavior. In the bar setting, the findings supported previous research suggesting that situational and emotional information (Baum et al., 1981), distraction (Worchel, 1978), and architectural and interior design (Baum and Valins, 1977) could influence approach/avoidance behavior. Examples of these are video, music, people watching, artifacts, and architectural/décor elements as well as other patrons. According to Hui and Bateson (1991), high density is associated with higher control and density can directly influence pleasure in a negative manner, but this can be counteracted by a positive association through perceived control. One example might be that people have different expectations between a bar and a bank, where perceived control is moderated by expectations of density.

Milliman (1986) examined the impact of music on restaurant patrons' approach/avoidance behavior. The study found variations in tempo and rhythm affected purchase intention and alcohol consumption. Slower tempo music contributed to longer stays and greater alcohol consumption. However, there was no increased food consumption dependent upon either fast or slow tempo music. Slower tempo background music elicited approach behaviors. However, this may be dependent on the type and style of restaurant as well as unique to the individual consumer. Hard Rock Café, as an example, plays music hard and loud as the name implies. Gueguen and Petr (2006) also examined the impact of olfactory cues on consumer behavior in a restaurant and found a significant effect of scents introduced into the restaurant on approach/avoidance behaviors. Casinos, other entertainment venues, and restaurants have used olfactory cues to elicit consumer responses in terms of spending more money and inducing appetite.

One of the most interesting trends in recent hotel development has been the emerging popularity of boutique accommodations. The transformation of city center hotels built before 1950s and the emergence of new brands such as ICON and W appeal to a different set of experiential criteria. The sameness of cookie cutter hotels built between the 1970s and 1990s no longer hold the same appeal to emerging markets with different needs and preferences. Emerging differences between different generations of consumers should be the criteria for researchers and developers. The sensation seeking tendencies of Generation Y and Generation X differ and the baby boomers appear to be a unique point of differentiation for new hotel development.

Service

The service encounter has received attention from an experiential perspective. Bloemer and de Ruyter (1999) examined customer loyalty in high and low involvement service settings and how positive emotions impacted service evaluations and loyalty. Two of the settings examined were a fast food restaurant and a fine dining restaurant. The researchers found that satisfaction and positive emotions had a positive effect on customer loyalty, and a higher ratio of return-intention resulted when the interaction elicited positive emotions. In a similar context, Mattila and Wirtz (2006) using a café scenario found satisfaction was dependent on the congruency between a customer's target arousal level and the actual arousal level experienced in the service environment. High congruency between expected arousal and actual arousal would enhance the customer's experience of pleasure and satisfaction. Incongruence between arousal and expectation had the opposite affect.

Mattila et al. (2003) examined the interplay of gender and affective tone in service encounter satisfaction. Previous work found a relationship between positive affective displays and service evaluation; however, the effect of gender had not been examined. Men and women were equally likely to be satisfied with affective exhibition in a normal service encounter. Men were less likely to negatively evaluate negative affective displays than women were. The outcome of research also suggests differences in men's orientation to outcomes and women's orientation to process in normal interactions. In situations with a negative outcome, men were highly influenced by negative affective displays and demonstrated avoidance. Female participants, on the other hand, were more likely to take service failure in their stride even when the employee's affective expression was negative. This suggests that women were more sensitive to emotional cues than men in their ability to identify with frontline employees and that they were able to accept service failure and a wider spectrum of affective tone from the employee in light of the failure.

Smith and Bolton (2002) examined the effect of customers' emotional responses to service failures based on their recovery effort evaluations and satisfaction judgments. The study was conducted in one focal hotel; however, multiple heterogeneous restaurant settings were used. While service failure in the hotel produced negative customer response, no emotional response was indicated when service failure occurred in the restaurant settings. The researchers attributed this to the heterogeneity of the restaurant settings. This may also be indicative of a greater zone of tolerance for service in a restaurant setting. When a service failure produces negative customer response, interactional justice is less likely to placate the guest than distributive justice. That is, the customer expects some form of substantive response in the form of a compliment. Apologies, attention, and empathy were significantly less effective in moderating customers' negative response to a service failure. Schoefer and Ennew (2005) examined the impact of perceived justice on the consumer's emotional responses to service complaint experiences in a problematic holiday check-in scenario. The researchers found positive or negative emotional responses based on the guest's evaluation of perceived justice. In this research the cognitive evaluation of complaint-handling based on perceived justice elicited an emotional response, which impacted the guest's satisfaction with complaint handling. Cognitive evaluation of perceived justice positively impacted overall service evaluation when distributive justice was present. Consistent with Smith and Bolton (2002), the researchers found positive feelings toward a distributive response over interactional responses.

Liljander and Mattsson (2002) evaluated the impact of the customer's pre-consumption mood on the evaluation of employee behavior in service encounters. Bank services, food bought over-the-counter and travel services were examined. The researchers identified three service personnel behavioral dimensions – concern, congeniality, and incivility (Winsted, 2000). Customers' positive and negative moods affected perception of the employee service. The researchers concluded managers should pay attention to both the behavioral dimensions demonstrated by employees and the customer's mood.

Grandey et al. (2005) examined authenticity of positive displays during service encounters, specifically smiling during a hotel check-in. The authenticity of the clerk improved guests' perceptions of friendliness, but with little impact on service evaluation. In a restaurant setting the researchers found positive authentic displays enhance service evaluation when the restaurant was quiet, but less so when the restaurant was busy. Unlike the case of the hotel, service evaluation was positively affected by positive authentic displays regardless of task performance in different settings.

Service has been a fertile area for the study of experiential consumption. The relationships examined have been loyalty with emotion, satisfaction with arousal, gender with affective tone, service failure with emotional response, customer mood with employee behavior, and authenticity with service evaluation. The results of these studies indicate that experiential aspects of the service encounter are information rich for further study and the implications will be discussed later in this chapter.

Tourism

Goossens (2000) examined tourism information and pleasure motivation. He proposed the following conceptual model (See Figure 12.2).
Goossens offers four propositions:

1. Enactive imagery elicits greater emotional responses and behavioral intent than static imagery.
2. Information with stimulus and hedonic factors will increase emotional responses and the resulting intention to purchase than information with stimulus factors alone.
3. Tourists use both affective choice modes in response to emotional and hedonic cues and information processing modes to evaluate pricing and other substantive variables in the proposition.
4. Visual and vivid information on pleasure destination characteristics increases buyers' involvement and their ability to differentiate between propositions in making the travel selection.

Goossens' model proposes that the pleasure travel choice process is a function of push and pull factors. Push factors are reflective of individual needs, motives, and drives. Pull factors are environmental cues received through advertising, the destination, and services. To the extent push and pull factors involve the customer's leisure travel desire through hedonic responses to imagery and emotions, the customer will be motivated to take the pleasure travel choice.

Yuksel (2007) examined tourist shopping habitat and its effects on emotions, shopping value, and approach behaviors. As a source of pleasure and entertainment in the tourism experience, shopping is central. The research found that shopping areas with a consistently themed environment were more likely to entice customers and that customers would spend more money there than environments without themes. Take, for example, the Forum Shops at Caesar's Palace in Las Vegas, a themed Roman street with period facades and a sunrise to sunset stared canopy that cycles every hour. These findings are consistent with the experience economy concept of Pine and Gilmore (1998). Pine and Gilmore sorted experience into four domains: entertainment, educational, aesthetic, and escapist. Customer participation in the experience lies on two intersecting continuum: passive to active and absorption to immersion. Passive participation might be going to a movie,

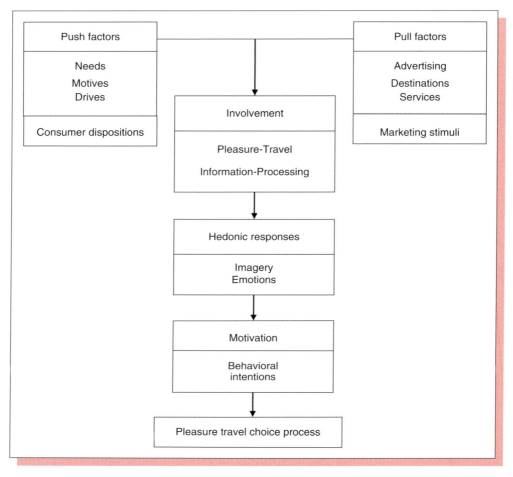

Figure 12.2
Tourism information and pleasure motivation (*Adapted from* Goossens (2000). Tourism information and pleasure motivation. *Annals of Tourism Research*, *27*(2), 304.)

while active participation, walking on a beach. In terms of absorption, one might become absorbed in the lives of the actors and immersed in the experience of fresh air, ocean breeze, and the sound of crashing waves. Places like Disney World bring both of these domains together and are able to create a 'sweet spot.' The same is true for tourism shopping experiences; attention should be paid to exterior environments of the shopping areas because the tourist will not enter into the interior when the exterior does not imply a good shopping experience. The researcher suggests that environmental perceptions drive approach behaviors and perception of shopping value. Pleasure and arousal are major motivators of shopping behavior in a tourist context.

White (2005) examined emotions and cross-cultural perspectives in destination visitation intentions and physical characteristics of the destination. The researcher sampled Italian and American respondents to determine the extent of emotional influence on destination visitation choice, perceptions of physical characteristics of a destination, and cultural differences across nationalities in destination perceptions. The study concluded that emotional response was a significant determinant in destination choice. However, differences between nationalities based on the intensity of their emotional response were insignificant.

Bigne and Andreu (2004) examined emotions in tourism segmentation. The results support emotion as a segmentation variable. Tourists experiencing higher pleasure and arousal were more likely to be satisfied, loyal, and less price sensitive. Pleasure was found to be more predictive than arousal in this study. Similarly, Qui and Wu (2005) conducted an experimental study on the influence of cognitive styles and negative emotions on tourism decision-making. While cognitive styles were not influential in tourism decision-making, negative emotions were. There was also significant difference in decision-making between persons whose emotions were negative toward a choice and persons whose emotions were neutral.

Tourism research in experiential consumption had been conducted on approach behaviors in shopping venues, cultural perspectives in visitation choice, emotions in market segmentation, and emotions in tourism decision-making. This section examined the travel choice process proposed by Goossens (2000), cultural perspectives on the nuances of approach behavior, segmentation of tourism based on emotional response, and the tourism decision-making process in terms of cognitive style.

Food

Food and pleasures of the body have for centuries been central to the expression and experience of pleasure and hedonism. Responding to recent attention to obesity and restaurant food, Geiliebter and Aversa (2003) examined influence of emotions on eating in overweight, normal weight, and underweight individuals. The research found underweight individuals ate less than both overweight and normal weight individuals during periods of emotional stress and ate more during positive emotional states. As predicted, overweight individuals ate more during negative emotional states.

Another emotional lens captures insights into the emotions of hospitality through special meal occasions (Lashley et al., 2005). The researchers examined participants' most memorable meal experiences. Both domestic and commercial settings were reported to elicit experiences of hospitality. Satisfaction through emotional fulfillment was a response to the occasion rather than rational evaluations found in the service quality management literature. In summarizing his review of emotional influences on food choice, Gibson (2006) concluded food could enhance mood which could in turn enhance food. In instances where the outcome was predictable in either direction, a re-enforcing learned behavior was in play. The eater was engaging in a food choice strategy enabling elevated mood or calming stress with foods having sensory characteristics that enhanced individual hedonic needs.

Alley and Burroughs (1991) examined gender preferences for hot, unusual and unfamiliar foods. Men had stronger preferences than women for hot spicy foods. The researchers' prediction that men would be more likely to try new and unusual foods was also supported. The research supported men's greater tendency toward sensation seeking than women's.

Macht et al. (2005, p. 153) examined the pleasure of eating. Their research results coincide with 'appetite gestalten' consisting of environmental stimuli, stimuli within, and response:

In the stimulus domain, the foods, features of the physical environment, and social factors; in the domain of the organism a specific somato-psychic state and an attitude towards hedonism; in the domain of responses preparatory activities, specific characteristics of eating behavior and positive sensations and emotions . . . the pleasures of eating depend on a variety of external and internal conditions. External conditions go far beyond the food itself. Physical features of the environment and social factors amplify food-induced positive affective reactions and embed them in an individually unique setting. Internal conditions include motivational, cognitive and behavioral factors. People who enjoy eating are physiologically ready to eat and they have the explicit intention to enjoy, they eat slowly and focus upon salient features of foods and environments. They also engage in social activities before, during, and after the meal.

Charters and Pettigrew (2005) examined wine consumption as an aesthetic experience. There are significant similarities between the appreciation of fine art and fine wine. Both experiences elicited sensory, emotional, and cognitive responses. Both were associated with trained cognitive responses which required a level of concentration and education to appreciate the experience and a commonality of beauty found in their enjoyment and experience.

Dube et al. (2005) examined affect asymmetry and comfort food consumption. Whereas women's comfort food consumption was motivated by negative emotions, men's comfort food consumption was motivated by positive emotions. Women felt guilty for indulgence. French Canadians' and older participants' indulgence was triggered by positive affect, whereas younger English participants reported more negative emotions prior to eating comfort food. Negative affects were alleviated by higher sugar and fat content foods and positive emotions were increased by low-calorie foods.

Bell and Marshal (2003) constructed a food involvement scale. The authors hypothesized individuals with a greater tendency toward food involvement would tend to be more discriminating between foods through affective and perceptive responses. The research found involvement influenced brand loyalty, product search and information processing, response to advertising, diffusion of innovations, and product choice. The hedonic scale examines both affective and perceptive relative judgments. The research resulted in a 12-item measure of food involvement with acceptable test–retest reliability and internal consistency within the two subscales.

Laros and Steenkamp (2005) examined emotions in consumer behavior in a food context. Genetically modified food, functional food (enriched or modified to make the product healthier or prevent diseases), organic food, and regular food were examined. Negative affect characterized by anger, fear, sadness, and shame were compared to positive affect characterized by contentment and happiness. When positive and negative affects were broken into their respective emotional components, it was the emotional components that provided a better context than positive or negative feeling constructs alone.

Experiential consumption of food was reviewed in this section. The food consumption experience was examined through the relationship of emotional response with weight, emotional response with special meal occasions, sensation seeking (spicy foods) with gender preference, hedonic response with wine consumption, emotional response with food fabrication processes.

Lodging and other related research

Barsky and Nash (2002) examined the role emotions played in hotel loyalty. The researchers identified a set of 'loyalty emotions' by market segment. The segments and their emotional response to each were presented by them as follows:

- Economy: comfortable – content – practical
- Mid-price: comfortable – secure – welcome
- Upscale: comfortable – important – welcome
- Luxury: pampered – relaxed – sophisticated
- Extended stay: comfortable – practical – respected

Those chains eliciting higher emotional loyalty scores had greater pricing flexibility than chains scoring lower. The authors suggested this understanding would enable identification of underserved market niches and profiling of emotional responses in support of price elasticity and return intention.

McIntosh and Siggs (2005) explored the experiential nature of boutique accommodation. Conversational style interviews were conducted with guests and operators/developers. Based on the researcher's analysis, the participants converged on five domains of experience in boutique hotels. They were unique character, personalization, homeliness, quality, and value addition. The guests characterized their emotional responses as warm, secure, homely, welcomed, comfortable, spoilt, delighted, charmed, serene, wonderful, peaceful, and at ease. The authors suggested boutique accommodation engendered a more genuine shared experience on an emotional level between the host and guest than found in standardized lodging products.

Pullman and Gross (2004) examined the ability of experience design elements to elicit emotions and loyalty behaviors in a VIP hospitality tent for a circus. They examined basic emotions and VIP emotions and their findings were consistent with Barsky and Nash's (2002) findings in that the emotions evoked were a strong indicator of loyalty behavior. Basic emotions and relational elements between actors and guests were more important to loyalty behavior than the VIP nature of the tent. There was little support for the role of VIP emotions in loyalty. Relational elements, such as participatory involvement by guests in the experience of the circus, were a strong indicator of customer loyalty, while physical attributes demonstrated resulted in mixed effects on customer loyalty.

Lodging remains significantly understudied in terms of understanding the guest's emotional triggers. However, there is an emerging body of work. Emotions and loyalty, the experiential nature of boutique accommodation, and experiential design elements were reviewed. Discussed in the next section are the relevant methodologies and future research potential.

Critical review of research methods

Based on the foundation of previous research, significant opportunities exist to examine the hospitality consumer's experiential realm. Table 12.1 represents selected articles reviewed in this chapter. The table is separated into six columns: author(s), year, study design and instrument used, methods of analysis employed, sampling methods, and the sample size reported. Results present a synopsis of the major findings of the study. Along with such a methodological review, suggestions for future research are presented.

The review summarized in Table 12.1 covers atmospherics, tourism, service, food, and lodging. The social scientists' empirical approach is evident in the reported studies. Experimental designs, survey research, student populations, and convenience sampling have thus far captured

Table 12.1 Methodological summary of reviewed studies

Author (Year)	Study design and instrument	Methods of analysis	Sampling	N	Key findings
Atmospherics					
Gueguen and Petr (2006)	Experimental	One-way ANOVA	Convenience	88	Olfactory cues in restaurants affect approach/avoidance behaviors.
Hui and Bateson (1991)	Experimental Slides/Scenario	Multi-sample structural equation modeling	Self-selected random assignment to treatments	115	Situational and emotional cues influence approach/avoidance behaviors under crowded conditions.
Milman (1986)	Experimental	T-test	Repeated randomized block design	1,392	Variation in tempo and rhythm of music affect purchase intention and alcohol consumption in restaurants.
Service					
Bloemer and de Ruyter (1999)	Positive affect–negative affect scale (PANAS)	T-tests Hierarchical regression analysis	Random Interview	924	Satisfaction and positive emotions had positive effects on customer loyalty and return intention.
Liljander and Mattsson (2002)	Self-report questionnaire	Factor Analysis Hierarchical regression analysis	Convenience sampling of students	173	Customer's moods affected perception of employee response in concern, congeniality, and incivility.

(Continued)

Table 12.1 (Continued)

Author (Year)	Study design and instrument	Methods of analysis	Sampling	N	Key findings
Mattila et al. (2003)	Video and scenario $2 \times 2 \times 2$ experimental design	ANOVA		145	Women were more sensitive to emotional cues than men and more able to accept service failure and a wider spectrum of affective tone in employee responses to service failure.
Mattila and Wirtz (2006)	Mehrabian and Russel PAD semantic differential scale Oliver's and Swan's satisfaction differentiation scale	Two-way ANOVA	Randomized convenience sampling of MBA students	178	Congruency between the desired arousal level and actual arousal level enhanced the customer's experience of pleasure and satisfaction.
Smith and Bolton (2002)	Self-developed questionnaire	Content analysis	Convenience sampling of students, restaurant customers, and hotel customers	904	Interactional justice is less likely to placate guests than distributive justice in cases of service failure.
Tourism					
Bigne and Andreu (2004)	Pleasure and arousal scale (Russel,1980) Universal scale of satisfaction (Oliver,1997)	ANOVA Cluster analysis	Mall interception	400	The higher the tourists experience of pleasure and arousal, the greater the satisfaction and loyalty and the lesser the price sensitivity.

Yuksel (2007)	Fisher's environmental aesthetic quality scale, Plutchik's (1980) differential emotions, and Mehrabian's and Russell's (1974) PAD	Structural equation modeling	Self-administered questionnaires	259	Perceived consistency of environmental cues drive approach behaviors and increased perception of shopping value.
Food				
Alley and Burroughs (1991)	Researcher-developed questionnaire	Pearson correlations Chi square	Self-selected student respondents	148	Men were more inclined toward sensation seeking than women in terms of trying spicy foods.
Charters and Pettigrew (2005)	Qualitative focus groups and one-on-one interviews	Content analysis	Self-selected samples	105	Wine and art elicited positive sensory, emotional, and cognitive responses and a commonality of beauty found in their enjoyment.
Dube et al. (2005)	Researcher-developed questionnaire	Multi-factorial ANOVA	Self selected web-enabled survey techniques	277	Women's comfort food consumption was associated with negative emotions and men's with positive emotions.

(Continued)

343

Table 12.1 (Continued)

Author (Year)	Study design and instrument	Methods of analysis	Sampling	N	Key findings
Laros and Steenkamp (2005)	Researcher-developed questionnaire	Randomized self-administered survey of Dutch consumers	Randomized self-administered questionnaire	645	Individual emotional components such as fear, shame, contentment, and happiness provided a better context to understand the affect of food than positive or negative feeling constructs alone.
Macht et al. (2005)	Semi-structured Interview	Content analysis	Self-selected student participants	16	People who enjoy eating are physiologically ready to eat and they have explicit intention to enjoy eating.
Lodging and other					
Barsky and Nash (2002)	MMHI	Frequencies	NCOP	30,000	Hotels eliciting higher emotional loyalty had greater pricing flexibility.
McIntosh and Siggs (2005)	Open-ended question format	Content Analysis	Convenience sampling	30	Boutique accommodation engendered a more genuine shared experience on an emotional level between the guest and host than standardized lodging.
Pullman and Gross (2004)	PANAS Scale and Mano's emotional domains	Principal component and confirmatory factor analysis	Convenience sampling	219	Emotions and relational elements between actors and guests were more important to loyalty behavior than the VIP nature of the event space.

the nature of experiential consumption. A variety of quantitative methods have been employed including ANOVA, structural equation modeling, t-tests, regression, cluster analysis, and factor analysis. Content analysis has also been employed in the study of hedonism. It is easier for the scientist to grasp and examine phenomena piecemeal rather than as an organic whole. But, how can we separate a tourist's shopping experience from the dining experience when at the end of the trip the visitor's return intention may well be predicated on the organic whole rather than the parts? What experiential components are hygienic in nature and what components are predictive of future purchase intention? Study design, methods of analysis, and sampling techniques employed in the limited research undertaken thus far leave significant opportunity for future research.

Directions for future research

Future research in the domain of atmospherics should address questions such as: How do atmospherics impact the emotional response of the guest and the employee? What are the impacts of atmospherics on employee turnover, guest loyalty, and evaluation of the service experience? What experiential triggers contribute to these outcomes? (One significant area not examined thus far is gender difference in approach/avoidance behaviors to 'servicescapes.') How does the emotional response to atmospherics impact price elasticity? How do rational and emotional responses vary given the nature of the servicescape, for example, between lodging brands within a particular segment? Which positive and negative emotional responses are determinative to outcomes of approach and avoidance behaviors?

There is an emerging body of research in the experiential components of service and their impact on guest behavior. Long after the field was dominated by a rational understanding of and approach to consumer behavior, recent studies have begun to focus on the hedonic aspects of the service experience. Studies on the impact of emotional triggers experienced in a service encounter and their relationship to service evaluation, price elasticity, service failure, and loyalty have been conducted. Management's orientation to a rational understanding of service evaluation is being expanded to include the impact of experience on the service encounter. In many cases inclusion of an experiential component in service evaluation has strengthened previous models relying solely on rational approaches. Management's orientation to standards, procedures, and scripting are gradually finding enlightenment with inclusion of the experiential/hedonic aspects of service. Mood of the guest, affective tone of employees in service recovery, and customer expectations of arousal in restaurants have all informed our understanding of experiential consumption. Service evaluation has long been examined through rational lenses. Interestingly, emotional responses are emerging as stronger predictors of outcomes in models that include both rational and experiential constructs.

This area of investigation offers new horizons and opportunities. Can guests be stratified based on emotional response to the service experience? Are emotional responses to the service experience predictive of loyalty and price acceptability? How do emotional cues from service providers impact the guest experience? Gender, cultural, and ethnic differences remain a viable and fertile area of exploration.

Tourism entails, by its nature, experiential consumption. Variations in sensation seeking are at the heart of the tourism experience. Segmenting tourists by sensation seeking and other experiential attributes remain on the horizon. Some studies have examined the relationship between advertising messages and emotional response, although much remains to be investigated further.

Certainly information-rich travel web sites and the emotions elicited deserve attention. Is destination selection a rational activity or an emotional activity? What are the significant predictors in either domain? Are there significant gender differences in tourists' selection processes based on emotional characteristics? What emotional push–pull experiences shape tourism choice? Rational classification models of destination and tourist characteristics exist. Including hedonic constructs can inform and extend these models. Tourism offers a rich environment to explore multiple facets of experiential consumption.

The phrases such as 'People eat with their eyes' and 'we sell the sizzle and not the steak' have long been guiding principles in restaurants and increasingly so in the retail sector. The underpinning principles appeal to the experiential nature of food consumption. Restaurateurs have long known that creating positive results rests on the success of an emotional invitation into the experience of dining. Management success rests on manipulation of the service product, the service delivery system, and the service setting. No matter whether consummating a business deal over lunch, celebrating an important passage, or merely satisfying hunger, the restaurateur's job is to provide the sought solution. One possible approach might be to evaluate rational and experiential factors related to food consumption and examine relative strength in terms of successful outcomes. Generalizable research has been scarce and much remains to be examined. Possible areas to examine are emotional triggers and motivations for dining. Some groundwork has been laid in examining relationship between weight and emotional response. Such studies should be carried over into a normative environment.

Lodging remains significantly understudied in terms of understanding emotional triggers of the customer. Research has examined pricing flexibility, emotional loyalty, boutique accommodation, and emotional triggers and a tangential study has examined relational elements between 'actors' and guests in the context of a VIP experience (see Table 12.1). It is apparent that security, safety, and comfort are paramount to the lodging experience. Examining these factors through experiential lenses will provide valuable insights. There are anecdotal classification schemes of the property and customer based on rational inputs. Examining relative strength of the experiential nature of lodging would improve our understanding and business models.

Application

This chapter on experiential consumption is merely an introduction. The view into the consumption experience is enriched by inclusion of hedonic constructs in exploration and research models. The question for the practitioner is how this information can be used to maximize the quality of customer experience. This chapter examined studies on experiential aspects of atmospherics, service, tourism, food, and lodging. Several examples were discussed and the experience aspects of the customer–employee encounter were examined.

Disneyworld, the Bellagio, Rainforest Café's, and Caesar's Forum Shops are examples of experientially designed venues. The challenge to practitioners is integration of both rational and hedonic aspects in experience planning. Product roll-out is preceded by extensive focus group input and testing. Employee selection, training, and development opportunities include structured interviews aimed at uncovering the candidate's temperament for service positions. Service recovery strategies are based upon customers' zone of service tolerance. Hygiene factors such as cleanliness, service competency, and product quality are designed to enhance the transparency of the guest's experience and are seamlessly integrated. Emotional service triggers are emerging as significant indicators in product choice, pricing, and customer loyalty. How can positive emotional triggers be built into the service system? Restaurant and hotel lobbies can be theatrically engineered to offer the guests new experiences. Web design is another area to be informed by experiential consumption. What elements of web design reduce risk and enhance product selection? Certainly there are rational criteria designers use in constructing web sites. The question remains: how can web sites be used as an invitation in the experience of a restaurant, hotel, or other hospitality venue by employing positive emotional triggers? Creative managers and operators will grasp the implications of experiential consumption and create the future.

Conclusions

Experiential consumption attempts to quantify the nature of affect through the relative evaluation of emotions, sensations, imaginations, and cognitions. The debate over the nature of affect as antecedent or precedent of a consumption evaluation has not been resolved. It is unlikely to be resolved, but rather will be more like a tennis match with the ball being exchanged interminably. There is emerging evidence to suggest that models of consumer behaviors without experiential elements do not capture the full meaning of the consumption phenomena. Two central themes emerge. One is that rational constructs and classification schemes are enhanced by including experiential constructs. The other is that hospitality is experiential by nature and failure to include experiential components in our study of the phenomena leaves us with half the question unanswered. Several scales have been used in previous research. Mehrabian's and Russell's (1974) Pleasure Arousal Dominance Scale (PAD) is a semantic differential scale examining emotional response to specified events. Swanson's (1978) Absorbing Experience Scale examines imagination and fantasy seeking tendencies. Zuckerman's (1994) Sensation Seeking Scale examines differences in approach and avoidance in terms of sensation seeking. Models of consumer behavior focusing on the rational may not be as strong as models of consumer behavior that account for experiential consumption. However, while the nature of hospitality research seems focused on quantification today, understanding the fullness of experiential consumption may take many systematic qualitative investigations. Experiential consumption by its nature is messy, confusing, conflicted, and downright difficult to grasp. But it is one of the frontiers in consumer behavior research and should not be ignored. Understanding the phenomena will take both qualitative and quantitative approaches. Understanding normative and maladaptive behaviors are critical from an ethical perspective and indeed the study of normative hedonism is informed by the pathological hedonism. Gradually, the exploration of experiential consumption has been populated since Hirschman and Holbrook (1982) first presented their ideas. Studies into the emotional nature of consumption have enlightened and strengthened models of consumer choice, evaluation, purchase intention, and loyalty. Little has been done relative to what remains to be discovered in the hospitality field.

References

Alley, T. R. and Burroughs, W. J. (1991). Do men have stronger preferences for hot, unusual, and unfamiliar foods? *Journal of General Psychology*, *118*(3), 201–213.

Barsky, J. and Nash, L. (2002). Evoking emotion: Affective keys to hotel loyalty. *Cornell Hotel and Restaurant Administration Quarterly*, (February), *43*(1), 39–46.

Baum, A. and Valins, S. (1977). Architecture and social behavior: Psychological studies of social density. Hillsdale, NJ: Erlbaum.

Baum, A., Fisher, J. D., and Solomon, S. K. (1981). Type of information, familiarity, and the reduction of crowing stress. *Journal of Personality and Social Psychology*, *40*(1), 11–23.

Becker, H. S. (1973). Art as a collective action. *American Sociological Review*, *39*(Spring), 767–776.

Bell, R. and Marshall, D. W. (2003). The construct of food involvement in behavioral research: Scale development and validation. *Appetite*, *40*(3), 235, 10p.

Bigne, J. E., and Andreu, L. (2004). Emotions in segmentation: An empirical study. *Annals of Tourism Research*, *31*(3), 682–696.

Bitner, M. J. (1992). Servicescapes: The impact of physical surroundings on customers and employees. *Journal of Marketing*, *56*(April), 57–71.

Bloemer, J. and de Ruyter, K. (1999). Customer loyalty in high and low involvement service settings: The moderating impact of positive emotions. *Journal of Marketing Management*, *15*, 315–330.

Charters, S. and Pettigrew, S. (2005). Is wine consumption an aesthetic experience? *Journal of Wine Research*, *16*(2), 121–136.

Cohen, J. B., Pham, M. T., and Andrade, E. B. (2008). The nature and role of affect in consumer behavior. In C. P. Haugtvedt, Herr, P. M., and Kardes, F. R., *Handbook of Consumer Psychology* (1st ed., pp. [in press at this time]). Mahwah, NJ: Lawrence Erlbaum Associates.

Crane, D. (1976). Reward systems in art, science and religion, In R. A. Peterson (ed.), *The Production of Culture*. Beverly Hills: Sage.

Damasio, A. R. (1994). *Descartes' Error: Emotion, Reason, and the Human Brain*. New York: G. P. Putnam's Sons.

Dichter, E. (1960). *The Strategy of Desire*. New York: Doubleday.

Dube, L., LeBel, J. L., and Lu, J. (2005). Affect asymmetry and comfort food consumption. *Physiology and Behavior*, *4*(15), 559–567.

Eagly, A. H. and Chaiken, S. (1993). *The Psychology of Attitudes*. Orlando, FL: Harcourt Brace Jovanovich.

Fishbein, M. and Ajzen, I. (1972). Attitudes and opinions. *Annual Review of Psychology*, *23*, 487–545.

Geiliebter, A., and Aversa, A. (2003). Emotional eating in overweight, normal weight, and underweight individuals. *Eating Behaviors*, *3*(4), 341–348.

Gibson, E. L. (2006). Emotional influences on food choice: Sensory, physiological and psychological pathways. *Physiology and Behavior*, *89*, 53–61.

Goossens, C. (2000). Tourism information and pleasure motivation. *Annals of Tourism Research*, *27*(2), 301–321.

Grandey, A. A., Fisk, G. M., Mattila, A. S. (2005). I 'service with a smile' enough? Authenticity of positive displays during service encounters. *Organizational Behavior and Human Decision Processes*, *96*(1), 38–55.

Grubb, E. L. and Grathwohl, H. L. (1967). Consumer self-concept, symbolism and market behavior: A theoretical approach. *Journal of Marketing*, *31*(October), 22–27.

Gueguen, N., and Petr, C. (2006). Odors and consumer behavior in a restaurant. *International Journal of Hospitality Management*, 25, 335–339.

Hirsch, P. M. (1972). Processing fads and fashions: An organization set analysis of cultural industry systems. *American Journal of Sociology*, 77(Winter), 639–659.

Hirschman, E. C., and Holbrook, M. B. (1982). Hedonic consumption: Emerging concepts, methods and propositions. *Journal of Marketing*, 46(Summer), 92–101.

Hui, M. K., and Bateson, J. E. G. (1991). Perceived control and the effects of crowding and consumer choice on the service experience. *Journal of Consumer Research*, 18(September), 174–184.

Jaeger, W. (1945). *Paideia: The Ideals of Greek Culture*, Vol. I, G. Highet (trans.), New York: Oxford University Press.

Laros, F. J. M., and Steenkamp, J. E. M. (2005). Emotions in consumer behavior: A hierarchical approach. *Journal of Business Research*, 58, 1437–1445.

Lashley, C., Morrison, A., and Randall, S. (2005). More than a service encounter? Insights into the emotions of hospitality through special meal occasions. *Journal of Hospitality and Tourism Management*, 12(1), 80–92.

Levy, S. J. (1959). Symbols for sale. *Harvard Business Review*, 37(July–August), 117–119.

Levy, S. J. (1963). Symbolism and lifestyle. In S. A. Greyser, (ed.), *Toward Scientific Marketing*. Chicago: American Marketing Association.

Liljander, V. and Mattsson, J. (2002). Impact of customer preconsumption mood on the evaluation of employee behavior in service encounters. *Psychology and Marketing*, 19(10), 837–860.

Liljander, V., and Strandvik, T. (1997). Emotions in service satisfaction. *International Journal of Service Industry Management*, 8(2), 148–169.

Lin, I. L. (2004). Evaluating a servicescape: The effect of cognition and emotion. *International Journal of Hospitality Management*, 23, 163–178.

Masters, R. A. (2000). Compassionate wrath: Transpersonal approaches to anger. *The Journal of Transpersonal Psychology*, 32(1), 31–51.

McIntosh, A. J., and Siggs, A. (2005). An exploration of the experiential nature of boutique accommodation. *Journal of Travel Research*, 44(August), 74–81.

Mano, H., and Oliver, R. L. (1993). Assessing the dimensionality and structure of the consumption experience: Evaluation, feeling and satisfaction. *Journal of Consumer Research*, 20(December), 451–466.

Mattila, A. S., Grandey, A. A., and Fisk, G. M. (2003). The interplay of gender and affective tone in service encounter satisfaction. *Journal of Service Research*, 6(2), 136–143.

Mattila, A. S., and Wirtz, J. (2006). Arousal expectations and service evaluations. *International Journal of Service Industry Management*, 17(3), 229–244.

Macht, M., Meininger, J., and Roth, J. (2005). The pleasures of eating: A qualitative analysis. *Journal of Happiness Studies, 6,* 137–160.

Mehrabian, A., and Russell, J. (1974). *An Approach to Environmental Psychology.* Cambridge, Mass.: MIT Press.

Milliman, R. E. (1986). The influence of background music on the behavior of restaurant patrons. *Journal of Consumer Research, 13*(September), 286–289.

Morris, J. D., Woo, C., Geason, J. A., and Kim, J. (2002). The power of affect: Predicting intention. *Journal of Advertising Research, 42*(3), 7–17.

Oliver, R. (1997). *Satisfaction: A Behavioral Perspective on the Consumer.* New York: McGraw-Hill.

Osgood, C. E., Suci, G. J., and Tannenbaum, P. H. (1957). *The Measurement of Meaning.* Urbana: University of Illinois Press.

Pine, B. J., and Gilmore, J. H. (1998). Welcome to the experience economy. *Harvard Business Review,* (July/August), *76*(4), 97–105.

Plutchik, R. (1980). *Emotion: A psychoevolutionary synthesis.* New York: Harper & Row.

Pullman, M. E., and Gross, M. A. (2004). Ability of experience design elements to elicit emotions and loyalty behaviors. *Decision Sciences, 35*(3), 551–578.

Qui, F., and Wu, M. (2005). An experimental research on the influence of cognitive styles and negative emotions on tourism decision-making. *Psychological Science, 28*(5), 1112–1114.

Reimer, A., and Kuehn, R. (2005). The impact of servicescape on quality perception. *European Journal of Marketing, 39*(7–8), 785–808.

Russell, J. A. (1980). A circumplex model of affect. *Journal of Personality and Social Psychology, 39*(6), 1161–1178.

Schoefer, K., and Ennew, C. (2005). The impact of perceived justice on consumer's emotional responses to service complaint experiences. *Journal of Services Marketing, 19*(5), 261–270.

Singer, J. L. (1966). *Daydreaming: An Introduction to the Experimental Study of Inner Experience.* New York: Random House.

Smith, A. K., and Bolton, R. N. (2002) The effect of customer's emotional responses to service failures on their recovery effort evaluations and satisfaction judgments. *Journal of the Academy of Marketing Science, 30*(1), 5–23.

SRI Consulting Business Intelligence. (2002). VALS: How do you create strategies for changing consumer dynamics.

Swanson, G. E. (1978). Travels through innerspace: Family structure and openness to absorbing experiences. *American Journal of Sociology, 83*(January), 890–919.

VeenHoven, R. (2003). Hedonism and happiness. *Journal of Happiness Studies, 4,* 437–457.

White, C. J. (2005). The role of emotions in destination visitation intentions: A cross-cultural perspective. *Journal of Hospitality & Tourism Management, 12*(2), 168–178.

Winsted, K. F. (2000). Service Behaviors that lead to satisfied customers. *European Journal of Marketing, 34*, 399–417.

Worchel, S. (1978). Reducing crowding without increasing space: Some applications of an attributional theory of crowding. *Journal of Population, 1(3)*, 216–230.

Yuksel, A. (2007). Tourist shopping habitat: Effects on emotions, shopping value and behaviors. *Tourism Management, 28*, 58–69.

Zhu, J., and Thagard, P. (2002). Emotion and action. *Philosophical Psychology, 15(1)*, 19–36

Zuckerman, M. (1994). *Behavioral Expressions and Biosocial Bases of Sensation Seeking.* Cambridge: Cambridge University Press.

CHAPTER 13

Psychology of pricing: A review and suggestions

H. G. Parsa and David Njite

Price is one of the important variables used by consumers in making purchase decisions. According to Kotler et al. (1999, p. 401), price is the only revenue-generating element in the four Ps (i.e., product, price, place, and promotion) of marketing mix. When calculating maximum utility of a product prior to a purchase decision, according to Monroe (1990, p. 46), consumers use product price and non-monetary sacrifices as the denominator and quality of goods and service as the numerator. By assessing product utility in this manner, consumers are able to effectively use monetary and non-monetary factors in deriving the final value of a product.

From an economics point of view, price is explained as a function of the interplay between demand and supply. The microeconomic theory of demand and supply describes and predicts price and quantity of goods and services sold in a perfectly competitive market, examining demand in terms of the customer and supply from a seller perspective. This can be graphically presented as in Figure 13.1. The supply and demand model in Figure 13.1 describes how prices vary as a result of a balance between product availability and demand. The graph depicts an increase in demand from D_1 to D_2 along with the consequent increase in price and quantity required to reach a new equilibrium point on the supply curve (S).

A great deal of economics theory on pricing is based on various assumptions. One assumption relates to the questions such as: what is the effect of altering price on sales volume? If the price is reduced, will the increase in sales volumes make up for the price reduction? Will a price increase lead to a reduction in demand? Will the extra dollars generated cover for the loss of sales volume? But this kind of

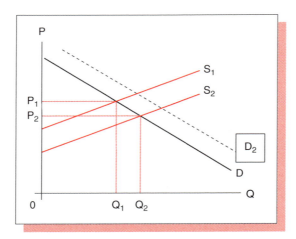

Figure 13.1
Relationship between supply, demand and price shifts

economics-based analytical approach to understanding pricing makes various assumptions about the consumer as well.

The most obvious assumption is the notion that consumers make rational decisions of utility maximization while making product purchases (Narasimhan, 1984). Thus, consumers keep rationalizing choices and the amount to buy in order to maximize utility. This classical economics theory assumes that consumers will only spend money on products that will give them the most happiness at the least cost. Thus, in general, price and demand will have an inverse relationship. Unfortunately, extant literature (literature in psychological pricing and conspicuous consumption in particular) shows that this is not necessarily true in all instances.

Consumer purchase is more complex than depicted by the economics theory. Thus, there are situations where consumers buy more as price increases. For example, literature identifies at least three kinds of consumption patterns that do not quite fit into the framework of traditional supply and demand. Some of them may include the *snob effect* where consumers want to distinguish themselves from other consumers (consume *niche* products) and the *bandwagon effect* where consumers want to be in the crowd and buy what everyone else is buying. The *Veblen effect* is another case in which consumers buy conspicuous goods that display a sense of belonging to the upper classes. According to these three effects, the traditional laws of supply and demand do not apply for some consumer products such as fashionable destinations, fancy restaurants, luxury cars, and any product that is priced at a high level not because of its high utility value but because of its affect value in the eyes of its consumers.

The concept of psychological pricing remains of interest and importance to both practitioners and academic researchers alike. This interest and importance is depicted by the continually emerging streams of literature and research related to psychological pricing. Generally, psychological pricing has been studied from many perspectives, the diversity of this examination matching that of the researchers involved. For example, papers published in the marketing literature have examined psychological price from both individual and household level models of reference price (Janiszewski and Lichtenstein, 1999; Krishnamurthi et al., 1992; Lattin and Bucklin, 1989). Other studies have examined psychological price from a framing perspective (e.g., Grewal et al., 1996; Naipaul and Parsa, 2001; Schindler, 1992; Thaler, 1985). The list is definitely unending. Even more recently, studies in psychological pricing have taken on a more interesting dimension by extending and examining pricing even further to include consumer psychology and culture. Simmons and Schindler (2002) and Hu et al. (2006) have examined the influence of consumers' cultural beliefs on pricing and price presentation.

Furthermore, empirical findings show that, consumer perception of product price is affected not only by the numerical value it represents but also by various other internal and external factors. Estelami (2001) demonstrated that price perceptions were influenced by the numeric format used and the arithmetic representation associated with the price. Coulter (2001) showed that placement of price information (left versus right) had a significant effect in product demand. Nagle and Holden (1995, p. 303) stated that consumers might *perceive* prices accurately but *might not* evaluate them in a perfectly rational manner. Monroe and Lee (1999, p. 46) noted, 'we still know little about how people process and remember numerical information (*prices*)' (emphasis added). Price perception is therefore more complex than depicted by the economics literature. To this point, therefore, it seems reasonable to rationalize that there is still so much to be learnt about psychological pricing.

This chapter is organized as follows. First, psychological pricing is defined, followed by an examination of theories that are applicable to the conceptualization of psychology of pricing. The next section of the chapter discusses psychological prices with a focus on reference prices. The last part of the chapter examines more recent developments in psychological pricing research (e.g., personality and cultural effects on the consumer's price perception). The concluding section of this chapter focuses on some challenges and prospects for researchers studying psychological pricing.

Conceptualization of psychological pricing

Hospitality managers face various pricing challenges everyday, including a question of how to price new products such as a new hotel package or a new menu item, or fix the price level of a new restaurant. Furthermore, managers are challenged when they have to set a new price for an existing product. Additional challenges exist when making a price adjustment, especially an increase when there is no noticeable increase in the quality of the product or accessories such as packaging. The intangible nature of hospitality products makes price setting and adjustment even more challenging.

Many price managers and consumers are aware of anomalies in pricing. Thus, there are pricing practices that depict a 'reverse' in the demand curve. For example, suppliers often offer price discounts during peak demand periods such as Christmas sales, happy hours at restaurants when demand is expected to be at the peak and no price increase when wait lines are long and seats are booked for months in advance. These are some of the examples of situations where psychological pricing is dominant. Interestingly, these pricing strategies do not comply with the traditional supply and demand rules of economics, and thus may even appear irrational from the economic perspective. Pricing managers are further challenged when they have to set a new price to meet the changing needs of the suppliers or distributors to reflect the changing costs of their capital requirements. It is even more interesting when pricing of products has to change to reflect the requirements of a local culture and available substitutes.

Psychology of pricing can be described as constituting an 'expansive subset of pricing research wherein prices and pricing are examined with respect to their human elements – that is, with respect to how humans attend to, perceive, process, and evaluate price information, as well as how they go about determining the price at which a particular item should be sold or purchased' (Miyazaki, 2003, p. 473). The psychological aspects of pricing encompass perception of price saving/discounts, perception of value, and perception of quality by the consumer of the price set by the sellers (Shapiro, 2000).

The behavioral pricing literature suggests that the attractiveness of a market price is determined by a comparison of the market price to an internal standard known as the *internal reference price* (Janiszewski and Lichtenstein, 1999; Kalwani and Yim, 1992, Krishnamurthi et al., 1992, p. 94; Kumar et al., 1998; Lattin and Bucklin, 1989). The notion of a reference price is grounded in considerations of the psychological dimension of price perception (Mazumdar et al., 2005). The theory of reference prices implies several phenomena that include the existence of a range of acceptable prices and an asymmetric market response to the reference price above and below the threshold (Raman and Bass, 2002).

These implications carry several managerial concerns in pricing hospitality products. Most important for managers to realize is that consumers do not have sufficient knowledge of the costs, profit margins, and even the true depth of discounts to appreciate what is a fair price. Due to this insufficiency, consumers may, for instance, be 'irrationally resistant' to a product or any improvement to a product that may carry a price increase. During price adjustments, managers must focus on two things: (1) the consumer's judgment of utility values; and (2) the consumer's judgment of transactional values, hence the issue of psychological considerations in pricing. Interestingly, consumers often tend to develop reference prices against which they measure any changes made to the current pricing strategies. Any significant deviation from the reference prices is likely to raise questions in consumers' mind.

Reference price

People view things in their environment through different perspectives. Consequently, there are always differing evaluations of the same conditions. Recall the example of a 'half empty glass' for a pessimist who looks at things from a loss perspective, while an optimist views the same phenomenon as 'a glass half full.' What is interesting is that the same glass and identical contents are perceived differently depending on the perspective of the consumer. Evaluative framing such as this has formed the core of discussion in social sciences (Ranyard et al., 2001).

In relation to pricing, it is generally accepted that consumers perceive the same price differently depending on various factors associated with their prior experience, the purchase environment, and the professional activities and demographics of the consumer. To illustrate this phenomenon, consider the following case. Thaler (1985) carried out a series of experiments in which respondents had to state the maximum price they would pay for a bottle of beer in the following hypothetical scenario (Thaler, 1985, p. 206):

You are lying on the beach on a hot day. All you have to drink is ice water. For the last hour you have been thinking about how much you would enjoy a nice cold bottle of your favorite brand of beer. A companion gets up to make a phone call and offers to bring back a beer from the only nearby place where beer is sold, a fancy resort hotel. He says that the beer might be expensive and so asks how much you are willing to pay for the beer. He says that he will buy the beer if it costs as much, or less than the price you state. But if it costs more than the price you state, he will not buy it. You trust your friend and there is no possibility of bargaining with the bartender. How much would you tell him?

Thaler (1985) gave this question to a group of participants in an executive development program who were regular beer drinkers. The median price given was $2.65 (1984 prices).

Another group was given a second version of the question in which the *fancy resort hotel* and the *Bartender* were replaced by a *small run-down store* and *store owner*. For this version, the median price given was $1.50. This difference in median prices is consistent with the view that respondents view things in the environment through different perspectives. This brings us to the discussion of psychological pricing and, in particular, reference pricing. Generally, it is accepted that consumers compare a market price to an internal reference price when judging the attractiveness of the product. For example, from the above study, Thaler stated that 'the measure of transactional utility depends on the price the individual pays compared to some reference price.' Similarly, Winer (1988, p. 205) explains that 'defining Po to be the observed retail price and Pr to be the individuals' internal reference price, the underlying assumption of this (behavioral pricing) is that the positive values of (Po − Pr) are perceived negatively and the negative values of (Po − Pr) are viewed positively.'

In an attempt to understand reference prices, various definitions have been offered. Monroe (1973) defines reference price as standards against which the purchase price of a product is judged. Another conceptualization of internal price offered by Briesch et al. (1997, p. 94) is, 'the predictive price expectation that is shaped by the consumer's prior experience and current purchase environment.' The definitions of reference price vary from those who view reference price as a point to those who view it as a range of acceptance/tolerance.

The theory of reference price offers a number of managerial implications:

1. The timing and magnitude of price promotions should ideally be influenced by the existence of reference prices and their effect on consumer demand (Kalyanaram and Winer, 1995).
2. The existence of reference prices and the manner in which they are formed influence brand choice and purchase quantity (Kumar et al., 1998).
3. Macro-economic factors such as inflation, unemployment, and interest rates impact reference price formation and hence should be considered in the evaluation of alternative pricing scenarios (Estelami et al., 2001).
4. The range of evoked prices moderates the effect of reference price, and hence has implications for pricing strategies such as 'every day low price' (EDLP) and 'high–low' pricing (Janiszewski and Lichtenstein, 1999).

Different conceptualizations of reference prices

Reference price, according to Monroe (2003, p. 641) is 'the price consumers use to compare the offered price of a product or service.' Reference price could be the price of a competitive product or from an ad for a comparable product noted by the consumer. In essence, reference price is used by consumers to psychologically maximize the utility in a transaction. The theoretical rationale for reference price comes from various perspectives including adaptation-level theory (Helson, 1964), social judgment theory (Sherif et al., 1965), and more recently the application of range theory (Janiszewski and Lichtenstein, 1999; Volkmann, 1951). In the pricing context, there are several conceptualizations of reference prices. As Garbarino and Slonim (2003, p. 230) posit, 'a preliminary step in discussing what reference price people use is showing that consumers are able to form distinct reference prices.' A number of researchers have proposed that there exist different reference prices (Klein and Oglethorpe, 1987). For example, Krause et al. (2006) discuss the existence of reservation price, market price, aspiration price, and the bargaining stance. Walton and McKersie (1965) discuss the existence of resistant price and target price. Chandrashekaran and Jagpal (1995) discuss different conceptualizations of reference prices (lowest price seen, normal, fair, and most willing to pay) based on consumer perception of value.

Theoretical background of pricing

The Weber–Fechner law

Developed by Weber and Fechner, the Weber law relates changes in a stimulus to the evoked response as follows: $\Delta S/S = C$ where S is a stimulus, ΔS is the just noticeable difference so that $S + \Delta S$ is perceived to be different from S, and C is a constant for each sensory stimulus. According to the above formula, the same level of response can be expected every time when the stimulus is increased by the same amount. The rate of change in the response is directly proportional to the rate of change in the stimulus.

Fechner added the mathematical part to the Weber law after analyzing subjective sensations using differential increments of stimulus to derive the Weber–Fechner law (see Laming, 1973). The Weber–Fechner law has been used by various researchers to demonstrate and investigate the concept of price threshold (Gabor and Granger, 1961; Monroe, 1973). The findings of these authors suggest that there exists an upper and a lower threshold point for any prices considered acceptable. The Weber–Fechner law provides a theoretical basis for determining such thresholds. Prices below the low threshold are considered too low that quality of the product becomes suspect; and prices above the high threshold are considered too high where incremental change in quality is not justified. This has been empirically tested by Monroe (2003).

Assimilation–contrast theory

Assimilation–contrast theory developed by Sheriff and Hovland (1961) proposes two concepts: *latitude of acceptance* and *price threshold*. The theory is related to the implications of the Weber–Fechner law. The 'latitude of acceptance' is similar to the acceptable range of prices discussed by Monroe (1973). Several marketing researchers have applied the theory of assimilation–contrast to examine pricing perception (Monroe, 1973, 2003; Sawyer and Dickson, 1984). Raman and Bass (1988, 2002) discuss the region of indifference about reference prices such that the prices within this region produce no change in perception. According to this theory, prices that are within the latitude of acceptance are assimilated and therefore acceptable. When prices fall outside the range, they are contrasted and their impact is strongly perceived.

Regarding the psychophysical phenomenon as it applies to pricing, it is important to refer to the work of Sherif et al. (1958). These authors conducted experiments to determine the effect of anchoring weight of a series of weights on people's judgments (concept explained in the next section). The assimilation effect is important since it provides the theoretical basis for latitude of acceptance (Raman and Bass, 2002). The assimilation–contrast theory suggests that the latitude of price acceptance will vary. For the customer who is exposed to a single price for a long time, the latitude is narrow. In contrast, when the consumer is exposed to various levels of prices during a certain time duration, that consumer may have wider latitude on price perception.

Adaptation level theory

Adaptation level theory can be used to motivate reference price and how consumers respond to new prices. Developed by Helson (1964), this theory hypothesizes that the perceived magnitude and effect of a stimulus at any given time depends on the relation of that stimulus to the preceding stimuli. The prior stimuli create an adaptation level and subsequent stimuli are judged in relation to it. The judgment and, consequently, the response to a stimulus depend on the relationship between the physical value of that stimulus and the value of the current adaptation level. The adaptation level is the value at which the scale of judgment is centered or anchored.

In the context of pricing and price response, the theory suggests that an adaptation level depends on the previous price experiences. The adaptation level is the reference price or what Emory (1970) calls the normal price. The reference price is an internal price that consumers have formed for a given product, but not necessarily what the seller is charging for the product (Raman and Bass, 2002).

Prospect theory

Some marketing authors have suggested that consumers may respond differently to price increases as compared to price reductions (Monroe, 1976; Raman and Bass, 1988). The suggestion is that consumers respond more negatively to price increases than they do positively to price decreases. Prospect theory by Kahneman and Tversky (1979) provides an explanation for this phenomenon. This theory was developed as an alternative to traditional utility theory in economics to explain the choice consumers face under risky conditions (Von Neuman and Morgensten, 1944). In the context of price response, it implies that an increase in price presents a loss in value and a decrease in the price leads to an increase in value.

Internal reference prices and correlates

Expected reference price

Also referred to as the market-framed price, the expected reference price is defined as the price the consumer or buyer expects the seller to charge for a given product (Bearden et al., 1992). It is commonly conceptualized based on historical prices in the marketplace

(Bearden et al., 1992). Since it is conceptualized as the market price, the expected reference price should be the market-framed price with no adjustment for personal preference (Garbarino and Slonin, 2003).

According to Krause et al. (2006), consumers rely on two fundamental types of information sources: private and public information. The private information is from within the firm, such as cost data and profit margins. Public information is the data from outside of the firm such as market price from various sources such as professional publications, annual reports, word-of-mouth (WOM), and the Internet. Both the private and public information contribute to the formation of the consumer's expected reference price.

In a market with many sellers and buyers, and where transactions are conducted in an anonymous manner, the expected price or market price represents the average price that maximizes social welfare (White et al., 1994, p. 441). In individual transactions, however, it is more appropriate to define the expected or market price as the 'average price for which comparable goods (products) have recently sold' (White et al., 1994, p. 441). Thus, the expected price may be used to evaluate the fairness of the purchase price.

Fair reference price

The following examples serve as an illustration of price fairness:

There is a commotion about the salary of managing director of a non-profit organization, 'De Hartstichting' (the 'Heart Foundation'), a foundation that combats heart diseases. In 2004, a newspaper reported that the managing director received a salary of over Ł170 000 annually.

Many contributors and collectors were furious and stopped their donations and their work for the foundation. According to them, the salary of the director was much too high and, therefore, unfair. The management of the foundation claimed that an experienced heart specialist was needed in order to lead the research and that experienced heart specialists often earn a lot more than Ł170 000. For many people, this explanation was insufficient. The foundation saw no other option than to discharge the managing director, who was not prepared to lower his salary. Despite this discharge, the reputation of 'De Hartstichting' was seriously damaged.

Also, the following excerption should enhance consumer perception of fair pricing (Krugman, 2004). Recently, it came to light that Amazon.com has been charging different customers different prices for movies, not books. The company insists that the price differentials were random, a way of testing the market. But many buyers accused the online retailer of tailoring its price to the consumer's characteristics. And even if Amazon's prices really were random, the outrage of those who had paid a few dollars extra suggests that 'dynamic pricing' is about to become a major consumer issue, and maybe even a political issue.

The issue of price fairness is very important since organizations need to understand whether consumers perceive prices and price adjustments as fair or unfair. Indeed, the issue of fairness has been addressed in various studies. Some of the findings reveal that when price is perceived unfair, consumers become unsatisfied (Oliver and Swan, 1989) and more price conscious (Sinha and Batra, 1999). Xia et al. (2004) report that if price is perceived unfair, consumers will complain and ask for refunds. Most interesting is the findings of Bougie et al. (2003) concerning price unfairness. These authors report that when consumers perceive the price to be unfair, they are likely to take punitive action against the company. The consumers will try to take revenge by not coming back, spreading negative WOM, or even using violence. Even more interesting is the research finding by Kahneman et al. (1986) who showed that in some cases people were even willing to disadvantage themselves in order to punish a seller who is perceived to be acting unfairly through their pricing systems. In brief, consumers may feel exploited.

Extant literature defines fair reference prices loosely, often referring to it as the judgment against a standard of fairness (Bearden et al., 1992) or a concept of what a good ought to cost (Winer, 1988). What is perceived as a fair price is therefore influenced by the market price (Bearden et al., 1992).

Various theoretical bases provide a conceptualization of price fairness. For example, the *dual entitlement principle* emphasizes that price should be a function of supply and demand changes and the seller's profit orientation (Kahneman and Thaler, 1986b). This principle suggests that consumers compare one price with another price or with a range of prices (Xia et al., 2004) and that this comparison price is what the consumers expect to pay, referred to as the expected reference price. The perceptions of price fairness are therefore based on a reference transaction and the belief that the transactor (e.g., the consumer, customer, employee, etc.) is entitled to the reference price and that the firm (e.g., merchant, employer, etc.) is likewise entitled to its reference profit (Campbell, 2006).

The dual entitlement principle hence implies that consumers should consider market prices that allow the seller some reasonable profit and the buyer, a reasonable value for money (Garbadino and Slonim, 2003, p. 230). From this presentation, it can be argued that fair price is not based on how attractive the product is, but on the value the buyer places on the product in the marketplace. But, because the seller's costs and profits are rarely known to the consumer, the consumer relies on previous experience and observations to develop fair prices. Garbadino and Slonim (2003, p. 230) suggest that '... because consumers will infer that even the lowest observed price leads to a reasonable profit, consumer perception of a fair price should be influenced by the lowest recently observed price *(unless in special occasions such as liquidation, etc.)'* (Italics added).

The context may also influence the perception of fair price (Mazumdar et al., 2005). The existence of different operation and profitability models for different organizations leads consumers to perceive fair price dependent on the context. For example, a consumer will expect the Hilton Hotel to charge differently for a room as compared to Motel 6. Thus, The Hilton may be looking at a high volume–high profit model versus Motel 6 operating on a high volume–low profit model. This does not prevent consumers from developing what is a fair price for each hotel or each operational model.

Another theoretical conceptualization of fair pricing derives from equity theory and distributive justice. Distributive justice is concerned with the fair allocation of resources among diverse members of a community. Fair allocation typically takes into account the total amount of goods to be distributed, the distributing procedure, and the pattern of distribution. Because societies have a limited amount of wealth and resources, a question arises as to how those benefits ought to be distributed. The common answer is that public assets should be distributed in a reasonable manner so that each individual receives a 'fair share.' Various principles might determine how goods are distributed. Equality, equity, and need are among the most common criteria. But the one most commonly applied to price is that equity should supersede. Thus, in any exchange relationship, people are entitled to receive a reward that is proportional to what they have invested in the relationship.

Reservation reference price

Reservation reference price is referred to as the least acceptable price to a party in a negotiation (Blount et al., 1996). From a buyer's perspective, it is the price above which the product will not be purchased and, consequently, it is the maximum that one is willing to pay (Garbarino and Slonim, 2003). Krause et al. (2006, p. 9) further describe the reservation price as that which '. . . represents the price at which a buyer will be indifferent about buying a good/product from a particular supplier or the *walk-away* from the negotiation.' Reservation price applies both to the consumer and the seller or supplier. At the reservation price, buyers consider going elsewhere or dealing with different suppliers based on the BATNA (Best Alternative to Negotiated Agreement: Fisher and Ury, 1981). To the seller, the reservation price is the lowest acceptable selling price and the point at which the seller will walk away from the negotiation and consider dealing with other buyers (see Figures 13.2 and 13.3 for positive and negative negotiation of a price

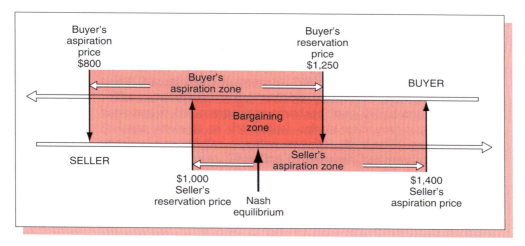

Figure 13.2
Positive bargaining/negotiation zone (*Adapted from* Krause et al., 2006)

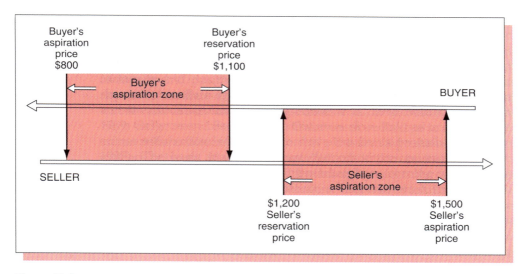

Figure 13.3
Negative bargaining/negotiating zone (*Adapted from* Krause et al. 2006)

between the consumer and supplier). From the consumer perspective, the reservation price or the highest price one is willing to pay is thought to be a function of the price substitutes available and personal factors such as income and preferences (Kristensen and Garling, 1997). From a supplier's perspective, many factors may affect the lowest price acceptable. For example, a seller or a supplier could consider selling below the cost price to keep the workers for a while. Therefore, the seller's reservation price is difficult for a buyer to determine (Krause et al., 2006, p. 9). Reservation price becomes important in purchase situations where bargaining and negotiation take place (e.g. purchase on the Internet: eBay, Priceline, Hotels.Com, etc.). Related to negotiation and reservation price is the concept of negotiation zone. The bargaining zone incorporates both the buyer and seller reservation prices (White et al., 1994, p. 441). The bargaining zone (see Figure 13.2) is the region between the buyer's and seller's reservation prices and is the region within which the settlement is likely to occur (Raiffa, 1992).

Figure 13.3 illustrates the discrepancy between the seller and the buyer. The two parties do not reach an agreement.

According to Garbarino and Slonim (2003), because reservation prices incorporate personal preferences, the level of reservation price should be influenced by the level of desire for a given product. If the consumer considers a given product important, then he or she is likely to have a reservation price that matches that of the supplier and a purchase is likely to occur. Otherwise, one of the parties in the purchase process will walk away. The reference prices discussed above are used by consumers at various times. The question arises as to what factors really influence the formation of these reference prices.

Price evaluations

Past experience

Lattin and Bucklin (1989) found that consumers use previous promotional prices as the reference prices. Promotional prices tend to influence the consumers' transactional utility (Thaler, 1985). Therefore, it can be argued that the greater the experience a consumer has had with promotions the lower the internal reference price developed for a particular product. This explains why frequently placing products on promotions could in the long run lead to reduced profitability. Also, Dickson and Sawyer (1990) found that the most recent prices encountered by consumers during a purchase are the more influential ones. Thus, the more recent prices have a greater influence on the formation of reference prices as compared to the older ones.

Atmospherics

The issue of content effect has been discussed extensively in psychology and marketing literature. That the environment in which an activity is taking place will influence its performance or outcome has been empirically demonstrated. Hotels and restaurants, for example, differ on the levels of service offered, location, menu range, and other factors. To illustrate, a room at The Hilton costing $190 a night will be perceived a good deal as compared to a room at Motel 6 costing $80 a night. Therefore, the content in which a price is charged determines what consumers will refer to as an acceptable or a fair price. It would be unfair to discuss psychological pricing without mentioning other aspects and perspectives of psychological pricing that impact pricing decisions and perceptions.

Personality types

Empirical evidence suggests that the use of price as a quality indicator is especially popular when consumers are unfamiliar with the brands or products being evaluated (Peterson, 1970; Venkataraman, 1981). Generally, higher prices are considered an indication of better quality products. To examine the two variables, image and performance, DeBono (2000) proposed that the way price is perceived in relation to these two variables depends on the individuals perceiving it. Thus, is it possible that different individuals are influenced to perceive the same product price differently? DeBono (2000) attempted to answer the question: Are there individuals who respond to price as an indicator of image and, conversely, are there individuals who are typically influenced by price because they perceive price as an indicator of quality and performance?

Earlier, Snyder (1974, 1979) proposed that there is a reason to believe that these contrasting individuals may be identified by the psychological construct of self-monitoring. According to the self-monitoring theory of social psychology, people differ substantially in the way they regulate their self in social situations (Snyder, 1974). The high self-monitors typically strive to be the person called for by different situations in which they find themselves (Snyder and Monson, 1975). Thus, they exert more expressive control over their social behavior and tend to adapt their appearance and acts to specific situations. The behavior of the high self-monitors will therefore display a marked difference depending on the situation shifts so as to convey the desirable images to others (Danheiser and Graziano, 1982).

According to Snyder and DeBono (1985), since these high self-monitoring individuals are concerned with being the right person in the right place and at the right time, they ought to be sensitive to their images of the self that they project in given situations. Due to this responsive characteristic, these individuals are likely to be attentive to and easily influenced by messages that convey information about images that they acquire and project by using products purchased at a certain price. Thus, if a high self-monitoring individual perceives that a certain price will enhance self-image, he or she will readily evaluate that product higher than one of a lower price. That is, a high self-monitoring individual will be willing to pay higher prices on a product so long as it helps him or her enhance self image.

On the contrary, low self-monitoring individuals do not attempt to mold their behavior to fit situational and personal considerations (Snyder and Monson, 1975). Thus, their self-presentation and expressive behavior seem, in a functional sense, to be controlled from within by their affective states (they express as they feel) and not as monitored, controlled, and molded by the situation (Snyder, 1974). Thus, low self-monitors typically display a substantial correspondence between their behaviors and their private attitudes in social contexts (Snyder and Swann, 1976). These low self-monitoring individuals tend to guide their behavior based on inner sources such as attitudes, feelings, and dispositions (Snyder and Tanke, 1976). Then the question arises whether high and low self-monitoring individuals would respond to the price differently.

This self-monitoring scale developed by Snyder and DeBono (1985) is known to divide individuals into high and low self-monitoring. The results indicate that the differential favorability of high and low self-monitoring individuals to image and quality appeals is accompanied by differences in the consumer's willingness to spend on a product. The results of this study showed that for the high self-monitoring individuals image was worth the price, while quality was what mattered to the low self-monitoring individuals. Thus, for the high self-monitors, image drives the price acceptance (Snyder and DeBono, 1985).

As described in Figure 13.4, personality types can be used effectively in understanding usage of types of currency in different hospitality contexts. Hu (2005) demonstrated that personality types, self-monitoring,

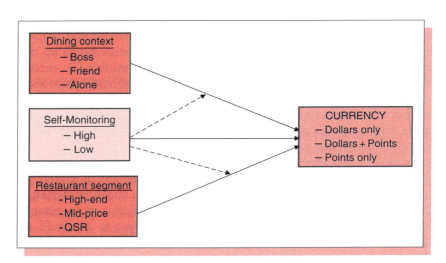

Figure 13.4
Personality types and currency usage in restaurant dining contexts

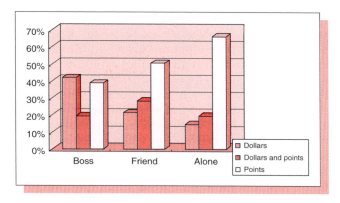

Figure 13.5
Currency preferences for companions when dining out

and need for cognition can significantly affect consumer choice for currencies: dollars only, points only, and combined points and dollars depending on the nature of dining context – dining with the boss, a friend, or alone. In her dissertation, Hu (2005) explored the application of personality types to pricing strategies in the hospitality field. Results of her study indicate that self-monitoring has a significant impact on the consumer's currency preference. High self-monitors were more likely to prefer to pay with dollars only than to pay with points only. Moreover, consumers who dine with boss were less likely to prefer to pay with dollars and points or points only as opposed to paying with dollars only, than the respondents who dine alone. Furthermore, the interaction effect of self-monitoring and companions was significantly associated with currency preference. High self-monitors dining with boss were more likely to prefer to pay with dollars only than pay with dollars and points or points only. This study provides the characteristics of customers dealing with the different currency options (see Figure 13.5). By understanding the individual personality differences of customers when using different currencies, restaurants could decide whether or not to implement different currency prices based on their target markets. Large restaurant chains may specifically target different personality types with specific promotional programs to meet their self-monitoring needs.

Cultural differences

Hofstede (1991) defines culture as the 'software of the mind' that guides us in our daily interactions. Hofstede goes further to indicate that every person carries within himself or herself patterns of thinking, feeling, and potential acting that were learned throughout their lifetime. Much of it has been acquired in early childhood, because at that time a person is most susceptible to learning and assimilating. As soon as certain patterns of thinking, feeling, and acting are established within a person's mind, the person must unlearn these before being able to learn something different, and unlearning is more difficult than learning for the first time.

Culture can be described as a shared set of basic assumptions and values, with resultant behavioral norms, attitudes, and beliefs that manifest themselves in systems and institutions as well as behavioral patterns and non-behavioral items (Dahl, 1998, 2000). There are various levels to culture, ranging from the easily observable outer layers (such as behavioral conventions) to the inner layers that are increasingly more difficult to grasp (such as assumptions and values). Culture is shared among members of a group or society, and has an interpretive function for the members of that group. Culture is situated between the human nature on the one hand and the individual personality on the other. Culture is not inheritable or genetic, but culture is learned. Although all members of a group or society share their culture, expressions of culture-resultant behavior are modified by the individual's personality.

Earlier studies had indicated that a majority of Chinese restaurants in the United States does not use 99 as a price ending. This resistance is attributed to the cultural and traditional beliefs about numbers and the meanings that they communicate in Chinese (Simmons and Schindler, 2002). For example, in the Chinese language, the word for digit 8 sounds similar to the word meaning 'rich' (Simmons and Schindler, 2002). Even today, according to Parsa and Hu (2003), the digit 8 is the most commonly used price ending digit in China and other Asian countries where Chinese culture has a strong influence. The digit 4 on the other hand is rarely used in Chinese culture as it is treated as a symbol of bad luck, similar to the assumptions about number 13 as a carrier of bad luck among Western cultures. In fact, in the Chinese language, the word for digit 4 is pronounced similar to the word 'death' in Chinese. Thus, usage of digit 4 has become a taboo in the Chinese culture (Simmons and Schindler, 2002) Hu and Parsa (2004).

To further illustrate this phenomenon, here are some examples from Taiwan. People prefer to begin business or get married on the 8th day of the month since digit 8 is considered a good luck number (Simmons and Schindler, 2002). Most hospitals and tall buildings in Taiwan avoid the use of digit 4 in identifying floors, consumers are reluctant to use digit 4 at the end of the telephone numbers or even as auto tags, and taxi cab companies avoid the use of digit 4 at the beginning or end of the number unlike in the United States where the one commonly noted on taxi cabs is (444–4444). Parsa and Hu (2003) hypothesized that there are significant differences in the usage of digits 1 through 9 as price endings in the Taiwanese restaurant menus. These authors further proposed that digit 4 would be the least used while digit 8 would be the most used in price endings. The data obtained showed that the least used digits were 1 and 4. The low usage of digit 4 was attributed to the cultural taboos associated with it (Parsa, 2004).

Later, Hu et al. (2006) investigated price-ending strategies of European restaurant menus and compared them to the strategies used in the United States and Taiwan. Their findings demonstrated that the pricing practices of European restaurants were different from those in the United States and were more akin to those used in Taiwan. Since the introduction of the Euro as the common European currency, Europeans have used price-ending digits in great diversity. The most commonly used price ending in the European restaurant industry was 0, with only slight usage of 5 and 9. The reason for the predominant usage of 0 may be 'the ease of communication,' because it is part of a more general phenomenon regarding the use of numbers in human communication (Suri et al., 2003). Still some American branded quick service restaurants such as McDonald's tended to use digit 9 predominantly.

Price-ending strategies and theoretical explanations

In spite of the extensive use of the odd–even psychological pricing strategy in the marketplace, very few studies have explored the theoretical rationale for this ubiquitous phenomenon. A study conducted by Parsa and Naipaul (2005) offers theoretical explanations and empirical support for this pricing strategy practiced in the fine-dining and quick-service restaurant segments. This study is particularly important because it offers theoretical rationale for the often-puzzling price-ending phenomenon. All four hypotheses posited by the Price-endings and Consumer Behavior Model (PCBM) from this study were empirically supported (Figure 13.6).

Interestingly in this study, restaurant operators stated that they do intentionally manipulate price endings using 00 and 99 for distinct purposes. Restaurant marketers from fine-dining restaurants intentionally use 00 as a pre-purchase signal of product and service quality, while marketers of quick-service restaurants promote high value attributes using 99 price endings. The findings of this study indicate that marketing incentives exist for both restaurant segments to use different signaling mechanisms through price-endings: quality (00 endings) for high end restaurants and value (99 endings) for quick service restaurants.

In conclusion, this study demonstrated that theoretical explanation for price-ending phenomenon can be understood when one considers *signaling theory* (Boulding and Kirmani, 1993; Chaiken, 1979; Spence, 1974) and the *persuasion knowledge model* (PKM) (Friestad and Wright, 1994). According to signaling theory, hospitality marketers *intentionally* use 0 price-endings to signal quality image of their products; and again *deliberately* use 9 endings when they have to signal high

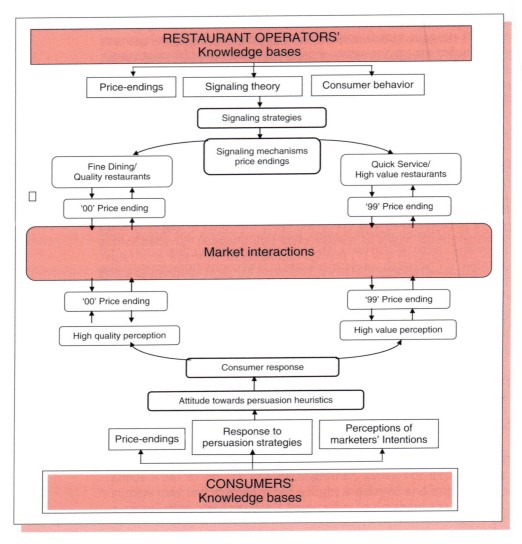

Figure 13.6
Price-endings and consumer behavior model (PCBM) (Naipaul and Parsa, 2002)

value attributes of their products. Further empirical support for this observation was provided by Schindler et al.'s (2006) working paper and Collins and Parsa (2006). The PKM model states that when consumers are exposed to selected marketing strategies repeatedly over a long period, they are more likely to relate the marketing message with the product attributes. When consumers are exposed to 99 price-endings for a long time with high value products, then they are most likely to associate 99 price-endings with high value products. It is schematically shown in Figure 13.6.

Agenda for pricing research in hospitality and tourism

The phenomenon of psychological pricing explains many of the anomalies observed in the pricing practices in the field of hospitality and tourism. The hospitality and tourism field is dominated by services with high heterogeneity, intangibility, production/consumption simultaneity, and shorter distribution channels. Under these conditions, it is difficult to simply adapt pricing strategies that are developed primarily in manufacturing industries. Thus, pricing of services has been a major challenge for many hospitality and tourism marketers. Many studies were undertaken recently focusing on pricing of services (Berry and Yadav, 1996; Guiltinan, 1989; Monroe 2003; Turley and Cabaniss, 1995). In the field of hospitality and tourism, research on pricing in general and pricing of services in particular has been sparse. Since the publication of Kreul's (1982) paper on price-endings in restaurants, research on pricing in this field did not receive enough attention. Numerous topics in this area remain unexplored.

In the field of hospitality and tourism, interested readers may want to follow the recent publications on pricing related topics by authors like, alphabetically, Canina, Crompton, Enz, Kim, Kime, Matilla, Oh, Parsa, Schwartz, and Shoemaker. The field of pricing is very interdisciplinary in nature with ample opportunities for further research. This chapter closes with some suggestions for future research on pricing in hospitality and tourism as listed below. These topics are presented only as possibilities for further exploration but not as tested paths of research.

- Possible mechanisms to influence reference prices by using marketing communication strategies
- Change in consumers' willingness to pay when service/product levels change
- Use of digital technology to communicate pricing choices in restaurants and making dynamic changes in restaurant pricing structures
- Effectiveness of dynamic pricing strategies that change according to the time of the day or day of the week in restaurants
- Price-ending strategies to maximize revenues at different levels of service
- Personality types and pricing strategies in tourism – the relationship between tourist profiles and price tolerance levels
- Cultural differences and pricing strategies in hospitality and tourism
- Cultural differences, cross-border travel, and pricing strategies in hospitality

- Effectiveness of price match guarantees in the field of hospitality and tourism
- Why busy restaurants and high-occupancy hotels do not raise prices in spite of obvious high demand?
- Pricing strategies for hospitality and tourism products for maximum returns on investment when atmospherics change
- Pricing strategies in the conventions and meeting planning industry
- Role of price discounts in revenue generation – identification of optimal discount points
- Price presentation and discount formats in hospitality. Effective price discounting strategies for various segments of the lodging industry – 'one glove doesn't fit all'.
- E-commerce and pricing strategies in hospitality and tourism: pricing strategies when hotel and travel reservations are made on-line.
- Price presentations and Internet hospitality purchases.
- Short-term pricing strategies and their effect on consumer satisfaction and loyalty.

References

Bearden, W. O., Kaicker, A., Smith de Borrero, M., and Urbany, J. E. (1992). Examining alternative operational measures of internal reference prices. In J. Sherry Jr. and B. Sternthal (Eds.), *Advances in Consumer Research, 19*, 629–635. Provo, UT: Association for Consumer Research.

Berry, L. L. and Yadav, M. S. (1996). Capture and communicate value in the pricing of services. *Sloan Management Review.* (*Summer*), 41–51.

Blount, S., Thomas-Hunt , M. C., and Neale, M. A. (1996). The price is right – or is it? A reference point model of dyadic price negotiations. *Organizational Behavior and Human Decision Processes, 68*, 1–12.

Bougie, J. R. G., Pieters, F. G. M., and Zeelenberg, M. (2003). Angry customers don't come back, they get back: The experience and behavioral implications of anger and dissatisfaction in services. *Journal of the Academy of Marketing Science, 31*, 377–393.

Boulding, W. and Kirmani, A. (1993). A consumer-side experimental examination of signaling theory. *Journal of Marketing, 20*, 111–123.

Briesch, R., Krishnamurthi, L., Mazumdar, T., and Raj, S. P. (1997). A comparative analysis of consumer internal reference price formulation. *Journal of Consumer Research, 24*, 202–214.

Campbell, M. (2006) *'Who Says?!': How the Source of Price Information and the Direction of Price Change Influence Perceptions of Price Fairness*. Retrieved August, 25, 2006, from http://www.gsb.uchicago.edu/kilts/research/workshop/WorkshopPapers/campbell.pdf

Chaiken, S. (1979). Communicator attractiveness and persuasion. *Journal of Personality and Social Psychology, 37*, 1387–1397.

Chandrashekaran, R. and Jagpal, H. S. (1995). Measuring internal reference price: some preliminary results. *Pricing Strategy and Practice*, 3, 28–34.

Collins, M. and Parsa, H. G. (2005). Pricing strategies to maximize revenues in the hotel industry. *International Journal of Hospitality Management*, 25, 91–107.

Coulter, K. S. (2001). Odd-ending price underestimation: An experimental examination of left-to-right processing effects. *Journal of Product and Brand Management*, 10 (5), 276–92.

Dahl, S. (1998). *Communications and Culture Transformation* [online]. Intercultural Research Index-MA Intercultural Communication (University of Luton) – EuropaCom Educational. Retrieved August 10, 2006, from http://www.stephweb.com/capstone/0.htm

Dahl, S. (2000). Introduction to intercultural communication. In Dahl, Stephan (Eds.) *Intercultural Skills for Business*, ECE, London.

DeBono, K. G. (2000). Attitude functions and consumer psychology: Understanding perceptions of product quality. In G. M. Maio and J. M. Olson (Eds.) *Why we Evaluate: The Functions of Attitudes* (pp. 195–221). Mahwah, NJ: Erlbaum.

Danheiser, P. R. and Graziano, W. G. (1982). Self-monitoring and cooperation as a self-presentational strategy. *Journal of Personality and Social Psychology*, 42, 495–505.

Dickson, P. R. and Sawyer, A. G. (1990). The price knowledge and search of supermarket shoppers. *Journal of Marketing*, 54, 42–53.

Emory, F. (1970). Some psychological aspects of price. In B. Taylor, G. Will (Eds.) *Pricing Strategy*. Princeton, NJ: Brandon/Systems Press. 98–111.

Estelami, H. (2001). An exploratory study of the effects of price presentation tactics on evaluation efforts and accuracy in multi-dimensional prices. Paper presented at the Annual Pricing Conference, Fordham University, New York.

Estelami, H., Lehmann, D. R., and Holden, A. C. (2001). Macroeconomic determinants of consumer price knowledge: a meta-analysis of our decades of research. *International Journal of Research in Marketing*, 18, 341–355.

Fisher, R. and Ury, W. (1981). *Getting to Yes*, London, UK: Business Books Ltd.

Friestad, M. and Wright, P. (1994). The persuasion knowledge model: How people cope with persuasion attempts. *Journal of Consumer Research*, 21, 1–31

Gabor, A. and Granger, C. (1961). On the price consciousness of consumers. *Applied Statistics*, 10 (3), 170–88.

Garbarino, E. and Slonim, R. L. (2003). Interrelationships and distinct effects of internal reference prices on perceived expensiveness and demand. *Psychology and Marketing*, 20 (3), 227–248.

Grewal, D., Marmorstein, H., and Sharma, A. (1996). Communicating price information through semantic cues: the effects of situation and discount size. *Journal of Consumer Research*, *23*, 148–55.

Guiltinan J. P. (1989). A classification of switching costs with implications for relationship marketing. In T. L. Childers, R. P. Bagozzi, and J. P. Peter (Eds.) *AMA Winter Educators' Conference: Marketing Theory and Practice*, Chicago, IL: AMA,

Guiltinan J. P. (1989). A conceptual framework for pricing consumer services. In Mary Jo Bitner and Lawrence a Crosby. (Eds) *Designing Winning Service Strategy*, Chicago, IL: American Marketing Association. 11–15.

Helson, H. (1964). *Adaptation-Level Theory*. New York, NY: Harper and Row.

Hu, H. H., Parsa, H. G., and Zhao, J. (2006). Magic of price-ending choices in European restaurants, and a comparison to USA and Taiwan. *International Journal of Contemporary Hospitality Management*, 18 (2 and 3), 110–123.

Hu, H. H. (2005) *Personality Types and Consumer Preferences for Multiple Currency Usages: A Study of the Restaurant Industry*. Unpublished doctoral dissertation submitted to the Hospitality Management, Ohio State University, Columbus, OH.

Hu, H. H. and Parsa, H. G. (2004). Pricing strategies and cultural differences in the foodservice industry: a study of three European countries. *EuroCHRIE Congress*, Ankara, Turkey (November).

Hofstede, G. (1991). *Cultures and Organizations*. Berkshire: McGraw-Hill Book Company, Europe.

Janiszewski, C. and Lichtenstein. D. R. (1999). A range theory account of price perception. *Journal of Consumer Research*, *25*, 353–368.

Kahneman, D., Knetsch, J., and Thaler, R. (1986b). Fairness as a constraint on profit seeking: Entitlements in the market. *American Economic Review*, *76*, 728–741.

Kahneman, D. and Tversky, A. (1979). Prospect theory: An analysis of decision under risk. *Econometrica*, *XVLII*, 263–291.

Kalwani, M. U. and Yim, C. K. (1992). Consumer price and promotion expectations: An experimental study. *Journal of Marketing Research*, *29*, 90–100.

Kalyanaram, G. and Winer, R. S. (1995). Empirical generalizations from reference price research. *Marketing Science*, *14*, 161–169.

Klein, N. M. and Oglethorpe, J. E. (1987). Cognitive reference points in consumer decision making. In M. Wallendorf, P. Anderson, (Eds.), *Advances in Consumer Research*, Association for Consumer Research, Provo, UT, *14*, 183–187.

Kotler, P., Bowen, J., and Makens, J. (1999). *Marketing for Hospitality and Tourism*, Upper Saddle River, NJ: Prentice Hall.

Krause, D., Terpend, R. and Petersen, K. (2006). Bargaining stances and outcomes in industrial negotiations. *Journal of Supply Chain Management*, *42* (3), 4–15.

Kreul, L. (1982). Magic numbers: psychological aspects of menu pricing. *Cornell HRA Quarterly*, 23, 70–5.

Krishnamurthi, L., Mazumdar, T., and Raj, S. P. (1992). Asymmetric response to price in consumer brand choice and purchase quantity decisions. *Journal of Consumer Research*, *19*, 387–400.

Kristensen, H. and Garling, T. (1997). The effects of anchor points and reference points on negotiation processes and outcome. *Organizational Behavior and Human Decision Processes*, *71*, 85–94.

Krugman, P. (2004). What Price Fairness? From the *New York Times*, October 4, 2000, p. A35. The New York Times Company. Retrieved January, 2007, from http://www2.sims.berkeley.edu/courses/is231/f02/amazon_pricing.pdf

Kumar, V., Karande, K. and Reinartz, W. J. (1998). The impact of internal and external reference prices on brand choice and the moderating role of contextual variables, *Journal of Retailing*, *74* (3), 401–425.

Laming, D. (1973). *Mathematical Psychology*. New York, NY: Academic Press.

Lattin, J. M. and Bucklin, R. E. (1989). Reference effects of price and promotion on brand choice behavior. *Journal of Marketing Research*, *26*, 299–310.

Mazumdar, T., Raj, S. P., and Sinha, I. (2005). Reference price research: Review and propositions. *Journal of Marketing*, *69* (4), 84–102.

Miyazaki, D. A. (2003). Guest editorial: The psychology of pricing on the internet. *Psychology and Marketing*, *20* (6), 471–476.

Monroe, K. B. (1973). Buyers' subjective perceptions of price. *Journal of Marketing Research*, *8* (2), 248–251.

Monroe, K. B. (1990), *Pricing: Making Profitable Decisions* (2nd ed.), New York, NY: McGraw-Hill.

Monroe, K. B. (2003) *Pricing: Making Profitable Decisions* (3rd ed.), New York, NY: McGraw-Hill.

Monroe, K. B. (1976). The influence of price differences and brand familiarity on brand preferences. *Journal of Consumer Research*, *3*, 42–49.

Monroe, K. B. and Lee, A. (1999). Remembering vs. knowing: Issues in buyers' processing price information. *Journal of the Academy of Marketing Science*, *27*, 207–225.

Nagle, T. T. and Holden, R. K. (1995), *The Strategy and Tactics of Pricing* (2nd ed.), Englewood Cliffs, NJ: Prentice-Hall.

Naipaul, S. and Parsa, H. G. (2001 February). 'Price Endings as Communication Cues, and Consumer Response Behavior: A Study of the Restaurant Industry,' *Cornell HRA Quarterly*, *42* (1), 26–37.

Naipaul, S. and Parsa, H. G. (2002). Role of quality and value perceptions in psychological pricing: a study of hospitality marketers. *Fifth Annual Pricing Conference*. Fordham University: New York.

Narasimhan, C. (1984). A price discrimination theory of coupons. *Marketing Science*, *3*, 128–147.

Oliver, R. L. and Swan, J. E. (1989). Consumer perceptions of interpersonal equity and satisfaction in transactions: Field survey approach. *Journal of Marketing*, *53*, 21–35.

Parsa, H. G. and Hu, H. H. (2003). Image communication, cultural differences and price ending practices: An analysis of restaurant menu from Taiwan. *International CHRIE Annual Conference*, *109*, Palm Spring. CA.

Parsa, H. G. and Hu, H. H. (2004). Price ending practices and cultural differences in the food service industry: a study of Taiwanese restaurants. *Food Service Technology*, *4*, 21–30.

Parsa, H. G. and Naipaul, S. (2005). Price-ending practices, marketing episodes and consumers' response behavior: a reciprocal relationship. *Advances in Hospitality and Leisure*, *1* (1), 77–82.

Naipaul, S. and Parsa, H. G. (2001). Menu price endings that communicate value and quality. *Cornell Hotel and Restaurant Administration Quarterly*, *42*, 26–37.

Peterson, R. A. (1970). The price-perceived quality relationship: Experimental evidence. *Journal of Marketing Research*, *1*, 525–528.

Raiffa, H. (1992). Game theory at the University of Michigan, 1948–1952. *Toward a History of Game Theory* (Annual Supplement to Volume 24, *History of Political Economy*), E. Roy Weintraub (Ed.) Duke University Press, Durham, 165–175.

Raman, K. and Bass, F. M. (1988). *A General Test of Reference Price Theory in the Presence of Threshold Effects*. Working paper, University of Texas, Dallas.

Raman, K. and Bass, F. M. (2002). A general test of reference price theory in the presence of threshold effects, *Tijdschrift voor Economie en Management*, *XLVII* (2), 205–226.

Ranyard, R., Charlton, J., and Williamson, J. (2001). The role of reference prices in consumers' willingness to pay judgments: Thaler's beer pricing task revisited. *Acta Psychologica*, *106*, 265–283.

Sawyer, A. G. and Dickson, P. (1984). Psychological perspectives on consumer response to sales promotion. In Katherine Jocz (Ed.) *Research on Sales Promotion: Collected Papers*, Cambridge, MA: Marketing Science Institute.

Schindler, R. M. (1992). A coupon is more than a low price: Evidence from a shopping-simulation study. *Psychology and Marketing*, *9*, 431– 451.

Schindler, R. M., Parsa, H. G., and Naipaul, S. (2006). Retail managers' price-ending beliefs. Working Paper. Dept of Marketing, Rutgers University, Camden, NJ.

Shapiro, B. P. (1968). The psychology of pricing. *Harvard Business Review*, *46*, 14–25 and 160.

Sherif, M. and Hovland, C. (1961). *Social Judgment*. New Haven, CT: Yale University Press.

Sherif, M., Taub, D., and Hovland, C. I. (1958). Assimilation and contrast effects of anchoring stimuli on judgments. *Journal of Experimental Psychology*, *55*, 150–155.

Sherif, C. W., Sherif, M., and Nebergall, R. E. (1965). *Attitude and Attitude Change: The Social Judgment-Involvement Approach*. Philadelphia: W. B. Saunders.

Simmons, L. and Schindler, R. (2002). Cultural superstitions and the price endings used in Chinese advertising. *Journal of International Marketing*, *11*, 101–11.

Sinha, I. R. and Batra, R. (1999). The effect of consumer price consciousness on private label purchases. *International Journal of Research in Marketing*, *16*, 237–251.

Suri, R., Anderson, R., and Kotlov, V. (2003). The use of 9-ending prices: contrasting United States with Poland. *European Journal of Marketing*, *38* (1), 56–72.

Snyder, M. (1974). Self–monitoring of expressive behavior. *Journal of Personality and Social Psychology*, *30* (4), 526–537.

Snyder, M. (1979). Self-monitoring processes. In L. Berkowitz (Ed.) *Advances in Experimental Social Psychology*. New York, NY: Academic Press. *12*, 85–125.

Snyder, M. and DeBono, K. G. (1985). Appeals to images and claims about quality: Understanding the psychology of advertising. *Journal of Personality and Social Psychology*, *49*, 586–597.

Snyder, M. and Monson, T. C. (1975). Persons, situations, and the control of social behavior. *Journal of Personality and Social Psychology*, *32*, 637–644.

Snyder, M. and Swann, W. B., Jr. (1976). When actions reflect attitudes: The politics of impression management. *Journal of Personality and Social Psychology*, *34*, 1034–1042.

Snyder, M. and Tanke, E. D. (1976). Behavior and attitude, some people are more consistent than others. *Journal of Personality*, *36* (5), 211–220.

Spence, A. M. (1974). *Market Signaling: Information Transfer in Hiring and Related Processes*. Harvard University Press. Cambridge, Massachusetts.

Thaler, R. (1985). Mental accounting and consumer choice. *Marketing Science*, *4* (3), 199–214.

Turley, L. W. and Cabannis, R. F. (1995). Price knowledge for services: an empirical investigation. *Journal of Professional Services Marketing*, *12* (1), 39–52.

Venkataraman, V. K .(1981). Price quality relationship in an experimental setting. *Journal of Advertising Research*, *21*, 49–52.

Volkmann, J. (1951). Scales of judgment and their implications for social psychology. In J. H. Rohrer, M. Sherif, (Eds.), *Social Psychology at the Crossroads* New York, (pp. 273–296). NY: Harper.

von Neumann, J. and Morgenstern, O. (1944). *Theory of Games and Economic Behavior*, Princeton University Press, Princeton NJ.

Walton, R. E. and McKersie, R. B. (1965). *A Behavioral Theory of Labor Negotiation*. New York: McGraw-Hill.

White, S. B., Valley, K., Bazerman, M., Neale M., and Peck, S. (1994). Alternative models of price behavior in dyadic negotiations: Market prices, reservation prices, and negotiator aspirations. *Organizational Behavior and Human Decision Processes*, 57, 430–447.

Winer, R. S. (1988). Behavioral perspective on pricing: buyers' subjective perceptions of price revisited. In T. M. Devinney (Eds.), *Issues in Pricing: Theory and Research*, Lexington Books, Lexington, MA.

Xia, L., Monroe, K. B., and Cox, J. L. (2004). The price is unfair! *Journal of Marketing*, 68, 1–15.

Part Four

Destination Marketing

CHAPTER 14

Destination branding and marketing: The role of marketing organizations

Chris Ryan and Huimin Gu

Introduction

The purpose of this chapter is to examine destination marketing and its relationship with branding. From this relationship, it is argued, complex and multi-layered implications arise whereby both image and marketing organizations become embroiled in wider social and environmental issues, while continuing to be funded on what, in effect, is only one of their several functions. The chapter first briefly reviews the academic literature, and then initially contests the concept that destination marketing actually exists – a stance that is adopted to (a) show the complexities of definition and (b) to argue that one primary function of destination marketing organizations is the manufacture of image and not product. However, subsequent discussion begins to modify this initial stance through the argument that tourism is about an experience of people, activities and interactions with the characteristics of place, thereby giving rise to the notion that image of place predicates expectation that in itself is a factor in the evaluation of experience. In short, the image, not the physical structure or nature of the activities, is the product generated by destination marketing organizations (DMOs). The chapter also draws attention to the different markets to which the DMO must direct its promotional efforts – different not only in terms of tourists as final consumers of place, but also in terms of other stakeholders who evaluate the promotional effort of the marketing organization for their own reasons. It also suggests that image creation has to be considered within a wider context of mobilities, and that again there are implications for the nature of the destination. Reference is made to Butler's destination life cycle, and amendments are suggested that relate the cycle to a process of localization, globalization and glocalization. From this arises the final section of the chapter wherein it is suggested that DMOs are increasingly being placed in a position where a further stakeholder group is important, as both they and tourism in general become subsumed into policies of economic and social development. This finally gives rise to possible future directions for further research.

The nature of destination image

There exists a significant amount of academic literature on destinations and their marketing, especially with reference to the creation and composition of place image. Image of place has been stated as possessing importance because of the nature of the purchase decision. It has been argued that visitors may possess little direct experience of destinations prior to their visit, and, by the very nature of tourism involving travel *to* a destination, are unable to try or test the place before purchase. Like many other examples in the services industry literature, tourism is characterized by purchases of the intangible. It is an experience that is purchased – as the tangible components such as hotel accommodation are not actually purchased; rather, what is purchased is a *right of use* for a period of time. In addition, such rented items often represent an ancillary or support role in the holiday or trip, and the experience (the intangible core of tourism) is born of the interaction between visitor and place, and the people of the place. These latter groups include not only local residents, but also industry intermediaries (the guides, bus drivers, and others who themselves may, or may not, be permanent residents) and other tourists. Indeed, image of place possesses importance in that for many tourists the main people with whom they travel and party will be other tourists – the people in the hotels, the others in the tour party, the fellow passengers on cruises, and the similar spirits on the adventure holiday. Consequently, given that a fulfilling sharing of experience can enhance the quality of that experience, it becomes important that fellow travelers/tourists possess similarities of outlook, background, and expectations. This degree of homogeneity within groups will create the harmonious relationships required for enhanced experiences (Trauer and Ryan, 2005).

Given the complex nature of place as tourism product, the composition of image has attracted significant attention from researchers. Hunt (1971) was among the first to identify the importance and role of image. Subsequently, there have been studies of both the composition and creation of image. Among the former, two of the most cited are those of Echtner and Ritchie (1991, 1993). They argued that destination image comprises locations on continua of (a) the place-specific attributes and the holistic impression, (b) the functional (tangibles) and the psychological (or more emotive and intangible), and (c) that which is unique to a place, and those things that it shares with others (the variable of commonality). The latter group of studies include that of Beerli and Martín (2004), who argue that the determinants of image formation include usage rates of information sources and the nature of those sources, whether tourists are first-time or repeat visitors, the motives for the trip, past experience of leisure trips, and socio-demographic variables that include age, gender, level of income, and country of origin. They found (in a Spanish context) that travel agents possessed significance as a source of information, and that past travel experience, motives, and congruence of place image and motive possessed importance.

A number of studies have sought to develop meta-narratives relating to formation and role of image. One of these is that of Gallarza et al. (2002), who surveyed what they considered to be 25 key studies. Their findings are summarized in Figure 14.1, which is an adaptation and not a replication of the original. On the left lie the different compositions of the tourist destination image. These include the cognitive, affective, and conative components of attitude, the acquisition of collective, shared image and personal impressions, the image as a gestalt or holistic image or as a total of individualistic, separate pictures.

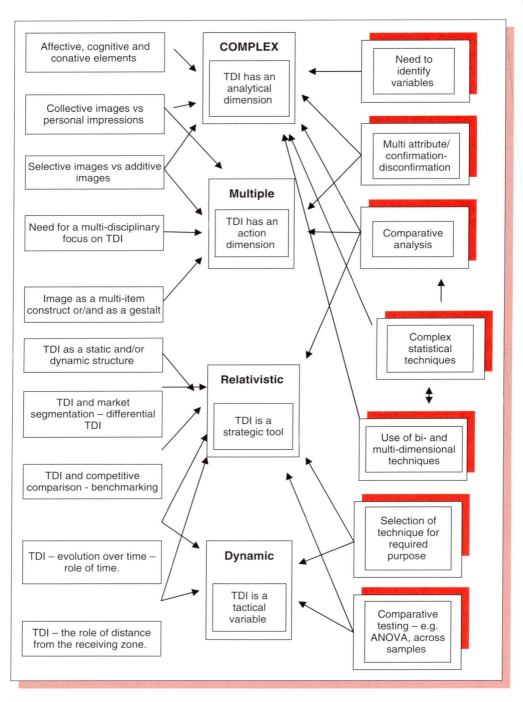

Figure 14.1
The Role of Image (*Modified from* Gallarza et al., 2002)

In addition, it is argued that images are dynamic; places are multiple products perceived differently by various market segments and are perceived differently over time, both by first-time and repeat visitors. Moreover, distance has an impact on place image, with those living furthest away possibly tending to ascribe more 'exotic' features to a destination based on concepts of difference and a greater gap between the tourist destination and the residential site which is familiar. Arising from the composition of image, there exist the roles and functions of destination image. These roles are listed in the centre of the diagram, with arrows linking *concepts* of image to the *roles* of image. Images can be acted upon in the generation of promotional campaigns, and they become strategic and tactical weapons in the establishment of brands that compete with other destinations. The images become means of establishing 'difference' and 'uniqueness' of place. The role of image is also discussed in much greater detail below. To the right of the Figure are shown some of the means by which images are operationalized and, in particular, measured. In the Gallarza et al. (2002) framework these techniques are overwhelmingly statistical in nature, but other techniques also exist, for example, comparative benchmarking, which can take many forms.

In another meta-study, Pike (2002) surveyed 142 studies and concluded that destination image research was overwhelmingly statistical in nature. Partly in reaction to this, Ryan and Cave (2005) specifically used semi-structured open-ended interviews by talking to respondents in cafes. They used textual analysis software to arrive at findings, which to a large extent confirmed the dimensions of place perceptions identified by other researchers, and were able to provide support for Gallarza et al. (2002) thesis that different market segments (in this instance based on nationality) occupied different spaces on underlying dimensions – the key ones in the case of Auckland being those of exciting vs. relaxing, and tense/frustrating vs. friendly. Another interesting aspect in recent years has been the role of the image in creating familiarity *with* places so that both Baloglu (2001) and Prentice (2004) suggested that tourists are not always seeking difference but are seeking to experience places made attractive through the familiarity of image portrayed. As discussed in more detail below, visitors select places and activities congruent with their own self-image, and thus seek place/activity made familiar through image consumption. Prebensen (2007) also found that familiarity through perception of place was a means of combating the role of distance – that is, destinations spatially far away are made perceptually near, thereby overcoming possible resistances to visit because of additional costs in terms of both money and time.

An alternative approach to image and destination marketing is to study the actual organizations charged with the creation of promotional campaigns – namely the DMOs themselves. Early studies that considered these issues include those of Pearce (1992) and Baum (1994), while

Pearce returned to this theme in looking how National Tourism Organizations (NTOs) can influence tourism policies in developing countries, in this instance, Samoa (Pearce, 1999). These studies tended to look at issues of formal functioning, characteristics, and responsibilities and drew distinctions between planning and promotional roles. A different approach was adopted by Ryan and Zahra (2004) and Zahra and Ryan (2005). In the former publication, they highlight the role of the informal and parochial in the allocation of funding and determination of promotional policies, while in the latter they trace the varying fortunes of DMOs in New Zealand and indicate, among other things, the degrees to which they are subject to the vagaries of political fortune, changing political environments, and election results. Another factor that is identified is the existence of organizational pressures within DMOs to continually revisit, re-appraise and amend destination marketing campaigns. Careers are based upon the introduction of new ideas and concepts, and rarely upon simply sustaining that done by predecessors. New managers wish to be seen to make a difference. In addition, other good reasons, apart from those of personal career enhancement, exist for such monitoring of place, markets, and messages about a destination. Destinations are not static, but evolve. Butler's (1980, 2006a,b) destination life cycle conceptualizes how a resort progresses through various stages from initial exploration and local involvement to development, consolidation, possible stagnation, and eventually, decline or rejuvenation. The implications of this cycle are many and include business mix, land use patterns, and size and composition of the tourist market, but it becomes evident that images of place can become dated and in need of amendment. These issues are discussed in more detail below.

The nature of destination marketing

What lessons can be learnt from this review? One possibly iconoclastic result suggests itself, namely, there is no destination marketing! There are national, regional, and district tourism organizations that promote destinations, and there are individual companies that market their individual products, but there is little destination marketing. This contention rests in part upon definitions of the two main terms 'destination' and 'marketing'. It is a cliché of marketing text books that marketing is more than simply promoting. At a basic level, the components of marketing are often summarized within an acronym such as the '5Ps' – which are described as 'product', 'place', 'promotion', 'price', and 'people' or some combination or amendment of this categorical approach to marketing. The essentials of this approach is that marketing is about the design of a product, for a given target group of potential customers, delivered at a given place via a distribution network at a price designed to generate both sales and profits, supported by advertising and service personnel. The acts of purchasing means that customers believe their transaction represents value for the money spent, that, in the terminology of economists, it permits *utility*, while for the entrepreneur the price is sufficient to earn the required profit that permits continuance in business. Immediately it can be seen that if this approach to marketing is applied to tourism destinations, various definitional problems arise. In tourism, the destination (place) is the product, and thus there arises the commonplace definition that tourism is an export unlike others, where the customer comes to the producing region to possibly, literally, consume the destination, given the reports about the environmental impacts generated by tourism.

Further consideration of terminology and definitions raises the question, how are destinations designed – indeed, how are they to be defined? Given there are national tourism marketing organizations such as VisitBritain or the Hong Kong Tourist Board, can it really be said that such organizations design the product that is Great Britain or Hong Kong? Obviously, these places, with their history, culture, architectural features, and life styles, are not produced by tourism marketing organizations but, on the other hand, it can be argued that the images that are promoted are manufactured, at least to some degree, by the tourism organizations. Or possibly, and more truthfully, a selective portrayal of image is undertaken where stereotypes perceived as being favorably received by potential clients are reinforced, while other images, thought less helpful, are not utilized in the promotional literature. Yet, while it can be argued that tourism marketing organizations seek to create favorable images, it cannot be argued that they produce the actual products that are consumed by the tourist. The marketing boards do not 'produce' the hotels, the adventure companies, the tour buses, or any of the other facilities used by the tourists. Equally, images are being created by organizations other than the tourism marketing boards. Tourists' images of place may be derived from television, films, books and magazines, and by reports of friends and relatives who may have visited those places. These different media may also have their own agendas. Television will promote images of place in programs that are designed to capture audiences specified by given characteristics so as to sell advertising spaces – which advertising creates the revenues that permit the television station to continue. Images of place may also be derived from news media, which again are selective in the ways in which they present the news. It has been argued that news media seek the spectacular image just as assiduously as the entertainment media, while the cynic might argue that by definition news is about conflict, dispute, and tension – aspects of human life not conducive to the image creation of places as being desirable to visit. On the other hand, the academic tourism literature does possess examples of 'hot spots' that attract visitors by reason of being 'exciting' and 'dangerous' places. Authors like Prideaux (2007) and Panakera (2007) have argued that tourism in places of 'hot conflict' can be initiated as participants such as troops or peace-keepers engaged in touristic pursuits such as the purchase of locally made 'exotic' souvenirs. Indeed, one might interpret the taking of pictures of degrading prisoners at Abu Ghraib, Iraq, by US military personnel as 'touristic behavior,' given the manner of the initial distribution of those pictures. Indeed, as Panakera (2007) highlights, the places of past conflict become the potential site of tourism premised upon veterans returning to the places of their youth to remember past comrades and actions and to honor the fallen.

Aware of the role of the mass media, tourism marketing organizations seek to influence the ways in which such media work. Many national and regional tourism boards have departments that engage in the following:

a) The creation or utilization of events and sporting occasions to generate positive image of place. Thus major cities bid for events like the Olympics in order to not only justify major infrastructure improvements, but also in the hope that subsequent years will bring a post-Olympic flow of visitors drawn by a wish to see the place previously seen only on television. Today the actual Olympics may be part of a longer-term strategy for the development of sporting facilities that not only host the Olympics but various World Championships of different sports or age groups, including Masters' Games. For example, Beijing in the period prior to 2008 hosted many different sports and athletics events of differing status as various national sporting organizations sought to provide an experience of Beijing for their elite athletes while gaining organizational experience of that city. Each such event helps justify the original expenditure on stadia, and each creates an economic impetus as competitors, media, and spectators are drawn to the venues. This process is also illustrated by the way in which tourism marketing organizations sponsor and aid sporting event organizers to make deals with television channels. One such example would be the way in which Tourism New Zealand provided support to the *Trans Southern Alps Traverse* Endurance Race to obtain coverage of New Zealand's scenery on the *Discovery* Television Channel – having concluded that viewers of that channel fitted the socio-demographic groups that Tourism New Zealand wished to attract (e.g., http://www.buddylevy.com/text%20pages/Discovery.html).

b) The provision of information sources and marketing aimed at film and television production channels and the identification of locations as appropriate sets for television and films. Riley et al. (1998), Beeton (2005), and others have provided examples of where films or television series have initiated tourism growth, whether it is a field in Iowa (from the Kevin Costner film *Field of Dreams*) or the development of a sheep farm now herding tourists through *Hobbiton* near the New Zealand small township of Matamata – a product made possible by Peter Jackson's film trilogy of *The Lord of the Rings*. Consequently, just as, for example, convention bureaus produce details of accommodation, conference, and event venues as to size of meeting rooms, lists of entertainers, styles of cuisine etc. on offer, DMOs can produce lists of historic sites, public venues, national parks, and much else with the information required by film production companies as to accessibility, catering support, etc. Thus, the observant filmgoer might have noticed that Hogwarts School in the first two Harry Potter films of 2001 and 2002 was exactly the same venue used in the film *Elizabeth* (in 1998). Indeed Alnwick Castle has been generating revenue from being a film and television set for over 40 years. Similarly Cypress Gardens near Charleston, South Carolina, was the site for not only the swamp scenes in the Mel Gibson film *The Patriot*, but also the setting for *The Notebook*. Even an office used by the first author once appeared briefly for a few seconds in a UK television series, the building having been identified by a regional tourism board as possessing the right characteristics for given lighting conditions.

c) Working with departments responsible for wider economic development. This function is discussed in more detail below.

d) Possession of research functions if not actual research departments. The DMO possesses many functions under this heading. First, it acts as a reviewer and disseminator of existing research as it prepares reports pertinent to its regional stakeholders by drawing on others' research and contextualizing those findings within the concerns of its own region. Second, it identifies problems to be researched, and commissions research to better understand those issues. Third, it might undertake research on its own accord from its own resource base.

The promotion of place to stakeholders

While tourism marketing organizations are responsible for constructing promotional materials and images of place, the truth is that generally they possess very little control over the nature and development of the destination. It might be said that destinations are neither static nor, in Western democracies, wholly controllable under a market system. Indeed, it might be further stated that it is the operation of free market systems that requires the establishment of the protection of natural areas as national parks wherein development is severely constrained if permitted at all. As Butler (1980) indicated, destinations possess a life cycle as described above. Within the different stages, important characteristics of the destination are subject to change. Land use patterns change as previous businesses become displaced, peripheral areas once on the boundary become subject to development, and destinations grow in size to cope with the influx of visitors, changing infrastructure and enduring population changes as migrant workers and prospective new residents are attracted to the increasingly 'desirable' location. Alongside these changes, other variations in business and capital structures occur when outside capital moves into the destination. In addition, the marketing of the developing resort begins to increasingly take place, not at the host zone, but in the tourist generating zones. Tourist destination marketing boards therefore accrue an increasingly more complex task as a destination develops. Indeed, its marketing effort may be directed at any number of stakeholders, and these include the following:

a) *Those who fund the destination marketing board.* These would normally include its commercial membership and the public sector. The membership generally comprises businesses in the private sector such as the accommodation, transport, and activities sectors. These may also conduct their own separate marketing initiatives. However, while large corporations such as hotel chains, airlines, and theme park operators exist with global brands instantly recognized by many throughout the world, it remains true in many countries that most businesses are small, proprietor-managed businesses, often based within a family business setting. Such businesses have limited marketing budgets and thus become dependent upon a few key marketing outlets such as, for example, accommodation guides and tourism marketing boards as well as the distribution of their own pamphlets and leaflets. Equally, with small budgets, there is little financial slack to misdirect their promotional effort and thus there is a continuous need to ensure that the marketing dollar is being spent effectively. Destination marketing boards therefore have to continually re-assure their commercial members that the efforts made on their behalf represent good value for their membership fees and the additional contributions they make for specific initiatives such as the establishment of booths at various tourism trade or public shows.

For many destination marketing organizations, the greater proportion of revenues is derived from the public sector. This is most notably the case for regional and district tourism organizations that often receive the bulk of their funding from local government. As Ryan and Zahra (2004) describe, this makes tourism marketing organizations continually sensitive to the need to demonstrate that their efforts represent good returns for investments derived from taxation, and to convince politicians (as elected guardians of the public purse) of this fact. However, Ryan and Zahra (2004) also argue that since such funding is often on an annual basis, it impedes longer-term planning, is susceptible to changing political fortunes and, particularly at a local level, is vulnerable to the whims of personalities and competing parochialisms. Thus, for many DMOs, a high proportion of their time is spent marketing themselves to their political funding sources to ensure their continued survival, thereby reducing their ability to perform other promotional activities.

It has been noted that DMOs do not produce products but manufacture modified place images. It should also be noted that the users of these place images are not simply holidaymakers, but can also include industry, local government and residents. Local government funds destination marketing companies not only for the economic impact that tourism can create, but also for other purposes. Positive place images can result in the following:

i) A high profile, positive place image makes easier the task of economic development officers within local authorities to attract other industries in that both businesses and employees are more likely to re-locate to places seen as desirable in preference to those perceived as either less desirable or possessing no strong brand image of their own.

ii) Positive images can aid the creation of local pride in a locale, for a region can be seen as desirable, dynamic, confident, and simply a 'good place' to live. In the United Kingdom, Bradford overcame an image of decaying and empty Victorian woolen mills through a proactive policy in the 1980s, and in Wellington, New Zealand, the success of the 'Absolutely Positively Wellington' campaign led to resident resistance in 2005–2006 to proposed changes when it was thought necessary to adopt new place promotional messages on the premise that the brand image had 'matured' to a point of having lost 'freshness.'

iii) Positive place images can create a virtuous circle in terms of attracting events, conferences, and meetings in that outside sporting organizations, delegates, speakers, and associations can more easily sell 'attractive' destinations to their audiences than less attractive places. For example, in the United States, while Charleston, South Carolina, is not the best place served by airlines, it competes successfully in the conference market by reason of the images of a historic city based on an eighteenth-century architectural and urban tradition with easy access to a seascape.

b) *Intermediaries in the distribution chain control.* This involves, to a greater or lesser extent, access to the market at the point of demand. It has been noted that tourism is an export and, like many exports, it requires access to the customer at the point of purchase. By the definition of a tourist as being someone traveling and requiring over-night accommodation away from home, this means the market place is outside the actual tourist destination zone. Indeed, the market might be on the other side of the globe. The DMO therefore finds it difficult to directly access that potential customer and might therefore become dependent upon other marketing companies who do have such access. These other companies include outbound tour operators in the tourists generating zone, inbound tour operators within the destination zone, airlines who might be persuaded to develop flight and accommodation packages, and hotel chains, travel agents, and specialist companies operating solely within specific forms of tourism. Consequently, the DMO has to promote product aimed at these intermediaries in a manner that not only informs them of the characteristics of place and its products, but also in a way that indicates how such place and products please their customers and profitably sustains the branding and images of the intermediaries. Accordingly, the DMO must possess knowledge of not only its own location and product and the pricing structures of those operators that it represents, and what represents profitable deals for them, but it must also know the market positioning of the intermediaries, possess insights into the clientele of those intermediaries, and be able to offer deals that are profitable for those intermediaries. It has to ensure that a complementary and supportive relationship exists between the brand and image of the given place and the brand and image of the on-selling tour operator, airline, or any other distribution chain intermediary.

There is, however, one way in which DMOs can directly access potential and actual clientele without a need to purchase expensive advertising space in the television and press used by tourists in the tourist generating zone, which purchases are often beyond the means of small DMOs. The alternative is to use the Internet. However, this too imposes further demands upon the DMO. While capital costs of accessing the Internet are comparatively low, the main costs are in terms of time, knowledge, and establishing and sustaining communications with a number of stakeholders. Time is required to obtain the data needed for the Internet pages and to ensure it remains valid. Time is needed to continually design and refresh content in different languages. Time and labor resources are required to ensure that if promises of direct customer contact are made, they can be kept and acted upon. Someone has to respond to the e-mail requests. In addition, responses to Internet pages are additional data about clientele and their preferences and nature – and the more effective use of the Internet includes data mining to better understand the potential market. Does a DMO possess these skills? Again the answer would be in the negative for the most part at levels below the national or larger regional tourism organizations.

Yet the Internet possesses significant benefits for a tourism market-ing organization. As already noted, it is very difficult for organizations funded on an annual basis to develop marketing strategies over longer time periods, given that these require not simply the development of a brand, but the pre-purchasing of advertising space into the future for periods when budgets might not yet be approved by public sector funding bodies. The Internet represents a means by which branding can be created, made consistent, developed and imposed upon a wide range of product that is otherwise outside the control of a destina-tion marketing company that promotes, but does not develop, actual product. As previously noted, destination marketing companies can 'manufacture' image or brand, and the Internet is one, perhaps the best, means they possess to do this. One oft-cited example of this process is the Tourism New Zealand's '100 percent pure' campaign prior to 2007. While it was carried over into poster and television advertising campaigns, it was primarily sustained through controlling image and access through the Internet.

One service that destination marketing companies can provide for both potential tourists and the commercial membership is to establish a Web presence whereby the marketing organization acts as a portal for individual operators. For example, the DMO represents a geographi-cal entity within which individual units of accommodation, activities, resources etc. can be found as structured in logical and aesthetically pleasing ways for the potential tourist, thereby making the search for specific wants within a place much easier to undertake. Research undertaken on Internet usage by tourists by using modifications of the Technology Acceptance Model (TAM) (see, for example, Xiang and Fesenmaier, 2004, and Wong and Law, 2005) shows that perceived ease of use and perceived value of outcomes of use are among the determi-nants of Internet use. Other secondary factors include confidence over security issues (especially important in making payments for advanced bookings), confidentiality and privacy.

c) *The final actual visitors*. The purpose of destination marketing is to attract visitors and, thus, DMOs need to market directly to the final consumer wherever possible. It has long been a criticism of DMOs that their main criterion of success has been the number of visitors. While not without some truth, it is a simplistic notion in that, for many years in the authors' separate experiences, at least two other criteria have been in common use: number of nights spent in an area as a measure of duration of stay and the total visitor expendi-ture. Many tourist marketing organizations thus break down market segments by domestic and international visitors, and the latter in turn are often segmented by main purpose of visit (holidays, busi-ness and visiting friends and relatives being common categories), nationality (or to be more precise, country of normal residence and country that issued the passport), and, to a lesser extent, some categories based on activities such as main type of accommodation used (e.g. backpackers in Australasia) and types of attractions patronized (e.g. skiers in Canada using Canadian Tourism Commission datasets). More recently, there has been a further evolution of market segmentation that commenced with discussion of targeting 'high yield' tourists, which initially meant high spending tourists (Getz, 1994), but which is now perceived as those tourists generating high profitability (Simmons, 2006).

However, given that many tourists utilize the services of tour operators and travel agents, as noted above, the contact between DMO and tourist is often indirect. But equally, it has been noted that the growth of the Internet has made possible contact with such visitors who may use the Internet to undertake their own search for information and who not wholly depend upon the services and materials produced by the intermediaries in the distribution chain.

Consequently, one category of visitor that attracts significant promotional effort by marketing organizations is the Free Independent Traveler (FIT). Such tourists are primarily characterized as determining their own itineraries with reference to place of stay, duration of stay and mode and time of transport. Such visitors engage in information search prior to embarking on their holidays and may or may not make various bookings in locales prior to departure; they will often retain some flexibility in travel plans subject to time and budgetary constraints whereby they can take new or amend previous decisions once at the destination. DMOs will thus seek to influence those decisions by the supply of information in persuasive as well as factual ways via various media such as advertising, brochures, pamphlets, and the Internet. In many countries there will also exist a strong link between DMOs in the public sector and networks of visitor information centers, as the latter are commonly used by such FIT visitors once in the tourist receiving zone. In many countries the relationship will be close because local government will often fund, at least in part, both visitor information provision services and the local tourism marketing organization, and in some instances the latter will be contracted by local government to organize and manage the visitor information centers (Ryan and Zahra, 2004).

The role of visitor information centers is not simply to supply data. They can make bookings and, while retaining neutrality between the products of competing private sector product suppliers, will seek to persuade tourists to stay longer in their area through tailoring as best they can the provision of information and support services to the specific needs of the person enquiring of them. Those working in visitor information services thus require the skills of detailed product knowledge, communication skills, an ability to quickly assess client need and match product to need, and empathetic and persuasive skills.In short, visitor information services might be said to be the direct retail arm of the DMO.

The role of image and ensuring quality

It has been noted that destination image is important because it is the beginning point that determines visitor expectations. Expectations are used when evaluating the visit experience in the sense that actual experiences are in part evaluated by reference to expectations. It has also been noted that DMOs seek to create images that are positive, thereby increasing expectation in order to appeal to visitors. The motives for visiting any destination have been generally divided into two categories – the 'push' and the 'pull'. It might be argued that 'push' factors are generic in nature – that is, they relate to general needs such as a need for difference, a need to escape the everyday familiarity of work and family, a need to fulfill intellectual curiosity, a need to be able to bond with family and friends through the sharing of an experience of 'out of the ordinary', a wish to develop possible skills and competencies, or a wish to find a place and situation in which to search for oneself freed from demands of daily life. It can be noted that for the most part these generic 'push' needs can be fulfilled by many different competing locations. An objection might be that intellectual curiosity can be about a specific place, culture, or history and, while this is true, it can also be observed that if curiosity is not place bound, many competing places might offer specific types of experiences whereby curiosity needs can be met. For example, an interest in Roman history might be satisfied by places other than Rome, while an interest in the American Civil War can be satisfied by visits to many different sites of that conflict.

Given that many places can meet generic holiday needs and wants, the specific attributes of place become important in determining the selection of any one site as the holiday destination. Attributes of place relate to a catalogue of features that include landscape, history, climate, pricing, accessibility, and range of activities on offer. Research (e.g., Woodside and Dubelaar, 2002) indicates that many holiday makers make their selection from a small range of evoked destinations – that is, destinations might be categorized as having no image, an inept image (one that is incomplete and/or negative), and an evoked set of desired attributes. There is also a need to recognize that in many instances tourist information searches are simplified by simply selecting favorite familiar places that command a high degree of patronage loyalty. That this is the case can be explained by reference to any number of factors. It is a cliché to observe that holiday purchase decisions relate to the buying of an intangible experience –experiences that tend to be both expensive and risky in the sense that a disappointing holiday has a high opportunity cost in terms of loss of time that cannot be reclaimed, loss of psychological refreshment that may be the purpose of the holiday, and possibly the potential to harm family and other social networks. The selection of a familiar place also need not be simply a replication of past experiences, as past learning and the changing nature of destinations may mean that past is never wholly repeated. The image of place thus represents a valuable function in determining purchase decisions, and positive images are important place assets.

The role of the image can be explained by reference to Figure 14.2. The origin of the diagram lies in Leiper's (1990) concept of the tourism system. Based on a geographical relationship, it linked the tourist generating zone to the tourist receiving zone (destination) via linkages of travel to encapsulate the key definition of tourism involving travel to a destination and back to the point of initial departure, thereby highlighting the temporary nature of the experience. It is this temporary nature that helps constitute the tourist trip as an out-of-the ordinary experience, while for many people, of course, it might be seen as travel for recreational purpose. However, while Leiper referred to geographical entities, in this diagram they have been replaced by concepts of 'The Tourism Supply System' and 'Tourism Demand' which is divided into two: 'Inter-personal demand' and 'intra-personal demand'.

'The tourism supply system' incorporates the linkages from the actual product, whether it is a hotel, a zoo, a theme park, or an activity in the destination zone to the high-street travel agent in the tourist generating zone. It can also incorporate the Internet. The supply system is therefore not geographically bound as in Leiper's (1990) original

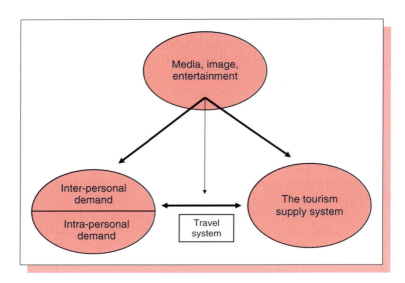

Figure 14.2
The Impact of Media and Destination Image Creation

formulation, and indeed can occupy cyber space. The components of that system include DMOs as well as actual activity, and specific attraction-site managers have a vested interest in product design, pricing, and communicating with the client to affect a sale. Of necessity, therefore, the system includes product at the destination and thus incorporates the original spatial elements of Leiper's notion. Figure 14.2 also includes the travel component as in the original Leiper model, and thus travel is not simply a function of transversing geographical space but is also a contributor to the tourist experience. Indeed, in some instances, the travel is the product, as in the *Venice Orient Express* or The Canadian Pacific's Royal *Canadian Rockies* train journey, or in those replications of past wagon trains in the American west.

Just as the supply system is not spatially bound, so too is 'Tourist Demand'. The demand can occur at both tourist generating and tourist receiving zones, but the key factor within the conceptualization represented by Figure 14.2 is the division between the social and the personal factors within demand. Of interest here, given the importance of branding, are those inter- and intra-personal aspects that relate to image. Inter-personal aspects can include the prestige factors associated with holidaying in given locations. Some locations are almost able to evoke images by the mere mention of their name – the Taj Mahal, Ayres Rock, Machu Pichu, for example. The visitor on returning home will elicit a series of often envious comments by reason of having visited these sites, thereby gaining social status of at least a temporary nature. Other social considerations relate to the nature of the place in forming and reinforcing relationships with significant others. Staying at a Butlin's Holiday Camp in the United Kingdom might not elicit positive social responses in some quarters, but may have generated excellent bonding with younger family members. A romantic weekend in Paris may reinforce bonds of intimacy between lovers. Inducing significant others to join in these holidays will in part be determined by the associated image such places possess.

As already noted, image is also important with reference to intra-personal concepts of self. As a consumer of a product, does the product equate with desired self-image? This is discussed below with reference to backpackers and adventure tourism product. It will also be noted that Figure 14.2 adds to the original Leiper diagram a third circle that represents the media and image creation. Image plays many specific roles that include:

a) Informing the supply systems of what to promote, how to promote, who to promote to and, for the actual product that is purchased, how to design that product;
b) Informing the tourist as to what to purchase and to what extent that purchase is consistent with needs and self-image. It also informs the tourist about how to behave and consume.

One example of this process at work is the adventure tourism industry. The producer of the product knows from experience that while many of the clientele will fall within a given age range, not all do so. The portrayal of older people in publicity material, the use of copy that appeals to a sense of adventure across all age ranges, the development of different versions of product that offer varying degrees of difficulty while sustaining the sense of adventure are all aided by images of who comprise the market. Through the utilization of those images, a self-confirming cycle is established whereby people who accept the images as applicable to themselves then buy the product. It also goes further with reference to aspects like clothing and the signage and the image they bestow on purchasers and wearers. Ferguson and Todd (2006) and Cater (2006) indicate the importance of signs through the example of clothing industry with reference to the New Zealand back-packer and adventure tourism industry centered upon Queenstown. Their findings can be generalized to many other regional adventure tourists such as surfers in Hawaii. Clothing possesses various ways of signing. Souvenir t-shirts indicate the activity done and signal the nature of the person to others as an 'adventurous' person. More specialized clothing such as wetsuits, cycle shirts, or casual clothing with specific logos signal degrees of involvement, expertise, and enduring commitment. The wearing of such clothing arguably bestows psychological benefits of self-esteem and prestige, including also affective rewards of being 'recognized' as an adventurous person. Ferguson and Todd (2006) demonstrate how attitudes towards the wearing of souvenir shirts are situational dependent on the sub-culture to which one belongs. They illustrate how the wearing of an A. J. Hackett souvenir t-shirt stating that one has bungee jumped is a statement of 'being cool' for the wearer, but from another hardened adventurer's perspective is simply being 'naff'. Cater (2006) has also shown how important clothing is, noting that economic power can be derived from the value of its sales to such an extent that it enables the sporting wear manufacturers to become an effective political stakeholder in US policies pertaining to the classification of natural areas and the economic consequences that subsequently flow from such categorization. T-shirts are but one way in which the search for self-statement, and the identification of interested others with whom one can share an enthusiasm and exchange knowledge about venues and activities, seemingly helps build expectations prior to participation. Therefore the signage and symbolizing of product consumption becomes important, and is part of the commoditization of experience by which the intangible is given a monetary value.

Various conclusions flow from this discussion. Experiences are signed. A market segment responds to the signing because it symbolizes some aspect of the segment members' own self-image, and a market transaction can result. Equally, the signage creates expectation, and the services literature is rich in confirmation–disconfirmation measures of service quality that argues expectations are important because (a) they are a criterion against which experiences are evaluated and (b) the expectation is itself a determinant of subsequent behaviors. These behaviors are not solely acts of purchase. They are also acts of role adoption. How does, for example, the white water rafter novice know how to act? While it is true there are instructions given by the guides, in all likelihood these instructions are acts of confirmation. They confirm what has been seen on the videos and television channels, and what has been learnt from word-of-mouth recommendations and the images in the brochures. By donning the wet suits and the helmets and picking up a paddle, the tourist becomes an actor adopting a role made familiar by images transmitted by the adventure tourism industry – the images which the tourist adopts by a predisposition to accept these roles. The image impacts upon the cognitive, affective, and conative dispositions of individual holidaymakers, thereby shaping purchases and behaviors. Hence there is little wonder that the tourism industry is engaged in image creation and storytelling. For some, the stories are comparatively simpler ones to tell, as perhaps is the case of the white water adventure operator. In other instances, they are more complex. DMOs are fully aware of these relationships, and in consequence, much advertising effort is directed not simply at the informational, but also at the emotive, brand reinforcement. An example of where, however, this approach has not always been perceived as successful was the Australian 'Where the Hell are You' 2006-campaign based on Australian self-imagery of irreverence, which was appropriate for market segments such as backpackers but which was apparently unable to bridge the gap to other market groups.

Challenges in destination marketing and future

Telling stories about destinations is a complex matter. When viewing the iconic images of many destinations – for example, Ayres Rock as representing Australia, Manhattan as representative of New York, Big Ben representing London – what is being viewed is, at best, selective truths. These images seek to encapsulate by definition what is unique and different and, thus, might also be said to be misleading and unrepresentative of the places in question. The not symbolized truth of daily life in these places is that most Australians live in suburbs, as do most Londoners and New Yorkers, and most do not frequently visit the iconic place – perhaps many do so only as often as the international tourist. For example, many Sydneysiders may not have actually entered the Sydney Opera House and view it as do the tourists, namely seeing it, and perhaps even having taken a photograph of it, from the Manly Ferry.

The promotion of place in a competitive global tourism industry, where the marketing organizations do not create for the most part the actual physical products (accommodation and activities undertaken by tourists), requires making statements of difference that are (a) unique to the destination and (b) are instantly recognizable as being of that destination. What the tourist consumes, however, is not simply the physical product, but also the experiences of being at the iconic, imaged, or imagined place that has taken shape within the neural networks of their brain. Hence, in marketing terms, the product is both the tangible and the intangible – something long recognized in the services marketing as well as the tourism literature.

However, the image, to be effective, has to evoke a positive response on the part of the tourist, and for the DMO it raises an issue in how to select an image. Most destinations are not simple or one product places but possess diversity that can appeal to different market segments. In addition, as Butler's Destination Life Cycle description implies, destinations are not static. As already noted, a destination possibly proceeds through the stages of exploration, involvement, development, consolidation, stagnation, and potential decline or rejuvenation (or even sequentially both of these latter stages) and in doing so changes in many ways. It has already been noted that changes can include variance in land use patterns and population composition. Added to this can be changes in the mix of tourism products with a general movement toward mass markets, externally-based capital provision, and a mix of local versus out-of-region-based businesses, with a trend toward more global brands entering local markets, and planning régimes. Even while there is a tendency to associate destination development as being initiated by tourists seeking the undeveloped, this is not wholly true as has been demonstrated by many studies. In addition, seasonal differences can exist. Ski fields may cater for different market segments during the summer, and Mediterranean resorts such as Mallorca similarly have different market segments from summer sun seekers to longer stay retired people from Northern Europe in the winter months. Another fallacy possibly implied in much of the academic literature is that market segments based upon psychographic studies are fixed and constant. The literature relates to segments such as adventure tourists, eco-tourists, culture tourists, hedonistic tourists, and fun loving tourists as if they are comprised of groups of people who remained fixed within these classifications. Yiannakis and Gibson (1992) pointed out, however, that these were roles, and tourists as actors can adopt and subsequently reject roles. In part, this is consistent with Urry's (2002) concept of the ludic tourist but, as Gibson and Yiannakis (2002) subsequently demonstrated, some of these role adoptions are partly determined by age and life cycle stage.

While destinations may possess certain fundamental characteristics as being, for example, rural or urban, inland or coastal, in many instances they also possess a range of products meeting the needs of different market segments. Thus, for example, a rural area might offer luxury lodges, farm stay accommodation, guided trout fishing holidays, off track adventure, and a range of other adventure products like rock climbing or kayaking holidays. There may be golf courses, rural events like agricultural shows, flower festivals, arts and crafts fairs and much else. All are rural tourism products, but not all appeal to the same market segments or have equal appeal to those who switch between market segments. Similar observations can be made of urban destinations that offer high-value and popular culture products, the refined and the seedy, luxurious shopping outlets, and colorful local markets. Given (a) that the destination can possess a range of products as described above, (b) that the range might be seasonal, (c) that the range of products have differential appeal to different classifications of tourists and hence (d) that the destination is a multi-produced place, it can be seen that the promotional task is complex in nature, might be dissipated over different points of tourist origin, and be constrained by resources insufficient to meet all these needs.

Other complexities also intrude. As tourism prepares itself for the emergent markets of China and India while assuming that energy resources and global warming will not impact much on future travel patterns, the truly cultural mix of the globe will commence and the future emphasis will no longer be upon a North American-European axis. Population changes arising from the declining birth rates of the developed world will require additional migrations from other parts of the world to sustain and create new patterns of demand (Ryan and Trauer, 2004). Tourism premised upon short duration trips is already being rivaled by new mobilities wherein the stay in lands other than that of one's birth becomes a sequence of homes of greater or shorter temporary natures. Destination marketing arguably is no longer simply an issue of attracting the temporary tourist but the migrant with the 'right' skills, for whom the destination may be little more than a career stage. Reference was earlier made to Butler's Destination Life Cycle. Ryan and Gu (2007a,b), based on studies of migration and businesses in a Beijing hutong and on expressed travel preferences between different national groupings (some of the research still in progress), have amended the Life Cycle model in an attempt to better reflect the new mobilities of the early twenty-first century. A summary of some of their arguments are shown in Figures 14.3 and 14.4.

Figure 14.3 is a conventional representation of the relationship between time, space, and travel patterns that illustrates the different mobilities that have existed for some time but are gaining more importance. Thus in their research in hutong in Beijing, Ryan and Gu found that many tourism businesses were initiated by migrants from other parts of China. Equally, British concerns being expressed in 2006 and 2007 about possible migration from new European Union states like

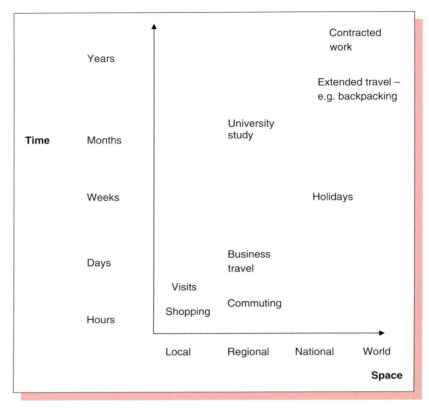

Figure 14.3
Time, Space and Travel Pattern

Bulgaria and Romania led to legislative restrictions on such travel. Yet such migrants are potentially drawn to new destinations on the basis of image just as surely as short-stay tourists are also drawn to many of the same places in the developed nations.

Figure 14.4 summarizes the arguments advanced by Ryan and Gu (forthcoming) that represent directions for future research. They observe that for many destinations the response to decline is a rejuvenation undertaken by government and parties local to the destination. Destinations successful in this process recognize that image is based upon local attributes that highlight either (a) difference or (b) access to a desired familiarity through travel to the destination. They argue that the destination life cycle can go through a process initially of an acquisition of global culture (and capital) where, for example, the multinational corporate and brand names 'legitimize' a developing resort area by processes of recognition and capital involvement. In this process, however, the destination has subsequently to develop a process of

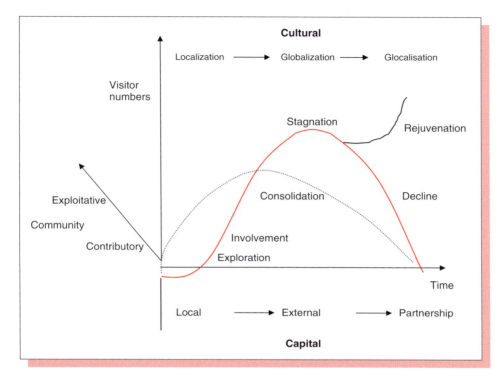

Figure 14.4
Amended destination Life Cycle

'glocalization' whereby what is local and unique has to be re-defined along with the global in order to better compete in international markets. Advertising and image creation for the Beijing Olympics is thus very interesting from this perspective in that the Chinese authorities simultaneously represent Beijing and China as being modern, but also as a place of tradition different from other parts of the world. Equally, there are messages of reassurance through the presentation of smiling faces, children playing, and a representation of ethnic and cultural diversity – images that offset the alternative image of authoritarian processes and social conformity to achieve desired ends. Images comprise what is represented and are also articulated by what is not said.

A further amendment to the destination life cycle model of Butler (1980) is represented by a third axis which indicates that 'glocalization' is contextualized within local communities. Initially tourism benefits local residents, but as it progresses and becomes more global, the resident increasingly ceases to play the role of host and becomes another tourism resource to be exploited as an employee, not as a business owner, as an extra in a spectacle, not as an artist-performer, and as colorful backdrop, not as an equal of the tourist. There exist the possibilities of local communities becoming marginalized as tourism develops in its globalization stages but, if success requires glocalization, local community exploitation is self defeating and such communities need to become involved in the sense of being participants in the benefits conferred by tourism. In processes of rejuvenation, given a propensity for external capital to leave to chase profits elsewhere, the local community and its representatives are required to step forward as both suppliers of capital and sources of difference that demarcate one destination from another. In some sense, they are 'rediscovered'. These concepts require research effort that is longitudinal, based upon constant monitoring, and that perhaps shape functions for academic institutions as partners for DMOs. Universities, too, are part of the local community and its resource base.

Implications for national, regional, and district tourism organizations

There are significant potential implications for regional organizations that arise from these patterns. DMOs used to be simply supported by local industry and government to better market their regions through the distribution of leaflets and brochures and to be present at trade shows for discussions with outward and inbound tour operators in a world, where most traveled using organized packages. Recent decades have brought new understandings in the face of environmental pressures, both natural and social. While responses have not been uniform across the world, various trends are discernable. At a regional level in the English speaking nations of Britain, New Zealand, and Australia, more holistic concepts of economic and social development have brought tourism organizations to the fore as glocalization is seized upon as means of progress. In New Zealand, amendments to local government legislation in the early twenty-first century reinforced a rolling five-year planning cycle by local authorities that required (a) public consultative processes and (b) specific duties and references to performance indicators of social and environmental objectives and progress. This has meant regional tourism organizations being reshaped and, in some instances, abolished to be reborn as part of a wider economic and social development program. This happened to Tourism Waikato in the case of Hamilton City Council. The destination must also be entrusted with social roles beyond the task of promotion of tourism as happened, arguably, in the case of Tourism Rotorua. In this latter instance, the City Council concluded that its Regional Tourism Organization (RTO) was the most experienced of all its offices in assessing residential and industry involvement, and environmental, social as well as economic implications of policies. It should perhaps be added that in this example Rotorua's tourism industry is a major employer in the town. Equally, perhaps in part because of the 2008 Olympic Games, the Beijing Tourism Administration is working closely with city and transport authorities on major infrastructure works such as developing new underground rail systems and equally developing policies designed to specifically combat the pollution, for which Beijing has become notorious. There is little doubt that these policies will have significant implications beyond the Games that should create positive social and environmental gain for the city's residents. In the United Kingdom, processes similar to those described for New Zealand exist. And various ironies can be traced. For example, the Birmingham City Council 2005 Annual Monitoring Report Contextual Summary fails to include the word 'tourism,' yet draws attention to the conservation management programs, the places of historic interest, the nationally listed buildings, and a whole range of recreational and tourism assets. The level of importance associated to that city's rolling 3-year local development scheme is implied by its acceptance at Cabinet level within the UK Government.

Tourism marketing organizations play important roles as advisory bodies in such processes. While the text books make much of processes of destination planning and management, it can be argued that there is actually little destination management from a tourism perspective other than possibly in national parks and their like. In urban areas, tourism bodies do not possess the means or legislative executive powers to dictate where hotels may or may not be built, how conservation areas are to be presented or interpreted, how pedestrian flows and transport patterns are to reflect tourists' and residents' needs. But through their creation and sustaining of image and through their linkages with the private commercial sector and the planning and environmental offices of the public sector, they occupy an important space in terms of acquiring expertise and knowledge of how these issues impact local communities and environments. They increasingly acquire the role of not only being promotional bodies but also advisory and representative bodies. The private sector commercial tourism interests expect the regional tourism organizations to represent their views to council, councils expect them to liaise with the private sector, and both expect them to provide advisory services as to flows and impacts of tourists and to interpret what international and national trends mean at local level.

Summary and conclusions

Apart from these organizational difficulties, the above discussion raises a number of questions about destination image. Tourism marketing organizations commonly seek a tag line to summarize the truth about a complex product called a region to meet the needs of diverse and different market segments that use a multi-produced zone for very different activities. Those activities may be subject to seasonal variance.

The destination itself does not remain static or constant as represented by the life cycle model of analysis, and changing stages have differing political implications because local communities may either feel exploited or be recipients of benefits. The image of place is also not only associated with short-term tourism but with longer-term movements of people – students, migrants, those developing global professional careers, refugees –are all drawn to places on the basis of an image and a hope of self betterment. Images are creations of selectivity – the positive is accentuated, whereas those aspects thought less appealing are silenced. But who makes judgments, and how are evaluations achieved as to what is or is not desirable about a place?

Image creation and promotion is an appeal to the cognitive, affective, and conative dispositions of potential market places. To be effective such appeals have to be based upon an understanding of both local product and different markets, thereby reinforcing the need for a research function. However, under trends toward incorporating tourism within wider economic and social policy development, dangers exist for such a research function. It either becomes, like much of tourism planning, lost in wider concerns as illustrated by the above mentioned example from Birmingham, UK, or, if retained, consistently needs to fight for funding. Similar observations might be made for the very basis of regional tourism organizations, caught as they often are in the eddies of local politics, personalities, and competing industry interests.

Given all these complexities, and the often low levels of funding associated with DMOs, not to mention the complexities involved in the actual construction of a successful brand image, one might say that the wonder is that many successful campaigns are mounted. To some extent, the tourism industry has had its task made easier by a combination of growing populations and increases in real disposable incomes that have occurred in the last 60 years or so. Economic models continually point to the importance of factors such as income growth, exchange rates, and population growth. While there have been fluctuations in trends due to exogenous shocks like SARS, 9/11 terrorist attacks, and similar natural and manmade disasters, the industry has a reputation of comparatively quick recovery. Indeed, so strong have been the underlying dynamics that one can ask the question, 'To what extent have demand patterns really been influenced by advertising campaigns mounted by DMOs?' Their promotional budgets set against the total volume of media outputs that engage potential clients daily is miniscule. Some organizations have proven more adept than others in using the way in which media work to their own ends by 'product placement' in films and on television, while the advent of the Internet promises to permit even the less well financially endowed regions to generate a presence in order to compete for attention. Yet it can be queried if these efforts generate little more than marginal movements around the broad trend lines. But, having conceded this may be the case, it can be argued that regional tourism organizations can make a real difference within the destination through the information services they often provide. If a visitor is detained an extra night within a region in serviced commercial accommodation, then additional marginal multiplier effects accrue. Possibly much of the academic literature on tourism destination marketing has been directed in the wrong direction. Traditionally it has looked at persuading visitors to come; perhaps, in reality, it is more important to look at efforts made to retain and direct visitors within regions once they have actually arrived. In short, profitability and long-term sustainability has as much to do with actual behaviors and activities upon arrival, as with the initial attempts to attract the tourist in the first place. There is also a need to better understand how DMOs actually work and how they adapt to the new roles thrust upon them. There is a need to assess career structures within these organizations and the way they use their resources. In short, there is a need to reappraise our literature and ask whether we have for far too long narrowly focused on image, and forgotten the world of politics, structures, and the wider concerns of local and national governments within which the bodies charged with image construction of place actually reside.

References

Baloglu, S. (2001). Image variations of Turkey by familiarity index: Informational and experiential dimensions. *Tourism Management*, 22(2), 127–133.

Baum, T. (1994). The development and implementation of national tourism policies. *Tourism Management*, 15(3), 185–192.

Beeton, S. (2005). *Film Induced Tourism*. Clevedon: Channel View Publications.

Beerli, A. and Martín, J.D. (2004). Factors influencing destination image. *Annals of Tourism Research*, 31(3), 657–681.

Butler, R. (1980). The concept of tourist area cycle of evolution: Implications for the management of resources. *Canadian Geographer*, 24, 5–12.

Butler, R. (ed.). (2006a). *The Tourism Area Life Cycle Vol. 2. Conceptual and Theoretical Issues*. Clevedon: Channel View Press.

Butler, R. (ed.). (2006b). *The Tourism Area Life Cycle Vol. 1. Applications and Modifications*. Clevedon: Channel View Press.

Cater, C. (2006). Looking the part: The relationship between adventure tourism and the outdoor fashion industry. In Ryan, C., Page, S.J., and Aicken, M. (eds.) *Taking Tourism to the Limits: Concepts, Issues and Management*. pp. 155–165, Oxford: Elsevier.

Echtner, C.M. and Ritchie, J.R.B. (1991). The meaning and measurement of destination image. *The Journal of Tourism Studies*, 2(2), 2–12.

Echtner, C.M., and Ritchie, J.R.B. (1993). The measurement of destination image: An empirical assessment. *Journal of Travel Research*, 31(4), 3–13.

Ferguson, S. and Todd, S. (2006). Acquiring status through the consumption of adventure tourism. pp. 149–154 in Ryan, C., Page, S.J., and Aicken, M. (eds.) *Taking Tourism to the Limits: Concepts, Issues and Management*. Oxford: Elsevier.

Gallarza, M.G., Saura, I.G., and García, H.C. (2002). Destination image: Towards a conceptual framework. *Annals of Tourism Research*, 29(1), 56–78.

Getz, D. (1994). Which tourists do we want? Keynote presentation. *Tourism Down Under Conference (1st New Zealand National Tourism and Hospitality Research Conference)*, Palmerston North, Massey University.

Gibson, H. and Yiannakis, A. (2002). Tourist roles: Needs and the lifecourse. *Annals of Tourism Research*, 29(2), 358–383.

Hunt, J.D. (1971). Image as a factor in tourism development. Cited in W.C. Gartner and J.D. Hunt (1987). An analysis of state image change over a twelve-year period (1971–1983). *Journal of Travel Research*, 13(3), 15–19.

Leiper, N. (1990). *Tourism Systems*. Department of Management Systems, Occasional Paper 2, Auckland, Massey University.

Panakera, C. (2007). World War II and tourism development in Solomon Islands. In Ryan, C. (ed.) *Battlefield Tourism: History, Place and Interpretation*. pp. 125–142, Oxford: Elsevier.

Pearce, D.G. (1992). *Tourist Organization*. Harlow, Longmans.

Pearce, D.G. (1999). Tourism development and national tourist organizations in small developing countries: The case of Samoa. In D.G. Pearce and R.W. Butler. (eds.) pp. 143–157, *Contemporary Issues in Tourism Development*. London, Routledge.

Pike, S. (2002). Destination image analysis – A review of 142 papers from 1973 to 2000. *Tourism Management*. 23(5), 541–549.

Prebensen, N.K. (2007). Exploring tourists' images of a distant destination. *Tourism Management*, 28(1), 747–756.

Prentice, R. (2004). Tourist familiarity and imagery. *Annals of Tourism Research*, 31(4), 923–945.

Prideaux, B. (2007). Echoes of war: Battlefield tourism. In Ryan, C. (ed) pp. 17–28. *Battlefield Tourism: History, Place and Interpretation*. Oxford: Elsevier.

Riley, R., Baker, D., and Van Doren, C.S. (1998). Movie induced tourism. *Annals of Tourism Research*, 25(4), 919–935.

Ryan, C. and Cave, J. (2005). Structuring destination image: A qualitative approach. *Journal of Travel Research*, 44(2), 143-150.

Ryan, C. and Gu, H. (2007a). The social impacts of tourism in Beijing Hutong: A case of environmental change. *China Tourism Research*, 3(2), 235–271.

Ryan, C. and Gu, H. (2007b). Spatial planning, motilities and culture: Chinese and New Zealand student differences for California travel. *International Journal of Tourism Research*, 9(3), 189–203.

Ryan, C. and Trauer, B. (2004). Ageing populations – trends and the emergence of the nomad tourist. In W. Theobald (ed.) *Global Tourism* (3rd edition). pp. 510–528, Oxford: Butterworth Heinemann.

Ryan, C. and Zahra, A. (2004). The politics of branding cities and regions: The case of New Zealand. In N. Morgan, A. Pritchard and R. Pride (eds.) pp. 79–110, *Destination Branding: Creating the Unique Destination Proposition*, Second Edition, Oxford: Butterworth Heinemann.

Simmons, D.G. (2006). *Enhancing Financial and Economic Yield in Tourism* FORST funded program. http://www.lincoln.ac.nz/story_images/911_yield_s3366.pdf. Accessed 22 January 2007.

Trauer, B. and Ryan, C. (2005). Destination image, romance and place experience – an application of intimacy theory in tourism. *Tourism Management*, 26(4), 481–492.

Urry, J. (2002). *The Tourist Gaze: Leisure & Travel in Contemporary Society*. Sage publications: London.

Wong, J. and Law, R. (2005). Analyzing the intention to purchase on hotel websites: A study of travelers to Hong Kong. *International Journal of Hospitality Management*, 24(3), 311–329.

Woodside, A. and Dubelaar, C. (2002). A general theory of tourism consumption systems: Conceptual framework and an empirical exploration. *Journal of Travel Research*, 40, 120–132.

Xiang, Z. and Fesenmaier, D.R. (2004). An analysis of two search engine interface metaphors for trip planning. *Information Technology and Tourism*, 7(2), 103–117.

Yiannakis, A. and Gibson, H. (1992). Roles tourists play. *Annals of Tourism Research*, 19(2), 287–303.

Zahra, A. and Ryan, C. (2005). National tourism organisations – Politics, functions and form: A New Zealand Case Study. *Anatolia: An International Journal of Tourism and Hospitality Research*, 16(1), 5–26.

CHAPTER 15

Push–pull dynamics in travel decisions

Muzaffer Uysal, Xiangping Li and Ercan Sirakaya-Turk

Introduction

Tourism researchers have long recognized the importance of studying reasons for travel, motivations, and attitudes toward tourism destinations to better understand and predict travel decisions and consumption behavior of tourists. They developed and applied a number of theories to explain tourist behavior. The sign–gestalt paradigm, better known as the 'push–pull factor' compendium theory by Tolman (1959) and later by Dann (1977), is perhaps the most recognized theory within the realm of tourism research. While models containing variables such as perceptions, images, attitudes, emotions, cultural conditioning, and learning contributed to an increased understanding of tourist behavior, motivation seems to be responsible for explaining much of the consumption behavior in tourism, thus making it a critical variable to study on its own right (Gnoth, 1997; Sirakaya et al., 2003). The authors of this chapter support the definition suggested by Fodness (1994), when he said '[it is] the driving force behind all behavior.' A motivated person acts on psychological or physiological stimuli in order to satisfy a felt need or achieve an anticipated goal (Dunn Ross and Iso-Ahola, 1991; Fodness, 1994; Gnoth, 1997).

An improved understanding of travel motivations would help in segmenting the markets, thereby allowing tourism marketers to allocate scarce tourism resources more efficiently. It has been suggested that the field of tourism would greatly benefit from a segmentation technique based on motivations because it could provide cues and/or insights that destination marketers could use in developing and promoting their tourism destinations. Crompton and McKay (1997) argued the importance of understanding motivations by giving three reasons: (1) understanding tourist motivations would pave the way for creating better products and services, (2) satisfaction with tourism experiences is intrinsically related to initial motives of tourists, and (3) motives must be identified and prioritized first before a destination marketer can understand tourist decision-making processes. Effective tourism marketing would be impossible without an understanding of consumers' motivation (Fodness, 1994). Thus, motivation seems to be a critical variable because it is the impelling and compelling force behind all behavior. Iso-Ahola (1980, 1982) also stated that motivation is one of the most important determinants of leisure travel. Therefore, understanding what motivates people to travel allows researchers to better define the value of tourism behavior, and ultimately predict or influence future travel patterns (Uysal and Hagan, 1993). Furthermore, delineation of underlying motivations offers useful insights into understanding the destination selection decision-processes (Crompton, 1979). Chapter 9 in this book has provided extensive reviews on motivation and its salient dimensions. This chapter is intended to provide in-depth discussion on the concept of push and pull motivation factors and their importance in and relationship to decision-making.

Dann (1977), following Tolman's work (1959), introduced the concept of push–pull of tourist motivation in tourism research. In answering the question 'What makes tourists travel?' he indicated that there is distinction between 'push' and 'pull' factors. Pull factors are those which attract the tourist to a given resort (e.g., sunshine, sea, etc.) and whose value is seen to reside in the object of travel, while push factors refer to the tourist as subject and deal with those factors predisposing him/her to travel (e.g., escape, nostalgia). This theory suggests that people travel because they are 'pushed' by internal and 'pulled' by external forces. In other words, these forces describe how individuals are pushed by motivational variables into making a travel decision and how they are pulled or attracted by the destination area (Uysal and Hagan, 1993).

Background - push and pull framework

The literature on tourist motivation indicates that the examination of motivations based on the push and pull factors has been generally accepted. The push factors, the needs and wants of the traveler, are the reasons why people want to get away from their regular place of residence. Pull factors are reasons for going to particular destinations. These factors have been generally characterized as relating two separate decisions made at two separate points in time. One focuses on whether to go and the other on where to go (Klenosky, 2002). Although these are separate decisions, many researchers have discussed these factors and described them as not operating independent of one another. One of the suggestions is that people travel because they are pushed by their own internal forces and simultaneously pulled by the external forces of a destination and its attributes (Uysal and Jurowski, 1994; Cha et al., 1995). Other researchers described the pull factors of a destination as corresponding to the motivational push (Uysal and Oh, 1995). Therefore, it is suggested that the attitude of a tourist toward a vacation destination may be a measure of that destination's ability to pull or attract the tourist. However, the hypothesis is that in order for a destination attribute to meaningfully respond to or reinforce the motivation to travel, it must be perceived and valued by the tourist as pulling him/her.

People travel or participate in leisure activities because they are 'pushed or pulled' by the forces of motivations and destination attributes. Push factors are considered to be the socio-psychological constructs of the tourists and their environment that predispose the individual to travel or to participate in leisure activities, thus influencing travel decisions and demand. Pull factors, on the other hand, are those that emerge as a result of the attractiveness of a destination and are thought to help establish the chosen destination. Uysal and Hagan (1993) emphasized that push factors are origin-related and refer to the intangible, intrinsic desires of the individual traveler, e.g., the desire for escape, rest and relaxation, adventure, health or prestige. Pull factors are mainly related to the attractiveness of a given destination and tangible characteristics such as beaches, accommodation, recreation facilities, and cultural and historical resources. Table 15.1 shows examples of push and pulls factors that motivate the individual to travel.

Dann (1981) also pointed out that tourist motivation should be examined in a two-tiered framework, 'push' and 'pull' domains. In this framework, the push domain focused on the 'why' question (socio-psychological predisposition to travel) and the pull domain focused on 'where to' issues (destination choice decision). This approach to motivations is from an interactions perspective, using destination 'pull' in response to motivational 'push'. The 'push' deals with tourist motivation per se. The 'pull' represents the specific attractions of the

Table 15.1 Push and pull framework of tourism motivations

Origin	Destination
Push factors	Pull factors
Motivations	**Destination attributes and type of facilities**
Escape	Climate
Rest and Relaxation	History sights
Self-esteem	Scenic beauty
Prestige	Sunshine
Health and fitness	Beaches
Adventure	Snow
Social interaction	Cultural events
Benefits	Recreational opportunities
Interests	Benefit expectations
Socioeconomic and demographic factors	**Accessibility**
Age, gender, income, education, family life-cycle and size, race/ethnic group, occupation, second home ownership	**Maintenance factors situational factors** (safety, security, seasonality)
Market knowledge	**Marketed image**
	Formed negative/positive destination images
	Quality of services
	Quality of facilities

Source: After Uysal and Hagan, (1993). Motivations of Pleasure Travel and Tourism In (Eds.), M. kahn, Olsen, M., and T.Var, *Encyclopedia of Hospitality and Tourism* (pp. 798–810). New York: Van Nostrand Reinhold.

destination that induces the traveler to go there once the prior decision to travel has been made. Pull factors relate to attributes of a travel destination, while push factors are internal to the individual and deal with tourist motivation. Push factors are thought to predispose individuals to travel, while pull factors help explain the destination selection decision.

In investigating motives of pleasure vacationers that influenced the selection of a destination, Crompton (1979) pointed out that disequilibrium in an individual's cultural, social, and psychological needs can be a primary motivation for travel. He suggested that individuals live in a social–psychological equilibrium, which may become unbalanced over time. This can occur during a period of routinized and repetitive action, such as at work or in the home environment. The need for change, relaxation, or escape from a perceived mundane environment results in psychological disequilibrium. The interaction between the two also has a behavioral dimension that includes not only reasons for travel but also perception of destination attributes. He empirically identified nine motives. Seven were classified as socio-psychological (push factors), namely, escape from a perceived mundane environment, exploration and evaluation of self, relaxation, prestige, regression, enhancement of kinship relationships, and facilitation of social interaction. The two remaining motives (pull factors) were novelty and education, which were at least partially aroused by the particular qualities of a destination.

Wilkie (1994) also pointed out that one of the key characteristics of motivation is that individuals are motivated by both internal and external forces. An internal force is socio-psychological impetus, while an external force comprises marketing stimuli and product attributes. The former concept is also known as 'primary motives' (mostly push motives) and the latter as 'selective motives' (mostly pull motives). The former is believed to be related to an individual's intention to use or not to use the entire class of products (e.g., in tourism, to take a trip or to do an alternative leisure activity). The latter, on the other hand, refers to consumer decisions related to particular alternatives from a product class (e.g., take a vacation trip either to Alaska or to Fiji).

In his model, Iso-Ahola (1982) suggested that there were two motivational forces that were the critical determinants of tourism behavior and simultaneously influence the individual. The two motivational forces are: (1) the desire to escape the everyday environments; and (2) the desire to seek psychological (intrinsic) rewards through travel in a contrasting (new or old) environment. In addition, both forces have a personal and interpersonal dimension. Therefore, the model has four sub-dimensions: seeking personal rewards, seeking interpersonal rewards, escaping personal environments, and escaping interpersonal environments. Recently, this model was empirically validated and tested for its structure and stability for tourism and recreation experiences by Snepenger and his colleagues (2006). The escaping and seeking dimensions of motivations may be analogous to those of some of the push and pull factors of travel behavior, respectively. For example, extrinsically goal-oriented reasons for travel may better correspond to those of measurable destination pull factors.

Similarly, Plog's psychocentric/allocentric model of motivation (1972, 1974, 1991) also implies the existing interaction between push and pull factors in travel behavior. Plog (1972, 1974) defined that at one extreme of the continuum are allocentrics, who prefer independent vacation experiences at destinations that have not yet developed a mass tourism market; at the other extreme are psychocentrics, who tend to visit well-developed tourist locations and prefer to travel with tour groups. Plog's model (1972, 1974) helps explain what types of people prefer which types of destinations based upon their psychographic characteristics. Both individual travelers and destinations can be defined along an allocentric/psychocentric continuum. Destinations that are new and distinctive in the marketplace are likely to appeal to allocentric travelers. Such destinations may include places like Tibet, China, and Africa. On the other hand, those destinations that are well established are likely to appeal to psychocentric travelers. Such destinations may include places like Coney Island and Miami Beach. Travelers feel comfortable, safe and secure with these places. The high degree of familiarity becomes a source of comfort. Plog (1991) extended the model by adding an energy dimension orthogonal to the allocentrism/psychocentrism dimension. This new dimension ranges from energy (high energy) to lethargy (low energy). The addition of this dimension allows the theory to account for variation in activity levels between travelers. This further emphasizes the importance of the interaction between psychological needs in travel behavior and how destinations would meet such needs in providing goods and services.

Empirical evidence between push and pull factors

Based on this push and pull framework, many studies have been conducted to investigate the effects of push and pull factors for several destinations, with different groups of respondents, and numerous push and pull factors have been generated. The means–end theory is used as a practical framework to examine the push and pull relationship (Klenosky, 2002). The 'means' refer to the pull attributes of a destination, while the 'ends' refer to the higher-level motivational forces important to the individual traveler in selecting potential destinations. Interviews with 53 undergraduates resulted in a series of means–end chains or ladders of meanings. The chains or ladders typically linked a particular destination pull factor or attribute with one or more benefits and ultimately with one or more values important to the individual. Analysis of the entire interview results provide useful insights into the relationship between the relatively concrete attributes or pull factors of a destination and the more abstract consequences/benefits and personal values that might also have served as push factors in motivating and guiding travel behavior.

Pyo et al. (1989) are among the first researchers who utilized canonical correlation analysis in simultaneous investigation of the push and pull factors of travel behavior. Canonical correlation analysis is recognized as a useful statistical tool to simultaneously examine the push and pull factors. The researchers identified 22 push items and 38 destination attributes or pull items. Canonical analysis of these two sets of variables was used to reveal any relationship, and the direction and extent of the relationship that may exist between the two. Empirically substantiated variates with their associated push and pull items formed the product bundles, meaning that the technique allowed the researchers to capture the commonality that existed between the two. Four product bundles were identified based on the significant variates. The first variate of attraction attributes includes first class superstructure and cultural components. The second variate indicated that tours to museums and galleries should appeal to intellectual needs. The third underlying dimension of the touring trip reflected two negatively correlated tourist market segments. The first segment is budget conscious people with kinship and relaxation motives. They also want a safe destination environment and good weather to travel. The other segment wants to experience different cultures. The fourth pair of variates implied that family oriented, health conscious people visit natural attractions, as opposed to those who want to be pampered by traveling to restaurants and enjoying nightlife activities.

Similarly, Oh et al. (1995) used an Australian sample to investigate the relationships between 52 destination attributes (pull items) and 30 trip motives (push items). Four significant variates/product bundles were identified based on the results of canonical analysis. In addition, once variates and their characteristics have been assessed and defined, respondents were assigned to the delineated variates, which in turn defined the size and type of segments. The four overlapping market segments were labeled safety/comfort seekers, culture/history seekers, novelty/adventure seekers, and luxury seekers. Baloglu and Uysal (1996) replicated Oh et al.'s (1995) study with a sample of German pleasure travelers. They identified 30 push and 53 pull items, and canonical analysis resulted in four significant variates/product bundles. Based on the variates, four overlapping segments were formed and labeled as sports/activity seekers, novelty seekers, urban-life seekers, and beach/resort seekers. These studies with canonical correlation analysis all demonstrate that there is a reciprocal interaction between push and pull factors of travel behavior.

Other empirical researches also used Pearson correlation and regression analysis to explore the relationship between the push and pull factors. Uysal and Jurowski (1994) pointed out that knowledge about the interaction of push and pull forces can aid marketers and developers of tourism destination areas in determining the most successful coupling of push and pull factors. They identified 26 push items and 29 pull items. Factor analyses of each set of items resulted in four push factors (re-experiencing family togetherness, sports, cultural experience, and escape) and four pull factors (entertainment/resorts, outdoor/nature, heritage/culture, and rural/inexpensive). To establish and delineate the nature and extent of the reciprocal relationship between the push and pull factors for pleasure travel, they were correlated and regressed against each other. Significant correlations between push and pull factors were found, indicating that a relationship did exist. A series of multiple regressions of push factors were regressed again onto the four pull factors, and all the models were significant.

Kim and Lee (2002) and Kim et al. (2003) replicated the study by Uysal and Jurowski (1994) by using a sample of visitors to national parks in South Korea. Twelve motivational items (push items) and 12 national parks attributes (pull items) were generated. Factor analyses of both motivational items and park attributes resulted in four push factors (family togetherness, appreciating natural resources and health, escaping from everyday routine, and adventure and building friendship) and three pull factors (various tourism resources and information, the convenience of facilities, and easy accessibility to national parks). Correlation analysis and regression analysis of the push and pull dimensions were conducted to examine the relationship between the push and pull factors. The results of the correlation analysis revealed that significant relationships were found between the four push and the three pull factor dimensions. In addition, in Kim and Lee (2002)'s study, as a method to confirm results of multiple regression analyses, a canonical correlation analysis was also used to identify interrelationships among a set of push and pull factors. The results of the analysis also supported those of the multiple regression analyses.

Bogari et al. (2003) also used the push–pull factors of travel behavior variables to understand travel motivations for Saudi Arabian tourists. Thirty-six push items of motivation for pleasure travel were identified; and 40 pull items of attractiveness of a destination were selected. The 36 push and 40 pull motivation items were subjected to factor analysis. Nine push factors were identified (cultural value, utilitarian, knowledge, social, economical, family togetherness, interest, relaxation, and convenience of facilities) and nine pull factors were derived (safety, activity, beach sports/activities, nature/outdoor, historical/cultural, religious, budget, leisure, and upscale). Similarly, correlation and regression analysis were used to examine the nature of the relationship between push and pull factors for pleasure tourism. The results proved that there exist significant relationships between the push and the pull factors.

Hanqin and Lam (1999) also adopted the push and pull model of motivation as a conceptual framework to identify motivations of Chinese travelers visiting Hong Kong. Twenty-two push motivation items and 26 pull items were factor-analyzed. The analysis delineated five push factors (knowledge, prestige, enhancement of human relationship, relaxation, and novelty) and six pull factors (hi-tech image, expenditure, accessibility, service quality and attitude, sightseeing variety, and cultural links). The results of factor analysis for both push and pull factors suggested that the conceptual framework of push and pull factors in the literature was generally supported and people's travel behavior is also driven by internal and external factors (push and pull factors).

Jang and Cai (2002) stated that knowledge of people's travel motivations and its association with destination selection plays a critical role in predicting future travel patterns. They attempted to uncover the underlying push and pull factors of motivation associated with British outbound pleasure travelers as well as to identify key motivational factors that have significant effects on destination choice. They identified 22 push items and 19 pull items. Factor analyses of the push and pull items resulted in six push factors (novel experience, escape, knowledge seeking, fun and excitement, rest and relaxation, and family and friend togetherness) and five pull factors (natural and historic environment, cleanliness and safety, easy-to-access and economical deal, outdoor activities, and sunny and exotic atmosphere). Seven logistic regression (logit) models identified the motivation factors that significantly affected destination choice by British travelers and showed that the British tend to visit the United States for 'fun and excitement' and 'outdoor activities,' Oceania for 'family and friend togetherness,' and Asia to seek a 'novel experience.'

Yuan and McDonald (1990) attempted to identify push motivations that predispose individuals to travel for pleasure overseas and specific pull factors (attractions) that induce tourists to visit overseas destinations. They also examined these push and pull factors across four countries: France, Japan, (West) Germany, and the United Kingdom. Five push or motivation factors were derived (escape, novelty, prestige, enhancement of kinship relationships, and relaxation/hobbies) from 29 items; and seven pull or attraction factors were derived (budget, culture and history, wilderness, ease of travel, cosmopolitan environment, facilities, and hunting) from 53 items. Analysis of variance (ANOVA) with multiple range tests was used to determine whether the four countries differed on each of the particular push and pull factors identified. The results indicated that individuals from each of the four countries travel to satisfy the same unmet needs (push factors); however, attractions for choosing a particular destination (pull factors) appear to differ among the countries. The results also indicated that the level of importance that individuals attach to the various factors in their decision-making differs among the countries.

Jamrozy and Uysal (1994) delineated the role and variations of the push and pull dimensions of travel and leisure behavior. They identified five travel groups and related them to the delineated factor groupings of motivational push-and-pull forces. The five groups were alone, wife/husband/girlfriend/boyfriend, family, friends, and organized tour groups. Thirty push items and 53 pull items were used and factor-analyzed. Factor analyses extracted eight push factors (escape; novelty, experience; family, friends togetherness; sports activities; adventure, excitement; familiar environment; luxury, doing nothing; and prestige) and eleven pull factors (active sports environment; unique natural environment; clean safe environment; sunshine environment; inexpensive environment; cultural activities; entertainment; sightseeing; local culture; different culture and cuisine; and small towns, villages, and mountains). ANOVA with multiple range tests determined whether variations in motivational push and pull factors occurred for different German travel groups. Results indicated that overseas travelers from Germany largely displayed variations in push motivations while traveling alone and in friendship groups, as opposed to traveling as families, couples, and tour groups. These findings further suggested that the items of push and pull motivations play a crucial role in decision-making with respect to sub-travel groups as well.

Another study by Turnbull and Uysal (1995) examined push and pull factors and types of information sources by destination types among German overseas visitors to North America, Latin America, and the Caribbean. Thirty push items and 53 pull items were used and factor-analyzed. Factor analyses extracted five push factors (cultural experiences; escape; re-experiencing family; sports; and prestige) and six pull factors (heritage/culture; city enclave; comfort–relaxation; beach resort; outdoor resources; and rural and inexpensive). ANOVA with multiple range tests revealed that the push factor of re-experiencing family was significantly more important for those who visited North America than those who chose the other two destinations. On the other hand, the pull factors of heritage–culture, beach-resort, and comfort–relaxation were significantly different and important among the visitors to the different destinations. The findings of this study also imply that push–pull factors of motivation are tied to destination preferences, and that these factors of motivation show variation from place to place.

You et al. (2000) used Dann's push and pull theory as a conceptual framework to test whether travelers from the United Kingdom and Japan had different travel motives and benefit seeking patterns (destination attributes). There were 17 push items and 53 pull items used in this study. The pull items were factor analyzed into ten factors (nature-based activities, outdoor sports activities, culture and heritage activities, city sightseeing and shopping, safety and hygiene, people-interactive activities, prices of restaurants and hotels, guiding services, exotic atmosphere and nice weather, and camping). ANOVA tests with multiple range tests were used to see whether UK and Japanese tourists differ in terms of their travel motives and benefits sought. The results supported that UK and Japanese long-haul travelers differed significantly on both push and pull forces, further attesting to the importance of push and pull factors in understanding the long-haul decision-making.

Lee et al. (2002) investigated how push and pull motivational forces influenced two of the most important travel decisions: destination choice and vacation activities pursued at a destination. Through factor analysis, six push factors and seven pull factors were extracted from 17 push items and 22 pull items, respectively. The push factors contained psychological motivation intrinsic to individual tourists such as escape and getaway, novelty seeking, relaxing, bragging about trip, and family togetherness. The seven pull factors were environmental quality, nature/ecology, ease and value, art and culture, atmosphere and weather, unique and different people, and outdoor activities. The study used regression analysis to assess the effect of each motivational factor on destination choice and vacation activity participation. The effect of other independent variables such as length of stay, travel budget, travel mode, and socio-demographics was also investigated. The results indicated that, in general, pull factors exerted more influence on destination choice than push factors, and different pull factors motivated travelers to select different destinations. Among all other variables under investigation, motivational push factors were the most significant determinants of destination choice. In addition, there was a relationship between motivational push and pull factors and vacation activity pursued at a chosen destination once travelers visited the place in a multiple activity–multiple destination context. Therefore, there is an underlying linkage between individual motivational factors (psychological push and destination pull factors) and pursuit of different thematic sets of vacation activities.

Kozak (2002) attempted to determine whether motivational differences existed between tourists from the same country who visited two different geographical destinations and across those from two different countries who visited the same destination. Two origin countries were Britain and Germany, while the two destinations were Mallorca and Turkey. Fourteen push items were used and the factor analysis resulted in four push factors (culture, pleasure seeking/fantasy, relaxation, and physical). On the other hand, open-ended questions were included in the analysis to explore specific factors influencing tourists' choice of Mallorca and Turkey (destination attractiveness). Content analysis indicated that accommodation facilities, weather, level of prices (cost), location of destination (or resort), and access to the sea and beaches were the most significant reasons given by British tourists for visiting both Mallorca and Turkey. The most important reasons for German tourists choosing Mallorca were weather, access to the sea and beaches, the length of flight time (accessibility of the destination), level of prices (cost) and the location of the destination/resort respectively. Weather, access to sea and beaches, level of prices, people/culture, and scenery and landscape were respectively the five most important reasons for those choosing Turkey. A series of independent t-tests and chi-square tests were used to compare push and pull motives between national-ities and places visited. Findings suggested, with few exceptions, that people from the same country but traveling to different destinations had different motivations. Table 15.2 presents a summary of some of the reviewed empirical studies that have specifically used the push and pull model of motivation.

Critical points in push and pull motivation studies

There are some critical issues and points that we need to keep in mind when conducting research using the push-pull framework of motivation.

- A closer examination of the studies of push and pull factors of motivations reveal that almost one-third of the reported empirical stud-ies utilized canonical correlation analysis to examine the commonality that exists between the two. Some studies used correlation analysis and regression analysis to establish the direction and magnitude of the relationship. Some other studies combined a multitude of statistical techniques including logit regression, ANOVA, or multivariate anal-ysis of variance (MANOVA) to analyze the push and pull factors of motivation. The use of statistical techniques appears to be a function of the main objective of the study and whether or not the factors of push and pull items are collectively or independently examined within the context of a given study.

- The examination of push and pull motivation studies also revealed that the number of pull factors included in the studies seem to be larger than the number of push factors. This observation may be attributed to the fact that pull items could be as large as the scope and nature of attributes that are associated with destinations and amenities. On the other hand, given the definition and meaning of push factors, they seem to be more stable and do not vary as much across destinations. In this respect, the 'push' deals with tourist motivation per se. The 'pull' represents the specific attributes of the destination. Thus, push factors are the ones that predispose individuals to travel, while pull factors help contribute to the formation of travel experiences and destination selection decisions.

Table 15.2 Empirical studies of push-pull framework

Authors	Push		Pull		Statistical analysis
	Items		**Items**		
Pyo et al. (1989)	22		38		Canonical correlation analysis between push and pull items (four product bundles are identified based on the significant variates with their associated push and pull items)
	Four variates: superstructure/cultural components; museums and galleries/intellectual needs; budget conscious/kinship and relaxation, safe destination environment and good weather; family oriented, health conscious/natural attractions				
Oh et al. (1995)	30		52		Canonical correlation analysis between push and pull items and the study developed an assignment scheme to create overlapping segments based on the significant and meaningful variates
	Four overlapping market segments: safety/comfort seekers, culture/history seekers, novelty/adventure seekers, and luxury seekers.				
Baloglu and Uysal (1996)	30		53		Canonical correlation analysis between push and pull items and the study developed an assignment scheme to create overlapping segments based on the significant and meaningful variates
	Four overlapping segments: sports/activity seekers; novelty seeker; urban-life seeker; beach-resort seeker				

Authors	Push		Pull		Statistical analysis
	Items	Factors	Items	Factors	
Uysal and Jurowski (1994)	26	Re-experiencing family togetherness, sports, cultural experience, and escape	29	Entertainment/resorts, outdoor/nature, heritage/culture, and rural/inexpensive	Pearson bivariate correlations between push and pull factors; A series of multiple regressions of push factors against the pull factors
Kim and Lee (2002)	12	Family togetherness and study, appreciating natural resources and health, escaping from everyday routine, and adventure and building friendship	12	Various tourism resources, information, the convenience of facilities, and easy accessibility to national parks	Correlation between push and pull factors; regression analysis to predict each pull factor using push factors
Bogari et al. (2003)	36	Cultural value, utilitarian, knowledge, social, economical, family togetherness, interest, relaxation, and convenience of facilities	40	Safety, activity, beach sports/activities, nature/outdoor, historical/cultural, religious, budget, leisure, and upscale	Correlation between push and pull factors; regression analysis

(Continued)

Table 15.2 (Continued)

Authors	Push		Pull		Statistical analysis
	Items	Factors	Items	Factors	
Lee et al. (2002)	17	Escape and getaway; novelty seeking; relaxing; bragging about trip; family togetherness	22	Environment and safety; natural/ecological sites; ease and value; art/culture and shopping; climate; unique people; outdoor activity for family	A multinomial logistic regression and OLS regression to assess the effect of each push and pull factor on destination choice and vacation activity participation.
Jang and Cai (2002)	22	Novel experience, escape, knowledge seeking, fun and excitement, rest and relaxation, and family and friend togetherness	19	Natural and historic environment, cleanliness and safety, easy-to-access and economical deal, outdoor activities, and sunny and exotic atmosphere	Seven logistic regression (logit) models were estimated to identify the motivation factors that significantly affected destination choice by British travelers
Yuan and McDonald (1990)	29	Escape, novelty, prestige, enhancement of kinship relationships, and relaxation/hobbies	53	Budget, culture and history, wilderness, ease of travel, cosmopolitan environment, facilities, and hunting	ANOVA to determine whether the four countries differed on each of the particular push and pull factors identified.

Jamrozy and Uysal (1994)	30	Escape, novelty, experience, family, friends togetherness, sports activities, adventure, excitement, familiar environment, luxury, doing nothing, and prestige	53	Active sports environment, unique natural environment, clean safe environment sunshine environment, inexpensive environment cultural activities entertainment, sightseeing, local culture, different culture and cuisine, and small towns, villages, and mountains	ANOVA to determine whether variations in motivational push and pull factors occurred for five different travel groups, using the resulting factors.
Turnbull and Uysal (1995)	30	Cultural experiences, escape, re-experiencing family, sports, and prestige	53	Heritage/culture, city enclave, comfort-relaxation, beach resort, outdoor resources, and rural and inexpensive	ANOVA on the resulting factors to see whether variation in push and pull factors existed between three destination types
Hanqin and Lam (1999)	22	Knowledge, prestige, enhancement of human relationship, relaxation, and novelty	26	Hi-tech image, expenditure, accessibility, service quality and attitude, sightseeing variety, and cultural links	ANOVA to examine whether significant differences existed between push or pull factors and demographic factors.

(Continued)

Table 15.2 (Continued)

Authors	Push			Pull		Statistical analysis
	Items	Factors	Items	Factors		
You et al. (2000)	17	No factor analysis was performed on the push items.	53	Nature-based activities, outdoor sports activities, culture and heritage activities, city sightseeing and shopping, safety and hygiene, people-interactive activities, prices of restaurants and hotels, guiding services, exotic atmosphere and nice weather, and camping		ANOVA to see whether significant difference existed between Japanese and UK travelers in terms of their push items and pull factors. Discriminant analyses to determine which push item and pull factors discriminate between Japanese and UK tourists better.
Kozak (2002)	14	Culture, pleasure seeking/fantasy, relaxation, and physical	Open-ended questions	Accommodation facilities, weather, level of prices (cost), location of destination (or resort), and access to the sea and beaches were the most significant reasons given by British tourists for visiting both Mallorca and Turkey. The most important reasons for German tourists choosing Mallorca were weather, access to the sea and beaches, the length of flight time (accessibility of the destination), level of prices (cost) and the location of the destination/resort respectively. Weather, access to sea and beaches, level of prices, people/culture, and scenery and landscape were respectively the five most important reasons for those choosing Turkey.		Content analysis of pull factors. A series of independent t-tests and chi-square tests to compare push and pull motives between nationalities and place visited.

• It is also important to mention that push factors may not change in themselves as individuals seek to find destinations to meet their unmet needs and fulfill their desires and expectations. However, the nature of pull factors may be a function of the nature of existing attractions and resources at the destination. Therefore, pulls factors show variation from place to place, signaling the importance of settings in which tourism activities and experience take place. This point is well supported in the recreation field under the concept of the Recreation Opportunity Spectrum (ROS) (Driver and Brown, 1978; Clark and Stanley, 1979). The assumption behind ROS is that people desire certain experiences from their recreation pursuits. To achieve those desired experiences, they participate in or choose activities within chosen settings that will facilitate the desired outcomes or experiences. Thus, visitors as consumers of products and services, will choose a combination of activities and settings that would lead them to achieve desired experiences. The implicit assumption of ROS is the strong connection between types of products one may consume and where those products may be consumed. This suggests that decision-making is strongly influenced by settings and its attributes that are conducive to creating the desired outcomes. ROS supports the notion that decision-making in travel behavior could not be examined without the consideration of the collective effects of push and pull variables on behavior, further supporting the importance of the push and pull framework of motivation in behavioral and choice-set models.

• Given the functional definition of push and pull factors, it appears that it is easier to define and measure pull factors since they are more tangible, evaluative, and concrete in their presence. On the other hand, push factors do not necessarily lend themselves to cognitive evaluation. They have affective and emotional connotations as they appeal to individuals' inner needs and emotional states. For the fulfillment of a need or emotional equilibrium, the interaction between the two seems essential.

• The challenge is not and should not be what push and pull factors are but the challenge is to capture the extent to which these factors interact. The commonality between the two is of interest to both practitioners and researchers. The second challenge lies in what we do once we have captured the commonality that exists between the two. For the push–pull framework of motivation to be useful, where and if possible, we as researchers should do a simultaneous examination of push and pull factors in the same research environment for two important reasons. First, we need to capture and delineate the commonality that exists between the two and know the magnitude of that shared variance. Second, once we know the nature and magnitude of the common variance shared between the two, we can start exploring the usefulness of the commonality in practical applications. For example, it is possible to assign individuals to the shared common variance as variates to match or create segments, and figure out the coupling of push and pull factors in order to develop appropriate product offerings.

- It is important to recognize that the common variance between the two factors of motivation is moderated by a host of intervening opportunities (distance, cost, substitutability, level of involvement in activities, availability of time etc) and external and effective marketing forces. Destination managers and marketers may attempt to establish some control over those opportunities in influencing the nature of demand that will be generated for the destination.

- A closer examination of the empirical studies on push and pull factors of motivations also implies that the quality of tourism experience, part of which may consist of push factors and tourists' perception of pull factors, relates to each other by sharing common variances between the two. This is an important implication for researchers to further validate and examine, for example, the notion of the relationship between destination competitiveness and tourism experience (Meng, 2006). Naturally, destination competitiveness, largely, depends on the ability of a destination to deliver better goods and services, which relate to the tourism experience considered important by tourists (Hassan, 2000; Dwyer et al., 2004).

- It is also important to mention that sometimes the distinction between the push and pull factors of motivation may not be as obvious, suggesting that these factors, as independent as they may appear, at times do collectively affect behavior. It is not suggested that one should attempt to develop some sort of a unified push and pull framework of motivation; rather researchers are urged to consider the duality and reciprocal nature of the interaction between push and pull factors in their applications and research efforts.

Push and pull dynamics in travel decision

Thus far, we have assessed the role and function of push and pull factors in explaining motivations for travel. They seem to be the necessary impetus that plays a role in choice decisions of a potential traveler. A systematic and in-depth understanding of tourists' destination-choice process is therefore central to any given consumer behavior study and the student of tourism studies. Ultimately what matters is the response to questions: 'where will the tourist go among many alternatives?', 'how does this selection process happen?', 'what is the role of push factors, travelers' psychological processes, during judgment or choice tasks?' and what push factors are more important on the judgment or on the choice of a specific destination?'

How individuals go about making travel decisions has been the focus of many studies in tourism since the late 1970s. We need to first recognize that decisions and the processes that lead up to ultimate site selection must consider the type of decision being made. What we know thus far in terms of these vacation site choice-decisions is that they are a little different from normal purchase decisions of manufactured goods. Most tourism service purchases are considered to be highly risky because of the relatively high cost, both monetary and non-monetary (e.g., time-investment), and thus require risk reduction strategies such as extensive information search. Making a bad vacation-decision means loosing a considerable monetary outlay and time as one cannot make these up, at least not until the next time around (Sirakaya and Woodside, 2005). We also know that, generally, tourists follow a funnel-like procedure of narrowing down choices from among a small set of alternative destinations, usually ranging from three to five destinations. These choices are affected by a number of variables. A synthesis of variables used in explaining choice decisions and the formation of choice-sets are usually categorized into four groups: (1) internal variables (i.e., push motivations, values, lifestyles, images, personality characteristics of a tourist); (2) external variables (i.e., pull factors of a destination, constraints, marketing mix, influences of family and reference groups, social class, household-related variables such as life-style, power structure, and group decision-making style); (3) the nature of the intended trip (party size, distance, time, and duration of trip); and (4) trip experiences (mood and feelings during the trip, post-purchase evaluations). The nature of interaction among all these variables determines the ultimate choice of a destination (Sirakaya and Woodside, 2005). But the question is, *how is this choice really being made*? Is there a structure involved in this process? We have learned through the years of investment into research in decision-making that tourist decision-making happens in phases; the phases can last anywhere from 'split second' to months, or even to years.

Tourist decision-making can be broken down into a series of well-defined stages: (a) recognition that there needs a decision to be made or what we call as a problem recognition stage, (b) formulation of travel goals and objectives, (c) generation of a set of alternative vacation destinations from which to choose, (d) search for information about the pull-properties of the alternatives under consideration, (e) ultimate judgment or choice among many alternative vacation destinations, (f) final selection of the vacation destination, and (g) post-travel evaluation and feedback for the next decision or what we call 'a post-purchase evaluation stage' (Engel et al., 1986; Carroll and Johnson, 1990). Marketing scholars believe that psychological mechanisms underlie each of these decision stages. For example, the first stage basically signifies a gap between tourists' desired conditions as to where he/she would like to be psychologically and his/her perceived state. It is during this present stage that push factors play a significant role in providing the necessary momentum for people to act upon the much needed change. They will be motivated to consider traveling as a medium to relieve that discrepancy between their current (e.g., mundane and boring conditions in a city) and desired state (e.g., being in an exciting and novel Mediterranean spot). During information search about destinations, alternative evaluation and selection, and post-purchase evaluation, the tourist unconsciously uses a number of push motivations as well as pull factors, among other variables such as their beliefs and attitudes about places. In the alternative evaluation stage, the tourist may use his/her own decision rules to evaluate and choose a final destination. Of course, these destinations are constantly evaluated, re-evaluated, and weighted for their pull-attributes in terms of their potential to fulfill the tourist's initial goals and needs, as new information becomes available to him/her. If the evaluation is not successful or complete, the search stays inconclusive and the tourist restarts from the beginning. After the vacation, the tourist continues evaluating his/her decision, which will provide inputs for future decisions.

As seen from the review of empirical studies, the push and pull framework is an intuitive approach for explaining the motivations that underlie a tourist behavior (Dann, 1977; Crompton, 1979). Push and pull factors of tourist motivation have a strong impact on overall travel just as with any consumer product. Push, being the internal drivers motivating an individual toward a vacation in general or a destination specifically, is usually the impetus factor in beginning the information search. An individual needs a break from the everyday life, wants to learn about a specific culture or history, is yearning for adventure, or simply wants to spend time by the water on a nice warm beach. These desires push the individual to search out areas that will satisfy these needs. That is where specific destinations with desirable attributes pull the individual to choose them over other competing destinations with less desirable attributes. By highlighting their specific advantages, they hope to lure the tourist toward them. The attributes the destination chooses to highlight are important, as they must match with the needs of the tourist performing the information search. The destination may have wonderful spa amenities, but if the individual is looking for a sparse, eco-friendly atmosphere, these amenities will mean nothing, or may have a negative meaning. This brings us to the point of attraction vs. attractiveness. These two terms are related, yet are also distinct from the perspective of a destination and determining demand. Both speak of the level of interest an individual has toward a specific destination. The level of attraction of a destination is determined by what that destination has to offer and how those aspects match with the desire of the tourist. If the individual has an interest in beautiful beaches and a great spa experience, their level of attraction is based on their perception of how that destination compares to what they expect in a destination. Attractiveness has a lot to do with attraction. An individual will not continue to the stage of determining attractiveness if he/she does not perceive the destination to hold an attraction. Once attraction is determined, the feasibility of actually traveling to the destination becomes a factor. Attractiveness of a destination includes all that attraction does plus all logistical necessities of actually taking the vacation. Attractiveness, differing from attraction in that destinations have little resource to improve it due to the 'en loco' effects of tourism, is what truly determines overall demand. Therefore, in order for a destination or site attribute to meaningfully respond to demand or reinforce push factors, it must be perceived and valued (Uysal and Hagan, 1993). Individuals as traveling consumers are likely to choose places that are in a better position to meet their needs and expectations at the destination.

Directions for future research

What is the advantage of applying the push–pull model of motivation in tourism and hospitality research in future? The advantage of approaching tourist motivation from the perspective of push and pull factors is that the researcher could provide information that would allow tourism and hospitality practitioners, destination managers, and planners to understand the relative importance of destination attributes as part of motivation factors and the degree to which they might have control over some of these factors. The information that could be obtained from such an approach to motivation would allow practitioners not to tolerate the poor performance of pull factors of destination attributes. Because of the tangibility nature of pull factors, planners and managers would be able to develop appropriate amenities and maintain them at the performance level that will be expected.

In today's highly competitive tourism market, managers can differentiate their products and amenities by knowing the degree to which they meet the needs and expectations of visitors. Knowing the usefulness of the simultaneous examination of push and pull factors would allow managers of destinations to remain competitive and increase their market share.

In future research efforts researchers and managers should also examine tourist destinations and their amenities from the perspective of a systems approach. A number of scholars have proposed models of the tourism system (Mill and Morrison, 1985; Gunn, 1988; Leiper, 1990). Tourism system, in its simplest form, consists of an origin and a destination (Fesenmaier and Uysal, 1990; Uysal, 1998). An origin represents the demand-side of tourism, the region or country generating tourists, while a destination refers to the supply-side of tourism.

Within this system of tourism, the main elements of motivation – pull and push attributes – represent two major components of the market place, namely, demand and supply. Some push factors are the behavioral results of an inner emotional state and pose opportunities for interaction and participation. These factors are the essence of travel motivation in the first place, representing the demand side of the equation. Thus, potential and actual visitors are the ones who seem to have more control over these attributes. The responses to the demand side or pull factors, including benefits sought at the destination or desired features in a hotel would then naturally represent the supply side of travel experience. Therefore, the pull factors are mainly maintenance attributes without which one may not achieve some degree of tourist satisfaction (Uysal, 2006).

It is clear from the studies reviewed on the interaction between push and pull factors of motivation that pull factors also influence the travel decision along with push factors. Laws (2002) points out that the appropriateness of the technical design delivery systems and product offerings along with an understanding of the meaning to customers of their experiences would be essential to develop a competitive position and maintain the advantages gained.

We know that the quality and availability of tourism supply resources are a critical element in meeting the needs of the ever-changing and growing tourism market. So, it is important that destination managements monitor visitors' satisfaction with pull factors such as facilities, programs, and services in order to maintain a sustained and expanding business.

Empirical studies on the push–pull model of motivation with respect to specific places as destinations and amenities within the destination help us understand the complexity of motivation as one of the elements of visitation behavior. Actual and potential markets can use these types of motivation studies to develop appropriate communication materials that would incorporate the relative importance of destination features as perceived by potential and actual consumers.

In the tourism industry, a destination is considered a consumer product and tourists are consumers who purchase a number of diverse tourism products and services. To market destinations and amenities within those destinations effectively, marketers need to understand what motivates an individual to travel and what destination attributes are important for an individual to select a product or amenity. If destination marketers have a clearer understanding of why their products are in demand for a given market segment or group, they will be able to tailor their products more closely to the needs of their customers with appropriate advertising and sales messages to inform and persuade consumers to buy products (Holloway and Plant, 2005). If several destinations or hotels have the same attraction attributes and physical amenities, preference is likely to be given to a destination

or a hotel that is perceived as most likely to match push motivations with pull attributes. Thus, understanding the nature of the commonality that exists between push and pull factors of motivations
would allow destination managers and marketers to better match a
destination's major attributes and physical amenities to the tourists'
diverse psychological needs. The framework of push and pull factors
of motivation should guide the future management and marketing
strategies.

Conclusion

Motivation is one of the variables that can explain travel decision-
making and travel behavior. A comprehensive review of studies on
tourist motivation within the concept of the push and pull model of
motivation indicates that the examination of motivations based on this
model has been generally well-received and accepted.

In order to understand the influence of the push–pull factors of motivation on decision-making and reducing uncertainty in decisions, one
needs to also examine the production systems of tourism goods and
services. In the system, the tourist and tourism attractions are the central aspects. The existence of tourism is based on the resources at the
destination and tourists' perceptions of those resources. Tourism occurs
as a function of the demand and supply interaction in space. In order
for a supply element (destination or site attribute) to meaningfully
respond to demand or reinforce affective factors, it must be perceived
and valued, leading to the examination of the market responses, thus
understanding the behavior of consumers (Uysal and Hagan, 1993). As
a result, there is a significant relationship between destination attributes
(pull forces) and tourist motives (push forces). Demand and supply factors collectively and simultaneously influence not only the production
and development of tourism goods and services but also the decision-
making process of travelers.. Therefore, it is the combined elements
of demand and supply – push and pulls items of motivation – that
influence the level of demand for a given destination and produce
the ultimate tourism experience. In general, all the empirical studies
mentioned in this chapter support and confirm the hypothesis that the
factors of push and pull share a common variance that can easily be
captured and capitalized on to develop 'product bundles' as implied
by the shared variance and create segments by assigning individuals
to the common variance that exists between the two. The commonality
that exist between push and pull factors have strong implications for
and relevance to decision-making. Thus, it is reasonable and very useful to examine the reciprocal interaction between the two phenomena
of push and pull items of motivation in the same context to better
understand tourist behavior (Uysal, 1998).

References

Baloglu, S. and Uysal, M. (1996). Market segments of push and pull motivations: A canonical correlation approach. *International Journal of Contemporary Hospitality Management, 8*(3), 32–38.

Bogari, N. B., Crowther, G., and Marr, N. (2003). Motivation for domestic tourism: A case study of the Kingdom of Saudi Arabia. *Tourism Analysis, 8*(2), 137–141.

Carroll, J. S. and Johnson, E. J. (1990). *Decision Research: A Field Guide*. Newbury Park: Sage Publications.

Cha, S., McCleary, K. W., and Uysal, M. (1995). Travel motivations of Japanese overseas travelers: A factor-cluster segmentation approach. *Journal of Travel Research, 34*(1), 33–39.

Clark, R. N. and Stanley, G. H. (1979). *The Recreation Opportunity Spectrum: A Framework for Planning, Management, and Research*: USDA Forest Service General Technical Report PNW-98.

Crompton, J. L. (1979). Motivations for pleasure vacation. *Annals of Tourism Research, 6*(4), 408–424.

Crompton, J. L. and McKay, S. L. (1997). Motives of visitors attending festival events. *Annals of Tourism Research, 24*(2), 425–439.

Dann, G. M. S. (1977). Anomie, ego-enhancement and tourism. *Annals of Tourism Research, 4*(4), 184–194.

Dann, G. M. S. (1981). Tourist motivation an appraisal. *Annals of Tourism Research, 8*(2), 187–219.

Driver, B. L. and Brown, P. J. (1978). *The Opportunity Spectrum Concept and Behavioral Information in Outdoor Recreation Resource Supply Inventories: A Rationale*. Fort Collins, Colorado: USDA Forest Service General Technical Report RM-55, Rocky Mountain Forest and Range Experiment Station.

Dunn Ross, E. L. and Iso-Ahola, S. E. (1991). Sightseeing Tourists' Motivation and Satisfaction. *Annals of Tourism Research, 18*(2), 226–237.

Dwyer, L., Mellor, R., Livaic, Z., et al. (2004). Attributes of destination competitiveness: A factor analysis. *Tourism Analysis, 9*(1–2), 91–101.

Engel, J. F., Blackwell, R. D., and Miniard, P. W. (1986). *Consumer Behavior* (5th ed.). Chicago: Dryden Press.

Fesenmaier, D. and Uysal, M. (1990). The tourism system: Levels of economic and human behavior. In J. B. Zeiger and L. M. Caneday (Eds.), *Tourism and Leisure: Dynamics and Diversity*. Alexandria, VA: National Recreation and Park Association.

Fodness, D. (1994). Measuring tourist motivation. *Annals of Tourism Research, 21*(3), 555–581.

Gnoth, J. (1997). Tourism motivation and expectation formation. *Annals of Tourism Research, 24*(2), 283–304.

Gunn, C. A. (1988). *Tourism Planning* (2nd, rev. & expand ed.). New York: Taylor and Francis.

Hanqin, Z. Q. and Lam, T. (1999). An analysis of Mainland Chinese visitors' motivations to visit Hong Kong. *Tourism Management, 20*(5), 587–594.

Hassan, S. S. (2000). Determinants of market competitiveness in an environmentally sustainable tourism industry. *Journal of Travel Research, 38*(3), 239–245.

Holloway, C., J. and Plant, R. V. (2005). *Marketing for Tourism*. London: Pitman.

Iso-Ahola, S. E. (1980). *The Social Psychology of Leisure and Recreation*. Dubuque, Iowa: W. C. Brown Co. Publishers.

Iso-Ahola, S. E. (1982). Toward a social psychological theory of tourism motivation: A rejoinder. *Annals of Tourism Research, 9*(2), 256–262.

Jamrozy, U. and Uysal, M. (1994). Travel motivation variations of overseas German visitors. *Journal of International Consumer Marketing, 6*(3/4), 135–150.

Jang, S. and Cai, L. (2002). Travel motivations and destination choice: A study of British outbound market. *Journal of Travel & Tourism Marketing 13*(3), 111–132.

Kim, S.-S. and Lee, C.-K. (2002). Push and pull relationships. *Annals of Tourism Research, 29*(1), 257–260.

Kim, S. S., Lee, C.-K. and Klenosky, D. B. (2003). The influence of push and pull factors at Korean national parks. *Tourism Management, 24*(2), 169–180.

Klenosky, D. B. (2002). The 'pull' of tourism destinations: A means-end investigation. *Journal of Travel Research, 40*(4), 385–395.

Kozak, M. (2002). Comparative analysis of tourist motivations by nationality and destinations. *Tourism Management, 23*(3), 221–232.

Laws, E. (2002). *Tourism Marketing: Quality and Service Management Perspectives*. London: Continuum.

Lee, G., O'Leary, J. T., Lee, S. H. and Morrison, A. (2002). Comparison and contrast of push and pull motivational effects on trip behavior: An application of a multinomial logistic regression model. *Tourism Analysis, 7*, 89–104.

Leiper, N. (1990). Tourist attraction systems. *Annals of Tourism Research, 17*(3), 367–384.

Meng, F. (2006). *An examination of Destination Competitiveness from the Tourists' Perspective: The Relationship between Quality of Tourism Experience and Perceived Destination Competitiveness*. Virginia Polytechnic Institute and State University, Blacksburg, VA 24061.

Mill, R. C. and Morrison, A. M. (1985). *The Tourism System : An Introductory Text*. Englewood Cliffs, N.J.: Prentice-Hall.

Oh, H. C., Uysal, M., and Weaver, P. A. (1995). Product bundles and market segments based on travel motivations: A canonical correlation approach. *International Journal of Hospitality Management 14*(2), 123–137.

Plog, S. (1972, October). *Why destination areas rise and fall in popularity*. Paper presented at the Travel Research Association Southern California Chapter, Los Angeles.

Plog, S. (1974). Why destination areas rise and fall in popularity.*The Cornell Hotel and Restaurant Administration Quarterly, 14*(4), 55–58.

Plog, S. (1991). *Leisure travel: making it a growth market . . . again!*: John Wiley and Sons, Inc.

Pyo, S., Mihalik, B. J., and Uysal, M. (1989). Attraction attributes and motivations: A canonical correlation analysis. *Annals of Tourism Research, 16*(2), 277–282.

Sirakaya, E., Uysal, M., and Yoshioka, C. F. (2003). Segmenting the Japanese Tour Market to Turkey. *Journal of Travel Research, 41*(3), 293–304.

Sirakaya, E. and Woodside, A. G. (2005). Building and testing theories of decision making by travelers. *Tourism Management, 26*(6), 815–832.

Snepenger, D., King, J., Marshall, E., and Uysal, M. (2006). Modeling Iso-Ahola's motivation theory in the tourism context. *Journal of Travel Research, 45*(2), 140–149.

Tolman, E. C. (1959). Principles of purposive behavior. In S. Koch (Ed.), *Psychology: A Study of a Science* (Vol. 2, pp. 92–157). New York: McGraw-Hill.

Turnbull, D. R. and Uysal, M. (1995). An exploratory study of German visitors to the Caribbean: Push and pull motivations. *Journal of Travel and Tourism Marketing 4*(2), 85–92

Uysal, M. (1998). The determinants of Tourism demand: A theoretical perspective. In D. Loannides and K. G. Debbage (Eds.), *The Economic Geography of the Tourist Industry* (pp. 79–98). London, England: Routledge.

Uysal, M. (2006). Factors of satisfactions: A case study of explorer park. In B. Prideaux, G. Moscardo and E. Laws (Eds.), *Managing Tourism and Hospitality Services : Theory and International Applications* (pp. 350–357). Wallingford, UK; Cambridge, MA: CABI Pub.

Uysal, M. and Hagan, L. A. (1993). Motivations of pleasure travel and tourism. In M. Khan, M. Olsen and T. Var (Eds.), *VNR's Encyclopaedia of Hospitality and Tourism* (pp. 798–810). New York: Van Nostrand Reinhold.

Uysal, M. and Jurowski, C. (1994). Testing the push and pull factors. *Annals of Tourism Research, 21*(4), 844–846.

Uysal, M. and Oh, H. C. (1995). *Product Bundles of Travel Motivations: A Canonical Correlation Approach to Segmentation*. Paper presented at the Structure and Process of Globalization in Business and Education (IMDA).

Wilkie, W. L. (1994). *Consumer behavior* (3rd ed.). New York: Wiley.

You, X., O'Leary, J., Morrison, A., and Hong, G.-S. (2000). A cross-cultural comparison of travel push and pull factors: United Kingdom vs. Japan. *International Journal of Hospitality and Tourism Administration, 1*(2), 1–26.

Yuan, S. and McDonald, C. (1990). Motivational determinates of international pleasure time. *Journal of Travel Research, 29*(1), 42–44.

CHAPTER 16

Group decision making

Alain Decrop

Introduction

Many hospitality and tourism decisions involve a group of individuals who will elaborate plans together, who will try to influence lodging or eating choices and, of course, who will participate in the consumption experience itself. Investigating how those travel parties make their decisions is worthwhile both from a research and an industry point of view. However, group decision-making (DM) has often been neglected in the hospitality and tourism literature. In many books and papers, the individual focus still prevails over a social perspective as it will be discussed below. In the same way, travel agencies as well as hotels, restaurants and tour operators often consider their customers on a one-to-one basis rather than developing strong one-to-many relationships. For example, when browsing travel brochures, individual packages and prices are easier to find than family or group offerings. Of course, some operators target niche segments such as school groups or single-parent families, but this is rather the exception than the rule. Most travel parties include more than one person. In the United States, couple/family leisure travel accounted for 69% of all domestic trips in 2004 and 31% of those travel parties included children (see Table 16.1;

Table 16.1   Travel party composition for US domestic travel in 2004 (TIA, 2005)

Domestic Household Trips

TOTAL (millions)	663.5
Solo Travelers (1 Adult)	41%
Adults Only	33%
Adults with Kids	26%
Domestic Leisure*	
TOTAL (millions)	490.1
Solo Travelers (1 Adult)	31%
Adults Only	38%
Adults with Kids	31%
Domestic Business**	
TOTAL (millions)	169.9
Solo Travelers (1 Adult)	73%
Adults Only	17%
Adults with Kids	10%

*Travel for visiting friends/relatives, outdoor recreation, entertainment/sightseeing, or other pleasure/personal reasons.
** Travel for business – either general reasons (e.g., consulting, service) or to attend a convention/conference/seminar or for combined business and pleasure purposes.

TIA, 2005). In Europe, families and groups represent up to 75% of the customers of Center Parks resorts which offer home-like cottages with multiple indoor and outdoor activities that are likely to satisfy group needs and make each family member happy.

This chapter focuses on issues related to social influences and group processes in hospitality and tourism DM. The major aspects that characterize group decisions may be found in Corfman's (1987) definition: 'a group decision is a decision made by two or more individuals who have the inclination and ability to influence the outcome and who are subject to a constraint or constraints preventing them from making independent decisions' (pp. 229–230). The fact that more people are involved in the process leads to a range of issues. Kirchler (1999) suggests three major aspects that are worthwhile investigating when analyzing decision-making processes (DMPs) in everyday life situations: the conceptualization of interactions among household members, the categorization of decision types, and the examination of the DMP itself. Ellis and Fisher (1994) further extend this list to include the following issues:

- Social and task dimensions (cohesiveness and productivity);
- Group structuration (networking);
- Communication and interaction processes within the group;
- Behavioral standards—roles and norms;
- Power and influence issues (e.g., leadership);
- Conflict and deviance (including the emergence of conflict situations and influence tactics that are used to resolve them).

Of course, these different issues are often addressed simultaneously in the same study. For example, many authors in tourism research have considered the following three questions together: (1) how roles and tasks are distributed across the household? (2) What is the relative influence of each member? (3) What is the specialization level of decisions?

In this chapter, group functions and group types will be defined first before going into issues of relevance when studying group DM. The next section will be devoted to the description of the different types of decision-making units (DMUs) in light of hospitality and tourism choices. Two major types will be discussed in more depth, that is, families and groups of friends. Extant literature on hospitality and vacation DM will be presented as well. Finally, the chapter closes with presentation of the major managerial implication of those extent studies. It should be noted that this chapter focuses on consumer groups or households and is not concerned with other types of DMUs such as organizational (e.g., buying center, board of directors) or institutional groups.

Group definitions and functions

Following Shaw (1976), a group involves members who share some-thing in common: 'two or more persons who are interacting with one another in such a manner that each person influences or is influenced by each other person' (p. 11). Blythe (1997) adds that those persons share a set of norms and maintain relationships that make their behav-ior dependent. In consumer behavior, the focus is often on the concept of reference group, defined as 'a person or a group of people that significantly influences an individual's behavior' (Beardon and Etzel, 1982, p. 184), rather than on group DM itself. Reference groups are thought to exert three types of influences on consumer choices: an informational, a comparative, and a normative influence (Assael, 1998). First, friends and relatives are often used as reliable sources of infor-mation or expertise when consumers lack knowledge and/or perceive a risk in buying a product. When we are making vacation plans, we often ask companions and family for recommendation, in addition to the advice of travel intermediaries. Second, friends and relatives have a comparative influence; consumers compare themselves with entities they consider important and 'judge whether the group would be sup-portive' (Assael, 1998, p. 547). For example, when looking for a tourism accommodation, we are more likely to choose a resort in which we will find customers similar (in age, household structure, or lifestyles) to our-selves, as these are more prone to reinforce our own values, attitudes, and behaviors. Self-maintenance and enrichment are the objectives of such an identification process. Finally, reference groups exert major normative influences on consumers' decisions and behaviors. In other words, the group strives to impose its norms, values, and behavior patterns on its members. Most of the time, this pressure toward group commitment and conformity is sustained by a reward and punishment system. For example, within the nightclub culture, Williams (2002) notices that 'individuals are aware of appropriate clothing, drinks and dance etiquette; those who do not conform are soon excluded' (p. 125). Of course, the individual's propensity to conform to group norms is influenced by a series of factors, such as his/her own value system and commitment to the reference group, the way he/she values individu-ality, and the motivation to comply.

Types of groups

When considering typologies of reference groups, particular types often come across. Blackwell et al. (2006) suggest three group dichotomies: primary vs. secondary; formal vs. informal; and aspirational vs. disso-ciative groups. A primary group is regarded as 'a social aggregation that is sufficiently intimate to permit and facilitate unrestricted direct interaction' (p. 523) and is characterized by a high level of cohesiveness. Primary groups are particularly important for hospitality and tourism providers since they share hobbies and spend most of their leisure activities with family, friends, or colleagues. In contrast, secondary groups are more occasional; they also bear face-to-face interaction but 'it is more sporadic, less comprehensive, and less influential in shaping thought and behavior' (p. 523). For example, members of the same choir or of the same sports club would constitute a secondary group. Faris (1953) does not use the idea of secondary group but rather makes the distinction between primary and institutional groups in which the former is 'held together by common traits and sentiments and tend to be spontaneous' (p. 160), whereas the latter 'exists to perform functions that may be other than those that bind the members of the group' (Corfman, 1987, p. 228). These are rather heterogeneous, externally formed and controlled. The cohesiveness of primary groups, such as families, is based on ascription, commitment, investment and attachment bonds whereas institutional groups tend to be united by instrumental bonds (McCall, 1970)[1].

Formal groups have a well-defined structure with established rules, a known list of members, and requirements for membership, while informal groups have a looser structure and are more likely to be based on friendship or common interests. Both types develop norms, which can have a pronounced effect on behavior and DM, and involve membership, that is, achieving a formal acceptance status in the group. A broad range of such formal structures exists within the hospitality and tourism sector. For example, a golf and country club may elaborate rules dictating the days when members may invite guests or when ladies may play, the dress code of the club, or the handicap level of visitors. Air France's Flying Blue Silver, Gold, or Platinum members can enjoy exclusive benefits, depending on the membership status and the number of miles traveled.

Finally, aspirational groups refer to groups with which the individual aspires to associate by adopting the group's norms, values, and behavior. In contrast, the individual will try to avoid any association with dissociative groups. From a marketing point of view, aspirational groups are of paramount importance because they can be used as a way to influence consumers, through the idea that buying certain products will result in membership in the group. For example, the timeshare and cruising industries often rely on such appeals, offering the aspiration to

---

[1] Ascription bonds stem from the status acquired by birth rather than by choice; attachment bonds arise when important personal needs are satisfied by the group and cannot be satisfied elsewhere. In contrast, instrumental bonds result from 'the group's ability to provide rewards for membership for fulfilling one's function in the group' (Corfman, 1987, p. 251).

own a property overseas or to be part of the affluent and elegant cruise customers. In contrast, some bars or restaurants may result in dissociative groups as individuals consider them not to be 'their kind of place.' 'Automatic' (Blythe, 1997) or 'associative' (Hoyer and MacInnis, 2004) groups are a last type of reference groups who represent the groups to which individuals actually and automatically belong (because of age, gender or education) and with whom they identify themselves. Of course, all these groups are not mutually exclusive. For example, people may belong to both formal (e.g., a family or a sport team) and informal groups (e.g., a group of friends or a crowd of sports fans) at the same time.

Issues of relevance in household decision-making

After having considered the characteristics of groups overall, we now focus on consumer groups or households and we present how they make their decisions together. Four major issues are discussed below: that is, interactions between members, types of decision processes going on, the way roles are distributed within the household and, finally, the issue of conflicts and influence tactics.

Interaction processes

Interaction processes depend on the structural characteristics of the household, that is, on the nature of relationships between members/partners. According to Kirchler (1999), mutual interactions may range from 'businesslike bartering to spontaneous altruism' (p. 297) and can be described by four principles: love, credit, exchange, and egoism. In love interactions, harmonious relationships prevail over power considerations to the extent that results of the decision are optimized for the mutual good, that is, for satisfying each other's needs and wants. When emotional ties between partners weaken, love often gets replaced by the credit principle. Although spouses may still make some efforts to find mutually satisfying solutions and to show consideration toward each other, they always wait for a return on their efforts and favors, granting the other spouse a kind of long-term 'credit.' If the quality of the relationship deteriorates further, interactions start to be guided by the equity principle. Acting like business partners, spouses strive to reach an equal distribution of costs and benefits in their decisions. Finally, when relationships become really poor, power differences in the household come to the fore, and interactions are dominated by the egoism principle. The person with the greater power manipulates decision situations and exchange transactions to his/her own advantage.

Types of decision processes

Kirchler (1999) proposes four dimensions in order to describe economic or purchase decisions: (1) uniqueness or frequency of repetition of a decision, (2) costs involved, (3) symbolic significance of the decision alternatives, and (4) effects of the decision on one or more household members. The combination of these dimensions will influence the decision variables, the decision mode that will be used, and the stakeholders of the DMP; 'the more expensive, socially prestigious and relevant a good is for all, the more likely it is that all members of the household will participate to the decision' (Kirchler, 1999, p. 298). Williams (2002) has developed a matrix in which major hospitality decisions are categorized into four types of decision processes (Table 16.2). Overall, group influences and the extent of group DM are more important in problem solving than in habit decision situations, and more important for high-involvement than for low-involvement purchases. As a result, the propensity to engage in group DM is the highest in extended problem solving situations (1 in Table 16.2) and the lowest when inertia prevails (4 in Table 16.2).

Table 16.2 suggests that most hospitality and tourism decisions are joint or syncretic in that they involve different members within a DMU (Fodness, 1992). Travel and vacation represent a major recurrent entry in many households' budget. Ryan (1995) points out that 'for many families, it is often the largest single repeated expenditure that occurs at frequent intervals' (pp. 94–95). As to tourism choices, Decrop (2006) has presented a list of 16 decision items (see Table 16.3). For each decision item, the last column of Table 16.3 indicates the extent to which social influences and group (rather than individual) DM is likely to take place.

Table 16.2 Categorization of hospitality decisions (*Adapted from* Williams, 2002)

	High-involvement purchase	Low-involvement purchase
Problem Solving (extensive information search)	1. EXTENDED PROBLEM SOLVING (EPS) (holidays, restaurants, theme parks)	3. LIMITED PROBLEM SOLVING (LPS) (beer brands, bowling alley, cinema)
Habit (limited information search)	2. BRAND LOYALTY (hotel chain, pub brand, fast-food outlet)	4. INERTIA (snacks in bars, beer brands)

Table 16.3 A typology of vacation decision items

Decision item	Definition	Likelihood of group DM
Accommodation	Includes not only lodging but also the general infrastructure (pool, tennis, disco, etc.) of the place to stay.	High
Accompaniment	People with whom one spends one's vacation.	High
Activities	What people do during their vacation time: sports, cultural visits, reading, entertainment, etc.	High
Attractions	Types of attractions the vacationer visits: museum, cities, monuments, national parks, events, etc.	High
Budget and expenses	Amount of money spent on vacation and the way it is spent.	Moderate
Destination	Place(s) where the vacation will be spent.	High
Duration	Length and timing of the trip.	Moderate
Formula	Global type of vacation: staying in one spot or touring sea or mountains, city or countryside, etc.	Moderate
Meals	Eating patterns (what and where one eats breakfast, lunch, and dinner).	High
Organization	The way the vacation is organized and reserved: by oneself, by a travel intermediary, by friends, etc.	Low
Period	Timing of the year for vacation.	Moderate
Purchases	Anything purchased and/or taken back home from one's vacation (souvenirs, self-gifts, postcards, photos, etc.).	Low
Route	Route followed to reach the vacation destination.	Low
Tour	Destination areas visited and route followed	Moderate
Transportation	Transportation modes used to reach the vacation destination and to make excursions there.	Low
Vacation style	Vacation lifestyle characterized particularly by the comfort level of the vacation and the level of integration in local life.	Low

Distribution of decision roles

Many authors have focused on the roles performed by the different household members. For consumer decisions, Kotler (2000) identifies up to five possible roles in any buying process, that is:

- *Initiator* or *gatekeeper*: the person(s) who first recognize(s) (and communicates) the need to go on vacation or to go out for dining.
- *Influencer*: the person(s) whose opinion is/are sought concerning criteria to use in purchases and whose preferences for alternatives are considered. For example, children may influence their parents to choose a place with a swimming pool or to go to McDonald.
- *Decider*: the individual(s) with the financial or moral authority to choose how the family's budget will be spent, on what products, and which brands.
- *Buyer*: the person(s) who act(s) as the purchasing agent (e.g., he/she visits the travel agency or web site to buy the vacation; he/she calls the restaurant or the hotel to book a table/room).
- *User*: the person(s) who actually experience(s) and benefit(s) from the product.

Of course, sometimes these five roles are performed by one and the same person and sometimes they are split over the different family members. Moreover, each role may be performed by one or more different members of the household, depending on factors such as household structure, gender statuses within the household, the type of product being consumed, and culture or religion.

Conflict and influence tactics

Most of the time, group DM involves a range of possible conflicts, starting from different involvement levels, motives, values, expectations, and preferences, since two or more people have to make choices. Decisions such as where to go for holiday, whether to go for a ride or to the cinema, and which films to see are often causes of household disagreements. Kirchler (1995) has introduced a distinction between three types of conflicts: value, preference, and distribution conflicts. Value conflicts arise when DMU members show fundamental differences in their goals resulting from different personality traits, product involvement, values, definitions, and motives. Preference conflicts mean that members share the same motives and involvement in the decision domain, but have different assessments about the attributes and alternatives involved in the choice. Finally, distribution conflicts result from situations in which the costs and benefits are perceived to be distributed unequally across DMU members.

Since human beings seldom like to stay in conflict situations, they will try to solve these in order to find harmony again. Zaichkowsky

(1985) suggests four broad types of techniques households may use to resolve purchase or consumption conflicts, namely:

- *Coercion*: It involves using authority, rewards and punishments, and gathering information and/or using outside expertise in order to force the other members to make a particular choice.
- *Persuasion*: It refers to the use of logical arguments in a reasonable manner or to the formation of a coalition within the household in order to influence the outcome of the decision. For example, children may collude against parents in order to influence the choice of a restaurant to one that offers a playground and gift material.
- *Bargaining and negotiation*: it involves strategies of give-and-take and of comparing benefits and costs wherein some household members seek to exert influence by exchanging a decision now for one later.
- *Manipulation*: It includes more psychological and emotional tactics that range from silence and sulking to withdrawal, all in an effort to pressure others into agreement.

Authors like Sheth and Cosmas (1975) or Kirchler (1995; 1999) have developed more detailed typologies of conflict resolving modes or influence tactics in consumer DM. These are paralleled in Table 16.4. Persuasion tactics include use of emotions, exertion of authority or physical force, presentation of (future) rewards or withdrawal of resources, insisting on one's desires or leaving the scene whenever the partner wants to impose his/her desires, strategic collection and use of information, and formation of coalitions. Family discussion involving offers of trade-offs and integrative bargaining are referred to as negotiation tactics. Reason stands for a cool logical argumentation in order to find the best solution. Finally, tactics may be developed in order to avoid any conflict within the household. These range from deciding autonomously to postponing the decision, through deciding or yielding according to established roles. Sheth and Cosmas' typology has been applied in a tourism context by Kang and Hsu (2004; 2005).

Types of hospitality and tourism DMUs

Consumers are usually involved in several types of DMUs when making product and service decisions. A distinction can be made between five usual types of DMUs for leisure and tourism products:

- Singles (individual deciding alone);
- Couples (married or non married);
- Families (two parents or single parent);
- Groups of friends; and
- Associative groups (sororities, school groups, charitable associations, cultural associations, sport clubs, etc.).

Table 16.4 Influence tactics in household decision making

Kirchler's general typology (1999)	Sheth and Cosmas's typology (1975)
Persuasion tactics	
1. Positive emotion (manipulation, humor)	
2. Negative emotion (threats, cynicism, ridicule)	
3. Helplessness (acting helpless or ill, crying)	
4. Aggression (constraints, hurt, violence)	1. Exertion of authority
5. Punishments (withdrawing resources)	
6. Insisting (insisting, discussing until the other yields)	
7. Rewards (offering services)	2. Future promise
8. Leaving the scene (resigning, yielding, leaving the scene)	
9. Overt information (talking openly about one's interest)	3. Information gathering
10. Distorted information (lying)	
11. Indirect coalition (reminding the other of children's needs)	4. Formation of coalition
12. Direct coalition (talking in the presence of others)	
Negotiation	
13. Trade-offs (book-keeping, reminding others of past favors)	5. Family discussion
14. Integrative bargaining (searching for an optimal solution which satisfies both partners)	
Reasoned argumentation	
15. Reason (talking in an emotionally neutral and objective way, logical argumentation)	
Conflict avoiding tactics	
16. Deciding autonomously (taking a decision without talking to the partner)	
17. Deciding according to roles (deciding autonomously according to role segregation)	6. Delegation to the most knowledgeable person
18. Yielding according to roles (the partner decides according to role segregation)	7. Delaying of decisions

Of course, the DMU may differ according to the product category. For example, the same consumer will go through the DMP alone for food or some beverage whereas he/she is more likely to get involved in a family DMU for the purchase of a new car and in a friend DMU for leisure activities. Moreover, it often happens that for the same product category, consumers are not always involved in the same type of DMU. For example, in addition to or in replacement of a family summer vacation, children may have their own vacation plans or parents can go for a mini-trip on their own. Groups of friends are also involved in other DMUs (family, couple or single) whereas the reverse is not always true. Finally, consumers may be involved in more projects with different types of DMU at the same time. For example, the same person may participate in more vacation projects at the same time (winter skiing, short breaks, summer vacation, camps, etc.). The next section focuses on discussing the two most relevant group DMUs as far as hospitality and tourism decisions are concerned: the family and the friend party.

Family: A major hospitality and tourism DMU

Families represent major consumer segments for hospitality and tourism industries (see Table 16.1). Many leisure activities and trips involve couples or families with children. A family may be defined as 'a group of two or more people living together who may be related by blood, marriage, or adoption' (Statt, 1997, p. 115). Families are characterized by intimate daily contacts, which allow their members to interact and behave as advisers, information providers, and DMUs. Once the decision is made, families also share much of their consumption, be it a dinner together or a holiday stay. The goal of family DM is not (always) to come to the best decision as possible for each individual but, 'families are seen to subordinate their individual needs to the needs of the family and, as a result, many purchases are seen not to act as satisfiers for individuals, but to satisfice the overall needs of the family' (Williams, 2002, p. 127). Of course, not all consumption situations involve family purchases; however, to quote Wilkie (1994), the family remains 'one of the most formidable areas in the entire field of consumer research' (p. 396). Wilkie further lists major reasons for this:

- Family purchase and consumption decisions are regular and continuous, making them difficult to generalize with confidence;
- Family decisions are made in private, which necessitates particular methods to approach them;
- Family decisions are not made independently from each other; for example, many trade-offs occur in leisure activities because of limited money and time budgets;

- Families have multiple and adaptive decision makers; the family DMU varies according to products and choice situations (see above);
- Family DM depends on the type of product/service involved; the decision to go to the cinema will not involve the same stakeholders as involved in the decision to go on a summer vacation.
- Families differ from each other, depending on variables such as life cycle, income, social affiliation, or psychographics.

All these dimensions make the study of family DM a complex and delicate enterprise.

The distribution of roles within the family is related to power and status issues. The question of relative influence and dominance in DM has led to many papers both in general marketing and in the hospitality literature. Davis and Rigaux's (1974) typology of influence in family DM is the most popular approach of the question to date. They make a distinction between four types of situations. In husband-dominant situations, the husband's opinions and preferences prevail all over the purchase decision and he makes the final choice, although the wife may have some influence regarding either problem recognition or the actual purchase decision. In contrast, a decision is characterized to be wife-dominant when the wife exerts primary influence over the purchase decision and makes the final choice although the husband has a (limited) role in problem recognition and final decision stages. In autonomic decisions, the final decision is made without much dialogue in the household, sometimes by one spouse and sometimes by the other; however considerable influence over the outcome may be exerted by the other spouse. Finally, a joint decision involves a syncretic process during which both spouses contribute to the DMP but neither dominates. The two parties may compromise, bargain, coerce, or persuade one another, but in the end both are responsible for the decision and agree more or less that it is the right one.

The family life-cycle

Consumers' age and family situation have a substantive influence on hospitality and tourism DM variables. The family life cycle (FLC) aims at incorporating these two variables in order to structure consumers' evolution over time in a number of typical, not compulsory, stages. It has received much consideration in the marketing and consumer behavior literature (e.g., Gilly and Enis, 1982; Murphy and Staples, 1979; Wells and Gubar, 1966). The typology of Table 16.5 is based on those studies as well as on Decrop (2006). Results have shown that position in the FLC has a major influence on income levels and on spending patterns. FLC also suggests a number of useful characteristics of DM relative to tourism and hospitality products. For example, it proves to be a better indicator of sport and culture participation and of

Table 16.5 A typology of vacationers based on the family life cycle (FLC)

Position in FLC	Definition
Younger single	People from 18 to 40 year old who no longer live with their parents; bachelor or divorced (but without children).
Younger couple	From 18 to 40 year old, married or non-married but without children.
Younger family	Head of household under 40 with young children (less than 12 years); includes both married and non-married households as well as newly made families.
Mid-life family	Head of household above 40 with (young and) older children (at least, one over 12 years), including married, non-married or newly made families. Sometimes, children have left the household while others still participate in family decisions.
Single parent family	Head of the household is divorced or widowed with children.
Older couple	More than 50 year old, without children anymore because they have left the household or with older children who no longer want to participate in activities with their parents.
Older single	More than 50 year old, old bachelor, widow and no children present or divorced.

leisure spending than age or social class (Williams, 2002). Other authors have shown that it is one of the best ways to segment vacationers (e.g., Fodness, 1992; Gitelson and Kerstetter, 1990).

Although the traditional family consisting of both parents living with child(ren) is still prevailing today, recent demographic and socio-cultural trends have a deep impact on the shape of the family in Western societies. Major trends have resulted in both an increase in the number of households and a decrease in the average household size along the following changes (Blackwell et al., 2006):

- Delayed marriage: In many industrialized countries, an increasing number of people are either postponing or avoiding getting married.
- Cohabitation: As a consequence of changing social norms, an increasing number of individuals decide to live with their partner outside marriage.
- The number of 'official' same-sex households is increasing as a result of a better social and political acceptance of gay and lesbian couples.
- Dual-careers: In more and more families, the two partners/spouses are working, which has a dramatic impact on household behavior,

norms and roles, especially as to housekeeping and bringing up children. In some cases, the woman is concerned about career advancement and personal fulfillment; in others, she works out of financial necessity.

- Divorce: Since 1960, the divorce rate in the United States has more than doubled (from 20 to 40%). Of course, divorces and separations represent major steps in the FLC (see Table 16.5) and have important implications for consumer, travel, and hospitality behavior.
- Change in values: Decreased influence of religion, increased influence of individualism and materialism, and concern for the future (overpopulation, etc).

These trends have resulted in the emergence of five types of 'modern' family structures in a growing importance: one-person households, reconstituted families, lone-parent households, cohabitating unmarried couples, and multi-person households. Of course, changing family structures have major consequences on consumer demand and behavior that should be taken into account when marketing hospitality and tourism products. For example, it is estimated that singles represent almost 50% of Club Med customers, a company that pioneered in offering tailor-made services and activities for singles. In the same way, major tour operators such as Neckermann, Thomas Cook, or Touristik Union International (TUI) now include lines of single-parent family packages.

Groups of friends: An increasingly important hospitality and tourism DMU

As a reference group, friends exert a major influence on most aspects of consumer behavior and, more particularly, on the DMP (Frenzen and Nakamoto, 1993; Peter and Olson, 1994). They provide information, reward or punish the decision maker for something he/she has done, and influence his/her values and self-concept. These three classical roles of friends have been well documented. However, few studies have focused on the group of friends as a DMU in itself (e.g., how friends make decisions together; what are the major characteristics of friend DMUs, etc.). Gitelson and Kerstetter (1994) have considered the DMP of travel parties visiting friends and relatives and the particular influence of the latter on the decisions made during the vacation stay. In a socio-cognitive study of group DMPs among the members of a sorority, Ward and Reingen (1990) concluded that social structure influences the individual's cognitive structure. Finally, Campbell (1998) has investigated DMPs between friends from a gender perspective. However, those works do not focus on friends as a DMU.

A group of friends can be defined as a set of persons sharing a mutual feeling of affection or sympathy that is based on neither blood ties nor sexual appeal. This is in line with Price and Arnould's (1999) definition of friendship as 'a voluntary, personal relationship, typically providing intimacy and assistance, in which the two parties like each other and seek each other's company' (p. 39). Friend parties may be involved in two major decision domains. The first involves 'inside' decisions, which arise when one or more members of the group recognize(s) a particular need to satisfy. These decisions may include convenience goods such as cigarettes or alcohol, or durables such as a car or an apartment. However, most decisions actually pertain to services and leisure activities: travel and vacation, restaurants, sport and cultural activities, evening or night out parties. In contrast, other decisions are triggered by 'outsiders' who require the group to make a decision. Those 'outside' decisions may include school tasks or activities related to youth movements, charities, or sororities. This emerging distinction may parallel with Faris' (1953) distinction between primary and institutional groups (see the earlier discussions). Of course, the DMP is not likely to be the same for these two types of decisions. This chapter focuses on the first decision domain (i.e., decisions involving a friend party held together spontaneously and not externally controlled) and, more particularly, on leisure decisions. Friend parties indeed represent large markets for the travel, movie, and catering industries. Most often, they are composed of younger consumers, be it a group of younger singles, a group of younger couples, or a mixed group (singles, couples and sometimes also a younger family).

Critical review of tourism and hospitality studies about group DM

In this chapter, the level of analytical interest is on the group rather than on the individual. This is much in contrast with the mainstream of hospitality and tourism research which focuses on the individual level both in conceptual models and in empirical studies. In many cases, researchers continue to collect data from only one of the individuals involved in the choice process. Studies addressing hospitality and tourism group DM are summarized in Table 16.6.

The first column of Table 16.6 indicates that most research so far has focused on the couple and the family. A series of studies have initially focused on the marital dyad (e.g., Filiatrault and Ritchie, 1980; Fodness, 1992; Jenkins, 1978; Nichols and Snepenger, 1988) from a role taxonomical perspective (i.e., who makes the decision within the couple?). A distinction between three typical situations has been suggested: husband-dominant, wife-dominant, and joint decisions. This distribution of roles has been investigated for different vacation sub-decisions (such as destination, accommodation, or budget) and typical DM stages (i.e., initiation of plans, information search, evaluation of alternatives,

Table 16.6 Extant literature related to leisure and tourism group DMP

	DMU	Types of decisions	Method (Sample size)	Group decision-making issues	Decision-making stages	Conclusions
Jenkins (1978)	Couple (married)	10 vacation subdecisions	Focus groups and survey (105)	Roles/relative influence Joint vs. dominated decisions (H–W–C)*	DMP overall Info collection Planning time Vacation behavior	The 10 purchase subdecisions are either husband-dominant or joint, none being wife-dominant.
Myers and Moncrief (1978)	Families	Destination Accommodation Trip route	Survey (478)	Roles/relative influence Joint vs. dominated decisions (H–W)	DMP overall	Destination and accommodation choices are found to be joint decisions; this is even more true for younger couples. Husbands exert more influence than wives on route decisions.
Filiatrault and Ritchie (1980)	Families	Generic decision to go on vacation Destination Lodging Budget Time period Duration Accompaniment (taking children or not)	Close-ended interviews (270)	Roles/relative influence Joint vs. dominated decisions (H–W)		

Crompton (1981)	Families	Holiday (overall) Destination and attractions Accompaniment	Unstructured interviews (39)	Interpersonal associations Group motivation Normative influences Socialization	DMP as a whole	There is a direct group influence on accompaniment and destination selection (children exerted a major influence); Social groups exerted a normative influence on destination and attraction choices; Socialization appeared to have some influence on the predisposition to vacation and to go to a particular destination.
Darley and Lim (1986)	Families (single vs. dual parents)	Three leisure activities: – motion picture attendance – family picnic outing – participant sports	Survey (106)	Child(ren) influence Locus of control	When to go How much to spend Where to go What type Gathering info Specific info Initial suggestion	Perceptions of child influence are product specific. Locus of control, child age and parental type are found to have differing impacts on the DMP.

(Continued)

Table 16.6 (Continued)

	DMU	Types of decisions	Method (Sample size)	Group decision-making issues	Decision-making stages	Conclusions
Nichols and Snepenger (1988)	Families (with or without children)	Transportation Expenditures Visits Accommodation Duration	Survey (1753)	Roles/relative influence Joint vs. dominated decisions (H–W)	Sociodemograhics Planning variables: time horizon, number of info sources Travel behaviors (leisure activities) Evaluation of the vacation experience	A majority of families (66%) used a joint decision-making mode. The three types of DM modes (H, W and joint) can be differentiated significantly using some sociodemographics, travel behaviors and post-experience evaluations.
Howard and Madrigal (1990)	Families	Recreation services		Roles/relative influence Joint vs. dominated decisions (H–W–C)	DMP as a whole	Mothers were found to play a dominant role in shaping the participation decisions of their children. Mothers actively screen the program before allowing the child to become involved in the final stage of the purchase decision.

Author (Year)	Sample	Context	Method	Focus	Variables	Findings
Fodness (1992)	Families (married couple with or without children)	Destination (Florida)	Survey (3585; 590)	Roles /relative influence Joint vs. dominated decisions (H–W)	FLC (5 stages) Info search Final decision	Stages in the FLC are found to be reflected both in info search and in the final decision.
Gitelson and Kerstetter (1994)	Individuals visiting friends and relatives	Sites to visit Length of stay Activities Eating choices Trip info Place to stay	Survey (71)	Roles/relative influence by friends and relatives	DM overall	Friends and relatives were found to play a dominant role or were the sole decision maker in 29 and 39% of all decisions respectively.
Seaton and Tagg (1995)	Families (parents and children)	Vacation overall	Survey (2824) in four European countries	Cross-cultural differences in decision influence (H–W–C) and in perception of decision outcomes	Children's role in: – consultation – influence – post-decisional approval – final decision – satisfaction – repeat intention	A majority of children in all countries had played some part in the vacation decision. In all countries, the vacation involves a syncretic decision; if not, mothers more likely to act as final decision-makers. Involving children in the DMP improves the satisfaction with decision outcomes.

(Continued)

Table 16.6 (Continued)

DMU	Types of decisions	Method (Sample size)	Group decision-making issues	Decision-making stages	Conclusions
Thornton et al. (1997)	Parents and children (0–16)	Activities	Diary (space–time budget) survey (143) and interviews (85)	Roles/relative influence	Activity behavior	Different generations have contrasting needs; children influence vacation activities either through their physical needs or through their ability to negotiate with parents.
Bohlmann and Qualls (2001)	Family triads (mother, father and teenager)	Destination	Longitudinal survey (56)	Preference revision through disconfirmation Individual vs. collective preferences Decision influences	Pre-discussion expectations and preferences Discussion Revised, post-experience preferences	Two types of significant disconfirmation effects are put into light: informational disconfirmation (when new product info is revealed in family discussion being different from one's prior beliefs) and preference disconfirmation (when a family member has incorrect expectations of another member's preferences).

Kang et al. (2003)	Families	Destination Particular location Duration Budget Activities Accommodation	Survey (297)	Dominant influence (individual, couple, one partner with child(ren), other joint and family)	Need recognition Info collection Info evaluation Final decision Actual purchasing	Couple joint decision was the most prevalent for the 10 decisions. Three market segments are generated based on common DM patterns: intergenerational, business-mixed-with-pleasure and visit friends and relatives travelers.
Decrop et al. (2004)	Groups of friends	Travel and vacation Leisure activities	In-depth interviews (18)	Functions of groups Group DMP Conflict and consensus Role distribution	Suggestion Discussion and evaluation Organization Post-experience evaluation	Groups of friends show particular characteristics when contrasted with families; these impact on the vacation DMP. DM is a long and chaotic process, and includes phenomena such as daydreaming, delegation and groupthink.
Kang and Hsu (2004)	Couple (married)	Destination	Survey (149)	Conflict arousal Influence strategies Satisfaction about decision and DMP	Family life cycle (FLC)	The level of overall conflict between spouses is moderate; Family life cycle and level of conflict between spouses are correlated with conflict solving strategies, which themselves influence satisfaction levels with the DMP.

(Continued)

461

Table 16.6 (Continued)

	DMU	Types of decisions	Method (Sample size)	Group decision-making issues	Decision-making stages	Conclusions
Litvin et al. (2004)	Couple (married)	10 vacation subdecisions (based on Jenkins, 1978)	Self-administered survey (215)	Roles/relative influence Joint vs. dominated decisions (H–W)	DMP overall Information collection	Most vacation subdecisions are joint. Only info collection appears to be more dominated by husbands.
Mottiar and Quinn (2004)	Couple (with or without children)	Holiday (overall) Budget to spend Travel agent Destination (country/resort) Accommodation Period	Survey (36)	Roles/relative influence Power relations	Initiation Info collection Specific decisions Booking	The overall consumption of a holiday is a joint decision whereas females have a dominant role in the early stages of the DMP.
Wang et al. (2004)	Parents and children (0–18)	Group package tour, including 13 subdecisions	Survey (240)	Roles/relative influence Joint vs. dominated decisions (H–W–C)	Problem recognition Info search Final decision	DM tends to be joint in the problem recognition and final decision stages whereas it tends to be dominated by wives in the info search stage.
Decrop (2005)	Couples, families and groups of friends	Holiday (overall) Destination	Longitudinal in-depth interviews (19)	Group cohesiveness Roles/relative influence Conflict and consensus	DMP overall Instigation Info search Preparation Reservation	Personal and interpersonal constraints have a major impact on group DM; Group processes may differ according to the type of DMU; in groups of friends, delegation and 'groupthink' often come across in the DMP.

| Kang and Hsu (2005) | Couple (married) | Destination | Survey (149) | Conflict arousal Influence strategies Satisfaction about decision and DMP | DMP overall | Four major dimensions of spousal conflict: interpersonal need, involvement, utility and power; Seven influencing strategies: family discussion, info gathering, delegation, delaying of decisions, coalition formation, future promise, and exertion of authority; Travelers' vacation experience positively impacts on conflict arousal. |

* H = Husband; W = Wife; C = Child or Children.

and booking). These studies have shown that most tourism decisions are joint decisions and that women have made an increasing influence in the last two decades due to the changing family structure discussed earlier. Recent papers have introduced more specific aspects of group DMPs, such as the role of disconfirmation in individual preference revisions arising from family interaction (Bohlmann and Qualls, 2001), the use of influence tactics in order to solve spousal conflicts in destination selection (Kang and Hsu, 2004; 2005), or power relationships within a couple (Mottiar and Quinn, 2004). The latter authors concluded that 'the overall consumption of a holiday is largely a joint decision, but when the purchase is broken down into different stages females have a dominant role in the early stages of the process, possibly making them the gatekeepers' (p. 149).

Originally ignored and later dismissed, the influence of children has been reassessed more recently. Some authors have limited the role of children to a passive indirect influence on vacation activities and on parents' attitudes and satisfaction levels (Cullingford, 1994; Filiatrault and Ritchie, 1980; Ryan, 1992). Other researchers have identified children as having a more active role as actual negotiators in DM (Howard and Madrigal, 1990; Seaton and Tagg, 1995; Thornton et al., 1997). Again, those studies have focused on which type of (pre-purchase) decision was most affected by children. For example, Thornton et al. (1997) have highlighted the influence of children on the activities of tourist parties while on holiday based on a space–time budget survey.

Table 16.6 shows that a large number of studies have been devoted to family DM. However, additional studies are still needed for two major reasons. First, the traditional family is changing (as discussed earlier) beyond the traditional husband–wife–children relationships. Single-parent families, recomposed families, or same-sex households should benefit from more consideration in future research. Second, issues other than decision roles, power, and relative influence should be approached. For example, topics such as decision strategies and rules and trade-offs with other (non travel) products and services deserve attention. The whole DMP of families should be investigated as well. By the time of writing this chapter, any paper presenting a thorough model of family DM for hospitality or tourism products could not be found. Finally, it would be worthwhile looking into the interconnectedness of different decision levels, including personal and interpersonal factors, and individual and group preferences/decisions (Ariely and Levav, 2000).

While couple and family have drawn considerable interests from marketing and tourism researchers, joint decisions by groups of friends have been ignored. As a solution, Gitelson and Kerstetter (1994) have proposed 'to include friends and/or relatives as potentially equal partners in the decision-making process' (p.65). However, their study did not focus on the friend party as a DMU in itself. They suggested that further research should incorporate when (prior, during, or after the trip) friends become influential. Decrop et al. (2004) and Decrop (2005) have tried to fill this gap to some extent by exploring the DMP of groups of friends through a qualitative study. They have showed that it dramatically departs from group DM in couples or families. First, most decisions involve all members of the friend party and not a sub-group of it; these are joint as opposed to autonomic decisions. Second, communication is less extensive. Groups of friends do not gather on such a regular basis as a family does. Next, personal and situational factors may strongly vary within the DMU, making it very trouble-some to find a compromising solution. As a consequence, DM takes place very late in the process, and leadership is often needed to carry out the project. A leader who triggers major decisions (destination, period, transportation, accommodation) emerges and acts on behalf of the group. Furthermore, participating in the group appears to be more important than the particular alternative that will be chosen. This may be related to group loyalty and 'groupthink' (Janis, 1983) which means that 'when a group is cohesive and in strong agreement about a decision, the opinions and preferences of the individuals in the group change to conform more to the preferences of the group as a whole' (Ellis and Fisher, 1994, p. 28). The group is more concerned with agree-ment and consensus than with the quality of the decision to be made, which leads to more extreme or poorer decisions.

However, more research is still needed to better understand how formal groups (sororities, sport clubs, etc.) and informal groups (friend parties) make their decisions together. Indeed such groups may repre-sent major segments for hotel, attraction, and tour operators. Moreover, the way 'outside' and 'inside' decisions are made needs further con-sideration.

Managerial implications of the studies

A series of suggestions for tourism and hospitality businesses may be elaborated based on the studies that have just been reviewed. Overall, tourism and hospitality customers should be addressed as groups and not only as individuals because (1) most of the time, DM is a joint process which involves several persons (two partners, parents and children, friends) and (2) social interaction is one of the major motives for leisure activities and for traveling. Members of a group like to benefit from the 'Saturday night fever' or from the holiday to meet again and to share activities. Operators should listen to group (and not only individual) needs/expectations/preferences, and be aware of the particular influence of each group member on decisions. In the same way, group values such as togetherness, friendship, trust, or confidence could be used in communication messages.

Because motives, constraints and decision modes are different in a couple, a family, and a party of friends, marketing strategies and tools should be adapted accordingly. In families, marketers should try to reach either women or men depending on the decision stage/role (see Table 16.6). Tour operators should develop packages with all-inclusive family prices and adapt to the evolving structure of many households (e.g., one parent + two children). Specialized operators such as OPF (One Parent Family) in the United Kingdom or Selectour in France nowadays offer the opportunity to one-parent households (or families in which only one parent can afford a vacation because the partner is working) to travel with small organized groups in order to share their vacation experience with other people in similar situations and not to be alone to care for children while holidaying. Those tour operators have adapted their offerings to the choice criteria that are usually used by such households, that is, being close to a beach, enjoying activities that are adapted to each age bracket (mini-clubs etc.), appropriate accommodation with special prices (children may stay in the same room for free), and so forth.

In groups of friends, leaders should be targeted. Of course, this would be easier in formal than in informal groups. In a formal group, such as a sport club or a cultural association, leaders can be identified easily based on yearbooks or directories and reached through direct marketing or personal selling. As to informal groups, occasions should be created for them to meet and to share leisure and travel activities, and communicated to through the mass media. Firms have already taken some steps in that direction. In the 'Coca-cola: Create your night' project, groups of two to four friends were invited to describe the party of their dreams and win a chance to live it out. More than 45,000 online votes were collected and considered by the jury! SN Brussels Airlines regularly offer special passes with favorable prices for (younger) groups of friends. In all cases, practitioners need to be careful regarding the measurement of expectations and preferences because group variables may differ from individual variables and not be the sum of it. It is especially not wise to predict choice on the basis of individual preferences as far as groups of friends are concerned. Adaptability should also be taken into account. Since many customers are involved in more projects and several DMUs at the same time, with different needs and desires, they should not be put in one exclusive segment. For example, promotional timing should be adapted according to the holiday DMU (e.g., early booking reductions for families and last-minute offers for couples or groups of friends).

Conclusion

Group decisions are not as easy as individual ones because of divergent personal constraints and conflicting values, expectations, or preferences. This chapter has presented the major aspects involved in such group DMPs for hospitality and tourism products. After the definition

of major group functions and types, the focus has been on issues associated with group DM, such as interaction processes, decision types,
conflict emergence, and resolution modes. Then, two major types of
DMUs were discussed in the context of leisure and hospitality choices,
that is, couples/families and groups of friends. Groups of friends are
atypical because they are based on informal friendship ties, which
are less binding than love and blood ties. Moreover, all members are
involved in other DMU types at the same time. As a result, group DM
in parties of friends is markedly different from group DM in couples or
families. Tourism and hospitality operators should incorporate these
differences to a larger extent in their strategies by segmenting different
types of groups and positioning their offerings accordingly.

References

Ariely, D., and Levav, J. (2000). Sequential choice in group settings:
Taking the road less travelled and less enjoyed. *Journal of Consumer
Research*, Vol. 27, 279–290.

Assael, H. (1998). *Consumer Behavior and Marketing Action*. Mason:
Southwestern.

Beardon, W. O., and Etzel, M. J. (1982). Reference group influence on
product and brand purchase decisions. *Journal of Consumer Research*,
9 (September), 178–196.

Blackwell, R. D., Miniard, P. W., and Engel, J. E. (2006). *Consumer
Behavior*, 10th ed. Cincinnati: Thomson South-Western.

Blythe, J. (1997). *The Essence of Consumer Behavior*. Upper Saddle River:
Prentice Hall.

Bohlmann, J. D., and Qualls, W. J. (2001). Household preference revisions and decision making: The role of disconfirmation. *International
Journal of Research in Marketing, 18*, 319–339.

Campbell, L. (1998). Decision-making processes between friends:
Speaker and partner gender effects. *Sex Roles, 39*, 125–133.

Corfman, K. P. (1987). Group decision making and relative influence when preferences differ. *Research in Consumer Behavior*, Vol. 2,
223–257.

Crompton, J. L. (1981). Dimensions of social group role in pleasure
vacations. *Annals of Tourism Research, 8* (4), 550–568.

Cullingford, C. (1994). Children's attitudes to holiday overseas. *Tourism
Management, 16*, 121–127.

Darley, W., and Lim, J. (1986). Family decision making in leisure-time
activities: An exploratory investigation of the impact of locus of control, child age influence factor and parental type on perceived child
influence. In R. Lutz (ed.), *Advances in Consumer Research* (Vol. 13,
pp. 370–374). Provo, UT: Association for Consumer Research.

Davis, H. L., and Rigaux, B. P. (1974). Perception of marital roles in
decision processes. *Journal of Consumer Research, 1*, 51–62.

Decrop, A. (2005). Group processes in vacation decision-making. *Journal of Travel and Tourism Marketing, 18* (3), 23–36.

Decrop, A. (2006). *Vacation Decision Making*. Wallingford: CABI.

Decrop, A., Pecheux, C., and Bauvin, G. (2004). Let's make a trip together: An exploration into decision making within groups of friends. *Advances in Consumer Research, 31*, 291–297.

Ellis, D. G., and Fisher, B. A. (1994). *Small Group Decision Making: Communication and the Group Process*. New York: McGraw-Hill.

Faris, R. E. (1953). Development of the small-group research movement. In M. Sherif and M. O. Wilson (eds.), *Group Relations at the Crossroads* (pp. 155–184). New York: Harper and Brothers.

Filiatrault, P., and Ritchie, J. R. (1980). Joint purchasing decisions: A comparison of influence structure in family and couple decision making units. *Journal of Consumer Research, 7*, 131–150.

Fodness, D. (1992). The impact of family life cycle on the vacation decision-making process. *Journal of Travel Research, 31*, 8–13.

Frenzen, J., and Nakamoto, K. (1993). Structure, cooperation, and the flow of market information. *Journal of Consumer Research, 20*, 360–375.

Gilly, M. C., and Enis, B. M. (1982). Recycling the family lifecycle. *Advances in Consumer Research, 9*, 271–276.

Gitelson, R., and Kerstetter, D. (1990). The relationship between socio-demographic variables, benefits sought, and subsequent vacation behavior: A case study. *Journal of Travel Research, 28* (3), 24–29.

Gitelson, R., and Kerstetter, D. (1994). The influence of friends and relatives in travel decision-making. *Journal of Travel and Tourism Marketing, 3* (3), 59–68.

Howard, D., and Madrigal, R. (1990). Who makes the decision: The parent or the child? The perceived influence of parents and children on the purchase of recreation services. *Journal of Leisure Research, 22*, 244–258.

Hoyer, W. D., and MacInnis, D. J. (2004). *Consumer Behavior*, 4th ed. Boston: Houghton Mifflin Company.

Janis, I. L. (1983). *Groupthink: Psychological Studies of Foreign Policy Decisions and Fiascoes*, 2nd ed. Boston: Houghton Mifflin.

Jenkins, R. L. (1978). Family vacation decision-making. *Journal of Travel Research, 16*, 2–7.

Kang, S. K., and Hsu, C. H. (2004). Spousal conflict level and resolution in family vacation destination selection. *Journal of Hospitality and Tourism Research, 28* (4), 408–424.

Kang, S. K., and Hsu, C. H. (2005). Dyadic consensus on family vacation destination selection. *Tourism Management, 26*, 571–582.

Kang, S. K., Hsu, C. H., and Wolfe, K. (2003). Family traveler segmentation by vacation decision-making patterns. *Journal of Hospitality and Tourism Research, 27* (4), 448–469.

Kirchler, E. (1995). Studying economic decisions within private households: A critical review and design for a 'couple experiences diary'. *Journal of Economic Psychology, 16*, 393–419.

Kirchler, E. (1999). Household decision making. In P. Earl and S. Kemp (eds.), *The Elgar Companion to Consumer Research and Economic Psychology* (pp. 296–304). Cheltenham: Edward Elgar.

Kotler, P. (2000). *Marketing Management.* The Millennium edition. Upper Saddle River, NJ: Prentice Hall International.

Litvin, S. W., Xu, G., and Kang, S. K. (2004). Spousal vacation-buying decision making revisited across time and place. *Journal of Travel Research, 43*, 193–198.

McCall, G. J. (1970). *Social Relationships.* Chicago: Aldine.

Mottiar, Z., and Quinn, D. (2004). Couple dynamics in household tourism decision-making: Women as the gatekeepers? *Journal of Vacation Marketing, 10*, 149–160.

Murphy, P. E., and Staples, W. (1979). A modernized family life cycle. *Journal of Consumer Research, 6* (June), 12–22.

Myers, P. B., and Moncrief, L. W. (1978). Differential leisure travel decision making between spouses. *Annals of Tourism Research, 5* (1), 157–165.

Nichols, C. M., and Snepenger, D. J. (1988). Family decision making and tourism behavior and attitudes. *Journal of Travel Research, 26* (Spring), 2–6.

Peter, J. P., and Olson, J. C. (1994). *Understanding Consumer Behavior.* Boston: Irwin.

Price, L. L., and Arnould, E. J. (1999). Commercial friendships: Service provider-client relationships in context. *Journal of Marketing, 63*, 38–56.

Ryan, C. (1992). The child a visitor. *World Travel and Tourism Review,* 135–139.

Ryan, C. (1995). *Researching Tourist Satisfaction: Issues, Concepts, Problems.* London: Routledge.

Seaton, A. V., and Tagg, S. (1995). The family vacation in Europe: Paedonomic aspects of choices and satisfactions. *Journal of Travel and Tourism Marketing, 4* (1), 1–21.

Shaw, M. E. (1976). *Group Dynamics: The Psychology of Small Group Behavior,* 2nd ed. New-York: McGraw-Hill.

Sheth, J. N., and Cosmas, S. (1975). *Tactics of conflict resolution in family buying behaviour.* Chicago: American Psychological Association.

Statt, D. A. (1997). *Understanding the Consumer.* Upper Saddle River: Prentice Hall.

Thornton, P. R., Shaw, G., and Williams, A. M. (1997). Tourist group holiday decision-making and behavior: The influence of children. *Tourism Management, 18*, 287–297.

TIA. (2005). *Domestic Travel Market Report.* Travel Industry Association of America.

Wang, K. -C., Hsieh, A. -T., Yeh, Y. -C., and Tsai, C. -W. (2004). Who is the decision-maker: The parents or the child in group package tours? *Tourism Management, 25*, 183–194.

Ward, J. C., and Reingen, P. H. (1990). Sociocognitive analysis of group decision making among consumers. *Journal of Consumer Research, 17,* 245–262.

Wells, W. D., and Gubar, G. (1966). The life cycle concept. *Journal of Marketing Research, 2,* 355–363.

Wilkie, W. L. (1994). *Consumer Behavior.* New York: John Wiley and Sons.

Williams, A. (2002). *Understanding the Hospitality Consumer.* Oxford: Butterworth-Heinemann.

Zaichkowsky, J. L. (1985). Measuring the involvement construct. *Journal of Consumer Research, 12,* 341–352.

Part Five

Special Topics

Internal marketing

Michael Davidson

Introduction and general issues

Prior to examining internal marketing (IM) in the hospitality and tourism industry, there is first a need to set this focus within the wider context of marketing and examine other elements of an organization's performance that shape how IM can be used. In the hospitality and tourism business environment, the marketing function concentrates upon the external customers rather than internal customers. Marketing and advertising campaigns, for example, are constructed after considerable market research to segment and target whom the marketing message is aimed at. Companies also have large and normally well-resourced marketing and sales departments to relate to external customers. As explained elsewhere in this book, there is now a level of sophistication in marketing to external customers that is aided by the use of computer technology that allows huge amounts of data to be stored and analyzed to ensure that marketing campaigns reach the desired market effectively. An important element of this marketing effort has been the increasing use of relationship marketing that has an IM component that uses organizational culture and values as the center of operations and strategy to link the organization to the customer (Sin et al., 2006).

The strategic focus of marketing is an integral part of any organization's overall strategy and business plan. Within the marketing domain, we are seeing an ever-increasing emphasis on relationship marketing that is based upon the direct linkage between the company and the customer. The external marketing focus for hospitality and tourism organizations is to get people to buy the product or service before sampling, whereas IM is concerned with ensuring that the yield from each customer is maximized when the service interactions are taking place. The time frame for service and opportunity for IM can vary enormously depending upon the time the customer will spend engaged with an organization, e.g., from buying a meal or staying at a hotel for several days. Many hospitality and tourism organizations see marketing and sales as essentially one function with two elements (Kotler et al., 2006). This chapter uses a similar approach.

Whilst, as noted above, there can often be an extended time period for customer interaction, especially while staying at a hotel, there is little focus from the marketing department given specifically to IM. The ongoing contact between the organization and the customer becomes the domain of operations and in turn is shaped by the service and marketing orientation of the employees. To a large extent, the IM during the customer contact phase is seen as operational selling.

This chapter will make the case that IM needs to be identified as a cogent and integrated part of the overall marketing strategy and the operational and human resource strategy. Many theorists have identified IM and its importance but very few have put forward this concept as part of overall organizational performance. To develop such a strategy requires the understanding of the interactions and perceptions of the employee, the organization, and the customer. Strong correlations have been established between employee attitudes and perceptions of service quality (Schneider and Bowen, 1995; Davidson et al., 2001). IM also refers to the employee relationship with marketing principles as it applies to the employees who provide the service for customers. An emphasis is also given to the notion of meeting the internal customers' needs and wants, that is, being able to satisfy the internal customers (fellow employees) so that they can satisfy the external customers' requirements (Lewis and Chambers, 2000).

Development of internal marketing

The term IM started to appear in the literature in the mid 1970s and has been the focus of a fairly continuous research stream for marketing, organizational, and operational theorists who are interested in services industries. Jones (1986) and Lewis (1989) were among the first to apply IM specifically to the hospitality and tourism industry. However, it was Berry et al. (1976) who are generally credited as the first to use the term 'Internal Marketing'. A brief overview is provided of some of the main theorists from a general marketing and management orientation as well as theorists from hospitality and tourism.

This section will provide a theoretical background and framework for IM and does not attempt to provide a fully comprehensive literature review. Berry et al. (1976) and Berry (1981, 1987) focused on linking jobs to employee satisfaction and to the re-engineering of jobs. Sasser and Arbeit (1976) linked job satisfaction and IM in examining front line employees and the retention of excellent service staff. Gronroos (1983, 1997) saw IM as a strategy to develop customer service effectiveness for the whole organization and it was integrated with the marketing strategy as all employees should have responsibility for marketing. Gummesson (1987) noted that IM, which is implemented through communication and cultural exchange, resulted in increased productivity and efficiency. George (1990) looked at effective internal exchanges that resulted from IM and the coordination of the human resources and marketing departments. Rafiq and Ahmed (2003); Ahmed et al. (2002) examined the alignment of IM as a cultural framework to facilitate the effectiveness of a marketing strategy by motivating employees though empowerment. Piercy (1995) also looked at strategic alignment of IM and how it facilitated the removal of department barriers. Rafiq and Ahmed (2000) examined how IM achieved employee satisfaction, customer satisfaction, and inter-functional coordination through empowerment. Naude et al. (2003) concluded that IM implementation produced increased job satisfaction in a service value chain and influenced individual and organizational characteristics. Lings and Greenly (2005) identified that IM was interchangeably used with internal-market orientation to improve organizational climate.

Themes that emerge from the above are that IM is linked to employees and their job satisfaction. It is not possible to effectively operate IM without the full participation of employees and, for this to occur, there must be a pre-condition of a high level of job satisfaction. This should also be underpinned by an organizational culture where there is good communication, which in turn requires that IM cannot be separated from the overall marketing strategy.

Hospitality and tourism researchers first started looking at IM in the 1980s with Jones (1986) noting that for internal marketers 'Product' was the employees, because of the branding and attributes they bring to the job. The 'Place' of external marketers is translated into the circumstances of the operations and systems used. The 'Promotion' aspect is seen as similar for both IM and external marketing, and finally, the 'Price' is characterized as remuneration and reward of employees. The approach taken by Lewis (1989) was to emphasize that the most important element of the hospitality product was the manner of service and not the tangible product such as a hotel room. The hospitality industry generally viewed marketing as an external activity, but because the customer experiences have the largest impact, the most effective marketing strategies are internal. Lewis et al. (1995) further developed this theme by focusing upon employees as an internal customer as they are buying their jobs. This means that, if they are satisfied with their jobs, they in turn will be able to satisfy the external customer. Hales and Mecrate-Butcher (1994) focused on IM in hotels as being aligned with human resources strategy rather than external marketing. They also noted that IM was used to a very limited extent in the hotel industry. The linkage of employees and IM is further supported by Bowen (1997) who saw hospitality employees as part of the product. The external marketing brings customers in but is of little good if the service is not appropriate. Marketing success in this case depends upon other constructs such as culture, service orientation, empowerment, and listening. These themes of linking human resource strategies and IM have been a constant for the above theorists and is also supported by the work of Paraskevas (2001), Arnett et al. (2002), Gounaris (2005), Hwang and Chi (2005), Varoglu and Eser (2006), and others.

The airline industry was examined by Czaplewski et al. (2001) who saw IM as treating frontline employees as internal customers to encourage them to provide excellent service. This also helped retain and energize employees. Crick (2003) has also looked at IM on a wider basis than a single or group of organizations. She used the concept to apply to a tourism area where there are multiple destination-marketing strategies to attract tourists and where IM is used as a focus for helping local residents to be more receptive to tourism, concluding that IM strategies are essential for destination marketing.

The theorists in hospitality, tourism, and other related areas have also reinforced that IM is an effective concept that can greatly assist the performance, whether it is at the individual organizational or corporate level. It is of concern that IM is not used more widely in hotels, although many researchers see IM as an integral part of the human resource strategy for all organizations.

Application of organizational culture and climate to IM

Organizational culture and climate are two theoretical constructs that are used by business organizations to assist with the efficiency of their operation. Culture has been described as the glue that keeps an organization together. It is characterized by the norms and the shared values that guide how the organization conducts its business. The organizational culture sets the frame of reference for the whole organization and its employees. It is created by myriad policies, documents, actions, and company guidelines, explicit and otherwise. Most organizations have a vision and/or mission statement that encapsulates how they see their business; this statement also serves as a starting point for building the culture. If the culture is dysfunctional, the likelihood of having a successful operation is extremely remote, and this is especially true when considering hospitality and tourism organizations as they are built upon high levels of employee and customer contacts. Of course, organizational culture varies between companies and is also affected by national and other cultural backgrounds but, at the very least, it must be positive in order to have a level of operation that is sustainable. Culture can be measured by a survey of employees to elicit what is understood by the range of organizational policies and practices, but the usual method for researchers is a detailed examination of the published documents that state the mission, vision, values, and goals of the organization. These documents are also reinforced by the training and standard operating procedures (SOP). Whilst these are the explicit manifestations of culture, there are also the norms and practices that encompass other shared beliefs that are often not written down.

Organizational climate is a snapshot of time that is measured by a psychologically based questionnaire that asks employees their perceptions of the organization and practices. Even though it is a separate theoretical construct from culture, the two are extrinsically linked. Organizational climate provides management with a reading on a range of dimensions that allows a judgment to be made on how their employees feel about the organization. Climate can be changed by specific management actions, whereas cultural change is a much slower process. Climate can also be used to measure other related constructs such as an orientation of employees to service quality, innovation, or IM.

Definitions of organizational culture and climate have seen some confusion as to precisely what these constructs represent, with Trice and Beyer (1993) defining culture in terms of what it is not. It is not climate, which is measured with researcher-based data, whereas culture is measured by intense data collection of an emic (contrastive) nature. The definitions of culture note that it has many unique indicators like myths, symbols, rites, and stories. A more controversial was the view expressed by Denison (1996) in arguing that it is not clear that culture and climate are examining distinct organizational phenomena. However, the literature refers to culture as being deeply rooted in the structure of an organization and based upon values, beliefs, and assumptions held by the members. Climate, however, tends to present social environments measured by a broad set of dimensions and can be considered as temporary and subject to a range of controls. Table 17.1 gives an outline of differences between the literatures using an epistemological approach – the point of view taken, methodology used, temporal orientation, level of analysis, and the discipline area.

Culture research studies were searching for what is unique in each setting and mainly used qualitative methods of data analysis, whereas climate research studies used quantitative methods and looked for dimensions that were generalizable across different settings. Many of the difficulties that seem to have plagued researchers in the 'climate' area can be traced to this desire to find generalizable dimensions that are applicable to all environments, to the extent that a multiplicity of dimensions, climate instruments, and underlying theoretical

Table 17.1 Organizational culture versus organizational climate

Research perspective	Cultural literature	Climate literature
Epistemological	Contextualized and idiographic	Comparative and nomothetic
ViewPoint	Emic (native view)	Etic (researcher's view)
Methodological	Qualitative observation	Quantitative data
Temporal Orientation	Historical evolution	Ahistorical snapshot
Level of Analysis	Underlying values and assumptions	Surface level manifestations
Discipline	Sociology	Psychology

Source: Denison (1996, p. 625).

assumptions have been produced by various researchers. Denison (1996, pp. 621–622) summed up this paradox:

Culture researchers were more concerned with the evolution of social systems over time... whereas climate researchers were generally less concerned with evolution but more concerned with the impact that organisational systems have on groups and individuals... Culture researchers argued for the importance of deep underlying assumptions... Climate researchers in contrast, typically placed greater emphasis on organisational members perceptions of observable practices and procedures that are closer to the surface of organisational life... and categorisation of these practices and perceptions into analytic dimensions defined by the researchers.

Most hospitality and tourism operations executives readily acknowledge that corporate culture plays a critical role in service quality. Often brand standards were seen as a way to implement corporate culture as opposed to the commonly held notion that culture is often developed unconsciously. The major role of senior management in hospitality and tourism is to create and maintain culture as is illustrated by the following quotations from two senior industry executives: 'Our company allows our property to be unique to adapt to city culture, but the company provides the guidelines'; 'Company culture is a major part of the Standard Operating Procedures' (Chacko et al., 2005).

Organizational culture and climate can be described as the bedrock upon which organizational performance is based. A poor organizational culture and climate will significantly impact service quality and customer satisfaction and hence performance. It is therefore critical for an IM environment to ensure that these are positive.

The IM process needs to be set within an operational framework to seek ways to ensure that the maximum gain is derived from what is essentially a captive market. It is the service interaction that allows staff members to have considerable contact with individual customers, and their attitude and behavior are critical to customer service (Susskind et al., 2000). It is apparent that the key to success in IM is being able to mobilize the employees to not only embrace but also actively pursue these marketing initiatives.

Relationship marketing is particularly pertinent to IM and organizational performance as it engages the three critical elements – the customer, the marketing department, and the employees. It is built upon rewarding the customer for loyalty to a particular organization such as hotel through reward and loyalty programs (Oh, 2000). Therefore, it is advantageous for all employees to have an understanding of relationship marketing as it is based upon service quality. If service quality is not achieved, there is no reason for the customer to have any interest in these loyalty programs. The use of loyalty programs in hospitality and tourism are facilitated by the use of technology that is now able to handle vast amounts of customer data (Geddie et al., 2002). Relationship marketing is built upon a long-term relationship between the organization, employees, and customers and is not limited to the marketing department (Kim et al., 2006), and it should not be seen as the only solution by hospitality marketers (Oh, 2002). This means that the customer dynamic and customer impression of the business are formed mainly from service interactions, which are shaped by organizational culture and climate.

Both of these theoretical constructs, organizational culture and climate, are fundamental to any successful hospitality and tourism operations as they shape the employee's performance and perceptions. Whilst these are theoretical constructs, they are very real and can be measured. Because of the nature of simultaneity of production and consumption, a feature of the industry, organizational culture and climate are the key underlying factors that have the ability to positively impact the level of service quality and customer satisfaction. It is simply not possible to inspect or check the vast array of service interactions that take place in hospitality and tourism operations. Of course there is pre-set SOP, but they can at best only cover a small proportion of the interactions. For example, a dish served in a restaurant will have a recipe, costing and there may well be a picture or diagram to show how it is to be presented. But,

- was the cooking process correct?
- was the serving temperature correct?
- how long did the customer have to wait?
- was the dish served in an appropriate manner?

The list of questions can go on.

Therefore, for the dish to be served correctly to the customer the hospitality organization is relying heavily upon individual employees completing the process. The employees need to have been successfully trained and follow SOP for the service to be of the highest level. Organizational culture and climate need to be supportive of the employee which in turn engenders that extra effort to achieve high levels of quality service.

Employees and IM

The employees are central to the examination of IM. It can be readily understood that those employees who have direct customer contact are of prime concern, but they are by no means the only employees that are crucial to IM. Indeed it is the contention of this chapter that *all employees need to be part of any IM strategy and this can only be achieved by a positive organizational culture and climate.*

Consider a brief hypothetical example: *A chef may have produced a special dish of the day; he or she will then have to ensure that some marketing collateral (daily menu boards or tent cards etc.) is in the restaurant to market the dish, and then there is the actual selling of the dish to customers by the wait staff. This requires cooperation between employees and departments, as the most critical aspect of the process, the last step, is the internal marketing to the customer. It is here that an enthusiastic wait staff is likely to have more success in selling the dish to the customers, as opposed to an unenthusiastic wait staff.*

Why should these employees and departments cooperate?

- it allows the kitchen to feature the dish for operational reasons
- it is likely to be more profitable for the organization
- it provides the customer with greater choice
- it is often unique and a point of difference from the competition
- it allows the wait staff to interact with and explain the dish to customers
- it fosters cooperation between departments and individuals
- it supports the economic viability of the restaurant for all staff
- a good organizational culture and climate supports and facilitates the process

The above illustration demonstrated that cooperation is an essential ingredient to the implementation of an IM strategy. This hypothetical example can be taken further to illustrate a possible supply chain: *The purchasing manager was contacted by one of the suppliers to say that there was an opportunity to purchase some prime cuts of beef at a very advantageous rate because of a cancelled order. He rang the chef who agreed to buy because they could feature the prime cuts as a special of the day on the menu to boost the weekly profit margins. The restaurant manager and wait staff were informed to ensure that the dish was marketed through the daily menu board and tent cards; yet for this to really work, it is essential that the wait staff can then do an enthusiastic sales job on the customers.* We have a supply chain with the supplier, the purchasing manager, chef, restaurant manager, wait staff, and, finally, the customer. This supply chain involves three internal departments and lots of staff plus two external links. A question to ask is:

Was this an operational decision to offer a special dish of the day? Or *Was it an IM decision to offer a special dish of the day?*

It is both, as very often the IM is driven by what is possible from an operational standpoint. This illustrates how critical the employees are in this series of decisions that eventually required the need for IM of the dish. This also illustrates another element of IM in that it can and often must react quickly to an operational decision if success is to be achieved and that requires cooperation between departments and employees.

The supplier was also a critical in the above example, although normally a supplier is thought of, in purely operational terms, as the deliverer of goods on time and of the right quality. But in this case the opportunity came about by the relationship between the purchasing manager and the supplier that presented a marketing outcome and a competitive edge in offering customers the special dish of the day.

What role does organizational culture and climate play? Culture and climate provide the background processes that facilitate and support a cooperative environment that allows employees to become enthusiastic. With a positive and supportive culture and climate, the above scenario becomes a seamless process between the external supplier, departments, and employees concerned in order that the dish of the day could be offered.

Organizational culture and climate in practice

Having introduced both constructs and their impact on service quality, IM and customer satisfaction, there is a need to have some deeper understanding. It is argued in this chapter that culture and climate are the basis of understanding organizational performance, especially in the area of IM.

Setting a company's (organizational) culture is seen as a fundamental step in promoting good performance. All companies have statements that indicate what sort of culture they are trying to embed. Table 17.2 presents three such examples.

The Marriott statement focuses upon values and associates (employees) and clearly recognizes that employees are critical to their success. Customer satisfaction and service quality simply cannot happen without the committed employees.

Southwest Airlines is perhaps the most outstanding example of putting employees at the center of their mission statement and linking it expressly to customer service. It further goes on to state that the culture and climate created for employees is exactly what they wish to create for the customers. This is not just rhetoric because the company has had 32 consecutive years of profitability and has also won numerous awards for customer service. This provides considerable evidence that the right organizational culture and climate generate outstanding organizational performance.

Starbucks asserts what their company purpose is and then very explicitly states that there are six guiding principles. These principles focus upon the employees with the explicit comment that they seek to 'provide a great work environment and treat each other with respect and dignity'. Starbucks realizes that 'developing enthusiastically satisfied customers all of the time' cannot be done without ensuring the appropriate organizational culture and climate.

Table 17.2 Examples of stated culture for hospitality and tourism organizations

Marriott Hotel Corporation	'The core values established by the Marriott family over 75 years ago have served our company well and will continue to guide our growth into the future. Foremost of these core values is the enduring belief that our associates are our greatest assets. There is a "Marriott Way." It's about serving the associates, the customer, and the community. Marriott's fundamental beliefs are enduring and the keys to its continued success. It's the Marriott experience. We do whatever it takes to provide our associates with the utmost opportunities, and our customers, with superior service.' (http://marriott.com/corporateinfo/culture)
Southwest Airlines	'The mission of Southwest Airlines is dedication to the highest quality of Customer Service delivered with a sense of warmth, friendliness, individual pride, and Company Spirit. We are committed to provide our Employees a stable work environment with equal opportunity for learning and personal growth. Creativity and innovation are encouraged for improving the effectiveness of Southwest Airlines. Above all, Employees will be provided the same concern, respect, and caring attitude within the organization that they are expected to share externally with every Southwest Customer. Jan. 1988.' (http://www.southwest.com/about_swa/)
Starbucks	Establish Starbucks as the premier purveyor of the finest coffee in the world while maintaining our uncompromising principles while we grow. The following six guiding principles will help us measure the appropriateness of our decisions: • Provide a great work environment and treat each other with respect and dignity. • Embrace diversity as an essential component in the way we do business. • Apply the highest standards of excellence to the purchasing, roasting and fresh delivery of our coffee. • Develop enthusiastically satisfied customers all of the time. • Contribute positively to our communities and our environment. • Recognize that profitability is essential to our future success. Corporate Social Responsibility: It's the way we do business Contributing positively to our communities and environment is so important to Starbucks that it's a guiding principle of our mission statement. We jointly fulfill this commitment with partners (employees), at all levels of the company, by getting involved together to help build stronger communities and conserve natural resources.' (http://www.starbucks.com/aboutus/environment.asp)

Similar statements can be found in many hospitality and tourism companies' brochures. However, there must be a match between the rhetoric of such statements and actions within the organization. These companies have certainly done this over many years setting an excellent organizational culture and climate. The Marriott Hotel Corporation was one of the first major hotel companies to introduce an organizational climate survey (Associate Opinion Survey) on a regular basis. These surveys are used to monitor employee perceptions of management and organizational performance and are taken very seriously. If falling or negative climate readings are obtained from departments, it will provide a basis for investigating what is happening operationally. In this way, Marriott demonstrated that the rhetoric from the organization is matched to the operations. Today, it is commonplace to find climate surveys conducted in the hospitality and tourism industry; yet many major companies still do not use this management tool.

Organizational climate and service quality perspective

Employees are an integral part in the development of service quality, and its implementation and success in turn allows IM strategies to be developed. Without an acceptable level of service quality in place, any effort expended on IM would be wasted as customers are not going to buy the goods or services offered. A climate for innovation needs to be developed in the context of a continuous improvement effort and to establish a quality culture that supports IM. Good examples of this can be seen in a number of upscale hotel chains such as the Four Seasons and the InterContinental Hotels Group where the stated practices and procedures for dealing with innovation and quality are centered on employees.

Four Seasons is dedicated to perfecting the travel experience through continuous innovations and the highest standards of hospitality. From the finest quality of elegant surroundings to caring, highly personalized 24-hour services, Four Seasons embodies a true home-away-from-home for those who know and appreciate the best. The deeply instilled Four Seasons culture is personified in its employees – people who share a single focus and are inspired to offer great service (http://www.fourseasons.com/about_us/).

InterContinental Hotels Group values and trusts its employees. This includes encouraging their contribution and investing in their development. It recognizes its employees are the company's best ambassadors and that their enthusiasm, energy and expertise are essential to the company's success (http://www.ihgplc.com/index.asp).

These examples provide more support for the notion that companies aspiring to offer the highest levels of service quality and customer satisfaction need to have published statements that give emphasis on how the culture and climate are linked to employee performance. These statements from leading companies give a clear indication of the importance of the role organizational climate plays in supporting any management initiative to enhance service quality. Again, it must be stressed that whilst making such statements lays the foundation, it is the translation into effective operations that produces results.

Measurement of organizational climate

Psychologists explain the behavior of people through the use of both nomothetic (group) and idiographic (individual) means (Mullins, 1996). A fundamental question inherent with organizational climate research is: What is the appropriate level of analysis; the organization, the department or sub-unit, the workgroup or the individual? Many researchers have conceptualized climate as an individual and psychological variable; however, the difficulty has been justifying the extrapolation of results from one level of analysis (i.e., the individual) to the broader context of the workgroup, the department, or to the total organization. The cross-level interference problems, together with the unit of analysis issue, have been addressed by a number of researchers (Glick, 1980; Mossholder and Bedeian, 1983; Glick and Roberts, 1984; Glick 1985).

The extrapolation of results from the individual level to the group level allows climate researchers to analyze and draw conclusions, in terms of whatever effectiveness parameter is being investigated, about the running of the total organization and for groups of people within the organization. Generally, researchers have sought to do this by calculating the average (usually a mean) of results for a particular climate survey and then seeking to discover the extent to which the results mapped into the structure and effectiveness of the organization, which is estimated by aggregating individual psychological climate scores. The multiple – level of unit of theory – is important because it may change the empirical approach. Whereas the term 'organizational climate' connotes an organizational-unit level of analysis, it does not refer to the individual, department, or workgroup. The debate on the unit of theory as being the organization is strengthened by the common practice of many researchers of using aggregation of psychological climate.

The argument for aggregating perceptually based climate scores (i.e., psychological climate scores) appears to rest heavily on three basic assumptions: first, psychological climate scores describe perceived situations; second, individuals exposed to the same set of situational conditions will describe these conditions in similar ways; and third, aggregation of psychological climate scores will emphasize perceptual similarities and minimize individual differences. (Jones and James, 1979, p. 206)

Schneider and Reichers (1983) discussed how climates form and why aggregation is a legitimate technique. They considered three approaches to the formation of climate: the structural perspective; selection, attraction, and attribution; and social interactionism. The structural perspective sees climate as arising from the structural characteristics of the organization. The selection, attraction, and attrition approach is where individuals create homogeneous organizational membership and have similar climate perceptions among individuals. Third, the social interactionism approach is where individuals check, suspend, regroup, and transform their own perceptions in light of their interactions. This approach seeks to explain differences in climate across workgroups in the same organization that are not explained by the other approaches.

A range of psychologically based questions and concepts are generated by a search of the organizational climate literature and studies completed by various theorists. These are then incorporated into survey instruments which are in turn completed by employees of an organization. It should be noted that these survey instruments are often modified to give a level of customization for a particular organization. This gives rise to the criticism that there is a multiplicity of dimensions for organizational climate, yet this is also a strength as each survey can more accurately reflect the setting in which it is going to be used. The answers to these questions are normally on a scaled response (1 = strongly disagree to 5 = strongly agree) and are subjected to factor analysis techniques to determine the underlying dimensions. Davidson et al. (2001) reported a study of organizational climate in four and five star hotels which used a 70-item climate instrument that produced seven dimensions of organizational climate:

- Leadership, facilitation, and support
- Professional and organizational esprit
- Conflict and ambiguity
- Regulations, organization, and pressure
- Job variety, challenge, and autonomy
- Workgroup cooperation, friendliness and warmth
- Job standards

Leadership, facilitation, and support dealt with issues of leadership, the facilitation of work and support given to employees. *Professional and organizational esprit* refers to organizational level characteristics that included planning, effectiveness, and the level of professional identification and pride. *Conflict and ambiguity* sought to elicit views on issues relating to the job and role, as well as job design and role conflict. *Regulations, organization, and pressure* examined the extent to which regulations impacted the job and functioning of the organization or created pressure. *Job variety, challenge, and autonomy* looked at the job and its characteristics and the level of autonomy. *Workgroup coopera-tion, friendliness and warmth* addressed the issue of workgroups and the social climate created. *Job standards* looked at how employees viewed the standards required and achieved. By far the most important dimen-sion in determining organizational climate was '*Leadership, facilitation and support*. This demonstrates that organizational climate is very much driven by the organizational leaders and managers, and how they act and interpret organizational requirements, together with their manage-ment style, shapes the organizational climate. Schneider et al. (2005) found in their recent study that specific kinds of service leadership is an aid to ensure that employees display organization citizenship behavior toward customers, and this enhances service quality.

Climate dimensions are dependent upon the organizational setting and can be used to target specific issues such as service, innovation, and training. Alternatively, they can be used to give a reading of overall organizational climate. Specific hospitality or tourism organizations can tailor the climate surveys to provide certain emphasis on critical issues. An example of a specifically tailored organizational climate survey is the Tracey and Tews (2004) study of unit performance of restaurants concentrated upon two climate dimensions (i.e., service and training) and how important these dimensions were for overall performance. However, when broad measures of climate are taken, leadership is the dimension that is always seen as critical, if a positive climate is to be achieved.

Another element that has attracted some research is that of organiza-tional burnout. There is evidence of the link between a non-supportive organizational climate and the burnout of service staff, sometimes termed 'emotional exhaustion of labour' (Van Dijk and Kirk Brown, 2006). This often occurs in companies that do not use a consulta-tive management style. One symptom of burnout is increased labour turnover; this in turn has an impact upon training and recruitment, which flows on to a negative impact on service quality. Quality pro-grams can be successful only when there is genuine staff and manage-ment commitment and a stable workforce. This demands considerable commitment from employees that can give rise to labour turnover as employees are simply unable to cope with the emotional strain of pro-viding the highest levels of service. Davidson and Timo (2006) have reported that human resource managers have rated attitude, personal-ity/appearance, and customer service orientation as the most important issues when recruiting staff.

A positive relationship between climate- and service-related issues are a prerequisite for any effective IM. Customer satisfaction has been clearly linked to the organizational climate created for the employ-ees of the organization (Davidson et al., 2001). Another study of the hotel industry found that if there were major divergences between management and employee service-quality ideals, it would have negative consequences for the quality of service (Ross, 1995). These issues are highly relevant for service managers in day-to-day operations and reinforce the need to ensure integration of both management and employees striving to meet the same service-quality objectives.

Service quality and customer satisfaction

Organizational practices have a direct impact on the people the organization serves, as well as on employee performance and attitudes. This stream of research can be traced back to Schneider and Bowen (1985), who were explicit about the importance of creating an organizational climate for service. They argue that consumers are better served if the policies, practices, and procedures of an organization meet the needs of, and satisfy, employees who then deliver a directly positive outcome in terms of service quality for the consumer. The creation of a climate for service is an example of organizational effectiveness and being responsive to its customers. The climate of the organization is an important factor in the creation of quality services as defined by the customer. There is also research in the early 1990s that called for the incorporation of the concept of employee satisfaction, in addition to the more widely used customer satisfaction, into the overall focus of the business. This is because the evidence shows that without an environment that supports the employee, it will be difficult to enlist the employee's support for the organizational objectives (Tracey and Tews, 2004).

This area of organizational research also complemented the considerable body of marketing research that has been completed on service quality, with the development of various instruments to measure the service quality construct. For example, Parasuraman et al. (1988) developed SERVQUAL; Mei et al. (1999) extended SERVQUAL to propose HOLSERV for use in the hotel industry; Stevens et al. (1995) developed DINESERV for the restaurant industry; and Knutson et al. (1990) developed LODGSERV for assessing service quality in the hotel industry. All of these instruments were designed to measure service quality though a gap analysis approach that sought to measure whether customer perceptions of service quality were met or not.

Customer satisfaction is a major issue for the hospitality and tourism industry as it is for most industries. It must be remembered that service quality is a construct different from, but related to, customer satisfaction. Its measurement in the hotel industry has been particularly difficult with many approaches being used, and these include pre- and post-customer surveys, in-room comment cards, focus groups, mystery shoppers, chat groups on the Internet, and total market surveys such as those conducted by US market research analysts like J.D. Power and Associates. There are now also Internet 'blog' sites where people express their opinions of service quality (e.g., tripadvisor.com). Many companies conduct customer satisfaction surveys themselves or commission market researchers to check their customer satisfaction rates.

In the hotel industry, it is still very common to use in-room guest comment and feedback forms as the major measure of customer satisfaction. These are normally read by the general manager and the executive team and passed on to individuals if necessary. This approach has been heavily criticized as the instruments used are often poorly designed and the results are an inadequate measure upon which to base any strategic decisions because of low response rates, which was estimated to be about 4%, and the resulting bias (Jones and Sasser, 1995; DeVeau et al., 1996; Gilbert and Horsnell, 1998;). The author's discussions with senior hotel and tourism executives in the United States, Asia, and Australia indicate that there is still a huge reliance upon the in-room comment card. At one level, this shows that there is a genuine interest and concern to get feedback and rectify any issues that may arise. However, given low response rates to in-house surveys, it is likely that some considerable level of service failure has occurred for a customer to be motivated to fill one out. This does not diminish the importance of reacting to issues raised by customers, but it cannot be seen as a reliable measure of the overall customer satisfaction rate.

There is one technique to measure customer satisfaction that would be very cost-effective, but is not used by most hospitality and tourism companies: ask the frontline employee to give an assessment of customer satisfaction. And as anyone who has ever been in a frontline service position will confirm, they are very close to the customer and are normally able to make a sound judgement as to the level of satisfaction of the customer. This view is supported by Schneider and Bowen (1985), Davidson et al. (2001), and others. So, why are companies not asking employees to give their perceived level of customer satisfaction on a regular basis? Of course, this technique should be used in conjunction with the other techniques outlined above. A partial application of this is often seen where employees automatically give feedback from customers, especially if negative, to their supervisors. But until such a technique becomes systematic, it must be seen as a wasted opportunity by the hospitality and tourism industry to obtain a customer satisfaction reading.

Organizational setting for IM

This chapter has put the case for employees being seen as the main agents and focus for IM. Employees are the deliverers of service and are able to form judgments as to the level of customer satisfaction. To achieve the highest levels of service quality and customer satisfaction, employees and departments need to have a marketing orientation and work in a cooperative manner to ensure the smooth and efficient running of the organization. However, this is not always the case with some departments being described as 'organizational silos' and not wishing to fully cooperate, which undermines efficiency. The hotel industry is a case in point where there are departments that have not always operated in this manner. It is not uncommon to find restaurants and kitchens, housekeeping, and front offices where there is conflict. It is interesting to note that these departments are reliant on one another to function efficiently, and therefore such behavior must be attributed to poor leadership and management practices. These departments are directly involved with customers, and, as previously noted, this can lead to employee burnout and a high content of emotional labor which can exacerbate conflict. This is of course totally counter-productive as the requirement to manage pressure, and still deliver quality service, is central to organizational performance.

When the mental silo occurs in an organization, this is often a symptom that both culture and climate settings are not appropriate and IM cannot be effective. These organization settings need to be changed and become positive if employees are to become market focused to deliver a high-level service and achieve customer satisfaction.

Where does IM fit? A conceptual model

There has been considerable discussion on culture, climate, service quality, and customer satisfaction and how they relate to IM. It should be noted that there are many other issues that also have a major impact upon organizational functioning, but discussions on them are beyond the scope of this chapter. However, *empowerment and training*, and *operating procedures*, and *resources* are critical elements that must be provided to ensure that an organization greatly enhances the likelihood of successful outcomes. The model below proposes a way of conceptualizing how the various elements relate.

The model shows organizational culture as bounding all of the organizational processes. As discussed, organizational culture takes time to develop and is affected by rules, norms, employee and management practices, and procedures. It has been described as the social glue, a frame of reference, or the shared values that shape how the organization and individuals act and react. Culture is therefore the basis of any functioning organization. Climate is shaped by the prevailing organizational culture and perceptions of employees, and can be measured by a process of scoring individuals on a climate survey and then aggregating the scores to the department and organization levels. It provides a snapshot of time that tells managers how the employees perceive the organization. Culture is slow to form and difficult to change, whereas climate is much more volatile and can be changed by many things within an organization. It is this malleability that makes it such a valuable management tool. By conducting regular surveys, often at six-month intervals, climate can be used to detect departments that have problems and then put in place corrective actions. Climate is also affected by the amount of empowerment and training, and operating procedures and resources. Both of these elements provide employees with the necessary tools to do their job well and react to individual customer requirements, thus enhancing service quality.

Empowerment in the organizational sense is a process whereby individual employees are allowed to make operational decisions without reference to a more senior manager. It is most commonly used in a situation where there has been a service failure and immediate remedial action must be taken for service recovery. If this is used properly, it enables employees to take more responsibility and make quick decision that facilitates both service quality and customer satisfaction. There are limits that need to be set because there will be costs that accrue to the organization.

Employees are allowed to use a specified monetary limit to satisfy a customer who is unhappy with the service quality or to offer an extra level of service to enhance reputation. An incident can be as simple as offering an additional cocktail if there has been a delay with a meal from the kitchen, or it may involve large sums if the customer was unsatisfied with other aspects of the service with genuine cause. Even using a modest sum of a $100 limit could be very expensive if there were many service failures. It involves employees in making significant judgement calls. Empowerment of employees cannot work in a vacuum but must be supported with culture and climate settings and appropriate training. Employees must also have confidence that they are able to make such judgement calls (right or sometimes wrong) without them being subject to management sanctions after the event. Empowerment allows employees to make a range of judgements to facilitate customer satisfaction. If culture and climate are positive and training has been provided, empowerment is a powerful tool for achieving customer satisfaction; however, it can readily be seen that there are major financial risks, if implemented poorly.

Training has been mentioned on a number of occasions as it provides the base for employees to be aware of the SOP and service standards of the organization. It can take the form of on-the-job training as a mentor, supervisor, or senior colleague can show a new employee or a promoted employee how a particular job is done, or it can be off-the-job; as the name implies, the training is completed in a non-work setting. Most new employees will be given induction training which is generally off-the-job to introduce an individual to the company, the culture, and their job. Additional training is often needed to lift the skill base and sometimes to train as multi-skill individuals. Induction training and ongoing training are seen as the main support processes that help an organization achieve and increase service levels. Linking training with a level of empowerment is essential for high-level organizational performance.

SOPs are the written-down standards and methods of doing a job. For relatively simple jobs it can be very explicit, but where there is a large number of elements of customer contact, there has to be interpretation and this is where the culture, climate, and training play an essential part. It is simply impossible to document every type of service interaction that might take place. Some set standards, such as the phone must be answered by the third ring, can be laid down and measured. Ongoing training and experience greatly enhance any SOPs and lift service quality.

It is self-evident that, for service quality and customer satisfaction to be achieved, employees must be given the right level of resources to complete their jobs. Ensuring that the appropriate equipment and human resources are available for an area or department is the responsibility of a manager. Here again, culture, climate, training, and SOPs all play an integral role to ensure that resources are used in the most effective manner across the organization.

The conceptual model (Figure 17.1) proposes that there is a direct link between organizational climate, service quality, customer satisfaction, and organizational performance. This is modified by various organizational processes; the extent and level of empowerment and training, the operating procedures, and resources facilitate and support service quality as an operational outcome. IM intervenes between service quality as an internal outcome and customer satisfaction; if the right organizational processes are not in place to support IM, a lower

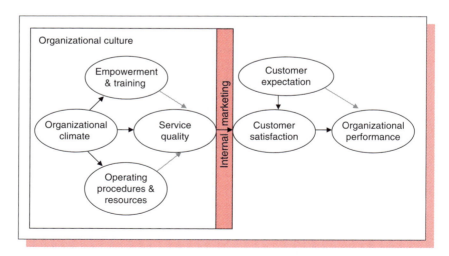

Figure 17.1
Culture/Climate-Service/Satisfaction-Performance (CSP) moderated by internal marketing (adapted from Davidson, 2003)

level of customer satisfaction will result. Customer satisfaction itself is also influenced by customer expectations which also impacts upon organizational performance.

Employees in hospitality and tourism

Employees are a major focus for any organization and they are especially important if that organization wishes to have an effective IM strategy in place. Another dynamic that has a major impact and must be taken into account is employee turnover. This is a particular problem for the hotel industry in developed countries. The positive impact of turnover maybe an infusion of fresh ideas and removing de-motivated employees. For employees, changing jobs may be a mechanism to cope with burnout (emotional labour) or mundane and boring jobs. However, there is a considerable cost to any organization, with loss of quality and efficiency in operations and service continuity. Organizations must regularly divert resources to training and re-training to maintain quality and service levels. Research has shown that up to 56.5% of staff and 48.3% of managers had two or less years of employment in a hotel. This is further complicated as 64.8% of managers have been in their jobs for 2 years or less (Davidson et al., 2006). To some extent this may be seen as positive because it opens up career path opportunities for ambitious managerial employees but the quality and depth of their understanding and experience in dealing with customers and other employees may be limited. In an industry where competitive advantage is based on cost and service quality, this presents problems.

The emphasis on training must be set in the context of employee turnover and job tenure figures. The high levels of training may be a necessity to adequately compensate for the ongoing loss of human capital due to the sheer volume of employee turnover. Obviously, such a high level of training also indicates that considerable resources are being expended not only for improvement in existing human capital levels, but as a 'stop gap' mechanism in order to remain competitive by maintaining service levels in a high turnover organization.

Summary

The chapter has provided a perspective of IM that is based upon a range of organizational processes. IM does not occur in isolation but is part of a web of inter-connected organizational and management practices. In particular, it is reliant upon several key elements, namely, culture and climate, empowerment and training, operating procedures and resources, and service quality. The relationship between these elements is shown in the conceptual model (Figure 17.1) and this has guided the discussion provided.

These organizational processes are interpreted through the employees who are the central focus for hospitality and tourism companies. This is amply demonstrated by the statements by such leading firms as Marriott, Four Seasons, InterContinental, South West Airlines, and Starbucks that make this employee focus absolutely explicit. These companies embed their employees focus with organizational culture and climate settings that are positive and supportive. It is only when this alignment of organizational process and employees is in place that service quality, customer satisfaction, and high-level organizational performance are attained. IM is a process that fits within the organization to assist in the maximization of yield from the customers, yet it cannot be effective unless the organizational processes and employees orientation is appropriate.

The formation of culture has been examined to show that it is a result of statements, policies, and procedures, and that it takes time to form and is generally slow to change. Climate is the result of individual employee perceptions, which are psychologically measured, to produce a reading on a range of dimensions or factors. The most important of these is leadership. A characteristic of climate is that it can be changed relatively quickly and hence it provides managers with an excellent tool in the understanding of their employees perceptions.

SOP and resources play a major role as they are the operations and context of what is being marketed. Empowerment has been shown to be a very powerful management tool to enhance customer satisfaction but, if not used appropriately, it can also pose significant risks for managers. Other major industry issues such as employee turnover, burnout, and emotional labour (exhaustion) all have an impact of requiring almost continuous training of employees. Turnover can have a significant negative impact on service quality and hence customer satisfaction.

Service quality can only be achieved if an organization has the right organizational processes in place and is supportive of its employees through the culture and climate. IM has been described as a lens through which service quality is viewed by the customer. The marketing orientation of the employees is the most significant aspect that allows them through service interaction with customers to internally market by up-selling the range of services and products offered by the hospitality and tourism industry.

Future research directions for IM

This chapter has highlighted the various research streams that impact on IM with a marketing focus upon service quality and customer satisfaction, on psychological processes examining organizational climate, on organizational studies focused upon culture, and on human resources emphasizing the employees as the most critical part of any business. A concern with the research in this area is that studies have focussed upon one issue and then extrapolated to include some other elements. Therefore, we have an array of instruments for climate, culture, service quality, and customer satisfaction with many researchers making links from IM to these other theoretical constructs. It is well-established that all of these elements are critical to a successful operation but there now needs to be a focus, for hospitality and tourism researchers, to draw these stands into a more comprehensive process that looks at this as a whole and not as the various constituent parts of IM. This is a challenge because in any complex organization, it is the norm for theoretical process to study the constituent parts (Ahmed and Rafiq, 2003). For managers, it is also much easier to manage by looking at individual elements rather than take a macro strategic approach to IM. Thus, both practitioners and researchers have the same tendency but this may not serve the best interests of the industry and further this research focus.

Of course there is only one opinion that really counts and that is of the customers; if they are not buying the product or service offered, the company will not survive. Given that the hospitality and tourism industry can design the products and services that are attractive to customers, it is logical to focus upon the delivery mechanism which is predominantly frontline staff. It is where the IM concept can make a significant impact upon customer satisfaction and company profit. However, whilst there is benefit in the somewhat piecemeal research approach, looking at the constituent parts, there is the possibility for theorists to integrate these processes into a macro approach to encompass the various parts and provide managers with a more effective model to implement IM.

Conclusion

A discussion on IM could have focused upon marketing collateral within the organization that highlights opportunities for customers to spend their money. It would have highlighted such things as whether the in-room marketing literature is eye-catching, whether the spa and gym have the right facilities, whether customers can access business centre services easily, whether the specials in the bar or restaurant are well publicized, whether every passenger has the in-flight magazine for duty free goods, and whether the memorabilia store is well located at the theme park. There of course could be many more examples but these are artefacts of the marketing processes and not the drivers of IM success.

The hospitality and tourism industry is a people business. It involves employees that have many service contacts from which judgements are made by customers as to the quality of the business, and their satisfaction is based upon these interactions. The gold taps and marble and the reclining sleeper seats in airplanes are becoming the norms and an expectation of customers that needs to be met. But the competitive advantage that is increasingly recognized by leading companies is the service level and customer satisfaction. The most important element of this is the service deliverer – the employee. The greater the understanding a company has of its employees and the better it treats and motivates them, the more profitable the business. It sounds simple, but it requires strong managerial commitment and time to ensure that this happens. IM is a process that relies very heavily upon the personal selling by employees in order that the company can maximize the yield from its customers. The foundations for this are the organizational culture and climate created and, therefore, managers must ensure that these are supportive and positive for employees.

References

Ahmed, P. K. and Rafiq, M. (1993). The scope of internal marketing: defining the boundary between marketing and human resource management. *Journal of Marketing Management, 9,* 219–232.

Ahmed, P. K., Rafiq, M., and Saad, M. N. (2002). Internal marketing, organizational competencies, and business performance. *American Marketing Association Conference Proceedings, 13,* 500–503.

Arnett, D. B., Laverie, D. A., and McLane, C. (April 2002). Using job satisfaction and pride as internal-marketing tools. *Cornell Hotel and Restaurant Administration Quarterly, 43,* 87–97.

Berry, L. L. (1981). The employee as customer. *Journal of Retail Banking, 3,* 25–28.

Berry, L. (1987). Big ideas in services marketing. *Journal of Services Marketing, 1,* 5–10.

Berry, L. L., Hensel, J. S., and Burke, M. C. (1976). Improving retailer capability for effective consumerism response. *Journal of Retail Marketing, 52,* 3–14.

Bowen, J. T. (1997). A market-driven approach to business development and service improvement in the hospitality industry. *International Journal of Contemporary Hospitality Management, 9,* 334–345.

Chacko, H., Davidson, M. C. G., and Green, Y. (2005). New Orleans customer service in hotels: The big easy or the hard ask? *Journal of Hospitality and Leisure Marketing, 13,* 181–203.

Crick, A. P. (2003). Internal marketing of attitudes in Caribbean tourism. *International Journal of Contemporary Hospitality Management, 15,* 161–169.

Czaplewski, A. J., Ferguson, J. M., and Milliman, J. F. (2001). Southwest Airlines: How internal marketing pilots success. *Marketing Management, 10,* 14–18.

Davidson, M. C. G. (2003). Does organizational climate add to service quality in hotels? *International Journal of Contemporary Hospitality Management, 15*, 206–213.

Davidson, M. C. G. and Timo, N. (2006). *Labor Turnover Costs in the Australian Accommodation Industry.* Tourism Transport Forum and the Sustainable Tourism Cooperative Research Centre, Sydney.

Davidson, M. C. G., Guilding, C., and Timo, N. (2006). Employment, flexibility and labor market practices of domestic and MNC chain luxury hotels in Australia. Where has accountability gone? *International Journal of Hospitality Management, 25*, 193–210.

Davidson, M. C. G., Manning, M., Timo, N., and Ryder, P. A. (2001). The dimensions of organizational climate in four and five start Australian hotels. *Journal of Hospitality and Tourism Research, 25*, 444–461.

Denison, D. R. (1996). What is the difference between organizational culture and organizational climate? A native's point of view on a decade of paradigm wars. *Academy of Management Review, 21*, 610–654.

DeVeau, L. T., DeVeau, P. M., and Downey, J. F. (1996). Earn good marks. *Lodging, April*, 77–80.

Four Seasons Hotels and Resorts (November 2006). Welcome to Four Seasons. Retrieved November 20, 2006, from http://www.fourseasons.com/about_us.

Geddie, M. W., DeFranco, A. L., and Geddie, M. F. (2002). From Guanxi to customer relationship marketing: How can the constructs of Guanxi can strengthen CRM in the hospitality industry. *Journal of Travel and Tourism Marketing, 13*, 19–33.

George, W. R. (1990). Internal marketing and organizational behavior: A partnership in developing customer conscious employees at every level. *Journal of Business Research, 20*, 63–70.

Gilbert, D. and Horsnell, S. (1998). Customer satisfaction measurement practice in United Kingdom hotels. *Journal of Hospitality and Tourism Research, 22*, 272–289.

Glick, W. H. (1980). Problems in cross level interference. *New directions for methodology of social and behavioural science, 6*, 17–30.

Glick, W. H. (1985). Conceptualising and measuring organizational and psychological climate: Pitfalls of multi-level research. *Academy of Management Review, 10*(3), 601–616.

Glick, W. H. and Roberts, K. H. (1984). Hypothesised interdependence, assumed independence. *Academy of Management Review, 9*, 772–735.

Gounaris, S. P. (2005). Internal-market orientation and its measurement. *Journal of Business Research, 59*, 432–448.

Gronroos, C. (1983). Strategic management and marketing in the service sector. Marketing Science Institute, Report no. 83–104. Massachusetts: Marketing Science Institute; 1983.

Gronroos, C. (1997). From marketing mix to relationship marketing-towards a paradigm shift in marketing. *Management Decisions, 35*, 318–340.

Gummesson, E. (1987). Lip service – a neglected area in service marketing. *Journal of Services Marketing, 1*, 19–24.

Hales, C. and Mecrate-Butcher, J. (1994). 'Internal marketing' and human resource management in hotel consortia. *International Journal Hospitality Management 13*, 313–326.

Hwang, I. and Chi, D. (2005). Relationships among Internal Marketing, Employee Job Satisfaction and International Hotel Performance: An Empirical Study. *International Journal of Management, 22*, 285–289.

InterContinental Hotels Group PLC (2006). *People*. Retrieved November 17, 2006, from http://www.ihgplc.com/index.asp.

Jones, A. P. and James, L. R. (1979). Psychological climate: Dimensions and relationships of individual and aggregated work environment perceptions. *Organizational Behaviour and Human performance, 23*, 201–250.

Jones, O. T. and Sasser, E., Jr. (1995). Why satisfied customers defect? *Harvard Business Review, 73*, 88–99.

Jones, P. (1986). Internal marketing. *International Journal Hospitality Management, 5*, 201–204.

Kim, W. O., Lee, Y., and Yoo, Y. (2006). Predictors of relationship quality and relationship outcomes in luxury restaurants. *Journal of Hospitality and Tourism Research, 30*, 43–169.

Knutson, B., Stevens, P., Wullaert, C., and Yokoyoma, F. (1990). LODSERV: A service quality index for the lodging industry. *Hospitality Research Journal, 14*, 227–284.

Kotler, P., Bowen, J., and Makens, J. C. (2006). *Marketing for Hospitality and Tourism*. Pearson International, Prentice Hall: Australia.

Lewis, R. C. (1989). Hospitality marketing: The Internal Approach, *Cornell Hotel and Restaurant Administration Quarterly, 30*, 41–45.

Lewis, R. C. and Chambers, R. E. (2000). *Marketing Leadership in Hospitality*, 3rd Ed., New York: John Wiley and Sons.

Lewis, R. C., Chambers, R. E., and Chacko, H. (1995). *Marketing Leadership in Hospitality*. 2nd Ed., New York: Van Nostrand Reinhold.

Lings, I. N. and Greenley, G. E. (2005). Measuring internal market orientation. *Journal of Services Research, 7*, 290–305.

Marriott International (2006). Core Values and Culture. Retrieved November 17, 2006 from http://marriott.com/corporteinfo/culture/coreValuesCulture.mi?

Mei, A. W., Dean, O. M. A., and White, C. J. (1999). Analyzing service quality in the hospitality industry. *Managing Service Quality, 9*, 136–143.

Mossholder, K. W. and Bedeian, A. G. (1983). Grass-level inference and organizational research: Perspectives on interpretation and application. *Academy of Management* Review, *8*, 547–558.

Mullins, L. J. (1996). *Management and Organizational Behaviour*. London: Pitman.

Naude, P., Desai, J., and Murphy, J. (2003). Identifying the determinants of internal marketing orientation. *European Journal of Marketing, 37*, 1205–1220.

Oh, H. (2000). The effect of brand class, brand awareness, and price on customer value and behavioral intentions. *Journal of Hospitality and Tourism Research, 24*, 136–162.

Oh, H. (2002). Transaction evaluations and relationship intentions. *Journal of Hospitality and Tourism Research, 26*, 278–305.

Paraskevas, A. (2001). Internal service encounters in hotels: An empirical study. *International Journal of Contemporary Hospitality Management, 13*, 285–293.

Parasuraman, A., Zeithaml, V. A., and Berry, L. L. (1988). A multiple-item scale for measuring customer perceptions of service quality. *Journal of Retail Marketing, Spring*, 12–40.

Piercy, N. (1995). Customer satisfaction and the internal market: marketing our customers to our employees. *Journal of Marketing Practice and Applied Marketing Science, 1*, 22–44.

Rafiq, M. and Ahmed, P. K. (2000). Advances in the internal marketing concept: definition, synthesis and extension. *The Journal of Services Marketing, 14*, 449–462.

Rafiq, M. and Ahmed, P. K. (2003). Internal marketing issues and challenges. *European Journal of Marketing, 37*, 1177–1187.

Ross, G. F. (1995). Management – employee divergences among hospitality industry employee service quality ideals. *International Journal of Hospitality Management, 18*, 61–79.

Sasser, W. E. and Arbeit, S. P. (1976). Selling jobs in the service sector. *Business Horizons, 19*(3), 61–65.

Schneider, B. and Bowen, D. E. (1985). Employee and customer perceptions of service in banks, replication and extension. *Journal of Applied Psychology, 70*, 423–433.

Schneider, B. and Bowen, D. E. (1993). The service organization: Human resources management is crucial. *Organizational Dynamics, Spring*, 39–52.

Schneider, B. and Bowen, D. E. (1995). *Winning the Service Game*. Boston: Harvard Business School Press.

Schneider, B., Ehrart, M., Mayer, D., et al. (2005). Understanding organization-customer links in service settings. *The Academy of Management Journal, 48*, 1017–1032.

Schneider, B. and Reichers, A. E. (1983). On etiology of climates. *Personnel Psychology, 36*, 19–39.

Sin, L. Y. M., Tse, A. C. B., Chan, H., et al. (2006). The effects of relationship marketing orientation on business performance in the hotel industry. *Journal of Hospitality and Tourism Research, 30*, 407–426.

Southwest Airlines, (1988, January). The Mission of Southwest Airlines. Retrieved November 17, 2006 from http://www.southwest.com/about_swa.

Starbucks (2006). Starbucks Mission Statement and Corporate Social Responsibility. Retrieved November 17, 2006 from http://www.starbucks.com/aboutus/environment.asp

Stevens, P., Knutson, B., and Patton, M. (1995). DINSERV: A tool for measuring service quality in restaurants. *The Cornell Hotel and Restaurant Administration Quarterly, 27*, 470–489.

Susskind, A. M., Borchgrevink, C. P., Brymer, R. A., and Kacmar, K. M. (2000). Customer service behavior and attitudes among hotel managers: A look at perceived support functions, standards, and service process outcomes. *Journal of Hospitality and Tourism Research, 24*, 373–397.

Tracey, J. B. and Tews, M. J. (2004). An empirical investigation of relationships among climate capabilities, and unit performance. *Journal of Hospitality and Tourism Research, 28*, 298–312.

Trice, H. M. and Beyer, J. M. (1993). *The cultures of work organizations.* New Jersey: Prentice Hall.

Van Dijk, P. A. and Kirk Brown, A. (2006). Emotional labor and negative job outcome evaluation of the mediating role of emotional dissonance. *Journal of Management and Organization, 12*, 101–116.

Varoglu, D. and Eser, Z. (2006). How service employees can be treated as internal customers in hospitality industry. *The Business Review Cambridge, 5*, 30–36.

CHAPTER 18

Strategic alliances

Karin Weber and
Prakash K. Chathoth

Introduction

Firms have used strategic alliances as a key source of competitive advantage. Numerous alliances have been formed worldwide with the objective of increasing the economic benefits of allying parties. Booz, Allen and Hamilton reported that the top 2000 companies in the world have benefited by using strategic alliances. These firms reported a return on investment of 17% (http://www.boozallen.com).

While the 1990s saw the increased use of strategic alliances, their effect on firms as a key source of competitive advantage has continued to grow during the past 6 years. Even stock exchanges have been engulfed in pursuing this strategy as seen recently in the case of the New York and Tokyo Stock Exchanges (Mills, 2007). Aircraft manufacturers such as Boeing and Lockheed Martin have also pursued this strategy to effectuate innovation in the field of air transportation in the United States (Airline Industry Information, 2007).

Alliances are effective in managing the business risk of firms, especially for those operating in an international business domain. Thus, alliances are not only vehicles for growth, but also provide avenues to mitigate risk. Specifically, alliances can address to a large extent environmental uncertainty (Burgers et al., 1993; Dickson and Weaver, 1997), assist in sharing costs of risky projects (Harrigan, 1985), and help businesses re-establish themselves in their competitive domain (Staber, 1996). Devlin and Bleackley (1988) suggested that firms seek alliances when confronted with mature, low-growth markets.

In a competitive setting, the role of alliances can be seen from the perspective of strategy formulation, allowing firms to keep up with the pace of new developments (Booz and Hamilton, 1996) with the objective of creating value for the firm. The scarcity of resources as well as the need to build strengths to sustain value has driven firms to use alliances as a key strategy to gain a competitive advantage. Notably, alliance networks with competitors, suppliers and customers, and firms in other industries have been used as key strategies for value creation (Lewis, 1990). The hospitality and tourism industry has made extensive use of this strategic option, and managers need to employ it even more in the future as an effective strategy to sustain the value addition in growing and mature markets.

This chapter provides an in-depth review of the concept of strategic alliances. In particular, it outlines various types of strategic alliances and details the strategic alliance formation process. The discussion of tourism and hospitality alliances provides a historical account of alliances' evolution and assesses the benefits that result from such collaborative arrangements. Despite the numerous benefits of strategic alliances, potential negative consequences of alliances have to be also acknowledged. The chapter assesses the current state of research in the field and offers directions for future research.

Background

What is a strategic alliance?

Strategic alliances have been defined in the literature from various perspectives. According to Parkhe (1993, p. 794) strategic alliances are 'relatively enduring, interfirm, cooperative arrangements, involving flows and linkages that use resources and/or governance structures from autonomous organizations, for the joint accomplishment of individual goals linked to the corporate mission of each sponsoring firm.' Business alliances, strategic partnerships, strategic networks, interorganizational linkages, interfirm cooperation, collaborative agreements, quasi-integration strategies, cooperative, coalition, and collective strategies, and corporate linkages are some of the alternative terminology used to study aspects of strategic alliances, as observed by Varadarajan and Cunningham (1995).

Strategic alliances can range from equity to non-equity alliances that involve two or more partners. Alliances provide firms with access to specialized assets and competencies within a relatively short period of time as compared to developing them internally or acquiring them through the market. The costs associated with internal development and acquisition would be much more than the alliance arrangement, which makes it a much more viable option in competitive and mature markets.

Equity participation and non-equity based cooperation constitute two modes that define the nature of the relationship (formal versus informal) between partnering firms. Formal relationships exist in joint ventures wherein two firms come together to create a new entity. Therefore, joint decision-making in the new venture becomes the basis of effective management in such an alliance (Harrigan, 1985). According to Faulkner (1995), a joint venture is appropriate when (1) the outcome of the partnership between firms results in a distinct business (which in some cases is a legal necessity to enter new markets); (2) alliance-specific assets are separable from the parent companies, and need to be managed jointly; and (3) the objectives of using the pooled assets are measurable.

Non-equity modes of alliance formation lead to cooperative arrangements that result in collaboration based on informal relationships rather than the use of formal governance methods. This type of cooperation does not involve either the creation of a new firm or one firm purchasing equity in the other(s). It may take the form of a partnership or network arrangement, licensing, or franchising. Such collaborations are appropriate when (1) task uncertainty exists between partnering firms of the cooperative venture; (2) flexibility between partners is essential to maintain the effectiveness of the collaboration; and (3) there are no distinct boundaries between the collaborating firms (Child and Faulkner, 1998). Collaborations are based on trust between partnering firms, resulting from awareness of its inherent benefits.

Thus, opportunistic behavior by partnering firms is rarely evident in such situations, as it may potentially jeopardize the realization of individual firms' objectives.

Ghemawat and colleagues (1986) suggested yet another way of classifying alliances, categorizing them as either 'x' or 'y'. 'X' alliances are those that involve vertical collaborations between allying partners that specialize in different functions. In contrast, 'y' alliances refer to horizontal collaborations, in which alliance partners specialize in similar functions. For instance, the collaboration between a buyer firm and a supplier firm is considered a vertical alliance, whereas the collaboration between two competitors is deemed a horizontal alliance. According to Pucik (1988), alliances can encompass technological relationships, co-production agreements, sales and distribution networks, product development ventures, and joint ventures.

Strategic alliances between firms, in both the manufacturing and service sector, have become prominent in the past decades. Fundamental changes in the competitive business environment contributed much to the accelerated pace of strategic alliance formation. Ohmae (1989) pointed to the growing domestic and international competition, shortening product life cycles, the rapid pace of technological change, convergence of consumer preferences across the world, rampant protectionism, and rising capital investment costs as key contributing factors. In the next section, the process in which alliances are formed is examined.

Strategic alliance formation process

The development of an alliance involves several stages. As stated previously, the fundamental principle of the alliance concept is based on the fact that distinctive resources of one company when held in combination with those of another create a set or bundle of resources that add more value than when the resources were held in isolation. This raises the barriers to imitation and presents a source of competitive advantage for the alliance partners. The strategic positioning resulting from combined resources is critical to the value creation process for alliance partners.

A firm's decision to adopt an alliance strategy is the first step to the alliance formation. Such a decision should be based on the firm's strategic orientation even if it does not possess the capabilities to carry the strategy forward (Child and Faulkner, 1998). Porter and Fuller (1986) suggested that ability in terms of scale (assets), technology, market access, and other factors that lead to a competitive advantage are essential screening criteria of potential alliance partners. Hence, screening becomes an important factor in the pre-alliance phase, with strategic and cultural fit being critical factors in partner selection. The former relates to value creation resulting from combined resources, whereby the synergistic effects ought to be superior to the competition. The latter refers to partners' ability to cope with each other's cultural differences. The key to such a fit lies in the willingness of alliance partners to compromise when they differ in orientation and action related to their joint activities.

Organizational screening results in a clear understanding of synergies among partners and the identification of partners that are most beneficial to achieving the alliance's overall objectives. Following the screening process is an assessment of organizational complementarity (Dyer and Singh, 1998), forming a basis for identifying mechanisms of access to each other's resources and the benefits related to resource complementarity. According to Dyer and Singh, the degree of compatibility among partner firms related to systems, processes, and culture impacts the value creation process. Identifying complementarity among prospective partners' resources is an essential part of this phase.

Finally, governance mechanisms sought during the inception and development phase of the alliance will impact the rate at which the alliance moves forward. Opportunism could be an impeding factor in the progress of the alliance. A firm may choose a formal governance structure to closely monitor actions of its partners. A more informal structure might develop as the alliance matures and trust develops (Chathoth and Heiman, 2004), potentially leading to the development of informal contractual relationships among partner firms.

Child and Faulkner (1998) proposed a taxonomy of alliance forms, which entails scope, size, and entity as three key factors that influence alliance formation. Scope is determined by the motive of partnering firms to form the alliance. It is a function of the type of resources partner firms decide to combine to achieve their objectives. The scope of the alliance could be focused in that it brings partner firms together to achieve a specific objective. Conversely, its scope could be complex, whereby partnering firms combine resources to meet objectives entailing a wide range of activities. The size of an alliance can range from two to several partners, with alliances that consist of more than two partners being referred to as 'consortiums'. These are effective when more than two firms' resources are required to create a competitive advantage. Depending on how alliance partners seek to manage their relationship, alliance entities can range from joint ventures to collaborations.

The criteria for partner selection (Figure 18.1) can be summarized as follows:

- Allying partners' unique competencies (skills and knowledge related to alliance-specific goals and objectives) (e.g., Yoshino and Rangan, 1995; Arino and Abramov, 1997)
- Resources that include tangible and intangible assets such as technical, managerial, and financial assets and reputation (e.g., Hitt et al., 2000)

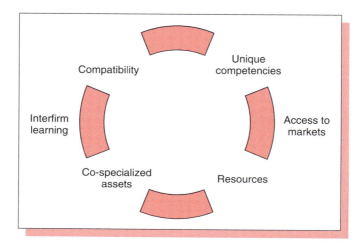

Figure 18.1
Alliance partner selection criteria

- Co-specialized assets and access to such assets (including complementarity of resources and capabilities; (e.g., Yoshino and Rangan, 1995; Klein and Dev, 1997; Dyer and Singh, 1998)
- Access to international/local markets (e.g., Child and Faulkner, 1998)
- Allying partners' compatibility including cultural fit and strategic fit as well as willingness to contribute to the alliance goals (e.g., Child and Faulkner, 1998)
- Potential for interorganizational learning to enhance own competencies (e.g., Kale et al., 2000)

Strategic alliances in the tourism and hospitality industry

Various types of strategic alliances found in the business environment in general can also be found in the tourism and hospitality industry. The most visible ones are the global airline alliances such as Star Alliance, Oneworld, and Skyteam. However, alliances have also been noted in other sectors of the industry. Several studies have assessed strategic alliances in the tourism destination marketing context (e.g., Hill and Shaw, 1995; Palmer and Bejou, 1995; Long, 1997; Apostolopoulos and Sonmez, 2000), while others have focused on hotels and/or restaurants (e.g., Dev and Klein, 1993; Morrison, 1994; Strate and Rappole, 1997; Preble et al., 2000; Chathoth and Olsen, 2003). Garnham (1996) and Go and Hedge (1994) adopted a broader view by assessing strategic alliances in several industry sectors. The discussion that follows will first examine strategic alliances in the tourism industry, in particular in the context of airlines, the travel distribution network, and tourism destinations before directing attention to the hospitality industry.

Strategic airline alliances

The number of airline alliances increased dramatically in the past few decades. Yet, it is not only the number but also the nature of alliances, now being more strategic in nature, that has changed. While previously allied airlines operated on the same route, they are now operating mostly on different routes (Burton and Hanlon, 1994). Gallacher and Odell (1994) reported that there were more than 280 alliances in 1994, based on the results of the annual airline alliance survey conducted by *Airline Business* magazine. About 60% of these alliances had been formed since 1992. The number of alliances increased to about 500 in 2006, involving 120 airlines (Airline Business, 2006). The most visible airline alliances are the global airline alliances, including Star Alliance, Oneworld, and Skyteam.

The environment in which airlines operated in the early 1990s contributed much to the acceleration in alliance formation. The combination of overcapacity, declining load factors, a worldwide recession, and a move away from first and business class travel resulted in severe financial losses (Bennett, 1997). The Economist (1993) noted that the losses of the world's scheduled airlines for the period of 1990–1992 amounted to US$11.5 billion – an amount greater than all net profits since services began 74 years before. The precarious financial situation was further compounded by structural changes in the industry, with the most prominent being deregulation and privatization. The globalization of the market place was an additional major force driving alliance formation (Faulkner, 1995).

Airline alliances are horizontal in nature and involve a high level of collaboration (e.g., Dresner and Windle, 1996). Bennett (1997) referred to tactical alliances as loose forms of collaboration that exist to gain marketing benefits, that do not involve major resource commitments, and that are relatively low-risk in nature. In contrast, a longer time frame, wider scope, and a higher level of commitment are distinguishing features of strategic alliances. They incorporate numerous elements of tactical/marketing alliances, even though there are now also many tactical alliances in their own right. Code-sharing, joint services, block seats, joint marketing, joint fares, franchise agreements, schedule coordination, frequent flyer benefits, airport slot sharing, joint purchase and repairs of spare parts, shared use of hangars, joint development of technical and training procedures, baggage handling, and ground maintenance represent the main features of strategic airline alliances (French, 1997; Rhoades and Lush, 1997; Li, 2000).

The proliferation of airline alliances in recent years has stimulated interest in researching various aspects of the phenomenon. Studies have traced the history of specific airline alliances (Simons, 2000), examined the motives to enter them (Youssef, 1992), proposed key factors contributing to their success (Bissessur, 1996), and suggested reasons for their failure (Li, 2000). Common to all these studies, indeed to the vast majority of studies on strategic alliances in the service sector in general, is the focus on issues relating to the organization, specifically, detailed descriptions of alliance partners, benefits accruing to them, and success factors for these alliances. More specifically, literature in airline alliances focused on a number of benefits of code-sharing practices that eventuate to the passenger (e.g., Burton and Hanlon, 1994; Youssef and Hansen, 1994; Beyhoff, 1995; Dresner and Windle, 1996), with the expansion of the route network, improved connections through the coordination of schedules, and greater frequency of services being the most prominent ones. In addition, shared airport facilities for check-in and lounges provide one stop check-in convenience and ease of transfers. Customers also benefit from combined sales operations, through fares, and the reciprocity of Frequent Flier Programs (FFPs). Improvements in service resulting from alliances are typically equated to the quantity of connections and their quality in terms of reduced layover time.

Alliances in the travel distribution network

The travel distribution sector was the last tourism sector to move toward alliances, evolving into a concentrated sector where the primary players hold major market shares (WTO, 2002). In order to successfully operate in an intensely competitive market environment that has seen profit margins decrease about 5%, tour operators tried to ensure profits by means of vertical integration whereby they could exercise some control over aircrafts, a network of agencies, cruise lines, or hotels. Control of the entire chain of distribution is particularly pronounced in Europe where the five largest groups account for more than 67% of total tour operator sales, estimated at US$30 billion.

As the travel industry experienced unprecedented changes due to the advances in information technology and telecommunications, and the increase in e-commerce, new channels of distributing travel products and services opened up (WTO, 2002). Trends reveal that tourism has become one of the dominant industries in retail e-commerce, with on-line sales of leisure and unmanaged business travel in the US of $65 billion in 2006. This is estimated to grow to $122 billion in 2009, with the projection that, by the year 2010, 46 percent of travel sales will be booked on-line (Grau, 2006). Thus, strategic alliances have been formed between travel agencies and IT companies to create customized services for consumers. Yet, while alliances in other sectors of the tourism industry have received considerable research attention, the same cannot be said for the travel distribution network (Huang, 2006). Moving from a single supplier perspective to a multiple supplier perspective, tourism destination alliances are assessed next.

Tourism destination marketing alliances

Several studies have assessed alliances relating to the tourism destination marketing context (e.g., Tosun et al., 2005; Wang and Fesenmaier, 2007). Tourism destination marketing involves numerous stakeholders, often with diverse interests and needs. As a result, the major marketing tasks are coordinated by convention and visitors bureaus (CVBs) who are charged with developing an image that will position their destinations in the marketplace as viable ones for meetings and visitors (Gartrell, 1994). In doing so, CVBs need to coordinate among the various stakeholders in the destination to attain the desired cohesive image. The collaborative marketing relationships can be further complicated by the fact that local tourism-related organizations and businesses in a destination may conduct marketing activities with others at different levels and in various dimensions (Ritchie and Crouch, 2003).

The effects of globalization have forced many destinations into a variety of economic, social, and political relationships. Tosun and colleagues (2005) noted that there were many positive implications of these developments; yet, at the same time, globalization is outpacing the structures and rules needed to manage it. Thus, in the process of globalization, cooperation and collaboration between countries are required to achieve sustainable development in tourism (Timothy, 1999). Potential benefits relate to tourism demand management and marketing growth strategies, including the diversification of products, reducing promotional costs, and creating new destinations. Numerous case studies highlight benefits of these collaborative arrangements. For example, Telfer (2001) pointed to the significance of horizontal and vertical linkages when examining formal and informal agreements between wineries, tour operators, and the food industry along the Niagara wine route. Selin and Myers (1998), investigating a regional alliance in the Eastern Sierra Nevada, suggested that effective collaborative planning required a shared vision, good working relationships, and effective communication in addition to strong leadership and administrative supports. Tosun and colleagues (2005) identified several strategies to increase the efficiency and effectiveness of cooperative tourism marketing strategies for the Greek–Turkish border region. They point to the importance of establishing a joint cross-border tourism organization, creating sufficient financial resources, and increasing involvement of business interest groups and non-government organizations from both sides of the border when implementing joint tourism marketing growth strategies. In the context of Ireland, Greer (2002) argued that tourism partnerships across national, regional, and local administrative boundaries could be maintained by formulating an inclusive and integrated tourism strategy, establishing partnership balance, understanding political sensitivities, and developing a participative partnership approach at the local level.

Wang and Fesenmaier (2007) proposed a framework for collaborative destination marketing. Based on interviews with CVB staff and industry representatives, they identified four core components: (1) preconditions for destination marketing alliances; (2) motivations for entering marketing alliances; (3) stages of marketing alliance formation; and (4) the outcomes of destination marketing alliances. Their findings indicate that the CVB is expected by the tourism industry in the local destination to provide leadership in initiating, managing, and maintaining the destination marketing networks in order to stay competitive. More importantly, they require the CVB to be skillful in coordinating partnerships between the public and private sectors, between normally competitive entities such as hotels, restaurants, and attractions, and other diverse constituents within the community.

Strategic alliances in the hospitality industry

Table 18.1 identifies various types of strategic alliances found in the hospitality industry, together with illustrative examples. Alliance strategies in the hospitality industry have primarily taken the form of franchise agreements. The agreement between the franchisor and the franchisee involves sharing of tangible and intangible assets. The franchisor provides the brand name and know-how related to the product, technology, marketing, and training whereas the franchisee provides the infrastructure. As a result, the risk exposure of the franchisee is more than the

Table 18.1 Types of hospitality alliances

Types of alliances	Examples
Management Contracts and Franchises	– Cendant, Marriott International, Hilton Hotels Corp., Hilton International
Supplier–supplier Alliances	– Sharp Electronics Corp. and Geac Restaurant Systems
Supplier–provider Alliances	– Marriott, AT&T and furniture, designer/manufacturer Steelcase Inc
Marketing Alliances	– Le Meridian and Nikko Hotels – Hilton International and Hilton Hotels Corp.
Technology-based Alliances	– Accor, Hilton, Starwood – Leading hotels of the world and Relais & Chateaux
Competitor Alliances	– Marriott, Starwood, Hilton, and Hyatt

Source: Chathoth and Olsen (2003).

franchisor. This is based on the fee arrangement related to the contract. The franchisor reduces the risk exposure by negotiating a fixed and variable fee component. Franchisors with more bargaining power are able to mitigate their risk exposure by being able to balance the fixed and variable components of the fee structure. Franchisees are exposed to higher risks as they depend on the cash flow generated by the operation. Examples of franchise operations that encompass such characteristics include Holiday Inn, Ramada, McDonalds, Burger King, etc.

A similar situation arises in the case of hospitality management contract set-ups in which it is the operator who provides management expertise while the property owner provides the required infrastructure. The operator is given exclusive rights to manage the property and in return earns management fees that are a percentage of revenues (Alexander and Lockwood 1996). The owner, on the other hand, assumes the venture's financial risks (e.g., Eyster, 1997) and is primarily concerned with net operating cash flows. Although the combining of specialized assets is with the overall objective of creating value at the interfirm level, the operator's know-how and expertise have greater perceived value than the owner's infrastructure-related resource commitments. Chathoth and Olsen (2003) noted that management contracts in the United States had evolved so as to bring about parity in the risk exposure to some extent, which, as supported by Eyster (1997), could lead to more balanced alliance contracts in the future.

Contractual agreements between hotels and restaurants have also become more popular in recent years. This is noted by Strate and Rappole (1997, p. 50), who suggest that the failure of hotel restaurants in terms of financial viability will lead to more strategic alliances between hotel and restaurant companies. This would enable hotel restaurants to be run by restaurant companies in a more profitable way. Such trends would result in the development of cross-segment alliances in order to minimize risk exposure of firms.

There are several alliances that reflect the growth of supplier–supplier and supplier–provider alliances. Supplier-supplier alliances such as Sharp Electronics Corp. and Geac Restaurant Systems provide support for resource commitments between allying parties and for complementarity of assets. In this case, Sharp Electronics Corp. and Geac Restaurant Systems combined their assets to provide integrated point-of-sale systems to hotels. Supplier–provider alliances as seen in the case of Marriott and AT&T, and Marriott and furniture designer/manufacturer Steelcase, Inc. are noteworthy. 'The resulting guest room workstations feature an ergonomically designed and fully adjustable chair; a two-level desk that provides lots of room for equipment and spreading out paperwork; two power outlets and a PC modem jack mounted in the desktop; and a light with elbow joints, so it adjusts to shine on the work. Such a room is available at no additional charge; other chains have set a $15–$20 premium' (Barker, 1995).

Through such alliances, Marriott is able to provide superior products and services to its customers.

Marketing alliances between firms have also been beneficial to allying firms. For example, the alliance agreement between McDonald's and Disney in 1996 helped promote each other's product in their outlets. By doing so, McDonald's helped promote Disney toys in its outlets and could increase its sales by 7%, becoming the largest distributor of Disney toys in the world (Fraim, 2000). Other marketing alliance agreements include Le Meridian and Nikko Hotels to create a 'one-stop' booking system for their customers by pooling-in resources related to sales, marketing, and reservation systems. In this case, the allying firms' objective was to increase customer satisfaction, brand awareness, trial, and repurchase.

Alliances have also been created between competing hotel firms within a given market as in the case of the Greater Greenspoint Management District in Texas. Threats to the market in terms of the declining hotel sales led to the alliance among hotels that created services for customers by combining each other's resources. Customers benefit from such alliances as they can avail of services such as free calls to alliance members and use of free shuttle services to the allied hotels. As a result, in 1995, occupancy within the district increased by approximately 6 percent, RevPAR rose by $9.53, and ADR grew by $9 (Whitford, 1998). The benefits include increased sales, decreased costs, and, above all, customers were provided superior services.

Looking at their evolution, alliances over the last three decades of the twentieth century have grown in distinct stages. In the 1970s, firms predominantly used alliances from a product perspective for market reach as well as raw material procurement. In the 1980s, alliances evolved to building economies of scale and scope and, in the 1990s, firms entered alliances to develop core competencies through innovation in technology and capabilities. Different types of alliances have emerged during the different stages of industry life cycle; even competitor alliances have been created to sustain value creation. From an industry life cycle perspective, marketing alliances are seen during the growth phase whereas alliances that lead to not only revenue generation but also cost reduction are seen during the consolidation and maturity phases. The evolution from marketing to cost reduction in the alliance objective will need a more collaborative agreement, which would benefit hospitality firms in markets where maturity has set in.

Current alliance research and future directions

Based on a review of research on alliances in the tourism and hospitality industry, two conclusions can be drawn about its current state. In the sections below, these will be discussed, potential problems outlined, and directions for future research offered.

Strategic alliances from the customer perspective

As detailed previously, research on strategic alliances to date has primarily focused on the supply side, whether it is tourism destinations or individual suppliers such as airlines, travel agencies, hotels, or restaurants. However, the demand side or consumer perspective of strategic alliances has been largely neglected. Questions that remain unanswered include: *How does the customer perceive alliances between individual firms?*; *What effect does the alliance of firms have on consumers' brand image?*; *Under what circumstances can negative impacts on a company's brand equity be expected?* Yet, potential effects on consumers' perceptions of, and behavior toward, a particular supplier resulting from its affiliation with an alliance partner and its services – who still has to be regarded as a competitor despite the membership in the same alliance – have to receive careful attention. Literature on brand alliances and service failure/recovery can shed some light on potential impacts of alliances resulting from exposure to alliance partners.

Brand alliance research

In brand alliances the intent is to capitalize on a brand's equity, that is, the value that a brand's name adds to a product or service. In recent years brand alliances have become a popular market entry strategy as marketers attempt to capitalize on the complementary features of different brands, with co-branding and dual branding representing the two most prominent branding alliance strategies. Much previous research has focused on the concept of co-branding in which two brands combine into a single product (e.g., Cathay Pacific Citibank Credit Card). However, of particular interest in the current context is the concept of dual branding – a strategy whereby two (or more) brands share the same facilities (typically restaurants, e.g., Arby's/Long John Silvers, Dunkin Donuts/Haagen-Dazs), providing consumers with the opportunity to use either one or both brands. The rationale for such an arrangement is similar to that of strategic airline alliances in that the service providers (restaurants/airlines) share expenses and facilities while providing greater variety and convenience to customers. There is, however, a question whether such a strategy can impair consumers' image of the core brands and dilute their brand equity (Farquhar, 1994), when consumers attribute a negative experience with one brand partner to the other. Impacts may even be more far-reaching, with potential impacts on customer satisfaction and repeat purchase intentions.

Several studies in the brand alliance context investigated the extent to which impressions of one brand are transferred to or are affected by impressions of the other brand to which it is strategically linked (Rao and Rueckert, 1994; Park et al., 1996; Simonin and Ruth, 1998; Rao et al., 1999). These studies are primarily placed in the consumer goods domain. In the few instances in which services were evaluated, service providers were assessed on specific standardized criteria only, without a consideration given to the variability in service delivery (Levin and Levin, 2000).

In general, studies investigating brand alliances have reported positive effects for partners. For example, brand alliances may trigger the transfer of consumer affect from a high-quality brand to a low-quality brand (Levin et al., 1996), improve the image of partners and signal greater product quality (Park et al., 1996), positively influence consumers' quality perceptions of unobservable product attributes of a partner brand (Rao et al., 1999), and contribute to the development of favorable attitudes toward the brand combination (Simonin and Ruth, 1998). However, detrimental effects of brand alliances have also been observed. Farquhar (1994) pointed to the possibility of consumers blaming a wrong brand for their dissatisfaction by attributing a negative experience with one brand partner to the other. Such asymmetries pose a risk of diluting brand associations. More recently, Janiszewski and van Osselaer (2000) found the timing of consumer exposure to individual brands versus the alliance to be a key factor influencing whether a brand alliance is beneficial to partnering brands or not. Apart from effects of non-experiential exposure to alliance brands, impacts of consumers' exposure to the services of alliance partners have to be investigated, in particular if the quality of services falls short of consumer expectations, as is the case for service failure situations.

Service failure and recovery (SF/R) in strategic alliances – impacts on consumer evaluation and behavior

Researchers have devoted considerable attention to the study of service failure and recovery in recent years (Tax et al., 1998; Smith et al., 1999; De Witt &and Brady, 2003) due to its critical impacts on customer satisfaction (McCollough et al., 2000), word-of-mouth (Blodgett et al., 1997), and repeat purchase intentions (Keaveney, 1995). A service failure occurs when customers' expectations are not met (Bell and Zemke, 1987). Similar to service quality and satisfaction, it is customers' perceptions that determine whether a service failure has occurred; even if the service is performed according to the provider's service blueprint (Shostack, 1992), a service failure takes place when customers perceive a deviation from their expectations. Consequently, a service failure is subjective as it depends on customers' perceptions and is not necessarily consistent with the service provider's perception of a service failure (Halstead et al., 1996; Bejou and Palmer, 1998; Michel, 2001). Service recovery, which is aimed at returning dissatisfied customers to a state of satisfaction, is a customer retention strategy that refers to the actions a service provider takes in response to a service failure (Groenroos, 1988).

The vast majority of previous research has concentrated on the impact of a single service failure event, in part facilitated by the critical incident technique. More recently, several researchers have begun to investigate how multiple service failure events over an extended time period influence consumer evaluations (e.g., Mittal et al., 1999, 2001), consistent with the notion of a distinction between encounter and cumulative satisfaction (e.g., Bitner and Hubbert, 1994). However, research to date has neglected the investigation of effects of SF/R in situations in which two or more service organizations are involved in the service provision, as is the case in strategic alliance settings. Yet, a better understanding of these dynamics is essential on three grounds. First, there is a continued focus on service excellence to build strong relationships with customers to gain a sustainable advantage in an increasingly competitive business environment (Bates et al., 2003). Potential benefits of strong, long-term relationships have been well documented in the literature (Morgan and Hunt, 1994) and, according to Reichheld and Sasser (1990), include continued patronage of loyal customers who display decreased price sensitivity over time, a concomitant reduction of marketing costs, and 'partnership' actions adopted by those customers. Reichheld and Sasser (1990) also demonstrated that an increase in customer retention results in a substantial increase in service providers' profits. Service failures, however, inhibit a firm's ability to develop long-term relationships with its customers. In a single service provider setting, the service firm has direct control over the quality of its service provision and relationship-building efforts. In a strategic alliance setting, however, a service provider relinquishes this direct control by encouraging its customers to use the services of the alliance partner (Weber, 2002).

Second, recent changes in the business environment also make it imperative to investigate consequences of service failures in strategic alliance settings. The dramatic increase in the past decade in the number of strategic alliances in general, and the airline industry in particular, has already been noted earlier. However, apart from the formal structure of strategic alliances underlying collaborative business arrangements, more loosely structured business networks have also emerged (Achrol and Kotler, 1999). Indeed, Drucker (1993) described the economy of the future as a network society. Achrol and Kotler (1999, p. 146) argued that, 'marketing outcomes are increasingly decided by competition between networks of firms rather than by competition among firms.' Vargo and Lusch (2004, p. 6), in their call for marketing's evolution to a services-dominant logic, stated that, 'firms can have long-term viability only if they learn in conjunction with and are coordinated with other channel and network partners.'

Third, despite changes in the business environment, the individual firm–customer dyad has remained a contextual focus of much of the extant services marketing research (Gittell, 2002). Only recently have service researchers begun to examine provider–provider relationships and the relationships' impact on consumer evaluations and behavior (Smith and Tax, 2005; Weber and Sparks, 2006). In order to ensure that a service firm's membership in a strategic alliance is beneficial, rather than compromises its competitive position in the long-term, understanding potential impacts of service failure events by an alliance partner is critical. These impacts, resulting from characteristics inherent in services, may be illustrated in the context of strategic airline alliances.

The services marketing literature affirms several characteristics that differentiate services from goods (e.g., Shostack, 1977; Thomas, 1978; Berry, 1980), namely, intangibility, perishability, inseparability, and variability. Variability in service provision is an issue that can occur with the same staff at different time periods and different staff at the same time within the same organization. However, potential problems, especially if a service failure occurs, are compounded if it happens across organizations. The notion of product fit becomes important in this context. Simonin and Ruth (1998) argued that fit in the alliance context refers to the relatedness of the product categories referred to, or implied by, the alliance, irrespective of the individual brands. In case of global airline alliances such as Star, Oneworld, and Skyteam, the issue of product fit is addressed with all partners in these alliances being primarily concerned with the transportation of passengers on routes that another may not service at all or service not to the same extent. However, in assessing the fit of brands, several observations on the composition of the three major global airline alliances can be made. The Star alliance, launched in May 1997, consists of Air Canada, Air New Zealand, All Nippon Airways, Asiana Airlines, Austrian, British Midland, LOT Polish Airlines, Lufthansa, Scandinavian Airlines, Singapore Airlines, South African Airways, Spanair, Swiss, TAP Portugal, Thai Airways, United Airlines, and US Airways. A broad geographical representation is also evident, albeit with fewer member airlines, for Oneworld and Skyteam. Oneworld was launched in February 1999 and consists of American Airlines, British Airways, Cathay Pacific, Finnair, Iberia, Lan Chile, Malev, Qantas, and Royal Jordanian. Skyteam, launched in June 1999, comprises Aeroflot, AeroMexico, Air France, KLM, Alitalia, Continental Airlines, CSA Czech Airlines, Delta, Korean Air, and Northwest Airlines.

In reviewing member airlines, it is apparent that in the desire to offer a global route network and facilitate seamless travels, global strategic airline alliances bring together airlines that have (1) traditionally a volume orientation (US airlines) versus airlines that have a service orientation (Asian and European airlines), and (2) very different cultural backgrounds. These alliances have introduced measures that aim to standardize policies and procedures dealing with service delivery, including recovery strategies following service failure events. For example, consideration has been given to on-board luggage allowances that often vary among alliance airlines and that can create difficulties for customers when traveling on multi-sector flights using various alliance airlines. Similarly, differences in the amount of compensation paid by alliance airlines in case of lost luggage may cause consumer anger. However, due to the recency of global airline alliance formation, such measures to standardize policies and procedures have not been adopted across various alliance partners, and even if they are fully implemented, the issue of variability of service delivery remains an issue to contend with.

Organizational perspective: focus on limited research areas

Previous studies that examined issues relating to alliances from the organization's perspective have centered around a limited number of research areas, namely, the history of specific alliances, detailed descriptions of alliance partners, motives of partners to enter an alliance, potential benefits, key factors contributing to their success, and reasons for their failure. In order to move research in the field forward, Chathoth and Olsen (2003) proposed a focus on a broader range of topics including the strategic alliance process and the direction of the evolution of hospitality alliances, especially that of non-equity alliances. The focus of such research should be on the level of complementarity of hospitality firms' related resources and capabilities to achieve a competitive advantage. Furthermore, research may be directed to verify whether competitor alliances are a source of competitive advantages to allying firms. Since technology has greatly impacted alliance formation, future research may further investigate the role of technology in sustaining the value-creation process in hospitality alliances. The combination of tangible and intangible assets required to achieve a competitive advantage for hospitality alliances represents another avenue for research. Since learning related to service systems and processes is at the crux of hospitality firms' ability to sustain value creation, it is essential to determine how such firms create, develop, and sustain superior systems in new and existing markets through alliances, while being able to internalize the knowledge, skills, and competencies related to such systems. Thus, knowledge creation and interorganizational learning represent a further area of research.

Conclusion

Strategic alliances have become and are likely to remain critical business arrangements that allow firms to manage risks in a highly competitive environment. They are cooperative arrangements whereby partnering firms gain access to specialized assets that they are unable to create internally or acquire through the market. In the tourism and hospitality industry, strategic alliances take various forms such as management contracts and franchises, supplier–supplier and supplier–customer alliances, marketing and technology-based alliances, and competitor alliances. Global airline alliances were discussed as the most visible strategic alliance examples, and potential negative impacts of strategic alliances on consumer evaluations and behaviour were illustrated in this context. Thus, in addition to research on the advantages and disadvantages of strategic alliances from an organizational perspective, future research needs to assess to a greater extent consumer perceptions of alliances and their impact on consumer evaluations and behaviour.

References

Achrol, R.S. and Kotler, P. (1999). Marketing in the network economy. *Journal of Marketing*, *63*, 146–163.

Airline Business (2006). Airline business alliance survey 2006. *Airline Business*, Sept., 50–87.

Airline Industry Information. (2007). Boeing and Lockheed Martin form strategic alliance, p.1. Obtained via ProQuest, *ABI Inform*. January

Alexander, N. and Lockwood, A. (1996). Internalization: A comparison of the hotel and retail sectors. *Service Industries Journal*, *16*(4), 458–473.

Apostolopoulos, Y. and Sonmez, S. (2000). New directions in Mediterranean tourism: Restructuring and cooperative marketing in the era of globalization. *Thunderbird International Business Review*, *42*(4), 381–392.

Arino, A. and Abramov, M. (1997). Partner selection and trust building in West European–Russian joint ventures. *International Studies Management Organization*, *27*(1), 19–37.

Barker, J. (1995). Hotels design rooms for serious business. *Successful Meetings*, *44*(6), 38.

Bates, K., Bates, H., and Johnston, R. (2003). Linking service to profit: The business case for service excellence. *International Journal of Service Industry Management*, *14*(2), 173–183.

Bejou, D. and Palmer, A. (1998). Service failure and loyalty: An exploratory empirical study of airline customers. *Journal of Services Marketing*, *12*(1), 7–22.

Bell, C.R. and Zemke, E.R. (1987). Service breakdown: The road to recovery. *Management Review*, *76*(10), 32–35.

Bennett, M.M. (1997). Strategic alliances in the world airline industry. *Progress in Tourism and Hospitality Research*, *3*(3), 213–223.

Berry, L.L. (1980). Services marketing is different. *Business*, *30*(May–June), 24–29.

Beyhoff, S. (1995). Code-sharing: A summary of the German study. *Journal of Air Transport Management*, *2*(2), 127–129.

Bissessur, A. (1996). *The Identification and Analysis of the Critical Success Factors of Strategic Airline Alliances.* Unpublished Ph.D. Dissertation, Cranfield University, Bedfordshire.

Bitner, M.J. and Hubbert, A.R. (1994). Encounter satisfaction versus overall satisfaction versus quality: The customer's voice. In R.T. Rust and R.L. Oliver (eds) *Service Quality: New Directions in Theory and Practice*, Thousand Oaks, CA: Sage Publication, 72–94.

Blodgett, J.G., Hill, D.J., and Tax, S.S. (1997). The effects of distributive, procedural and interactional justice on service complaint behavior. *Journal of Retailing*, *73*(2), 185–210.

Booz, A. and Hamilton, H. (1996). Strategic alliances: Gaining a competitive advantage, Conference Board Report # 1168, Author.

Burgers, W.P., Hill, C.W.L., and Chan, K. (1993). A Theory of global strategic alliances: The case of the global auto industry. *Strategic Management Journal*, *14*(6), 419–432.

Burton, J. and Hanlon, P. (1994). Airline alliances: Cooperating to compete? *Journal of Air Transport Management*, *1*(4), 209–227.

Chathoth, P.K. and Heiman, B. (2004). Governance costs in alliances: Combining the evolutionary and transaction cost economics views, Jan 8–11 2004, *Proceedings of the International Business and Economy Conference*, San Francisco, California.

Chathoth, P.K. and Olsen, M.D. (2003). Strategic alliances: A hospitality industry perspective. *International Journal of Hospitality Management*, *22*(4), 419–434.

Child, J. and Faulkner, D. (1998). *Strategies of Cooperation: Managing Alliances, Networks, and Joint Ventures*, Oxford, New York: Oxford University Press.

Dev, C.S. and Klein, S. (1993). Strategic alliances in the hotel industry. *Cornell Hotel and Restaurant Administration Quarterly*, *34*(4), 42–45.

Devlin, G. and Bleackley, M. (1988). Strategic alliances-guidelines for success. *Long Range Planning*, *21*(5), 18–23.

DeWitt, T. and Brady, M.K. (2003). Rethinking service recovery strategies. *Journal of Service Research*, *6*(2), 193–207.

Dickson, P.H. and Weaver, K.M. (1997). Environmental determinants and individual-level moderators of alliance use. *The Academy of Management Journal*, *40*(2), 404–425.

Dresner, M.E. and Windle, R.J. (1996). Alliances and code-sharing in the international airline industry. *Built Environment*, *22*(3), 201–211.

Drucker, P.F. (1993). *Concept of the Corporation*. New Brunswick, NJ: Transaction Publishers.

Dyer, J.H. and Singh, H. (1998) Relational view: Cooperative strategy and sources of interorganizational competitive advantage. *Academy of Management Review*, *23*(4), 660–679.

Eyster, J.J. (1997). Hotel management contracts in the US: The revolution continues. *Cornell Hotel and Restaurant Administration Quarterly*, *38*(3), 14–20.

Farquhar, P.H. (1994). Strategic challenges for branding. *Marketing Management*, 3(2), 8–15.

Faulkner, D. (1995). *International Strategic Alliances: Co-operating to Compete*. London: McGraw-Hill.

Fraim, J. (2000). The entertainment economy. *Journal of Marketing*, 64(1), 113–117.

French, T. (1997). Global trends in airline alliances. *Travel and Tourism Analyst*, 4, 81–101.

Gallacher, J. and Odell, M. (1994). Tagging along. *Airline Business*, 25–42.

Garnham, B. (1996). Alliances and liaisons in tourism: Concepts and implications. *Tourism Economics*, 2(1), 61–77.

Gartrell, R.B. (1994). *Destination Marketing for Convention and Visitor Bureaus*. (2nd ed.) Dubuque, IA: Kendall/Hunt Publishing.

Ghemawat, P., Porter, M.E., and Rowlinson, A. (1986). Patterns of international coalition activities. In M.E. Porter (ed.) *Competition in Global Industries*, Boston, MA: Harvard Business School Press.

Gittell, J.H. (2002). Relationships between service providers and their impact on customers. *Journal of Service Research*, 4(4), 299–311.

Go, F.M. and Hedge, A. (1994). Strategic alliances. In S.F. Witt and L. Moutinho (eds), *Tourism Marketing and Management Handbook*, pp. 166–175. London: Prentice Hall.

Grau, J. (2006). On-line travel sales to boom, obtained from http://www.imediaconnection.com/content/9953.asp

Greer, J. (2002). Developing trans-jurisdictional tourism partnerships – insights from the Island of Ireland. *Tourism Management*, 23(4), 355–366.

Groenroos, C. (1988). Service quality: The six criteria of good perceived service quality. *Review of Business*, 9(Winter), 3–32.

Halstead, D., Morash, E.A., and Ozment, J. (1996). Comparing objective service failures and subjective complaints: An investigation of domino and halo effects. *Journal of Business Research*, 36(2), 107–115.

Harrigan, K.R. (1985). *Strategic Flexibility*, Lexington, MA: Lexington Books.

Hill, T. and Shaw, R.N. (1995). Co-marketing tourism internationally: Bases for strategic alliances. *Journal of Travel Research*, 34(1), 25–32.

Hitt, M.A., Dacin, T.M., Levitas, E. et al. (2000). Partner selection in emerging and developed market contexts: Resource-based and organizational learning perspectives. *Academy of Management Journal*, 43, 449–467.

Huang, L. (2006). Building up a B2B e-commerce strategic alliance model under an uncertain environment for Taiwan's travel agencies. *Tourism Management*, 27(6), 1308–1320.

Janiszewski, C. and van Osselaer, S.M.J. (2000). A connectionist model of brand-quality associations. *Journal of Marketing Research*, 37(3), 331–350.

Kale, P., Singh, H., and Perlmutter, H. (2000). Learning and protection of proprietary assets in strategic alliances: Building relational capital. *Strategic Management Journal*, *21*, 217–237.

Keaveney, S.M. (1995). Customer switching behavior in service industries: An exploratory study. *Journal of Marketing*, *59*(April), 71–82.

Klein, S. and Chekitan, D. (1997). Partner selection in market-driven strategic alliance. *South African Journal of Business Management*, *28*(3), 97–106.

Levin, A.M., Davis, J.C., and Levin, I.P. (1996). *Theoretical and empirical linkages between consumers' responses to different branding strategies*. (eds.) K. Coffman and J. Lynch. Vol. 23, *Advances in Consumer Research*: Provo, UT: Association for Consumer Research, 296–300.

Levin, I.P. and Levin, A.M. (2000). Modeling the role of brand alliances in the assimilation of product evaluations. *Journal of Consumer Psychology*, *9*, 43–52.

Lewis, J.D. (1990). *Partnerships for Profit*, New York: Free Press.

Li, M.Z.F. (2000). Distinct features of lasting and non-lasting airline alliances. *Journal of Air Transport Management*, *6*(2), 65–73.

Long, P.E. (1997). Researching tourism partnership organizations: From practice to theory to methodology. In P.E. Murphy (ed.), *Quality Management in Urban Tourism*, pp. 235–251. London: Wiley & Sons.

McCollough, M.A., Berry, L.L., and Yadav, M.S. (2000). An empirical investigation of customer satisfaction after service failure and recovery. *Journal of Service Research*, *3*(2), 121–137.

Michel, S. (2001). Analyzing service failures and recoveries: A process approach. *International Journal of Service Industry Management*, *12*(1), 20–33.

Mills, D. (2007). New York, Tokyo stock exchanges to form strategic alliance; [National Edition] *National Post*, Feb. 1. p. FP.9

Mittal, V., Katrichis, J.M., and Kumar, P. (2001). Attribute performance and customer satisfaction over time: Evidence from two field studies. *Journal of Services Marketing*, *15*(4/5), 343–356.

Mittal, V., Kumar, P., and Tsiros, M. (1999). Attribute performance, satisfaction, and behavioral intentions over time: A consumption system approach. *Journal of Marketing*, *63*(2), 88–101.

Morgan, R. and Hunt, S.D. (1994). The commitment-trust theory of relationship marketing. *Journal of Marketing*, *58*(July), 20–38.

Morrison, A.J. (1994). Marketing strategic alliances: The small hotel firm. *International Journal of Contemporary Hospitality Management*, *6*(3), 25–30.

Ohmae, K. (1989). The global logic of strategic alliances. *Harvard Business Review*, *67*(2), 143–154.

Palmer, A. and Bejou, D. (1995). Tourism destination marketing alliances. *Annals of Tourism Research*, *22*(3), 616–629.

Park, C.W., Jun, S.Y., and Shocker, A.D. (1996). Composite branding alliances: An investigation of extension and feedback effects. *Journal of Marketing Research*, *33*(November), 453–466.

Parkhe, A. (1993). Strategic alliance structuring: A game theoretic and transaction cost examination of interfirm cooperation. *Academy of Management Journal*, 36(August), 794–829.

Preble, J.F., Reichel, A., and Hoffman, R.C. (2000). Strategic alliances for competitive advantage: Evidence from Israel's hospitality and tourism industry. *International Journal of Hospitality Management*, 19(3), 327–341.

Porter, M.E. and Fuller, M.B. (1986). Coalitions and global strategy. In M.E. Porter (ed.) *Competition in Global Industries*, pp. 315–344. Boston: Harvard Business School Press.

Pucik, V. (1988). Strategic alliances, organizational learning and competitive advantage: The HRM agenda. *Human Resources Management*, 27(1), 77–93.

Rao, A.R. and Ruekert, R.W. (1994). Brand alliances as signals of product quality. *Sloan Management Review*, 36(Fall), 87–97.

Rao, A.R., Qu, L., and Ruekert, R.W. (1999). Signaling unobservable quality through a brand ally. *Journal of Marketing Research*, 36(36), 258–268.

Reichheld, F.F. and Sasser, W.E. (1990). Zero defections: Quality comes to services. *Harvard Business Review*, 68(September/October), 105–111.

Rhoades, D.L. and Lush, H. (1997). A typology of strategic alliances in the airline industry: Propositions for stability and duration. *Journal of Air Transport Management*, 3(3), 109–114.

Ritchie, J.R.B. and Crouch, G.I. (2003). *The Competitive Destination*, Wallingford: CABI Publishing.

Selin, S.W. and Myers, N.A. (1998). Tourism marketing alliances: Member satisfaction and effectiveness attributes of a regional initiative. *Journal of Travel and Tourism Marketing*, 7(3), 79–94.

Shostack, G.L. (1977). Breaking free from product marketing. *Journal of Marketing*, 41(April), 73–80.

Shostack, G.L. (1992). Understanding services through blueprinting. In T.A. Swartz, D.E. Bowen and S.W. Brown (eds) *Advances in Services Marketing and Management: Research and Practice*, Greenwich, CT: JAI Press.

Simonin, B.L. and Ruth, J.A. (1998). Is a company known by the company it keeps? Assessing the spillover effects of brand alliances on consumer brand attitudes. *Journal of Marketing Research*, 35(1), 30–42.

Simons, M.S. (2000). Global airline alliances – reaching out to new galaxies in a changing competitive market – The Star Alliance and Oneworld. *Journal of Air Law and Commerce*, 65(2), 313–325.

Smith, A.K. and Tax, S.S. (2005). A pound of flesh, but from whom? Assessing failure and recovery in a service network. Paper read at 2005 SERVSIG Conference, at Singapore.

Smith, A.K., Bolton, R.N., and Wagner, J. (1999). A model of customer satisfaction with service encounters involving failure and recovery. *Journal of Marketing Research*, 36(3), 356–372.

Staber, U.H. (1996). The social embeddedness of industrial district networks. In U.H. Staber, N.V. Schaefer, and B. Sharma (eds), *Business Networks: Prospects for Regional Development*, pp. 148–174, Berlin and New York: de Gruyter.

Strate, R.W. and Rappole, C.L. (1997). Strategic alliances between hotels and restaurants. *Cornell Hotel and Restaurant Administration Quarterly*, *38*(3), 50–61.

Tax, S.S., Brown, S.W., and Chandrashekaran, M. (1998). Customer evaluations of service complaint experiences: Implications for relationship marketing. *Journal of Marketing*, *62*(April), 60–76.

Telfer, D.J. (2001). Strategic alliances along the Niagara Wine Route. *Tourism Management*, *22*(1), 21–30.

The Economist (Oct 30, 1993). Shooting for the Moon, *329*(7835), 65–70.

Thomas, D.R.E. (1978). Strategy is different in service businesses. *Harvard Business Review*, *56*(July–August), 158–165.

Timothy, D. (1999). Cross-border partnership in tourism resource management. *Journal of Sustainable Tourism*, *7*(3/4), 182–205.

Tosun, C., Timothy, D., Parpairis, A., and MacDonald, D. (2005). Cross-border cooperation in tourism marketing growth strategies. *Journal of Travel and Tourism Marketing*, *18*(1), 5–23.

Varadarajan, P.R. and Cunningham, M.H. (1995). Strategic alliances: A synthesis of conceptual foundations. *Journal of the Academy of Marketing Science*, *23*(4), 282–296.

Vargo, S.L. and Lusch, R.F. (2004). Evolving to a new dominant logic in services marketing. *Journal of Marketing*, *68*(January), 1–17.

Wang, Y. and Fesenmaier, D.R. (2007) Collaborative destination marketing: A case study of Elkhart county, Indiana, *Tourism Management*, *28*(3), 863–875

Weber, K. (2002). Consumer perceptions and behavior: Neglected dimensions in research on strategic airline alliances. *Journal of Travel and Tourism Marketing*, *13*(4), 27–46.

Weber, K. and Sparks, B. (2006). When service fails: Does customers' identification with a firm matter? *Annals of Tourism Research*, *3*(3), 859–863.

Whitford, M. (1998). Houston hotels join forces to attract business. *Hotel and Motel Management*, *213* (7), 7.

World Tourism Organization. (2002). Tourism in the age of alliances, mergers and acquisitions. Author. Spain, Madrid.

Yoshino, M. and Rangan, U.S. (1995). Strategic alliance: An entrepreneurial approach to globalisation. Boston: Harvard Business School Press.

Youssef, W. (1992). *Causes and Effects of International Airline Equity Alliances*. Unpublished Ph.D. Dissertation, University of California, Berkeley, CA.

Youssef, W. and Hansen, M. (1994). Consequences of strategic alliances between international airlines: The case of Swissair and SAS. *Transportation Research A*, *28A(5)*, 415–431.

Research on the casino industry

Kathryn Hashimoto

Introduction

As the only industry research chapter in this marketing handbook, this last chapter will explore what research has been done so far, by examining each of the marketing sections of this handbook by placing them within the setting of gaming as an industry. However, unlike most other industries, gambling, as a product, has had a very bad reputation. Historically, it has been considered to be one of the major sins of living. As economic hardships have befallen different geographic areas of America, however, politicians have recognized the immediate monetary advantages of casinos on taxes, employment, and regional development. Therefore, legalized gaming jurisdictions have multiplied as government budgets have been squeezed by their need for more money. The casinos have provided needed revenues for state and local governments and, as a result, governments have come to rely heavily on gaming revenues. During this process, attitudes have slowly changed and despite their controversial nature, the casinos of today are very popular. In America, for example, casinos have had three times more attendees than major league baseball games and five times more than skiing and other sporting events (Nealon, 2006).

Social responsibility and ethics

Gambling has had a difficult history. Aristocrats did not want peasants to gamble because their losses would deplete the taxable income the aristocrats needed. As a result, gambling was kept illegal. Another reason to keep the fun of gambling limited to the aristocracy was that it was considered a form of divine intervention. Aristocrats typically used a form of dice cast by priests to aid in difficult decisions such as going to war. Later, gambling was banned because winning money that was not earned through hard labor was considered to be a sin by the church and sanctioned as an evil, as the devil's work or pastime. As lotteries crossed over into America, greedy lottery organizers were chased out of town when citizens were corrupted by the massive wealth they could gain. Gambling was not only considered sinful, but it also created thieves. Then, when the Mafia took over running the casinos in Las Vegas, gambling reached its pinnacle of social disgrace.

As a result of this history, social responsibility and ethics play a very important part in the casino industry today. With every new jurisdiction that considers legalizing gambling, the opposition cites social problems as a reason against the legislation. Gambling has also been blamed for higher crime rates (Piscitelli and Albanese, 2000; Stitt et al., 2003a; Moufakkir, 2005; Grinols and Mustard, 2006). According to conventional wisdom, when casinos come to town, crime rates increase. However, once the number of tourists is taken into account compared to the entire population, research suggests that crime rates increase for the first several years, but then drop below the pre-casino numbers. Similarly, the demise of local restaurants has also been cited as a reason not to allow casinos in a region (Hashimoto and Fenich, 2003; Fenich and Hashimoto, 2004). Folklore says that local restaurants that operate outside the casinos go out of business when casinos come to town. In fact, using government data, the same pattern occurs as in crime rates: restaurant numbers diminish for a couple of years after the opening of casinos, but then the number of restaurants increases, the number of employees goes up, and wages increase. Other negative factors such as personal bankruptcy (Nichols et al., 2000; de la Viña and Bernstein, 2002) and suicides (Lester and Jason, 1989; McCleary et al., 2002; Nichols et al., 2004) have been studied for links to gambling. However, there is not enough research on these topics because the findings have been contradictory. There is also a very large research database on gambling addiction, which will not be explored here because of its size. With all of these negative or controversial perceptions about casinos and gaming, marketers must be alert for opportunities to create positive images and to educate the public on the differences between folklore and objective research findings when making decisions about gaming issues.

Because of these claims, proprietary, regional, and state studies all extensively explore the various aspects of life in a community before and after gaming is legalized there. In exploring the issues of quality of life, theories such as tourism development cycles and social disruption theories have been used to evaluate quality of life issues before, after, and in projected trends of casino development (Perdue et al., 1999; D'Hauteserre, 2001b; Stitt, Nicholas, and Giacopassi, 2002; Foley, 2005; Stitt et al., 2005). Tourism development cycle theories in general explain that the social carrying capacity of a region has an initial positive change that occurs during the early stages of development and then reverts back to a negative change as the community reaches its 'carrying capacity.' On the other hand, social disruption theory believes that there is an initial negative change in quality of life but then grows positive as the community adapts to its new environment. Disruptive influences in social disruption theory are defined not only as more than just crime, bankruptcy, and addiction, but also as publicly visible nuisance crimes, the physical decay of the communities, the presence of litter on streets, homelessness, and traffic congestion. There appear to be mixed findings in impact studies on these theories, depending on the community, type of disruptive influence, and whether the respondent is a gambler or not. Many states and regions have asked market researchers to develop these impact studies so that they can evaluate strategies on whether to allow casinos to operate, what circumstances should be created to control the process, and how residents feel about the casinos.

This type of consumer research has explored both the perceptions about gaming (Spears and Boger, 2002; Brown et al., 2003) as well as the perceptions about gaming impact (Carmichael and Peppard, 1996; Hsu, 2000; Schmelzer et al., 2002; Lee and Back, 2003; Janes and Collison, 2004; Kwan and McCartney, 2005). One of the consistent results from this research is that the more people gamble and spend time at a casino, the more positive their perceptions are of the impact of casinos on local life. Another constant finding is that perceptions of gambling can be subdivided by religious affiliations. Catholics tend to have a more positive attitude towards gambling than Protestants, which is reflected in studies on participation in gambling activities and the level or frequency of gambling. On the other hand, sects like Southern Baptists, Mormons, Jehovah's Witnesses, and Muslims tend to discourage gambling and casinos. This type of information is important to marketers as they assess whether to have gambling in a region and also evaluate what kind of marketing should be used and where advertising should be placed in various media. In addition, perceptions about gaming change as people are more or less in tune with their church. For example, issues have been raised about whether it is appropriate for Mormons to manage casinos, or why there is a very successful casino city on the border of Utah and Nevada. Perceptions are difficult to assess and more difficult to change. Even when presented with objective data, people tend to maintain their beliefs.

Because of these negative claims against gambling, casinos have higher taxes than other industries (from 5% to 70%), and special fees to pay for additional police protection. In another example, New Jersey casinos pay an additional Casino Reinvestment Development Authority (CRDA) tax of 1.25% to help re-build Atlantic City. Harrah's Casino in New Orleans funds $2 million to help market the city and another $2 million for 'social funds.' In addition to taxes and special fees, casinos also fund, promote, and work with Gamblers Anonymous and other social programs. The negative image of casinos is difficult to change. More research needs to be conducted on target markets that might be influenced by the growing positive findings in objective research. Keep in mind that people tend to block information that is contrary to their current belief system. Because of their history and reputation, casinos work hard with various groups so that no one can say that they have shirked their social responsibility to the community.

Functions and strategies

There has been limited research on the functions and strategies of casinos. This has partially been due to a problem of access; casinos have been reluctant to allow researchers into their secrets of operation. Given that there have been many who would use this information to write negative research on gaming, their concerns are understandable. However, as casinos have opened their doors, service quality/corporate performance articles have begun to appear (Ference, 2001; Brandmeir and Baloglu, 2004; Chen et al., 2005). Because the casino industry is an oligopoly in the United States, the issues of branding (d'Hauteserre, 2001a) and physical distribution (Meyer-Arendt, 1995; Dowd, 2005) are important, but research is limited. In addition, the government also carefully sets up requirements and regulations to control the actions of casinos. In 1934, Congress passed the Communications Act that bans any advertisement or paid information for anything offering prizes dependent on a lottery or a game of chance. Until 1999 when the Supreme Court lifted the ban on casino advertising, promotional campaigns were limited in their options. Therefore, there has been very little research conducted on the effectiveness of casino advertising (Seonmi Youn et al., 2000; Lucas and Bowen, 2002; Lucas, 2004; Lucas et al., 2005). As a result, casinos have primarily focused on database marketing and relationship marketing to attract customers. Once again, however, because of the concern for privacy, very little research on this has been conducted. Also, as Mother Nature has been on a rampage in recent years, crisis management has come into focus for the industry. Especially with Hurricane Katrina destroying casinos on the Gulf Coast, more gambling establishments and hospitality ventures are re-examining strategic plans for implementation. Because of this new trend, there are articles on disasters (Cheung and Law, 2006) and their impact on tourism (Higgins, 2005a; Hashimoto and O'Brien, 2006).

The most research in strategic planning has been conducted in the area of market segmentation and positioning. College students (Brown, 2006; Caswell, 2006) are quite often used in discussions of underage gambling, and they are an easily accessible demographic group for study. However, for segmentation, most research focuses on tourists, seniors, and locals. Tourists are primarily overnight stay visitors, or weekend and weeklong vacationers. Locals are defined as 'driving distance' gamblers who usually can gamble during the week and go out for evening recreation. Tourists were the first demographic segment to be studied in the context of casinos (Morrison and Braunlich, 1996; Reece, 2001; Dense and Barrow, 2003; Wynne and Shaffer, 2003; Hong and Jang, 2004; Moufakkir et al., 2004). Although there is a lot of research on tourists, there appears to be no demographic profile that can reliably identify who will be a gambler and who will not. As a result, one of the ways that casinos identify new players is through loyal, regular customers. For example, regular guests are often offered a cruise or party in which they can invite their 10 or 20 closest friends. When the new friends arrive, they are given a player's club card so that they can be given offers.

In order to assess economic impact, tourism research has focused on how much tourists spend and what they spend on. Volume segmentation is a process that has adopted usage rate principle segmentation and segmented travel markets based on either their length of stay or the volume of their trip expenditures (Pizam and Reichel, 1979; Woodside et al., 1987; Spotts and Mahoney, 1991). Moufakkir, et al. (2004) have taken these volume usage principles and expanded them to test the folklore that gamblers only spent money in the casinos and not in the community. According to their research, heavy spenders had higher expenditure levels for non-gaming products than the light and medium users. However, this varied in terms of age and household income. Overall, the heavy spenders were younger, more affluent, and first time visitors on their own, not on charters. In fact, their spending accounted for over 90% of the total spending by the three segments. These findings reinforce the trend for casinos to seek younger, more affluent gamblers by designing entertainment venues for the younger and re-designing the bars to reflect a youthful fashion taste. The question has been: does this 20–30 years old market have enough money and numbers to be a viable segment? On the other hand, most of the local casinos have the Frank Sinatra style entertainers for the seniors, and entertainers from the 1960s–1970s such as Creedence Clearwater Revisited and Tina Turner for the baby boomers. In order to break out of the crowd and create new sustainable guests, marketers must explore new target markets.

In assessing the changes in target markets, it is important to look back at the different behavioral patterns in the volume segmentation of gamblers. Historians have suggested that Las Vegas was originally built so that people in California would have an adult playground where they could do whatever they wanted that they could not in their hometown as it might jeopardize their reputations or families. While that has not been a popular theory in Las Vegas, it would now be supported by the slogan 'What happens in Vegas, stays in Vegas.' Since Las Vegas is surrounded by desert, people had to drive a long distance to get there, which meant that in the early days of casinos, it was assumed that the most important gamblers would be from outside the normal commuting distance. Tourists brought outside money and bolstered the local economy. While some drove to and from Las Vegas in a day, the majority of gamblers spent at least one night in the hotels. As Las Vegas became the Mecca of gambling, it drew tourists who expanded their plans to include spending their weekends and holidays there. As the competitive environment from riverboats and Native American casinos grew, Las Vegas expanded beyond casinos to become an entertainment destination in order to keep tourists coming. Museums, Broadway-like productions and, of course, shopping areas such as Caesars Forum and Desert Passage created new reasons to come, in addition to the standard attractions of internationally recognized entertainers. As a result, gamblers and non-gamblers alike went to Vegas to spend their weekends and vacations.

As casinos spread beyond Las Vegas to Atlantic City, a different tourist segment has emerged. Atlantic City is situated perfectly within a two-hour commute to the most densely populated area of America – between Philadelphia and New York City. In addition, it is within 3–5 hours of Boston and Washington, DC. As a result, Atlantic City developed the fine art of bussing guests to the location. For a relatively inexpensive fee, people could board a bus that had food, beverages, and video entertainment, and relax until they got to the casino. As the buses picked up people from farther and farther away, people could sleep on the bus before and after their activities.

However, Atlantic City was also a place where people could drive in and play. Gamblers could choose from 12 casinos to drive to for dinner, a show, or some gambling and then leave. This was the beginning of the locals market. The smaller casino operations outside the two major gambling cities were not able to draw enough tourists to their sites because they did not have the synergistic effect of Las Vegas, nor did they have an easily accessible casino where large numbers of visitors could come like in Atlantic City. Therefore, as riverboats and Native American casinos grew in numbers, they looked toward local patrons. Researchers (Campbell and Ponting, 1984; Smith, 1992; Hinch and Walker, 2005) have studied the differences between tourists and local patrons. According to this research, tourists who tended to have higher educational levels were more likely to have jobs in management/professional areas and were more motivated by the social environment of casinos. Local patrons tended to be motivated by the excitement associated with the risks or rush of gambling.

Shoemaker and Zemke (2005) studied the 'local' markets because they found there were relatively little empirical data on this segment. Their study identified reasons why people would visit a particular casino, how they decided their gambling budget, thetime they spent on gambling, and their favorite games. As gambling growth exploded, Steve Wynn, a prominent casino developer, convinced people that 'Gambling is only another form of recreation.' According to this argument, locals have a choice on how they spend their weekly recreation budget. They can go to the movies, go out to dinner, go bowling, or go to a casino on Saturday night. Going to a casino was no longer a major decision like where to spend the weekend or a vacation. It was a simple alternative to other activities available in the area. While previous tourist research focused on economic impact and destination attractiveness, recent locals research (Brown 2001) began to explore how often gamblers could come and how they spent their money. Adding new variables to the concept of repeat visitors, Shinnar et al. (2004) explored the impact that visiting friends and family have on the frequency of casino visits. When friends and family visited, 65.8% of the sample said, the visitors would accompany them to casinos if they went. In fact, 17% of locals would go to casinos only when visitors came. Therefore, new strategies had to be developed.

Because the highest percentage of gamblers belongs to seniors, some researchers have studied why they gamble (McNeilly and Burke, 2001; Hope and Havir, 2002; Stitt et al., 2003b; Loroz, 2004a, b; Zaranek and Chapleski, 2005). Hope and Havir (2002) used social exchange theory to explain why seniors gamble. This theory explains social change and stability as a process of negotiated exchanges between parties. It suggests that all social relationships are perceived from the use of a subjective cost–benefit analysis and the comparison of alternatives. In this case, seniors derive pleasure out of the social interactions when they go to the casino, and it gives them a topic of conversation and shared rapport with all ages. Thus, it is a good trade-off for them between the money and the interactions received. On the other hand, Zaranek and Chapleski (2005) used a Russian cultural–historical theory from the 1920–1930s to analyze urban elders' desire to gamble. This theory, known as activity theory, suggests that the human mind can only be analyzed by understanding the context of meaningful, goal-oriented, and socially determined interactions between human beings and their material environment. It consists of a set of basic principles concerning how to develop a conceptual framework to study people's motivation in their lives and in their activities. In this case, gambling provides a meaningful goal-oriented activity for urban elders. For example, in New York City, many elders are concerned about their safety when walking around the city and, thus, a bus trip to Atlantic City for a day gives them the freedom to walk around, enjoy the ocean, be with other seniors, and obtain some excitement by gambling. In addition, according to Loroz (2004a), gambling reinforces and enhances seniors' self-image.

Other research (Higgins, 2001; Moseley et al., 2003; Higgins, 2005b) explores issues of seniors' trips to the casino. Attracting seniors to gambling has become a social issue as younger people feel the need to protect their parents. For example, in New York City, politicians in the 1990s tried to block casino buses. The rationale was that seniors were not mentally capable of making those decisions because it was believed that they were becoming addicted and spending their life savings on going to Atlantic City to gamble. The very strong response to this action was that seniors were not senile and that they had budgeted their own money for longer than these politicians had been alive. They had lived through the Depression and, as a result, older people were quite capable of making their own decisions and managing their own money. Research from Stitt et al. (2003b) supported this viewpoint. Their results indicated that

casino gambling is not a major threat to the elderly and it does not prey on the aged and lead them to destructive gambling practices... elderly, although visiting casinos more frequently than younger gamblers, generally exercise better money management and experience proportionately fewer gambling problems than the general population.

(p. 199)

Higgins (2005b) looks at the senior trips from a political framework. Many senior centers have developed field trips to different destinations including casinos. Therefore, municipal funding is supplied by local and state tax dollars to develop, organize, and run these trips to the casinos. There are many people who still believe that gambling is not an ethical, moral, or religiously appropriate activity. Therefore, they believe that tax dollars should not be used to support any trips to a casino. However, this is a two-sided sword, since local and state governments are increasingly dependent on gambling and gambling related tax revenue as a source of support for their programs including senior centers. There is a dilemma on whether senior centers should 'support' casinos by planning and providing transportation for these trips using tax money even though the source of the tax money is the gambling venues.

Relationship marketing

From the first casino in New Orleans in 1827, managers have understood the importance of developing relationships with their guests. Copying from the upper class European casinos, John Davies created a casino where 'comps' (loss leaders of food and lodging) were standard operating procedures. He understood that people who knew where they were going to sleep and had good food were more likely to stay where they were – in the casino gambling. It was easy to 'comp' a high roller (someone who spends a lot of money betting) because they were few and easy to identify. To keep the high rollers happy, management assigned each high roller a casino host, who specialized in making sure the guest had everything he/she wanted.

As casinos became more hi-tech, database marketing meant that it was easy to keep track of the high rollers including how much money they spent, how often they came, how long they stayed, and what their preferences were (Lucas et al., 2002). Databases also opened the door for the casino to track any customer who wanted to receive 'comps.' This allowed the casino to identify segments of the market and create a new relationship with their patrons (Baloglu, 2002; Sui and Baloglu, 2003). For example, Johnson (2002a) used the critical incident technique to assess gaming customer satisfaction. The Critical Incident Technique (or CIT) is a set of procedures that rely on collecting data by only observing as guests interact with employees; a database keeps track of these as incidents which are used to solve practical problems.

Sui and Baloglu (2003) found that the most influential of the behavioral variables in loyalty were based on trust and emotional attachment. Phillips et al. (2004) took the concept of relationship marketing one step further by creating a segmentation strategy based on the value of relationship strength. They used a combination of attitudinal and behavioral measurements to identify customers who might be over-looked due to the stage in their relationship development. 'For example, individuals who visited the casino infrequently (i.e., have weak bonds to the casino in terms of "behavioral" measures) . . . [are] likely to be overlooked by the casino if only behavioral indicators are used to segment customers. Yet as these attitudinal bonds are nurtured and strengthened, this type of customer is likely to remain a loyal patron' (http://web105.epnet.com.ezproxy.uno.edu/, accessed 5/2/06). Therefore, Sui and Baloglu have developed an Attitudinal and Behavioral Measures Matrix to analyze different stages of the process and to offer advice on how casinos might use this information. The new emphasis on gaining inroads into these delicate, emotional issues might be a path toward increased guest loyalty. After all, the traditional 'comps' are nice but they can be duplicated and they do not necessarily instill emotional attachment.

CRM (customer relationship management) is the new buzzword that attempts to address these issues. One way to define CRM is as a holistic process of identifying, attracting, differentiating, and retaining customers (Strauss and Frost, 2001). Another more precise definition is 'tracking customer behavior in order to develop marketing and relationship-building programs that bond consumers to a brand often by development of software systems to provide one-on-one contact between the marketing business and their customer' (http://www.commerce-database.com/crm.htm). However, CRM, like service, must involve the entire corporation from the top down. It is a corporate commitment to providing a consistent, high-quality experience to guests, which in turn boosts customer satisfaction and ultimately shareholder value. On a practical level, CRM simply means establishing individual relationships with guests and treating customers differently based on their preferences and spending patterns. While the technological environment has made CRM a highly sophisticated process, ultimately some would say that it is another name for one-to-one or relationship marketing. The principles are the same, only the data dredging has changed.

Harrah's uses its CRM data warehouse as a marketing workbench to track 20 million guests visiting any of its casinos, restaurants, hotels, or entertainment locations. Its patented WIN network allows the company to analyze customer preferences, predict visit frequency and desired rewards, manage promotions and personalized offers, and, most importantly, drive marketing campaigns that have effectively generated over 20% growth in profitability since implementing the CRM strategy. On January 15, 1998, Harrah's stock traded at around

$19.50. On January 15, 2003, it traded as high as $38.49, almost twice the price, at a time when the market value of the industry as whole had declined by more than 25%.

(Kale, 2003, p.43)

As casinos multiplied throughout the United States, the competitive environment forced them to strategize new ways of working with their potential guests. CRM became the new buzzword to attract and keep customer loyalty (Kale, 2003; Hendler and Hendler, 2004; Kale, 2005; Krell, 2006). However; according to Kale (2005), while many casinos are still investing in CRM, the failure rate of CRM attempts still hovers around 70%. 'Given that many casino strategy decisions are driven by the underlying odds, one would expect casinos to shy away from projects offering a mere 30% chance of success' (Kale, 2005, p. 55).

Consumer behavior

With the colorful past of gambling, casino management has never been sure about what information to allow the public to have access to. In the past, the press has frequently taken information from casinos and written negative articles using this information as a backup. Therefore, obtaining information about internal operations has been difficult, especially when it concerns employees and guests. As a result, the research focus has been external to the casino in three main areas: attitude/motivation/beliefs, product selection, and customer satisfaction.

Since the early 1900s, theorists have tried to answer the question of why people gamble. Researchers have become interested in gambling behavior as more Americans embrace the idea of casinos. For example, in 2003 Americans spent more in commercial casinos than they did on amusement parks and movies combined. For an average gambler this figure translated into $87.17 per bettor in a commercial casino. In fact, more than 53.4 million Americans visited casinos in 2003, compared to 51.2 million in 2002. That works out to an average of 5.8 casino trips per gambler. Gamblers also make up 26% of the US adult population (AGA, 2004).

However, despite the volume of play, decisions to gamble are largely a volitional process for casual participants (Oh and Hsu, 2001). While Oh and Hsu used Fishbein and Ajzen's theory of reasoned/planned action to study volitional and non-volitional aspects of gambling behavior, Chantal et al. (1995) used self-determination theory to evaluate volitional motivations. The theory of reasoned/planned action suggests that a person's voluntary behavior is predicted by his/her attitude toward that behavior and how other people would view him/her if he/she performed the behavior. A person's attitude, combined with his/her subjective norms, forms his/her behavioral intention. Self-determination theory focuses on the degree to which people endorse their actions at the highest level of reflection and engage in the actions with a full sense of choice. While the two studies used different theories, both theoretical applications reached the same conclusion that the decision to gamble is a voluntary, rational process for casual visitors.

To understand why people gamble, the fields of economics, psychology, and the interdisciplinary nature of work and play have each developed theories.

Economics

Economists (Conlisk, 1993; Woodland and Woodland, 1999; Dickinson, 2003; Ziegelmeyer et al., 2004) believe that people are rational beings and that they evaluate *all* alternatives before making a decision. Therefore, one theory about gambling behavior is that people do not know the probabilities of winning. After all, a rational person would not deliberately make the choice to gamble knowing that they were likely to lose. However, this is too simplistic an explanation and doesn't explain the reality that there are many people who know the odds and still bet. In a study by Williams and Connolly (2006), students in a statistics class learned about probabilities of different games in the casino and they calculated the odds. The students receiving the information still demonstrated above average ability in calculating gambling odds as well as resistance to gambling fallacies six months after the class. However, the increased math knowledge had no correlation to decreases in actual gambling behavior. Economist Milton Friedman (1949) developed the 'utility of wealth' theory. He argued that rational people will gamble if they place a high enough value on the chance of achieving wealth. In other words, a person realizes the true probabilities, but he wants the rewards so much that he will risk losing. This theory might explain the results of Williams and Connolly's study.

The psychological theories of gambling

Psychology (from the ancient Greek: *psyche* = soul and *logos* = word) is the study of behavior, mind, and thought. Two of the simplest psychological theories on why people gamble are that: (1) life is boring and the excitement of the game confirms that one is alive, and (2) people want to win money. Both of these theories are based on universal needs, which may explain why there is not a demographic profile or combination of personality characteristics that can isolate potential gamblers. Even in gender research, for example, motivation is more complex. Walker et al. (2005) found that there were two types of male gamblers: men who were motivated by the emotional 'rush,' and others who wanted the communing experience. In comparison, the research found that there were three types of female gamblers: women who were motivated by escaping everyday problems, those wanted the communing experience, and those who wanted to commune alone (such as gaining time away from family responsibilities).

Applying general psychological theories to gambling offers an additional series of gambling motives. Attribution theory suggests that people attribute their success to themselves, their skill, or their luck (e.g., a gambler is on a winning streak or his/her luck is hot tonight). Their losses are, however, blamed on something else – because the dealer was crooked, their companion had bad karma, the moon was in the wrong phase, or any other reason that might come to mind. Because losses are not the player's fault, it is easy to forget them or write them off as a fluke. It has been suggested that men tend to use this type of attribution more than women. Research indicates that women are more likely to explain winning on outside factors, such as 'My good fairy was with me,' or 'The slot machine was ready to hit and I happened by.' On the other hand, losing tends to be attributed to a personal failure: 'I picked the wrong machine,' or 'I have a bad luck stream running today.' This kind of thinking may explain why males' self-perceptions of their winnings are higher than females' perceptions. However, both views tend to be inflated.

This attribution of wins and losses allows people to believe that they have some kind of control over their fate (Chantal et al., 1995). For example, younger gamers have more of a feeling of control, which is why they tend to have greater win perceptions than older players. If one listens to people talk about their gambling experiences, everyone talks about the big win they had. Nobody talks about how much they played and lost before they won the pot. This little game played in gamblers' minds keeps them feeling as tomorrow is another day to win. Several studies (Langer, 1975; Langer and Roth, 1975; Davis et al., 2000) have explored this illusion of control in chance encounters. Whether it was cards, racetracks, lotteries or flipping coins, when the players felt that they had some control, whether from early success, perceived skill, familiarity of the game, or even involvement, they had inappropriately higher expectations than the objective probability would warrant. In support of this 'control' theory, Davis et al. (2000) went to a craps table to observe players acting out their beliefs. As expected, when players felt they had some 'control,' like blowing on the dice, they placed larger and more complex bets than other players. Superstitions are very important to gamblers because it gives them that 'edge' or 'illusion of control.' They believe that the big score is just around the corner.

Behavioral psychologists believe that these mental games are interesting, but it is really what people do and how they behave that is important. Given a particular stimulus, people are programmed to respond in the same way each time. This response pattern is based on the person's previous reinforcement to a stimulus. If Sam puts a coin in a slot machine, and he is rewarded with a 'hit;' this sets up a pattern of behavior. When Skinner (1969) developed his variable schedule of reinforcement (rewards were given at totally random times), the reaction of the animals to this stimulus–response cycle was predictable. The birds rapidly hit a key without slowing down until they were rewarded. Then they immediately began the cycle again. Watching people play at two or three slot machines at a time has a remarkable resemblance to Skinner's experiments.

Interdisciplinary study of play and leisure

Interdisciplinary research integrates concepts across different disciplines. The casino gaming industry is a complex and multi-faceted interdisciplinary field. Understanding the needs, wants, and motivations of both casino patrons and non-patrons is essential for the continued growth and success of this industry. Today, thanks to Steve Wynn, casino gaming competes with many other forms of play and leisure activities. Americans made nearly three times as many trips to casinos during 2003 as they did to professional baseball games (310 million trips to casinos vs. 106.5 million trips to baseball games (American Gaming Association's, 2004). Understanding the leisure preferences of casino patrons can enable the industry to position itself as a viable alternative to other competing forms of leisure activities.

What makes a person pick a casino destination instead of a destination such as Disneyland? When competing with other vacation spots, casinos can compete based on affordable rooms and good, inexpensive food. Many locations have great entertainment both on stage and off. Places like Las Vegas have every type of tourist attraction a person could want: art museums, amusement parks, theaters, cultural events, and shopping. In addition, players take a shot at changing their lives when they sit down at a table or a slot machine. Gambling is the only recreation where a person could literally walk away in a different economic position.

Other research on gambling consumer behavior

Other than motivational research, the other aspects of consumer behavior research focus on the games themselves (Shapiro, 1982; Davis et al., 2000; Titz et al., 2002; MacLin and Dixon, 2004). In particular, slot machine design tends to motivate people to stay longer. Proprietary research suggests that color, sounds, and design all play a role in attracting and keeping gamers at machines. People tend to look at slot machines as simple hand pull devices, but in fact they are based on very complex information processing cues (Côté et al., 2003; Dixon and Schreiber, 2004; Christopherson and Weatherly, 2006). For example, Dixon and Schreiber (2004) explored the win estimations when the slot machines had near-misses such as two out of three symbols lined up or three symbols showing up with one just a half roll from even. Even though bettors did not get a reward in these near-misses, many treated the near-miss as close to a 'win,' resulting in a positive reinforcement of playing the machine.

Recent research also explores the complex issue of atmospherics and motivation (Hirsch, 1995; Mayer and Johnson, 2003; Lucas, 2003; Johnson et al., 2004). Mayer and Johnson (2003) supported the folklore that slot players will stay longer and spend more money when they like the layout and design of the area. The higher the interaction between the casino and the guest, the more likely the player would view the facility as the service they want. In addition, the physical surroundings change the perception of the level of service competence. As a result, the more positive the emotional response to the atmospherics, the more time and money the guest will spend. In this regard, Hirsch (1995) studied the effects of ambient odors on slot machine usage. It was found that people enjoyed the ambient odors and spent more time at their machines in those areas than in others. As a result of this research, people were concerned that casinos were taking advantage of the players. However, it should be noted that bakeries in malls blow the scents of baking cookies and breads through the ventilation systems because they know that people will become hungry from the scents, and their sales will go up. Upscale department stores such as Saks Fifth or Lord and Taylor have a different scent in the air than a Wal-Mart. Therefore, retail has been using scented products for a long time, and casinos are just investigating this phenomenon. This information reinforces the study by Johnson et al. (2004) that there is a strong need for casino management to create an inviting atmosphere that will maximize customer satisfaction, with specific attention to those aspects that players appear to value the most.

There is a major discrepancy between the casino industry focus and research in terms of customer service, service failure, and service recovery. Casinos have always realized the importance of service in keeping their customers returning. However, especially in the past decade, since competition from Native American, riverboats, and land-based casinos has grown, managers have begun to focus on service, although they needed a connection to profits in order to invest in service improvement. Heskett et al. (1994) provided a seminal work on 'Putting the Service-Profit Chain to Work' in which they developed a series of links between the management of service and the profitability of a company. This was the first step in demonstrating a logical flow of effective steps from management and the corporate culture it creates through the employees to the guests, ending with the profits. This article gives logical guiding steps for creating a successful business. One of the authors, Gary Loveman, was hired by Harrah's Entertainment to become Chief Operating Officer in 1998, in large part to operationalize this theoretical framework. 'Most people thought I'd leave in 2 years and go back to Harvard,' Loveman recalls. 'They thought this would be like a kidney stone: It would hurt for a while and then it would pass' (Becker, 2003, p. 46). For Harrah's Entertainment, the theory works. In 2003, the Board appointed Loveman as CEO and the company's performance has led to its inclusion in the Dow Jones Sustainability Index, a group of international companies noted for creating long-term shareholder value for four consecutive years. Institutional Investor magazine named Loveman gaming and lodging's best CEO in 2004, 2005, and 2006 (www.harrahs.com). However, despite the strong focus on service, casino research has not followed suit. Part of the problem has been gaining access to the casino's proprietary information. Casino management has been reluctant to allow detailed information in the public domain.

Summary and conclusion

This chapter has explored the casino industry by combining the practical issues and the research that has either reinforced casinos' daily practices or gone off in new directions. The negative image of the casino industry must always be a part of a discussion of gambling because it has created so much research on the pros and cons of regulating gaming as well as its effect on marketing strategies. In addition, the image of gaming must naturally be a constant background factor when assessing casino decisions because it is in the back of the minds of the stakeholders. For example, the fact that until 1999 casinos could not advertise their product was an issue because of the public's general negative perception of them. These negative factors have also created a corporate casino environment of mistrust, creating the need for proprietary research that is rarely available to the public. As a result, research agendas have focused on issues that do not require confidential information from the casinos, such as the impact of the casino on the community, market segmentation, consumer motivation, and design/atmospherics. However, as gambling has become more accepted as a part of people's everyday lives, casino managers have eased their restrictions. As a result, researchers have developed networking with casino personnel, and the possibility of studying other internal issues has become feasible. Following are some of the pending issues calling for research:

- Because advertising was limited by legislation, there is very little research on the effectiveness of casino advertising. Currently, advertising shows people playing the tables and winning. Is it true that people gamble only to win? What motivates people to gamble? What promotional message should be used?

- As Mother Nature continues her rampage, disaster planning on an operational as well as corporate level has come to the forefront. These are issues that span many levels from maintaining power during a thunderstorm to hurricanes destroying the casino. What is the impact of these issues on guests? How should managers and employees handle power outages or threats from major storms? When should a casino shut down?

- The failure rate for CRM is 70%. Why? What are planners doing wrong? What would be a more successful program? The concept is good, but somewhere there is a piece missing that causes these plans to fail.

- Folklore suggests that people go to a casino and never leave until it is time to go home. Is that truly the case? Should local businesses be concerned that all the casino guest traffic will never come to their businesses? Can casinos be used as the core of a major regional tourism development plan, or is it not feasible because people go directly to the casino and then go directly home?

- Folklore suggests that local restaurants go under when casinos arrive. Yet, research suggests that is not the case. What type of local restaurants go under? Why? What type of restaurants replace them? Do national chains replace the local operators? If so, what factors allow chains to compete more effectively than the local operator? Who survives? What strategies do they use that differ from those of restaurants that fail?

- The American Gaming Association is calling for an independent study to explore Internet gambling issues. While this chapter has only explored casino research, Internet gambling is a new and relatively open area for study. There is one academic journal on Internet Gaming Law published by Mary Ann Liebert (www.liebertpub.com).

- The casino industry is pushing for responsible gambling. The American Gaming Association has affiliated with the National Center for Responsible Gaming (NCRG) to become more proactive on handling the positive impact of research in casino communities nationwide. Therefore, there are many opportunities to develop and provide research on implementation programs.

- Although some researchers have tried, there has never been a cost–benefit model that accurately assesses all aspects of the pros and cons of casinos on a region.

Studying the casino industry is a multi-faceted venture, and because of its relative newness to public acceptance, there are many avenues to explore. As much of the research has shown, matching up the special nuances of the casino industry and theories from hospitality, business, psychology, sociology, and economics will allow this area of marketing to be extremely fruitful.

References

American Gaming Association's (AGA) (2004). State of the States annual report Retrieved August 8, 2006, from http://www.americangaming.org/assets/files/2004_Survey_for_Web.pdf

Baloglu, S. (2002). Dimensions of customer loyalty: Separating the friends from the well wishers. *Cornell Hotel and Restaurant Administration Quarterly*, *43*(1), 47–60.

Becker, D.O. (2003). Gambling on customers. *Mckinsey Quarterly*, (2), 46–59.

Brandmeir, K. and Baloglu, S. (2004). Linking employee turnover to casino restaurant performance: A cross-sectional and time-lagged correlation analysis. *Journal of Foodservice Business Research*, *7*(2), 25–39.

Brown, D. (2001). A sociodemographic and trip profile of Kentucky visitors based on their gaming activity and destination-specific behaviour. *Journal of Vacation Marketing*, *7*(1), 41–50.

Brown, D., Roseman, M., and Ham, S. (2003). Perceptions of a Bible Belt State's proposed casino gaming legislation by religious affiliation: The case of Kentucky residents. *UNLV Gaming Research and Review Journal*, *7*(1), 49–59.

Brown, S. (2006). The surge in online gambling on college campuses. *New Directions for Student Services*, *113*, 53–61.

Campbell, C. and Ponting, J.R. (1984) The evolution of casino gambling in Alberta. *Canadian Public Policy*, *10*(2), 142–155.

Carmichael, B. and Peppard Jr., D. (1996). Megaresort on my doorstep: Local resident attitudes toward. *Journal of Travel Research*, *34*(3), 9–18.

Caswell, J. (2006). Listening to their stories: Students' perspectives about campus gambling. *New Directions for Student Services*, 113, 25–32.

Chantal, Y., Vallerand, R., and Vallières, E. (1995). Motivation and gambling involvement. *Journal of Social Psychology*, *135*(6), 755–763.

Chen McCain, S., (Shawn) Jang, S., and Hu, C. (2005). Service quality gap analysis toward customer loyalty: practical guidelines for casino hotels. *International Journal of Hospitality Management*, *24*(3), 465–472.

Cheung, C. and Law, R. (2006). How can hotel guests be protected during the occurrence of a Tsunami? *Asia Pacific Journal of Tourism Research*, *11*(3), 289–295.

Christopherson, K. and Weatherly, J. (2006). The effect of visual complexity when playing a slot-machine simulation: The role of computer experience, computer anxiety, and optimism. *Computers in Human Behavior*, *22*(6), 1072–1079.

Commerce-Database.com (n.d.) Business Terms Dictionary (www document), retrieved 2nd January, 2004, from http://www.commerce-database.com/crm.htm.

Conlisk, J. (1993). The utility of gambling. *Journal of Risk and Uncertainty*, *6*(3), 255–275.

Côté, D., Caron, A., Desrochers, J. and Ladouceur, R. (2003). Near wins prolong gambling on a video lottery terminal. *Journal of Gambling Studies*, *19*(4), 433–438.

D'Hauteserre, A. (2001a). Destination branding in a hostile environment. *Journal of Travel Research*, *39*(3), 300–308.

D'Hauteserre, A. (2001b). Representations of rurality: Is foxwoods casino resort threatening the quality of life in southeastern Connecticut? *Tourism Geographies*, *3*(4), 405–429.

Davis, D., Sundahl, I., and Lesbo, M. (2000). Illusory personal control as a determinant of bet size and type in casino craps games. *Journal of Applied Social Psychology*, *30*(6), 1224–1242

de la Viña, L. and Bernstein, D. (2002). The impact of gambling on personal bankruptcy rates. *Journal of Socio-Economics*, *31*(5), 503–510.

Dense, J. and Barrow, C. (2003). Estimating casino expenditures by out-of-state patrons: Native American gaming in Connecticut. *Journal of Travel Research*, *41*(4), 410–416.

Dickinson, D. (2003). Illustrated examples of the effects of risk preferences and expectations on bargaining outcomes. *Journal of Economic Education*, *34*(2), 169–180.

Dixon, M. and Schreiber, J. (2004). Near-miss effects on response latencies and win estimations of slot machine players. *Psychological Record*, *54*(3), 335–348.

Dowd, M. (2005). Suitable casino sites in Mississippi: What are they? Why? What about the future? *Gaming Law Review*, *9*(4), 325–332.

Fenich G. and Hashimoto, K. (2004) Perceptions of cannibalization: What is the real effect of land-based casinos on local restaurants?. *Gaming Law Review*. 8(4), 247–259.

Ference, G. (2001). Improving organizational performance. *Cornell Hotel and Restaurant Administration Quarterly*, *42*(2), 12–28.

Foley, D. (2005). The heartland chronicles revisited: The casino's impact on settlement life. *Qualitative Inquiry*, *11*(2), 296–320.

Friedman, M. (1949). The marshallian demand curve. *The Journal of Political Economy*, *57*(6), 463–495.

Grinols, E. and Mustard, D. (2006). Casinos, crime, and community costs. *Review of Economics and Statistics*, *88*(1), 28–45.

Hashimoto, K. and Fenich, G. (2003) Does casino development destroy local food and beverage operations? Development of casinos in Mississippi. *Gaming Law Review*.7(2), 101–109.

Hashimoto, K. and O'Brien, J. (2006) The aftermath of Hurricane Katrina and its impact on crisis planning on casinos. *Casino and Gaming International*. 3, 77–88.

Hendler, R. and Hendler, F. (2004). Revenue management in fabulous Las Vegas: Combining customer relationship management and revenue management to maximise profitability. *Journal of Revenue and Pricing Management*, *3*(1), 73–79.

Heskett, J., Jones, T., Loveman, G. et al. (1994). Putting the Service-Profit Chain to work. *Harvard Business Review*, *72*(2), 164–170.

Higgins, B. (2005a). The storms of summer: Lessons learned in the aftermath of the hurricanes of '04. *Cornell Hotel and Restaurant Administration Quarterly, 46*(1), 40–46.

Higgins, J. (2001). A comprehensive policy analysis of and recommendations for senior center gambling trips. *Journal of Aging and Social Policy, 12*(2), 73–92.

Higgins, J. (2005b). Exploring the politics and policy surrounding senior center gambling activities. *Journal of Aging Studies, 19*(1), 85–107.

Hinch, T. and Walker, G. (2005). Casino markets: A study of tourist and local patrons. *Tourism and Hospitality Research, 6*(1), 72–87.

Hirsch, A. (1995). Effects of ambient odors on slot-machine usage in a Las Vegas casino. *Psychology and Marketing, 12*(7), 585–594.

Hong, S. and Jang, H. (2004). Segmentation of early casino markets: An exploratory study. *Tourism Management, 25*(6), 801–805.

Hope, J. and Havir, L. (2002). You bet they're having fun! Older Americans and casino gambling. *Journal of Aging Studies, 16*(2), 177–198.

Hsu, C. (2000). Residents' support for legalized gaming and perceived impacts of riverboat casinos: Changes in five years. *Journal of Travel Research, 38*(4), 390–396.

Janes, P. and Collison, J. (2004). Community leader perceptions of the social and economic impacts of Indian gaming. *UNLV Gaming Research and Review Journal, 8*(1), 13–30.

Johnson, L. (2002a). An application of the critical incident technique in gaming research. *Journal of Travel and Tourism Marketing, 12*(2/3), 45. Retrieved Friday, January 19, 2007 from the Hospitality and Tourism Complete database.

Johnson, L. (2002b). Using the Critical Incident Technique to assess gaming customer satisfaction. *UNLV Gaming Research and Review Journal, 6*(2), 1–14.

Johnson, L., Mayer, K., and Champaner, E. (2004). Casino atmospherics from a customer's perspective: A re-examination. *UNLV Gaming Research and Review Journal, 8*(2), 1–10.

Kale, S. (2003). CRM in gaming: It's no crapshoot!. *UNLV Gaming Research and Review Journal, 7*(2), 43–54.

Kale, S. (2005). Change management: Antecedents and consequences in casino CRM. *UNLV Gaming Research and Review Journal, 9*(2), 55–67.

Krell, E. (2006). CRM a gamble no more!. *Baylor Business Review, 24*(2), 21–23.

Kwan, F. and McCartney, G. (2005). Mapping resident perceptions of gaming impact. *Journal of Travel Research, 44*(2), 177–187.

Langer, E. (1975). The illusion of control. *Journal of Personality and Social Psychology, 32*(2), 311–328.

Langer, E. and Roth, J. (1975). Heads I win, tails it's chance: The illusion of control as a function of the sequence of outcomes in a purely chance task. *Journal of Personality and Social Psychology, 32*(6), 951–955.

Lee, C. and Back, K. (2003). Pre- and post-casino impact of residents' perceptions. *Annals of Tourism Research*, 30(4), 868–885.

Lester, D. and Jason, D. (1989). Suicides at the casino. *Psychological Reports*, 64(1), 337–338.

Loroz, P. (2004a). Golden-age gambling: Psychological benefits and self-concept dynamics in aging consumers' consumption experiences. *Psychology and Marketing*, 21(5), 323–349.

Loroz, P. (2004b). Casino gambling and aging consumers: Overcoming barriers and reaping the benefits of experiential leisure consumption. *Journal of Hospitality and Leisure Marketing*, 11(2/3), 115–138.

Lucas, A. (2003). The determinants and effects of slot servicescape satisfaction in a Las Vegas hotel casino. *UNLV Gaming Research and Review Journal*, 7(1), 1–20.

Lucas, A. (2004). Estimating the impact of match-play promotional offers on the blackjack business volume of a Las Vegas hotel casino. *Journal of Travel and Tourism Marketing*, 17(4), 23–33.

Lucas, A. and Bowen, J. (2002). Measuring the effectiveness of casino promotions. *International Journal of Hospitality Management*, 21(2), 189–203.

Lucas, A., Kilby, J., and Santos, J. (2002). Assessing the profitability of premium players. *Cornell Hotel and Restaurant Administration Quarterly*, 43(4), 65–79.

MacLin, O. and Dixon, M. (2004). A computerization simulation for investigating gambling behavior during roulette play. *Behavior Research Methods, Instruments, and Computers*, 36(1), 96–100.

Mayer, K. and Johnson, L. (2003). A customer-based assessment of casino atmospherics. *UNLV Gaming Research and Review Journal*, 7(1), 21–32.

McCleary, R., Chew, K., Merrill, V., and Napolitano, C. (2002). Does legalized gambling elevate the risk of suicide? An analysis of U.S. counties and metropolitan areas. *Suicide and Life-Threatening Behavior*, 32(2), 209–216.

McNeilly, D. and Burke, W. (2001). Gambling as a social activity of older adults. *International Journal of Aging and Human Development*, 52(1), 19–29.

Meyer-Arendt, K. (1995). Casino gaming in Mississippi: Location, location, location. *Economic Development Review*, 13(4), 27–34.

Morrison, A. and Braunlich, C. (1996). A profile of the casino resort vacationer. *Journal of Travel Research*, 35(2), 55–62.

Moseley, C., Schwer, K., and Thompson, W. (2003). Elderly casino gambling behavior: Marketing implications. *Journal of Hospitality and Leisure Marketing*, 10(1/2), 87–100.

Moufakkir, O. (2005). An assessment of crime volume following casino gaming development in the City of Detroit. *UNLV Gaming Research and Review Journal*, 9(1), 15–28.

Moufakkir, O., Singh, A., Moufakkir-van der Woud, A., and Holecek, D. (2004). Impact of light, medium and heavy spenders on casino destinations: Segmenting gaming visitors based on amount of non-gaming expenditures. *UNLV Gaming Research and Review Journal*, *8*(1), 59–71.

Nealon, J.T.(2006) Take me out to the slot machines: Reflections on gambling and contemporary American culture. *South Atlantic Quarterly*, *105*(2), 465–474.

Nichols M., Stitt, B., and Giacopassi, D. (2000). Casino gambling and bankruptcy in new United States casino jurisdictions. *Journal of Socio-Economics*, *29*(3), 247–262.

Nichols, M., Stitt, B., and Giacopassi, D. (2004). Changes in suicide and divorce in new casino jurisdictions. *Journal of Gambling Studies*, *20*(4), 391–404.

Oh, H. and Hsu, C. (2001). Volitional degrees of gambling behaviors. *Annals of Tourism Research*, *28*(3), 618–637.

Perdue, R., Long, P., and Kang, Y. (1999). Boomtown tourism and resident quality of life: The marketing of gaming to host community residents. *Journal of Business Research*, *44*(3), 165–177.

Phillips, J., Tandoh, M., Noble, S., and Bush, V. (2004). The value of relationship strength in segmenting casino patrons: An exploratory investigation. *Journal of Interactive Advertising*, *4*(3), N.PAG. Retrieved Friday, January 19, 2007 from the Business Source Complete database.

Piscitelli, F. and Albanese, J. (2000). Do casinos attract criminals? A study at the Canadian-U.S. border. *Journal of Contemporary Criminal Justice*, *16*(4), 445–457.

Pizam, A. and Reichel, A. (1979). Big spenders and little spenders in U.S. tourism. *Journal of Travel Research*, *18*, 42–43.

Reece, W.S. (2001) Travelers to Las Vegas and to Atlantic City. *Journal of Travel Research*, *39*(3) 275–285.

Lucas, A., Dunn, W., and Singh, A. (2005). Estimating the short-term effect of free-play offers in a Las Vegas hotel casino. *Journal of Travel and Tourism Marketing*, *18*(2), 53–68.

Schmelzer, C., Revelas, D., and Brown, D. (2002). Casino gaming from a border state perspective: Impact on the hospitality industry. *UNLV Gaming Research and Review Journal*, *6*(2), 29–43.

Youn, S.K., Faber, R., and Shah, D. (2000). Restricting gambling advertising and the third-person effect. *Psychology and Marketing*, *17*(7), 633–649.

Shapiro, G. (1982). Reference for gambling at slot machines, Keno, Blackjack and craps: Who and why. In *The Gambling papers: Gambling Research: Proceedings of the Fifth National Conference on Gambling and Risk Taking*. (pp. 34–60). Reno, NV: University of Nevada Press.

Shinnar, R., Young, C., and Corsun, D. (2004). Las Vegas locals as gamblers and hosts to visiting friends and family: Characteristics and gaming behavior. *UNLV Gaming Research and Review Journal*, *8*(2), 39–48

Shoemaker, S. and Zemke, D. (2005). The 'Locals' market: An emerging gaming segment. *Journal of Gambling Studies*, *21*(4), 379–410.

Skinner, B.F. (1969). Contingency management in the classroom. *Education*, *90*(2), 93–101.

Smith, G. (1992) *The gambling attitudes and behaviors of Albertans*. Population Research Laboratory, Department of Sociology, Edmonton, Canada: University of Alberta.

Spears, D. and Boger Jr., C. (2002). Residents' perceptions and attitudes toward Native American gaming (NAG) in Kansas: Proximity and number of trips to NAG activity. *UNLV Gaming Research and Review Journal*, *6*(2), 13–28.

Spotts, D.M. and Mahoney, E.M. (1991) Segmenting visitors to a destination region based on the volume of their expenditures. *Journal of Travel Research*, *29* (4), 24–31.

Stitt, M., Nicholas, B. and Giacopassi, D. (2002). Community assessment of the effects of casinos on quality of life. *Social Indicators Research*, *57*(3), 229–263.

Stitt, B., Nichols, M., and Giacopassi, D. (2003a). Does the presence of casinos increase crime? An examination of casino and control communities. *Crime and Delinquency*, *49*(2), 253–285.

Stitt, B., Nichols, M., and Giacopassi, D. (2003b). Gambling among older adults: A comparative analysis. *Experimental Aging Research*, *29*(2), 189–203.

Stitt, B., Nichols, M., and Giacopassi, D. (2005). Perception of casinos as disruptive influences in USA communities. *International Journal of Tourism Research*, *7*(4/5), 187–200.

Strauss, J. and Frost, R. (2001) *E-marketing*. Upper Saddle River, NJ: Prentice Hall.

Sui, J. and Baloglu, S. (2003). The role of emotional commitment in relationship marketing: An empirical investigation of a loyalty model for casinos. *Journal of Hospitality and Tourism Research*, *27*(4), 470–490.

Titz, K., Andrus, D., and Miller, J. (2002). Hedonistic differences between mechanical game players and table game players: An exploratory investigation on the road to comprehensive theory for gambling. *Gaming Research and Review Journal*, *6*(1), 23–33.

Walker, G., Hinch, T., and Weighill, A. (2005). Inter- and intra-gender similarities and differences in motivations for casino gambling. *Leisure Sciences*, *27*(2), 111–130.

Williams, R. and Connolly, D. (2006). Does learning about the mathematics of gambling change gambling behavior? *Psychology of Addictive Behaviors*, *20*(1), 62–68.

Woodland, B. and Woodland, L. (1999). Expected utility, skewness, and the baseball betting market. *Applied Economics*, *31*(3), 337–345.

Woodside, A.G., Cook, V.J. and Mindak, W. (1987). Profiling the heavy travel segment. *Journal of Travel Research*, *25*, 9–14.

Wynne, H. and Shaffer, H. (2003). The socioeconomic impact of gambling: The Whistler symposium. *Journal of Gambling Studies*, *19*(2), 111–121.

Zaranek, R. and Chapleski, E. (2005). Casino gambling among urban elders: Just another social activity? *Journals of Gerontology Series B: Psychological Sciences and Social Sciences*, *60*B(2), S74–S81.

Ziegelmeyer, A., Broihanne, M., and Koessler, F. (2004). Sequential parimutuel betting in the laboratory. *Journal of Risk and Uncertainty*, *28*(2), 165–186.

Index